Realty Bluebook®

EDITION 32

Robert de Heer

**Real Estate
Education Company®**
a division of Dearborn Financial Publishing, Inc.

This publication is designed to provide accurate and authoritative information in regard to the subject matter covered. It is sold with the understanding that the publisher is not engaged in rendering legal, accounting or other professional service. If legal advice or other expert assistance is required, the services of a competent professional person should be sought.

Publisher: Carol L. Luitjens
Executive Editor: Diana Faulhaber
Managing Editor: Ronald J. Liszkowski
Art Manager: Lucy Jenkins

© 1998 by Dearborn Financial Publishing, Inc.®

Published by Real Estate Education Company,®
a division of Dearborn Financial Publishing, Inc.®
155 North Wacker Drive
Chicago, IL 60606-1719

All rights reserved. The text of this publication, or any part thereof, may not be reproduced in any manner whatsoever without permission in writing from the publisher.

Printed in the United States of America.

98 99 00 10 9 8 7 6 5 4 3 2 1

CONTENTS

FINANCING
Promissory Note A-1
Finance Instruments A-1

Types of Mortgages A-8

**The Secondary Mortgage
Market A-25**

Conventional Financing A-53

FHA Financing A-73

VA Financing A-115

HIGH-TECH SELLING

Modern Technology B–1

Listing Techniques B–14

CHECKLISTS

Checklists E-1

ACKNOWLEDGMENTS

The author would like to acknowledge valuable assistance from the staff of Fannie Mae, FHA, the Department of Veterans Affairs, as well as from educators and authors John W. Reilly, John P. Wiedemer and Dr. Joan M. Harrison.

Thanks are also extended to the following people who served as reviewers of the *Realty Bluebook®:* Edward O'Donnell, The Real Estate School; Rose S. Bock, Arvida Realty Sales, Ltd.; John A. Hamilton, Regional Director, Polley Associates; Vernon Hoven, CPA, Vern Hoven Tax Seminars; James M. Kinney, President, Rubloff Residential Properties; Judith Meadows; Jane Rosen, President, ACS, Assessment & Compliance Services; Barbara J. Stepp, Coldwell Banker School of Real Estate; and Michael L. White, President, Deed Transfer Report.

Special thanks are extended to the Hawaii Association of REALTORS® for permission to reproduce "Disclosure of Environmental Hazards," a section of its Risk Management Course.

Finally, comments and suggestions from many real estate professionals nationwide are sincerely appreciated.

PREFACE

The *Realty Bluebook®*, updated annually, has been a standard reference of the real estate profession since 1966.

The information in the *Realty Bluebook®* has been compiled from authoritative sources and reviewed by qualified legal and other specialists in the various fields to which the book has reference.

The *Realty Bluebook®* is not intended to provide legal, tax or other advice. Readers are encouraged to consult appropriate experts for specific advice.

HOW TO USE THIS BOOK

The ***Realty Bluebook®*** is designed as a day-to-day reference tool. To become familiar with the wide variety of topics in the book read the tables of contents. Just open one of the six thumb indexes to locate the contents of a section. In addition, the alphabetical cross index at the end of the book provides instant access to any topic. The text is easy to understand and provides detailed essential information.

The convenient size and organization make the ***Realty Bluebook®*** a walking memory! Let it be your constant companion in both field and office.

FINANCING

To receive advance notice of the
next *Realty Bluebook*® edition
(and information about
what's new), please call
1-800-428-3846
to register your name and address,
or visit the Bluebook Web Page at
www.deheer.com/bluebook

CONTENTS

FINANCING
Promissory Note A-1
Finance Instruments A-1

Types of Mortgages A-8

The Secondary Mortgage Market A-25

Conventional Financing A-53

FINANCE INSTRUMENTS

PROMISSORY NOTE

A *promissory note* is an unconditional written promise to pay a certain sum of money to another at a future specified time. In real estate financing, the note is evidence of the debt secured by a mortgage or deed of trust upon the property. The person signing the promissory note is called the maker, the person to whom the promise is made is the payee.

Most promissory notes in real estate financing are negotiable instruments. To be negotiable, the note must be made to a person or order or bearer, which enables the lender to endorse and transfer the note.

SECURITY INSTRUMENTS

A security instrument is a contract between lender and borrower by which property is given as security for repayment of a loan, evidenced by a note or bond.

In some states, the mortgage (in other states the deed of trust) is used as a real property security instrument. In a *mortgage,* the borrower is called the *mortgagor* and the lender, the *mortgagee.* In a *deed of trust,* the borrower is called the *trustor;* the lender is the *beneficiary;* and the property is conveyed to the trustee (often a title company or bank) that holds title as security for repayment of the loan for the benefit of the beneficiary.

The *installment land contract,* also known as the *contract of sale* or *contract for deed,* is an installment-type contract between buyer and seller, whereby the buyer obtains the right to occupy but the seller retains legal title to the real property as security for payment of the purchase price. The seller agrees to convey title to the buyer upon fulfillment of certain conditions. During the term of the contract the buyer is said to have an *equitable ownership interest* in the property. A contract of sale is both a marketing instrument (like a sale/purchase agreement) and a security instrument (like a mortgage or deed of trust). Because a contract of sale is also a security instrument, brokers should not use such a form without having it reviewed by the buyer's legal counsel.

PRIORITY

An executed security instrument is a lien upon the property it secures, and the priority of a lien, in relationship to other liens, is determined by the date and time it is entered into the public records. A mortgage recorded before another mortgage is said to be prior or senior to a mortgage recorded later; a mortgage recorded after another mortgage is said to be junior or subordinate to one that is recorded earlier.

SUBORDINATION

A *subordination* clause in a mortgage or deed of trust is an agreement by the lender to subordinate its lien upon the property to a prior lien for the benefit of another creditor.

Subordination provisions are most commonly used when the holder of the mortgage agrees to subordinate its lien to a construction loan. A subordination clause may also be used when the holder of a second lien subordinates to a new, increased first lien used to improve the property and thus enhance the value of the lender's security.

To be enforceable, the courts ordinarily require that the lien to which subordination is granted be clearly and specifically described.

A partial release, partial satisfaction or reconveyance clause is used when the lender has agreed to reconvey a portion of the real property that secures its debt when a portion of that debt has been paid. Such clauses are common when the parties contemplate that the real property, which furnishes security for the mortgage or the deed of trust, will be subdivided and that portions will be sold to third parties. The creditor needs to be certain that the remaining property is sufficient to secure the remaining portion to the debt and that the reconveyance will not adversely affect the value of the remaining property. For example, when a large parcel of real property is being developed, it is common to include in the reconveyance provisions that the property reconveyed will be contiguous to other property that is reconveyed and that there be sufficient access to the property remaining subject to the encumbrance so that it will retain its value.

A real estate broker should not undertake to negotiate the provisions of either a subordination clause or a reconveyance clause. Such clauses are important contractual matters that should be drafted by legal counsel.

FORECLOSURE

Foreclosure is a procedure prescribed by law whereby real property, pledged as security for repayment of a debt, is sold to pay the debt in the event of default.

In the event the borrower defaults, the lender's remedy is foreclosure. The debtor, or any other person having an interest in the property (such as a junior lienholder), has the right to redeem the property any time after the obligation is due and before his or her right of redemption ends. The length of the redemption period varies from state to state.

Judicial foreclosure is a foreclosure ordered by a court following the filing of an action for that purpose by the holder of a mortgage or deed of trust. This procedure is used in states where there is no power of sale included in the mortgage or deed of trust, or where there is a controversy about the terms of the mortgage or the deed of trust or the amount due. In some states, a deficiency judgment is allowed only in connection with a judicial foreclosure. In some states, the debtor has the right to redeem the property from sale within a specified period by paying the buyer the purchase price, interest and expense of maintaining the property.

Nonjudicial foreclosure proceedings are allowed in some states under a power of sale contained in a mortgage or deed of trust. The proceedings are conducted without the filing of any court proceeding. The lender, or the lender's trustee, has the right to sell the property upon default following the procedure set forth in state law and the terms of the mortgage or deed of trust. The procedure normally allows the debtor a period in which to cure the default under the secured obligation, and requires that the sale be made at a public auction following proper notice. In some states, the creditor cannot obtain a deficiency judgment if foreclosure proceedings take place without the aid of a court.

A *deficiency judgment* is a judgment against a debtor, endorser, guarantor or other party who may be liable for the debt when the security for the loan is insufficient to satisfy the debt because the sale proceeds are less than the amount due. A deficiency judgment may not be available in some states where the sale was made under a power of sale contained in the mortgage or deed of trust. Where available, a deficiency judgment can only be granted in a court proceeding. In some states, the court makes an independent determination with respect to whether or not the property was sold for less than its fair value at the foreclosure sale.

ACCELERATION—DUE ON SALE

The term *acceleration clause*, also called *alienation clause*, refers to a provision in a note and deed of trust or mortgage requiring immediate payment of the entire unpaid balance of principal and interest upon the occurrence of a specified event or events.

One of the two common types of acceleration clauses, contained in most notes, makes the entire amount of unpaid principal and interest become immediately due and payable upon default, at the option of the lender. Although this right of the lender is usually stated without qualification, in most states there are laws that permit the borrower to reinstate his or her right upon payment within a specified time and upon reimbursement to the lender of costs incurred.

The other type of acceleration clause, referred to as a *due-on-sale* or *alienation clause*, makes the entire amount of unpaid principal and interest immediately due and payable upon the sale, transfer and sometimes further encumbrance of the property or any part thereof or interest therein, at the option of the lender.

Acceleration is at the option of the lender; but without an acceleration clause, the lender cannot accelerate the obligation upon default or transfer.

The due-on-sale clause enables the lender to exercise or waive its option to accelerate the payment date. The lender can, therefore, approve or disapprove of a buyer wishing to assume the loan; the lender can forbear its right to accelerate in return for an increased interest rate.

ASSUMING—TAKING SUBJECT TO A MORTGAGE

A mortgage loan is *assumed* when a written assumption agreement is executed between the lender and the purchaser of the property. Thus, the primary responsibility for repayment of the loan is placed upon the new owner.

In the event no due-on-sale clause is provided in the mortgage or trust deed, the lender cannot require a purchaser to sign an assumption agreement, nor can the lender raise the interest rate or make any other demands. In such event, the purchaser is said to buy the property subject to the mortgage loan, rather than to assume it.

In some states, either by statute or court decisions, due-on-sale clauses were made unenforceable.

The U.S. Supreme Court held in 1982 that a due-on-sale clause in a mortgage or deed of trust securing a note to a federal savings and loan association was enforceable notwithstanding state laws to the contrary.

Life insurance companies, due to the long-term nature of their investment objectives, rarely provide due-on-sale clauses in their mortgages. On the contrary, they charge high prepayment penalties and often lock in a mortgage during the initial portion of the term, which means that the loan may not be paid off under any circumstances.

From the seller's point of view, when a mortgage is assumed, the assumption agreement between the lender and the new owner places the primary responsibility for repayment of the mortgage upon the new owner. If, on the other hand, the property is sold subject to the mortgage, the person primarily responsible for repayment of the mortgage debt is the original maker of the note. The fact that the new owner makes the payments after the sale is consummated does not place the obligation to pay off the mortgage debt upon the new owner because he or she never agreed to do so in writing; the only party with whom the lender has a contractual relationship is the original borrower. Sellers who allow buyers to purchase subject to the mortgage should be aware of their contingent liability. In the event of default, the lender would foreclose, and as long as the property can be sold for sufficient net proceeds to satisfy the balance of the mortgage, the lender is satisfied and the original borrower is released of all obligations with respect to the mortgage. Only if the property does not bring sufficient net proceeds to pay off the balance of the loan will the lender have legal recourse to recover the deficiency. Some states do not permit deficiency judgments against the original borrower when the loan was made for the purpose of acquisition of the borrower's home or when the lender exercises its right to foreclose without a court proceeding.

PREPAYMENT

A *prepayment penalty* or *fee* in a loan document requires the borrower to pay a penalty for paying off the loan before maturity.

Where prepayment fees are not prohibited, the borrower cannot prepay a real estate loan before maturity unless the lender consents or unless expressly permitted by the terms of the note (stating periodic payments of a certain sum or more). Therefore, unless the mortgage note permits unlimited payments or provides for a specific prepayment fee, the lender is in a position to negotiate the charge it will accept in return for consent to an early payoff. This may be of particular concern in the case of private loans, including those financed by the seller.

FHA, VA, Fannie Mae and Freddie Mac do not allow prepayment fees in their loan documents.

TYPES OF MORTGAGES

To increase available financing options to cover various financial situations, government agencies and the lending and real estate industries continue to create new alternative mortgage instruments and financing techniques.

ALTERNATIVE MORTGAGE INSTRUMENTS

Fixed Rate Mortgage (FRM)

A *fixed rate mortgage* provides for repayment of the principal amount (the unpaid balance of a loan) over a specified number of years in equal monthly payments, which include interest. Monthly interest is computed on the outstanding principal balance. The difference between the note payment and the interest reduces the principal. As the principal of the loan is reduced, the interest portion of the monthly payment becomes smaller while the principal payment increases each month.

Biweekly Mortgage

A *biweekly mortgage* provides for payments amounting to one half the monthly payments and are due every two weeks. Because there are 52 weeks in a year, the program results in 26 biweekly payments or the equivalent of 13 monthly payments per year. The result is a considerable reduction in the term of the mortgage, as well as a savings in total interest paid. As an example, the monthly payments necessary to amortize a $70,000 mortgage at 8% interest over a term of 30 years amount to $513.64. Biweekly payments of $256.82 would amortize the same mortgage in 22 years and 7 months.

	Monthly Payments	*Biweekly Payments*
Loan amount	$70,000	$70,000
Interest rate	10%	10%
Payments	$614.30	$307.15
Number of payments per year	12	26
Total of amount paid per year	12 × $614.30 = $7,371.60	26 × $307.15 = $7,985.90
Terms in years	**30 years**	**20.96 years**
	$7,371.60 × 30 =	$7,985.90 × 20.96 =
Total payments	$221,148	$167,384
Minus principal	-$70,000	-$70,000
Total interest	$151,148	$97,384
Interest savings	$151,148 – $97,384 = $53,764	

Adjustable Rate Mortgage (ARM)

The concept of variable rate financing calls for the borrower to share with the lender the risks of a fluctuating economy.

An ARM, or *adjustable rate mortgage*, is a mortgage that provides for interest rate adjustments that are tied to an independent index.

Although the terms of ARM programs vary widely, there are several characteristics common to most adjustable rate financing plans:

1. **The index** is an indicator of current economic conditions and is used to calculate the new interest rate. Following are the only requirements a lender must meet in selecting an index.
   a. The index must be beyond the control of the lender.
   b. The index must be readily available to, and verifiable by, the public. Rate increases are at the option of the lender while rate decreases are mandatory.

Indices used by lenders include: One-Year Treasury Bill Rates, Three- and Five-Year Treasury Note Rates, Federal Reserve Discount Rates, Eleventh District Cost of Funds Index and LIBOR (London InterBank Offer Rate), the rate at which commercial banks lend money to one another in the international market.

Cost of Funds. The national median cost of funds to SAIF-insured institutions as reported by the Office of Thrift Supervision, Washington, D.C., (202) 906-6000.

Contract Rate. The national average contract interest rate for major lenders as reported by the Federal Housing Finance Board, Washington, D.C., (202) 408-2500.

Eleventh District Cost of Funds. The cost of funds for the 11th District as released by the Federal Home Loan Bank of San Francisco (415) 616-2600.

One-Year Treasury Securities (T-Bills). The one-year constant maturity yield on U.S. Treasury securities as reported by the Federal Reserve Board, Washington, D.C., (202) 452-3400.

2. **The margin,** also referred to as the spread or differential, is the percentage added to the index rate in order to arrive at what is referred to as the *full indexed rate*. The margin should be clearly stated in the note and should remain constant throughout the term of the loan. At each adjustment interval, the interest rate is recalculated by adding the margin to the index rate. The margin varies with lender, type of index and market conditions.

CAUTION: When selecting an ARM, buyers should be cautioned about so-called incentive teaser rates offered by many lenders to help qualify the buyer. These are introductory below-market rates, referred to as *initial note rates,* in effect for a limited time (typically 6 or 12 months). At the end of that period, the interest rate is adjusted to the *full indexed rate.* In the event of a large difference between the teaser rate and the full indexed rate, the increase in monthly payments could be a shocking experience to a home owner. (Fannie Mae's refusal to buy such loans has made them much less of a factor.)

3. **The adjustment interval** is the frequency with which the interest rate and/or the monthly payment amount can be reset. There is a wide variety of ARM loans in the market today with adjustment intervals ranging from several months to a number of years. Adjustments to the consumer's mortgage interest rate can only occur on a predetermined time schedule. Fannie Mae and Freddie Mac will not purchase loans that adjust more often than annually. The interest rate and payment adjustments may or may not be scheduled to change at the same time. For example, the interest rate on some plans changes more frequently than the monthly payment, which may result in negative amortization. This means that the additional interest is added to the principal balance of the loan and may accrue additional interest itself.

4. **The cap** is a restriction on the periodic or lifetime change in interest rate or payment amount. A *periodic cap* limits the percentage of change at periodic or annual intervals. A *lifetime cap* sets a maximum on the percentage the interest rate can change from the initial note rate over the entire term of the loan. Typical caps for conventional loans are 2% annually and 6% lifetime. FHA and VA loans have caps of 1% and 5% respectively.

Negative Amortization. Although interest caps offer protection to the borrower, payment caps without corresponding interest caps can result

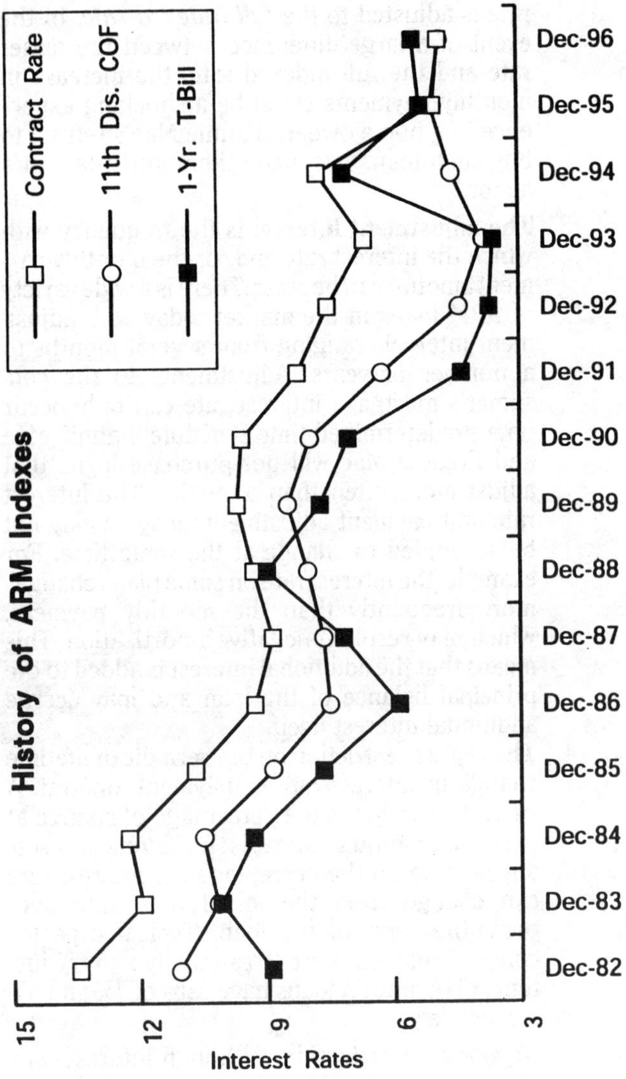
History of ARM Indexes
Contract Rate
11th Dis. COF
1-Yr. T-Bill
Dec-96
Dec-95
Dec-94
Dec-93
Dec-92
Dec-91
Dec-90
Dec-89
Dec-88
Dec-87
Dec-86
Dec-85
Dec-84
Dec-83
Dec-82
15
12
9
6
3
Interest Rates

in considerable negative amortization in which the interest portion not covered by payments is added to the balance of the loan. This can result in the borrower owing more than the original loan amount. Fannie Mae and Freddie Mac refuse to buy ARM loans with negative amortization.

Lenders may restrict the amount of negative amortization by recasting the loan every few years, or whenever the loan balance has increased a certain percentage over and above the original loan amount. When a loan is recast, the monthly payment—regardless of any payment cap—is refigured based on the then-remaining loan balance, the remaining term of the loan and the interest rate then in effect. This can result in very considerable payment increases, as much as 30%.

As a result, it may be difficult to obtain secondary financing from lenders and sellers carrying back seconds behind assumed first loans with negative amortization.

The following example of interest rate adjustments incorporates a 2% annual interest cap.

Year	Index	+	Margin	=	Calc. Rate	New Rate
1	4.50	+	2.75	=	7.25	7.25
2	6.00	+	2.75	=	8.75	8.75
3	9.00	+	2.75	=	11.75	10.75
4	5.50	+	2.75	=	8.25	8.75
5	5.50	+	2.75	=	7.25	7.25

Yr 1: Lender and borrower agreed to a contract rate of 7.25% for the first year, with annual adjustments based on the index plus a margin of 2.75%.

Yr 2: The index increases 1.5% (from 4.5% to 6%). *Index + Margin* = 7.25%. Because the increase is less than the 2% annual cap, the new rate is 8.75%.

Yr 3: The index increases 3% (from 6% to 9%). *Index + Margin* = 11.75%; however, because of the 2% annual interest cap, the new rate is only 10.75%.

Yr 4: The index decreases 3.5% (from 9% to 5.50%). *Index + Margin* = 8.25%. The annual 2% interest cap, however, limits the interest decrease, and the rate is 8.75%.

Yr 5: The index remains the same as in previous year. *Index + Margin* = 8.25%. This is within the annual 2% cap, so the new interest rate decreases to 7.25%.

Advantages of ARMs

1. The initial interest rate is generally quite a bit below the going fixed rate, which means that the monthly payments are lower and more buyers can afford them.

2. It may be easier to qualify borrowers for an ARM because the initial rate is lower. Borrowers may have a much harder time qualifying for a fixed rate mortgage because their monthly payments are higher, which may put their income-to-debt ratio beyond the maximum. (Most lenders follow Fannie Mae guidelines and require borrowers to qualify at the initial rate plus 2%.)

3. Lenders usually permit assumptions, provided the new buyer meets credit standards. This is not nearly as common with a fixed rate mortgage.

4. Generally, there are no prepayment penalties.

Convertible ARMs

Convertible ARMs were introduced to the market by Fannie Mae in 1987. This type of ARM allows the borrower to convert to a fixed rate mortgage, usually any time from the 13th through the 60th month.

When a borrower converts, the new interest rate is usually ⅝% over Fannie Mae's 60-day posted yield for fixed rate mortgages. The borrower is sometimes charged a conversion fee of about 1% of the original principal balance plus a processing fee that may not exceed $250.

A borrower's cost to convert may be substantially less than the cost of refinancing, but this is not always true.

Lenders must provide borrowers with an adjustable rate program disclosure upon discussing any adjustable program.

Potential borrowers should be cautioned to carefully analyze the wide differences between ARMs before committing themselves to this type of financing.

Growing Equity Mortgage (GEM)

A *GEM* provides for a gradual increase in monthly payments with all of the increase being applied to the principal balance, resulting in a relatively rapid accumulation of equity and an accelerated maturity.

GEMs offer borrowers an affordable starting monthly payment based on 30-year amortization and predetermined increases, usually 3% to 5% annually, for a specified period.

Because the payment increases are applied to principal only, the mortgage balance is reduced more quickly than usual. Homebuyers who expect to earn rising incomes, or who are interested in paying off their loan in less time than with a traditional loan, find GEMs appealing.

DATE: _____	LENDER 1	LENDER 2
Name of Lender	_____	_____
Loan amount	$_____	$_____
Points charged	_____%	_____%
Index used	_____	_____
Current index rate	_____%	_____%
Margin used	_____%	_____%
Contract rate	_____%	_____%
Contract rate guaranteed as of:		
❑ Submission date	_____	_____
❑ Loan approval date	_____	_____
❑ Closing date	_____	_____
Fee (if any) to lock in rate earlier	_____%	_____%
Initial monthly payment	$_____	$_____
APR	_____%	_____%
APR of fixed rate loan	_____%	_____%
Initial discounted rate, if any	_____%	_____%
Term of discounted rate	_____mos.	_____mos.
Interest rate when discount rate ends:		
❑ Contract rate	_____	_____
❑ Adjusted rate	_____	_____
First interest rate adjustment date		
First interest rate adjustment %, assuming no index change	_____%	_____%

First payment adjustment date _____ _____

Regular rate adjustment period _____mos. _____mos.

Regular payment adjustment _____mos. _____mos.
period

Lifetime interest cap, if any _____% _____%

Periodic interest cap, if any _____% _____%

Can interest rate increase in excess _____ _____
of cap be carried over to next
adjustment?

Does periodic interest cap apply to _____ _____
index decreases?

Does lifetime interest cap apply to _____ _____
index decreases?

Method of calculating interest rate if index decreases:

❑ Interest rate bottoms at contract _____ _____
rate

❑ Interest rate declines same % as _____ _____
index

❑ Other _____ _____

Lifetime payment cap, if any _____ _____

Periodic payment cap, if any _____ _____

Can negative amortization occur? _____ _____

When is loan recast to pay off increase in principal balance due
to negative amortization:

❑ Periodically _____yrs _____yrs

❑ When balance exceeds _____% _____%
original by

Does payment cap apply to payment increases resulting from recasting of the loan due to negative amortization?

   _____   _____

Can ARM be converted to fixed rate?

   _____   _____

Can loan term be extended?

   _____   _____

Open end (add on) feature?

   _____   _____

Is ARM assumable?

   _____   _____

Assumable for one time only?

   _____   _____

Assumption conditions:

❑ Customary credit standards

   _____   _____

❑ Assumption fee

   _____   _____

❑ Original periodic caps remaining?

   _____   _____

❑ Original lifetime cap remaining?

   _____   _____

Prepayment penalty, if any

   _____   _____

Graduated Payment Mortgage (GPM)

The interest rate remains fixed throughout the term of the loan, but the monthly payments start out at a low level and gradually increase (for example, at 3% a year) until they rise above the level at which a standard fixed rate mortgage would have been written.

The amount of house a family can buy depends upon its current income, and so the GPM is particularly attractive to the young family buying its first home, because the income requirements to qualify for a GPM are significantly less than those for a fixed rate mortgage. A GPM enables a family to raise its housing standard to a level that averages out more accurately with its expected lifetime income.

A major drawback of the GPM is that a family's income may not increase in line with the rate of increase in the payments.

Graduated Payment Adjustable Rate Mortgage (GPARM)

The GPARM is a blend of the GPM and ARM. Buyers can take advantage of the initial low payments of a GPM while lenders get the flexible rate advantage of the ARM. The GPARM is not accepted by Fannie Mae.

EQUAL™ Mortgage

The EQUAL™ mortgage combines a fixed rate interest, buydown, graduated payments without negative amortization and a known payment schedule.

- *Buydown:* By enabling the borrower to buy down the interest rate, the initial rate is substantially reduced from the note rate, thus producing lower monthly payments on which to qualify.
- *One- or Two-Year Initial Payments:* At the borrower's option, the initial payment is maintained for the first year or the first two years of the mortgage.
- *Yearly Increased Payments:* After one or two years the monthly payments are adjusted upward by 7.5% per year until level payments are reached to amortize the mortgage over the balance of its term.
- *EQUAL™ Mortgages:* Available for 15- or 30-year terms.
- *Down Payment:* 20%
- *Other:* No prepayment penalty, limited documentation, no income verification.

Rate Improvement Mortgage (RIM)

A *RIM* is a 30-year fixed rate mortgage with a one-time interest rate improvement option. Lenders charge a conversion fee and a processing fee.

Pledged Account Mortgage (PAM) or Flexible Loan Insurance Program (FLIP)

The *pledged account mortgage* is a form of GPM. In order to reduce the monthly payments during the first years of the loan, the buyer places part of the cash intended for the down payment into a pledged interest-bearing savings account. The lender makes a fixed rate mortgage. During the early years of the loan the borrower makes monthly payments considerably smaller than the payment that would amortize the fixed rate mortgage. The deficit is made up of monthly withdrawals from the pledged savings account. The borrower's portion of the payments increases and the withdrawals decline annually until the pledged account is exhausted at the end of the graduation period.

Example

Purchase price	$100,000
Available cash	20,000
Deposit in pledged account	15,000
Down payment	5,000
Fixed rate mortgage (with private mortgage insurance) @ 8% interest for 30 years, payable $697 per month	95,000
First year's monthly payments	500
First year's monthly pledged account withdrawal	197

Reverse Mortgage

In the past, senior citizen homeowners have faced the problem of not being able to utilize the equity in their homes without mortgaging again, or selling their homes and moving.

Today, a number of government-backed and private reverse mortgage programs enable seniors to convert the equity in their homes into cash without the need of making monthly payments. In some programs all the money can be taken out in a single *lump sum* of cash, and some programs combine a lump sum at closing with a credit line or monthly advances; they can be *term advances* (for a fixed period), *tenure advances* (for as long as the recipient lives in the home), or *lifetime advances* (for as long as the recipient lives, wherever he or she lives).

Lifetime advances can be guaranteed by combining a reverse mortgage with an *annuity* (a contract with a life insurance company to pay a fixed amount for the rest of one's life).

The following reverse mortgage programs, available now, offer these choices:

	Single Lump Sum	Credit Line	Term Advances	Tenure Advances	Lifetime Advances
HUD/ HECM[1]	YES	YES	YES	YES	NO
Fannie Mae[2]	YES	YES	NO	YES	NO
Household	YES	YES	NO	NO	NO
Home First	YES	YES	YES	NO	YES
Freedom	YES	NO	YES	NO	YES
Fixed Term	NO	NO	YES	NO	NO

Note 1   HECM = Home Equity Conversion Mortgage (see FHA FINANCING)

Note 2   Home Keeper Mortgage (see CONVENTIONAL FINANCING)

The nonprofit National Center of Home Equity Conversion (NCHEC), the leading authority on reverse mortgages, publishes *Your New Retirement Nest Egg–A Consumer Guide to The New Reverse Mortgages* (2nd edition, 352 pages, 1996) by Ken Scholen. The book features the first independent analysis of the new Fannie Mae plan, "Home Keeper Mortgage," and compares it in detail to the other reverse mortgage plans. Also included is a nationwide list of Reverse Mortgage Lenders with telephone numbers. The book is available for $24.95 plus $4.50 shipping directly from NCHEC, 7373 147th Street West, Suite 115, Apple Valley, MN 55124; telephone 1-800-247-6553. The list of Reverse Mortgage Lenders may also be obtained separately from NCHEC by sending a self-addressed, stamped business envelope and $1.00 to NCHEC Locator, 7373 147th St., Apple Valley, MN 55124.

Zero Percent Mortgage (ZPM)

With a typical *ZPM*, the buyer makes a large cash down payment, perhaps one-third of the purchase price, with the remaining balance payable in equal monthly installments over five years with no interest. The payments are comparable with those of a fixed rate 30-year mortgage at current interest rates.

Example

	ZPM	Fixed Rate Mortgage
Price	$100,000	$100,000
Down payment	33,000	20,000
Loan amount	67,000	80,000
Term of loan	5 years	30 years
Interest	0%	17%
Monthly payments	$1,100	$1,140

Taxation of ZPM Payments

For federal income tax purposes, when there is a sale of property and a portion of the purchase price is deferred, interest is imputed when no interest is stated or when the interest is less than the minimum allowable. (See Imputed Interest in the Tax Information section.) Interest is imputed at the lower of 9% or the applicable federal rate. Consequently, a portion of each payment is interest income to the seller and constitutes deductible interest to the buyer, subject to the limitations of the Internal Revenue Code.

Pros and Cons

To the buyer, the advantages of a ZPM are a home completely paid for in five years and avoidance of the high cost of interest. The problem, of course, is the requirement of a large down payment.

The seller has the advantage of facilitating the sale of his or her home, or in the case of a builder, moving his or her inventory. The disadvantage to the seller is the deferment of the receipt of the full purchase price without interest while incurring tax liability for imputed interest.

However, the interest-free benefit to the buyer may be illusory if the purchase price has been adjusted by adding a premium as an alternative to the stated interest. The buyer should compare the price of the property if purchased on an all-cash basis against the price with the ZPM.

Variations of ZPMs

Any number of variations to ZPMs have been devised by homebuilders. In one variation, a buyer with a low down payment is offered a ZPM and a second mortgage at current interest rates accumulating for five years with no monthly payments. After five years, when the ZPM is paid off, the buyer begins making payments on the second mortgage in the same amount as the payments on the ZPM.

Example

Purchase price:	$100,000
Down payment:	$15,000
ZPM:	$65,000, payable @ $1,084 for five years
Second mortgage:	$20,000, accumulating interest @ 8%

With a negative amortization of 8% per year for five years, the principal of the second mortgage has increased to $29,400. With monthly payments of $1,084 including interest at 8%, the second mortgage will be retired in less than three years.

Shared Equity Mortgage (SEM)

Through a sale-leaseback arrangement called a *shared equity mortgage*, parents sell their home to their children or to other investors, then lease it back for the remainder of their lives. Sales proceeds are invested in a life annuity on behalf of the parents. After deduction of rent, the annuity payments go to the parents.

Shared Appreciation Mortgage (SAM)

Under a *SAM,* the lender offers a below-market interest rate in return for a percentage in the appreciation of the property. Typically, the home is appraised in five years, with the lender being entitled to 40% of the increase (which is added to the mortgage balance).

Unsecured Loan

A very well-qualified borrower can obtain an *unsecured loan* or line of credit, which may be used for almost any purpose, from a lending institution. The individual must have outstanding income, savings and credit. Unsecured loans are not normally committed for more than a year at a time, and the interest rate is generally stated as the lender's prime rate plus an agreed upon percentage above that rate. Although this money could be used to purchase a home and would not appear as a lien against the property, an unsecured loan is not normally suitable for financing real estate, other than perhaps as an interim loan or construction loan.

THE SECONDARY MORTGAGE MARKET

The *secondary mortgage market* is an investor market in which blocks of residential mortgage loans, originated by lending institutions, are purchased and assembled into mortgage pools for the issuance of mortgage-backed securities. The main players among these so-called poolers are Fannie Mae, Freddie Mac, investment bankers, a few large commercial banks and some state and local housing agencies. By purchasing mortgages, these investors provide local lenders new funds to make more home loans, thereby assuring homebuyers a continual supply of credit.

Pool underwriting procedures began in the early 1970s on a small scale, reaching a peak level by 1982. There are now four agencies involved in this activity:

1. Fannie Mae (FNMA)
2. Freddie Mac (FHLMC)
3. Ginnie Mae (GNMA) and
4. Farmer Mac (FAMC)

Since 1992, these agencies have held in portfolio or issued underwriting guaranties on more than 45% of all residential mortgage debt in the United States. Because the ability to sell a mortgage loan into any of the agency pools represents good liquidity (the ability to convert any asset into immediate cash), many loan originators tend to follow agency requirements whether they expect to sell the loan immediately or not.

Investors of mortgage-backed securities look not only for yields in comparison with other investments, but also for safety and salability. The safety factor is provided by government backing of FHA, VA and conventional loans. Salability and liquidity have been accomplished through standardization of mortgage instruments, terms and credit standards brought about by Fannie Mae and Freddie Mac. To make their loans salable in the secondary market, lending institutions incorporate these standards into their underwriting guidelines.

THE FOUR FEDERAL UNDERWRITING AGENCIES

Fannie Mae, Freddie Mac, Ginnie Mae and Farmer Mac differ somewhat in how they function and in how congressional authority within each of these agencies must work.

Fannie Mae, Freddie Mac and *Farmer Mac* are publicly owned by stockholders, but maintain close ties to the federal government. *Ginnie Mae* is a government agency operating under the U.S. Department of Housing and Urban Development (HUD).

Fannie Mae and Freddie Mac are authorized either to purchase loans for their own portfolio or to underwrite loans, whereas Ginnie Mae and Farmer Mac are limited to approving loan pools and issuing guaranty certificates based upon approved pools. Neither makes outright purchases of mortgage loans.

Only one federal agency, Ginnie Mae, carries the authority to issue a government guaranty on its certificates, meaning the full faith and credit of the U.S. government. The other three issue "agency guaranties."

FEDERAL NATIONAL MORTGAGE ASSOCIATION (FANNIE MAE)

Fannie Mae was founded as a government agency in 1938 to purchase (not underwrite) FHA loans. In 1944, VA loans were added to its approved list of loans. All these loans were held in portfolio. In 1954, Fannie Mae was rechartered and granted authority to sell its mortgage loans with purchases made at discount prices rather than at par. In 1968, Fannie Mae became a private corporation through a partitioning that created the Government National Mortgage Association (Ginnie Mae). In 1972, Fannie Mae enlarged its mortgage operations by adding conventional loans.

To make the purchase of conventional loans practical, it was necessary to create a uniform pattern of documents, qualifying requirements and insurance against loan default, which was accomplished in cooperation with Freddie Mac. The result, called a conforming loan, is a standardized conventional loan written on uniform documents that meets the purchase requirements of both agencies.

Today, Fannie Mae is authorized to purchase FHA, VA and conventional loans that conform to its requirements. Loan purchases are made for two separate purposes:

1. its own portfolio and
2. creation of mortgage pools.

The guaranty securities Fannie Mae issues, backed by its mortgage pools, are called MBSs (mortgage-backed securities) in financial markets.

FEDERAL HOME LOAN MORTGAGE CORPORATION (FREDDIE MAC)

Freddie Mac was created in 1970 and placed under the administration of the Federal Home Loan Bank Board. In 1989, the FHLBB was abolished and Freddie Mac was shifted to a new regulator and new management.

Almost from its inception, Freddie Mac purchased loans for the purpose of creating its own mortgage pools. A Freddie Mac pool generally is made up of a large, geographically diverse block of residential loans. Each designated pool collateralizes a series of mortgage participation certificates, called PCs in financial markets. In 1983, Freddie Mac issued the first collateralized mortgage obligation (CMO).

GOVERNMENT NATIONAL MORTGAGE ASSOCIATION (GINNIE MAE)

Ginnie Mae was created when Fannie Mae was restructured in 1968. Ginnie Mae operates as a part of HUD. Of the four federal underwriting agencies, Ginnie Mae is the only true government entity, and it continues to serve as the government's agency whenever Congress authorizes housing assistance programs.

Ginnie Mae is limited to underwriting only VA and certain FHA loans.

Unlike Fannie Mae and Freddie Mac, Ginnie Mae does not purchase loans to create pools. It does set its own requirements for loans that can be accepted into a mortgage pool, then subsequently approves loan poolers who are committed to complying with those requirements. The loan poolers can be any Ginnie Mae-approved company, such as investment bankers, finance companies, mortgage companies, homebuilders, real estate brokers, insurance companies or others.

The poolers then either originate or buy qualified mortgage loans from other loan originators across the country. When a pool is designated, Ginnie Mae is asked to grant its underwriting certificate, called a Ginnie Mae. The servicing (collecting monthly payments and handling the escrow accounts) of individual loans remains with the loan originator or a specialized servicing company.

FARM SERVICE AGENCY (F.S.A.–Formerly Known as Farmer Mac)

The Agricultural Credit Act of 1987 established Farmer Mac as a separate agency within the Farm Credit System to develop a secondary market in farm real estate loans.

To qualify for a pool, a loan must be collateralized by agricultural real estate in the United States that can include a home costing not more than $100,000 that is in a rural community with a population of 2,500 or less. The maximum loan is the larger of $2.5 million or that secured by no more than 1,000 acres.

LENDING SOURCES

INSTITUTIONAL LENDERS

Savings Associations (Formerly Savings and Loan Associations)

The deregulation of the savings and loan industry, brought about by the Depository Institutions' Deregulation and Monetary Control Act of 1980 and the Garn-St. Germain Depository Act of 1982, was intended to give relief from the adversities thrifts experienced in the 1970s. As a result, S&Ls were allowed to branch out from their traditional role as residential real estate lenders into nonresidential loans and consumer financing. A new downturn of the economy in the mid-1980s gradually led to riskier investments that resulted in growing numbers of thrift failures. It culminated in the dramatic S&L crisis, which cost taxpayers more than $100 billion.

In 1989, Congress passed the Financial Institutions Reform, Recovery and Enforcement Act (FIRREA), which eliminated the Federal Home Loan Bank Board and the Federal Savings and Loan Insurance Corporation. They were replaced by the Federal Housing Finance Board, the Office of Thrift Supervision and the Savings Association Insurance Fund. At the same time, FIRREA changed the name savings and loan association to *savings association*. The reorganized Federal Deposit Insurance Corporation (FDIC) now controls the Savings Association Insurance Fund (SAIF), which insures deposits in savings associations, and the Bank Insurance Fund (BIF), which insures deposits in commercial banks and savings banks.

FIRREA also imposed new restrictions on savings associations to reverse the practice of high-risk investments and to encourage more residential lending. The dominating market position savings associations once held in residential lending is now shared to a large extent by mortgage bankers and also by commercial banks.

Today, most savings associations invest the majority of their assets in residential mortgages and home equity loans, and generally adhere to underwriting guidelines of the secondary market.

Savings Banks

Savings banks, traditionally located in the Northeast, generally provide the same services as savings associations.

Mortgage Companies (Mortgage Bankers)

Mortgage bankers or *mortgage companies,* now the largest force in residential lending, generally specialize in originating FHA, VA and conventional loans, using strict underwriting guidelines. They generally obtain financing from commercial banks via lines of credit and sell their portfolios in the secondary market. Mortgage companies also represent insurance companies and large pension funds as loan correspondents, originating and servicing loans for these investors.

Commercial Banks

Commercial banks remain major participants in the mortgage market by supplying lines of credit to mortgage companies. Commercial banks have surpassed savings associations in market share of residential lending. Most banks sell their residential loans on the secondary market. They tend to give preferential treatment to depositors because customers' deposits constitute most of their assets. Traditionally, banks are a good source for office and apartment building loans, also for commercial construction loans.

Mortgage Brokers

Mortgage brokers originate loans but send them to an institutional lender for underwriting and funding. A mortgage broker's profit is derived from wholesale fees that are built into the retail fees charged by the lender.

Often, mortgage brokers have the most competitive rates because they work with a pool of lenders and programs (some brokers have more than 500 programs to choose from), and they are aware of the lowest interest rates available. Also, they are capable of sending a borrower's loan package to two or three different lenders at the same time, locking in the best rates and securing quicker approval.

After the mortgage broker and the borrower select a program, the loan is processed and the completed package is sent to the lender for underwriting. Documents are drawn, and the lender funds the loan at closing.

Life Insurance Companies

Life insurance companies are regulated by the state in which they operate, as well as by the state in which the company is incorporated. They are usually represented by loan correspondents. A borrower must have an excellent credit payment history to qualify, but insurance companies sometimes allow higher debt-to-income ratios than other lenders.

Pension Funds

Pension funds generally have abundant funds available for investment. Comparatively high yields and their safety factor make mortgages ideal investments for their portfolios. Pension funds buy large blocks of mortgages on the secondary market, or they invest in large mortgages, usually through mortgage bankers.

Pension fund administrators include trust departments of commercial banks and life insurance companies, trustees of union pension funds and boards of trustees of government employee pension funds.

Endowment Funds

Many commercial banks and mortgage bankers handle investments for *endowment funds*. Endowment funds of hospitals, universities, colleges, charitable foundations and other endowed institutions offer a good source of financing for commercial and industrial properties.

Credit Unions

In the past, *credit unions* have specialized in short-term consumer loans for their members, but today they are playing an increasing role in the residential mortgage market by financing homes for their members.

"Wall Street" and Other Private Investors

"Wall Street" and other private investors often form pools for themselves or for public or private partnerships for the purpose of buying and selling mortgages both directly and in the secondary mortgage market, thus creating another source of mortgage funds.

Private individuals are also a source for second mortgage money. Much higher interest rates coupled with discounts render excellent yields to an investor.

LOAN UNDERWRITING

Underwriting a real estate loan is the process of evaluating an applicant as a credit risk and ascertaining that the property is sufficient security for the mortgage.

The underwriting procedure includes the following seven steps:

1. Evaluation of the applicant's stable monthly income;
2. Verification of liquid assets available for down payment, closing costs and reserves;
3. Determination of the applicant's monthly financial obligations;
4. Use of income ratios to compare proposed housing expense with applicant's income;
5. Evaluation of the applicant's credit history (credit report);
6. Valuation of the property pledged as collateral (appraisal); and
7. Establishment of the loan-to-value ratio (LTV) from the maximum loan for which the applicant qualifies (step 4) and the valuation of the property (step 6).

INCOME

In evaluating the borrower's income, the underwriter looks at three aspects:

1. amount of monthly income,
2. dependability of the income source and
3. continuity of stable monthly income.

Acceptable Types of Income

Income from Regular Employment

The borrower should have a history of receiving stable income from employment, have been employed full-time for two full years preceding the loan application and have a reasonable expectation for employment income to continue in the foreseeable future. (To the FHA this means through the first three years of the loan.)

A borrower who changes jobs frequently to advance within the same line of work should receive favorable consideration. On the other hand, job-hopping without advancement, or from one line of work to another, may indicate an inability to master a job and could lead to unstable income.

Borrowers who have recently entered the job market may be considered favorably if adequate future income can be anticipated due to their education and training.

Allowances for seasonal employment, typical in the building and other trades, may be made.

Commission Income

As a general rule, the lender develops an average of two years' commission income. The annual earnings trend is an important consideration.

Overtime and Bonus Income

As a general rule, the lender develops an average of two years' income and requires verification from the employer that such income will in all probability continue.

Part-Time Income or Second Job

Income should be uninterrupted for two years and have a strong likelihood of continuing.

Verification of Employment Income

There are two alternatives:

1. the lender mails a *Verification of Employment* form directly to the employer; or
2. the borrower furnishes W-2 forms for the preceding two years, plus payroll stubs for the previous 30-day period, which the lender confirms with the employer by telephone.

If commission, bonus or overtime income exceeds 25% of the borrower's total income from the employer, the lender requires copies of signed income tax returns for the preceding two years.

Retirement Income

Retirement income may be verified by letters from the organization providing the income, copies of the retirement award letters, tax returns or W-2 forms. (If benefits expire within about five years, the FHA considers this income only a compensating factor.)

Alimony, Child Support, Spousal Maintenance

These types of income must continue for at least three years (five years for the FHA). Acceptable verification is a copy of the divorce decree or separation agreement, which must specify the amount of the award and the period over which it will be received. The borrower must provide evidence that the funds have been received for the last 12 months in the form of deposit slips, canceled checks, court records or tax returns.

Public Assistance Payments

Unemployment and welfare benefits may be considered acceptable income if they are properly documented by the paying agency showing the amount, frequency and duration of the payments. (FHA requires that the income be expected to continue for approximately five years.)

Notes Receivable

Payments must continue for at least three years. Evidence required is a copy of the note showing amount and length of payment, plus deposit slips, canceled checks or tax returns showing funds have been received during the last 12 months.

Interest and Dividends

Such investment income is counted, provided the investment is not cashed in to provide funds for closing. Photocopies of tax returns must show funds have been received for the past two years.

Rental Income

A stable pattern of rental income must be verified by submitting authenticated copies of the property's books showing gross rental income and operating expenses for the previous two years, as well as two years' income tax returns. Lenders generally add only 75% of the verified income to the borrower's stable income.

For qualifying purposes, estimated tax savings from depreciation deductions may be added. Positive rental income is considered gross income; negative rental income must be treated as a recurring liability.

Self-Employment Income

Any individual who has at least a 25% ownership interest in a business is considered to be self-employed and requires the following documentation:

- signed individual federal income tax returns, including Schedule C for sole ownership or partnership business, and other applicable schedules for the most current two years;
- signed corporate federal income tax returns for the most current two years with all applicable schedules, if the business is an S corporation;
- a business credit report, in addition to the individual credit report, if the business is a corporation, an S corporation or a partnership;
- a year-to-date profit and loss statement regardless of the type of entity; and
- a balance sheet for the previous two years if the business is a sole proprietorship.

Knowledge of the structure of the business and the length of time the self-employed borrower has successfully operated the business are important considerations. (The FHA requires the borrower to be self-employed for two or more years, unless the borrower has past employment experience, formal education or training in his or her occupation.)

VA Benefits

Direct compensation, such as for a service-related disability, is acceptable if documented by the VA and if it will continue for at least three years.

Mortgage Credit Certificates and Differential Payments

If the employer or a government entity subsidizes the mortgage payments, either through direct payments or through tax rebates, these payments can be considered acceptable income if verified in writing. Either type of subsidy may be added to gross income before calculating gross ratios.

Trust Income

Income from trusts may be used if guaranteed, constant payment will continue for at least three years (for the FHA, five years). The documentation includes a copy of the trust agreement or trustee's statement confirming amount, frequency and duration of payments.

Unacceptable Types of Income

- Expense account payments, except for any excess of receipts over expenditures
- Retained earnings in a company
- Rent from boarders in a single-family property that is also the borrower's primary residence or second home
- Temporary employment

ASSETS AVAILABLE FOR DOWN PAYMENT AND CLOSING

The underwriter verifies that the borrower has sufficient funds or liquid assets for closing and adequate reserves to handle financial emergencies, such as unexpected bills or interruption of income. Cash equal to at least two mortgage payments is considered an adequate reserve.

Typical Sources of Liquid Assets

Earnest Money Deposit on Purchase Contract

The required documentation is a canceled check and/or verification of deposit.

Bank Accounts

The request for verification of deposit is used to verify each checking and savings account. The underwriter checks the verifications for

- any information that does not conform to the statements in the loan application,
- recently opened accounts and
- any large increases in existing accounts.

Stocks and Bonds

Stocks and bonds must be properly verified.

IRA/Keogh Accounts

Only the net withdrawal amount may be counted.

Trust Account

Trust account funds can be used if the applicant has access to them and if they can be verified.

Gifts or Grants

If the applicant is short of funds for closing, gifts may be used to supplement the funds needed for closing, provided the donor is a relative, church, municipality or nonprofit organization, and provided further that the applicant makes a down payment of at least 5% of the purchase price.

A gift from a relative, evidenced by a signed letter, must

- specify the amount of the gift and the date the funds were transferred;
- indicate the donor's name, address, telephone number and relationship to the borrower; and
- include the donor's statement that no repayment is expected.

A gift (or grant) from a church, municipality or nonprofit organization must be evidenced by either a copy of the letter awarding the gift or grant, or a copy of the legal agreement that specifies the terms and conditions of the gift or grant.

The donor of the gift may not be a person or entity with an interest in the sale of the property, such as the seller, real estate agent or broker, builder or any entity associated with them.

Sales Proceeds

Proceeds from the sale of a currently owned home are a common and acceptable source for the down payment and closing costs on a new house, as well as for the required reserve. A photocopy of the fully executed settlement statement on the sale of the home, showing sufficient net cash proceeds to consummate the purchase of the new home, must be used to verify the source of these funds.

Anticipated Sales Proceeds

If the borrower's currently owned home is listed for sale but has not yet been sold, the lender may temporarily qualify the applicant on the basis of his or her anticipated equity.

Formula to determine the equity in a house sold but not yet closed:

Sales Price – Sales Costs – All Liens = Equity

Formula to determine the equity in a house listed for sale:

*Listing Price – 10% of Listing Price –
All Liens = Equity*

Bridge Loans

Bridge, or *swing, loans* are secured by the borrower's present home, which is usually for sale. By using funds from a bridge loan, the borrower can close on a new house before selling his or her existing house. This type of financing is acceptable if

- the purchaser has the ability to carry the payment on the new home, the payment on other obligations, the payment on the current home and the payment on the bridge loan; and
- the bridge loan is not cross-collateralized against the new property.

Construction Loans

For the purpose of financing the construction of a home on a lot owned by the applicant, any equity in the lot may be applied toward the down payment.

Example

Estimated construction costs	$100,000
Lot value	+ 20,000
Total property value	$120,000
Maximum loan at 80% LTV	− 96,000
Down payment	$ 24,000
Lot value	$ 20,000
Mortgage against lot	− 5,000
Equity in lot	$ 15,000
Down payment	$ 24,000
Equity in lot	− 15,000
Remaining down payment in cash	$ 9,000

Trade Equity

Property equity as part of the down payment when the seller takes a borrower's existing property in trade is acceptable as long as the borrower has made a 5% cash down payment and the equity contribution is a true-value consideration. This is determined as follows:

The lesser of the trade property's appraised value or agreed trade-in-value *minus* outstanding loan balance *minus* transfer costs.

The appraisal must be a residential appraisal (conventional, FHA or VA) not more than six months old.

Lease with Option to Purchase

Fannie Mae accepts as part down payment rental payments that exceed the market rent if a valid lease/purchase agreement is in effect, a copy of which must be attached to the loan application. The original term of the lease must have been at least 12 months. The appraiser must develop the market rent figure, and the lender must obtain copies of canceled checks or money order receipts to document the rental payments for the last 12 months.

Real Estate Sales Commission

If the borrower is entitled to a real estate commission from the sale of the property being purchased, that amount may be used as part of the down payment.

Sweat Equity

FHA and VA (not Fannie Mae) consider labor performed on the property being purchased or materials furnished by the borrower before closing as the equivalent of a cash investment to the extent of the estimated cost of the work or materials. (Sweat equity may be "gifted.")

LIABILITIES

Recurring Obligations

Recurring obligations include all installment loans, revolving charge accounts, real estate loans, alimony, child support, spousal maintenance and all other continuing obligations, extending beyond ten months for conventional financing (beyond six months for FHA financing).

For each liability, the lender verifies the unpaid balance, terms and the borrower's payment history.

Contingent Liabilities

A contingent liability exists if a borrower is a cosigner on an obligation or a coborrower on a mortgage.

NET WORTH

Net worth is the excess of assets over liabilities. Accumulation of net worth, particularly in the form of liquid assets, is a strong indication of creditworthiness. A borrower who accumulates net worth solely from earnings and savings demonstrates a strong ability to manage his or her financial affairs. If the net worth is in a liquid form, it can be used to service the debt, to pay unexpected obligations that may occur or to protect against short-term interruptions of income. Therefore, large liabilities may be offset by liquid assets.

QUALIFYING RATIOS

Qualifying ratios are used to compare the borrower's anticipated monthly housing expense and the total monthly obligations to his or her monthly gross income to determine whether the borrower will be able to meet the expenses involved in home ownership.

These ratios vary between conventional, FHA and VA financing and are discussed in detail under these respective headings.

CREDIT HISTORY

Lenders generally require a residential mortgage credit report from an independent consumer reporting agency. For self-employed borrowers doing business as a corporation or partnership, a business credit report is required to supplement the individual credit report. The borrower's credit history should demonstrate past willingness and ability to meet credit obligations in a way that enables the lender to draw a logical conclusion about the borrower's commitment to making payments on the new loan.

Fannie Mae is more concerned about a borrower's overall payment pattern than about a few individual occurrences. Unless the borrower's credit history over the last 24 months raises some serious concerns or there are major indications of derogatory credit (undisclosed debts, judgments, bankruptcies, etc.) at any time during the last seven years, the lender generally considers a borrower's credit history as acceptable if, over the last 12 months, the borrower has had

- no payments 60 days or more past due and no more than two payments 30 days past due—for all of his or her *revolving credit accounts* (credit cards, etc.);
- no payments 60 days or more past due and no more than one payment 30 days past due—for all of his or her *installment credit accounts* (car loans, etc.); and
- no payments past due—for all of his or her *housing debt* (first or second mortgage, rent, etc.).

Major Indications of Derogatory Credit

The following items remain on credit reports for seven years.

Undisclosed Debt

If the credit report reveals significant debt not disclosed on the application, the borrower may have attempted to conceal liabilities to qualify for the mortgage.

Judgments, Garnishments or Liens

Any judgments, garnishments or liens must be paid in full before closing. The borrower must have re-established good credit.

Bankruptcy

A bankruptcy must be fully discharged, and the borrower must have re-established good credit for a period of at least two years between the discharge of the bankruptcy and the mortgage application.

Foreclosure of Real Property

Generally, Fannie Mae will not purchase a mortgage if the borrower has been a defendant in mortgage foreclosure proceedings completed in the past three years.

However, if the foreclosure was the result of extenuating circumstances beyond the control of an owner-occupant borrower—such as a serious, long-term illness; death of the principal wage earner; loss of employment because of factory slowdowns or shut-downs; reductions-in-force; etc.—Fannie Mae will purchase the mortgage as long as the lender's underwriting confirms the borrower has re-established good credit and has demonstrated an ability to manage his or her financial affairs.

PROPERTY APPRAISAL

As a direct result of the 1989 bailout of insolvent thrifts, a federal appraiser law requires all states to license or certify any appraiser who works on loans of $250,000 or more, and is involved with federally regulated lending institutions.

Three different levels of appraisal reporting are now in effect.

1. The Self-Contained Appraisal Report. This is the most detailed and encompassing of the three report formats. The length and descriptive details in such a report should fully support (in a self-contained format) the reasoning and conclusions of the appraiser.

2. The Summary Report. This report is less detailed than a self-contained report. Rather than describing in detail the information considered and the appraisal procedures followed, such information may be summarized.

3. The Restricted Report. This is the least detailed of the reporting options, with minimal presentation of information. It is intended for use only by a client. A restricted report must contain a prominent use restriction that limits reliance on the report to the client and warns that the report cannot be properly comprehended without addi-

tional information from the work file of the appraiser.

The Federal Reserve Board issued a rule, which became mandatory June 6, 1994, that requires residential mortgage loan creditors to provide certain applicants with either of two alternatives: (1) provide all covered applicants with copies of the appraisal no later than when notice of action taken on the application is given or (2) advise the applicant of the right to an appraisal upon receipt by the creditor of a written request from the applicant.

Because the valuation of real property is an integral part of loan underwriting, a basic discussion of the three appraisal methods is in order. They are

1. sales comparison approach to value,
2. cost-depreciation approach to value, and
3. income approach to value.

Sales Comparison Approach to Value

The sales comparison approach to value, also referred to as the market data approach, is an analysis of recently sold properties that are comparable to the subject property. This is the method most relied upon for appraising single-family residences.

Factors Considered in Comparing Properties

- Date of sale—Should be within the preceding six months
- Location—Proximity to transportation, shopping, schools, churches, recreational facilities
- Physical characteristics—Size, construction, quality, design, floor plan, amenities, energy efficiency
- Site—Lot size, topography, view, landscaping
- Terms of sale—Cash, seller financing, buydowns, closing costs paid by seller
- Arm's-length transaction—Assumes that both buyer and seller are informed about the local real estate market and are under no unusual pressure to buy or sell, that no conflict of interest exists between agents and principals, and that the prop-

erty has been exposed to the market for a reasonable time.

Cost-Depreciation Approach to Value

Residential appraisers use the cost-depreciation approach as a check to verify the result obtained from the sales comparison method. This approach measures the value of a property in a three-step process.

1. Estimating the cost of reproducing the improvements. A valid estimate of production cost per square foot is multiplied by the square footage of the improvements.
2. Subtracting accrued depreciation. There are three principal types of depreciation: (1) physical depreciation, or deterioration, in the physical condition of the property; (2) functional depreciation, or obsolescence, caused by poor design; and (3) external depreciation, or economic obsolescence, caused by negative influences outside the property, such as a deteriorating neighborhood, expressways or industrial developments in the proximity of the subject property.
3. Adding the value of the lot. Appraisers use the sales comparison approach to arrive at the lot value, assuming the lot is vacant and available to be developed to its highest and best use. Market value of the property is obtained by adding the lot value to the estimated reproduction cost of the improvements minus depreciation.

Income Approach to Value

The income approach to value is based on the assumption that market value is related to the net operating income of the property (market rent minus operating expenses.)

The appraiser adjusts actual rents to market rent, adjusts expenses to a realistic operating expense and obtains a capitalization rate by dividing the net income of the comparable property by the sales price.

An appropriate cap rate is then applied to the subject property.

Although the income approach is of dubious value for appraising small residential income properties, gross multipliers are in common use. The *gross rent multiplier* (GRM) is arrived at by dividing the sale price of a comparable property by its total monthly gross rent. Conversely, a property value may be established by multiplying the total monthly gross rent by an appropriate GRM. In lieu of gross rental multipliers, the appraiser may use *gross income multipliers* (GIMs), which simply use annual gross rent, rather than monthly gross rent.

In an appraisal, a gross rent multiplier (or gross income multiplier) is determined for each of a number of comparable properties. Using these multipliers, the appraiser establishes a GRM (or GIM) for the subject property, making adjustments for differences between the properties. If necessary, the appraiser may adjust the actual rents of the subject property up or down to bring them into line with market rents. Finally, a property valuation is arrived at by multiplying the adjusted total gross rent for the subject property by its GRM (or GIM).

Example

Property	Sale Price	Annual Gross Rent	GIM
1	$100,000	$ 8,300	12.05
2	150,000	12,400	12.10
3	125,000	9,920	12.60
4	140,000	11,400	12.28
5	115,000	8,960	12.83

If in the appraiser's judgment a GIM of 12.15 were appropriate, and assuming an adjusted annual gross rental income of $10,000, the appraised value of the subject property would be $121,500.

Final Reconciliation

In the final analysis, the appraiser must reconcile the reasonability and reliability of each approach to value and the reasonability and validity of the indicated values and the available data, and then select and report the approach or approaches that were given the most weight. Simply averaging the indicated values is not a proper appraisal technique.

Low Appraisals

Appraisal valuations that are less than the contract price are a continuous problem for real estate agents, buyers and sellers alike. Sales often fall apart due to low appraisals, when the buyer is not willing or able to complete the transaction, and the seller is unwilling to reduce the price to the appraised value.

In many cases, the problem can be avoided by listing the property at a fair market price, preparing a competitive market analysis for the seller when listing the property and offering a copy of the analysis to the appraiser. The agent should make every effort to be present when the appraiser inspects the property to answer any questions and to make sure the appraiser knows what the sale price is. Agents should be aware that items of personal property, which may be part of the transaction, are not included in the appraisal.

In the event comparable sales indicate that an appraisal is low, a request for reconsideration should be submitted to the lender. The request should be accompanied by an analysis of three recent sales of comparable properties, providing information along the lines of Fannie Mae's Uniform Residential Appraisal Report (see Sales Comparison Analysis on the following page).

Sales Comparison Analysis

Item	Subj. Prop.	Comp. 1	Comp. 2	Comp. 3
Address				
Sales price				
Terms of sale				
Data source				
Date of sale				
Location				
Site/view				
Design/appeal				
Quality of construction				
Age				
Condition				
Total no. of rooms				
No. of bedrooms				
No. of baths				
Family room				
Square feet, living area				
Heating/cooling				
Garage/carport				
Patio, pool, etc.				
Energy efficiency				
Fireplaces				
Built-in kitchen equipment				
Other				

Uniform Residential Appraisal Report (URAR)

The following appraisal reports are mandatory for all loans involving Fannie Mae, Freddie Mac, FHA and VA loans:

- Uniform Residential Appraisal Report (Fannie Mae form 1004, Freddie Mac form 70) for residential income properties;
- Small Residential Income Property Appraisal Report (Fannie Mae form 1025, Freddie Mac form 72) for two- to four-family units; and
- Individual Condominium Unit Appraisal Report (Fannie Mae form 1073, Freddie Mac form 465).

AUTOMATED UNDERWRITING

Automated underwriting systems (the application of technology in evaluating mortgage risk) allow lenders to make quicker, more accurate and more consistent underwriting decisions of mortgage applications that have varying degrees of risk, and also let them approve more mortgages without increasing risk.

Accurate prediction of probable loan default has become a reality due to combining a risk based computerized model with a database drawing on the experience of a vast number of loans.

An important tool in streamlining mortgage underwriting is *credit scoring* (a system using numerical values to measure an applicant's credit risk), used in automated underwriting systems including Fannie Mae's "Desktop Underwriter" and Freddie Mac's "Loan Prospector."

Real estate agents are now able to take information required for a mortgage loan and process an original application through a computer terminal. The information can be submitted directly to a lender, or to a person possessing adequate knowledge of the market, plus having access to various lenders. Some agents perform this service without charging a fee simply to expedite the closing, while others earn an origination fee. Such a fee is not considered a "kick-back" or as "steering" a borrower, both of which are prohibited by federal law. Federal restrictions require a broker to inform the borrower of all fees charged for the service and to state who is required to pay them (usually the borrower). The borrower must acknowledge and approve of the fees in writing. There is no dollar restriction on the fees, other than they must be reasonable. Because mortgage lending is a very specialized field, licensees who wish to participate in lending and in providing competent advice need to become proficient in this specialty. Many licensees take courses or rely on sound advice from an experienced mortgage lender.

CONVENTIONAL FINANCING

A conventional loan is any loan made by an institutional lender that is not insured or guaranteed by a governmental agency.

Most conventional loans on residential properties of one to four units conform to the underwriting criteria established by Fannie Mae and Freddie Mac, the secondary market agencies that purchase conventional loans and mortgage-backed securities.

Loans that deviate from the criteria, called nonconforming loans, are made by lenders that keep loans in their portfolio rather than sell them in the secondary market.

Unless otherwise noted, underwriting guidelines for conventional mortgages discussed under this heading are criteria set by Fannie Mae or Freddie Mac.

DOCUMENTATION

Credit documents must not be more than 120 days old (180 days for new construction) on the date the note is signed. Appraisals must not be more than 180 days old (360 days for new construction).

- *Uniform Underwriting and Transmittal Summary* (Fannie Mae form 1008/Freddie Mac form 1077). Effective December 1992, Fannie Mae and Freddie Mac combined their forms under this new title.
- *Residential Loan Application* (form 1003)
- *Residential Mortgage Credit Report* and a *Business Credit Report* for self-employed borrowers if their business is a corporation, S corporation or partnership
- *Verification of Deposit* (form 1006)
- *Verification of Employment* (form 1005)
- *Federal income tax returns* (both individual and business returns) for past two years, with all applicable schedules; plus for self-employed borrowers and all business entities a year-to-date profit and

loss statement and balance sheet for previous two fiscal years

- A year-to-date profit and loss statement for self-employed borrower's business, if the loan application is dated more than 120 days after the end of the business's tax year
- A balance sheet for the previous two fiscal years for a self-employed borrower's business that is held as a sole proprietorship
- *Self-Employed Income Analysis* (form 1084A or 1088B)
- *Comparative Income Analysis* (form 1088) for self-employed borrowers
- A self-employed borrower's written permission to request copies of his or her federal income tax returns for the past two years directly from the IRS if they are needed for quality control purposes
- Purchase agreement and amendments
- Escrow instructions
- Verification of payment history on previous mortgages
- Any other documentation needed to make a prudent underwriting decision

Under the FDIC Improvement Act of 1991, there is no ceiling on the following loans: permanent residential and home equity loans on owner-occupied one- to four-family properties, except that loans over 90% must have private mortgage insurance; FHA and VA loans; problem loans that must be renewed, refinanced or restructured; and loans that facilitate the sale of foreclosed properties.

ELIGIBLE MORTGAGES

First mortgages can be fixed rate or adjustable rate, purchase money or refinance loans.

Second mortgages must be secured by properties that are owner-occupied principal residences. The second loan must be a fixed rate interest loan and have a minimum term of five years. The borrower must make a cash down payment of at least 10%. The underlying first mortgage must be an institutional loan with a loan-to-value (LTV) ratio not to exceed 75% and cannot permit negative amortization. A second mortgage can be a purchase money, refinance or home improvement loan.

Fixed rate first mortgages can be secured by properties that are owner-occupied principal residences (including one- to four-family properties), second homes or investment properties.

Adjustable rate first mortgages must be secured by owner-occupied principal residences or second homes. The maximum LTV for ARMs is 90%. The lifetime interest cap is 6%; the annual interest cap, 2%. They may not permit negative amortization.

ELIGIBLE BORROWERS

U.S. citizens and aliens who are lawful residents of the United States and who have reached the age at which the mortgage note can be legally enforced in the jurisdiction in which the property is located qualify as eligible borrowers.

A *coborrower* may be any party who does not have an interest in the property sales transaction. A coborrower must occupy the property if the LTV is over 90%. An occupant coborrower must have ratios of 35%/43% after the income and expenses of a non-occupying coborrower have been excluded. If the LTV is over 80%, the occupant coborrower must make the first 5% of the down payment from his or her own funds.

Nonpermanent resident aliens (not foreign nationals without lawful residency status) with a maximum LTV of 75% who have an established two-year credit history in the U.S., or shorter if it can be supplemented by credit histories established in the country from which the borrower immigrated.

ELIGIBLE PROPERTIES

Mixed-use property—eligible under the following criteria:

- It must be a one-family property the borrower occupies as his or her principal residence.
- The mixed use of the property must represent a legal, permissible use of the property under the local zoning requirements.
- The borrower must be both the owner and the operator of the business.
- The property must be primarily residential in nature.
- The market value of the property must be primarily a function of its residential characteristics, rather than of the business use or any special business-use modifications that were made.

Principal residence—a one- to four-family property that is the borrower's primary residence.

Second home—a single-family property that the borrower occupies in addition to his or her principal residence. (Rental income may not be used to qualify the borrower.)

Investment property—a one- to four-family property that the borrower does not occupy.

Multiple mortgages—When a mortgage delivered to Fannie Mae is secured by a one- to four-family property that is the borrower's principal residence, Fannie Mae does not impose any limitations on the number of mortgages the borrower can currently be financing. But if the mortgage is secured by a second home or an investment property, the borrower may not own more than four properties that are currently being financed. In these cases, the borrower's principal residence must be counted toward the limitation. Properties not being financed are excluded from this limitation.

MAXIMUM LOAN AMOUNTS

The following maximum amounts for Fannie Mae or Freddie Mac mortgages are in effect for 1997.

No. of Units	Maximum Loan	Alaska and Hawaii
1	$214,600	$321,900
2	$274,550	$411,825
3	$331,850	$497,775
4	$412,450	$618,675
Second mortgages	$107,300	$160,950

Loans exceeding these ceilings are *nonconforming jumbo loans*.

DOWN PAYMENT

A minimum down payment of 5% must come from the borrower's savings or liquid assets. The remainder of a larger down payment may come from other sources (e.g., gift, trade equity, rent credit). If the LTV is 80% or less, the entire down payment may come from a gift or grant from a relative, church, municipality or nonprofit organization.

With secondary financing, the minimum down payment is 10% of the lesser of appraised value or purchase price.

The property seller may take the borrower's existing property, or an asset other than real estate, in trade as part of the down payment as long as the borrower has made a 5% cash payment and his or her equity contribution for the traded property is a true value consideration supported by a current, full appraisal.

In the event of a lease purchase option, the property seller may give the purchaser credit toward the down payment for a portion of previous rent payments he or she made under a documented lease purchase agreement that had a minimum original term of at least 12 months in an amount up to the difference between the market rent and the actual rent paid. (The appraiser must determine "market" rent.)

The buyer, in such case, does not have to make a 5% minimum cash down payment in order for the rental payments to be credited toward the down payment.

Cash Reserves

Borrowers are generally required to have at least two months of *liquid reserves* as a cushion for unforeseen financial problems after paying the down payment, closing costs and prepaid expenses related to the mortgage.

LOAN-TO-VALUE RATIOS (LTV)

Loan-to-value ratios are determined by dividing the loan amount by the property value.

Example

The LTV of a property appraised at $100,000, secured by a loan of $90,000, is 90%.

Maximum LTVs

	Units	Max. LTV	With Secondary Fin.
Primary residences	1	95%	75%
	2	90%	
	3	80%	
Investor (fixed rate only)		70%	

80% loans–Loans with an LTV of 80% or less

90% loans–Loans with an LTV of over 80%, but not more than 90%

95% loans–Loans with an LTV of over 90%, but not more than 95%

High-ratio loans are loans with LTVs over 80%. Due to the risk involved, private mortgage insurance (PMI) is required for high-ratio loans.

ESCROW ACCOUNT

At the option of the borrower, the lender may maintain an escrow account from which to pay property taxes, hazard insurance and homeowners' association fees. HUD established guidelines for lenders to compute escrow charges, which became mandatory October 27, 1997. Under these rules, lenders can require monthly escrow contributions equal to $\frac{1}{12}$ of the annual property taxes and hazard insurance. The lender may add a cushion equal to two months' worth of escrow charges.

PRIVATE MORTGAGE INSURANCE (PMI)

There are risks of varying degrees associated with mortgages, depending upon the loan-to-value ratio and other factors. *Private mortgage insurance companies* insure lending institutions against loss due to borrower default. The insurance covers the lender for the upper portion of the loan, typically 25% of the outstanding balance. For example, with a sales price of $100,000, a down payment of $5,000 and PMI coverage of 25%, the lender's exposure is calculated as follows:

Sales price	$100,000
Down payment	$- 5,000
Loan amount	$ 95,000
Coverage	× 25%
Amount of coverage	$ 23,750

The lender's exposure is $100,000 - $23,750 = $76,250.

Fannie Mae requires PMI coverage for high-ratio conventional mortgages (LTVs higher than 80%). Taking into consideration a lower risk factor associated with fully amortizing, fixed rate mortgages with an original term of 20 years or less, the PMI coverage requirement has been sharply reduced for these mortgages, as shown in the following chart.

Premiums usually increase at intervals of 5% of LTV; so 85%, 90% and 95% loans have progressively higher premiums due to increased risk.

Borrowers may include the one-time PMI in the amount financed for first purchase money mortgages secured by owner-occupied properties. The one-time

PMI Coverage Requirements
(Effective December, 1996)

Mortgage Terms	LTV 0–85%	LTV 85–90%	LTV 90–97%
10, 15, 20 yr. Fixed Rate	6%	12%	25%
25 & 30 yr. Fixed Rate	12%	25%	30%
15 & 30 yr. ARM	12%	25%	30%
7 yr. Balloon	12%	25%	30%

PMI is added to the loan before the monthly payment is calculated.

PMI is eligible for cancellation after two years if (1) the LTV, based on a current appraisal, is 80% or less due to an addition or improvement of the property; (2) the LTV, based on a current appraisal, is 75% or less due to appreciation of the property; or (3) the loan has amortized to 80% or less (no appraisal required).

In an effort to reduce cash requirements at closing, private mortgage insurance companies began offering monthly premium payment plans rather than annual or single payment plans. Insurers are now reporting nearly half their new insurance business is in monthly premium payments.

Borrowers who are uncertain about the length of time they will keep their mortgage are well advised to choose the monthly payment plan, rather than the up-front private mortgage insurance. The up-front premium is not refunded for conventional loans in case of early payoff.

QUALIFYING RATIOS

Two ratios are used to determine whether the borrower can reasonably be expected to meet expenses involved in home ownership. Fannie Mae's current benchmark ratios are:

1. Housing expense = max. 28% of gross income
2. Total obligations = max. 36% of gross income*

*With temporary buydowns, Fannie Mae's requirement for total obligations is 33% of gross income.

Housing expense means the monthly payment for principal, interest, hazard insurance, real estate taxes, mortgage insurance premium and any owners' association dues.

Total obligations means the sum of (1) housing expenses and (2) monthly recurring obligations on installment loans and revolving charge accounts extending beyond ten months, nonincome producing real estate loans, alimony, child support, spousal maintenance and payments on all other debts of a continuing nature.

Gross income means stable monthly income, reasonably expected to continue for at least three years.

Example of Qualifying a Buyer for Conventional Financing

Jim Miller wants to buy a home. His gross income is $5,000. He has monthly recurring obligations of $800. Calculate the maximum monthly housing expense for which he can qualify.

Gross income	$5,000	
	× 0.28	
Max. housing expense	$1,400	(Ratio 1)

Gross income	$5,000	
	× 0.36	
Max. total obligations	$1,800	
Recurring obligations	− 800	
Max. housing expense	$1,000	(Ratio 2)

Because the result of Ratio 2 is lower, the maximum monthly housing expense Mr. Miller qualifies for is $1,000.

High-Ratio Mortgages

For high-ratio mortgages (above 80% LTV), lenders look beyond the total obligations-to-income ratio to determine the borrower's eligibility, particularly with respect to the

- adequacy of the borrower's reserves after closing—cash that equals at least two mortgage payments represents adequate reserves;
- borrower's demonstrated ability to make monthly housing payments equal to or greater than the proposed monthly housing expense;
- borrower's ability to accumulate savings and to demonstrate prompt payment of debts;
- borrower's demonstrated capability for increased earnings in future years, based on his or her employment history (this is especially true for ARM borrowers); and
- borrower's ability to maintain an acceptable credit history.

Compensating Factors

Fannie Mae's debt-to-income benchmark ratios may be exceeded when compensating factors are present. The strongest compensating factor is a borrower's demonstrated history (12 to 24 months) of paying previous housing expenses equal to or greater than the proposed monthly housing expense, while successfully handling other debt obligations. In such cases, lenders may approve the application of an otherwise qualified borrower even if Fannie Mae's benchmark ratios are exceeded. Additional compensating factors are a borrower's

- making a large down payment toward the purchase of the property;
- purchasing a property that qualifies as an energy-efficient dwelling;
- demonstrating the ability to devote a greater portion of income to basic needs, such as housing expenses;
- demonstrating the ability to accumulate savings and to maintain a good credit history or a debt-free position;
- having a potential for increased earnings and advancement because of education or job train-

ing, even though he or she has just entered the job market;

- having short-term income (such as Social Security income, alimony child support, notes receivable, mortgage differential payments, trust income, VA benefits) that could not be counted as stable income because it would not continue to be received for at least three years beyond the date of the mortgage application;

- purchasing the home as a result of corporate relocation of the primary wage-earner, and the secondary wage-earner, who has a history of employment in the previous location, is expected to return to work (even if he or she has not yet obtained employment in the new location); and

- having a net worth substantial enough to evidence the ability to repay the mortgage.

In order to qualify under the higher ratios for mortgages with loan-to-value ratios above 90%, not only must borrowers fall into one of the above categories, but one of the following conditions must also exist:

- The borrower must have financial reserves that can be used to carry the mortgage debt for two to three months.

- The borrower must have a demonstrated ability to devote a greater portion of his or her income to housing expenses, an excellent payment history on any prior mortgage obligation and an acceptable credit history.

- The borrower must have a total obligation-to-income ratio (at the time of the application) of 30% or less, an excellent payment history on any prior mortgage obligation, and an acceptable credit history.

SECONDARY FINANCING

The source of *secondary financing* is generally the seller who accepts a note for part of the purchase price, secured by a mortgage on the property. This is referred to as a *purchase money mortgage*. Secondary financing may also be obtained from a private third party or from an institutional lender (that may or may not be the lender making the first loan).

Most lenders have the following seven requirements for second loans (regardless of the source) in conjunction with conventional financing:

1. 10% minimum cash down payment. The combined first and second loans may not exceed 90% of the lesser of the appraised value or purchase price.
2. 75% maximum LTV for first mortgage.
3. Minimum term 5 years, maximum 30 years.
4. No prepayment penalty.
5. Regular scheduled payments. May be amortized or interest only, may provide for balloon payment, may be monthly, quarterly, and so on, but must be regular payments.
6. No negative amortization.
7. Buyer must qualify for combined payments of first and second loans. For qualification purposes, lenders base monthly payments of the second mortgage on an interest rate not less than 2% below the market rate for second loans.

REFINANCING

Lenders' guidelines for refinancing are somewhat similar to purchase guidelines. Some differences follow.

- Seasoning, or age of loan, is important. Many lenders ask for at least one year's and sometimes two years' seasoning.
- An excellent payment history on the present mortgage is important, with no late mortgage payments reported.

Cash-Out Refinances

Cash-out refinance mortgages must be secured by properties that will be owner-occupied principal residences only. Mortgage proceeds may include the unpaid principal balance of the existing first mortgage, closing costs, points, the outstanding balance of existing liens and additional cash the borrower may use for any purpose.

Limited Cash-Out Rate/Term Refinances

Limited cash-out rate/term refinances may be secured by owner-occupied principal or second homes or investment properties. Mortgage proceeds may include the unpaid principal balance of the existing first mortgage, closing costs, points, the outstanding balance of existing liens and additional cash to the borrower not to exceed 1% of the principal amount of the new mortgage.

No Cash-Out Rate/Term Refinances

No cash-out rate/term refinances must be secured by owner-occupied principal residences only. The mortgage must be fully amortizing and fixed-rate. When deciding to refinance for the purpose of reducing the rate of interest, a general rule of thumb is that the new interest rate should be approximately two percentage points lower than the current rate, and the borrower should plan to own the home for at least three more years. Of course, this rule does not apply where the borrower is mainly interested in refinancing for purposes other than interest rate reduction, such as converting an ARM to a fixed rate loan, retiring existing liens, making repairs or improvements, or obtaining cash for other purposes.

A. Limited Cash-Out Rate/Term Transaction

- *Owner-occupied principal residence*
  - —One- to two-family first mortgage — 90%
  - —Three- to four-family first mortgage — 80%
- *Second home*
- *Investment property* — 70%
  — 70%

B. No Cash-Out Rate/Term Transaction — 95%

C. Cash-Out Transaction

- One- to four-family first mortgage — 75%
- One- to four-family second mortgage — 70%

FINANCING PROGRAMS

Freddie Mac Lease Purchase Option

Freddie Mac's Plan allows a renter to make a lease purchase agreement for a set number of years with a sponsoring nonprofit group or housing finance agency that purchases the home financed by a conventional loan. The tenant makes monthly rental payments, part of which are set aside toward the down payment and closing costs. When the accumulated funds total the required 5 percent down payment, the tenant can assume the mortgage from the sponsoring agency and Freddie Mac will buy the loan.

Fannie Mae Reverse "Home Keeper Mortgage"

The new *Home Keeper Mortgage*, announced by Fannie Mae, is a compilation of all the best features of reverse mortgage products on the market, including the FHA-insured Home Equity Conversion Mortgage.

Basic Requirements:

I. All owners of the home must be aged 62 or over.
II. At least one owner must occupy the home as his or her principal residence.

III. The home must be a single-family residence or part of a HUD-approved condominium or Planned Unit Development (PUD).
IV. The borrower must attend a consumer education session approved by Fannie Mae.
 V. Maximum loan $207,000 ($310,500 for Alaska, Hawaii, Virgin Islands, Guam).

Benefits:

The borrower has the choice of taking the loan as:

* a single lump sum of cash, or
* a credit line, or
* monthly cash advances for as long as the borrower lives in the home, or any combination of the above options.

The nonprofit National Center of Home Equity Conversion (NCHEC), the leading authority on reverse mortgages, publishes *Your New Retirement Nest Egg–A Consumer Guide to The New Reverse Mortgages* (2nd edition, 352 pages, 1996) by Ken Scholen. The book features the first independent analysis of the new Fannie Mae plan, "Home Keeper Mortgage," and compares it in detail to the other reverse mortgage plans.

Also included is a nationwide list of Reverse Mortgage Lenders with telephone numbers. The book is available for $24.95 plus $4.50 shipping directly from NCHEC, 7373 147th Street West, Suite 115, Apple Valley, MN 55124; telephone 1-800-247-6553. The list of Reverse Mortgage Lenders may also be obtained separately from NCHEC by sending a self-addressed, stamped business envelope and $1.00 to NCHEC Locator, 7373 147th St., Apple Valley, MN 55124.

Transamerica Homefirst Reverse Mortgages

The only reverse mortgage providing lifetime monthly cash advances even if the borrower sells or moves out of the residence.

Maximum $750,000 in CA, CO, CT, DC, FL, GA, IL, MD, MI, NJ, NY, OH, OR, PA, VA, and WA. Details: 1-800-538-5569, Dept. W206.

Community Lending Programs

Many lenders are now playing a positive role in the revitalization of neighborhoods to reverse historic patterns of neglect and decay. Fannie Mae supports development of other community lending programs that combine acceptable risk with the flexibility required to make home finance opportunities available to low- and moderate-income households. Two community lending models are currently in place: The *Community Home Buyer's Program* model, generally available only to borrowers with incomes of not more than 100% of the median income for their locality, and the *Enhanced Fannie Neighbors* model, which opens up the Community Home Buyer's Program model to a wider range of borrowers by using as its qualifying criterion the location of the security property. Additional models (or changes to these models) may be announced from time to time.

Community Home Buyer's Program (CHBP)

Eligible borrowers. Mortgages are made to natural persons (not entities). But for certain types of transactions, borrowers may be nonprofit organizations or public agencies. A borrower's income generally may not exceed 100% of the median area income published by HUD.

Mortgages. CHBP mortgages are conventional fully amortizing first mortgages obtainable with a minimum investment. The one exception is the *start-up mortgage*, a graduated payment mortgage with interest-only payments for the first year. Payments increase 2% annually until the mortgage becomes fully amortizing. There is no negative amortization. Mortgages may have 15-, 20-, 25- or 30-year terms with either monthly or biweekly payments. Qualifying guidelines for CHBP mortgages are 33% for the monthly housing expense-to-income ratio and 36% for the total obligations-to-income ratio.

Properties. CHBP mortgages generally must be secured by one-family properties, including units in eligible condominium, PUD and cooperative projects. The properties may be new, existing or rehabilitated. Borrowers must occupy the security property as a principal residence and cannot concurrently have any ownership interest in any other residential dwelling. In addition, all coborrowers whose names appear on the mortgage note must occupy the security property as their principal residence.

Down payment options. Three down payment options are available.

1. *Regular down payment option.* Minimum down payment required under this option is 5% of the sales price of the property. Generally, this entire 5% must come from the borrower's own funds.

2. *3/2 Option.* Minimum down payment required under this option is 5% of the sales price of the property. However, the borrower only needs to make a 3% down payment from his or her own funds. The remaining 2% down payment may be obtained through a gift from a relative; a gift, grant or unsecured loan from a nonprofit organization or a public agency; or a secured loan from a public agency.

3. *Fannie 97.* Minimum down payment required under this option is 3% of the sales price of the property. This entire 3% generally must come from the borrower's own funds. However, the borrower may pool funds with a relative who lives with the borrower.

Homebuyer Education Requirement

Fannie Mae requires that all borrowers who obtain a start-up mortgage or who use the 3/2 Option or the Fannie 97 Down Payment Option participate in prepurchase homebuyer education sessions. These sessions provide information on selecting a home, obtaining a mortgage, budgeting to meet monthly costs and maintaining a home. This requirement may not be waived unless the borrower

- has previously owned a home;
- makes at least a 5% cash down payment from his or her own funds (and does not rely on a gift, loan or grant to obtain any portion of the down payment); and
- has cash reserves after closing that are at least equal to two monthly mortgage payments.

Education sessions generally must take the form of face-to-face tutorial or classroom or workshop sessions and may be conducted by a member of the lender's staff, a representative of a mortgage insurance company or a counselor using an approach and curriculum acceptable to the lender. Lenders that originate either a Fannie 97 Mortgage or a start-up mortgage must offer early delinquency intervention counseling to the borrower.

Community Living Group Homes

Fannie Mae announced that Community Living mortgages may be used to finance group homes designed to house individuals who have any disability. Maximum Loan-to-Value ratio for purchase money mortgages and limited cash-out rate/term refinance is 90%.

COMMERCIAL AND INVESTMENT PROPERTIES

Financing Sources

Generally, the best sources for financing of commercial properties are commercial banks, insurance companies and pension funds. Private investors are a good source for smaller properties and short-term loans. Many commercial loans are placed through loan brokers who represent insurance companies, pension funds and other lenders.

Property Qualification

Lenders require a positive cash flow, expressed as a *net operating income to annual debt service ratio*, to qualify commercial properties. The ratio is typically stated as 1:1, 1:3, and so on. A 1:3 ratio means the property must have a net operating income of $1.30 for each $1 of debt service. Most projects are expected to have a ratio between 1:1 and 1:5.

The cash down payment required for commercial property can range from 20 to 25%; office buildings, warehouses and shopping centers generally require from 25 to 35%. For unimproved commercial land, lenders often require a 50% down payment.

The quality of tenants and terms and safety of leases are other important criteria. Many lenders require 65% or more preleasing prior to funding. Lenders often require estoppel certificates, wherein tenants state the amount of their rent, any advance payments, security deposits and any defaults or modifications of their leases.

In contrast to financing of residential property, most lenders retain commercial loans in their own portfolio. For that reason, they are not only more selective in the projects they fund, but also favor particular types of properties in accordance with the lender's past experience. The size of loan is another criterion some lenders take into account. A lender may fund a loan of $5 million but turn down one of $800,000.

The term of most commercial loans does not exceed 10 years, although payments may be amortized over 30 years with a due date of 10 years or less. On the other hand, some commercial loans, such as insurance company loans, may have a high prepayment penalty or even a lock-in clause stating that the loan cannot be prepaid under any circumstances.

Construction

Construction loans are interim or short-term loans, normally about 12 months, at interest only. Usually, a sum of money is set aside in a special account for the borrower, who may be a builder, developer or future homeowner. Money is drawn out in installments as needed and as construction progresses. The monthly interest payment is calculated on the amount of funds disbursed, not on the overall amount of the loan. With this type of financing the lender often lends up to 90% of construction cost, provided that figure does not exceed 75% to 80% of the appraised value. At the end of the construction period, the borrower must obtain permanent financing, also referred to as a take-out, permanent or construction-permanent loan.

FHA FINANCING

The Federal Housing Administration (FHA) was created by Congress in 1934 as part of the National Housing Act.

FHA, a division of HUD, insures mortgage loans, secured by residential property, against default and foreclosure and compensates approved lending institutions for losses resulting from borrower default.

LOAN UNDERWRITING

Also refer to the main financing section Loan Underwriting.

Effective March 1995, FHA underwriting guidelines were revised as follows to enhance homebuying opportunities for a substantial number of American families.

- *Elimination of five-year test for income stability.* The number of years for which income is reasonably expected to continue for qualifying purposes has been changed from five years to three years.
- *Recognition of overtime and bonus income.* Overtime and/or bonus income received for less than a full two years is now acceptable when the lender determines there are reasonable prospects of its continuance.
- *Recognition of part-time income.* Part-time income, defined as income from jobs taken in addition to the normal, regular employment to supplement a borrower's income, received for less than two years, may be included as effective income, provided the lender determines there are strong indications of its continuance.
- *Definition of long-term obligations extended from six to ten months.* Only those debts extending ten or more months need to be included in the debt-to-income ratios.
- *Mortgage credit certificates (MCCs).* Lenders may now consider the tax credit resulting from

MCCs as a direct reduction in housing expense (Principal, Interest, Taxes, Insurance, or PITI), although the tax credit results in an increase in the borrower's net monthly income. This reduces the borrower's qualifying ratios and increases the size of the mortgage.

- *Elimination of child care as recurring debt.* The cost of child care is no longer considered in the computation of debt-to-income ratios. (Court-ordered or voluntary child support payments must continue to be counted as recurring debts.)
- *Unnecessary repair requirements on FHA appraisals.* HUD acknowledges some repair requirements should be eliminated. Lenders should exercise their authority to delete conditions that have little or nothing to do with the safety or soundness of the property.

Bridal Registry Savings Accounts for Down Payment

Effective October, 1996, FHA announced an initiative encouraging couples planning to get married to establish a bridal registry savings account in order to help them accumulate the down payment necessary for purchasing their first home together. This initiative formalizes FHA's policy to permit cash gifts to be used as an acceptable source of funds for down payment.

Upon request, participating lenders would set up an interest bearing account with a financial institution in the borrower's name. The lender and borrower must certify to the best of their knowledge that the deposits were (1) from friends that do not have a financial interest in the transaction, and (2) not from participants (seller, builder, real estate agent, etc.) with a financial interest in the transaction.

DOCUMENTATION

Credit documents must not be more than 120 days old (180 days for proposed construction) at the time the loan closes. Verification forms must pass directly between lender and creditor without being handled by any third party. Credit documents and verification forms include the following:

- Uniform Residential Loan Application (HUD-92900-A).
- Nontraditional Mortgage Credit Report. To establish a credit history for borrowers who do not use credit or whose history on traditional reports is insufficient. NMCRs include history of verified payments for rental housing, utilities, insurance premiums, payments to local stores, medical bills, school tuition, child care, documented debt payments to individuals and verifications of personal property tax payments. NMCRs were to be available by credit reporting repositories effective January 1, 1996, as announced by Fannie Mae 7/1/95.
- Borrower's Notification and Interest Rate Disclosure Statement (HUD-92900-B).
- Mortgage Credit Analysis Worksheet (HUD-92900-WS) and Attachment A if seller financing concessions are involved.
- Picture identification and evidence of Social Security number for each borrower.
- Residential Mortgage Credit Report on all borrowers who will be obligated on the note.
- Verification of Employment (VOE) and most recent pay stub. (In lieu of VOE, lenders may choose alternative method.)
- Verification of Deposit (VOD) and most recent bank statement. (In lieu of VOD, lenders may use original bank statements covering most recent three months.)
- Federal income tax returns for the past two years for commissioned individuals. For self-employed borrowers, both individual and business returns with all applicable schedules. All business entities must also provide profit and loss statements and evidence of quarterly tax payments.

- Purchase (sales) agreement and amendments or other agreements, plus certification unless the agreement contains a clause stating that the document contains the entire agreement of the parties and supersedes all prior agreements and representations with respect to the property not expressed in writing in the agreement.
- Verification of payment history of previous mortgages, used in the credit report.
- Uniform Residential Appraisal Report (URAR) and Conditional Commitment/DE Statement of Appraised Value (HUD-92800.5-B), or VA Certificate of Reasonable Value (CRV).

Alternative Documentation

As of January 2, 1992, FHA can accept alternative documents to verify employment and assets. To verify employment, the past two years of original IRS W-2 forms (meaning any copy of the form not attached to the borrower's income tax form) along with original paycheck stubs for the most recent 30-day period can be used. Income must be computed over the 24-month period represented by the W-2s.

To verify assets, original bank statements for the most recent three months may be used. These statements may not be averaged.

A signed copy of IRS Form 4506, Request for Copy of Tax Form, must be submitted on all loans. During loan processing, the tax return must be reviewed by the lender, who must report any discrepancies between that and documents furnished by the borrower.

The new procedures are intended to make loan processing faster and less expensive. Employment verifications have sometimes been slow or difficult to obtain, and some banks are now charging fees to verify deposits.

MAXIMUM LOAN AMOUNTS

Under most FHA programs, the maximum insurable loan is the lesser of (1) the statutory loan limit for the geographical area; (2) the applicable loan-to-value ratio; and (3) the applicable loan-to-appraised-value limit.

Statutory Loan Limits

In accordance with legislation effective October 1994, FHA mortgage limits are indexed to annual Fannie Mae/Freddie Mac limits. Base limits *(floors)* are indexed at 38% and limits for high cost areas *(ceilings)* at 75% of the Fannie Mae/Freddie Mac limits, adjusted January 1 of each year (usually announced by the end of November or beginning of December).

Freddie Mac Loan Limits for 1997

1-unit properties	$214,000
2-unit properties	274,550
3-unit properties	331,850
4-unit properties	412,450

FHA Base Limits (38% of Freddie Mac)

1-unit properties	$ 81,548
2-unit properties	104,329
3-unit properties	126,103
4-unit properties	156,731
1-condominium unit	81,548

FHA Limits for High-Cost Areas (75% of Freddie Mac)

1-unit properties	$160,950
2-unit properties	205,912
3-unit properties	248,887
4-unit properties	309,337

FHA Ceilings for Alaska, Guam, Hawaii and the Virgin Islands

1-unit properties	$241,425
2-unit properties	308,868
3-unit properties	373,330
4-unit properties	464,005

A complete schedule of mortgage limits for high-cost areas is available through the Internet: www.hud.gov/fha/fhahome.html. Under "Business" select "Single Family," then page down to "Development," then "FHA Maximum Mortgage Limits."

Contact your local FHA office for limits applicable to your county. The mortgage amount must be a multiple of $50 for a mortgage that does not include financing of a mortgage insurance premium.

Maximum Loan-to-Value Ratios (LTVs)

The following *LTVs* establish an additional limit for individual loans effective in 1994. The new limits are 98.75% for loans of up to $50,000; 97.65% for loans between $50,000 and $125,000; and 97.15% for loans of more than $125,000 of appraised value or sale price, whichever is lower.

Closing costs may not be financed, but the mortgage insurance premium may be added to the loan after the down payment calculation is made.

Example

The maximum mortgage amount for a property eligible for maximum financing with a value of $150,000 (including closing costs) is:

$150,000 - 125,000 = $25,000 → $25,000 × 97.15% = $24,287.50
$125,000 - 50,000 = $75,000 → $75,000 × 97.65% = $73,237.50
$ 50,000 - 50,000 = $75,000

For properties under construction, and properties less than one year old not approved by and built under FHA or VA inspection and without a ten-year homeowners warranty, the maximum LTV is 90% of appraised value (or sales price, whichever is less) including closing costs.

For eligible veterans, the maximum LTV is 100% of the first $25,000 plus 95% of the amount between $25,000 and $125,000, and 90% of the amount over $125,000 (or sales price, whichever is less) including closing costs.

Nonoccupying coborrowers: When there are two or more borrowers, but one or more will not occupy the property as a principal residence, the LTV is usually limited to 75%. However, maximum financing is available for blood-related borrowers, or for unrelated individuals who can document evidence of a family-type, long and substantial relationship *not arising out of the loan transaction.* The occupant borrower must sign the security instrument and mortgage note.

Loan-to-Appraised-Value Limit

The 1990 housing legislation requires that the amount of any insured mortgage not exceed 97.75% of the appraised value of the property excluding closing costs (or 98.75% if the value is $50,000 or less).

If the amount determined by the applicable LTV limit is less than the amount determined by the LTV ratio, the amount of closing costs that can be financed must be reduced by the amount the LTV ratio exceeds the LTV limit.

Calculating the Maximum Loan

1. Start with the lesser of the sales price or appraised value.
2. Add 100% of the borrower's closing costs shown on the good faith estimate form.
3. Add any repairs and improvements required by the appraiser to be paid by the borrower.
4. Add energy-related weatherization items to be paid by the borrower.
5. Subtract any closing costs paid by the seller.
6. Subtract any seller-paid sales concessions.
7. If the total of seller-paid closing costs and other financing concessions exceeds 6% of the selling price, subtract the excess.
8. The result is the mortgage basis, which is multiplied by the appropriate loan-to-value ratio.
9. The lesser of the amount thus obtained or the statutory LTV limit (without closing costs) is the maximum obtainable loan.

Closing costs may not include discount points or prepaid items. In the event the lender pays the borrower's closing costs by charging a premium interest rate or additional discount points, these closing costs may not be added to the sales price.

Repairs and improvements, if required by the appraiser as essential for property eligibility, are to be paid by the borrower. The sales agreement must identify the borrower as responsible for performing these repairs or improvements. The appraised value will already reflect these repairs and improvements.

Energy-related weatherization items, if the borrower is responsible for the payment of these items, include thermostats, insulation, storm windows and doors, weather stripping, caulking, and so forth.

Seller-paid sales concessions include prepaid items (tax and insurance escrows, association dues, etc.), personal property items, buyer-broker fees, decorating allowances, moving costs, payment of buyer's sales commission on present residence, excess rent credits, and so forth. Sales concessions must be subtracted dollar-for-dollar from the sales price before computing the loan amount.

Seller-paid financing concessions include closing costs, discount points, interest rate buydowns and other payment supplements, and payment of the UFMIP (up-front mortgage insurance premium). Financing concessions are not subtracted dollar-for-dollar from the sales price, but any excess of financing concessions over 6% of the sales price must be deducted before computing the loan amount.

Calculating the Cash Requirement

1. Start with the mortgage basis.
2. Subtract the maximum loan.
3. Add back the seller-paid sales concessions.
4. Add back any excess of seller-paid financing concessions over 6% of sales price.
5. Add buyer-paid discount points, UFMIP, prepayable expenses.

6. Subtract items financed in the mortgage.
7. Subtract proceeds of a second mortgage, if any.
8. The result is the minimum cash requirement (including any earnest money deposit).

It is permissible to use gift funds for all or part of the cash investment, provided the donor is the borrower's employer, a close relative or a close friend with a clearly defined interest in the borrower.

With a *lease option* (lease with option to purchase), any rent over and above the market rent for the area may be applied toward the cash investment.

Three- and four-unit properties must be self-sufficient, regardless of occupancy. The maximum mortgage is limited, so monthly mortgage payments (PITI and owners' association fees) do not exceed the net rental income based on the appraiser's estimate of fair market rent less HUD's allowance for vacancies and maintenance.

Items That May Be Added Directly to the Loan Amount

1. Solar energy systems may increase the maximum mortgage amount. In addition, the statutory loan limit may be exceeded by 20%.
2. Buyer-broker fees may be added directly to the loan amount if the broker has been the exclusive agent of the buyer and a written agreement is submitted with the loan application.

FHA Maximum Loan Worksheet for properties with sales prices and appraised value of more than $50,000 is shown on the next page with information from the following example:

John Smith bought a home for $60,000 with an appraised value of $62,000. The seller paid the buyer's closing costs amounting to $2,500, discount points amounting to $1,500 and $500 of the buyer's prepaid expenses.

FHA MAXIMUM LOAN WORKSHEET
WITH APPR. VAL. OVER $50,000
TRANSACTION DATA

1	Sales price		$60,000
2	Appraised value		62,000
3	Total closing costs		2,500
4	Seller–paid closing costs	−	2,500
5	Buyer–paid closing costs (Line 3 − 4)	=	$0
6	Other financing concessions		1,500
7	Total financing concessions (Line 4 + 6)		4,000
8	Financing concessions exceeding 6% of price		400
9	Seller–paid sales concessions		500
10			
11	**MAXIMUM LOAN CALCULATION**		
12	The lower of sales price or appraised value		$60,000
13	Buyer–paid closing costs (Line 5)	+	0
14	Seller–paid sales concessions (Line 9)	−	500
15	Financing concession > 6% of price (Line 8)	−	400
16	Mortgage basis (Lines 12 + 13 −14 −15)	=	$59,100
17	97% × 25,000		24,250
18	95% × (Line 16 betw. 25,000 × 125,000)	+	32,395
19	90% × (Line 16 in excess of 125,000)	+	0
20	Maximum LTV (Lines 17 + 18 + 19)	=	$56,645
21	Max. LTV for new constr.: 90% × Line 16		
22	Mortgage limit: (97.75% × Line 2)		60,605
23	Max. loan (the lesser of 20 [21] or 22)		56,645
24	**CASH REQUIREMENT**		
25	Required cash investment (Line 16 − 23)		$2,455
26	Sales concessions (Line 14)	+	500
27	Financing concessions > 6% of price (15)	+	400
28	Discount points paid by buyer	+	0
29	Prepayable expenses paid by buyer	+	800
30	UFMIP paid in cash	+	
31	Total invested (25 + 26 + 27 + 28 + 29 + 30)	=	$4,155
32	Items financed in mortgage	−	1,788
33	Amount paid in cash (Line 31 − 32)	=	$2,367
34	Second mortgage proceeds (if applicable)	−	
35	Assets available (Line 33 − 34)	=	$2,367

SECONDARY FINANCING FROM FAMILY MEMBERS

Effective 10/23/96, FHA permits family members (children, parents, grandparents of the borrower or the borrower's spouse, including legally adopted children and foster children) to lend on a secured or unsecured basis 100% of the homebuyer's required cash investment, which may include the down payment, closing costs, prepaid expenses and discount points.

Requirements

The combined amount of financing may not exceed 10% of the lesser of the property's value or sales price, plus normal closing costs, prepaid expenses and discount points.

If periodic payments of the secondary financing are required, the combined payments may not exceed the borrower's reasonable ability to pay. The secondary financing payments are to be included in the total debt payment-to-income ratio for qualifying purposes.

The second lien may not provide for balloon payment within five years from the date of execution.

If the family member providing the secondary financing borrows those funds, the source may not be any entity with an identity-of-interest in the sale of the property, including the seller, builder, loan officer or real estate agent.

An executed copy of the document outlining the terms of the secondary financing must be maintained in the lender's file.

CLOSING COSTS

Legislation, effective October 1992, rescinded the 57% limit on financeable closing costs.

Allowable Closing Costs

- Title examination and title insurance fee

- Escrow fee
- Document preparation fee (if performed by a third party not controlled by lender)
- Attorney fee
- Credit report (actual cost)
- Appraisal fee
- Loan origination fee
- Deposit verification fees
- Recording fees
- Home inspection fees (up to $200)
- Survey fee
- Test and verification fees

Costs that may not be financed include discount points, local transfer fees and prepaid expenses (impounds for property taxes, hazard insurance and prorated interest).

The seller is permitted to pay all or part of the buyer's closing costs or prepaid expenses to help the buyer qualify for the loan.

Lenders may pay the borrower's closing costs (and prepaid items) by charging a premium interest rate or additional discount points to the borrower.

QUALIFYING RATIOS

Two ratios are used to determine whether the borrower can reasonably be expected to meet the expenses involved in home ownership and otherwise provide for the family:

1. Mortgage payment expense = maximum 29% of gross effective income
2. Total fixed payments = maximum 41% of gross effective income

Mortgage payment expense means the monthly payment for principal, interest, hazard insurance, real estate taxes, one twelfth of the annual MIP, any owners' association fees and payments for any acceptable secondary financing.

Total fixed payments means the sum of (1) mortgage payment expense and (2) monthly recurring obligations on installment loans and revolving charge accounts extending beyond ten months, substantial monthly payments ($200 or more) extending for less than six months, real estate loans, alimony, child support, spousal maintenance and payments on all other debts of a continuing nature.

Gross effective income is the applicant's monthly gross income from all sources that can be expected to continue for the first five years of the loan term. Effective income includes salary, bonuses, commissions, overtime pay, interest, rent and other verified income. Any income, other than the principal salary, must be supported with a two-year verified history. If the borrower has changed employment within the last two years, both present and previous jobs must be verified. For salaried borrowers, lenders must obtain two years' original W-2 forms and pay stubs (photocopies are not acceptable).

Energy efficient homes (EEH) when purchased or refinanced are allowed both ratios to be exceeded by up to 2%. The local HUD office determines if a property qualifies for the EEH designation.

Condominium fees with proper documentation, such as that available from the utility company, are allowed that portion of the condominium fee clearly attributable to utilities to be subtracted from the mortgage payment before computing ratios.

Compensating Factors

Ratios in excess of the above may be acceptable if significant compensating factors are presented. Typically, for borrowers with limited recurring expense, greater latitude is permissible on the mortgage payment ratio than on the total fixed payment ratio. The compensating factors include the following situations:

- The borrower makes a large down payment toward the purchase of the property (at least 10%).

- The borrower has demonstrated a conservative attitude toward the use of credit and an ability to accumulate savings.
- Previous credit history shows that the borrower has the ability to devote a greater portion of income to housing expenses.
- The borrower receives compensation of income not reflected in effective income, but directly affecting the ability to pay the mortgage.
- There is only a small increase (10% or less) in the borrower's housing expense.
- The borrower has substantial nontaxable income.
- The borrower has potential for increased earnings as indicated by job training or education in the borrower's profession.

Example of Qualifying a Buyer for FHA Financing

Sandra Johnson wants to buy a home. Her gross effective income is $5,000. She has monthly recurring obligations of $800. Calculate the maximum monthly mortgage payment expense for which she can qualify.

Gross effective income	$5,000
	$\times 0.29$
Max. mortgage payment expense	$1,450 (Ratio 1)

Gross effective income	$5,000
	$\times 0.41$
Max. total fixed payments	$2,050
Recurring obligations	– 800
Max. mortgage payment expense	$1,250 (Ratio 2)

The maximum monthly mortgage payment expense Ms. Johnson qualifies for is $1,250 (the lower of Ratio 1 or Ratio 2).

MORTGAGE INSURANCE PREMIUMS (MIP)

For most FHA programs the borrower pays a one-time (up-front) premium plus annual premiums.

Up-Front MIP (UFMIP)

Effective September 3, 1996, the UFMIP was lowered from 2.25% to 2.00% of the base loan amount for first-time homebuyers who receive housing counseling.

For *first-time homeowners*, HUD reduced the UFMIP from 2.00% to 1.75%, effective June 12, 1997. To qualify for the premium reduction, prospective first-time homeowners must successfully complete the Homebuyer Education and Learning Program (HELP), a 16-hour course that covers such topics as how to select the right house and mortgage, household budgeting, managing credit, and maintenance and repair.

The one-time MIP can be paid in cash at time of closing or it may be financed. If financed, the MIP is added to the base loan amount and becomes part of the total amount financed. Financing of the one-time MIP does not in any way affect the maximum loan amount for purposes of loan qualification.

A person, other than the borrower, may pay the one-time MIP, but only if the entire MIP is paid in cash at closing.

If the MIP is paid in cash at closing, the lender is required to round down the base loan amount to the nearest $50.

Upon payment in full of the principal obligation of the mortgage, HUD refunds all of the unearned one-time MIP paid.

There is an exception to the reduced UFMIP that applies to streamlined refinancing of loans originated before July 1, 1991. For these refinanced loans, the premium remains at 3.8%.

Annual Premium

In addition to the one-time MIP, there is an annual premium of 0.5% of the outstanding loan balance, which is divided by 12 and added to the monthly payments.

The annual premium is charged for a period of years, depending on the down payment. Since October 1, 1994, the following terms apply:

Down Payment	Term
More than 10%	11 years
10% or less	30 years

UFMIP and Annual MIP for Loans over 15 Years, as of October 12, 1994

UFMIP	LTV	Annual MIP	Years
2.25%	Up to 90%	0.5%	7%
2.25	90–95%	0.5	30

UFMIP and Annual MIP for Loans of 15 Years or less, as of October 12, 1994

UFMIP	LTV	Annual Premium	Years
2.00%	Up to 90%	None	n/a
2.00	90–95%	.25%	4

DISCOUNT POINTS

Restrictions regarding *discount points* paid by the borrower were removed as of November 30, 1983. The 1% loan origination fee was not affected.

INTEREST RATES

Since November 30, 1983, FHA interest rates have been free from HUD control, except for Section 235 loans.

The interest rate on a fixed rate FHA loan is not raised after an assumption.

MAXIMUM LOAN TERM

The maximum term for most FHA-insured mortgages is 30 years.

MONTHLY PAYMENTS

Under FHA financing, it is the lender's responsibility to ascertain that property taxes and hazard insurance premiums are paid when due. Lenders, therefore, insist that the monthly payments include proportionate amounts for taxes and insurance.

Escrow Account

Under FHA financing the lender is required to maintain an escrow account from which to pay property taxes, hazard insurance and Mortgage Insurance Premiums (MIPs). HUD has established guidelines for lenders to compute escrow charges, which became mandatory October 27, 1997. Under the new rules, lenders can require monthly escrow contributions equal to $\frac{1}{12}$ of the annual property taxes, hazard insurance, and homeowners' association dues. The lender may add a cushion equal to 2 months' worth of escrow charges.

PREPAYMENT

There is no penalty for full or partial prepayment of FHA loans insured on or after August 2, 1985. However, FHA loans provide for collection of interest to the first of the month following payment in full.

NOTE: If an FHA loan is paid off early, the borrower may be entitled to a refund of part of the up-front mortgage insurance premium (UFMIP).

REFINANCING

Refinancing is permitted for the purpose of retiring existing liens, making repairs and improvements to the property, obtaining a reduction in interest rates, paying off a mortgage subject to a balloon payment, paying a divorced spouse as a result of a court-ordered property settlement, paying heirs to settle an estate, or obtaining cash to finance family related expenditures, such as a college education.

Streamline refinances are designed to reduce interest on a current FHA mortgage and may not include cashback to the borrower. No appraisal or credit approval is necessary. The term of the mortgage is the lesser of 30 years or the unexpired term of the mortgage plus 12 years.

Cashback refinances are permitted for owner-occupied principal residences owned more than one year, and are limited to 85% of appraised value plus closing costs.

NOTE: If an FHA loan is refinanced, the borrower may be entitled to a refund of part of the up-front mortgage insurance premium (UFMIP).

OPEN-END CLAUSE

An FHA home loan may contain an *open-end clause* by which the outstanding balance may be increased by amounts advanced to the borrower for improvements, alterations or repairs to the property. Such advances may not increase the outstanding balance to an amount greater than the original loan amount unless they are used to add rooms or other enclosed space to the dwelling. For the loan increase, monthly payments can be raised or the term can be extended.

ASSUMPTIONS

Loans Originated Prior to December 1, 1986

FHA loans originated prior to December 1, 1986, are freely assumable, which means a buyer can title subject to the mortgage without the lender's approval, in which case the seller remains liable for repayment of the mortgage debt.

Assumptions with release of liability are granted only if the assumptor is creditworthy and willing to execute an agreement to assume and pay the mortgage debt.

Loans Originated Between December 1, 1986, and December 15, 1989

Some FHA mortgages executed during this period contain language that is not enforced due to later congressional action, and such loans are now freely assumable despite any restrictions stated in the mortgage.

Restrictions of the HUD Reform Act of 1989

FHA loans originated after December 15, 1989, contain due-on-sale clauses, which means they can only be assumed by an owner-occupant buyer found creditworthy who executes an agreement to assume and pay the mortgage debt. Lenders cannot refuse release of liability if an acceptable borrower assumes the loan. The due-on-sale clause is triggered whenever an owner's name is deleted from title, except when that party's interest is transferred by devise, descent or in other circumstances when transfer cannot legally lead to acceleration of the mortgage debt.

Any Mortgage Originated Before January 27, 1991

If the original borrower is an owner-occupant and the assumptor is purchasing the property as a second home, the seller can obtain release of liability only if the remaining balance is paid down to 85% LTV.

Allowable Assumption Charges

- A maximum of $500, plus cost of credit report, based on the lender's actual costs. Half of the fee must be refunded if the borrower is found creditworthy, but settlement does not occur for reasons beyond the borrower's control.
- Nonrefundable fees or charges for credit reports and VOEs or VODs, which are collected by the lender.
- Closing fees, such as document preparation fees, attorney fees, recording fees, and so forth.

BUYER PROTECTION CLAUSES

Amendatory Clause

The following amendatory clause must be part of the purchase agreement unless the borrower has been informed of the appraised value prior to signing the agreement.

> *It is expressly agreed that notwithstanding any other provisions of this contract, the purchaser shall not be obligated to complete the purchase of the property described herein or to incur any penalty by forfeiture of earnest money deposits or otherwise unless the purchaser has been given, in accordance with HUD/ FHA or VA requirements, a written statement by the Federal Housing Commissioner, VA or a direct endorsement lender, setting forth the appraised value of the property of not less than $[_____]. The purchaser shall have the privilege and option of proceeding with consummation of the contract without regard to the amount of the appraised valuation. The appraised valuation is arrived at to determine the maximum mortgage the Department of Housing and Urban Development will insure. HUD does not warrant the value nor the condition of the property. The purchaser should satisfy himself or herself that the price and condition of the property are acceptable.*

Importance of Home Inspections

Since December 6, 1996, the EPA pamphlet "Protect Your Family From Lead in Your Home" has become the official lead-based paint disclosure in conjunction with FHA loans. That disclosure is the responsibility of the owner selling or renting the property.

In addition, FHA has developed the following form to be signed and dated by the borrower(s) on or before the date that the sales contract is executed, for all transactions involving FHA mortgage insurance on existing property.

IMPORTANCE OF HOME INSPECTIONS

While FHA requires the lender to have an appraiser determine the value of the property, it is an estimate only and is used to determine the amount of mortgage FHA will insure and if the condition of the property makes it eligible for FHA mortgage insurance. It is not, however, a guarantee that the property is free of defects.

As the purchaser, YOU should carefully examine the property or have it inspected by a qualified home inspection company to make sure that the condition is acceptable to you. You should do this before you sign the sales contract or make the contact contingent on the inspection. If repairs are needed, you may negotiate with the owner about having the faults corrected.

There is no requirement that you hire an inspector. If you choose to, the cost of the inspection up to $200 may be included in your mortgage loan. Names of home inspection companies can be found in the yellow pages of your telephone directory under the heading "Home Inspection Services."

I/We have carefully read this notice and fully understand that FHA will not perform a home inspection nor guarantee the price or condition of the property we are purchasing.

_____ *I/We choose to have a home inspection performed.*

_____ *I/We do not choose to have a home inspection performed.*

Borrower_____ Date_____

Coborrower_____ Date_____

FHA LOAN PROGRAMS

Section 203(b) Fixed Rate One- to Four-Family Dwellings

The objective of Section 203(b) is to finance the acquisition or the refinance of one- to four-family units for owner-occupants. 203(b) loans are available for (1) new construction approved by and built under FHA or VA inspection, (2) new construction not built under FHA/VA inspection but with a ten-year home-owner's warranty and (3) existing construction more than one year old.

Section 203(b)(2) FHA Loans to Veterans

The objective of Section 203(b)(2) is to finance, at special low cash requirements, the acquisition or refinance of single-family units for owner-occupant veterans.

Loan-to-Value Ratio (LTV)

The maximum LTV is 100% of the first $25,000, plus 95% of the amount between $25,000 and $125,000, and 90% of the amount over $125,000 of appraised value (or sales price, whichever is less), plus allowable closing costs.

The minimum cash investment is $750 less for veterans than for regular 203(b) borrowers of properties in excess of $50,000.

Eligibility Requirements

To be eligible for an FHA 203(b)(2) loan, the veteran must have served 90 days of continuous active duty (which includes active duty training) in any branch of the U.S. armed forces, including the National Guard and U.S. Coast Guard. This service could have been at any time, not necessarily in time of war. If a veteran can establish that he or she served under hazardous duty conditions, he or she is eligible with service of less than 90 days.

Veterans who have used their eligibility to obtain a VA home loan are still eligible for this program. Veterans who were eligible for a VA home loan and did not use their eligibility are still eligible for the FHA program.

Use of the FHA program does not cause veterans to lose their VA eligibility for future use. Veterans who use the FHA program may use it again an unlimited number of times, provided certain other requirements are met.

Application

In addition to the normal application forms required for a regular Section 203(b) FHA loan, the veteran must furnish a *Certificate of Veterans Status* (VA Form 26-8261), which must be obtained from the Department of Veterans Affairs. *Requests for Certificate of Veterans Status* must be made by filling out VA Form 26-8261A and mailing it to the VA regional office, together with separation and discharge papers. Real estate brokers can expedite the process by obtaining a supply of these 26-8261A forms from the nearest VA office, and by assisting the veteran in filling out the form.

Section 203(i) Single-Family Mortgage Insurance for Outlying Areas

Section 203(i) provides mortgage insurance for a person to purchase a principal residence in a rural area.

Eligibility Requirements

A borrower must meet standard FHA credit qualifications.

Eligible properties are one-to-four unit structures, including farm housing located on two acres or more of land adjacent to an all-weather road.

The maximum mortgage amount for a single family unit is 75% of the Section 203(b) limit.

Section 203(h) Single-Family Home Mortgage Insurance for Disaster Victims

Section 203(h) provides mortgage insurance for a person to purchase a principal residence after being displaced by a disaster. The residence to be purchased need not be located in the disaster area.

Eligibility Requirements

A borrower must meet standard FHA credit qualifications.

A borrower's previous residence must have been destroyed or damaged to such an extent that reconstruction or replacement is necessary. The borrower may be the owner or a renter of the property destroyed.

The borrower is eligible for 100% financing. No down payment is required. The up-front mortgage insurance premium can be financed into the mortgage, and the borrower will pay an annual premium.

The borrower must purchase a one-family unit; two, three and four-unit properties may not be purchased under this program.

ARMs cannot be used with this program.

Mortgage limits are the same as for a Section 203(b) loan.

The borrower's application for the mortgage insurance must be submitted within one year of the President's disaster declaration.

Section 203(k) Rehabilitation Home Mortgage Insurance

Section 203(k) provides mortgage insurance to:

- rehabilitate an existing one- to four-family dwelling (completed for more than a year) that will be used for residential purposes;
- rehabilitate such a structure and refinance the outstanding indebtedness;
- purchase and rehabilitate such a structure; and
- rehabilitate a dwelling after it has been moved from another site to a new foundation.

Section 203(k) should not be used unless the rehabilitation or improvement costs total a minimum of $5,000.

Eligible improvements include such items as structural alterations, additions, reconstruction, remodeling, new siding, plumbing, heating, air conditioning, electrical systems, roofing, flooring, carpeting, energy conservation improvements, and major landscape work.

Maximum Insurable Mortgage: Based on the expected value of the property with the work completed.

Minimum Cash Investment: Same as Section 203(b) for owner occupants; 15% for investors.

Term: Same as Section 203(b).

Mortgage Insurance Premium: Monthly.

Refinancing: Permitted in conjunction with rehabilitation.

Permanent Construction Loans

Purpose–To assist approved FHA builders in obtaining construction financing by allowing borrowers to be approved prior to start of construction.

Closing–In name of borrower prior to start of construction.

Mortgage amount–Same as any other FHA loan. Appraisal from plans and specifications with requirement for completion inspection. Builder must supply HOW warranty policy to enable borrower to obtain an LTV in excess of 90%.

MIP–To be paid within 15 days of closing.

Documents–Construction documents must contain a provision that the construction terms cease to be effective and the FHA terms become effective at time of final inspection or certificate of occupancy.

Section 221(d)(2) Mortgage Insurance for Low and Moderate Income Buyers

Provides mortgage insurance for a person of low or moderate income, or one displaced by disaster or urban renewal, to purchase or refinance a low cost principal residence.

Eligibility Requirements

- A displaced borrower can purchase a house with only a $200 cash investment.
- Eligible properties are one-to-four-unit structures.

- Maximum mortgage amount for a single-family unit is $36,000. Lesser limits may be applicable in some areas.

Section 234(c) Condominiums

This section provides mortgage insurance for a person to purchase or refinance a principal residence in a condominium project.

Eligibility Requirements

- The project must be approved by HUD to be eligible for insurance.
- Maximum mortgage amount for a condominium unit is $155,250. Lesser limits may be applicable in some areas.

Occupancy Requirements

At least 80% of the units on which there are HUD-insured mortgages in a project must be owner-occupied before HUD can make insured financing available on additional units.

Guidelines

The project in which the unit is located must conform to the following guidelines:

1. The unit must be in a condominium project that provides for undivided ownership of common areas by the unit owners.
2. The project must be more than one year old. All units and all common elements and improvements must have been completed. (Exception: VA-approved complexes)
3. Satisfactory completion of all improvements must have been made, including the common areas and facilities. (Exception: VA-approved complexes)
4. Eighty percent of the total number of units must be occupied by unit purchasers. No more than 40% of the units shall be insured under Section

235. (If the VA has issued approval subject to a higher presale requirement, reconsideration must be sought through the VA.)

5. Parking and recreational facilities must be a legal part of the project and owned by unit owners. However, leasing of these facilities is permitted provided the lessors can terminate with no more than 90-days notice any contract entered into with the lessee.

6. The developer must have no special rights with respect to the project or common areas other than the marketing of unsold units. The project must not be subject to future expansion at the option of the developer.

   Any special rights of the developer (as developer and not as a unit owner) to do any and all of the following must have expired or have been waived in a recorded instrument:
   a. add land or units to the condominium;
   b. convert common elements into additional units or limited common elements;
   c. withdraw land from the condominium;
   d. use easements through the common elements for the purpose of making improvements within the condominium or within any adjacent land; or
   e. convert a unit into two or more units, common elements, or into two or more units and common elements.

7. Each unit owner, his/her successors and assigns, upon acceptance of the unit deed, automatically must become members of the association. Each unit member must have a proportionate vote at association meetings and must be responsible to pay a proportionate share of the expenses of the association.

8. The project must demonstrate good management, maintenance and financial stability. There must be an adequate reserve fund for the peri-

odic maintenance, repair and replacement of the common elements.

9. The master deed, bylaws and any other similar documents must be in accordance with current state law. The legal documents clearly must designate
   a. unit composition, description of common areas and the party responsible for repair and maintenance of the property;
   b. a mechanism for amendment of the documents;
   c. the allocation on an equitable basis of the unit owner's voting rights and responsibilities for assessments; and
   d. the methods to be used in operating and governing the condominium.
10. Each condominium unit owner should have a clearly specified interest in the common area.
11. The association must have a master or blanket policy, protecting against loss or damage by fire and other hazards, sufficient to cover the replacement cost of the common areas of the project, and a comprehensive public liability insurance policy covering the common areas. If the project is in a flood zone, flood insurance also is required.
12. The project will not qualify if circumstances or conditions concerning the project will have a substantially adverse effect upon the project or be a contributing cause for the unit mortgage to become delinquent.

Application Forms and Exhibits

Application for an appraisal must be submitted on Form HUD-92800, *Application for Property Appraisal and Commitment.*

The application on the first unit submitted for HUD insurance in an existing condominium project must be accompanied by the following exhibits:

1. Master deed or equivalent document (including amendments), with the recordation date of the project.
2. Bylaws for the association.
3. Recorded plat, plan, survey or map (including amendments) of projects.
4. Articles of incorporation, if any, executed in connection with the establishment of the association.
5. Mortgagee's certification that
   a. the deed of the family unit and the deed or other recorded instrument committing the project to a plan of condominium ownership comply with all legal requirements of the jurisdiction;
   b. the mortgagor has good marketable title to the family unit, subject only to the mortgage, which is a valid first lien on the same; and
   c. the family unit is assessed and subject to assessment for taxes pertaining only to that unit.
6. Statement of insurance and fidelity bond coverage for the common areas.
7. The project's annual income, expenses and budget. The reserve funds for commonly owned replacements must be sufficient to meet current costs. Submission must include copies of the minutes of the last two meetings of the council of co-owners.
8. Certification from the association that 70% of the units are owner occupied.
9. Certification from the mortgagee's attorney that legal documents submitted for review meet HUD's objectives.

Condominium Conversions

Units in any project (including VA approved) converted from rental housing to condominiums less than one year prior to the application for insurance are not acceptable unless

1. the mortgagor or comortgagor was a tenant of that rental housing or
2. the conversion of the property is sponsored by a bona fide tenants' organization representing a majority of the households.

Condominium Projects Approved by the FNMA and VA

The approval of condominium projects by the FNMA and/or VA will waive the requirement for project approval procedures as a condition of accepting applications (i.e., appraisal requests will be taken, but evidence of approval must accompany the first application). Form 1028* must be submitted by the lender demonstrating that the project was approved by FNMA and evidence that the project is more than one year old. The CRV will be accepted as evidence of approval by the VA. The VA project is not limited to the one-year age restriction. Specific requirements to meet eligibility criteria established in the regulations will be made conditions of the commitment.

Any other documentation is not acceptable. FNMA's streamlined procedure is not acceptable, and submission of the above documentation is required.

Section 251 Adjustable Rate Mortgage (ARM)

Section 251 provides mortgage insurance for a person to purchase or refinance a principal residence.

Eligibility Requirements

- ARMs can only be used in conjunction with Sections 203(b), 234(c) and 203(k).
- Eligible properties are one- to four-unit structures.

Interest Rate Keyed to Index

Changes in the interest rate must correspond to changes in the weekly average yield on U.S. Treasury securities adjusted to a constant maturity of one year. Weekly average yields are published in the Federal Reserve Bulletin, easily obtained from the Federal Reserve Board by requesting to be placed on a mail-

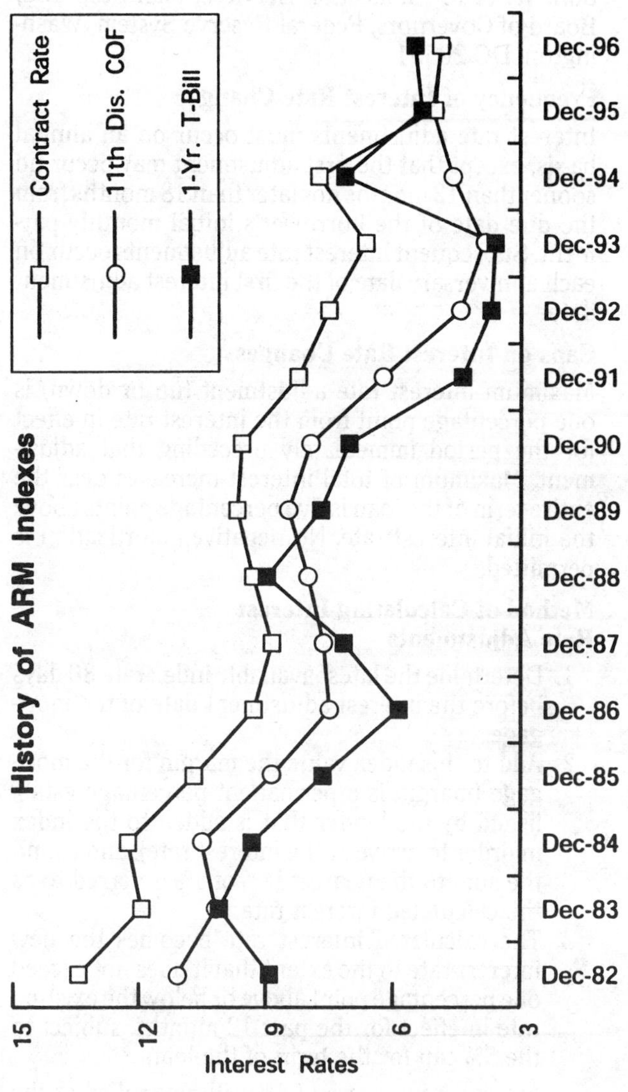
History of ARM Indexes
Contract Rate
11th Dis. COF
1-Yr. T-Bill
Interest Rates
15
12
9
6
3
Dec-82
Dec-83
Dec-84
Dec-85
Dec-86
Dec-87
Dec-88
Dec-89
Dec-90
Dec-91
Dec-92
Dec-93
Dec-94
Dec-95
Dec-96

ing list for receipt of the weekly H.15(519) publication. Write to Publication Services, Mail Stop 138, Board of Governors, Federal Reserve System, Washington, DC 20551.

Frequency of Interest Rate Change

Interest rate adjustments must occur on an annual ba-sis, except that the first adjustment may occur no sooner than 12 months nor later than 18 months from the due date of the borrower's initial monthly payment. Subsequent interest rate adjustments occur on each anniversary date of the first interest adjustment date.

Caps on Interest Rate Changes

Maximum interest rate adjustment (up or down) is one percentage point from the interest rate in effect for the period immediately preceding that adjustment. Maximum of total interest increases over the entire term of the loan is five percentage points above the initial interest rate. No negative amortization is permitted.

Method of Calculating Interest Rate Adjustments

1. Determine the latest available index rate 30 days before the interest adjustment date of the mortgage.
2. Add to this index value the margin for the mortgage (margin is a permanent percentage established by the lender that is added to the index in order to arrive at the interest rate), and round the sum to the nearest ⅛% of 1%, referred to as the calculated interest rate.
3. The calculated interest rate becomes the new interest rate to the extent that it does not exceed one percentage point above or below the existing rate in effect for the past 12 months, subject to the 5% cap for the term of the loan.

   Increases in excess of 1% will be applied at the next adjustment date (subject to both caps) if the calculated interest rate remains at or above the existing interest rate. (Decreases in excess of 1% also are applied at the next adjustment date if the calculated interest rate remains at or below the existing interest rate.)

Year	Index	+ Margin	=	Calc. Rate	New Rate
1	N/A	+ N/A	=	N/A	7.25
2	6.00	+ 2.75	=	8.75	8.25
3	9.00	+ 2.75	=	11.75	9.25
4	5.25	+ 2.75	=	8.00	8.25
5	4.75	+ 2.75	=	7.50	7.25

Yr 1: Lender and borrower agreed to an initial interest rate of 7.25% for the first year with annual adjustments based on the index plus a margin of 2.75%.

Yr 2: Calculated interest rate (*Index* + *Margin*) is 8.75%. Because this is more than 1% above the initial interest rate, the new rate is 8.25%.

Yr 3: The index increases 3% (from 6% to 9%) bringing the calculated rate to 11.75%. However, because of the 1% annual interest cap, the new rate is only 9.25%.

Yr 4: The index decreases 2.75% (from 9% to 5.25%). After adding the margin, the calculated rate becomes 8.00%, which is more than 1% below the existing rate of 9.25%. Therefore, the new rate can only decrease to 8.25%.

Yr 5: The index decreased 0.50% (from 5.25% to 4.75%). After adding the margin, the calculated rate becomes 7.50%, a decrease of 0.75% from the previous year. However, because there was a decrease of 0.25% in excess of the 1% annual cap in year 4, the excess decrease of 0.25% is applied to year 5, bringing the new rate down to 7.25%, still within the annual 1% cap.

4. The new interest rate is then used to adjust the monthly payment to fully amortize the remaining principal balance as of the adjustment date over the remaining term of the loan. The adjusted monthly payment becomes effective 30 days after the interest adjustment date. This eliminates negative amortization.

Loan Disclosure

The lender is required to give the borrower a complete written explanation of the loan terms, including a hypothetical monthly payment schedule that shows a worst case scenario of the first five years of the loan. Such a scenario shows what the monthly payments would be if the interest rate rose by 1% each year for five years to the maximum allowed total increase of 5%.

Additionally, the lender is obligated to inform the borrower at least 30 days in advance of any adjustment to the monthly payment of (1) the new interest rate and the amount of the monthly payment, (2) the current index figure and how the payment adjustment was calculated and (3) the method any interest rate change in excess of the cap is carried over to the next adjustment interval.

Section 255 Home Equity Conversion Mortgage (HECM) (Mortgage Insurance for Reverse Mortgages)

Section 255 provides mortgage insurance for elderly homeowners to convert the equity in their homes into monthly streams of income and/or a line of credit, to be repaid when they no longer occupy the home.

Borrower Requirements

- Minimum 62 years of age, based on youngest borrower
- Must occupy property as principal residence
- Must participate in a consumer information session

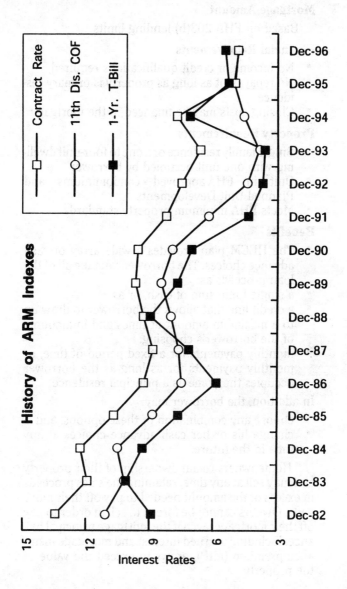

History of ARM Indexes

Legend:
- Contract Rate (□)
- 11th Dis. COF (○)
- 1-Yr. T-Bill (■)

Y-axis (right side): Dec-82, Dec-83, Dec-84, Dec-85, Dec-86, Dec-87, Dec-88, Dec-89, Dec-90, Dec-91, Dec-92, Dec-93, Dec-94, Dec-95, Dec-96

X-axis (Interest Rates): 3, 6, 9, 12, 15

Mortgage Amount

Based on FHA 203(b) lending limits

Financial Requirements

- No income or credit qualifications required
- No repayment as long as property is primary residence
- Closing costs may be financed in the mortgage

Property Requirements

- Single-family residence or a one to four-unit dwelling with one unit occupied by borrower
- Unit in FHA-approved condominiums and Planned Unit Developments
- Meets FHA minimum property standards

Benefits

- The HECM plan provides a wide array of cash advance choices. The borrower can take all of the loan proceeds as:
- a single lump sum of cash, or as
- a credit line that allows the borrower to draw up to a maximum amount at times and in amounts of the borrower's choosing;
- monthly payments for a fixed period of time, or monthly payments for as long as the borrower occupies the home as a principal residence.

In addition, the borrower may:

- choose any combination of these options, and
- change his or her cash advance choices at any time in the future.

Homeowners retain ownership of their property and may sell at any time, retaining the sales proceeds in excess of the amount needed to pay off their mortgage. Owners cannot be forced to sell in order to pay off their mortgage, even if the mortgage principal balance, including accrued interest and mortgage insurance premium (MIP), grows to exceed the value of the property.

HUD protects the borrower against the lender's failure to make the required payments under the mortgage. When the mortgage becomes due, the lender's recovery from the borrower's estate is limited to the value of the home; i.e., there is no deficiency against the borrower or the estate.

Energy Efficient Mortgages

These provide mortgage insurance for a person to purchase or refinance a principal residence and incorporate the cost of energy efficient improvements into the mortgage.

Eligibility Requirements

- Eligible properties are one- to two-unit existing and new construction.
- The cost of the energy-efficient improvements eligible for financing into the mortgage is the greater of 5% of the property's value (not to exceed $8,000) or $4,000.
- The total cost of the improvements must be less than the total present value of the energy saved over the useful life of the energy improvement.
- The cost of the energy improvements and estimate of the energy savings must be determined by a home energy rating system (HERS) or energy consultant.

The maximum mortgage amount for a single-family unit is $155,250, plus the cost of the eligible energy efficient improvements. Lesser limits may be applicable in some areas.

Title I Mobile Homes

The objective is to finance the acquisition of a new or used mobile home, which the borrower must occupy as his or her primary residence.

Qualifications

The mobile home must be new (not previously occupied); or a used mobile home sold by a person who financed it with an FHA mobile home loan; or occupied by the purchaser under a government lease after having been displaced from previous housing by a disaster.

The mobile home must be constructed according to standards prescribed by the American National Standards Institute, and placed on a lot owned by the borrower that complies with certain standards, or be in an approved mobile home park.

The mobile home must have a minimum floor space of 400 square feet.

Maximum Loan and Term

Multisection	$40,500
Multisection with lot	54,000
Lot only	13,500
Maximum term of loan	20 years

Minimum Cash Down Payment

The minimum cash down payment is 5% of the first $3,000 of the purchase contract amount, plus 10% of any excess. A used mobile home with a blue book value of at least the required minimum down payment may be acceptable in lieu of a cash down payment.

Interest Rate

Interest on loans may vary depending on the amount and term of the loan.

FHA Title I Manufactured Homes

Effective April 6, 1983, new or existing manufactured homes on a permanent site are eligible for insured financing under Title II, subject to the following criteria:

1. They must have a minimum floor area of 400 square feet.
2. They must be constructed after June 15, 1976, in conformance with the Federal Manufactured Home Construction and Safety Standards, evidenced by an affixed certification label.

3. They must be classified and subject to taxation as real estate.
4. The mortgage must cover the manufactured home and its site, and shall have a term not to exceed 30 years.
5. The finished grade elevation beneath the manufactured home or, if a basement is used, the lowest finished exterior grade adjacent to the perimeter enclosure, shall be at or above the 100-year return frequency flood elevation.

In addition to the above general requirements applicable to all manufactured homes, the following specific requirements apply to existing or proposed construction.

Existing Manufactured Homes

Existing units permanently erected on a site more than one year prior to the date of application for mortgage insurance shall

1. be permanently anchored to and supported by permanent footings (anchoring straps or cables affixed to ground anchors other than footings will not meet this requirement);
2. have permanently installed utilities that are protected from freezing;
3. have the space beneath the dwelling properly enclosed as a crawlspace that provides for adequate crawlspace ventilation;
4. have been installed or occupied only at the location for which a mortgage is being requested; and
5. have a site, site improvements and all other features of the mortgaged property not addressed by the Federal Manufactured Home Construction and Safety Standards that meet or exceed applicable provisions of the requirements for existing housing one- to four-family living units.

Existing manufactured homes erected on a site less than one year prior to date of application for mortgage insurance that were not approved by HUD prior to their construction may not have been installed or occupied at any other site. Such homes shall comply with items 1 through 8 listed below for proposed construction. Such units are subject to a loan-to-appraised value ratio of 90% unless the unit is covered by a builder's warranty (as listed in item 10 below under proposed construction) and an insured ten-year protection plan accepted by HUD, in which case the unit could qualify for high ratio (97–95%) loans.

Proposed Construction

In addition to the general requirements listed above, manufactured homes shall meet the following requirements to qualify for proposed construction.

1. Be erected with or without a basement on a site-built permanent foundation that meets or exceeds applicable requirements of the Minimum Property Standards for One- and Two-Family Dwellings (MPS)
2. Be permanently attached to that foundation by anchoring devices adequate for all loads identified in the MPS, which includes resistance to ground movements, seismic shakings, potential shearing, overturning and uplift loads caused by wind, and so forth
3. Have the towing hitch or running gear, which includes tongues, axles, brakes, wheels, lights and other parts of the chassis that operate only during transportation, removed
4. Have any crawlspace beneath the manufactured home properly ventilated and enclosed by continuous permanent foundation-type construction designed to resist all forces to which it may be subject without transmitting to the building superstructure movements or any effects caused by frost heave, soil settlement or consolidation, or shrinking or swelling of expansive soils
5. Have the crawlspace perimeter enclosure, if separate from the supporting foundation, ade-

quately secured to the perimeter of the manufactured home and constructed of materials that conform to MPS requirements for foundations

6. Be insulated so that envelope Uo values (the rate of heat loss through floors, walls, windows, doors and ceilings, measured in BTUs per hour per square foot of surface per degrees Fahrenheit difference between indoor and outdoor temperatures) do not exceed:

   a. 0.145 in Climatic Zone I, which includes the states of Alabama, Arkansas, Arizona, California, Florida, Georgia, Hawaii, Louisiana, Mississippi, New Mexico, North Carolina, Oklahoma, South Carolina, Tennessee and Texas.

   b. 0.087 in Climatic Zone III, which includes Alaska, Maine, Michigan, Minnesota, Montana, New Hampshire, North Dakota, South Dakota, Vermont, Wisconsin and Wyoming.

   c. 0.099 in Climatic Zone II, which includes the remainder of the states.

7. Have a site, site improvements and all other features of the mortgaged property not addressed by the Federal Manufactured Home Construction and Safety Standards that meet or exceed applicable requirements of the MPS except paragraph 311-2.2

8. Have had the manufactured home itself braced and stiffened before it leaves the factory to eliminate racking and potential damage during transportation

9. Be eligible for high-ratio (97–95%) financing, for which purpose the beginning of construction will be interpreted as the commencement of on-site work even though the manufactured home itself may have been produced and temporarily stored prior to the date of application for insured financing

10. Have submitted with the application for insured financing an agreement to execute a *Builder's Warranty,* Form HUD 92544, plus an addendum warranting that the manufactured home property substantially complies with the plans and specifications, and that the manufactured home sustained no hidden damage during transportation and, if the manufactured home was manufactured in separate sections, the sections were properly joined and sealed. The agreement must provide that upon the sale or conveyance of the dwelling and delivery of the warranty, the seller/ builder will promptly furnish the local HUD office with a copy of the warranty. This copy must be signed and dated by the purchaser to evidence that the original warranty was received.

VA FINANCING

VA loans are administered by the U.S. Department of Veterans Affairs (VA).

PURPOSE

VA is authorized to guarantee loans made to eligible veterans for the following purposes:

1. To purchase or construct a dwelling to be owned and occupied by a veteran
2. To purchase a farm on which there is a farm residence to be owned and occupied by a veteran
3. To purchase and occupy a one-family residential unit in a condominium housing development approved by the VA
4. To purchase a manufactured home, permanently affixed to its lot, provided that the laws of the state provide that the manufactured home is considered real property
5. To purchase a manufactured home
6. To repair, alter or improve a dwelling owned and occupied by a veteran and to install energy conservation improvements in a home, including solar heating or solar cooling

   A veteran who purchases an existing home will be informed of the opportunity to include energy conservation improvements in the financing.

7. To refinance an existing mortgage secured by a lien of record on a dwelling owned and occupied by a veteran as a home
8. To refinance an existing VA loan for the purpose of interest rate reduction

TYPES OF LOANS

1. Fixed rate mortgage
2. Adjustable rate mortgage (ARM)
3. Graduated payment mortgage (GPM)
4. Growing equity mortgage (GEM)
5. Buydown

AUTOMATIC APPROVAL SYSTEM

Lenders are classified by the VA as supervised and nonsupervised. *Supervised lenders* are lending institutions that are subject to examination and supervision by an agency of the United States or of any state or territory, including the District of Columbia. *Nonsupervised lenders* are not supervised by any federal or state agency.

Loans that are automatically guaranteed without requiring specific prior VA approval may be made by supervised lenders and also by nonsupervised lenders that are specifically authorized by the VA to close loans on an automatic basis.

In the event the borrower defaults, the lender is compensated for the loss to the extent of the VA loan guaranty.

UNDERWRITING GUIDELINES

A VA loan may not be guaranteed unless the veteran is a satisfactory credit risk and the contemplated loan payments bear a proper relation to the veteran's present and anticipated income and expenses.

Please refer to the Underwriting Guidelines section for information on acceptable types of income and liquid assets available for down payment.

The VA has additional requirements with respect to active duty applicants and recently discharged veterans.

Active duty applicants. A Leave & Earnings Statement (LES) is required in addition to employment verification. Each active duty applicant must be counseled through the use of a Counseling Checklist for Military Home Buyers (VA Form 26-0592).

Recently discharged veterans. Special attention is given to veteran applicants recently discharged or retired who have little or no employment experience other than their military occupation.

DOCUMENTATION

Documents may be obtained before starting the loan application.

- The veteran needs to submit a Request for Determination of Eligibility and Available Loan Entitlement (Form 26-1880) together with discharge or separation papers in order to obtain a Certificate of Eligibility (Form 26-8320).
- The veteran, seller or lender may also request an appraisal of the property to obtain a Certificate of Reasonable Value (Form 26-1843).

Important documents required for loan underwriting include a(n):

- Certificate of Reasonable Value (CRV) (Form 26-1843);
- Certificate of Eligibility (Form 26-8320);
- Uniform Residential Loan Application (URLA) with a revised HUD/VA addendum (Form 26-1802a);
- Loan Analysis (Form 26-6393);
- Original credit report and related documents;
- Request for Verification of Deposit (Form 26-8497a);
- Request for Verification of Employment (or equivalent) (Form 26-8497) and original pay stubs; verification of other income (e.g., tax returns, profit and loss statement and balance sheet);
- Purchase (sales) agreement (earnest money contract);
- Counseling Checklist for Military Home Buyers (if applicable) (Form 26-0592); and
- Interest Rate Reduction Refinancing Worksheet (if applicable) (Form 26-8923).

ELIGIBLE VETERANS

A veteran is defined as a person who served in the active military, naval, or air service, and who, except for a service member on active duty, was discharged or released from active duty under conditions other than dishonorable. The unremarried surviving spouse of a veteran is also considered a veteran for certain benefits under title 38 of the U.S. Code. For a spouse of a POW or MIA, eligibility is based on the spouse's basic qualifications.

Service Eligibility

To be eligible the veteran must have served on active duty for the minimum required periods listed below, except if discharged because of a service-connected disability.

Era	Dates	On Active Duty
World War II	09/16/40-07/25/47	90 days
Peacetime	07/26/47-06/26/50	181 days[1]
Korean	06/27/50-01/31/55	90 days
Post-Korean	02/01/55-08/04/64	181 days[1]
Vietnam	08/05/64-05/07/75	90 days
Post Vietnam– Enlisted	05/08/75-09/07/80	181 days[1]
Post Vietnam– Officer	05/08/75-10/16/81	181 days[1]
Peacetime– Enlisted	09/07/80-open	24 months[1]
Peacetime–Officer	10/16/81-open	181 days[2]
Pers. Gulf–Enlisted	08/02/90-open	24 months[2]
Pers. Gulf–Officer	08/02/90-open	90 days[2]

[1]continuous days

[2]Eligibility may also be established if discharged due to hardship or a service-connected disability, or for the convenience of the government after completing at least the full period for which ordered to active duty (90 days).

Members of the Reserves or National Guard are eligible (until Oct. 28, 1999) upon completion of six years service in the selected Reserve, or upon discharge because of a service-connected disability before completing six years of service. Also eligible are unremarried surviving spouses of reservists who die of service-connected causes.

ENTITLEMENT

In accordance with the VA Housing Act of 1970, all loan guaranty entitlement is available until used (it does not expire), whether derived from World War II, the Korean War or any other period. The act also revived unused, expired loan guaranty entitlement.

Restoration (Substitution) of Entitlement

The Veterans Housing Act of 1974 permits *restoration* (also called reinstatement) of a veteran's entitlement to the full extent of the current maximum guaranty if the property has been disposed of and the loan paid in full, or if the property is sold to another eligible, creditworthy veteran with entitlement equal to or greater than the loan's guaranty amount, and who assumes the VA loan and agrees to substitute his or her entitlement for the seller's.

Under the Veterans Benefits Improvement Act of 1994, a veteran's entitlement may be restored *one time only* if the veteran has repaid the prior VA loan in full, even if he or she is not disposing of the property securing the loan. Future restoration requires disposal of the property financed with that loan.

Remaining (Available or Partial) Entitlement

A veteran who has used up his or her entitlement and wishes to keep and rent the VA-financed home, or who sold it without substitution of entitlement by another creditworthy veteran, or to a nonveteran, can still obtain a VA loan to finance the purchase of a new home by using any remaining entitlement. A veteran who used his or her entitlement several years ago is likely to have remaining entitlement now because VA guaranties have increased as property values have increased. (See the table below.) Remaining entitlement can be determined by subtracting the amount of entitlement used for prior guaranteed loans from the current maximum guaranty.

Maximum Guaranty

The VA sets no maximum loan ceilings but issues maximum loan guaranties. A veteran is entitled to the current maximum guaranty minus any entitlement used for prior guaranteed loans that have not been restored. As property values have increased over the years, so have VA guaranties, as shown in the following table.

History of Maximum Guaranties

Beginning of program	$ 2,000
12/28/45	4,000
04/20/50	7,500
05/07/68	12,500
12/31/74	17,500
10/01/78	25,000
10/01/80	27,500
02/01/88	46,000
10/13/94	50,750

Current Maximum Guaranty, as of December 1994

Loan Amount	Maximum Guaranty
Up to $45,000	50% of loan amount
$ 45,000 to $ 56,250	$22,500
$ 56,251 to $144,000	40% of loan amount
$144,001 to $184,000	25% of loan amount
$184,001 to $203,000	*25% of loan amount

*Loans made for the purchase or construction of a home, to purchase a residential unit in a condominium or to refinance an existing VA-guaranteed loan for interest rate reduction. Cash-out refinances are limited to a maximum $36,000 guaranty.

Maximum Obtainable VA Loans

The VA does not set maximum loan amounts, except for the requirement that loans cannot exceed the CRV or the purchase price, whichever is less.

The veteran can obtain a larger loan by making a down payment. The loan amount is arrived at by multiplying the sum of the down payment and guaranty by four (see item 2 of the following example).

Examples

1. Veteran Louise Brading bought a home in 1982 and used her maximum entitlement of $27,500. She sold her home in 1987 to a buyer who took title to the property subject to the existing VA loan. In May 1988, the veteran wanted to purchase a new home with a CRV of $80,000. What was the maximum obtainable VA loan?

   Answer: The veteran was entitled to the maximum guaranty of $46,000 (as of May 1988) minus used entitlement of $27,500 = $18,500. The maximum obtainable VA loan, therefore, was 4 × $18,500 = $74,000.

2. Veteran Brading (from the previous example) has saved $10,000, which she wants to use as down payment on her new house. How does this affect her maximum obtainable VA loan?

   Answer: Her available entitlement of $18,500 plus her $10,000 down payment = $28,500, multiplied by 4 = $114,000, the maximum obtainable loan.

3. A veteran wants to purchase a house for $210,000. What is the maximum obtainable VA loan, and how much would he or she need for down payment?

   Answer: The maximum loan is four times the maximum guaranty of $50,750 = $203,000. Her or his down payment would be $210,000 − $203,000 = $7,000.

4. Veteran Larry Lombard bought a home in 1979 and used his entitlement of $25,000. In 1995, he sold his home to veteran Miller, who agreed to substitute his available entitlement for that of Lombard. Lombard wants to buy a house with a CRV of $190,000. What is the maximum obtainable VA loan?

Answer: Because Lombard's entitlement is reinstated, his available entitlement is the applicable guaranty of $50,750. The maximum loan obtainable would be 4 × $50,750 = $203,000 if it were not limited by the CRV of $190,000.

5. Had veteran Lombard (from the previous example) sold his home with release of liability, but to a nonveteran, what would his available entitlement be? What would the maximum obtainable VA loan be for the purchase of a home with a CRV of $190,000?

Answer: Lombard's available entitlement would be the applicable guaranty of $50,750 minus the used entitlement of $25,000 = $25,750. The maximum obtainable VA loan would be 4 × $25,750 = $103,000.

ENERGY EFFICIENT MORTGAGES

The VA authorizes an addition to the purchase loan for the cost of energy efficient improvements up to $3,000, or $6,000 if the increase in the monthly payments for principal and interest does not exceed the likely reduction on monthly utility costs resulting from the energy efficiency improvements.

For a refinancing loan, the loan may not exceed 90% of the CRV plus the cost of the energy efficient improvements (CRV × .90 + cost of improvements).

Example

If a veteran has $20,000 remaining entitlement and applies for a loan of $80,000, plus $6,000 in energy efficient improvements, the VA will guarantee 25% of the full loan amount of $86,000. Thus, the dollar amount of the guaranty is $21,500, even though the veteran's entitlement is only $20,000. (See Model Energy Code.)

QUALIFYING GUIDELINES

Lenders must follow two separate qualification guidelines based on (1) ratio of total obligations to income and (2) residual income (cash flow) for family support.

Ratio of Total Obligations to Income

The ratio is determined by dividing the total monthly obligations by gross income. Total monthly obligations include housing expenses (principal, interest, taxes, insurance, maintenance, utilities, homeowners' fees and special assessments) and recurring obligations (payments on debts with more than six months to go and other monthly obligations, such as alimony and child support). Generally, the ratio should not exceed 41%.

Twenty Percent Rule

If the residual income (cash flow) exceeds the guidelines by at least 20%, lenders may approve loans with ratios in excess of 41%.

Example

Veteran Larry Halladay and his wife, Joan, are interested in buying a home and want to know the VA loan amount Larry can qualify for. Larry's monthly gross income is $3,500. They are making $200 monthly payments on a car with ten months to go and have other monthly obligations of $250.

Monthly gross income	$3,500
Multiply by ratio	× .41
Remaining for total obligations	$1,435
Recurring obligations	− 450
Remaining for housing expense	$ 985
Assume that taxes, insurance, utilities and maintenance amount to	− 125
Remaining for principal & interest	$ 860

At a VA rate of 7%, the veteran qualifies for a loan of about $141,000

Residual Income (Cash Flow) for Family Support

Residual income is determined by subtracting from the monthly gross income not only the total monthly obligations (including housing expenses and recurring obligations), but also all federal, state and local taxes. A family's residual income should be at least the applicable amount in the following table.

The table shows minimum residual income for family expenditures of such standard items as food, health care, apparel and gasoline. The amounts are based on the loan amount, the region of the country where the veteran lives and family size.

Residual Family Incomes by Region
Loan Amounts Below $70,000

Family Size	Northeast	Midwest	South	West
1	$375	$367	$367	$409
2	629	616	616	686
3	758	742	742	826
4	854	835	835	930
5	886	867	867	965
6	961	942	942	1,040
7	1,031	1,017	1,017	1,115

Loan Amounts of $70,000 up

Family Size	Northeast	Midwest	South	West
1	$433	$424	$424	$472
2	726	710	710	791
3	874	855	855	952
4	986	964	964	1,074
5	1,021	999	999	1,113
6	1,101	1,079	1,079	1,193
7	1,181	1,159	1,159	1,273

Northeast:	Connecticut, Maine, Massachusetts, New Hampshire, New Jersey, New York, Pennsylvania, Rhode Island, Vermont
Midwest:	Illinois, Indiana, Iowa, Kansas, Michigan, Minnesota, Missouri, Nebraska, North Dakota, Ohio, South Dakota, Wisconsin
South:	Alabama, Arkansas, Delaware, District of Columbia, Florida, Georgia, Kentucky, Louisiana, Maryland, Mississippi, North Carolina, Oklahoma, Puerto Rico, South Carolina, Tennessee, Texas, Virginia, West Virginia
West:	Alaska, Arizona, California, Colorado, Hawaii, Idaho, Montana, Nevada, New Mexico, Oregon, Utah, Washington, Wyoming

Example

The Halladays from the previous example live in Phoenix, Arizona, and have three children. They saw a house they like with a CRV of $150,000. The payments, including principal and interest at 7% for a $150,000 loan, would be about $917. At the 41% total obligations-to-income ratio, they would not be able to qualify (the maximum for principal and interest in the previous example was only $860). However, they may have a chance to qualify for a higher loan if their residual income exceeds the guidelines by at least 20%.

Here is how to calculate their residual income:

Monthly gross income	$3,500
Principal and interest for a $150,000 loan at 7%	–917
Property taxes, insurance, utilities, maintenance	–140
Recurring obligations	–450
Federal, state and local taxes	–600
Residual income	$1,393

The minimum residual income for a loan in excess of $70,000 for a family of five living in Arizona is $1,113. Because the Halladays' residual income exceeds that amount by $280, in fact by more than 20%, they should have a good chance to qualify, providing, of course, that their credit history is satisfactory.

Compensating Factors

No single factor is a final determinant in an applicant's qualification for a VA-guaranteed loan. The residual income and ratio guidelines are never intended to be absolute determinants in deciding whether a VA loan should be approved, but must be used only with discretion in conjunction with other factors. These factors become especially important when reviewing marginal loans with respect to residual income or the debt-to-income ratio. The following are examples of compensating factors.

- Excellent long-term credit
- Conservative use of consumer credit
- Minimal consumer debt
- Long-term employment
- Significant liquid assets
- Down payment or the existence of equity in refinancing loans
- Little or no increase in shelter expense
- Military benefits
- Satisfactory home ownership experience
- High residual income
- Low debt-to-income ratio

The VA's intention to advance veterans' best interests is perhaps best expressed in this advice to lenders: "When making a credit determination for a VA-guaranteed loan, keep in mind that a veteran's benefit is involved. However, it serves no purpose to approve or make a loan to a veteran who would be unable to meet the repayment terms or is not a satisfactory credit risk. Such an approval would be, in fact, a disservice since it could well result in the veteran losing the home, a debt being owed to the U.S. government, and an adverse effect on the veteran's credit standing."

The latest addition to the VA Lender's Handbook encourages underwriters to recognize that there are those whose lifestyle, minority status or location require consideration of extraordinary, yet valid, factors in the underwriting process, and to give consideration to every possible appropriate factor in seeking a proper basis for approving loan applications for every qualified veteran.

LOCK-IN AGREEMENTS

The VA will accept agreements between lender and borrower to lock in an interest rate when the VA maximum interest rate is expected to change prior to settlement.

Lock-in agreements must be in writing and unconditional, except for contingencies for approval of the property and of the borrower's income and credit. The agreement must be signed by both the veteran and the lender. The agreement must be for a specific rate of interest and must not exceed the effective rate on the date of the agreement.

The agreement may specify either the interest rate only or the interest rate and the number of discount points payable by the seller (or by the veteran in case of refinancing loans).

Lock-in agreements are typically valid for 45, 60 or 90 days. Prior to the expiration of a lock-in agreement, a lender and borrower may agree to extend the duration of the agreement.

No fee or charge may be imposed against the veteran for an interest rate lock-in agreement.

FEATURES AND REQUIREMENTS OF VA LOANS

Occupancy

Veterans are required to certify that they intend to occupy the home as their principal place of residence. Occupancy by the spouse of a veteran on active duty as a member of the armed forces meets the requirement.

In the event the veteran moves to another home at a later date, he or she may rent the old home financed by the VA-guaranteed loan.

Down Payment

No down payment is required by the VA except on GPMs. However, in the event the veteran agrees to a purchase price in excess of the CRV, the veteran is required to pay cash for such excess. The lender may require that the sum of the available entitlement and the down payment be at least 25% of the CRV.

Secondary Financing

The VA does not preclude second mortgages in conjunction with the VA first loan to obtain funds for closing costs, provided the following conditions are met.

1. The sum of the VA and the second loans may not exceed the amount of the CRV.
2. The veteran meets the qualification requirements based on payments of both loans.
3. The interest rate on the second loan does not impose an undue burden on the veteran.
4. The conditions of the second loan do not impose an undue burden on the veteran.

Interest Rate

VA home loans are guaranteed at an interest rate negotiated between the veteran and the lender.

Discount Points

Discount points may be paid by the veteran and are negotiable. Discount points may not be included in the loan, except that in Interest Rate Reduction Refinancing Loans (IRRRLs) a maximum of 2 points may be financed. Veterans may pay more than 2 points on IRRRLs, but must pay in cash.

Closing Costs

Closing costs may be included in the loan, except for prepaid items and refinancing purposes.

Schedule of Allowable Fees for Loans under U.S.C. 1810

1. Appraisal and compliance inspection fees, and special inspections at request of a veteran to satisfy concerns about condition of the property
2. Recording fees
3. Credit report
4. That portion of taxes, assessments and similar items for the current year chargeable to the borrower and the initial lump-sum payment for the tax and insurance account
5. Hazard insurance
6. Survey, if required by the the lender or veteran
7. Title examination and title insurance
8. VA funding fee
9. Lenders may charge a maximum loan fee of 1% of the loan amount, which is in lieu of all other charges for loan origination.

Funding Fee Table

Loan Type		Active Duty or Veteran	National Guard/ Reservists
Purchase/ construction	0% down	2.00%	2.75%
Purchase/ construction	5% down	1.50	2.25

Purchase/	10% down	1.25	2.00
construction			
Cash-out refinance		2.00	2.75
Rate reduction refinance		0.50	0.50
Native American direct loan		1.25	1.25
Manufactured homes		1.00	1.00
Assumption		0.50	0.50
Vendee loans		1.00	1.00
Second or subsequent use—		3.00	3.00
Does not apply on IRRRLs or on purchase or construction loans with 5% or more down payment			

Permissible Charges and Fees for Refinancing Loans

1. Reasonable discount points
2. Title insurance (no escrow fees)
3. Recording fees for release of prior loans
4. Cost of repair and inspections
5. Cost of termite inspections and clearances

Maximum Term of Loan

The maximum term of VA loans is the economic life of the property not to exceed 30 years and 32 days. In most cases, this allows for the first payment not later than 60 days after closing and an even 360 payments.

Monthly Payments

All VA loans, with the exception of term loans, GPMs and GEMs, must be amortized with approximately equal monthly payments. Under VA financing, it is the lender's responsibility to ascertain that property taxes and hazard insurance premiums are paid when due. Lenders, therefore, insist that the monthly payments include proportionate amounts for taxes and insurance.

Escrow Account

Lenders deposit the property tax and hazard insurance portion of the monthly payments into an escrow account from which to pay taxes and insurance premiums when due. In order to ascertain that sufficient funds are in the escrow account to make the first tax payment after the loan has been funded, the lender requires that the buyer deposit a certain sum into the escrow account at closing. The VA has revised its procedures with respect to surpluses in escrow accounts so that they are in line with the Cranston-Gonzalez National Affordable Housing Act of 1990. The new policy allows a loanholder/servicer to release surplus escrow accounts offering borrowers a choice of options: (1) a lump-sum refund, (2) the surplus to be used to reduce or pay the next monthly payment(s) or (3) the surplus to be used to reduce principal or several other options.

Refinancing

The VA allows two types of refinancing: (1) refinancing of an existing mortgage secured by a lien on a dwelling owned and occupied by the veteran and (2) an interest rate reduction refinancing loan (IRRRL), which permits restoration of used entitlement.

With interest rate reduction refinancing loans, the lender may pay all closing costs and set an interest rate high enough to recover the advance of costs (but the rate must be lower than the loan being refinanced). A fixed rate loan may be refinanced with an ARM as long as the initial ARM rate is lower than the fixed rate.

Under the Veterans Benefits Improvement Act of 1994, veterans may obtain an IRRRL to convert their existing VA-guaranteed ARM to fixed rate loans even if the interest rate is higher than the rate of the ARM. The interest rate on the new fixed rate loan may be negotiated between the veteran and the lender. A maximum of 2 discount points may be included in IRRRLs.

Under the act, IRRRLs may include additional funds for energy efficiency improvements.

The following table shows additional features of IRRRLs.

Comparison of VA Loan Refinancing

	Liens Other than VA	IRRRL*
Guaranty entitlement required	Yes	25% of loan, regardless of guaranty on the original VA loan, even if loan exceeds $184,000
Cash to veteran	Yes	No
Loan limit	90% of CRV plus funding fee	VA loan balance + closing costs + 0.5% funding fee, but no discount points
Must veteran own property?	Yes	Yes
Must veteran occupy property?	Yes	No (must have once occupied)
Maximum loan term	30 years + 32 days	Existing VA loan term + 10 yrs, not to exceed 30 yrs and 32 days
Lien of record required	Yes	Yes
OK to finance other liens	Yes	No
Appraisal required	Yes	No
Credit package required	Yes	No

The program permits restoration of used entitlement for the purpose of refinancing the same property with a new VA-guaranteed loan.

Veteran's Liability

Even though the lender is compensated by the VA for any loss up to the amount of the guaranty, the veteran remains liable for the full amount of his or her debt to the U.S. government in the event of default and foreclosure.

Assumption

Prior approval. The VA requires prior approval to any transfer of property securing VA loans committed or closed after March 1, 1988, unless the loan is paid in full at the time of transfer.

VA loans for which commitments were made before March 1, 1988, remain freely assumable, even by nonveteran buyers.

Release of liability. Upon approval of the prospective purchaser as an acceptable credit risk, and upon full assumption of liability for repayment of the loan by the transferee and completion of the sale, the veteran is released from personal liability to the government.

Substitution of entitlement. Receiving an approved release of liability will not restore the veteran-seller's loan guaranty entitlement unless the purchaser is a veteran who has sufficient entitlement to substitute for that of the seller and consents to use his or her entitlement to the same extent the entitlement of the veteran-transferor had been used originally. In addition, the veteran-buyer must certify that he or she will occupy the property as his or her principal residence.

Prepayment. There is no prepayment penalty if a VA loan is partially or fully prepaid at any time.

Transfers Requiring No VA Approval

1. Creation of a lien subordinate to the lender's mortgage, which does not transfer right of occupancy
2. Creation of a purchase money security interest for household appliances

3. Transfer by devise, descent or operation of law on the death of a joint tenant or tenant by the entirety
4. Granting of a lease of three years or less not containing an option to purchase
5. Transfer to a relative resulting from the death of a borrower
6. Transfer when the spouse or children of the borrower become joint owner(s) of the property with the borrower
7. Transfer resulting from divorce, legal separation or property settlement
8. Transfer into an inter vivos trust, which does not relate to a transfer of occupancy rights, in which the borrower remains a beneficiary
9. Installment contracts of sale calling for transfer of title after a certain period, provided that VA approval is required at time of actual transfer

Joint Loans

To determine whether income and credit requirements are met for joint loans, the VA considers the income and credit of both the veteran and the other person joining in title. Income and assets of each party are combined to determine whether there is sufficient total income available to repay the loan (if the veteran alone cannot qualify) and adequate liquidity to cover any required down payment. This policy also applies to loans in which two or more veterans intend to use their entitlement and take title jointly. The only exception is a joint loan involving a veteran and a nonveteran who is not the veteran's spouse, when the veteran's income must be sufficient to repay at least that portion of the loan allocable to the veteran's interest in the property, and the nonveteran's income must be adequate to cover the balance of the payment obligation.

Option Agreement

The following agreement must be included in or presented as an amendment to purchase agreements providing for VA-guaranteed financing.

In the event of VA financing, it is expressly agreed that, notwithstanding any other provisions of this contract, the Buyer shall not incur any penalty by forfeiture of earnest money or otherwise be obligated to complete the purchase of the property, described herein, if the contract purchase price or cost exceeds the Reasonable Value of the property established by the VA. The Buyer shall, however, have the privilege and option of proceeding with the consummation of this contract without regards to the amount of the Reasonable Value established by the VA. Escrow fee to be paid by Seller.

MANUFACTURED-HOME FINANCING

A manufactured home that has been permanently affixed to the land on a permanent foundation is eligible for guaranty as is any other home. The unit must have been built in conformance with the Federal Manufactured Home Construction and Safety Standards, or must comply with the VA's minimum property requirements as applicable. The home and land must be taxed as real property under each state's real property laws. The same interest rates, loan amounts, and so forth, are specified as on any other VA home loan.

The VA is authorized to guarantee loans for the following purposes:

1. the purchase of a manufactured home to be permanently affixed to a lot already owned by the veteran,
2. the purchase of a manufactured home and a lot to which the home will be permanently affixed,
3. the refinance of an existing VA-guaranteed loan that is secured by a manufactured home permanently affixed to a lot owned by the veteran, and

4. the refinance of an existing loan made for the purchase of, and secured by, a manufactured home permanently affixed to a lot, and the purchase of the lot to which the home is affixed.

Manufactured homes are eligible for guarantee by the VA under a separate program that includes

- a loan of 95% of the purchase price,
- a maximum guarantee of $20,000,
- a maximum guarantee of 40% of the loan,
- a maximum interest rate permitted that is higher than that for normal VA loans, and
- maximum loan terms of 15 to 25 years.

GRADUATED PAYMENT MORTGAGE (GPM)

Since November 1981, the VA has been authorized to guaranty graduated payment mortgages, allowing lower monthly payments than for a fixed payment mortgage during the first year and increasing annually by a fixed percentage for a stated graduation period. At the end of the graduation period, the payments remain level for the remainder of the loan. The reduction in the initial monthly payments is accomplished by deferring a portion of the interest due and adding that interest to the principal balance. This causes the outstanding balance to increase during the graduation period, an effect known as negative amortization.

Provisions Applying to VA GPMs

- The initial principal amount of the loan may not exceed the reasonable value of the property at the time the loan is made.
- The principal amount of the loan thereafter (including the amount of all interest deferred and added to principal) may not at any time be scheduled to exceed the projected value of the property.
- The projected value of the property may be calculated by increasing the reasonable value of the

property from the time the loan is made at a rate not in excess of 2.5% per year, but not to exceed 115% of the reasonable value. This value projection is applicable only to new construction or existing homes not previously occupied.

- GPMs are limited to the acquisition of single-family units. This includes the purchase of new or existing homes, condominium units in VA-approved projects and existing homes for which the loan also includes funds for energy conservation improvements.

Amortization Plan

Plan III under FHA Section 245 is the only amortization plan authorized for VA GPMs. This plan provides for increasing loan payments at a rate of 7.5% per year for the first five years, increasing at annual intervals. At the beginning of the sixth year, the payments become level for the remaining term of the loan.

Down Payment

Because the outstanding loan balance increases during the graduation period, a down payment is required to prevent the loan balance from exceeding the CRV. The down payment must be paid in cash from the veteran's own resources. For existing homes, the amount of the down payment is equal to the highest amount of negative amortization that occurs during the graduation period. For new homes, the maximum VA GPM loan amount is 97.5% of the CRV or the purchase price, whichever is less, at the time the loan is made.

Computing the Amount of Down Payment

1. Find the GPM factor for the applicable interest rate on the following table.

Int. Rate	GPM Factor	Int. Rate	GPM Factor
7¾%	1.0280728		
8	1.0309550	12%	1.0787075
8¼	1.0341945	12¼	1.0815692
8½	1.0373748	12½	1.0843740
8¾	1.0404961	12¾	1.0871336
9	1.0435617	13	1.0898424
9¼	1.0465678	13¼	1.0925044
9½	1.0495186	13½	1.0951202
9¾	1.0524197	13¾	1.0976904
10	1.0552637	14	1.1002174
10¼	1.0580559	14¼	1.1026993
10½	1.0607998	14½	1.1051467
10¾	1.0635966	14¾	1.1075476
11	1.0667347	15	1.1099107
11¼	1.0698110	15¼	1.1122353
11½	1.0728295	15½	1.1145245
11¾	1.0757962	15¾	1.1167789

2. Find the maximum original loan amount by dividing the reasonable value of the property by the GPM factor, and round down to the nearest dollar.
3. The minimum down payment equals the reasonable value minus the maximum original loan amount found in Step 2.

Credit Underwriting

In determining whether a veteran-applicant meets statutory income requirements for a GPM, the loan analysis is based on the first year's payment only when there are strong indications that the income to support the application can be reasonably expected to keep pace with increases in monthly mortgage payments. In the absence of such strong indications, the GPM is underwritten based on the payment that would apply if the loan were a fixed rate loan at the current maximum VA interest rate.

BUYDOWN PROGRAM

Under the buydown program, sellers (usually builders) may temporarily reduce buyers' loan payments during the initial years of a mortgage by depositing buydown funds into a third party escrow without recourse. The buydown funds must be beyond the reach of prospective creditors of the builder-seller, lender or borrower. The funds must be used to reduce the buyer's loan payment and may not be used to pay past due monthly loan payments. The maximum loan may not exceed the CRV and funding fee.

Credit Underwriting

Underwriting based on full payment amount. Credit underwriting for loans with buydown plans is based on the full payment amount, except when there are strong indicators that the purchaser's income used to support the application can reasonably be expected to keep pace with the increases in the monthly mortgage payments.

Underwriting based on the first year's payment amount. For loans based on the first year's payment amount (the buydown rate), there must be strong indications that income used to support the application will increase to cover the yearly increases in loan payments, and the following criteria must be met.

Assistance payments will run for a minimum of one year. Scheduled reductions in the assistance payments must occur annually on the anniversary of the first mortgage payment. The annual payment increases must be in equal, or approximately equal, amounts. Alternately, when the subsidy is calculated by setting the veteran's initial payments to a lower interest rate, the reduction in the assistance payments may be accomplished through equal annual increases in that interest rate.

SELLER CONCESSIONS

For VA purposes, a seller concession is defined as anything of value added to the transaction by the builder-seller for which the buyer pays nothing additional and that the builder-seller is not customarily expected or required to pay or provide.

Such concessions include payment by the seller of the buyer's VA funding fee, prepaid taxes and insurance, gifts such as a television set or microwave oven, extra discount points paid to provide temporary interest rate buydowns, or the payoff of credit balances on behalf of the buyer.

Any concession or combination of concessions that exceeds 4% of the established reasonable value of the property is considered excessive for VA loan purposes. Normal discount points and payment of the buyer's closing costs are not considered a concession for purposes of determining if total concessions are within the established limit.

SELLER FINANCING

Although seller financing may be in the best interest of a seller in certain circumstances, such as spreading tax on profit from the sale over a number of years or for investment reasons, it is usually done to induce a sale by assisting the buyer in some way.

Seller financing can take many different forms, including purchase-money mortgage, buydown, wraparound mortgage, lease with option to purchase, installment sale or various degrees of seller-paid contributions.

CONTRIBUTIONS

A *contribution* (also called *financing concession*) is the payment of a cost typically paid by the buyer, but is instead paid by the seller or a third party. Contributions can include title insurance premiums, discount points, mortgage insurance premium, surveys, recording fees, attorney's fees, prepaid items, decorating allowances, moving costs, personal property, and seller-paid buydowns or financing costs.

Lenders may also make contributions to cash-poor but otherwise qualified buyers in return for a higher interest rate, which is called *premium pricing*. In a market of increasing interest rates when fewer buyers can qualify, lenders may rely more on premium pricing to capture a larger market share.

BUYDOWNS

Buydown is a form of seller contribution to help a buyer qualify for a new institutional loan by paying the lender a lump sum in return for reducing the buyer's interest rate, either for the life of the loan (permanent buydown) or for a period of years (temporary buydown). The lump-sum payment increases the lender's yield and has an effect similar to collecting discount points in lieu of a lower interest rate.

Permanent Buydown

The generally used rule of thumb is that it takes a lump-sum payment of 8% to reduce the interest rate of a 30-year loan by 1%. Thus, $8,000 is required to reduce the rate of a $100,000, 30-year loan by 1%.

Temporary Buydown

Temporary buydowns reduce the interest rate, either by level payments or progressively increasing payments over the first few years of a loan. Buydown contributions may come from the seller, borrower, lender or other interested third party.

Borrowers must justify the increase in payments by the likelihood of increased income, and limitations are imposed for conventional, FHA and VA loans, as shown in the chart below.

Fannie Mae Limitations of Buydown Contributions

Occupancy Type	LTV	Contr. Limited to
Investment Property	Fixed Rate— Regardless of LTV	2% of Sales Price or Appr. Value
Principal Residence	LTV over 90%	3% of Sales Price or Appr. Value
Principal Residence	LTV 90% or less	6% of Sales Price or Appr. Value
Second Home	LTV 80% or less	6% of Sales Price or Appr. Value

If seller contributions exceed the limits, the excess must be deducted from the sales price or appraised value before calculating the maximum loan amount.

FHA Limitations of Buydown Contributions

1. It must be a fixed rate loan on an owner-occupied principal residence.

2. The underwriting is based on a maximum interest rate reduction of 2% below note rate.
3. The increase in interest rate is limited to 1% once a year.
4. The lender must establish that the eventual increase in payments will not adversely affect the borrower and likely lead to default. One of the following criteria must be met.
   a. Potential for increased income to offset scheduled payment increases, as indicated by job training or education in the borrower's profession or by a history of advancement in the borrower's career with attendant increases in earnings
   b. A demonstrated ability to manage financial obligations in such a way that a greater portion of income may be devoted to housing expense
   c. Substantial assets to cushion the effect of increased payments
   d. Borrower's cash investment that substantially exceeds the minimum required

VA Buydown Requirements

Under the VA buydown program, sellers may temporarily reduce buyers' loan payments during the initial years of a mortgage by depositing buydown funds into a third party escrow without recourse. The buydown funds must be beyond the reach of prospective creditors of the builder-seller, lender or borrower. The funds must be used to reduce the buyer's loan payment and may not be used to pay past due monthly loan payments. The maximum loan may not exceed the CRV.

There must be strong indications that income used to support the application will increase to cover the yearly increases in loan payments, and the following criteria must be met.

• Assistance payments will run for a minimum of one year.

- Scheduled reductions in the assistance payments must occur annually on the anniversary of the first mortgage payment.
- The annual payment increases must be in equal or approximately equal amounts.

PURCHASE-MONEY MORTGAGE

When a seller accepts a note that is secured by a mortgage or deed of trust on the property for all or part of the purchase price, it is referred to as a purchase-money mortgage.

Primary Seller Financing

A seller whose property is free and clear of any mortgages or other liens may consider carrying a first note secured by a mortgage or deed of trust on the property, or a contract of sale, either for tax reasons (as described in the tax section of the *Realty Bluebook*® under the heading Installment Sales) or as an investment.

Although the seller may benefit from financing the entire purchase, the buyer benefits in saving origination fees, discount points, flexibility in terms to suit the buyer's needs and more lenient qualification. Consequently, a seller who offers these benefits can usually command a higher price.

Secondary Seller Financing

Secondary seller financing is generally used as a marketing tool to supplement a buyer's required cash for down payment and closing costs, but also to help a buyer qualify for a new first loan from an institutional lender.

In structuring the second purchase-money mortgage, the broker needs to be aware of restrictions imposed by Fannie Mae, FHA and VA as shown in the following summary of requirements for second loans on page A-145.

Summary of Requirements for Second Loans in Conjunction with New First Loans

Conventional	FHA	VA
Sum of First and Second may not exceed 90% of Appraised Value or Price. whichever is the lesser. The LTV of the First Loan may not exceed 75%	Sum of FHA and Second may not exceed HUD's maximum mortgage amount for area—Secondary financing to obtain the required Cash Investment is PROHIBITED	Sum of VA and Second may not exceed the CRV
Buyer must Qualify for Combined Payments of First and Second Loans	Buyer must Qualify for Combined Payments of First and Second Loans	Buyer must Qualify for Combined Payments of First and Second Loans
Minimum 5 yrs. max. 30 yrs.	No balloon payment before 10 years	
Regular Scheduled Payments—May be amortized, interest only, monthly, quarterly, etc. Balloon payment OK	Any periodic payments made on account of the Second must be made on a monthly basis in substantially the same amount	The conditions of the Second may not be more stringent than those of the VA loan
For qualification purposes, payments on Second are based on interest rate not less than 2% below market rate for seconds		Interest Rate on Second may not exceed the rate of the VA loan
No Negative Amortization	No Negative Amortization	No Negative Amortization
No Prepayment Penalty	No Prepayment Penalty	No Prepayment Penalty

Examples

A particular buyer has 10% cash for down payment but cannot qualify for a new first loan. The seller offers to carry a second mortgage with the following types of financing:

- Conventional financing. The seller offers to carry a second for 15% of the appraised value, thus reducing the LTV of the first loan from 90% to 75% (the maximum LTV allowed with secondary financing). Additionally, the seller accepts interest payments only and a balloon payment in five years (permitted with conventional financing). The result is that the sum of monthly payments on both first and second is reduced to enable the buyer to qualify.
- FHA financing. A similar scenario could be structured with the combined amount of first and second limited to the maximum FHA loan amount (see section on FHA Financing under the heading Calculating the Maximum Loan) and the balloon payment not due before ten years.
- The VA may approve secondary seller financing, provided that the sum of the VA loan and the second does not exceed the certificate of reasonable value, and that the interest rate of the second does not exceed the rate of the VA loan.

Note that in all three cases the buyer must qualify for the combined payments of first and second loans.

Seller's Risk and Broker's Liability

Needless to say, the seller's risk in carrying a mortgage increases proportionately with the amount of the note, the buyer's cash investment, the degree of the buyer's creditworthiness, the amount of periodic payments and the maturity of the loan. The broker structuring the transaction (down payment, the buyer's creditworthiness and qualification, interest rate, loan term, balloon payment, insurance coverage, etc.) may be held liable for errors and should take the utmost care in the performance of his or her duties. A seller entering into such a sale should be aware of the effect the transaction may have on his or her tax liability, and the real estate broker or agent should advise the seller to consult his or her legal counsel before entering into such a transaction. Such a disclaimer should also be included in the purchase agreement.

Market for Purchase-Money Mortgages

Notes secured by a first or second deed of trust (or mortgage) on real property are negotiable instruments and have a cash value that is normally lower than the face value of the note. The difference between the face value and cash value of the note is called the *discount*. Brokers can usually find private investors who buy such notes, provided the borrower's equity in the property and his or her creditworthiness meet the investor's standards, at a discount in order to realize a required return (yield) on their cash investment.

The discount needed to obtain the required yield depends upon the following terms included in the note:

1. interest rate;
2. payoff rate (the amount of monthly payments expressed as a percentage of the face value of the note);
3. due date (the date the remaining balance becomes due and payable in full, referred to as a *balloon payment*); and
4. transferability (whether the note includes a due-on-sale clause).

Equity is the difference between the fair market value of the property and the total amount of outstanding loans against the property. Equity, therefore, represents the capital investment a borrower has in the property. Equity is an essential factor in determining the marketability of a note. The smaller the equity, the greater the risk for the holder of the note. When the equity is too small, foreclosure and resale costs could easily exceed the equity in the event the borrower were to default.

Examples

1. Smith purchases a home from Brown for $100,000.
2. Smith obtains a new conventional loan of $70,000 for 30 years payable at $829.50 per month including interest at 14% per annum.
3. Smith executes a note secured by a second deed of trust in favor of Brown for $10,000, payable at $150 per month or more including interest at 13%, due and payable eight years from date of note or upon sale of the property.
4. Smith pays Brown the balance of $20,000 in cash.
5. Smith has a good credit rating, has no current debts, has a dependable monthly salary of $2,000 and has been employed for five years.
6. Three weeks after the close of escrow, Brown decides to sell the note and asks his broker how much cash he can get for the note.
7. In view of the terms of the note, Smith's credit standing, his income and his equity in the property, the broker finds investor Green, who offers to buy the note at a discount of 10%, giving Smith a yield of about 16% on his investment.

To protect the buyer in the above example, the broker structured the terms of the second loan so that the buyer could make the balloon payment from the proceeds of refinancing the first loan at the time the balloon payment came due. This is demonstrated in the following scenario.

Eight years after purchasing the property, Smith faces a balloon payment of $3,025. The unpaid balance of the first loan at the end of eight years is $67,760. The combined total outstanding balance of first and second loans is, therefore, $70,785, which is the amount needed to refinance at the end of eight years to eliminate the second loan. Note that this is about the same amount as that of the original first loan.

As an alternative, Smith could have eliminated any balloon payment by increasing his monthly payments on the second mortgage from $150 to $168.

WRAPAROUND OR ALL-INCLUSIVE DEED OF TRUST

A *wraparound mortgage* includes the remaining balance of an existing first mortgage (to which it is subordinate) plus an additional amount carried by the seller. It is similar to a contract of sale, except that title to the property is actually transferred and may be insured by a policy of title insurance. When a deed of trust is used rather than a mortgage instrument, it is usually referred to as an *all-inclusive deed of trust,* but has also been known as a *hold-harmless, overriding* or *overlapping deed of trust.*

When Can a Wraparound Not Be Used?

A wraparound cannot be used unless there is no acceleration or any other alienation clause in any of the mortgages or deeds of trust that are to remain on the subject property. Sometimes these may be removed by agreement with the beneficiary.

The use of a wraparound when the underlying loan is an ARM should also be avoided.

When Is It Desirable To Use a Wraparound?

1. When there is a locked-in loan on the subject property
2. When the seller is anxious to sell but has a poor-risk buyer with a small down payment who is willing to purchase the property
3. When there is an overpriced property and the seller is firm as to the price, but not as to the terms of sale

4. When the seller does not want to lose the benefit of a present low-interest loan but is still anxious to sell, thereby retaining the use of funds already provided by the present financing
5. When there is little time to shop for loans and/or little likelihood of the new buyer qualifying for same
6. When there is insufficient cash down payment offered and the seller must carry back a large purchase-money trust deed

Advantages to Seller

1. Retains the good terms of the present financing should it become necessary to repossess the subject property at some future date
2. Probably is the only practical way of disposing of a property that has a locked-in loan against it without being forced to negotiate with the same lender for additional funds or for loan assumption
3. Can get a much higher *effective interest* on the true value of the all-inclusive trust deed
4. Can cash out the all-inclusive trust deed at a lower discount rate than a similar purchase-money trust deed because of the higher effective rate of interest generated
5. Can get a higher price for the property because seller can afford to give better terms on the balance (apparent terms)
6. Better than a contract of sale because property may be repossessed by trustee sale, while a contract sometimes requires a court judgment in order to be canceled

Advantages to Buyer

1. Can acquire a much larger property for the same down payment
2. Can now purchase property for which he or she normally could not qualify were it necessary to apply for new financing

3. Can generate greater tax benefits through adjustment of price and terms
4. Saves cost of new loan appraisal fees, new loan points and loan escrow fees
5. Saves time required to make application, or shop, for new loans
6. Can tailor the cash spendable return to suit his or her needs more easily
7. Gets title to the subject property with an owner's policy of title insurance; while with a contract of sale, he or she would not
8. Can afford to overpay for the property by adjusting the terms of the all-inclusive trust deed to compensate for the overpayment
9. Is responsible for only one loan payment, rather than two or more

Precautions for Protection of Seller

1. Impound sufficient funds to cover cost of taxes and insurance.
2. Have the right to approve all leases that might have a detrimental effect on the value of the property (i.e., leases with prepaid rent provisions where the buyer may take the funds and then walk away from the property).
3. Provide for the availability of funds when required to meet due dates of the senior loans remaining on the property.
4. Limit or forbid the use of another all-inclusive trust deed on resale.
5. Have the right to refinance the property at any time, or at a specified time should certain events occur (e.g., expiration of lock-in clause on existing loan).
6. Assume the present loans at some time.
7. Spell out the exact circumstances that will bring about default, the exact amount that will be in default and the exact procedure to be followed upon foreclosure.

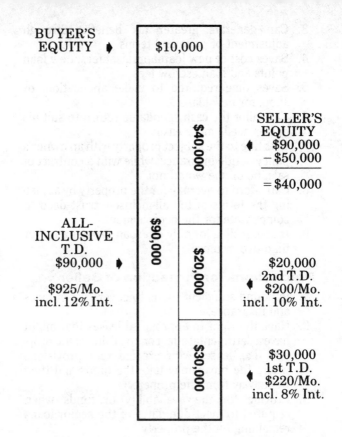

BUYER'S EQUITY ▸ $10,000

SELLER'S EQUITY
$90,000
− $50,000
───────
= $40,000 ◂ $40,000

ALL-INCLUSIVE T.D.
$90,000 ▸

$925/Mo.
incl. 12% Int.

$90,000

$20,000 ◂ $20,000
2nd T.D.
$200/Mo.
incl. 10% Int.

$30,000 ◂ $30,000
1st T.D.
$220/Mo.
incl. 8% Int.

Seller gets 12% × $90,000 = $10,800 Int.
and pays   10% × $20,000
           8% × $30,000 = $ 4,400 Int.
Seller nets . . . . $ 6,400 Int.
on T.D. Equity of $40,000 or

16% Effective Interest

Precautions for Protection of Buyer

1. Have some method of preventing the property from being lost through the failure of the seller to meet the payments or other terms of the senior loans of record.
2. Desirable to make the payments of the all-inclusive trust deed payable to a neutral collection agency, such as a bank or to a trust specifically set up for that purpose. Cost of setting up these arrangements must be considered, as well as who shall be billed for same.
3. Should the payment on the all-inclusive trust deed not be sufficient to cover the payments needed to pay the senior remaining loans of record, some provision to provide them.
4. Desirable for the buyer to have the right to assume one or all of the senior loans of record upon a certain event, such as a lump-sum payment of X dollars.

Procedure To Set Up an All-Inclusive Trust Deed

1. Examine the existing trust deeds and notes, and ascertain the following:
   a. Is there any acceleration clause that becomes effective upon the change of ownership of the property? (Alienation clause). If there is, then stop right here. The all-inclusive may not be used unless this clause is removed. You might be able to pay it off, or renegotiate it.
   b. Note the exact balance of each trust deed as of the projected transfer date.
   c. Note the monthly payments, interest rate and dates and amounts of any balloon payments due (both partial balloon payments or final).
   d. Determine the amount of monthly payments necessary to make the payments on all of the senior loans in addition to funds necessary to cover the tax and insurance impounds (if required by seller).

2. Decide what the monthly payments on the all-inclusive trust deed shall be and draw up a schedule for same, including the
   a. total value of the all-inclusive (total price minus down payment);
   b. interest rate to be charged on the all-inclusive trust deed; and
   c. partial balloon payment or total balloon payments and due dates of remaining senior loans.
3. Decide who is to collect and disburse the payments on the all-inclusive trust deed: the seller, bank, other collection agency, or a trust set up specifically for that purpose.
4. Decide who will pay for the cost of the collections or for the setting up and administration of the trust.
5. Decide on the exact procedure for handling the funds when received.
6. Spell out the exact circumstances that will bring about default on the all-inclusive trust deed and the exact amount that will be in default.
7. Spell out the exact procedure to be followed in case of default and subsequent foreclosure.

Preparation Is Essential

8. Provide your attorney with all of the above data as well as all of the documents involved. Your attorney will then be able to draw up the necessary phraseology that will be acceptable to the title company providing the policy of title insurance.

NOTE: Title insurance companies in California have drafted and printed standard forms of all-inclusive notes secured by deeds of trust. If these forms are used, the title company will provide title insurance.

Note that the purchaser takes the property subject to the existing lien or liens, so that the seller remains the trustor. Obviously, this can only be done if the notes secured by such liens do not contain an enforceable due-on-sale clause. The all-inclusive deed of trust is recorded as a junior lien, subject to the existing liens.

The purchaser may later become the trustor of the deeds of trust that are prior to the all-inclusive deed of trust by assuming these liens in the form of assumption agreements; at such time, the seller must reconvey the all-inclusive deed of trust. It is strongly suggested that all-inclusive deeds of trust and contracts providing for their use be prepared by legal counsel.

NOTE: See Finance Instruments under the heading Assuming—Taking Subject to a Mortgage.

LEASE WITH OPTION TO PURCHASE

A *lease with option to purchase* is another tool sellers can use to induce a sale when the buyer lacks sufficient funds for down payment and closing costs.

A lease with option to purchase, also referred to as *lease option*, entitles the lessee to purchase the leased property for a price and upon terms provided in the agreement by exercising the option within a specified time (often a year). The lessee/buyer is referred to as the *optionee*, the lessor/seller as the *optionor*. The optionee pays the optionor up front a nonrefundable *option consideration*, which is usually applied toward the purchase price in the event the option to purchase is exercised. Lease options generally provide that a portion of the rent is applied toward the purchase if the option is exercised, referred to as *rent credit*.

Example

John Seller has a house on the market for $100,000. Jim Buyer wants to buy the house but does not have enough funds to qualify for a new loan. Instead of a purchase agreement, Seller and Buyer enter into a lease with option to purchase that includes the following terms: Buyer pays Seller a nonrefundable option consideration of $4,000, which is to be applied toward the purchase price if the option to purchase is exercised; Buyer agrees to lease the property for 12 months, at which time he may exercise the option to purchase the property for $100,000; Buyer agrees to pay rent of $1,200 per month, of which $200 is to be applied to the purchase price if the option is exercised.

If Buyer decides to exercise the option after 12 months, he pays $100,000 minus the $4,000 option consideration, minus $2,400 (12 months rent credit at $200), amounting to $100,000 - $6,400 = $93,600.

Institutional lenders accept rent credits as part of the down payment if rental payments exceed the market rent and if a valid lease/purchase agreement is in effect, a copy of which must be attached to the loan application.

Advantages of Lease Option to the Optionee

* Low cash requirement
* Partial rent credit applied toward down payment
* Lock-in of purchase price at today's market value
* Time to plan and prepare for the finance of the purchase
* Possibility to sell the option (unless prohibited by the terms of the agreement)

Advantages of Lease Option to the Optionor

* Monthly rent higher than market rent (reducing negative cash flow)
* Top market value for property
* Optionee is likely to treat the property as an owner would
* Tax-free use of option consideration until the option expires or is exercised
* Continued tax deductions for expenses and depreciation during the option period

TRUTH-IN-LENDING ACT

Truth in Lending is a federal law enacted to promote the informed use of consumer credit by requiring creditors (lenders) to disclose various terms and conditions of credit. The law is enforced and administered by the Federal Trade Commission. Regulation Z, issued by the Board of Governors of the Federal Reserve System, implements this law that applies to individuals and businesses that regularly offer or extend credit to consumers for personal, family or household purposes.

Disclosures (12 Code of Fed. Regs. Sec. 226)—The Truth-in-Lending Act requires a creditor to furnish certain disclosures to the consumers before a permanent contract for loan is made. With respect to real estate loans, a creditor is a person who in any calendar year extends credit more than 25 times or more than 5 times for loans secured by a dwelling used as the borrower's residence, when the credit extended is subject to a finance charge or is payable by written agreement in more than four installments (excluding the down payment). A dwelling is defined as a residential structure including a mobile home or trailer that contains one- to four-family housing units.

REQUIRED ITEMS OF DISCLOSURE

Items of disclosure required of creditors by Regulation Z for real estate loans are summarized below. (The first four disclosures listed below must also have simple descriptive phrases of explanation similar to those shown.)

1. Amount financed—the amount of credit provided to you or on your behalf
2. Finance charge—the dollar amount the credit will cost you
3. Annual percentage rate—the cost of your credit as a yearly rate

4. Total of payments—the amount you will have paid when you have made all the scheduled payments
5. Identity of the creditor making the disclosure
6. Written itemization of the amount financed or a statement that the consumer has a right to receive a written itemization and a space in the statement for the consumer to indicate whether or not the itemization is requested
7. Payment schedule to include number, amount and timing of payments
8. Demand feature of the loan excluding borrower default or due-on-sale clause
9. Loan payment penalties—if not charged by the lender or if uncertainty exists, a statement to that effect; rebate penalty disclosure
10. Late payment charge stated either as a percentage or dollar amount
11. Description of the security interest that will be retained by the lender as security for the loan
12. Insurance and whether or not premiums are included in the finance charge
13. Certain security interest charges or fees, such as taxes or other fees paid to public officials or the premium for insurance in lieu of perfecting the security interest, to be excluded from the finance charge
14. Specific reference to terms of the contract related to nonpayment, default, acceleration or prepayment penalties
15. A statement that a due-on-sale clause or other conditions about the loan assumption policy are contained in the loan documents; a statement as to whether the lender will allow subsequent purchasers to assume the remaining obligation
16. Whether there is a required deposit by the borrower as a condition of the loan, and a statement that the annual percentage rate does not reflect the effect of any such required deposit

ARM Disclosure Rules

Effective October 1, 1988, the Federal Reserve Board implemented an amendment to Regulation Z. These rules apply to lenders that offer adjustable rate mortgages (ARMs) to borrowers. ARMs subject to the rules are for purchase money, refinance, house improvement, closed-end equity second mortgages and any consumer purpose transaction secured by a principal dwelling.

At the time an application form is provided or before the consumer pays a nonrefundable fee, whichever comes first, certain information must be given to the consumer-borrower. The initial disclosures must be delivered or placed in the mail not later than three business days following receipt of the consumer's application.

At the time an ARM is initiated, lenders must make available the following information:

1. An educational brochure about ARMs, either the "Consumer Handbook on Adjustable Rate Mortgages," published jointly by the Federal Reserve Bank and the Federal Home Loan Bank, or a suitable substitute.

2. A loan program disclosure for each adjustable rate program in which a consumer expresses an interest. The disclosure information must reveal that the interest rate or term of the loan can change, identify the index applied and the source of information for that index, plus provide an explanation of how the index is adjusted. A statement must be included advising the consumer to ask about the current margin value, the current interest rate and the amount of discount, if any.

3. An historic example must be given illustrating how payments on a $10,000 loan would have changed in response to actual historical data on the index to be applied. The consumer must be provided with an explanation of how to calculate payment amounts for the loan.

4. A statement reporting the initial and maximum interest rates and payments for a $10,000 loan originated at the most recent rate in the historic example.

At time of settlement (close of escrow), the following disclosures must be made:

1. The transaction contains an adjustable rate feature.
2. A statement that the adjustable rate disclosures have been provided earlier.

Right of Rescission

The *right of rescission* with respect to real estate loans applies to consumer credit transactions in which the lender will retain or acquire a security interest in the consumer's principal dwelling, including in many cases a mobile home (even if treated as personal property). The creditor must notify each consumer entitled to rescind under the provisions of this law with written notice to rescind. The consumer has the right to rescind under the provisions of this law with written notice of the right to rescind without penalty until midnight of the third business day following the later of these events:

- consummation of the loan transaction;
- delivery of all material truth-in-lending disclosures; or
- delivery of two copies of the notice of the right to rescind.

Advertising

Regulation Z also requires that anyone who places an advertisement for consumer credit (including solicitation by mail or telephone) must comply with the advertising requirement of the Truth-in-Lending Act summarized as follows:

- The finance charge must be expressed as an annual percentage rate (APR), and if applicable, a statement that the APR is subject to increase after the loan is made.

- The variable rate mortgage ads should state the number and timing of payments, the amount of the largest and smallest of those payments and the fact that payments will vary between the two amounts after close of escrow.
- Buydowns or reduced interest rate advertisements must show the limited term to which the reduced interest rate applies, as well as the annual percentage rate determined in accordance with Section 226.17c of Regulation Z.

Failure to comply with the Truth-in-Lending Act may subject the creditor or advertiser to criminal and civil liability.

Exempt Transactions

- Credit for agricultural purposes
- Credit for business and/or commercial purposes
- Credit over $25,000 not secured by real property
- Credit to government agencies and other entities not considered "natural persons"
- Credit for nonoccupied rental housing if the owner does not occupy for more than 14 days

IS THE REAL ESTATE BROKER SUBJECT TO THE TRUTH-IN-LENDING ACT?

Because a residential mortgage transaction is exempt from the act, a broker involved in an ordinary sale will not be concerned with the purchaser's right to rescind.

Effective September 17, 1982, the following regulatory amendment was adopted in order to clarify the definition of *arrangement of credit:*

"Real estate brokers—The general definition does not include a person (such as a real estate broker or salesperson) who, as part of the process of arranging the sale of real property or a dwelling, arranges for the seller to totally or partly finance the purchase, even if the obligation by its terms is simultaneously assigned by the seller to another person. However, a broker or salesperson is not exempt from coverage in all transactions. For example, the real estate broker may be a creditor in the following situations:

"The broker acts as a loan broker to arrange for someone other than the seller to extend credit, provided that the extender of credit (the person to whom the obligation is initially payable) does not meet the 'creditor' definition.

"The broker extends credit itself, provided that the broker otherwise meets the 'creditor' definition.

"Under the revised regulation, a broker would not be required to make the disclosures required by the act, unless the broker is involved in more than five transactions in the current or preceding calendar year wherein he acts as a loan broker for a third party who is not a creditor or extends credit himself. Where loans are made by persons coming within the definition of creditor, the broker will not be responsible for the disclosures."

Amendments to Regulation Z, effective October 1, 1995, impose new disclosure requirements by lenders making certain high risk loans. These new requirements do not apply to a residential mortgage transaction. Such a transaction is defined in 12 CFR ¶b6226.2(24) as a "transaction in which a mortgage, deed of trust, purchase money security interest arising under an installment sales contract, or equivalent consensual security interest is created or retained in the consumer's principal dwelling to finance the acquisition or initial construction of that dwelling." This would clearly appear to eliminate seller financing from the requirements of the amendments.

REAL ESTATE SETTLEMENT AND PROCEDURES ACT (RESPA)

The Real Estate Settlement and Procedures Act of 1974 is a federal law administered by the U.S. Department of Housing and Urban Development (HUD). RESPA is designed to protect homebuyers during the settlement phase of the purchase. Settlement (in many states referred to as *close of escrow*) is the process whereby the ownership of real property passes from the seller to the buyer. RESPA provides specific procedures, forms for settlement and detailed information that enable buyers to shop for settlement services and make informed decisions.

Originally, RESPA applied to federally related sale transactions in which a new first lien would be placed against residential one- to four-family dwellings, including condominiums, cooperatives and manufactured homes.

In 1992, the Housing and Community Development Act of 1992 extended coverage of RESPA to (a) junior liens, (b) refinance transactions, and (c) home improvement loans; and HUD issued revised regulations affecting three areas of primary concern to REALTORS®: Controlled Business Arrangement (CBA), Prohibitions against Kickbacks, and Computer Loan Origination (CLO).

Exemptions from RESPA include

- a loan secured by property of 25 acres or more;
- loans primarily for business, commercial or agricultural purposes;
- temporary financing, such as construction loans (not take-out loans);
- bridge loans or swing loans; and
- loans secured by unimproved property.

Disclosure requirements by providers of credit include the following:

- *HUD's special information booklet* describes and explains the settlement process. This booklet must be provided not later than three business days after the application is received or prepared. In the case of a home equity line of credit, the brochure entitled "When Your Home Is on the Line: What You Should Know about Home Equity Lines of Credit" is provided.

- *A good faith estimate* listing the amount of, or range of, charges for the specific settlement services the borrower is likely to incur. The good faith estimate must be provided to loan applicants within three business days after the loan application is received or prepared. Terminology must conform to the HUD's Uniform Settlement Statement (HUD-1), and lenders are encouraged to use the same item numbers that appear on the HUD-1.

CONTROLLED BUSINESS ARRANGEMENT

A controlled business arrangement is a situation in which a person such as a real estate licensee has an affiliate relationship or a direct beneficial relationship of at least 1% in a provider of settlement services, and directly or indirectly refers sellers or buyers to a settlement service provider (such as a title, escrow, or pest control company) that is owned in whole or in part by the referring licensee.

If a controlled business arrangement is determined to exist, the referring party must meet all three conditions below to avoid a RESPA problem:

1. The referring licensee must provide to a buyer or seller, no later than the time of referral, a Controlled Business Arrangement Disclosure Statement form that shows the nature of the relationship between the referring party and the

provider of services, and the range of charges for the referred business.

2. The buyer or seller may not be required to use the services of an affiliated provider, subject to certain exceptions.

3. Nothing of value can be received by the referring licensee beyond a "return on ownership or franchise interest," or payments otherwise allowed under other exemptions.

Effective October 7, 1996, HUD issued a new rule on compensation in controlled business arrangements (CBAs) among settlement service providers. The new rule revokes an existing exemption for employee compensation in CBAs. The new rule exempts from RESPA's antikickback prohibition three types of employee compensation for referring business:

I. Managerial employees can be paid for referrals to an affiliated entity. The rule makes it clear that qualifying managers are employees who do not routinely deal with the public. Their compensation can be based on performance criteria, such as profitability or capture rate, but cannot be directly calculated as a multiple of the number or the value of transactions.

II. Employees who do not perform settlement services in a transaction can receive referral compensation, provided that the consumer first receives a new CBA disclosure statement. The referral must be to an affiliated settlement service provider or entity in which the employer has a direct or beneficial ownership interest. HUD specifically states that, for the purposes of this exemption, marketing a settlement service or gathering information—including taking an application—does not constitute performing a settlement service. Examples of such employees are bank tellers and marketing staff.

III. Employers can pay their own employees for generating business for the employer itself.

TRANSFER OF SERVICING RIGHTS

At the time of application, lenders are required to disclose to the applicant whether the servicing rights may be assigned, sold or transferred to any other person or entity at any time during which the loan is outstanding.

DISCLOSURE REQUIREMENTS FOR ESCROW ACCOUNTS

Within 45 days of closing, borrowers are to be furnished an initial escrow statement clearly itemizing the estimated taxes, insurance premiums and charges that may be assessed, and the anticipated dates of such payments during the first 12 months of the escrow account. Annual escrow account statements must also be provided, and a final escrow statement must be furnished within 45 days of termination of the escrow account.

COMPUTERIZED LOAN ORIGINATION (CLO)

Effective June 7, 1996, HUD published a new policy statement defining CLOs as systems used by consumers or on behalf of consumers to choose among alternative products or settlement service providers. A CLO's capabilities can range from simply providing information to prequalifying borrowers or actually originating and processing applications. "To the extent that a CLO performs 'settlement services,' it is a settlement service provider," the statement says.

The statement makes clear that consumers can be charged for CLO services, and that these payments must be reported on disclosure statements.

The statement also provides that service providers can pay a CLO, provided that the payment bears a reasonable relationship to the value of the goods, facilities or services provided. An example of an unearned fee is payment for access to a CLO that only provides basic information about the products offered by one settlement service provider.

CLOs used in the context of controlled business arrangements are subject to RESPA's CBA limitations.

SELECTED
FINANCIAL TABLES

MONTHLY PAYMENT TO
AMORTIZE A LOAN OF $1,000

The following table shows monthly payments for loans of $1,000. To find the payment for a loan of any amount, multiply the number found in the body of the table by the loan amount and divide by 1,000.

Example

What is the monthly payment necessary to amortize a $90,000 loan at 8½% interest per year over a 30-year term?

Answer: Locate the point of intersection of the 30-year column and the line for 8½% interest. The number at that point of intersection is 7.6891, which is the monthly payment for a $1,000 loan at 8½% for 30 years. To find the monthly payment for a 30-year $90,000 loan at 8½%: 7.6891 × 90 = $692.02.

Amortization Table for $1000 Loans

	30 yr.	25 yr.	20 yr.	15 yr.	10 yr.	5 yr.
5	5.3682	5.8459	6.5996	7.9079	10.607	18.871
5⅛	5.4449	5.919	6.6688	7.9732	10.668	18.929
5¼	5.522	5.9925	6.7384	8.0388	10.729	18.986
5⅜	5.5997	6.0665	6.8085	8.1047	10.791	19.044
5½	5.6779	6.1409	6.8789	8.1708	10.853	19.101
5⅝	5.7566	6.2157	6.9497	8.2373	10.915	19.159
5¾	5.8357	6.2911	7.0208	8.3041	10.977	19.217
5⅞	5.9154	6.3668	7.0924	8.3712	11.039	19.275
6	5.9955	6.443	7.1643	8.4386	11.102	19.333
6⅛	6.0761	6.5196	7.2366	8.5062	11.165	19.391
6¼	6.1572	6.5967	7.3093	8.5742	11.228	19.449
6⅜	6.2387	6.6742	7.3823	8.6425	11.291	19.508
6½	6.3207	6.7521	7.4557	8.7111	11.355	19.566
6⅝	6.4031	6.8304	7.5295	8.7799	11.419	19.675
6¾	6.486	6.9091	7.6036	8.8491	11.482	19.683
6⅞	6.5693	6.9883	7.6781	8.9185	11.547	19.742
7	6.653	7.0678	7.753	8.9883	11.611	19.801
7⅛	6.7372	7.1477	7.8282	9.0583	11.675	19.86
7¼	6.8218	7.2281	7.9038	9.1286	11.74	19.919
7⅜	6.9068	7.3088	7.9797	9.1992	11.805	19.979
7½	6.9921	7.3899	8.0559	9.2701	11.87	20.038
7⅝	7.0779	7.4714	8.1325	9.3413	11.936	20.097
7¾	7.1641	7.5533	8.2095	9.4128	12.001	20.157
7⅞	7.2507	7.6355	8.2868	9.4845	12.067	20.217
8	7.3376	7.7182	8.3644	9.5565	12.133	20.276
8⅛	7.425	7.8012	8.4424	9.6288	12.199	20.336
8¼	7.5127	7.8845	8.5207	9.7014	12.265	20.396
8⅜	7.6007	7.9682	8.5993	9.7743	12.332	20.456
8½	7.6891	8.0523	8.6782	9.8474	12.399	20.517
8⅝	7.7779	8.1367	8.7575	9.9208	12.466	20.577
8¾	7.867	8.2214	8.8371	9.9945	12.533	20.637
8⅞	7.9564	8.3065	8.917	10.068	12.6	20.698
9	8.0462	8.392	8.9973	10.143	12.668	20.758
9⅛	8.1363	8.4777	9.0778	10.217	12.735	20.819
9¼	8.2268	8.5638	9.1587	10.292	12.803	20.88
9⅜	8.3175	8.6502	9.2398	10.367	12.871	20.941
9½	8.4085	8.737	9.3213	10.442	12.94	21.002
9⅝	8.4999	8.824	9.4031	10.518	13.008	21.063
9¾	8.5915	8.9114	9.4852	10.594	13.077	21.124

	30 yr.	25 yr.	20 yr.	15 yr.	10 yr.	5 yr.
9⅞	8.6835	8.999	9.5675	10.67	13.146	21.186
10	8.7757	9.087	9.6502	10.746	13.215	21.247
10⅛	8.8682	9.1753	9.7332	10.823	13.284	21.309
10¼	8.961	9.2638	9.8164	10.9	13.354	21.37
10⅜	9.0541	9.3527	9.9	10.977	13.424	21.432
10½	9.1474	9.4418	9.9838	11.054	13.493	21.494
10⅝	9.241	9.5312	10.068	11.132	13.564	21.556
10¾	9.3348	9.6209	10.152	11.209	13.634	21.618
10⅞	9.4289	9.7109	10.237	11.288	13.704	21.68
11	9.5232	9.8011	10.322	11.366	13.775	21.742
11⅛	9.6178	9.8916	10.407	11.445	13.846	21.805
11¼	9.7126	9.9824	10.493	11.523	13.917	21.867
11⅜	9.8077	10.073	10.578	11.603	13.988	21.93
11½	9.9029	10.165	10.664	11.682	14.06	21.993
11⅝	9.9984	10.256	10.751	11.761	14.131	22.055
11¾	10.094	10.348	10.837	11.841	14.203	22.118
11⅞	10.19	10.44	10.924	11.921	14.275	22.181
12	10.286	10.532	11.011	12.002	14.347	22.244
12⅛	10.382	10.675	11.098	12.082	14.419	22.308
12¼	10.479	10.717	11.186	12.163	14.492	22.371
12⅜	10.576	10.81	11.273	12.244	14.565	22.434
12½	10.673	10.904	11.361	12.325	14.638	22.498
12⅝	10.77	10.997	11.45	12.407	14.711	22.562
12¾	10.867	11.091	11.538	12.488	14.784	22.625
12⅞	10.964	11.184	11.627	12.57	14.857	22.689
13	11.062	11.278	11.716	12.652	14.931	22.753
13⅛	11.16	11.373	11.805	12.735	15.005	22.817
13¼	11.258	11.467	11.894	12.817	15.079	22.881
13⅜	11.356	11.562	11.984	12.9	15.153	22.945
13½	11.454	11.656	12.074	12.983	15.227	23.01
13⅝	11.553	11.751	12.164	13.066	15.302	23.074
13¾	11.651	11.847	12.254	13.15	15.377	23.139
13⅞	11.75	11.942	12.345	13.234	15.452	23.203
14	11.849	12.038	12.435	13.317	15.527	23.268
14⅛	11.948	12.133	12.526	13.402	15.602	23.333
14¼	12.047	12.229	12.617	13.486	15.677	23.398
14⅜	12.146	12.325	12.708	13.57	15.753	23.463
14½	12.246	12.422	12.8	13.655	15.829	23.528
14⅝	12.345	12.518	12.892	13.74	15.905	23.594
14¾	12.445	12.615	12.984	13.825	15.981	23.659
14⅞	12.545	12.711	13.076	13.91	16.057	23.724

MONTHLY PAYMENT NECESSARY
TO AMORTIZE A $1,000 LOAN

INTEREST► YEARS	6%	6⅛%	6¼%	6⅜%	6½%	6⅝%	6¾%	6⅞%	MOS
.5	169.5955	169.6568	169.7181	169.7794	169.8407	169.9020	169.9633	170.0246	6
1.0	86.0665	86.1239	86.1814	86.2389	86.2965	86.3540	86.4116	86.4692	12
1.5	58.2318	58.2883	58.3449	58.4015	58.4582	58.5148	58.5715	58.6283	18
2.0	44.3207	44.3770	44.4334	44.4898	44.5463	44.6028	44.6594	44.7160	24
2.5	35.9790	36.0354	36.0919	36.1484	36.2050	36.2617	36.3184	36.3751	30
3.0	30.4220	30.4787	30.5354	30.5922	30.6491	30.7060	30.7630	30.8200	36
3.5	26.4563	26.5133	26.5703	26.6274	26.6847	26.7419	26.7993	26.8567	42
4.0	23.4851	23.5424	23.5999	23.6574	23.7150	23.7727	23.8305	23.8883	48
4.5	21.1769	21.2347	21.2925	21.3505	21.4085	21.4666	21.5249	21.5832	54
5.0	19.3329	19.3910	19.4493	19.5077	19.5662	19.6248	19.6835	19.7423	60
5.5	17.8263	17.8849	17.9437	18.0025	18.0615	18.1206	18.1798	18.2391	66
6.0	16.5729	16.6320	16.6912	16.7505	16.8100	16.8696	16.9293	16.9891	72
6.5	15.5143	15.5738	15.6335	15.6933	15.7532	15.8133	15.8735	15.9339	78
7.0	14.6086	14.6686	14.7287	14.7890	14.8495	14.9101	14.9708	15.0317	84
7.5	13.8253	13.8858	13.9464	14.0072	14.0682	14.1293	14.1905	14.2519	90
8.0	13.1415	13.2024	13.2635	13.3248	13.3863	13.4479	13.5097	13.5716	96
8.5	12.5395	12.6010	12.6626	12.7243	12.7863	12.8484	12.9108	12.9733	102
9.0	12.0058	12.0677	12.1298	12.1921	12.2546	12.3172	12.3801	12.4431	108
9.5	11.5295	11.5919	11.6545	11.7173	11.7803	11.8435	11.9068	11.9704	114
10.0	11.1021	11.1650	11.2281	11.2913	11.3548	11.4186	11.4825	11.5466	120
10.5	10.7165	10.7799	10.8435	10.9073	10.9713	11.0355	11.0999	11.1646	126
11.0	10.3671	10.4309	10.4950	10.5593	10.6238	10.6886	10.7535	10.8187	132
11.5	10.0491	10.1134	10.1780	10.2428	10.3078	10.3731	10.4386	10.5043	138
12.0	9.7586	9.8234	9.8884	9.9537	10.0193	10.0850	10.1511	10.2173	144
12.5	9.4922	9.5575	9.6231	9.6889	9.7549	9.8212	9.8878	9.9546	150
13.0	9.2473	9.3131	9.3791	9.4454	9.5120	9.5788	9.6459	9.7132	156
13.5	9.0214	9.0876	9.1541	9.2209	9.2880	9.3553	9.4229	9.4908	162
14.0	8.8124	8.8791	8.9462	9.0134	9.0810	9.1489	9.2170	9.2854	168
14.5	8.6187	8.6859	8.7534	8.8212	8.8892	8.9576	9.0262	9.0952	174
15.0	8.4386	8.5063	8.5743	8.6426	8.7111	8.7800	8.8491	8.9186	180
15.5	8.2709	8.3391	8.4075	8.4763	8.5454	8.6147	8.6844	8.7544	186
16.0	8.1144	8.1831	8.2520	8.3212	8.3908	8.4607	8.5309	8.6013	192
16.5	7.9681	8.0372	8.1066	8.1763	8.2464	8.3168	8.3875	8.4585	198
17.0	7.8311	7.9006	7.9705	8.0407	8.1113	8.1821	8.2533	8.3248	204
17.5	7.7025	7.7725	7.8429	7.9136	7.9846	8.0559	8.1276	8.1997	210
18.0	7.5817	7.6522	7.7230	7.7942	7.8657	7.9375	8.0097	8.0822	216
18.5	7.4680	7.5389	7.6102	7.6819	7.7539	7.8262	7.8989	7.9719	222
19.0	7.3609	7.4323	7.5040	7.5761	7.6486	7.7214	7.7946	7.8681	228
19.5	7.2598	7.3317	7.4039	7.4765	7.5494	7.6227	7.6964	7.7704	234
20.0	7.1644	7.2367	7.3093	7.3824	7.4558	7.5296	7.6037	7.6782	240
20.5	7.0741	7.1468	7.2200	7.2935	7.3673	7.4416	7.5162	7.5912	246
21.0	6.9886	7.0618	7.1354	7.2093	7.2837	7.3584	7.4335	7.5089	252
21.5	6.9076	6.9813	7.0553	7.1297	7.2045	7.2797	7.3552	7.4312	258
22.0	6.8308	6.9049	6.9793	7.0542	7.1294	7.2051	7.2811	7.3575	264
22.5	6.7578	6.8323	6.9073	6.9826	7.0583	7.1344	7.2108	7.2877	270
23.0	6.6885	6.7635	6.8388	6.9145	6.9907	7.0672	7.1442	7.2215	276
23.5	6.6226	6.6980	6.7737	6.8499	6.9265	7.0035	7.0809	7.1587	282
24.0	6.5598	6.6356	6.7118	6.7884	6.8655	6.9429	7.0208	7.0990	288
24.5	6.5000	6.5763	6.6529	6.7299	6.8074	6.8853	6.9636	7.0423	294
25.0	6.4431	6.5197	6.5967	6.6742	6.7521	6.8304	6.9092	6.9883	300
25.5	6.3887	6.4657	6.5432	6.6211	6.6994	6.7782	6.8574	6.9369	306
26.0	6.3368	6.4143	6.4922	6.5705	6.6492	6.7284	6.8080	6.8880	312
26.5	6.2873	6.3651	6.4434	6.5222	6.6013	6.6809	6.7609	6.8414	318
27.0	6.2399	6.3182	6.3969	6.4760	6.5556	6.6356	6.7161	6.7969	324
27.5	6.1946	6.2733	6.3524	6.4319	6.5119	6.5924	6.6732	6.7545	330
28.0	6.1513	6.2303	6.3099	6.3898	6.4702	6.5510	6.6323	6.7140	336
28.5	6.1098	6.1893	6.2692	6.3495	6.4303	6.5116	6.5932	6.6754	342
29.0	6.0701	6.1499	6.2302	6.3110	6.3922	6.4738	6.5559	6.6384	348
29.5	6.0320	6.1123	6.1929	6.2741	6.3557	6.4377	6.5202	6.6031	354
29.8	6.0075	6.0880	6.1690	6.2504	6.3322	6.4145	6.4972	6.5804	358
30.0	5.9956	6.0762	6.1572	6.2387	6.3207	6.4032	6.4860	6.5693	360
35.0	5.7019	5.7861	5.8708	5.9560	6.0416	6.1277	6.2142	6.3012	420
40.0	5.5022	5.5896	5.6774	5.7658	5.8546	5.9439	6.0336	6.1238	480

MONTHLY PAYMENT NECESSARY
TO AMORTIZE A $1,000 LOAN

INTEREST↓ YEARS	7%	7⅛%	7¼%	7⅜%	7½%	7⅝%	7¾%	7⅞%	MOS
.5	170.0860	170.1473	170.2087	170.2701	170.3315	170.3929	170.4543	170.5157	6
1.0	86.5268	86.5844	86.6421	86.6998	86.7575	86.8152	86.8729	86.9307	12
1.5	58.6850	58.7418	58.7987	58.8555	58.9124	58.9694	59.0263	59.0833	18
2.0	44.7726	44.8293	44.8860	44.9428	44.9996	45.0565	45.1134	45.1704	24
2.5	36.4320	36.4888	36.5457	36.6027	36.6597	36.7168	36.7739	36.8311	30
3.0	30.8771	30.9343	30.9916	31.0489	31.1063	31.1637	31.2212	31.2788	36
3.5	26.9143	26.9718	27.0295	27.0872	27.1450	27.2029	27.2609	27.3189	42
4.0	23.9463	24.0043	24.0625	24.1207	24.1790	24.2373	24.2958	24.3543	48
4.5	21.6416	21.7001	21.7588	21.8175	21.8763	21.9352	21.9942	22.0533	54
5.0	19.8012	19.8603	19.9194	19.9787	20.0380	20.0975	20.1570	20.2167	60
5.5	18.2985	18.3581	18.4178	18.4775	18.5374	18.5975	18.6576	18.7178	66
6.0	17.0491	17.1091	17.1694	17.2297	17.2902	17.3508	17.4115	17.4723	72
6.5	15.9944	16.0550	16.1158	16.1767	16.2377	16.2989	16.3602	16.4216	78
7.0	15.0927	15.1539	15.2152	15.2767	15.3383	15.4001	15.4620	15.5241	84
7.5	14.3135	14.3752	14.4371	14.4992	14.5614	14.6237	14.6863	14.7489	90
8.0	13.6338	13.6961	13.7585	13.8211	13.8839	13.9469	14.0100	14.0733	96
8.5	13.0359	13.0988	13.1618	13.2250	13.2884	13.3519	13.4156	13.4795	102
9.0	12.5063	12.5697	12.6333	12.6971	12.7611	12.8252	12.8895	12.9541	108
9.5	12.0342	12.0982	12.1623	12.2267	12.2912	12.3560	12.4209	12.4860	114
10.0	11.6109	11.6754	11.7402	11.8051	11.8702	11.9356	12.0011	12.0669	120
10.5	11.2295	11.2945	11.3598	11.4253	11.4911	11.5570	11.6232	11.6895	126
11.0	10.8842	10.9498	11.0157	11.0817	11.1481	11.2146	11.2813	11.3483	132
11.5	10.5703	10.6365	10.7029	10.7696	10.8364	10.9036	10.9709	11.0385	138
12.0	10.2839	10.3506	10.4176	10.4848	10.5523	10.6200	10.6880	10.7562	144
12.5	10.0216	10.0889	10.1565	10.2243	10.2923	10.3606	10.4292	10.4980	150
13.0	9.7808	9.8486	9.9168	9.9851	10.0538	10.1226	10.1918	10.2612	156
13.5	9.5589	9.6273	9.6960	9.7650	9.8341	9.9036	9.9733	10.0433	162
14.0	9.3541	9.4230	9.4922	9.5617	9.6315	9.7015	9.7718	9.8424	168
14.5	9.1644	9.2338	9.3036	9.3737	9.4440	9.5146	9.5855	9.6566	174
15.0	8.9883	9.0584	9.1287	9.1993	9.2702	9.3413	9.4128	9.4845	180
15.5	8.8246	8.8952	8.9661	9.0372	9.1087	9.1804	9.2524	9.3248	186
16.0	8.6721	8.7432	8.8146	8.8863	8.9583	9.0306	9.1032	9.1761	192
16.5	8.5298	8.6014	8.6733	8.7456	8.8181	8.8910	8.9641	9.0376	198
17.0	8.3967	8.4688	8.5413	8.6140	8.6871	8.7605	8.8343	8.9083	204
17.5	8.2720	8.3447	8.4177	8.4910	8.5646	8.6386	8.7128	8.7874	210
18.0	8.1551	8.2283	8.3018	8.3756	8.4498	8.5243	8.5991	8.6742	216
18.5	8.0453	8.1190	8.1930	8.2674	8.3421	8.4171	8.4924	8.5681	222
19.0	7.9420	8.0162	8.0907	8.1656	8.2408	8.3164	8.3923	8.4685	228
19.5	7.8447	7.9194	7.9945	8.0699	8.1456	8.2217	8.2981	8.3749	234
20.0	7.7530	7.8282	7.9038	7.9797	8.0560	8.1326	8.2095	8.2868	240
20.5	7.6665	7.7422	7.8183	7.8947	7.9715	8.0486	8.1261	8.2039	246
21.0	7.5848	7.6610	7.7375	7.8144	7.8917	7.9693	8.0473	8.1257	252
21.5	7.5075	7.5841	7.6612	7.7386	7.8164	7.8945	7.9730	8.0518	258
22.0	7.4343	7.5115	7.5890	7.6669	7.7452	7.8238	7.9028	7.9821	264
22.5	7.3650	7.4426	7.5206	7.5990	7.6778	7.7569	7.8364	7.9162	270
23.0	7.2992	7.3773	7.4558	7.5347	7.6139	7.6936	7.7735	7.8539	276
23.5	7.2369	7.3154	7.3944	7.4737	7.5535	7.6336	7.7140	7.7948	282
24.0	7.1776	7.2567	7.3361	7.4159	7.4961	7.5767	7.6576	7.7389	288
24.5	7.1214	7.2009	7.2807	7.3610	7.4417	7.5227	7.6041	7.6859	294
25.0	7.0678	7.1478	7.2281	7.3088	7.3900	7.4715	7.5533	7.6356	300
25.5	7.0169	7.0973	7.1781	7.2593	7.3408	7.4228	7.5051	7.5878	306
26.0	6.9684	7.0493	7.1305	7.2121	7.2941	7.3765	7.4593	7.5425	312
26.5	6.9222	7.0035	7.0852	7.1672	7.2497	7.3325	7.4158	7.4994	318
27.0	6.8782	6.9599	7.0420	7.1245	7.2074	7.2907	7.3744	7.4584	324
27.5	6.8362	6.9183	7.0008	7.0838	7.1671	7.2508	7.3349	7.4194	330
28.0	6.7961	6.8787	6.9616	7.0450	7.1287	7.2129	7.2974	7.3823	336
28.5	6.7579	6.8408	6.9242	7.0080	7.0921	7.1767	7.2617	7.3470	342
29.0	6.7214	6.8047	6.8885	6.9727	7.0573	7.1422	7.2276	7.3134	348
29.5	6.6864	6.7702	6.8544	6.9390	7.0240	7.1094	7.1951	7.2813	354
29.8	6.6640	6.7481	6.8325	6.9174	7.0026	7.0883	7.1743	7.2608	358
30.0	6.6531	6.7372	6.8218	6.9068	6.9922	7.0780	7.1642	7.2507	360
35.0	6.3886	6.4765	6.5647	6.6534	6.7425	6.8319	6.9218	7.0120	420
40.0	6.2144	6.3054	6.3968	6.4886	6.5808	6.6733	6.7662	6.8595	480

MONTHLY PAYMENT NECESSARY
TO AMORTIZE A $1,000 LOAN

INTEREST↓ YEARS	8%	8⅛%	8¼%	8⅜%	8½%	8⅝%	8¾%	8⅞%	MOS
.5	170.5771	170.6385	170.7000	170.7614	170.8229	170.8844	170.9459	171.0074	6
1.0	86.9884	87.0462	87.1041	87.1619	87.2198	87.2777	87.3356	87.3935	12
1.5	59.1403	59.1974	59.2544	59.3116	59.3687	59.4259	59.4831	59.5404	18
2.0	45.2273	45.2843	45.3414	45.3985	45.4557	45.5129	45.5701	45.6274	24
2.5	36.8883	36.9456	37.0030	37.0604	37.1178	37.1753	37.2329	37.2905	30
3.0	31.3364	31.3941	31.4518	31.5096	31.5675	31.6255	31.6835	31.7416	36
3.5	27.3770	27.4352	27.4934	27.5517	27.6102	27.6686	27.7272	27.7858	42
4.0	24.4129	24.4716	24.5304	24.5893	24.6483	24.7074	24.7665	24.8257	48
4.5	22.1124	22.1717	22.2311	22.2906	22.3501	22.4098	22.4696	22.5294	54
5.0	20.2764	20.3363	20.3963	20.4563	20.5165	20.5768	20.6372	20.6977	60
5.5	18.7782	18.8386	18.8992	18.9599	19.0208	19.0817	19.1428	19.2040	66
6.0	17.5332	17.5943	17.6556	17.7169	17.7784	17.8400	17.9017	17.9636	72
6.5	16.4832	16.5449	16.6068	16.6688	16.7309	16.7931	16.8555	16.9181	78
7.0	15.5862	15.6486	15.7111	15.7737	15.8365	15.8994	15.9625	16.0257	84
7.5	14.8117	14.8747	14.9378	15.0011	15.0646	15.1282	15.1919	15.2558	90
8.0	14.1367	14.2003	14.2641	14.3280	14.3921	14.4564	14.5208	14.5854	96
8.5	13.5436	13.6078	13.6722	13.7368	13.8016	13.8666	13.9317	13.9970	102
9.0	13.0187	13.0836	13.1487	13.2139	13.2794	13.3450	13.4108	13.4767	108
9.5	12.5513	12.6168	12.6826	12.7485	12.8145	12.8808	12.9473	13.0140	114
10.0	12.1328	12.1990	12.2653	12.3318	12.3986	12.4655	12.5327	12.6000	120
10.5	11.7560	11.8228	11.8898	11.9570	12.0244	12.0920	12.1599	12.2279	126
11.0	11.4154	11.4829	11.5505	11.6183	11.6864	11.7547	11.8232	11.8919	132
11.5	11.1063	11.1743	11.2426	11.3110	11.3797	11.4487	11.5178	11.5872	138
12.0	10.8245	10.8932	10.9621	11.0312	11.1006	11.1701	11.2400	11.3100	144
12.5	10.5670	10.6362	10.7057	10.7755	10.8455	10.9157	10.9862	11.0569	150
13.0	10.3307	10.4006	10.4708	10.5412	10.6118	10.6827	10.7538	10.8252	156
13.5	10.1135	10.1840	10.2548	10.3258	10.3970	10.4686	10.5403	10.6124	162
14.0	9.9132	9.9843	10.0557	10.1273	10.1992	10.2713	10.3438	10.4164	168
14.5	9.7280	9.7997	9.8717	9.9440	10.0165	10.0893	10.1623	10.2356	174
15.0	9.5565	9.6288	9.7014	9.7743	9.8474	9.9208	9.9945	10.0684	180
15.5	9.3973	9.4702	9.5434	9.6168	9.6906	9.7646	9.8389	9.9135	186
16.0	9.2493	9.3227	9.3965	9.4706	9.5449	9.6195	9.6945	9.7697	192
16.5	9.1113	9.1854	9.2597	9.3344	9.4093	9.4846	9.5601	9.6359	198
17.0	8.9826	9.0572	9.1321	9.2074	9.2829	9.3588	9.4349	9.5113	204
17.5	8.8622	8.9375	9.0130	9.0888	9.1649	9.2413	9.3181	9.3951	210
18.0	8.7496	8.8254	8.9015	8.9779	9.0546	9.1316	9.2089	9.2865	216
18.5	8.6441	8.7204	8.7970	8.8740	8.9513	9.0289	9.1068	9.1850	222
19.0	8.5450	8.6219	8.6991	8.7766	8.8545	8.9326	9.0111	9.0899	228
19.5	8.4519	8.5294	8.6071	8.6852	8.7636	8.8423	8.9214	9.0007	234
20.0	8.3644	8.4424	8.5207	8.5993	8.6782	8.7575	8.8371	8.9170	240
20.5	8.2820	8.3605	8.4393	8.5185	8.5980	8.6778	8.7579	8.8384	246
21.0	8.2043	8.2833	8.3627	8.4424	8.5224	8.6028	8.6835	8.7645	252
21.5	8.1310	8.2105	8.2904	8.3706	8.4512	8.5321	8.6133	8.6949	258
22.0	8.0618	8.1418	8.2222	8.3030	8.3841	8.4655	8.5472	8.6293	264
22.5	7.9964	8.0769	8.1578	8.2391	8.3207	8.4026	8.4849	8.5675	270
23.0	7.9345	8.0156	8.0970	8.1788	8.2609	8.3433	8.4261	8.5092	276
23.5	7.8760	7.9575	8.0394	8.1217	8.2043	8.2873	8.3706	8.4542	282
24.0	7.8205	7.9026	7.9850	8.0677	8.1508	8.2343	8.3181	8.4022	288
24.5	7.7680	7.8505	7.9334	8.0166	8.1002	8.1841	8.2684	8.3530	294
25.0	7.7182	7.8012	7.8845	7.9682	8.0523	8.1367	8.2214	8.3065	300
25.5	7.6709	7.7543	7.8381	7.9223	8.0069	8.0917	8.1770	8.2625	306
26.0	7.6260	7.7099	7.7942	7.8788	7.9638	8.0491	8.1348	8.2209	312
26.5	7.5833	7.6677	7.7524	7.8375	7.9230	8.0088	8.0949	8.1814	318
27.0	7.5428	7.6276	7.7128	7.7983	7.8842	7.9705	8.0570	8.1440	324
27.5	7.5043	7.5895	7.6751	7.7611	7.8474	7.9341	8.0211	8.1085	330
28.0	7.4676	7.5533	7.6393	7.7257	7.8125	7.8996	7.9871	8.0749	336
28.5	7.4327	7.5188	7.6053	7.6921	7.7793	7.8668	7.9547	8.0429	342
29.0	7.3995	7.4860	7.5729	7.6601	7.7477	7.8357	7.9240	8.0126	348
29.5	7.3678	7.4547	7.5420	7.6297	7.7177	7.8061	7.8948	7.9838	354
29.8	7.3475	7.4347	7.5223	7.6102	7.6985	7.7871	7.8761	7.9654	358
30.0	7.3376	7.4250	7.5127	7.6007	7.6891	7.7779	7.8670	7.9564	360
35.0	7.1026	7.1936	7.2849	7.3766	7.4686	7.5610	7.6536	7.7466	420
40.0	6.9531	7.0471	7.1414	7.2360	7.3309	7.4262	7.5217	7.6175	480

MONTHLY PAYMENT NECESSARY
TO AMORTIZE A $1,000 LOAN

INTEREST↓ YEARS	9%	9⅛%	9¼%	9⅜%	9½%	9⅝%	9¾%	9⅞%	MOS
.5	171.0689	171.1304	171.1920	171.2535	171.3151	171.3766	171.4382	171.4998	6
1.0	87.4515	87.5095	87.5675	87.6255	87.6835	87.7416	87.7997	87.8578	12
1.5	59.5977	59.6550	59.7123	59.7697	59.8271	59.8846	59.9420	59.9995	18
2.0	45.6847	45.7421	45.7995	45.8570	45.9145	45.9720	46.0296	46.0873	24
2.5	37.3482	37.4059	37.4637	37.5215	37.5794	37.6373	37.6953	37.7533	30
3.0	31.7997	31.8579	31.9162	31.9746	32.0330	32.0914	32.1499	32.2085	36
3.5	27.8445	27.9033	27.9621	28.0211	28.0801	28.1392	28.1983	28.2575	42
4.0	24.8850	24.9444	25.0039	25.0635	25.1231	25.1829	25.2427	25.3026	48
4.5	22.5894	22.6494	22.7096	22.7698	22.8301	22.8906	22.9511	23.0117	54
5.0	20.7584	20.8191	20.8799	20.9408	21.0019	21.0630	21.1242	21.1856	60
5.5	19.2652	19.3266	19.3882	19.4498	19.5116	19.5734	19.6354	19.6975	66
6.0	18.0255	18.0876	18.1499	18.2122	18.2747	18.3373	18.4000	18.4629	72
6.5	16.9807	17.0435	17.1065	17.1696	17.2328	17.2961	17.3596	17.4232	78
7.0	16.0891	16.1526	16.2162	16.2800	16.3440	16.4081	16.4723	16.5367	84
7.5	15.3199	15.3841	15.4485	15.5130	15.5777	15.6425	15.7075	15.7726	90
8.0	14.6502	14.7151	14.7802	14.8455	14.9109	14.9765	15.0422	15.1081	96
8.5	14.0624	14.1281	14.1939	14.2599	14.3260	14.3923	14.4588	14.5255	102
9.0	13.5429	13.6093	13.6758	13.7425	13.8094	13.8764	13.9437	14.0111	108
9.5	13.0808	13.1479	13.2151	13.2825	13.3502	13.4180	13.4859	13.5541	114
10.0	12.6676	12.7353	12.8033	12.8714	12.9398	13.0083	13.0770	13.1460	120
10.5	12.2961	12.3646	12.4332	12.5021	12.5712	12.6404	12.7099	12.7796	126
11.0	11.9608	12.0299	12.0993	12.1689	12.2386	12.3086	12.3788	12.4493	132
11.5	11.6568	11.7267	11.7967	11.8670	11.9375	12.0082	12.0791	12.1503	138
12.0	11.3803	11.4508	11.5216	11.5925	11.6637	11.7352	11.8068	11.8787	144
12.5	11.1279	11.1991	11.2705	11.3422	11.4141	11.4862	11.5586	11.6312	150
13.0	10.8968	10.9687	11.0408	11.1131	11.1857	11.2586	11.3316	11.4049	156
13.5	10.6846	10.7572	10.8300	10.9030	10.9763	11.0498	11.1236	11.1976	162
14.0	10.4894	10.5626	10.6360	10.7097	10.7837	10.8579	10.9324	11.0071	168
14.5	10.3092	10.3831	10.4572	10.5316	10.6062	10.6811	10.7562	10.8316	174
15.0	10.1427	10.2172	10.2919	10.3670	10.4422	10.5178	10.5936	10.6697	180
15.5	9.9884	10.0635	10.1389	10.2146	10.2905	10.3668	10.4432	10.5200	186
16.0	9.8452	9.9209	9.9970	10.0733	10.1499	10.2268	10.3039	10.3813	192
16.5	9.7120	9.7884	9.8651	9.9420	10.0193	10.0968	10.1746	10.2527	198
17.0	9.5880	9.6651	9.7423	9.8199	9.8978	9.9760	10.0544	10.1331	204
17.5	9.4724	9.5500	9.6280	9.7062	9.7847	9.8634	9.9425	10.0219	210
18.0	9.3644	9.4427	9.5212	9.6000	9.6791	9.7585	9.8382	9.9182	216
18.5	9.2635	9.3423	9.4214	9.5008	9.5806	9.6606	9.7409	9.8215	222
19.0	9.1690	9.2484	9.3281	9.4081	9.4884	9.5690	9.6499	9.7311	228
19.5	9.0804	9.1604	9.2406	9.3212	9.4021	9.4833	9.5648	9.6466	234
20.0	8.9973	9.0778	9.1587	9.2398	9.3213	9.4031	9.4852	9.5675	240
20.5	8.9192	9.0003	9.0817	9.1635	9.2455	9.3279	9.4105	9.4935	246
21.0	8.8458	8.9275	9.0094	9.0917	9.1743	9.2573	9.3405	9.4240	252
21.5	8.7768	8.8590	8.9415	9.0243	9.1075	9.1909	9.2747	9.3588	258
22.0	8.7117	8.7945	8.8775	8.9609	9.0446	9.1286	9.2129	9.2975	264
22.5	8.6505	8.7337	8.8173	8.9012	8.9855	9.0700	9.1548	9.2400	270
23.0	8.5927	8.6765	8.7606	8.8450	8.9297	9.0148	9.1002	9.1858	276
23.5	8.5381	8.6224	8.7071	8.7920	8.8772	8.9628	9.0487	9.1349	282
24.0	8.4866	8.5714	8.6566	8.7420	8.8277	8.9138	9.0002	9.0869	288
24.5	8.4380	8.5233	8.6089	8.6948	8.7811	8.8676	8.9545	9.0417	294
25.0	8.3920	8.4777	8.5638	8.6502	8.7370	8.8240	8.9114	8.9990	300
25.5	8.3484	8.4347	8.5212	8.6081	8.6953	8.7829	8.8707	8.9588	306
26.0	8.3072	8.3939	8.4810	8.5683	8.6560	8.7440	8.8323	8.9209	312
26.5	8.2682	8.3554	8.4429	8.5307	8.6188	8.7072	8.7960	8.8850	318
27.0	8.2313	8.3189	8.4068	8.4950	8.5836	8.6725	8.7617	8.8512	324
27.5	8.1962	8.2843	8.3726	8.4613	8.5503	8.6396	8.7293	8.8192	330
28.0	8.1630	8.2515	8.3403	8.4294	8.5188	8.6086	8.6986	8.7890	336
28.5	8.1315	8.2204	8.3096	8.3991	8.4890	8.5791	8.6696	8.7604	342
29.0	8.1016	8.1909	8.2805	8.3705	8.4607	8.5513	8.6421	8.7333	348
29.5	8.0732	8.1629	8.2529	8.3433	8.4339	8.5249	8.6162	8.7077	354
29.8	8.0551	8.1450	8.2353	8.3259	8.4169	8.5081	8.5996	8.6914	358
30.0	8.0462	8.1363	8.2268	8.3175	8.4085	8.4999	8.5915	8.6835	360
35.0	7.8399	7.9335	8.0274	8.1216	8.2161	8.3109	8.4059	8.5012	420
40.0	7.7136	7.8100	7.9066	8.0035	8.1006	8.1980	8.2956	8.3934	480

MONTHLY PAYMENT NECESSARY TO AMORTIZE A $1,000 LOAN

INTEREST ▶ YEARS	10%	10⅛%	10¼%	10⅜%	10½%	10⅝%	10¾%	10⅞%	MOS
.5	171.5614	171.6230	171.6846	171.7462	171.8079	171.8695	171.9312	171.9929	6
1.0	87.9159	87.9740	88.0322	88.0904	88.1486	88.2068	88.2651	88.3234	12
1.5	60.0571	60.1147	60.1723	60.2299	60.2876	60.3453	60.4030	60.4607	18
2.0	46.1449	46.2026	46.2604	46.3182	46.3760	46.4339	46.4919	46.5498	24
2.5	37.8114	37.8696	37.9278	37.9860	38.0443	38.1027	38.1611	38.2195	30
3.0	32.2672	32.3259	32.3847	32.4435	32.5024	32.5614	32.6205	32.6796	36
3.5	28.3168	28.3762	28.4356	28.4952	28.5547	28.6144	28.6742	28.7340	42
4.0	25.3626	25.4227	25.4828	25.5431	25.6034	25.6638	25.7243	25.7849	48
4.5	23.0724	23.1332	23.1941	23.2551	23.3162	23.3774	23.4387	23.5000	54
5.0	21.2470	21.3086	21.3703	21.4320	21.4939	21.5559	21.6180	21.6801	60
5.5	19.7597	19.8220	19.8845	19.9470	20.0097	20.0725	20.1354	20.1984	66
6.0	18.5258	18.5889	18.6522	18.7155	18.7790	18.8426	18.9063	18.9701	72
6.5	17.4869	17.5508	17.6148	17.6790	17.7432	17.8077	17.8722	17.9369	78
7.0	16.6012	16.6658	16.7306	16.7956	16.8607	16.9259	16.9913	17.0568	84
7.5	15.8379	15.9034	15.9690	16.0347	16.1006	16.1666	16.2328	16.2992	90
8.0	15.1742	15.2404	15.3068	15.3733	15.4400	15.5069	15.5739	15.6411	96
8.5	14.5923	14.6593	14.7265	14.7938	14.8613	14.9290	14.9969	15.0649	102
9.0	14.0787	14.1465	14.2144	14.2826	14.3509	14.4193	14.4880	14.5568	108
9.5	13.6225	13.6910	13.7598	13.8287	13.8978	13.9671	14.0366	14.1062	114
10.0	13.2151	13.2844	13.3539	13.4236	13.4935	13.5636	13.6339	13.7043	120
10.5	12.8494	12.9195	12.9898	13.0603	13.1310	13.2018	13.2729	13.3442	126
11.0	12.5199	12.5907	12.6618	12.7330	12.8045	12.8761	12.9480	13.0201	132
11.5	12.2216	12.2932	12.3650	12.4370	12.5093	12.5817	12.6543	12.7272	138
12.0	11.9508	12.0231	12.0957	12.1684	12.2414	12.3146	12.3880	12.4617	144
12.5	11.7040	11.7771	11.8503	11.9239	11.9976	12.0716	12.1458	12.2202	150
13.0	11.4785	11.5523	11.6263	11.7005	11.7750	11.8497	11.9247	11.9999	156
13.5	11.2718	11.3463	11.4211	11.4961	11.5713	11.6467	11.7224	11.7984	162
14.0	11.0820	11.1572	11.2327	11.3084	11.3843	11.4605	11.5370	11.6136	168
14.5	10.9073	10.9832	11.0593	11.1358	11.2124	11.2893	11.3665	11.4439	174
15.0	10.7461	10.8227	10.8995	10.9766	11.0540	11.1316	11.2095	11.2876	180
15.5	10.5970	10.6743	10.7518	10.8297	10.9077	10.9860	11.0646	11.1434	186
16.0	10.4590	10.5370	10.6152	10.6937	10.7724	10.8514	10.9307	11.0102	192
16.5	10.3310	10.4096	10.4885	10.5677	10.6471	10.7268	10.8067	10.8869	198
17.0	10.2121	10.2914	10.3709	10.4507	10.5308	10.6112	10.6918	10.7727	204
17.5	10.1015	10.1814	10.2616	10.3420	10.4228	10.5038	10.5851	10.6666	210
18.0	9.9984	10.0790	10.1598	10.2409	10.3223	10.4039	10.4858	10.5680	216
18.5	9.9023	9.9835	10.0649	10.1467	10.2287	10.3110	10.3935	10.4763	222
19.0	9.8126	9.8944	9.9764	10.0588	10.1414	10.2243	10.3075	10.3909	228
19.5	9.7287	9.8111	9.8937	9.9767	10.0599	10.1434	10.2272	10.3113	234
20.0	9.6502	9.7332	9.8164	9.9000	9.9838	10.0679	10.1523	10.2370	240
20.5	9.5767	9.6603	9.7441	9.8282	9.9126	9.9973	10.0823	10.1675	246
21.0	9.5078	9.5919	9.6763	9.7610	9.8460	9.9313	10.0168	10.1026	252
21.5	9.4432	9.5278	9.6128	9.6980	9.7836	9.8694	9.9555	10.0419	258
22.0	9.3825	9.4677	9.5532	9.6390	9.7251	9.8114	9.8981	9.9850	264
22.5	9.3254	9.4112	9.4972	9.5836	9.6702	9.7571	9.8443	9.9318	270
23.0	9.2718	9.3581	9.4447	9.5315	9.6187	9.7061	9.7938	9.8818	276
23.5	9.2214	9.3082	9.3952	9.4826	9.5703	9.6582	9.7465	9.8350	282
24.0	9.1739	9.2612	9.3488	9.4366	9.5248	9.6133	9.7020	9.7910	288
24.5	9.1292	9.2169	9.3050	9.3934	9.4820	9.5710	9.6602	9.7497	294
25.0	9.0870	9.1753	9.2638	9.3527	9.4418	9.5312	9.6209	9.7109	300
25.5	9.0473	9.1360	9.2250	9.3143	9.4040	9.4938	9.5840	9.6744	306
26.0	9.0098	9.0990	9.1885	9.2782	9.3683	9.4586	9.5492	9.6401	312
26.5	8.9744	9.0640	9.1540	9.2442	9.3347	9.4255	9.5165	9.6079	318
27.0	8.9410	9.0311	9.1214	9.2121	9.3030	9.3943	9.4857	9.5775	324
27.5	8.9094	8.9999	9.0907	9.1818	9.2732	9.3648	9.4567	9.5489	330
28.0	8.8796	8.9705	9.0618	9.1533	9.2450	9.3371	9.4294	9.5220	336
28.5	8.8514	8.9428	9.0344	9.1263	9.2185	9.3109	9.4036	9.4966	342
29.0	8.8248	8.9165	9.0085	9.1008	9.1934	9.2862	9.3793	9.4727	348
29.5	8.7996	8.8917	8.9841	9.0768	9.1697	9.2630	9.3564	9.4502	354
29.8	8.7835	8.8759	8.9686	9.0615	9.1547	9.2482	9.3419	9.4358	358
30.0	8.7757	8.8682	8.9610	9.0541	9.1474	9.2410	9.3348	9.4289	360
35.0	8.5967	8.6925	8.7886	8.8848	8.9813	9.0781	9.1750	9.2722	420
40.0	8.4915	8.5897	8.6882	8.7868	8.8857	8.9847	9.0840	9.1834	480

MONTHLY PAYMENT NECESSARY
TO AMORTIZE A $1,000 LOAN

INTEREST⟶ YEARS	11%	11⅛%	11¼%	11⅜%	11½%	11⅝%	11¾%	11⅞%	MOS
.5	172.0545	172.1162	172.1779	172.2397	172.3014	172.3631	172.4248	172.4866	6
1.0	88.3817	88.4400	88.4983	88.5567	88.6151	88.6735	88.7319	88.7903	12
1.5	60.5185	60.5764	60.6342	60.6921	60.7500	60.8080	60.8660	60.9240	18
2.0	46.6078	46.6659	46.7240	46.7821	46.8403	46.8985	46.9568	47.0151	24
2.5	38.2781	38.3366	38.3953	38.4539	38.5127	38.5714	38.6303	38.6892	30
3.0	32.7387	32.7979	32.8572	32.9166	32.9760	33.0355	33.0950	33.1546	36
3.5	28.7939	28.8538	28.9139	28.9740	29.0342	29.0944	29.1547	29.2151	42
4.0	25.8455	25.9063	25.9671	26.0280	26.0890	26.1501	26.2113	26.2725	48
4.5	23.5615	23.6230	23.6847	23.7464	23.8083	23.8702	23.9322	23.9944	54
5.0	21.7424	21.8048	21.8673	21.9299	21.9926	22.0554	22.1183	22.1813	60
5.5	20.2615	20.3247	20.3881	20.4515	20.5151	20.5788	20.6426	20.7065	66
6.0	19.0341	19.0982	19.1624	19.2267	19.2912	19.3557	19.4204	19.4853	72
6.5	18.0017	18.0666	18.1317	18.1969	18.2622	18.3277	18.3933	18.4590	78
7.0	17.1224	17.1882	17.2542	17.3202	17.3865	17.4528	17.5193	17.5860	84
7.5	16.3657	16.4323	16.4991	16.5661	16.6332	16.7004	16.7678	16.8354	90
8.0	15.7084	15.7759	15.8436	15.9114	15.9794	16.0475	16.1158	16.1842	96
8.5	15.1330	15.2014	15.2699	15.3386	15.4074	15.4764	15.5456	15.6150	102
9.0	14.6259	14.6950	14.7644	14.8339	14.9037	14.9735	15.0436	15.1138	108
9.5	14.1761	14.2461	14.3163	14.3867	14.4572	14.5280	14.5989	14.6700	114
10.0	13.7750	13.8459	13.9169	13.9881	14.0595	14.1312	14.2029	14.2749	120
10.5	13.4157	13.4873	13.5592	13.6313	13.7035	13.7760	13.8486	13.9215	126
11.0	13.0923	13.1648	13.2375	13.3104	13.3835	13.4568	13.5303	13.6040	132
11.5	12.8003	12.8736	12.9471	13.0208	13.0947	13.1688	13.2431	13.3177	138
12.0	12.5356	12.6096	12.6839	12.7584	12.8332	12.9081	12.9833	13.0586	144
12.5	12.2948	12.3697	12.4448	12.5201	12.5956	12.6713	12.7473	12.8235	150
13.0	12.0753	12.1509	12.2268	12.3029	12.3792	12.4557	12.5325	12.6095	156
13.5	11.8745	11.9509	12.0276	12.1044	12.1815	12.2588	12.3364	12.4142	162
14.0	11.6905	11.7677	11.8451	11.9227	12.0006	12.0786	12.1570	12.2355	168
14.5	11.5215	11.5994	11.6776	11.7559	11.8345	11.9134	11.9925	12.0718	174
15.0	11.3660	11.4446	11.5234	11.6026	11.6819	11.7615	11.8413	11.9214	180
15.5	11.2225	11.3018	11.3814	11.4613	11.5413	11.6216	11.7022	11.7830	186
16.0	11.0900	11.1700	11.2503	11.3309	11.4117	11.4927	11.5740	11.6555	192
16.5	10.9674	11.0481	11.1291	11.2103	11.2918	11.3736	11.4556	11.5378	198
17.0	10.8538	10.9352	11.0169	11.0988	11.1810	11.2634	11.3461	11.4290	204
17.5	10.7484	10.8305	10.9128	10.9954	11.0782	11.1613	11.2447	11.3283	210
18.0	10.6505	10.7332	10.8162	10.8994	10.9830	11.0667	11.1507	11.2350	216
18.5	10.5594	10.6428	10.7264	10.8103	10.8945	10.9789	11.0635	11.1484	222
19.0	10.4746	10.5586	10.6429	10.7274	10.8122	10.8972	10.9825	11.0681	228
19.5	10.3956	10.4802	10.5651	10.6502	10.7356	10.8213	10.9072	10.9933	234
20.0	10.3219	10.4071	10.4926	10.5783	10.6643	10.7506	10.8371	10.9238	240
20.5	10.2530	10.3388	10.4249	10.5112	10.5978	10.6847	10.7718	10.8591	246
21.0	10.1887	10.2751	10.3617	10.4486	10.5358	10.6232	10.7109	10.7988	252
21.5	10.1285	10.2155	10.3027	10.3901	10.4779	10.5658	10.6541	10.7426	258
22.0	10.0722	10.1597	10.2475	10.3355	10.4237	10.5123	10.6011	10.6901	264
22.5	10.0195	10.1075	10.1958	10.2843	10.3731	10.4622	10.5515	10.6411	270
23.0	9.9701	10.0586	10.1474	10.2365	10.3258	10.4154	10.5052	10.5953	276
23.5	9.9237	10.0128	10.1021	10.1917	10.2815	10.3716	10.4619	10.5525	282
24.0	9.8803	9.9698	10.0596	10.1497	10.2400	10.3306	10.4214	10.5125	288
24.5	9.8395	9.9295	10.0198	10.1103	10.2011	10.2922	10.3835	10.4751	294
25.0	9.8011	9.8916	9.9824	10.0734	10.1647	10.2562	10.3480	10.4400	300
25.5	9.7651	9.8561	9.9473	10.0388	10.1305	10.2225	10.3147	10.4072	306
26.0	9.7313	9.8227	9.9144	10.0063	10.0984	10.1909	10.2835	10.3764	312
26.5	9.6994	9.7913	9.8834	9.9757	10.0683	10.1612	10.2543	10.3476	318
27.0	9.6695	9.7618	9.8543	9.9471	10.0401	10.1333	10.2268	10.3205	324
27.5	9.6413	9.7340	9.8269	9.9201	10.0135	10.1072	10.2011	10.2952	330
28.0	9.6148	9.7079	9.8012	9.8948	9.9886	10.0826	10.1769	10.2714	336
28.5	9.5898	9.6833	9.7770	9.8710	9.9652	10.0596	10.1542	10.2491	342
29.0	9.5663	9.6601	9.7542	9.8486	9.9431	10.0379	10.1329	10.2281	348
29.5	9.5441	9.6383	9.7328	9.8275	9.9224	10.0175	10.1129	10.2085	354
29.8	9.5301	9.6245	9.7192	9.8141	9.9093	10.0046	10.1002	10.1960	358
30.0	9.5232	9.6178	9.7126	9.8077	9.9029	9.9984	10.0941	10.1900	360
35.0	9.3696	9.4672	9.5649	9.6629	9.7611	9.8594	9.9579	10.0566	420
40.0	9.2829	9.3827	9.4826	9.5826	9.6828	9.7832	9.8836	9.9843	480

MONTHLY PAYMENT NECESSARY TO AMORTIZE A $1,000 LOAN

INTEREST ▸ YEARS	12%	12⅛%	12¼%	12⅜%	12½%	12⅝%	12¾%	12⅞%	MOS
.5	172.5484	172.6101	172.6719	172.7337	172.7955	172.8573	172.9192	172.9810	6
1.0	88.8488	88.9073	88.9658	89.0243	89.0829	89.1414	89.2000	89.2586	12
1.5	60.9820	61.0401	61.0982	61.1564	61.2146	61.2728	61.3310	61.3893	18
2.0	47.0735	47.1319	47.1903	47.2488	47.3073	47.3659	47.4245	47.4831	24
2.5	38.7481	38.8071	38.8662	38.9253	38.9844	39.0436	39.1029	39.1622	30
3.0	33.2143	33.2740	33.3338	33.3937	33.4536	33.5136	33.5737	33.6338	36
3.5	29.2756	29.3362	29.3968	29.4575	29.5183	29.5791	29.6400	29.7010	42
4.0	26.3338	26.3953	26.4568	26.5183	26.5800	26.6417	26.7036	26.7655	48
4.5	24.0566	24.1189	24.1813	24.2438	24.3064	24.3691	24.4318	24.4947	54
5.0	22.2444	22.3077	22.3710	22.4344	22.4979	22.5616	22.6253	22.6891	60
5.5	20.7705	20.8347	20.8989	20.9633	21.0278	21.0923	21.1570	21.2218	66
6.0	19.5502	19.6153	19.6804	19.7458	19.8112	19.8767	19.9424	20.0082	72
6.5	18.5249	18.5909	18.6570	18.7232	18.7896	18.8561	18.9228	18.9896	78
7.0	17.6527	17.7197	17.7867	17.8539	17.9212	17.9887	18.0563	18.1241	84
7.5	16.9031	16.9709	17.0389	17.1070	17.1753	17.2437	17.3123	17.3810	90
8.0	16.2528	16.3216	16.3905	16.4596	16.5288	16.5982	16.6677	16.7374	96
8.5	15.6845	15.7541	15.8240	15.8940	15.9641	16.0344	16.1049	16.1756	102
9.0	15.1842	15.2548	15.3256	15.3965	15.4676	15.5388	15.6102	15.6818	108
9.5	14.7413	14.8128	14.8844	14.9563	15.0283	15.1004	15.1728	15.2453	114
10.0	14.3471	14.4194	14.4920	14.5647	14.6376	14.7107	14.7840	14.8574	120
10.5	13.9945	14.0678	14.1412	14.2148	14.2886	14.3626	14.4368	14.5111	126
11.0	13.6779	13.7520	13.8263	13.9007	13.9754	14.0503	14.1254	14.2006	132
11.5	13.3924	13.4674	13.5425	13.6179	13.6934	13.7692	13.8451	13.9213	138
12.0	13.1342	13.2100	13.2860	13.3622	13.4386	13.5152	13.5920	13.6690	144
12.5	12.8999	12.9765	13.0533	13.1303	13.2076	13.2851	13.3627	13.4406	150
13.0	12.6867	12.7641	12.8417	12.9196	12.9977	13.0760	13.1545	13.2332	156
13.5	12.4922	12.5704	12.6488	12.7275	12.8064	12.8855	12.9648	13.0443	162
14.0	12.3143	12.3933	12.4725	12.5520	12.6317	12.7116	12.7917	12.8721	168
14.5	12.1513	12.2311	12.3111	12.3913	12.4718	12.5525	12.6334	12.7146	174
15.0	12.0017	12.0822	12.1630	12.2440	12.3252	12.4067	12.4884	12.5703	180
15.5	11.8640	11.9453	12.0268	12.1086	12.1906	12.2728	12.3552	12.4379	186
16.0	11.7373	11.8193	11.9015	11.9840	12.0667	12.1496	12.2328	12.3162	192
16.5	11.6203	11.7030	11.7859	11.8691	11.9526	12.0362	12.1201	12.2043	198
17.0	11.5122	11.5956	11.6792	11.7631	11.8473	11.9316	12.0162	12.1011	204
17.5	11.4121	11.4962	11.5806	11.6652	11.7500	11.8350	11.9203	12.0059	210
18.0	11.3195	11.4043	11.4893	11.5745	11.6600	11.7457	11.8317	11.9179	216
18.5	11.2336	11.3190	11.4047	11.4906	11.5767	11.6631	11.7497	11.8366	222
19.0	11.1539	11.2399	11.3262	11.4127	11.4995	11.5865	11.6738	11.7613	228
19.5	11.0798	11.1664	11.2533	11.3405	11.4279	11.5155	11.6034	11.6915	234
20.0	11.0109	11.0981	11.1856	11.2734	11.3614	11.4496	11.5381	11.6268	240
20.5	10.9467	11.0346	11.1227	11.2110	11.2996	11.3885	11.4775	11.5668	246
21.0	10.8870	10.9754	11.0641	11.1530	11.2422	11.3316	11.4212	11.5111	252
21.5	10.8313	10.9203	11.0095	11.0990	11.1887	11.2787	11.3689	11.4593	258
22.0	10.7794	10.8689	10.9587	11.0487	11.1390	11.2294	11.3202	11.4111	264
22.5	10.7309	10.8210	10.9113	11.0018	11.0926	11.1836	11.2748	11.3663	270
23.0	10.6856	10.7762	10.8670	10.9581	11.0494	11.1409	11.2326	11.3246	276
23.5	10.6434	10.7344	10.8257	10.9173	11.0091	11.1011	11.1933	11.2857	282
24.0	10.6038	10.6954	10.7872	10.8792	10.9714	11.0639	11.1566	11.2495	288
24.5	10.5668	10.6589	10.7511	10.8436	10.9363	11.0293	11.1224	11.2158	294
25.0	10.5322	10.6247	10.7174	10.8104	10.9035	10.9969	11.0905	11.1843	300
25.5	10.4999	10.5928	10.6859	10.7793	10.8729	10.9667	11.0607	11.1550	306
26.0	10.4695	10.5629	10.6565	10.7503	10.8443	10.9385	11.0329	11.1276	312
26.5	10.4411	10.5349	10.6289	10.7231	10.8175	10.9121	11.0070	11.1020	318
27.0	10.4145	10.5087	10.6030	10.6977	10.7925	10.8875	10.9827	11.0781	324
27.5	10.3895	10.4841	10.5789	10.6739	10.7690	10.8644	10.9600	11.0558	330
28.0	10.3661	10.4611	10.5562	10.6516	10.7471	10.8429	10.9388	11.0350	336
28.5	10.3442	10.4395	10.5350	10.6307	10.7266	10.8227	10.9190	11.0155	342
29.0	10.3236	10.4192	10.5151	10.6112	10.7074	10.8039	10.9005	10.9973	348
29.5	10.3043	10.4003	10.4964	10.5928	10.6894	10.7862	10.8832	10.9803	354
29.8	10.2920	10.3883	10.4847	10.5813	10.6781	10.7751	10.8722	10.9696	358
30.0	10.2861	10.3824	10.4790	10.5757	10.6726	10.7697	10.8669	10.9644	360
35.0	10.1555	10.2545	10.3537	10.4531	10.5525	10.6522	10.7520	10.8519	420
40.0	10.0850	10.1859	10.2869	10.3880	10.4892	10.5905	10.6920	10.7935	480

MONTHLY PAYMENT NECESSARY
TO AMORTIZE A $1,000 LOAN

INTEREST YEARS	13%	13⅛%	13¼%	13⅜%	13½%	13⅝%	13¾%	13⅞%	MOS
.5	173.0429	173.1047	173.1666	173.2285	173.2903	173.3522	173.4142	173.4761	6
1.0	89.3173	89.3759	89.4346	89.4933	89.5520	89.6108	89.6695	89.7283	12
1.5	61.4476	61.5059	61.5643	61.6227	61.6811	61.7396	61.7981	61.8566	18
2.0	47.5418	47.6006	47.6593	47.7182	47.7770	47.8359	47.8949	47.9539	24
2.5	39.2215	39.2810	39.3404	39.4000	39.4595	39.5192	39.5788	39.6386	30
3.0	33.6940	33.7542	33.8145	33.8749	33.9353	33.9958	34.0563	34.1170	36
3.5	29.7621	29.8232	29.8844	29.9457	30.0071	30.0685	30.1300	30.1916	42
4.0	26.8275	26.8896	26.9517	27.0140	27.0763	27.1387	27.2012	27.2638	48
4.5	24.5577	24.6207	24.6839	24.7471	24.8104	24.8739	24.9374	25.0010	54
5.0	22.7531	22.8171	22.8813	22.9455	23.0098	23.0743	23.1388	23.2035	60
5.5	21.2868	21.3518	21.4170	21.4822	21.5476	21.6131	21.6787	21.7444	66
6.0	20.0741	20.1401	20.2063	20.2726	20.3390	20.4055	20.4721	20.5389	72
6.5	19.0565	19.1235	19.1907	19.2579	19.3254	19.3929	19.4606	19.5284	78
7.0	18.1920	18.2600	18.3282	18.3965	18.4649	18.5335	18.6022	18.6710	84
7.5	17.4499	17.5189	17.5881	17.6574	17.7268	17.7964	17.8662	17.9361	90
8.0	16.8073	16.8773	16.9474	17.0177	17.0882	17.1588	17.2295	17.3004	96
8.5	16.2464	16.3174	16.3885	16.4598	16.5312	16.6028	16.6746	16.7465	102
9.0	15.7536	15.8255	15.8976	15.9699	16.0423	16.1149	16.1877	16.2606	108
9.5	15.3180	15.3909	15.4640	15.5372	15.6106	15.6842	15.7579	15.8318	114
10.0	14.9311	15.0049	15.0789	15.1531	15.2274	15.3020	15.3767	15.4516	120
10.5	14.5857	14.6604	14.7354	14.8105	14.8858	14.9612	15.0369	15.1128	126
11.0	14.2761	14.3518	14.4276	14.5036	14.5799	14.6563	14.7329	14.8097	132
11.5	13.9976	14.0742	14.1509	14.2279	14.3050	14.3823	14.4598	14.5376	138
12.0	13.7463	13.8237	13.9013	13.9791	14.0572	14.1354	14.2138	14.2925	144
12.5	13.5187	13.5970	13.6755	13.7542	13.8331	13.9122	13.9915	14.0710	150
13.0	13.3121	13.3912	13.4706	13.5502	13.6299	13.7099	13.7901	13.8704	156
13.5	13.1241	13.2041	13.2843	13.3647	13.4453	13.5261	13.6071	13.6883	162
14.0	12.9526	13.0334	13.1144	13.1956	13.2771	13.3587	13.4406	13.5226	168
14.5	12.7959	12.8775	12.9593	13.0413	13.1236	13.2060	13.2887	13.3715	174
15.0	12.6524	12.7348	12.8174	12.9002	12.9832	13.0664	13.1499	13.2335	180
15.5	12.5208	12.6039	12.6873	12.7708	12.8546	12.9386	13.0228	13.1073	186
16.0	12.3999	12.4837	12.5678	12.6521	12.7367	12.8214	12.9064	12.9916	192
16.5	12.2886	12.3732	12.4580	12.5431	12.6283	12.7138	12.7995	12.8854	198
17.0	12.1861	12.2714	12.3570	12.4427	12.5287	12.6149	12.7013	12.7879	204
17.5	12.0916	12.1776	12.2638	12.3503	12.4369	12.5238	12.6109	12.6982	210
18.0	12.0043	12.0910	12.1779	12.2650	12.3523	12.4399	12.5276	12.6156	216
18.5	11.9236	12.0109	12.0985	12.1863	12.2742	12.3624	12.4509	12.5395	222
19.0	11.8490	11.9369	12.0251	12.1135	12.2021	12.2910	12.3800	12.4693	228
19.5	11.7798	11.8684	11.9572	12.0462	12.1354	12.2249	12.3146	12.4044	234
20.0	11.7158	11.8049	11.8943	11.9839	12.0737	12.1638	12.2541	12.3445	240
20.5	11.6563	11.7461	11.8360	11.9262	12.0166	12.1072	12.1981	12.2891	246
21.0	11.6011	11.6915	11.7820	11.8727	11.9637	12.0549	12.1463	12.2379	252
21.5	11.5499	11.6408	11.7318	11.8231	11.9146	12.0063	12.0983	12.1904	258
22.0	11.5023	11.5937	11.6853	11.7771	11.8691	11.9613	12.0538	12.1464	264
22.5	11.4580	11.5499	11.6420	11.7343	11.8269	11.9196	12.0125	12.1057	270
23.0	11.4168	11.5092	11.6018	11.6946	11.7876	11.8808	11.9743	12.0679	276
23.5	11.3784	11.4713	11.5644	11.6577	11.7512	11.8449	11.9388	12.0329	282
24.0	11.3427	11.4360	11.5296	11.6233	11.7173	11.8114	11.9058	12.0003	288
24.5	11.3094	11.4032	11.4972	11.5914	11.6858	11.7804	11.8751	11.9701	294
25.0	11.2784	11.3726	11.4670	11.5616	11.6564	11.7515	11.8467	11.9420	300
25.5	11.2494	11.3441	11.4389	11.5339	11.6292	11.7246	11.8202	11.9160	306
26.0	11.2224	11.3175	11.4127	11.5082	11.6038	11.6996	11.7956	11.8917	312
26.5	11.1973	11.2927	11.3883	11.4841	11.5801	11.6763	11.7727	11.8692	318
27.0	11.1738	11.2696	11.3656	11.4618	11.5581	11.6547	11.7514	11.8483	324
27.5	11.1518	11.2480	11.3444	11.4409	11.5376	11.6345	11.7316	11.8288	330
28.0	11.1313	11.2279	11.3246	11.4214	11.5185	11.6157	11.7131	11.8107	336
28.5	11.1122	11.2091	11.3061	11.4033	11.5007	11.5982	11.6959	11.7938	342
29.0	11.0943	11.1915	11.2889	11.3864	11.4841	11.5819	11.6799	11.7781	348
29.5	11.0776	11.1751	11.2728	11.3706	11.4686	11.5667	11.6650	11.7635	354
29.8	11.0671	11.1648	11.2626	11.3606	11.4588	11.5572	11.6556	11.7543	358
30.0	11.0620	11.1598	11.2577	11.3559	11.4541	11.5525	11.6511	11.7499	360
35.0	10.9519	11.0521	11.1524	11.2529	11.3534	11.4541	11.5549	11.6557	420
40.0	10.8951	10.9969	11.0987	11.2006	11.3026	11.4047	11.5069	11.6091	480

MONTHLY PAYMENT NECESSARY
TO AMORTIZE A $1,000 LOAN

INTEREST → YEARS	14%	14⅛%	14¼%	14⅜%	14½%	14⅝%	14¾%	14⅞%	MOS
.5	173.5380	173.5999	173.6619	173.7239	173.7858	173.8478	173.9098	173.9718	6
1.0	89.7871	89.8459	89.9048	89.9637	90.0225	90.0815	90.1404	90.1993	12
1.5	61.9152	61.9738	62.0324	62.0910	62.1497	62.2084	62.2672	62.3260	18
2.0	48.0129	48.0720	48.1311	48.1902	48.2494	48.3087	48.3680	48.4273	24
2.5	39.6984	39.7582	39.8181	39.8780	39.9380	39.9981	40.0582	40.1183	30
3.0	34.1776	34.2384	34.2992	34.3600	34.4210	34.4820	34.5430	34.6041	36
3.5	30.2532	30.3150	30.3768	30.4386	30.5006	30.5626	30.6247	30.6868	42
4.0	27.3265	27.3892	27.4521	27.5150	27.5780	27.6410	27.7042	27.7674	48
4.5	25.0647	25.1285	25.1924	25.2563	25.3204	25.3846	25.4488	25.5132	54
5.0	23.2683	23.3331	23.3981	23.4631	23.5283	23.5935	23.6589	23.7244	60
5.5	21.8102	21.8761	21.9421	22.0083	22.0745	22.1409	22.2074	22.2740	66
6.0	20.6057	20.6727	20.7398	20.8071	20.8744	20.9419	21.0095	21.0772	72
6.5	19.5963	19.6644	19.7326	19.8009	19.8693	19.9379	20.0066	20.0754	78
7.0	18.7400	18.8091	18.8784	18.9478	19.0173	19.0870	19.1568	19.2267	84
7.5	18.0061	18.0763	18.1466	18.2170	18.2876	18.3584	18.4293	18.5003	90
8.0	17.3715	17.4427	17.5141	17.5856	17.6573	17.7291	17.8010	17.8731	96
8.5	16.8186	16.8909	16.9633	17.0358	17.1085	17.1814	17.2544	17.3276	102
9.0	16.3337	16.4070	16.4804	16.5540	16.6277	16.7016	16.7757	16.8499	108
9.5	15.9059	15.9802	16.0546	16.1292	16.2040	16.2789	16.3540	16.4293	114
10.0	15.5266	15.6019	15.6773	15.7529	15.8287	15.9046	15.9807	16.0570	120
10.5	15.1888	15.2650	15.3414	15.4180	15.4947	15.5717	15.6488	15.7261	126
11.0	14.8867	14.9638	15.0412	15.1187	15.1964	15.2743	15.3524	15.4307	132
11.5	14.6155	14.6936	14.7719	14.8503	14.9290	15.0079	15.0869	15.1661	138
12.0	14.3713	14.4503	14.5295	14.6089	14.6885	14.7683	14.8483	14.9284	144
12.5	14.1507	14.2306	14.3107	14.3911	14.4716	14.5522	14.6331	14.7142	150
13.0	13.9510	14.0318	14.1128	14.1940	14.2754	14.3570	14.4387	14.5207	156
13.5	13.7698	13.8514	13.9333	14.0153	14.0976	14.1800	14.2627	14.3455	162
14.0	13.6049	13.6874	13.7701	13.8529	13.9360	14.0193	14.1028	14.1865	168
14.5	13.4546	13.5379	13.6214	13.7051	13.7890	13.8731	13.9575	14.0420	174
15.0	13.3174	13.4015	13.4858	13.5703	13.6550	13.7399	13.8250	13.9104	180
15.5	13.1919	13.2768	13.3619	13.4471	13.5326	13.6183	13.7042	13.7903	186
16.0	13.0770	13.1626	13.2484	13.3345	13.4207	13.5071	13.5938	13.6806	192
16.5	12.9716	13.0579	13.1445	13.2312	13.3182	13.4054	13.4928	13.5804	198
17.0	12.8748	12.9618	13.0491	13.1366	13.2242	13.3121	13.4002	13.4885	204
17.5	12.7858	12.8735	12.9615	13.0496	13.1380	13.2266	13.3153	13.4043	210
18.0	12.7038	12.7922	12.8809	12.9697	13.0587	13.1480	13.2374	13.3271	216
18.5	12.6284	12.7174	12.8067	12.8962	12.9859	13.0757	13.1658	13.2561	222
19.0	12.5588	12.6485	12.7384	12.8285	12.9188	13.0093	13.1000	13.1909	228
19.5	12.4945	12.5848	12.6753	12.7660	12.8570	12.9481	13.0394	13.1309	234
20.0	12.4352	12.5261	12.6172	12.7085	12.8000	12.8917	12.9836	13.0756	240
20.5	12.3804	12.4718	12.5635	12.6554	12.7474	12.8397	12.9321	13.0247	246
21.0	12.3297	12.4217	12.5139	12.6063	12.6989	12.7917	12.8847	12.9778	252
21.5	12.2827	12.3753	12.4680	12.5609	12.6541	12.7474	12.8409	12.9346	258
22.0	12.2393	12.3323	12.4256	12.5190	12.6126	12.7065	12.8004	12.8946	264
22.5	12.1990	12.2926	12.3863	12.4802	12.5743	12.6686	12.7631	12.8578	270
23.0	12.1617	12.2557	12.3500	12.4443	12.5389	12.6337	12.7286	12.8237	276
23.5	12.1271	12.2216	12.3163	12.4111	12.5061	12.6013	12.6967	12.7922	282
24.0	12.0950	12.1900	12.2851	12.3803	12.4758	12.5714	12.6672	12.7632	288
24.5	12.0653	12.1606	12.2561	12.3518	12.4477	12.5437	12.6399	12.7363	294
25.0	12.0376	12.1334	12.2293	12.3254	12.4216	12.5181	12.6146	12.7114	300
25.5	12.0119	12.1081	12.2044	12.3009	12.3975	12.4943	12.5913	12.6884	306
26.0	11.9881	12.0846	12.1813	12.2781	12.3751	12.4723	12.5696	12.6671	312
26.5	11.9659	12.0628	12.1598	12.2570	12.3544	12.4519	12.5496	12.6474	318
27.0	11.9453	12.0425	12.1399	12.2375	12.3351	12.4330	12.5310	12.6291	324
27.5	11.9262	12.0237	12.1214	12.2193	12.3173	12.4155	12.5138	12.6122	330
28.0	11.9084	12.0062	12.1043	12.2024	12.3007	12.3992	12.4978	12.5965	336
28.5	11.8918	11.9900	12.0883	12.1868	12.2854	12.3841	12.4830	12.5820	342
29.0	11.8764	11.9749	12.0735	12.1722	12.2711	12.3701	12.4693	12.5686	348
29.5	11.8621	11.9608	12.0597	12.1587	12.2579	12.3571	12.4566	12.5561	354
29.8	11.8531	11.9520	12.0510	12.1502	12.2496	12.3490	12.4486	12.5483	358
30.0	11.8487	11.9477	12.0469	12.1462	12.2456	12.3451	12.4448	12.5445	360
35.0	11.7567	11.8578	11.9590	12.0603	12.1617	12.2632	12.3647	12.4664	420
40.0	11.7114	11.8138	11.9162	12.0187	12.1213	12.2240	12.3267	12.4294	480

APR TABLE
(Effective Interest Rate including Discount Points)

The table shows the effective interest rate of a mortgage loan taking into account the actual interest rate and the points (loan fee) required to obtain the loan. It is useful for comparing the actual cost of several mortgages over a given number of years, expressed as an Annual Percentage Rate.

PROBLEM:

Mr. and Mrs. Buyer are faced with a choice between two mortgage loans offered by different lenders. Both loans are for $150,000, to be amortized over a 10 year period.

Mortgage "A": 11¾% Interest, with a loan fee of 3 points.

Mortgage "B": 12½% Interest, with a loan fee of 1 point.

QUESTION:

If the Buyers expect to keep the property for 10 years, which loan offers the lower APR?

ANSWER:

MORTGAGE "A" – Find the block of 11¾% in the INTEREST RATE column at the far left of the table. In the DISCOUNT POINTS column select the line of 3 Points. At the intersection of that line and the 10-YEAR column you find the APR of 12.51%.

MORTGAGE "B" – Find the block of 12½% in the INTEREST RATE column at the far left of the table. In the DISCOUNT POINTS column select the line of 1 Point. At the intersection of that line and the 10-YEAR column you find the APR of 12.75%.

Mortgage "A" has the lower APR.

INTEREST RATE	DISCOUNT POINTS	5 YEARS	10 YEARS	15 YEARS	20 YEARS	25 YEARS	30 YEARS
6%	1	6.42	6.22	6.16	6.13	6.11	6.09
	2	6.84	6.45	6.32	6.25	6.21	6.19
	3	7.27	6.68	6.48	6.38	6.32	6.29
	4	7.71	6.91	6.64	6.51	6.44	6.39
	5	8.15	7.15	6.81	6.65	6.55	6.49
6¼%	1	6.67	6.47	6.41	6.38	6.36	6.35
	2	7.10	6.70	6.57	6.50	6.47	6.44
	3	7.53	6.93	6.73	6.63	6.58	6.54
	4	7.97	7.16	6.90	6.77	6.69	6.64
	5	8.41	7.40	7.07	6.90	6.81	6.74
6½%	1	6.92	6.72	6.66	6.63	6.61	6.60
	2	7.35	6.95	6.82	6.76	6.72	6.70
	3	7.78	7.18	6.99	6.89	6.83	6.80
	4	8.22	7.42	7.15	7.02	6.95	6.90
	5	8.66	7.66	7.32	7.16	7.06	7.00
6¾%	1	7.17	6.98	6.91	6.88	6.86	6.85
	2	7.60	7.21	7.07	7.01	6.97	6.95
	3	8.03	7.44	7.24	7.14	7.09	7.05
	4	8.47	7.67	7.41	7.28	7.20	7.15
	5	8.92	7.91	7.58	7.41	7.32	7.26
7%	1	7.42	7.23	7.16	7.13	7.11	7.10
	2	7.85	7.46	7.33	7.26	7.23	7.20
	3	8.29	7.69	7.49	7.40	7.34	7.30
	4	8.73	7.93	7.66	7.53	7.46	7.41
	5	9.17	8.17	7.83	7.67	7.58	7.52
7¼%	1	7.67	7.48	7.41	7.38	7.36	7.35
	2	8.10	7.71	7.58	7.51	7.48	7.45
	3	8.54	7.94	7.75	7.65	7.59	7.56
	4	8.98	8.18	7.92	7.79	7.71	7.67
	5	9.43	8.42	8.09	7.93	7.83	7.77
7½%	1	7.92	7.73	7.66	7.63	7.61	7.60
	2	8.36	7.96	7.83	7.77	7.73	7.71
	3	8.79	8.20	8.00	7.90	7.85	7.81
	4	9.24	8.44	8.17	8.04	7.97	7.92
	5	9.69	8.68	8.35	8.19	8.09	8.03
7¾%	1	8.18	7.98	7.92	7.88	7.87	7.85
	2	8.61	8.21	8.08	8.02	7.98	7.96
	3	9.05	8.45	8.25	8.16	8.10	8.07
	4	9.49	8.69	8.43	8.30	8.23	8.18
	5	9.94	8.94	8.60	8.44	8.35	8.29
8%	1	8.43	8.23	8.17	8.14	8.12	8.11
	2	8.86	8.47	8.34	8.27	8.24	8.21
	3	9.30	8.70	8.51	8.41	8.36	8.32
	4	9.74	8.95	8.68	8.55	8.48	8.44
	5	10.20	9.19	8.86	8.70	8.61	8.55
8¼%	1	8.68	8.48	8.42	8.39	8.37	8.36
	2	9.11	8.72	8.59	8.53	8.49	8.47
	3	9.55	8.96	8.76	8.67	8.61	8.58
	4	10.00	9.20	8.94	8.81	8.74	8.69
	5	10.45	9.45	9.12	8.96	8.86	8.81

ANNUAL PERCENTAGE RATES

INTEREST RATE	DISCOUNT POINTS	5 YEARS	10 YEARS	15 YEARS	20 YEARS	25 YEARS	30 YEARS
8½%	1	8.93	8.73	8.67	8.64	8.62	8.61
	2	9.36	8.97	8.84	8.78	8.74	8.72
	3	9.80	9.21	9.02	8.92	8.87	8.83
	4	10.25	9.46	9.19	9.07	8.99	8.95
	5	10.71	9.70	9.37	9.21	9.12	9.07
8¾%	1	9.18	8.98	8.92	8.89	8.87	8.86
	2	9.62	9.22	9.09	9.03	9.00	8.97
	3	10.06	9.46	9.27	9.18	9.12	9.09
	4	10.51	9.71	9.45	9.32	9.25	9.21
	5	10.96	9.96	9.63	9.47	9.38	9.32
9%	1	9.43	9.24	9.17	9.14	9.12	9.11
	2	9.87	9.48	9.35	9.28	9.25	9.23
	3	10.31	9.72	9.52	9.43	9.38	9.34
	4	10.76	9.96	9.70	9.58	9.51	9.46
	5	11.22	10.21	9.89	9.73	9.64	9.58
9¼%	1	9.68	9.49	9.42	9.39	9.38	9.36
	2	10.12	9.73	9.60	9.54	9.50	9.48
	3	10.56	9.97	9.78	9.68	9.63	9.60
	4	11.01	10.22	9.96	9.83	9.76	9.72
	5	11.47	10.47	10.14	9.99	9.90	9.84
9½%	1	9.93	9.74	9.67	9.64	9.63	9.62
	2	10.37	9.98	9.85	9.79	9.76	9.73
	3	10.82	10.23	10.03	9.94	9.89	9.85
	4	11.27	10.47	10.21	10.09	10.02	9.98
	5	11.73	10.73	10.40	10.24	10.16	10.10
9¾%	1	10.18	9.99	9.93	9.90	9.88	9.87
	2	10.62	10.23	10.10	10.04	10.01	9.99
	3	11.07	10.48	10.29	10.19	10.14	10.11
	4	11.52	10.73	10.47	10.35	10.28	10.23
	5	11.98	10.98	10.66	10.50	10.41	10.36
10%	1	10.44	10.24	10.18	10.15	10.13	10.12
	2	10.88	10.48	10.36	10.30	10.26	10.24
	3	11.32	10.73	10.54	10.45	10.40	10.37
	4	11.78	10.98	10.72	10.60	10.53	10.49
	5	12.24	11.24	10.91	10.76	10.67	10.62
10¼%	1	10.69	10.49	10.43	10.40	10.38	10.37
	2	11.13	10.74	10.61	10.55	10.52	10.50
	3	11.58	10.99	10.79	10.70	10.65	10.62
	4	12.03	11.24	10.98	10.86	10.79	10.75
	5	12.49	11.50	11.17	11.02	10.93	10.88
10½%	1	10.94	10.74	10.68	10.65	10.63	10.62
	2	11.38	10.99	10.86	10.80	10.77	10.75
	3	11.83	11.24	11.05	10.96	10.91	10.88
	4	12.29	11.49	11.24	11.11	11.05	11.01
	5	12.75	11.75	11.43	11.27	11.19	11.14
10¾%	1	11.19	10.99	10.93	10.90	10.89	10.88
	2	11.63	11.24	11.11	11.06	11.02	11.00
	3	12.08	11.49	11.30	11.21	11.16	11.13
	4	12.54	11.75	11.49	11.37	11.30	11.26
	5	13.01	12.01	11.68	11.53	11.45	11.40

ANNUAL PERCENTAGE RATES

INTEREST RATE	DISCOUNT POINTS	5 YEARS	10 YEARS	15 YEARS	20 YEARS	25 YEARS	30 YEARS
11%	1	11.44	11.25	11.18	11.15	11.14	11.13
	2	11.88	11.49	11.37	11.31	11.28	11.26
	3	12.34	11.75	11.56	11.47	11.42	11.39
	4	12.80	12.00	11.75	11.63	11.56	11.52
	5	13.26	12.26	11.94	11.79	11.71	11.66
11¼%	1	11.69	11.50	11.43	11.40	11.39	11.38
	2	12.14	11.75	11.62	11.56	11.53	11.51
	3	12.59	12.00	11.81	11.72	11.67	11.64
	4	13.05	12.26	12.00	11.88	11.82	11.78
	5	13.52	12.52	12.20	12.05	11.97	11.92
11½%	1	11.94	11.75	11.69	11.66	11.64	11.63
	2	12.39	12.00	11.87	11.81	11.78	11.76
	3	12.84	12.25	12.06	11.98	11.93	11.90
	4	13.30	12.51	12.26	12.14	12.08	12.04
	5	13.77	12.78	12.46	12.31	12.23	12.18
11¾%	1	12.19	12.00	11.94	11.91	11.89	11.88
	2	12.64	12.25	12.13	12.07	12.04	12.02
	3	13.10	12.51	12.32	12.23	12.18	12.16
	4	13.56	12.77	12.51	12.40	12.33	12.30
	5	14.03	13.03	12.71	12.57	12.49	12.44
12%	1	12.44	12.25	12.19	12.16	12.14	12.13
	2	12.89	12.50	12.38	12.32	12.29	12.27
	3	13.35	12.76	12.57	12.49	12.44	12.41
	4	13.81	13.02	12.77	12.65	12.59	12.55
	5	14.28	13.29	12.97	12.82	12.74	12.70
12¼%	1	12.69	12.50	12.44	12.41	12.40	12.39
	2	13.15	12.76	12.63	12.57	12.54	12.53
	3	13.60	13.02	12.83	12.74	12.69	12.67
	4	14.07	13.28	13.03	12.91	12.85	12.81
	5	14.54	13.55	13.23	13.08	13.00	12.96
12½%	1	12.95	12.75	12.69	12.66	12.65	12.64
	2	13.40	13.01	12.88	12.83	12.80	12.78
	3	13.86	13.27	13.08	13.00	12.95	12.92
	4	14.32	13.53	13.28	13.17	13.11	13.07
	5	14.79	13.80	13.49	13.34	13.26	13.22
12¾%	1	13.20	13.00	12.94	12.91	12.90	12.89
	2	13.65	13.26	13.14	13.08	13.05	13.03
	3	14.11	13.52	13.34	13.25	13.21	13.18
	4	14.58	13.79	13.54	13.42	13.36	13.33
	5	15.05	14.06	13.74	13.60	13.52	13.48
13%	1	13.45	13.26	13.19	13.17	13.15	13.14
	2	13.90	13.51	13.39	13.33	13.30	13.29
	3	14.36	13.78	13.59	13.51	13.46	13.44
	4	14.83	14.04	13.79	13.68	13.62	13.59
	5	15.31	14.32	14.00	13.86	13.78	13.74
13¼%	1	13.70	13.51	13.45	13.42	13.40	13.39
	2	14.15	13.77	13.64	13.59	13.56	13.54
	3	14.62	14.03	13.85	13.76	13.72	13.69
	4	15.09	14.30	14.05	13.94	13.88	13.85
	5	15.56	14.57	14.26	14.12	14.04	14.00

ANNUAL PERCENTAGE RATES

INTEREST RATE	DISCOUNT POINTS	5 YEARS	10 YEARS	15 YEARS	20 YEARS	25 YEARS	30 YEARS
13½%	1	13.95	13.76	13.70	13.67	13.65	13.65
	2	14.41	14.02	13.90	13.84	13.81	13.80
	3	14.87	14.28	14.10	14.02	13.97	13.95
	4	15.34	14.55	14.31	14.19	14.14	14.10
	5	15.82	14.83	14.52	14.38	14.30	14.26
13¾%	1	14.20	14.01	13.95	13.92	13.91	13.90
	2	14.66	14.27	14.15	14.09	14.07	14.05
	3	15.12	14.54	14.35	14.27	14.23	14.21
	4	15.59	14.81	14.56	14.45	14.39	14.36
	5	16.07	15.09	14.77	14.64	14.56	14.52
14%	1	14.45	14.26	14.20	14.17	14.16	14.15
	2	14.91	14.52	14.40	14.35	14.32	14.31
	3	15.38	14.79	14.61	14.53	14.48	14.46
	4	15.85	15.07	14.82	14.71	14.65	14.62
	5	16.33	15.34	15.03	14.89	14.82	14.78
14¼%	1	14.70	14.51	14.45	14.42	14.41	14.40
	2	15.16	14.78	14.66	14.60	14.57	14.56
	3	15.63	15.05	14.86	14.78	14.74	14.72
	4	16.10	15.32	15.08	14.97	14.91	14.88
	5	16.58	15.60	15.29	15.15	15.08	15.05
14½%	1	14.95	14.76	14.70	14.68	14.66	14.66
	2	15.42	15.03	14.91	14.86	14.83	14.81
	3	15.88	15.30	15.12	15.04	15.00	14.97
	4	16.36	15.58	15.33	15.22	15.17	15.14
	5	16.84	15.86	15.55	15.41	15.34	15.31
14¾%	1	15.21	15.01	14.95	14.93	14.91	14.91
	2	15.67	15.28	15.16	15.11	15.08	15.07
	3	16.14	15.56	15.37	15.29	15.25	15.23
	4	16.61	15.83	15.59	15.48	15.43	15.40
	5	17.10	16.11	15.81	15.67	15.60	15.57
15%	1	15.46	15.27	15.21	15.18	15.17	15.16
	2	15.92	15.54	15.42	15.36	15.34	15.32
	3	16.39	15.81	15.63	15.55	15.51	15.49
	4	16.87	16.09	15.84	15.74	15.69	15.66
	5	17.35	16.37	16.07	15.93	15.86	15.83
15¼%	1	15.71	15.52	15.46	15.43	15.42	15.41
	2	16.17	15.79	15.67	15.62	15.59	15.58
	3	16.64	16.06	15.88	15.80	15.77	15.74
	4	17.12	16.34	16.10	16.00	15.94	15.92
	5	17.61	16.63	16.32	16.19	16.12	16.09
15½%	1	15.96	15.77	15.71	15.68	15.67	15.66
	2	16.42	16.04	15.92	15.87	15.84	15.83
	3	16.90	16.32	16.14	16.06	16.02	16.00
	4	17.38	16.60	16.36	16.25	16.20	16.17
	5	17.86	16.88	16.58	16.45	16.39	16.35
15¾%	1	16.21	16.02	15.96	15.94	15.92	15.92
	2	16.68	16.29	16.18	16.12	16.10	16.09
	3	17.15	16.57	16.39	16.32	16.28	16.26
	4	17.63	16.85	16.61	16.51	16.46	16.43
	5	18.12	17.14	16.84	16.71	16.65	16.61

ANNUAL PERCENTAGE RATES

INTEREST RATE	DISCOUNT POINTS	5 YEARS	10 YEARS	15 YEARS	20 YEARS	25 YEARS	30 YEARS
16%	1	16.46	16.27	16.21	16.19	16.17	16.17
	2	16.93	16.55	16.43	16.38	16.35	16.34
	3	17.40	16.83	16.65	16.57	16.53	16.51
	4	17.89	17.11	16.87	16.77	16.72	16.69
	5	18.38	17.40	17.10	16.97	16.91	16.88
16¼%	1	16.71	16.52	16.46	16.44	16.43	16.42
	2	17.18	16.80	16.68	16.63	16.61	16.59
	3	17.66	17.08	16.90	16.83	16.79	16.77
	4	18.14	17.37	17.13	17.03	16.98	16.95
	5	18.63	17.66	17.36	17.23	17.17	17.14
16½%	1	16.96	16.77	16.72	16.69	16.68	16.67
	2	17.43	17.05	16.93	16.89	16.86	16.85
	3	17.91	17.33	17.16	17.08	17.05	17.03
	4	18.40	17.62	17.38	17.28	17.24	17.21
	5	18.89	17.91	17.62	17.49	17.43	17.40
16¾%	1	17.21	17.03	16.97	16.94	16.93	16.93
	2	17.69	17.30	17.19	17.14	17.12	17.10
	3	18.16	17.59	17.41	17.34	17.30	17.29
	4	18.65	17.88	17.64	17.54	17.49	17.47
	5	19.14	18.17	17.87	17.75	17.69	17.66
17%	1	17.47	17.28	17.22	17.19	17.18	17.18
	2	17.94	17.56	17.44	17.39	17.37	17.36
	3	18.42	17.84	17.67	17.59	17.56	17.54
	4	18.90	18.13	17.90	17.80	17.75	17.73
	5	19.40	18.43	18.13	18.01	17.95	17.92
17¼%	1	17.72	17.53	17.47	17.45	17.44	17.43
	2	18.19	17.81	17.70	17.65	17.62	17.61
	3	18.67	18.10	17.92	17.85	17.82	17.80
	4	19.16	18.39	18.16	18.06	18.01	17.99
	5	19.66	18.68	18.39	18.27	18.21	18.18
17½%	1	17.97	17.78	17.72	17.70	17.69	17.68
	2	18.44	18.06	17.95	17.90	17.88	17.87
	3	18.92	18.35	18.18	18.11	18.07	18.06
	4	19.41	18.64	18.41	18.32	18.27	18.25
	5	19.91	18.94	18.65	18.53	18.47	18.45
17¾%	1	18.22	18.03	17.97	17.95	17.94	17.93
	2	18.70	18.32	18.20	18.15	18.13	18.12
	3	19.18	18.61	18.43	18.36	18.33	18.31
	4	19.67	18.90	18.67	18.57	18.53	18.51
	5	20.17	19.20	18.91	18.79	18.73	18.71
18%	1	18.47	18.28	18.23	18.20	18.19	18.19
	2	18.95	18.57	18.46	18.41	18.39	18.38
	3	19.43	18.86	18.69	18.62	18.59	18.57
	4	19.92	19.16	18.93	18.83	18.79	18.77
	5	20.42	19.46	19.17	19.05	19.00	18.97
18¼%	1	18.72	18.53	18.48	18.45	18.44	18.44
	2	19.20	18.82	18.71	18.66	18.64	18.63
	3	19.69	19.11	18.94	18.87	18.84	18.83
	4	20.18	19.41	19.18	19.09	19.05	19.03
	5	20.68	19.71	19.43	19.31	19.26	19.23

Selected Financial Tables **A-185**

ANNUAL PERCENTAGE RATES

INTEREST RATE	DISCOUNT POINTS	5 YEARS	10 YEARS	15 YEARS	20 YEARS	25 YEARS	30 YEARS
18½%	1	18.97	18.79	18.73	18.71	18.70	18.69
	2	19.45	19.07	18.96	18.92	18.90	18.89
	3	19.94	19.37	19.20	19.13	19.10	19.08
	4	20.43	19.67	19.44	19.35	19.31	19.29
	5	20.94	19.97	19.69	19.57	19.52	19.49
18¾%	1	19.22	19.04	18.98	18.96	18.95	18.94
	2	19.70	19.33	19.22	19.17	19.15	19.14
	3	20.19	19.62	19.45	19.39	19.36	19.34
	4	20.69	19.92	19.70	19.61	19.57	19.55
	5	21.19	20.23	19.95	19.83	19.78	19.76
19%	1	19.48	19.29	19.23	19.21	19.20	19.20
	2	19.96	19.58	19.47	19.42	19.40	19.40
	3	20.45	19.88	19.71	19.64	19.61	19.60
	4	20.94	20.18	19.96	19.86	19.82	19.81
	5	21.45	20.49	20.20	20.09	20.04	20.02
19¼%	1	19.73	19.54	19.48	19.46	19.45	19.45
	2	20.21	19.83	19.72	19.68	19.66	19.65
	3	20.70	20.13	19.97	19.90	19.87	19.86
	4	21.20	20.44	20.21	20.12	20.08	20.07
	5	21.70	20.75	20.46	20.35	20.30	20.28
19½%	1	19.98	19.79	19.74	19.71	19.70	19.70
	2	20.46	20.09	19.98	19.93	19.91	19.90
	3	20.95	20.39	20.22	20.16	20.13	20.11
	4	21.45	20.69	20.47	20.38	20.34	20.33
	5	21.96	21.00	20.72	20.61	20.56	20.54
19¾%	1	20.23	20.04	19.99	19.97	19.96	19.95
	2	20.71	20.34	20.23	20.19	20.17	20.16
	3	21.21	20.64	20.48	20.41	20.38	20.37
	4	21.71	20.95	20.73	20.64	20.60	20.59
	5	22.22	21.26	20.98	20.87	20.83	20.81
20%	1	20.48	20.29	20.24	20.22	20.21	20.21
	2	20.97	20.59	20.48	20.44	20.42	20.41
	3	21.46	20.90	20.73	20.67	20.64	20.63
	4	21.96	21.20	20.98	20.90	20.86	20.85
	5	22.47	21.52	21.24	21.13	21.09	21.07
20¼%	1	20.73	20.55	20.49	20.47	20.46	20.46
	2	21.22	20.85	20.74	20.70	20.68	20.67
	3	21.71	21.15	20.99	20.92	20.90	20.89
	4	22.22	21.46	21.24	21.16	21.12	21.11
	5	22.73	21.78	21.50	21.39	21.35	21.33
20½%	1	20.98	20.80	20.74	20.72	20.71	20.71
	2	21.47	21.10	20.99	20.95	20.93	20.92
	3	21.97	21.41	21.24	21.18	21.15	21.14
	4	22.47	21.72	21.50	21.42	21.38	21.37
	5	22.99	22.03	21.76	21.66	21.61	21.59
20¾%	1	21.23	21.05	21.00	20.97	20.97	20.96
	2	21.72	21.35	21.24	21.20	21.19	21.18
	3	22.22	21.66	21.50	21.44	21.41	21.40
	4	22.73	21.97	21.76	21.67	21.64	21.62
	5	23.24	22.29	22.02	21.92	21.87	21.85

BI-WEEKLY, WEEKLY & MONTHLY
PAYMENT SCHEDULES

INTEREST RATE	WEEKLY PAYMENT	WEEKLY TERM IN YRS	BI-WEEKLY PAYMENT	BI-WEEKLY TERM IN YRS	MONTHLY PAYMENT	MONTHLY TERM IN YRS
6.00%	1.498877	24.50	2.997753	24.54	5.995506	30
6.25%	1.539293	24.31	3.078587	24.35	6.157173	30
6.50%	1.580170	24.12	3.160341	24.15	6.320681	30
6.75%	1.621495	23.90	3.242991	23.92	6.485981	30
7.00%	1.663256	23.69	3.326513	23.73	6.653025	30
7.25%	1.705441	23.48	3.410882	23.50	6.821763	30
7.50%	1.748037	23.27	3.496073	23.31	6.992146	30
7.75%	1.791031	23.06	3.582062	23.08	7.164123	30
8.00%	1.834412	22.83	3.668823	22.85	7.337646	30
8.25%	1.878167	22.60	3.756334	22.62	7.512667	30
8.50%	1.922284	22.37	3.844568	22.38	7.689135	30
8.75%	1.966751	22.13	3.933503	22.15	7.867005	30
9.00%	2.011557	21.90	4.023114	21.92	8.046227	30
9.25%	2.056689	21.67	4.113378	21.69	8.226755	30
9.50%	2.102136	21.42	4.204272	21.46	8.408543	30
9.75%	2.147886	21.19	4.295773	21.23	8.591545	30
10.00%	2.193929	20.94	4.387858	20.96	8.775716	30
10.25%	2.240253	20.71	4.480507	20.73	8.961013	30
10.50%	2.286848	20.46	4.573697	20.50	9.147393	30
10.75%	2.333704	20.21	4.667407	20.23	9.334814	30
11.00%	2.380809	19.98	4.761617	20.00	9.523234	30
11.25%	2.428154	19.73	4.856307	19.77	9.712614	30
11.50%	2.475729	19.48	4.951458	19.54	9.902915	30
11.75%	2.523525	19.25	5.047049	19.27	10.094098	30
12.00%	2.571532	19.00	5.143063	19.04	10.286126	30
12.25%	2.619741	18.77	5.239483	18.81	10.478965	30
12.50%	2.668145	18.52	5.336289	18.58	10.672578	30
12.75%	2.716733	18.29	5.433467	18.31	10.866933	30
13.00%	2.765499	18.06	5.530998	18.08	11.061996	30
13.25%	2.814434	17.83	5.628868	17.85	11.257736	30
13.50%	2.863531	17.60	5.727061	17.62	11.454122	30
13.75%	2.912782	17.37	5.825563	17.38	11.651126	30
14.00%	2.962180	17.15	5.924359	17.19	11.848718	30
14.25%	3.011718	16.92	6.023436	16.96	12.046871	30
14.50%	3.061390	16.71	6.122780	16.73	12.245560	30
14.75%	3.111190	16.48	6.222379	16.54	12.444758	30
15.00%	3.161110	16.27	6.322221	16.31	12.644441	30
15.25%	3.211147	16.06	6.422293	16.12	12.844586	30
15.50%	3.261293	15.87	6.522585	15.88	13.045170	30
15.75%	3.311543	15.65	6.623086	15.69	13.246172	30
16.00%	3.361893	15.46	6.723785	15.50	13.447570	30
16.25%	3.412337	15.27	6.824674	15.31	13.649347	30
16.50%	3.462870	15.08	6.925741	15.12	13.851481	30
16.75%	3.513489	14.88	7.026978	14.92	14.053956	30

NET AND GROSS SELLING PRICE

Net	Gross at 3% Commission	Gross at 3½% Commission	Gross at 4% Commission	Gross at 4½% Commission	Gross at 5% Commission	Gross at 5½% Commission	Gross at 6% Commission	Gross at 6½% Commission
25000	25773	25907	26042	26178	26316	26455	26596	26738
26000	26804	26943	27083	27225	27368	27513	27660	27807
27000	27835	27979	28125	28272	28421	28571	28723	28877
28000	28866	29016	29167	29315	29474	29630	29787	29947
29000	29897	30052	30208	30366	30526	30688	30851	31016
30000	30928	31088	31250	31414	31579	31746	31915	32086
31000	31959	32124	32292	32461	32632	32804	32979	33155
32000	32990	33161	33333	33508	33684	33862	34043	34225
33000	34021	34197	34375	34555	34737	34921	35106	35294
34000	35052	35233	35417	35602	35789	35979	36170	36364
35000	36082	36269	36458	36649	36842	37037	37234	37433
36000	37113	37306	37500	37696	37895	38095	38298	38503
37000	38144	38342	38542	38743	38947	39153	39362	39572
38000	39175	39378	39583	39791	40000	40212	40426	40642
39000	40206	40415	40625	40838	41053	41270	41489	41711
40000	41237	41451	41667	41885	42105	42328	42553	42781
41000	42268	42487	42708	42932	43158	43386	43617	43850
42000	43299	43523	43750	43979	44211	44444	44681	44920
43000	44330	44560	44792	45026	45263	45503	45745	45989
44000	45361	45596	45833	46073	46316	46561	46809	47059
45000	46392	46632	46875	47120	47368	47619	47872	48128
46000	47423	47668	47917	48168	48421	48677	48936	49198
47000	48454	48705	48958	49215	49474	49735	50000	50267
48000	49485	49741	50000	50262	50526	50794	51064	51337
49000	50515	50777	51042	51309	51579	51852	52128	52406
50000	51546	51813	52083	52356	52632	52910	53191	53476
51000	52577	52850	53125	53403	53684	53968	54255	54545
52000	53608	53886	54167	54450	54737	55026	55319	55615
53000	54639	54922	55208	55497	55789	56085	56383	56684
54000	55670	55959	56250	56545	56842	57143	57447	57754
55000	56701	56995	57292	57592	57895	58201	58511	58824
56000	57732	58031	58333	58639	58947	59259	59574	59893
57000	58763	59067	59375	59686	60000	60317	60638	60963
58000	59794	60104	60417	60733	61053	61376	61702	62032
59000	60825	61140	61458	61780	62105	62434	62766	63102
60000	61856	62176	62500	62827	63158	63492	63830	64171
61000	62887	63212	63542	63874	64211	64550	64894	65241
62000	63918	64249	64583	64921	65263	65608	65957	66310
63000	64948	65285	65625	65969	66316	66667	67021	67380
64000	65979	66321	66667	67016	67368	67725	68085	68449
65000	67010	67358	67708	68063	68421	68783	69149	69519
66000	68041	68394	68750	69110	69474	69841	70213	70588
67000	69072	69430	69792	70157	70526	70899	71277	71658
68000	70103	70466	70833	71204	71579	71958	72340	72727
69000	71134	71503	71875	72251	72632	73016	73404	73797
70000	72165	72539	72917	73298	73684	74074	74468	74866
71000	73196	73575	73958	74345	74737	75132	75532	75936
72000	74227	74611	75000	75393	75789	76190	76596	77005
73000	75258	75648	76042	76440	76842	77249	77660	78075
74000	76289	76684	77083	77487	77895	78307	78723	79144
75000	77320	77720	78125	78534	78947	79365	79787	80214
76000	78351	78756	79167	79581	80000	80423	80851	81283
77000	79381	79793	80208	80628	81053	81481	81915	82353
78000	80412	80829	81250	81675	82105	82540	82979	83422
79000	81443	81865	82292	82723	83158	83598	84043	84492
80000	82474	82902	83333	83770	84211	84656	85106	85561
81000	83505	83938	84375	84817	85263	85714	86170	86631
82000	84536	84974	85417	85864	86316	86772	87234	87701
83000	85567	86010	86458	86911	87368	87831	88298	88770
84000	86598	87047	87500	87958	88421	88889	89362	89840
85000	87629	88083	88542	89005	89474	89947	90426	90909
86000	88660	89119	89583	90052	90526	91005	91489	91979
87000	89691	90155	90625	91099	91579	92063	92553	93048
88000	90722	91192	91667	92147	92632	93122	93617	94118
89000	91753	92228	92708	93194	93684	94180	94681	95187
90000	92784	93264	93750	94241	94737	95238	95745	96257
91000	93814	94301	94792	95288	95789	96296	96809	97326
92000	94845	95337	95833	96335	96842	97354	97872	98396
93000	95876	96373	96875	97382	97895	98413	98936	99465
94000	96907	97409	97917	98429	98947	99471	100000	100535
95000	97938	98446	98958	99476	100000	100529	101064	101604
96000	98969	99482	100000	100524	101053	101587	102128	102674
97000	100000	100518	101042	101571	102105	102645	103191	103743
98000	101031	101554	102083	102618	103158	103704	104255	104813
99000	102062	102591	103125	103665	104211	104762	105319	105882
100000	103093	103627	104167	104712	105263	105820	106383	106952

NET AND GROSS SELLING PRICE

Net	Gross at 3% Commission	Gross at 3½% Commission	Gross at 4% Commission	Gross at 4½% Commission	Gross at 5% Commission	Gross at 5½% Commission	Gross at 6% Commission	Gross at 6½% Commission
101000	104124	104663	105208	105759	106316	106878	107447	108021
102000	105155	105699	106250	106806	107368	107937	108511	109091
103000	106186	106736	107292	107853	108421	108995	109574	110160
104000	107216	107772	108333	108901	109474	110053	110638	111230
105000	108247	108808	109375	109948	110526	111111	111702	112299
106000	109278	109845	110417	110995	111579	112169	112766	113369
107000	110309	110881	111458	112042	112632	113228	113830	114439
108000	111340	111917	112500	113089	113684	114286	114894	115508
109000	112371	112953	113542	114136	114737	115344	115957	116578
110000	113402	113990	114583	115183	115789	116402	117021	117647
111000	114433	115026	115625	116230	116842	117460	118085	118717
112000	115464	116062	116667	117277	117895	118519	119149	119786
113000	116495	117098	117708	118325	118947	119577	120213	120856
114000	117526	118135	118750	119372	120000	120635	121277	121925
115000	118557	119171	119792	120415	121053	121693	122340	122995
116000	119588	120207	120833	121466	122105	122751	123404	124064
117000	120619	121244	121875	122513	123158	123810	124468	125134
118000	121649	122280	122917	123560	124211	124868	125532	126203
119000	122680	123316	123958	124607	125263	125926	126596	127273
120000	123711	124352	125000	125654	126316	126984	127660	128342
121000	124742	125389	126042	126702	127368	128042	128723	129412
122000	125773	126425	127083	127749	128421	129101	129787	130481
123000	126804	127461	128125	128796	129474	130159	130851	131551
124000	127835	128497	129167	129843	130526	131217	131915	132620
125000	128866	129534	130208	130890	131579	132275	132979	133690
126000	129897	130570	131250	131937	132632	133333	134043	134759
127000	130928	131606	132292	132984	133684	134392	135106	135829
128000	131959	132642	133333	134031	134737	135450	136170	136898
129000	132990	133679	134375	135079	135789	136508	137234	137968
130000	134021	134715	135417	136126	136842	137566	138298	139037
131000	135052	135751	136458	137173	137895	138624	139362	140107
132000	136082	136788	137500	138220	138947	139683	140426	141176
133000	137113	137824	138542	139267	140000	140741	141489	142246
134000	138144	138860	139583	140314	141053	141799	142553	143316
135000	139175	139896	140625	141361	142105	142857	143617	144385
136000	140206	140933	141667	142408	143158	143915	144681	145455
137000	141237	141969	142708	143455	144211	144974	145745	146524
138000	142268	143005	143750	144503	145263	146032	146809	147594
139000	143299	144041	144792	145550	146316	147090	147872	148663
140000	144330	145078	145833	146597	147368	148148	148936	149733
141000	145361	146114	146875	147644	148421	149206	150000	150802
142000	146392	147150	147917	148691	149474	150265	151064	151872
143000	147423	148187	148958	149738	150526	151323	152128	152941
144000	148454	149223	150000	150785	151579	152381	153191	154011
145000	149485	150259	151042	151832	152632	153439	154255	155080
146000	150515	151295	152083	152880	153684	154497	155319	156150
147000	151546	152332	153125	153927	154737	155556	156383	157219
148000	152577	153368	154167	154974	155789	156614	157447	158289
149000	153608	154404	155208	156021	156842	157672	158511	159358
150000	154639	155440	156250	157068	157895	158730	159574	160428
151000	155670	156477	157292	158115	158947	159788	160638	161497
152000	156701	157513	158333	159162	160000	160847	161702	162567
153000	157732	158549	159375	160209	161053	161905	162766	163636
154000	158763	159585	160417	161257	162105	162963	163830	164706
155000	159794	160622	161458	162304	163158	164021	164894	165775
156000	160825	161658	162500	163351	164211	165079	165957	166845
157000	161856	162694	163542	164398	165263	166138	167021	167914
158000	162887	163731	164583	165445	166316	167196	168085	168984
159000	163918	164767	165625	166492	167368	168254	169149	170053
160000	164948	165803	166667	167539	168421	169312	170213	171123
161000	165979	166839	167708	168586	169474	170370	171277	172193
162000	167010	167876	168750	169634	170526	171429	172340	173262
163000	168041	168912	169792	170681	171579	172487	173404	174332
164000	169072	169948	170833	171728	172632	173545	174468	175401
165000	170103	170984	171875	172775	173684	174603	175532	176471
166000	171134	172021	172917	173822	174737	175661	176596	177540
167000	172165	173057	173958	174869	175789	176720	177660	178610
168000	173196	174093	175000	175916	176842	177778	178723	179679
169000	174227	175130	176042	176963	177895	178836	179787	180749
170000	175258	176166	177083	178010	178947	179894	180851	181818
171000	176289	177202	178125	179058	180000	180952	181915	182888
172000	177320	178238	179167	180105	181053	182011	182979	183957
173000	178351	179275	180208	181152	182105	183069	184043	185027
174000	179381	180311	181250	182199	183158	184127	185106	186096
175000	180412	181347	182292	183246	184211	185185	186170	187166
176000	181443	182383	183333	184293	185263	186243	187234	188235

NET AND GROSS SELLING PRICE

Net	Gross at 3% Commission	Gross at 3½% Commission	Gross at 4% Commission	Gross at 4½% Commission	Gross at 5% Commission	Gross at 5½% Commission	Gross at 6% Commission	Gross at 6½% Commission
177000	182474	183420	184375	185340	186316	187302	188298	189305
178000	183305	184456	185417	186387	187368	188360	189362	190374
179000	184536	185492	186458	187435	188421	189418	190426	191444
180000	185567	186528	187500	188482	189474	190476	191489	192513
181000	186598	187565	188542	189529	190526	191534	192553	193583
182000	187629	188601	189583	190576	191579	192593	193617	194652
183000	188660	189637	190625	191623	192632	193651	194681	195722
184000	189691	190674	191667	192670	193684	194709	195745	196791
185000	190722	191710	192708	193717	194737	195767	196808	197861
186000	191753	192746	193750	194764	195789	196825	197872	198930
187000	192783	193782	194792	195812	196842	197884	198936	200000
188000	193814	194819	195833	196859	197895	198942	200000	201070
189000	194845	195855	196875	197906	198947	200000	201064	202139
190000	195876	196891	197917	198953	200000	201058	202128	203209
191000	196907	197927	198958	200000	201053	202116	203191	204278
192000	197938	198964	200000	201047	202105	203175	204255	205348
193000	198969	200000	201042	202094	203158	204233	205319	206417
194000	200000	201036	202083	203141	204211	205291	206383	207487
195000	201031	202073	203125	204188	205263	206349	207447	208556
196000	202062	203109	204167	205236	206316	207407	208511	209626
197000	203093	204145	205208	206283	207368	208466	209574	210695
198000	204124	205181	206250	207330	208421	209524	210638	211765
199000	205155	206218	207292	208377	209474	210582	211702	212834
200000	206186	207254	208333	209424	210526	211640	212766	213904
201000	207216	208290	209375	210471	211579	212698	213830	214973
202000	208247	209326	210417	211518	212632	213757	214894	216043
203000	209278	210363	211458	212565	213684	214815	215957	217112
204000	210309	211399	212500	213613	214737	215873	217021	218182
205000	211340	212435	213542	214660	215789	216931	218085	219251
206000	212371	213471	214583	215707	216842	217989	219149	220321
207000	213402	214508	215625	216754	217895	219048	220213	221390
208000	214433	215544	216667	217801	218947	220106	221277	222460
209000	215464	216580	217708	218848	220000	221164	222340	223529
210000	216495	217617	218750	219895	221053	222222	223404	224599
211000	217526	218653	219792	220942	222105	223280	224468	225668
212000	218557	219689	220833	221989	223158	224339	225532	226738
213000	219588	220725	221875	223037	224211	225397	226596	227807
214000	220619	221762	222917	224084	225263	226455	227660	228877
215000	221649	222798	223958	225131	226316	227513	228723	229947
216000	222680	223834	225000	226178	227368	228571	229787	231016
217000	223711	224870	226042	227225	228421	229630	230851	232086
218000	224742	225907	227083	228272	229474	230688	231915	233155
219000	225773	226943	228125	229319	230526	231746	232979	234225
220000	226804	227979	229167	230366	231579	232804	234043	235294
221000	227835	229016	230208	231414	232632	233862	235106	236364
222000	228866	230052	231250	232461	233684	234921	236170	237433
223000	229897	231088	232292	233508	234737	235979	237234	238503
224000	230928	232124	233333	234555	235789	237037	238298	239572
225000	231959	233161	234375	235602	236842	238095	239362	240642
226000	232990	234197	235417	236649	237895	239153	240426	241711
227000	234021	235233	236458	237696	238947	240212	241489	242781
228000	235052	236269	237500	238743	240000	241270	242553	243850
229000	236082	237306	238542	239791	241053	242328	243617	244920
230000	237113	238342	239583	240838	242105	243386	244681	245989
231000	238144	239378	240625	241885	243158	244444	245745	247059
232000	239175	240414	241667	242932	244211	245503	246808	248128
233000	240206	241451	242708	243979	245263	246561	247872	249198
234000	241237	242487	243750	245026	246316	247619	248936	250267
235000	242268	243523	244792	246073	247368	248677	250000	251337
236000	243299	244560	245833	247120	248421	249735	251064	252406
237000	244330	245596	246875	248168	249474	250794	252128	253476
238000	245361	246632	247917	249215	250526	251852	253191	254545
239000	246392	247668	248958	250262	251579	252910	254255	255615
240000	247423	248705	250000	251309	252632	253968	255319	256684
241000	248454	249741	251042	252356	253684	255026	256383	257754
242000	249485	250777	252083	253403	254737	256085	257447	258824
243000	250515	251813	253125	254450	255789	257143	258511	259893
244000	251546	252850	254167	255497	256842	258201	259574	260963
245000	252577	253886	255208	256544	257895	259259	260638	262032
246000	253608	254922	256250	257592	258947	260317	261702	263102
247000	254639	255959	257292	258639	260000	261376	262766	264171
248000	255670	256995	258333	259686	261053	262434	263830	265241
249000	256701	258031	259375	260733	262105	263492	264894	266310
250000	257732	259067	260417	261780	263158	264550	265957	267380
251000	258763	260104	261458	262827	264211	265608	267021	268449
252000	259794	261140	262500	263874	265263	266667	268085	269519

Net	Gross at 3% Commission	Gross at 3½% Commission	Gross at 4% Commission	Gross at 4½% Commission	Gross at 5% Commission	Gross at 5½% Commission	Gross at 6% Commission	Gross at 6½% Commission
253000	260825	262176	263542	264921	266316	267725	269149	270588
254000	261856	263212	264583	265969	267368	268783	270213	271658
255000	262887	264249	265625	267016	268421	269841	271277	272727
256000	263918	265285	266667	268062	269474	270899	272340	273797
257000	264948	266321	267708	269110	270526	271958	273404	274866
258000	265979	267358	268750	270157	271579	273016	274468	275936
259000	267010	268394	269792	271204	272632	274074	275532	277005
260000	268041	269430	270833	272251	273684	275132	276596	278075
261000	269072	270466	271875	273298	274737	276190	277660	279144
262000	270103	271503	272917	274346	275789	277249	278723	280214
263000	271134	272539	273958	275393	276842	278307	279787	281283
264000	272165	273575	275000	276440	277895	279365	280851	282353
265000	273196	274611	276042	277487	278947	280423	281915	283422
266000	274227	275648	277083	278534	280000	281481	282979	284492
267000	275258	276684	278125	279581	281053	282540	284043	285561
268000	276289	277720	279167	280628	282105	283598	285106	286631
269000	277320	278756	280208	281675	283158	284656	286170	287701
270000	278351	279793	281250	282723	284211	285714	287234	288770
271000	279381	280829	282292	283770	285263	286772	288298	289840
272000	280412	281865	283333	284817	286316	287831	289362	290909
273000	281443	282902	284375	285864	287368	288889	290426	291979
274000	282474	283938	285417	286911	288421	289947	291489	293048
275000	283505	284974	286458	287958	289474	291005	292553	294118
276000	284536	286010	287500	289005	290526	292063	293617	295187
277000	285567	287047	288542	290052	291579	293122	294681	296257
278000	286598	288083	289583	291099	292632	294180	295745	297326
279000	287629	289119	290625	292147	293684	295238	296808	298396
280000	288660	290155	291667	293194	294737	296296	297872	299465
281000	289691	291192	292708	294241	295789	297354	298936	300535
282000	290722	292228	293750	295288	296842	298413	300000	301604
283000	291753	293264	294792	296335	297895	299471	301064	302674
284000	292783	294301	295833	297382	298947	300529	302128	303743
285000	293814	295337	296875	298429	300000	301587	303191	304813
286000	294845	296373	297917	299476	301053	302645	304255	305882
287000	295876	297409	298958	300524	302105	303704	305319	306952
288000	296907	298446	300000	301571	303158	304762	306383	308021
289000	297938	299482	301042	302618	304211	305820	307447	309091
290000	298969	300518	302083	303665	305263	306878	308511	310160
291000	300000	301554	303125	304712	306316	307936	309574	311230
292000	301031	302591	304167	305759	307368	308995	310638	312299
293000	302062	303627	305208	306806	308421	310053	311702	313369
294000	303093	304663	306250	307853	309474	311111	312766	314439
295000	304124	305699	307292	308901	310526	312169	313830	315508
296000	305155	306736	308333	309948	311579	313227	314894	316578
297000	306186	307772	309375	310995	312632	314286	315957	317647
298000	307216	308808	310417	312042	313684	315344	317021	318717
299000	308247	309845	311458	313089	314737	316402	318085	319786
300000	309278	310881	312500	314136	315789	317460	319149	320856
301000	310309	311917	313542	315183	316842	318519	320213	321925
302000	311340	312953	314583	316230	317895	319577	321277	322995
303000	312371	313990	315625	317277	318947	320635	322340	324064
304000	313402	315026	316667	318325	320000	321693	323404	325134
305000	314433	316062	317708	319372	321053	322751	324468	326203
306000	315464	317098	318750	320419	322105	323810	325532	327273
307000	316495	318135	319792	321466	323158	324868	326596	328342
308000	317526	319171	320833	322513	324211	325926	327660	329412
309000	318557	320207	321875	323560	325263	326984	328723	330481
310000	319588	321244	322917	324607	326316	328042	329787	331551
311000	320619	322280	323958	325654	327368	329101	330851	332620
312000	321649	323316	325000	326702	328421	330159	331915	333690
313000	322680	324352	326042	327749	329474	331217	332979	334759
314000	323711	325389	327083	328796	330526	332275	334043	335829
315000	324742	326425	328125	329843	331579	333333	335106	336898
316000	325773	327461	329167	330890	332632	334392	336170	337968
317000	326804	328497	330208	331937	333684	335450	337234	339037
318000	327835	329534	331250	332984	334737	336508	338298	340107
319000	328866	330570	332292	334031	335789	337566	339362	341176
320000	329897	331606	333333	335079	336842	338624	340426	342244
321000	330928	332642	334375	336126	337895	339683	341489	343316
322000	331959	333679	335417	337173	338947	340741	342553	344385
323000	332990	334715	336458	338220	340000	341799	343617	345455
324000	334021	335751	337500	339267	341053	342857	344681	346524
325000	335052	336788	338542	340314	342105	343915	345745	347594
326000	336082	337824	339583	341361	343158	344974	346808	348663
327000	337113	338860	340625	342408	344211	346032	347872	349733
328000	338144	339896	341667	343455	345263	347090	348936	350802

NET AND GROSS SELLING PRICE

Net	Gross at 3% Commission	Gross at 3½% Commission	Gross at 4% Commission	Gross at 4½% Commission	Gross at 5% Commission	Gross at 5½% Commission	Gross at 6% Commission	Gross at 6½% Commission
329000	339175	340933	342708	344503	346316	348148	350000	351872
330000	340206	341969	343750	345550	347368	349206	351064	352941
331000	341237	343005	344792	346597	348421	350265	352128	354011
332000	342268	344041	345833	347644	349474	351323	353191	355080
333000	343299	345078	346875	348691	350526	352381	354255	356150
334000	344330	346114	347917	349738	351579	353439	355319	357219
335000	345361	347150	348958	350785	352632	354497	356383	358289
336000	346392	348187	350000	351832	353684	355556	357447	359358
337000	347423	349223	351042	352880	354737	356614	358511	360428
338000	348454	350259	352083	353927	355789	357672	359574	361497
339000	349485	351295	353125	354974	356842	358730	360638	362567
340000	350515	352332	354167	356021	357895	359788	361702	363636
341000	351546	353368	355208	357068	358947	360847	362766	364706
342000	352577	354404	356250	358115	360000	361905	363830	365775
343000	353608	355440	357292	359162	361053	362963	364894	366845
344000	354639	356477	358333	360209	362105	364021	365957	367914
345000	355670	357513	359375	361257	363158	365079	367021	368984
346000	356701	358549	360417	362304	364211	366138	368085	370053
347000	357732	359585	361458	363351	365263	367196	369149	371123
348000	358763	360622	362500	364398	366316	368254	370213	372193
349000	359794	361658	363542	365445	367368	369312	371277	373262
350000	360825	362694	364583	366492	368421	370370	372340	374332
351000	361856	363731	365625	367539	369474	371429	373404	375401
352000	362887	364767	366667	368586	370526	372487	374468	376471
353000	363918	365803	367708	369633	371579	373545	375532	377540
354000	364948	366839	368750	370681	372632	374603	376596	378610
355000	365979	367876	369792	371728	373684	375661	377660	379679
356000	367010	368912	370833	372775	374737	376720	378723	380749
357000	368041	369948	371875	373822	375789	377778	379787	381818
358000	369072	370984	372917	374869	376842	378836	380851	382888
359000	370103	372021	373958	375916	377895	379894	381915	383957
360000	371134	373057	375000	376963	378947	380952	382979	385027
361000	372165	374093	376042	378010	380000	382011	384043	386096
362000	373196	375130	377083	379058	381053	383069	385106	387166
363000	374227	376166	378125	380105	382105	384127	386170	388235
364000	375258	377202	379167	381152	383158	385185	387234	389305
365000	376289	378238	380208	382199	384211	386243	388298	390374
366000	377320	379275	381250	383246	385263	387302	389362	391444
367000	378351	380311	382292	384293	386316	388360	390426	392513
368000	379381	381347	383333	385340	387368	389418	391489	393583
369000	380412	382383	384375	386387	388421	390476	392553	394652
370000	381443	383420	385417	387435	389474	391534	393617	395722
371000	382474	384456	386458	388482	390526	392593	394681	396791
372000	383505	385492	387500	389529	391579	393651	395745	397861
373000	384536	386528	388542	390576	392632	394709	396808	398930
374000	385567	387565	389583	391623	393684	395767	397872	400000
375000	386598	388601	390625	392670	394737	396825	398936	401070
376000	387629	389637	391667	393717	395789	397884	400000	402139
377000	388660	390674	392708	394764	396842	398942	401064	403209
378000	389691	391710	393750	395812	397895	400000	402128	404278
379000	390722	392746	394792	396859	398947	401058	403191	405348
380000	391753	393782	395833	397906	400000	402116	404255	406417
381000	392783	394819	396875	398953	401053	403175	405319	407487
382000	393814	395855	397917	400000	402105	404233	406383	408556
383000	394845	396891	398958	401047	403158	405291	407447	409626
384000	395876	397927	400000	402094	404211	406349	408511	410695
385000	396907	398964	401042	403141	405263	407407	409574	411765
386000	397938	400000	402083	404188	406316	408466	410638	412834
387000	398969	401036	403125	405236	407368	409524	411702	413904
388000	400000	402073	404167	406283	408421	410582	412766	414973
389000	401031	403109	405208	407330	409474	411640	413830	416043
390000	402062	404145	406250	408377	410526	412698	414894	417112
391000	403093	405181	407292	409424	411579	413757	415957	418182
392000	404124	406218	408333	410471	412632	414815	417021	419251
393000	405155	407254	409375	411518	413684	415873	418085	420321
394000	406186	408290	410417	412565	414737	416931	419149	421390
395000	407216	409326	411458	413613	415789	417989	420213	422460
396000	408247	410363	412500	414660	416842	419048	421277	423529
397000	409278	411399	413542	415707	417895	420106	422340	424599
398000	410309	412435	414583	416754	418947	421164	423404	425668
399000	411340	413471	415625	417801	420000	422222	424468	426738
400000	412371	414508	416667	418848	421053	423280	425532	427807
401000	413402	415544	417708	419895	422105	424339	426596	428877
402000	414433	416580	418750	420942	423158	425397	427660	429947
403000	415464	417617	419792	421990	424211	426455	428723	431016
404000	416495	418653	420833	423037	425263	427513	429787	432086

FACTORS TO COMPUTE INTEREST PORTION OF MONTHLY LOAN PAYMENTS

Annual Interest %	Monthly Interest %	Annual Interest %	Monthly Interest %	Annual Interest %	Monthly Interest %
6	0.5000	11	0.9167	16	1.333
6¼	0.5208	11¼	0.9375	16¼	1.354
6½	0.5417	11½	0.9583	16½	1.375
6¾	0.5625	11¾	0.9792	16¾	1.396
7	0.5833	12	1.0000	17	1.417
7¼	0.6042	12¼	1.0208	17¼	1.438
7½	0.6250	12½	1.0417	17½	1.458
7¾	0.6458	12¾	1.0625	17¾	1.479
8	0.6667	13	1.0833	18	1.500
8¼	0.6875	13¼	1.1042	18¼	1.521
8½	0.7083	13½	1.1250	18½	1.542
8¾	0.7292	13¾	1.1458	18¾	1.563
9	0.7500	14	1.1667	19	1.583
9¼	0.7708	14¼	1.1875	19¼	1.604
9½	0.7917	14½	1.2083	19½	1.625
9¾	0.8125	14¾	1.2292	19¾	1.646
10	0.8333	15	1.2500	20	1.667
10¼	0.8542	15¼	1.2708	20¼	1.688
10½	0.8750	15½	1.2917	20½	1.708
10¾	0.8958	15¾	1.3125	20¾	1.729

EXAMPLE:

Loan Balance $19,866.66

Interest 10% p/yr. or 0.8333 p/mo.

Monthly Payment $300.00

Interest: 0.8333% X 19,866.66 .... (165.55)

Payment toward principal 134.45
New Loan Balance $19,732.21

Monthly Payment $300.00

Interest: 0.8333% X 19,732.21 .... (164.43)

Payment toward principal 135.57
New Loan Balance $19,596.64

AGE OF LOAN	2.0	3.0	5.0	8.0	10.0	12.0	15.0	16.0	17.0	18.0	19.0	20.0	AGE OF LOAN
1	51.7	69.0	82.7	90.3	92.8	94.5	96.1	96.5	96.8	97.1	97.4	97.6	1
2	0.0	35.7	64.1	80.0	85.2	88.6	91.9	92.7	93.4	94.0	94.6	95.1	2
3	0.0	0.0	44.2	68.8	76.9	82.2	87.4	88.7	89.8	90.7	91.6	92.3	3
4	0.0	0.0	22.9	56.9	68.1	75.4	82.6	84.3	85.8	87.2	88.4	89.4	4
5	0.0	0.0	0.0	44.1	58.6	68.1	77.4	79.7	81.6	83.4	84.9	86.3	5
6	0.0	0.0	0.0	30.4	48.5	60.0	71.9	74.7	77.1	79.3	81.2	82.9	6
7	0.0	0.0	0.0	15.7	37.6	51.9	65.9	69.3	72.3	74.9	77.2	79.3	7
8	0.0	0.0	0.0	0.0	25.9	42.5	59.5	63.6	67.1	70.2	73.0	75.4	8
9	0.0	0.0	0.0	0.0	13.4	33.3	52.7	57.5	61.6	65.2	68.4	71.2	9
10	0.0	0.0	0.0	0.0	0.0	23.0	45.4	50.9	55.6	59.8	63.5	66.8	10
11	0.0	0.0	0.0	0.0	0.0	11.9	37.5	43.8	49.2	54.0	58.2	62.0	11
12	0.0	0.0	0.0	0.0	0.0	0.0	29.1	36.2	42.4	47.8	52.6	56.9	12
13	0.0	0.0	0.0	0.0	0.0	0.0	20.1	28.1	35.1	41.2	46.6	51.4	13
14	0.0	0.0	0.0	0.0	0.0	0.0	10.4	19.4	27.2	34.0	40.1	45.5	14
15	0.0	0.0	0.0	0.0	0.0	0.0	0.0	10.0	18.7	26.4	33.2	39.1	15
16	0.0	0.0	0.0	0.0	0.0	0.0	0.0	0.0	9.7	18.2	25.7	32.4	16
17	0.0	0.0	0.0	0.0	0.0	0.0	0.0	0.0	0.0	9.4	17.7	25.1	17
18	0.0	0.0	0.0	0.0	0.0	0.0	0.0	0.0	0.0	0.0	9.2	17.3	18
19	0.0	0.0	0.0	0.0	0.0	0.0	0.0	0.0	0.0	0.0	0.0	8.9	19

AGE OF LOAN	21.0	22.0	23.0	24.0	25.0	26.0	27.0	28.0	29.0	30.0	35.0	40.0	AGE OF LOAN
1	97.8	98.0	98.2	98.3	98.5	98.6	98.7	98.8	98.9	99.0	99.3	99.5	1
2	95.5	95.9	96.2	96.5	96.8	97.1	97.3	97.5	97.7	97.9	98.6	99.0	2
3	93.0	93.6	94.1	94.6	95.1	95.5	95.8	96.2	96.5	96.7	97.8	98.5	3
4	90.3	91.2	91.9	92.6	93.2	93.7	94.2	94.7	95.1	95.5	96.9	97.9	4
5	87.5	88.5	89.5	90.4	91.2	91.9	92.5	93.1	93.6	94.1	96.0	97.3	5
6	84.4	85.7	86.9	88.0	89.0	89.9	90.7	91.4	92.1	92.7	95.0	96.6	6
7	81.1	82.7	84.2	85.5	86.7	87.7	88.7	89.6	90.4	91.1	94.0	95.9	7
8	77.5	79.5	81.2	82.8	84.2	85.4	86.6	87.7	88.6	89.5	92.9	95.1	8
9	73.7	76.0	78.0	79.9	81.5	83.0	84.3	85.6	86.7	87.7	91.7	94.3	9
10	69.7	72.3	74.6	76.7	78.6	80.3	81.9	83.3	84.6	85.8	90.4	93.4	10
11	65.3	68.3	71.0	73.4	75.6	77.5	79.3	80.9	82.4	83.8	89.0	92.5	11
12	60.6	64.0	67.1	69.8	72.3	74.5	76.5	78.4	80.0	81.6	87.5	91.4	12
13	55.6	59.4	62.9	65.9	68.7	71.2	73.5	75.6	77.5	79.2	85.9	90.3	13
14	50.2	54.5	58.4	61.8	64.9	67.8	70.3	72.6	74.8	76.7	84.2	89.2	14
15	44.5	49.2	53.5	57.4	60.9	64.0	66.9	69.5	71.8	74.0	82.4	87.9	15
16	38.3	43.6	48.4	52.6	56.5	60.0	63.2	66.1	68.7	71.1	80.4	86.6	16
17	31.7	37.5	42.8	47.5	51.8	55.7	59.2	62.4	65.3	68.0	78.3	85.1	17
18	24.5	31.0	36.8	42.1	46.8	51.1	55.0	58.5	61.7	64.7	76.1	83.6	18
19	16.9	24.1	30.5	36.2	41.4	46.2	50.4	54.3	57.9	61.1	73.7	81.9	19
20	8.7	16.6	23.6	30.0	35.7	40.9	45.6	49.8	53.7	57.3	71.1	80.1	20
21	0.0	8.6	16.3	23.2	29.5	35.2	40.3	45.0	49.3	53.2	68.3	78.2	21
22	0.0	0.0	8.4	16.0	22.9	29.1	34.7	39.8	44.5	48.8	65.3	76.2	22
23	0.0	0.0	0.0	8.3	15.8	22.5	28.7	34.3	39.4	44.1	62.1	74.0	23
24	0.0	0.0	0.0	0.0	8.1	15.5	22.3	28.4	33.9	39.0	58.7	71.6	24
25	0.0	0.0	0.0	0.0	0.0	8.0	15.3	22.0	28.0	33.6	55.0	69.1	25
26	0.0	0.0	0.0	0.0	0.0	0.0	7.9	15.2	21.7	27.8	51.1	66.4	26
27	0.0	0.0	0.0	0.0	0.0	0.0	0.0	7.8	15.0	21.5	46.8	63.5	27
28	0.0	0.0	0.0	0.0	0.0	0.0	0.0	0.0	7.7	14.8	42.3	60.4	28
29	0.0	0.0	0.0	0.0	0.0	0.0	0.0	0.0	0.0	7.7	37.5	57.1	29
30	0.0	0.0	0.0	0.0	0.0	0.0	0.0	0.0	0.0	0.0	32.2	53.5	30
31	0.0	0.0	0.0	0.0	0.0	0.0	0.0	0.0	0.0	0.0	26.7	49.7	31
32	0.0	0.0	0.0	0.0	0.0	0.0	0.0	0.0	0.0	0.0	20.7	45.6	32
33	0.0	0.0	0.0	0.0	0.0	0.0	0.0	0.0	0.0	0.0	14.2	41.2	33
34	0.0	0.0	0.0	0.0	0.0	0.0	0.0	0.0	0.0	0.0	7.4	36.4	34
35	0.0	0.0	0.0	0.0	0.0	0.0	0.0	0.0	0.0	0.0	0.0	31.4	35
36	0.0	0.0	0.0	0.0	0.0	0.0	0.0	0.0	0.0	0.0	0.0	25.9	36
37	0.0	0.0	0.0	0.0	0.0	0.0	0.0	0.0	0.0	0.0	0.0	20.1	37
38	0.0	0.0	0.0	0.0	0.0	0.0	0.0	0.0	0.0	0.0	0.0	13.9	38
39	0.0	0.0	0.0	0.0	0.0	0.0	0.0	0.0	0.0	0.0	0.0	7.2	39

AGE OF LOAN	2.0	3.0	5.0	8.0	10.0	12.0	15.0	16.0	17.0	18.0	19.0	20.0	AGE OF LOAN
1	51.8	69.0	82.8	90.4	92.9	94.6	96.2	96.6	96.9	97.2	97.5	97.7	1
2	0.0	35.8	64.3	80.1	85.3	88.7	92.1	92.9	93.6	94.2	94.7	95.2	2
3	0.0	0.0	44.4	69.1	77.2	82.5	87.6	88.9	90.0	90.9	91.8	92.5	3
4	0.0	0.0	23.0	57.2	68.4	75.7	82.9	84.6	86.1	87.5	88.6	89.7	4
5	0.0	0.0	0.0	44.4	58.9	68.5	77.8	80.0	82.0	83.7	85.2	86.6	5
6	0.0	0.0	0.0	30.6	48.8	60.7	72.3	75.1	77.5	79.7	81.6	83.3	6
7	0.0	0.0	0.0	15.9	37.9	52.3	66.3	69.8	72.8	75.4	77.7	79.7	7
8	0.0	0.0	0.0	0.0	26.2	43.3	60.0	64.1	67.6	70.7	73.4	75.9	8
9	0.0	0.0	0.0	0.0	13.5	33.6	53.2	57.9	62.1	65.7	68.9	71.7	9
10	0.0	0.0	0.0	0.0	0.0	23.2	45.8	51.3	56.1	60.3	64.0	67.3	10
11	0.0	0.0	0.0	0.0	0.0	12.0	37.9	44.2	49.7	54.6	58.8	62.6	11
12	0.0	0.0	0.0	0.0	0.0	0.0	29.5	36.6	42.9	48.4	53.2	57.4	12
13	0.0	0.0	0.0	0.0	0.0	0.0	20.3	28.4	35.5	41.7	47.1	51.9	13
14	0.0	0.0	0.0	0.0	0.0	0.0	10.5	19.6	27.6	34.5	40.6	46.0	14
15	0.0	0.0	0.0	0.0	0.0	0.0	0.0	10.2	19.0	26.8	33.6	39.7	15
16	0.0	0.0	0.0	0.0	0.0	0.0	0.0	0.0	9.9	18.5	26.1	32.8	16
17	0.0	0.0	0.0	0.0	0.0	0.0	0.0	0.0	0.0	9.6	18.0	25.5	17
18	0.0	0.0	0.0	0.0	0.0	0.0	0.0	0.0	0.0	0.0	9.3	17.6	18
19	0.0	0.0	0.0	0.0	0.0	0.0	0.0	0.0	0.0	0.0	0.0	9.1	19

AGE OF LOAN	21.0	22.0	23.0	24.0	25.0	26.0	27.0	28.0	29.0	30.0	35.0	40.0	AGE OF LOAN
1	97.9	98.1	98.2	98.4	98.5	98.6	98.8	98.9	98.9	99.0	99.4	99.6	1
2	95.6	96.0	96.4	96.7	96.9	97.2	97.4	97.6	97.8	98.0	98.7	99.1	2
3	93.2	93.8	94.3	94.8	95.2	95.6	96.0	96.3	96.6	96.9	97.9	98.6	3
4	90.6	91.4	92.2	92.8	93.4	94.0	94.4	94.9	95.3	95.7	97.1	98.0	4
5	87.8	88.5	89.8	90.7	91.5	92.2	92.8	93.4	93.9	94.4	96.2	97.4	5
6	84.8	86.1	87.3	88.4	89.3	90.2	91.0	91.7	92.4	93.0	95.3	96.8	6
7	81.5	83.1	84.6	85.9	87.1	88.1	89.1	90.0	90.8	91.5	94.3	96.1	7
8	78.0	79.9	81.7	83.2	84.6	85.9	87.0	88.1	89.0	89.9	93.2	95.4	8
9	74.3	76.5	78.5	80.4	82.0	83.5	84.8	86.0	87.2	88.2	92.1	94.6	9
10	70.2	72.8	75.2	77.3	79.2	80.9	82.4	83.9	85.1	86.3	90.8	93.8	10
11	65.9	68.9	71.6	74.0	76.1	78.1	79.9	81.5	83.0	84.3	89.5	92.9	11
12	61.2	64.6	67.7	70.4	72.9	75.1	77.1	79.0	80.6	82.2	88.0	91.9	12
13	56.2	60.1	63.5	66.6	69.4	71.9	74.2	76.3	78.1	79.9	86.5	90.8	13
14	50.9	55.2	59.0	62.5	65.6	68.4	71.0	73.3	75.5	77.4	84.8	89.7	14
15	45.1	49.9	54.2	58.1	61.6	64.7	67.6	70.2	72.6	74.7	83.1	88.5	15
16	38.8	44.2	49.0	53.3	57.2	60.7	63.9	66.8	69.5	71.9	81.1	87.2	16
17	32.2	38.1	43.4	48.2	52.5	56.4	60.0	63.2	66.1	68.8	79.1	85.8	17
18	25.0	31.5	37.4	42.7	47.5	51.8	55.7	59.3	62.5	65.5	76.9	84.3	18
19	17.2	24.5	31.0	36.8	42.1	46.9	51.2	55.1	58.7	61.9	74.5	82.7	19
20	8.9	16.9	24.1	30.5	36.3	41.5	46.3	50.6	54.5	58.1	71.9	80.9	20
21	0.0	8.8	16.6	23.7	30.0	35.8	41.0	45.8	50.1	54.0	69.2	79.1	21
22	0.0	0.0	8.6	16.3	23.3	29.6	35.3	40.5	45.3	49.6	66.2	77.1	22
23	0.0	0.0	0.0	8.5	16.1	23.0	29.3	34.9	40.1	44.8	63.0	74.9	23
24	0.0	0.0	0.0	0.0	8.3	15.9	22.7	28.9	34.6	39.7	59.6	72.6	24
25	0.0	0.0	0.0	0.0	0.0	8.2	15.7	22.5	28.6	34.2	55.9	70.1	25
26	0.0	0.0	0.0	0.0	0.0	0.0	8.1	15.5	22.2	28.3	52.0	67.4	26
27	0.0	0.0	0.0	0.0	0.0	0.0	0.0	8.0	15.3	22.0	47.7	64.5	27
28	0.0	0.0	0.0	0.0	0.0	0.0	0.0	0.0	7.9	15.2	43.1	61.4	28
29	0.0	0.0	0.0	0.0	0.0	0.0	0.0	0.0	0.0	7.9	38.2	58.1	29
30	0.0	0.0	0.0	0.0	0.0	0.0	0.0	0.0	0.0	0.0	33.0	54.5	30
31	0.0	0.0	0.0	0.0	0.0	0.0	0.0	0.0	0.0	0.0	27.3	50.6	31
32	0.0	0.0	0.0	0.0	0.0	0.0	0.0	0.0	0.0	0.0	21.2	46.5	32
33	0.0	0.0	0.0	0.0	0.0	0.0	0.0	0.0	0.0	0.0	14.6	42.0	33
34	0.0	0.0	0.0	0.0	0.0	0.0	0.0	0.0	0.0	0.0	7.6	37.3	34
35	0.0	0.0	0.0	0.0	0.0	0.0	0.0	0.0	0.0	0.0	0.0	32.1	35
36	0.0	0.0	0.0	0.0	0.0	0.0	0.0	0.0	0.0	0.0	0.0	26.6	36
37	0.0	0.0	0.0	0.0	0.0	0.0	0.0	0.0	0.0	0.0	0.0	20.6	37
38	0.0	0.0	0.0	0.0	0.0	0.0	0.0	0.0	0.0	0.0	0.0	14.2	38
39	0.0	0.0	0.0	0.0	0.0	0.0	0.0	0.0	0.0	0.0	0.0	7.4	39

AGE OF LOAN	ORIGINAL TERM IN YEARS												AGE OF LOAN
	2.0	3.0	5.0	8.0	10.0	12.0	15.0	16.0	17.0	18.0	19.0	20.0	
1	51.9	69.1	82.9	90.5	93.0	94.7	96.2	96.6	97.0	97.3	97.5	97.8	1
2	0.0	35.8	64.4	80.3	85.5	88.9	92.2	93.0	93.7	94.3	94.9	95.3	2
3	0.0	0.0	44.5	69.3	77.4	82.7	87.8	89.1	90.2	91.1	92.0	92.7	3
4	0.0	0.0	23.1	57.4	68.6	76.0	83.2	84.9	86.4	87.7	88.9	89.9	4
5	0.0	0.0	0.0	44.6	59.2	68.8	78.1	80.4	82.3	84.0	85.6	86.9	5
6	0.0	0.0	0.0	30.8	45.1	61.0	72.6	75.5	77.9	80.1	82.0	83.6	6
7	0.0	0.0	0.0	16.0	38.2	52.7	66.8	70.2	73.2	75.8	78.1	80.1	7
8	0.0	0.0	0.0	0.0	26.4	43.6	60.4	64.5	68.1	71.2	73.9	76.3	8
9	0.0	0.0	0.0	0.0	13.7	33.9	53.6	58.4	62.6	66.2	69.4	72.3	9
10	0.0	0.0	0.0	0.0	0.0	23.4	46.3	51.8	56.6	60.9	64.6	67.9	10
11	0.0	0.0	0.0	0.0	0.0	12.2	38.3	44.7	50.2	55.1	59.3	63.1	11
12	0.0	0.0	0.0	0.0	0.0	0.0	29.8	37.0	43.3	48.9	53.7	58.0	12
13	0.0	0.0	0.0	0.0	0.0	0.0	20.6	28.8	35.9	42.2	47.7	52.5	13
14	0.0	0.0	0.0	0.0	0.0	0.0	10.7	19.9	27.9	34.9	41.1	46.6	14
15	0.0	0.0	0.0	0.0	0.0	0.0	0.0	10.3	19.3	27.2	34.1	40.2	15
16	0.0	0.0	0.0	0.0	0.0	0.0	0.0	0.0	10.0	18.8	26.5	33.3	16
17	0.0	0.0	0.0	0.0	0.0	0.0	0.0	0.0	0.0	9.7	18.3	25.9	17
18	0.0	0.0	0.0	0.0	0.0	0.0	0.0	0.0	0.0	0.0	9.5	17.9	18
19	0.0	0.0	0.0	0.0	0.0	0.0	0.0	0.0	0.0	0.0	0.0	9.3	19

AGE OF LOAN	ORIGINAL TERM IN YEARS												AGE OF LOAN
	21.0	22.0	23.0	24.0	25.0	26.0	27.0	28.0	29.0	30.0	35.0	40.0	
1	98.0	98.1	98.3	98.5	98.6	98.7	98.8	98.9	99.0	99.1	99.4	99.6	1
2	95.8	96.1	96.5	96.8	97.1	97.3	97.5	97.7	97.9	98.1	98.7	99.1	2
3	93.4	94.0	94.5	95.0	95.4	95.8	96.1	96.5	96.8	97.0	98.0	98.7	3
4	90.8	91.7	92.4	93.0	93.6	94.2	94.7	95.1	95.5	95.9	97.3	98.2	4
5	88.1	89.2	90.1	91.0	91.7	92.4	93.1	93.6	94.1	94.6	96.4	97.6	5
6	85.1	86.5	87.6	88.7	89.7	90.5	91.3	92.0	92.7	93.3	95.5	97.0	6
7	81.9	83.5	85.0	86.3	87.5	88.5	89.5	90.3	91.1	91.8	94.6	96.4	7
8	78.5	80.4	82.1	83.7	85.1	86.3	87.5	88.5	89.4	90.3	93.5	95.7	8
9	74.8	77.0	79.0	80.9	82.5	84.0	85.3	86.5	87.6	88.6	92.4	94.9	9
10	70.8	73.4	75.7	77.8	79.7	81.4	83.0	84.4	85.6	86.8	91.2	94.1	10
11	66.5	69.5	72.1	74.6	76.7	78.7	80.5	82.1	83.5	84.8	89.9	93.2	11
12	61.8	65.2	68.3	71.0	73.5	75.7	77.7	79.6	81.2	82.7	88.6	92.3	12
13	56.8	60.7	64.1	67.2	70.0	72.5	74.8	76.9	78.8	80.5	87.1	91.3	13
14	51.4	55.8	59.7	63.1	66.3	69.1	71.7	74.0	76.1	78.0	85.4	90.2	14
15	45.6	50.5	54.8	58.7	62.2	65.4	68.3	70.9	73.3	75.4	83.7	89.0	15
16	39.4	44.8	49.6	54.0	57.9	61.4	64.6	67.5	70.2	72.6	81.8	87.8	16
17	32.6	38.6	44.0	48.9	53.2	57.2	60.7	63.9	66.9	69.5	79.8	86.4	17
18	25.4	32.0	38.0	43.3	48.2	52.5	56.5	60.0	63.3	66.3	77.6	85.0	18
19	17.5	24.9	31.5	37.4	42.7	47.5	51.9	55.5	59.4	62.7	75.3	83.4	19
20	9.1	17.2	24.5	31.0	36.9	42.2	47.0	51.3	55.3	58.9	72.7	81.7	20
21	0.0	8.9	16.9	24.1	30.5	36.4	41.7	46.5	50.8	54.8	70.0	79.8	21
22	0.0	0.0	8.8	16.6	23.7	30.2	36.0	41.2	46.0	50.4	67.1	77.9	22
23	0.0	0.0	0.0	8.6	16.4	23.4	29.8	35.6	40.8	45.6	63.9	75.7	23
24	0.0	0.0	0.0	0.0	8.5	16.2	23.2	29.5	35.2	40.4	60.5	73.5	24
25	0.0	0.0	0.0	0.0	0.0	8.4	16.0	22.9	29.2	34.9	56.8	71.0	25
26	0.0	0.0	0.0	0.0	0.0	0.0	8.3	15.8	22.7	28.9	52.8	68.3	26
27	0.0	0.0	0.0	0.0	0.0	0.0	0.0	8.2	15.7	22.5	48.6	65.4	27
28	0.0	0.0	0.0	0.0	0.0	0.0	0.0	0.0	8.1	15.5	43.9	62.4	28
29	0.0	0.0	0.0	0.0	0.0	0.0	0.0	0.0	0.0	8.0	39.0	59.0	29
30	0.0	0.0	0.0	0.0	0.0	0.0	0.0	0.0	0.0	0.0	33.6	55.4	30
31	0.0	0.0	0.0	0.0	0.0	0.0	0.0	0.0	0.0	0.0	27.9	51.6	31
32	0.0	0.0	0.0	0.0	0.0	0.0	0.0	0.0	0.0	0.0	21.7	47.4	32
33	0.0	0.0	0.0	0.0	0.0	0.0	0.0	0.0	0.0	0.0	15.0	42.9	33
34	0.0	0.0	0.0	0.0	0.0	0.0	0.0	0.0	0.0	0.0	7.7	38.0	34
35	0.0	0.0	0.0	0.0	0.0	0.0	0.0	0.0	0.0	0.0	0.0	32.8	35
36	0.0	0.0	0.0	0.0	0.0	0.0	0.0	0.0	0.0	0.0	0.0	27.2	36
37	0.0	0.0	0.0	0.0	0.0	0.0	0.0	0.0	0.0	0.0	0.0	21.1	37
38	0.0	0.0	0.0	0.0	0.0	0.0	0.0	0.0	0.0	0.0	0.0	14.6	38
39	0.0	0.0	0.0	0.0	0.0	0.0	0.0	0.0	0.0	0.0	0.0	7.6	39

AGE OF LOAN	2.0	3.0	5.0	8.0	10.0	12.0	15.0	16.0	17.0	18.0	19.0	20.0	AGE OF LOAN
					ORIGINAL TERM IN YEARS								
1	51.9	69.2	83.C	90.6	93.1	94.7	96.3	96.7	97.0	97.3	97.6	97.8	1
2	0.0	35.9	64.6	80.5	85.7	89.1	92.4	93.2	93.9	94.5	95.0	95.5	2
3	0.0	0.0	44.7	69.5	77.6	82.9	88.1	89.3	90.4	91.4	92.2	92.9	3
4	0.0	0.0	23.2	57.7	68.9	76.3	83.4	85.2	86.7	88.0	89.2	90.2	4
5	0.0	0.0	0.0	44.9	59.5	69.1	78.4	80.7	82.7	84.4	85.9	87.2	5
6	0.0	0.0	0.C	31.1	45.4	61.4	73.0	75.9	78.3	80.5	82.3	84.0	6
7	0.0	0.0	0.0	16.1	38.4	53.0	67.2	70.6	73.6	76.2	78.5	80.6	7
8	0.0	0.0	0.0	0.0	26.6	44.0	60.9	65.0	68.5	71.7	74.4	76.8	8
9	0.0	0.0	0.0	0.0	13.8	34.2	54.1	58.9	63.1	66.7	69.9	72.8	9
10	0.0	0.0	0.C	0.0	0.0	23.7	46.7	52.3	57.1	61.4	65.1	68.4	10
11	0.0	0.0	0.0	0.0	0.0	12.3	38.7	45.2	50.7	55.6	59.9	63.7	11
12	0.0	0.0	0.C	0.C	0.0	0.0	30.1	37.5	43.8	49.4	54.3	58.6	12
13	0.0	0.0	0.C	0.0	0.0	0.C	20.9	29.2	36.4	42.7	48.2	53.1	13
14	0.0	0.0	0.C	0.C	0.0	0.C	10.8	20.2	28.3	35.4	41.6	47.1	14
15	0.0	0.0	0.C	C.C	C.0	0.C	0.0	10.5	19.6	27.5	34.5	40.7	15
16	0.0	0.0	0.C	0.C	0.0	0.0	0.0	0.0	10.2	19.1	26.9	33.8	16
17	0.0	0.0	0.0	0.0	C.0	0.0	0.0	0.C	0.0	9.9	18.6	26.3	17
18	0.0	0.C	0.C	0.0	0.0	0.0	0.0	0.0	0.0	0.0	9.7	18.2	18
19	0.0	0.0	0.0	0.0	C.0	0.C	0.0	0.0	0.0	0.0	0.0	9.4	19

AGE OF LOAN	21.0	22.0	23.0	24.0	25.0	26.C	27.0	28.0	29.0	30.0	35.0	40.0	AGE OF LOAN
					ORIGINAL TERM IN YEARS								
1	98.0	98.2	98.4	98.5	98.6	98.8	98.9	99.C	99.0	99.1	99.4	99.6	1
2	95.9	96.3	96.6	96.9	97.2	97.4	97.6	97.8	98.0	98.2	98.8	99.2	2
3	93.6	94.2	94.7	95.2	95.6	96.0	96.3	96.6	96.9	97.1	98.1	98.8	3
4	91.1	91.9	92.6	93.3	93.9	94.4	94.9	95.3	95.7	96.0	97.4	98.3	4
5	88.4	89.5	90.4	91.2	92.0	92.7	93.3	93.9	94.4	94.8	96.6	97.8	5
6	85.5	86.8	88.0	89.1	90.0	90.9	91.6	92.3	93.0	93.6	95.8	97.2	6
7	82.4	84.0	85.4	86.7	87.8	88.5	89.8	90.7	91.5	92.2	94.9	96.6	7
8	79.0	80.9	82.6	84.1	85.5	86.7	87.9	88.5	89.8	90.7	93.9	95.9	8
9	75.3	77.5	79.6	81.4	83.0	84.4	85.8	87.0	88.0	89.0	92.8	95.2	9
10	71.3	73.9	76.3	78.4	80.2	81.9	83.5	84.9	86.1	87.3	91.6	94.4	10
11	67.1	70.1	72.7	75.1	77.3	79.2	81.0	82.6	84.1	85.4	90.4	93.6	11
12	62.4	65.8	68.9	71.6	74.1	76.3	78.3	80.2	81.8	83.3	89.0	92.7	12
13	57.4	61.3	64.8	67.9	7C.7	73.2	75.5	77.5	79.4	81.1	87.6	91.8	13
14	52.0	56.4	60.3	63.8	67.0	69.8	72.4	74.7	76.8	78.7	86.0	90.7	14
15	46.2	51.1	55.5	59.4	62.9	66.1	69.0	71.6	74.0	76.1	84.3	89.6	15
16	39.9	45.4	50.3	54.7	58.6	62.2	65.4	68.3	70.9	73.3	82.5	88.4	16
17	33.1	39.2	44.6	49.5	53.9	57.9	61.4	64.7	67.6	70.3	80.5	87.0	17
18	25.8	32.5	38.6	44.0	48.9	53.2	57.2	60.8	64.1	67.0	78.4	85.6	18
19	17.8	25.3	32.C	38.0	43.4	48.2	52.6	56.6	60.2	63.5	76.0	84.1	19
20	9.3	17.5	24.9	31.5	37.5	42.8	47.7	52.1	56.1	59.7	73.5	82.4	20
21	0.0	9.1	17.2	24.5	31.1	37.0	42.4	47.2	51.6	55.6	70.8	80.6	21
22	0.0	0.0	8.9	17.0	24.2	3C.7	36.6	41.9	46.7	51.1	67.9	78.7	22
23	0.0	0.0	0.0	8.8	16.7	23.9	30.4	36.2	41.5	46.3	64.8	76.6	23
24	0.0	0.0	0.C	0.C	8.7	16.5	23.6	30.0	35.9	41.1	61.4	74.3	24
25	0.0	0.0	0.0	0.0	C.0	8.6	16.3	23.4	29.7	35.5	57.7	71.9	25
26	0.0	0.0	0.0	0.0	0.0	0.0	8.5	16.2	23.1	29.5	53.7	69.2	26
27	0.0	0.0	0.C	0.C	C.0	0.C	0.0	8.4	16.0	22.9	49.4	66.4	27
28	0.0	0.0	0.0	0.0	0.0	0.C	0.0	0.0	8.3	15.9	44.8	63.3	28
29	0.0	0.0	0.C	0.0	0.0	0.C	0.0	0.C	0.0	8.2	39.8	60.0	29
30	0.0	0.0	0.C	0.C	C.0	0.0	0.0	0.C	0.0	0.0	34.3	56.4	30
31	0.0	0.0	0.0	0.0	0.0	0.C	0.0	0.0	0.0	0.0	28.5	52.5	31
32	0.0	0.0	0.C	0.0	0.0	0.0	0.0	0.0	0.0	0.0	22.2	48.3	32
33	0.0	0.0	0.0	0.0	0.0	0.0	0.0	0.0	0.0	0.0	15.3	43.8	33
34	0.0	0.0	0.0	0.0	0.0	0.0	0.0	0.0	0.0	0.0	8.0	38.9	34
35	0.0	0.0	0.C	0.0	0.0	0.C	0.0	0.0	0.0	0.0	0.0	33.6	35
36	0.0	0.0	0.C	0.0	0.0	0.0	0.0	0.0	0.0	0.0	0.0	27.8	36
37	0.0	0.0	0.0	0.0	0.0	0.0	0.0	0.0	0.0	0.C	0.0	21.7	37
38	0.0	0.0	0.0	0.0	0.0	0.0	0.0	0.0	0.0	0.0	0.0	15.0	38
39	0.0	0.0	0.0	0.0	0.0	0.0	0.0	0.0	0.0	0.0	0.0	7.8	39

AGE OF LOAN	2.0	3.0	5.0	8.0	10.0	12.0	15.0	16.0	17.0	18.0	19.0	20.0	AGE OF LOAN
1	52.0	69.3	83.1	90.7	93.2	94.8	96.4	96.8	97.1	97.4	97.7	97.9	1
2	0.0	36.0	64.7	80.6	85.8	89.2	92.5	93.3	94.0	94.6	95.1	95.6	2
3	0.0	0.0	44.8	69.7	77.8	83.1	88.3	89.5	90.6	91.6	92.4	93.1	3
4	0.0	0.0	23.3	57.9	69.2	76.6	83.7	85.4	86.9	88.3	89.4	90.4	4
5	0.0	0.0	0.0	45.1	59.8	69.4	78.8	81.0	83.0	84.7	86.2	87.5	5
6	0.0	0.0	0.0	31.3	49.7	61.7	73.4	76.2	78.7	80.8	82.7	84.4	6
7	0.0	0.0	0.0	16.2	38.7	53.4	67.6	71.0	74.0	76.6	78.9	81.0	7
8	0.0	0.0	0.0	0.0	26.8	44.3	61.3	65.4	69.0	72.1	74.9	77.3	8
9	0.0	0.0	0.0	0.0	13.9	34.5	54.5	59.3	63.5	67.2	70.4	73.3	9
10	0.0	0.0	0.0	0.0	0.0	23.9	47.1	52.7	57.6	61.9	65.6	68.9	10
11	0.0	0.0	0.0	0.0	0.0	12.4	39.1	45.6	51.2	56.1	60.4	64.2	11
12	0.0	0.0	0.0	0.0	0.0	0.0	30.5	37.9	44.3	49.9	54.8	59.2	12
13	0.0	0.0	0.0	0.0	0.0	0.0	21.1	29.5	36.8	43.1	48.7	53.7	13
14	0.0	0.0	0.0	0.0	0.0	0.0	11.0	20.4	28.7	35.8	42.1	47.7	14
15	0.0	0.0	0.0	0.0	0.0	0.0	0.0	10.6	19.9	27.9	35.0	41.2	15
16	0.0	0.0	0.0	0.0	0.0	0.0	0.0	0.0	10.3	19.3	27.3	34.3	16
17	0.0	0.0	0.0	0.0	0.0	0.0	0.0	0.0	0.0	10.0	18.9	26.7	17
18	0.0	0.0	0.0	0.0	0.0	0.0	0.0	0.0	0.0	0.0	9.8	18.5	18
19	0.0	0.0	0.0	0.0	0.0	0.0	0.0	0.0	0.0	0.0	0.0	9.6	19

AGE OF LOAN	21.0	22.0	23.0	24.0	25.0	26.0	27.0	28.0	29.0	30.0	35.0	40.0	AGE OF LOAN
1	98.1	98.3	98.4	98.6	98.7	98.8	98.9	99.0	99.1	99.2	99.5	99.6	1
2	96.0	96.4	96.7	97.0	97.3	97.5	97.7	97.9	98.1	98.3	98.9	99.3	2
3	93.8	94.3	94.9	95.3	95.7	96.1	96.4	96.8	97.0	97.3	98.2	98.8	3
4	91.3	92.1	92.9	93.5	94.1	94.6	95.1	95.5	95.9	96.2	97.5	98.4	4
5	88.7	89.7	90.7	91.5	92.3	93.0	93.6	94.1	94.6	95.1	96.8	97.9	5
6	85.8	87.2	88.3	89.4	90.3	91.2	91.9	92.6	93.3	93.8	96.0	97.4	6
7	82.8	84.4	85.8	87.1	88.2	89.2	90.2	91.0	91.8	92.5	95.1	96.8	7
8	79.4	81.3	83.0	84.6	85.9	87.2	88.3	89.3	90.2	91.0	94.2	96.2	8
9	75.8	78.0	80.0	81.8	83.4	84.9	86.2	87.4	88.5	89.4	93.1	95.5	9
10	71.9	74.5	76.8	78.9	80.8	82.4	84.0	85.3	86.6	87.7	92.0	94.8	10
11	67.6	70.6	73.3	75.7	77.9	79.8	81.5	83.1	84.6	85.9	90.8	94.0	11
12	63.0	66.4	69.5	72.2	74.7	76.9	78.9	80.7	82.4	83.9	89.5	93.1	12
13	58.0	61.9	65.4	68.5	71.3	73.8	76.1	78.1	80.0	81.7	88.1	92.2	13
14	52.6	57.0	60.9	64.5	67.6	70.4	73.0	75.3	77.4	79.3	86.6	91.2	14
15	46.8	51.7	56.1	60.1	63.6	66.8	69.7	72.3	74.6	76.8	84.9	90.1	15
16	40.5	46.0	50.9	55.3	59.3	62.8	66.1	69.0	71.6	74.0	83.1	88.9	16
17	33.6	39.8	45.2	50.2	54.6	58.6	62.2	65.4	68.4	71.0	81.2	87.6	17
18	26.2	33.0	39.1	44.6	49.5	53.9	57.9	61.5	64.8	67.8	79.1	86.2	18
19	18.1	25.7	32.5	38.6	44.0	48.9	53.3	57.4	61.0	64.3	76.8	84.7	19
20	9.4	17.8	25.3	32.0	38.1	43.5	48.4	52.8	56.8	60.5	74.3	83.1	20
21	0.0	9.3	17.5	24.9	31.6	37.6	43.0	47.9	52.3	56.4	71.6	81.4	21
22	0.0	0.0	9.1	17.3	24.6	31.2	37.2	42.6	47.5	51.9	68.7	79.5	22
23	0.0	0.0	0.0	9.0	17.1	24.3	30.9	36.8	42.2	47.1	65.6	77.4	23
24	0.0	0.0	0.0	0.0	8.9	16.8	24.1	30.6	36.5	41.8	62.2	75.2	24
25	0.0	0.0	0.0	0.0	0.0	8.8	16.7	23.8	30.3	36.2	58.5	72.8	25
26	0.0	0.0	0.0	0.0	0.0	0.0	8.7	16.5	23.0	30.0	54.5	70.1	26
27	0.0	0.0	0.0	0.0	0.0	0.0	0.0	8.6	16.3	23.4	50.2	67.3	27
28	0.0	0.0	0.0	0.0	0.0	0.0	0.0	0.0	8.5	16.2	45.6	64.2	28
29	0.0	0.0	0.0	0.0	0.0	0.0	0.0	0.0	0.0	8.4	40.5	60.9	29
30	0.0	0.0	0.0	0.0	0.0	0.0	0.0	0.0	0.0	0.0	35.0	57.3	30
31	0.0	0.0	0.0	0.0	0.0	0.0	0.0	0.0	0.0	0.0	29.1	53.4	31
32	0.0	0.0	0.0	0.0	0.0	0.0	0.0	0.0	0.0	0.0	22.6	49.2	32
33	0.0	0.0	0.0	0.0	0.0	0.0	0.0	0.0	0.0	0.0	15.7	44.6	33
34	0.0	0.0	0.0	0.0	0.0	0.0	0.0	0.0	0.0	0.0	8.1	39.6	34
35	0.0	0.0	0.0	0.0	0.0	0.0	0.0	0.0	0.0	0.0	0.0	34.3	35
36	0.0	0.0	0.0	0.0	0.0	0.0	0.0	0.0	0.0	0.0	0.0	28.5	36
37	0.0	0.0	0.0	0.0	0.0	0.0	0.0	0.0	0.0	0.0	0.0	22.2	37
38	0.0	0.0	0.0	0.0	0.0	0.0	0.0	0.0	0.0	0.0	0.0	15.4	38
39	0.0	0.0	0.0	0.0	0.0	0.0	0.0	0.0	0.0	0.0	0.0	8.0	39

AGE OF LOAN	2.0	3.0	5.0	8.0	1C.0	12.0	15.0	16.0	17.0	18.0	19.0	20.0	AGE OF LOAN
1	52.0	69.4	83.1	90.8	93.3	94.9	96.5	96.9	97.2	97.5	97.7	97.9	1
2	0.0	36.1	64.8	80.8	86.0	89.4	92.7	93.4	94.1	94.7	95.3	95.7	2
3	0.0	0.0	45.0	69.9	78.1	83.4	88.5	89.7	90.8	91.8	92.6	93.3	3
4	0.0	0.0	23.4	58.1	69.5	76.8	84.0	85.7	87.2	88.5	89.7	90.7	4
5	0.0	0.0	0.0	45.3	6C.1	69.8	79.1	81.3	83.3	85.0	86.5	87.8	5
6	0.0	0.0	0.0	31.4	50.0	62.1	73.8	76.6	79.1	81.2	83.1	84.7	6
7	0.0	0.0	0.0	16.4	35.0	53.7	68.0	71.5	74.4	77.1	79.4	81.4	7
8	0.0	0.0	0.0	0.0	27.0	44.7	61.7	65.9	69.4	72.6	75.3	77.7	8
9	0.0	0.0	0.0	0.0	14.1	34.8	54.9	59.8	64.0	67.7	70.9	73.8	9
10	0.0	0.0	0.0	0.C	C.0	24.2	47.6	53.2	58.1	62.4	66.2	69.5	10
11	0.0	0.0	0.C	0.0	0.0	12.6	39.5	46.1	51.7	56.6	61.0	64.8	11
12	0.0	0.0	0.C	0.0	C.0	C.C	30.8	38.3	44.8	50.4	55.4	59.7	12
13	0.0	0.0	0.C	0.0	0.0	C.0	21.4	29.9	37.2	43.6	49.3	54.2	13
14	0.0	0.0	0.C	C.C	0.0	0.0	11.1	20.7	29.0	36.3	42.6	48.2	14
15	0.0	0.0	0.C	0.0	C.0	0.C	0.0	10.8	20.1	28.3	35.4	41.8	15
16	0.0	0.0	0.0	0.0	0.0	0.0	0.0	0.0	10.5	19.6	27.6	34.7	16
17	0.0	0.0	0.C	0.C	C.0	0.0	0.0	0.0	0.0	10.2	19.2	27.1	17
18	0.0	0.0	0.0	0.0	0.C	0.C	0.0	0.0	0.0	0.C	10.0	18.8	18
19	0.0	0.0	0.0	0.0	C.0	0.0	0.0	0.0	0.0	0.0	0.0	9.8	19

AGE OF LOAN	21.0	22.0	23.0	24.0	25.0	26.C	27.0	28.0	29.0	30.0	35.0	40.0	AGE OF LOAN
1	98.1	98.3	98.5	98.6	98.7	98.9	99.0	99.0	99.1	99.2	99.5	99.7	1
2	96.1	96.5	96.8	97.1	97.4	97.6	97.8	98.0	98.2	98.3	98.9	99.3	2
3	93.9	94.5	95.0	95.5	95.9	96.3	96.6	96.9	97.2	97.4	98.3	98.9	3
4	91.6	92.4	93.1	93.7	94.3	94.8	95.3	95.7	96.0	96.4	97.7	98.5	4
5	89.0	90.0	91.0	91.8	92.5	93.2	93.8	94.3	94.8	95.3	97.0	98.0	5
6	86.2	87.5	88.7	89.7	9C.6	91.5	92.2	92.9	93.5	94.1	96.2	97.5	6
7	83.2	84.7	86.2	87.4	88.6	89.6	90.5	91.3	92.1	92.8	95.4	97.0	7
8	79.9	81.8	83.5	85.0	86.3	87.6	88.7	89.7	90.6	91.4	94.5	96.4	8
9	76.3	78.5	80.5	82.3	83.9	85.3	86.6	87.8	88.9	89.8	93.5	95.8	9
10	72.4	75.0	77.3	79.4	81.3	82.9	84.5	85.8	87.0	88.2	92.4	95.1	10
11	68.2	71.2	73.9	76.3	78.4	80.3	82.1	83.6	85.1	86.4	91.2	94.3	11
12	63.6	67.C	70.1	72.8	75.3	77.5	79.5	81.3	82.9	84.4	90.0	93.5	12
13	58.6	62.5	66.0	69.1	71.9	74.4	76.7	78.7	80.6	82.3	88.6	92.6	13
14	53.2	57.6	61.6	65.1	68.3	71.1	73.7	76.0	78.1	79.9	87.1	91.6	14
15	47.4	52.3	56.8	60.7	64.3	67.5	70.3	72.9	75.3	77.4	85.5	90.6	15
16	41.0	46.6	51.5	56.C	60.0	63.5	66.8	69.7	72.3	74.7	83.7	89.4	16
17	34.1	40.3	45.8	50.8	55.3	59.3	62.9	66.1	69.1	71.7	81.8	88.2	17
18	26.6	33.5	39.7	45.2	5C.2	54.6	58.6	62.3	65.6	68.5	79.8	86.8	18
19	18.4	26.1	33.0	39.1	44.6	49.6	54.1	58.1	61.7	65.0	77.5	85.4	19
20	9.6	18.1	25.7	32.5	38.6	44.1	49.1	53.5	57.6	61.2	75.1	83.8	20
21	0.0	9.4	17.8	25.4	32.1	38.2	43.7	48.6	53.1	57.1	72.4	82.1	21
22	0.0	0.0	9.3	17.6	25.0	31.8	37.8	43.2	48.2	52.7	64.6	80.2	22
23	0.0	0.0	0.0	9.1	17.4	24.8	31.4	37.4	42.9	47.8	66.4	78.2	23
24	0.0	0.0	0.C	0.0	9.0	17.2	24.5	31.1	37.1	42.5	63.1	76.0	24
25	0.0	0.0	0.0	0.0	0.0	8.9	17.0	24.3	30.8	36.8	59.4	73.6	25
26	0.0	0.0	0.C	0.C	0.0	0.0	8.8	16.8	24.1	30.6	55.4	71.0	26
27	0.0	0.0	0.C	0.0	0.0	0.C	0.0	8.7	16.7	23.9	51.1	68.2	27
28	0.0	0.0	0.0	0.0	C.0	0.C	0.0	0.0	8.7	16.5	46.3	65.1	28
29	0.0	0.0	0.C	0.C	0.0	0.0	0.0	0.0	0.0	8.6	41.2	61.8	29
30	0.0	0.0	0.C	0.0	0.0	0.0	0.0	0.0	0.0	0.0	35.7	58.2	30
31	0.0	0.0	0.0	0.0	C.0	C.C	0.0	0.0	0.0	0.0	29.7	54.3	31
32	0.0	0.0	0.0	0.0	C.0	0.C	0.C	0.0	0.0	0.0	23.1	50.0	32
33	0.0	0.0	0.0	0.0	0.0	0.0	0.0	0.C	0.0	0.0	16.0	45.4	33
34	0.0	0.0	0.0	0.0	0.0	0.0	0.0	0.0	0.0	0.0	8.3	40.4	34
35	0.0	0.0	0.0	0.0	C.0	0.C	0.0	0.0	0.0	0.0	0.0	35.0	35
36	0.0	0.0	0.C	0.0	0.0	0.0	0.0	0.0	0.0	0.0	0.0	29.1	36
37	0.0	0.0	0.0	0.0	C.0	0.C	0.C	0.0	0.0	0.0	0.0	22.7	37
38	0.0	0.0	0.0	0.0	0.0	0.0	0.0	0.0	0.0	0.C	0.0	15.7	38
39	0.0	0.0	0.0	0.0	0.0	C.C	0.0	0.0	0.0	0.0	0.0	8.2	39

Selected Financial Tables **A-199**

REMAINING BALANCE
IN PERCENT OF ORIGINAL LOAN AMOUNT

AGE OF LOAN	2.0	3.0	5.0	8.0	10.0	12.0	15.0	16.0	17.0	18.0	19.0	20.0	AGE OF LOAN
1	52.1	69.4	83.2	90.9	93.4	95.0	96.6	96.9	97.3	97.5	97.8	98.0	1
2	0.0	36.2	65.0	81.0	86.1	89.5	92.8	93.6	94.3	94.9	95.4	95.8	2
3	0.0	0.0	45.1	70.1	78.3	83.6	88.7	89.9	91.0	91.9	92.8	93.5	3
4	0.0	0.0	23.5	58.4	69.7	77.1	84.3	86.0	87.5	88.8	89.9	90.9	4
5	0.0	0.0	0.0	45.6	60.4	70.1	79.4	81.7	83.6	85.3	86.8	88.1	5
6	0.0	0.0	0.0	31.7	50.3	62.4	74.2	77.0	79.4	81.6	83.4	85.1	6
7	0.0	0.0	0.0	16.5	39.3	54.1	68.4	71.9	74.9	77.5	79.8	81.8	7
8	0.0	0.0	0.0	0.0	27.3	45.0	62.2	66.3	69.9	73.0	75.9	78.2	8
9	0.0	0.0	0.0	0.0	14.2	35.2	55.4	60.3	64.5	68.2	71.4	74.3	9
10	0.0	0.0	0.0	0.0	0.0	24.4	48.0	53.7	58.6	62.9	66.7	70.0	10
11	0.0	0.0	0.0	0.0	0.0	12.7	39.9	46.5	52.2	57.2	61.5	65.3	11
12	0.0	0.0	0.0	0.0	0.0	0.0	31.2	38.7	45.2	50.9	55.9	60.3	12
13	0.0	0.0	0.0	0.0	0.0	0.0	21.7	30.2	37.7	44.1	49.8	54.8	13
14	0.0	0.0	0.0	0.0	0.0	0.0	11.3	21.0	29.4	36.7	43.2	48.8	14
15	0.0	0.0	0.0	0.0	0.0	0.0	0.0	10.9	20.4	28.7	35.9	42.3	15
16	0.0	0.0	0.0	0.0	0.0	0.0	0.0	0.0	10.6	19.9	28.0	35.2	16
17	0.0	0.0	0.0	0.0	0.0	0.0	0.0	0.0	0.0	10.4	19.5	27.5	17
18	0.0	0.0	0.0	0.0	0.0	0.0	0.0	0.0	0.0	0.0	10.1	19.1	18
19	0.0	0.0	0.0	0.0	0.0	0.0	0.0	0.0	0.0	0.0	0.0	9.9	19

AGE OF LOAN	21.0	22.0	23.0	24.0	25.0	26.0	27.0	28.0	29.0	30.0	35.0	40.0	AGE OF LOAN
1	98.2	98.4	98.5	98.7	98.8	98.5	99.0	99.1	99.2	99.2	99.5	99.7	1
2	96.2	96.6	96.9	97.2	97.5	97.7	97.9	98.1	98.3	98.4	99.0	99.4	2
3	94.1	94.7	95.2	95.6	96.0	96.4	96.7	97.0	97.3	97.5	98.4	99.0	3
4	91.8	92.6	93.3	93.9	94.5	95.0	95.4	95.8	96.2	96.6	97.8	98.6	4
5	89.3	90.3	91.2	92.1	92.8	93.4	94.0	94.6	95.1	95.5	97.1	98.2	5
6	86.5	87.8	89.0	90.0	90.9	91.8	92.5	93.2	93.8	94.3	96.4	97.7	6
7	83.6	85.1	86.5	87.8	88.9	89.9	90.8	91.7	92.4	93.1	95.6	97.2	7
8	80.3	82.2	83.9	85.4	86.7	88.0	89.0	90.0	90.9	91.7	94.7	96.6	8
9	76.8	79.0	81.0	82.8	84.4	85.8	87.1	88.2	89.3	90.2	93.8	96.0	9
10	72.9	75.5	77.8	79.9	81.8	83.4	84.9	86.3	87.5	88.6	92.8	95.3	10
11	68.7	71.7	74.4	76.8	78.9	80.9	82.6	84.2	85.6	86.8	91.6	94.6	11
12	64.2	67.6	70.7	73.4	75.9	78.1	80.1	81.8	83.5	84.9	90.4	93.8	12
13	59.2	63.1	66.6	69.7	72.5	75.0	77.3	79.3	81.2	82.8	89.1	93.0	13
14	53.8	58.2	62.2	65.7	68.9	71.7	74.3	76.6	78.7	80.6	87.6	92.1	14
15	47.9	52.9	57.4	61.4	64.9	68.1	71.0	73.6	76.0	78.1	86.1	91.0	15
16	41.5	47.2	52.2	56.6	60.6	64.2	67.5	70.4	73.0	75.4	84.3	89.9	16
17	34.6	40.9	46.5	51.5	55.9	60.0	63.6	66.8	69.8	72.5	82.5	88.7	17
18	27.0	34.0	40.3	45.8	50.8	55.3	59.4	63.0	66.3	69.3	80.5	87.4	18
19	18.7	26.6	33.5	39.7	45.3	50.3	54.8	58.8	62.5	65.8	78.2	86.0	19
20	9.8	18.4	26.2	33.1	39.2	44.8	49.8	54.3	58.3	62.0	75.8	84.5	20
21	0.0	9.6	18.2	25.8	32.7	38.8	44.3	49.3	53.8	57.9	73.2	82.8	21
22	0.0	0.0	9.5	17.9	25.5	32.3	38.4	43.9	48.9	53.4	70.4	81.0	22
23	0.0	0.0	0.0	9.3	17.7	25.2	32.0	38.1	43.6	48.5	67.3	79.0	23
24	0.0	0.0	0.0	0.0	9.2	17.5	25.0	31.7	37.8	43.2	63.9	76.8	24
25	0.0	0.0	0.0	0.0	0.0	9.1	17.3	24.7	31.4	37.5	60.2	74.4	25
26	0.0	0.0	0.0	0.0	0.0	0.0	9.0	17.2	24.5	31.2	56.2	71.9	26
27	0.0	0.0	0.0	0.0	0.0	0.0	0.0	8.9	17.0	24.3	51.9	69.1	27
28	0.0	0.0	0.0	0.0	0.0	0.0	0.0	0.0	8.9	16.9	47.2	66.0	28
29	0.0	0.0	0.0	0.0	0.0	0.0	0.0	0.0	0.0	8.8	42.0	62.7	29
30	0.0	0.0	0.0	0.0	0.0	0.0	0.0	0.0	0.0	0.0	36.4	59.1	30
31	0.0	0.0	0.0	0.0	0.0	0.0	0.0	0.0	0.0	0.0	30.3	55.2	31
32	0.0	0.0	0.0	0.0	0.0	0.0	0.0	0.0	0.0	0.0	23.6	50.9	32
33	0.0	0.0	0.0	0.0	0.0	0.0	0.0	0.0	0.0	0.0	16.4	46.3	33
34	0.0	0.0	0.0	0.0	0.0	0.0	0.0	0.0	0.0	0.0	8.5	41.2	34
35	0.0	0.0	0.0	0.0	0.0	0.0	0.0	0.0	0.0	0.0	0.0	35.7	35
36	0.0	0.0	0.0	0.0	0.0	0.0	0.0	0.0	0.0	0.0	0.0	29.7	36
37	0.0	0.0	0.0	0.0	0.0	0.0	0.0	0.0	0.0	0.0	0.0	23.2	37
38	0.0	0.0	0.0	0.0	0.0	0.0	0.0	0.0	0.0	0.0	0.0	16.1	38
39	0.0	0.0	0.0	0.0	0.0	0.0	0.0	0.0	0.0	0.0	0.0	8.4	39

AGE OF LOAN	2.0	3.0	5.0	8.0	10.0	12.0	15.0	16.0	17.0	18.0	19.0	20.0	AGE OF LOAN
					ORIGINAL TERM IN YEARS								
1	52.2	69.3	83.3	91.0	93.5	95.1	96.0	97.0	97.3	97.6	97.9	98.1	1
2	0.0	36.3	65.1	81.1	86.3	89.7	92.9	93.7	94.4	95.0	95.5	96.0	2
3	0.0	0.0	45.3	70.4	78.5	83.8	88.9	90.1	91.2	92.1	92.9	93.7	3
4	0.0	0.0	23.6	58.6	70.0	77.4	84.5	86.2	87.7	89.0	90.2	91.2	4
5	0.0	0.0	0.0	45.8	60.7	70.4	79.7	82.0	83.9	85.6	87.1	88.4	5
6	0.0	0.0	0.0	31.9	50.6	62.8	74.5	77.3	79.8	81.9	83.9	85.4	6
7	0.0	0.0	0.0	16.6	39.5	54.5	68.8	72.3	75.3	77.9	80.2	82.2	7
8	0.0	0.0	0.0	0.0	27.5	45.4	62.6	66.8	70.3	73.5	76.2	78.6	8
9	0.0	0.0	0.0	0.0	14.3	35.5	55.8	60.7	65.0	68.7	71.9	74.7	9
10	0.0	0.0	0.0	0.0	0.0	24.7	48.4	54.1	59.1	63.4	67.2	70.5	10
11	0.0	0.0	0.0	0.0	0.0	12.9	40.3	47.0	52.7	57.7	62.0	65.9	11
12	0.0	0.0	0.0	0.0	0.0	0.0	31.5	39.1	45.7	51.4	56.4	60.8	12
13	0.0	0.0	0.0	0.0	0.0	0.0	21.9	30.6	38.1	44.6	50.3	55.4	13
14	0.0	0.0	0.0	0.0	0.0	0.0	11.4	21.3	29.8	37.2	43.7	49.4	14
15	0.0	0.0	0.0	0.0	0.0	0.0	0.0	11.1	20.7	29.0	36.4	42.8	15
16	0.0	0.0	0.0	0.0	0.0	0.0	0.0	0.0	10.8	20.0	28.4	35.7	16
17	0.0	0.0	0.0	0.0	0.0	0.0	0.0	0.0	0.0	10.5	19.8	27.9	17
18	0.0	0.0	0.0	0.0	0.0	0.0	0.0	0.0	0.0	0.0	10.3	19.4	18
19	0.0	0.0	0.0	0.0	0.0	0.0	0.0	0.0	0.0	0.0	0.0	10.1	19

AGE OF LOAN	21.0	22.0	23.0	24.0	25.0	26.0	27.0	28.0	29.0	30.0	35.0	40.0	AGE OF LOAN
					ORIGINAL TERM IN YEARS								
1	98.3	98.4	98.6	98.7	98.8	98.9	99.0	99.1	99.2	99.3	99.5	99.7	1
2	96.4	96.7	97.0	97.3	97.6	97.8	98.0	98.2	98.3	98.5	99.1	99.4	2
3	94.3	94.9	95.3	95.8	96.2	96.5	96.9	97.1	97.4	97.6	98.5	99.1	3
4	92.0	92.8	93.5	94.1	94.7	95.2	95.6	96.0	96.4	96.7	97.9	98.7	4
5	89.6	90.6	91.5	92.3	93.0	93.7	94.3	94.8	95.3	95.7	97.3	98.3	5
6	86.9	88.2	89.3	90.3	91.2	92.1	92.8	93.4	94.0	94.6	96.6	97.8	6
7	83.9	85.5	86.9	88.2	89.3	90.3	91.2	92.0	92.7	93.4	95.8	97.3	7
8	80.7	82.6	84.3	85.8	87.1	88.3	89.4	90.4	91.3	92.0	95.0	96.8	8
9	77.2	79.5	81.5	83.2	84.8	86.2	87.5	88.6	89.7	90.6	94.1	96.2	9
10	73.4	76.0	78.3	80.4	82.3	83.9	85.4	86.7	87.9	89.0	93.1	95.6	10
11	69.3	72.3	75.0	77.3	79.5	81.4	83.1	84.6	86.0	87.3	92.0	94.9	11
12	64.7	68.2	71.3	74.0	76.4	78.6	80.6	82.4	84.0	85.4	90.8	94.2	12
13	59.8	63.7	67.2	70.3	73.1	75.6	77.9	79.9	81.7	83.4	89.5	93.4	13
14	54.4	58.9	62.8	66.4	69.5	72.4	74.9	77.2	79.3	81.1	88.1	92.5	14
15	48.5	53.5	58.0	62.0	65.6	68.8	71.7	74.3	76.6	78.7	86.6	91.5	15
16	42.1	47.7	52.8	57.3	61.3	64.9	68.1	71.1	73.7	76.0	84.9	90.4	16
17	35.0	41.4	47.1	52.1	56.6	60.6	64.3	67.5	70.5	73.1	83.1	89.3	17
18	27.4	34.5	40.8	46.5	51.5	56.0	60.1	63.7	67.0	70.0	81.1	88.0	18
19	19.0	27.0	34.0	40.3	45.9	50.9	55.5	59.5	63.2	66.5	78.9	86.6	19
20	9.9	18.7	26.6	33.6	39.8	45.4	50.5	55.0	59.1	62.8	76.6	85.1	20
21	0.0	9.8	18.5	26.2	33.2	39.4	45.0	50.0	54.6	58.6	74.0	83.5	21
22	0.0	0.0	9.6	18.2	25.9	32.8	39.0	44.6	49.6	54.2	71.2	81.7	22
23	0.0	0.0	0.0	9.5	18.0	25.7	32.5	38.7	44.2	49.3	68.1	79.7	23
24	0.0	0.0	0.0	0.0	9.4	17.8	25.4	32.2	38.4	43.9	64.7	77.6	24
25	0.0	0.0	0.0	0.0	0.0	9.3	17.7	25.4	32.0	38.1	61.1	75.2	25
26	0.0	0.0	0.0	0.0	0.0	0.0	9.2	17.5	25.0	31.7	57.1	72.7	26
27	0.0	0.0	0.0	0.0	0.0	0.0	0.0	9.1	17.4	24.8	52.7	69.9	27
28	0.0	0.0	0.0	0.0	0.0	0.0	0.0	0.0	9.0	17.2	47.9	66.9	28
29	0.0	0.0	0.0	0.0	0.0	0.0	0.0	0.0	0.0	9.0	42.7	63.6	29
30	0.0	0.0	0.0	0.0	0.0	0.0	0.0	0.0	0.0	0.0	37.1	60.0	30
31	0.0	0.0	0.0	0.0	0.0	0.0	0.0	0.0	0.0	0.0	30.9	56.1	31
32	0.0	0.0	0.0	0.0	0.0	0.0	0.0	0.0	0.0	0.0	24.1	51.8	32
33	0.0	0.0	0.0	0.0	0.0	0.0	0.0	0.0	0.0	0.0	16.8	47.1	33
34	0.0	0.0	0.0	0.0	0.0	0.0	0.0	0.0	0.0	0.0	8.7	42.0	34
35	0.0	0.0	0.0	0.0	0.0	0.0	0.0	0.0	0.0	0.0	0.0	36.4	35
36	0.0	0.0	0.0	0.0	0.0	0.0	0.0	0.0	0.0	0.0	0.0	30.3	36
37	0.0	0.0	0.0	0.0	0.0	0.0	0.0	0.0	0.0	0.0	0.0	23.7	37
38	0.0	0.0	0.0	0.0	0.0	0.0	0.0	0.0	0.0	0.0	0.0	16.5	38
39	0.0	0.0	0.0	0.0	0.0	0.0	0.0	0.0	0.0	0.0	0.0	8.6	39

AGE OF LOAN	2.0	3.0	5.0	8.0	10.0	12.0	15.0	16.0	17.0	18.0	19.0	20.0	AGE OF LOAN
						ORIGINAL TERM IN YEARS							
1	52.2	69.6	83.4	91.1	93.5	95.1	96.7	97.1	97.4	97.7	97.9	98.1	1
2	0.0	36.4	65.3	81.3	86.5	89.8	93.1	93.9	94.5	95.1	95.6	96.1	2
3	0.0	0.0	45.4	70.6	78.7	84.0	89.1	90.3	91.4	92.3	93.1	93.8	3
4	0.0	0.0	23.7	58.9	70.3	77.7	84.8	86.5	88.0	89.3	90.4	91.4	4
5	0.0	0.0	0.0	46.1	61.0	70.7	80.1	82.3	84.2	85.9	87.4	88.7	5
6	0.0	0.0	0.0	32.1	50.9	63.1	74.9	77.7	80.2	82.3	84.1	85.8	6
7	0.0	0.0	0.0	16.7	35.8	54.8	69.2	72.7	75.7	78.3	80.6	82.6	7
8	0.0	0.0	0.0	0.0	27.7	45.7	63.0	67.2	70.8	73.9	76.7	79.1	8
9	0.0	0.0	0.0	0.0	14.5	35.8	56.3	61.2	65.4	69.1	72.4	75.2	9
10	0.0	0.0	0.0	0.0	0.0	24.9	48.9	54.6	59.6	63.9	67.7	71.0	10
11	0.0	0.0	0.0	0.0	0.0	13.0	40.8	47.4	53.2	58.2	62.6	66.4	11
12	0.0	0.0	0.0	0.0	0.0	0.0	31.9	39.6	46.2	51.9	57.0	61.4	12
13	0.0	0.0	0.0	0.0	0.0	0.0	22.2	31.0	38.5	45.1	50.9	55.9	13
14	0.0	0.0	0.0	0.0	0.0	0.0	11.6	21.5	30.1	37.6	44.2	49.9	14
15	0.0	0.0	0.0	0.0	0.0	0.0	0.0	11.3	21.0	29.4	36.8	43.3	15
16	0.0	0.0	0.0	0.0	0.0	0.0	0.0	0.0	11.0	20.5	28.8	36.1	16
17	0.0	0.0	0.0	0.0	0.0	0.0	0.0	0.0	0.0	10.7	20.1	28.3	17
18	0.0	0.0	0.0	0.0	0.0	0.0	0.0	0.0	0.0	0.0	10.5	19.7	18
19	0.0	0.0	0.0	0.0	0.0	0.0	0.0	0.0	0.0	0.0	0.0	10.3	19

AGE OF LOAN	21.0	22.0	23.0	24.0	25.0	26.0	27.0	28.0	29.0	30.0	35.0	40.0	AGE OF LOAN
						ORIGINAL TERM IN YEARS							
1	98.3	98.5	98.6	98.8	98.9	99.0	99.1	99.2	99.2	99.3	99.6	99.7	1
2	96.5	96.8	97.1	97.4	97.7	97.9	98.1	98.3	98.4	98.6	99.1	99.4	2
3	94.5	95.0	95.5	95.9	96.3	96.7	97.0	97.3	97.5	97.8	98.6	99.1	3
4	92.3	93.0	93.7	94.3	94.9	95.4	95.8	96.2	96.5	96.9	98.0	98.8	4
5	89.8	90.9	91.8	92.6	93.3	93.9	94.5	95.0	95.5	95.9	97.4	98.4	5
6	87.2	88.5	89.6	90.6	91.5	92.3	93.1	93.7	94.3	94.8	96.8	98.0	6
7	84.3	85.9	87.3	88.5	89.6	90.6	91.5	92.3	93.0	93.6	96.0	97.5	7
8	81.2	83.1	84.7	86.2	87.5	88.7	89.8	90.7	91.6	92.4	95.2	97.0	8
9	77.7	79.9	81.9	83.7	85.2	86.6	87.9	89.0	90.0	91.0	94.4	96.5	9
10	74.0	76.5	78.9	80.9	82.7	84.4	85.8	87.2	88.4	89.4	93.4	95.9	10
11	69.8	72.8	75.5	77.9	80.0	81.9	83.6	85.1	86.5	87.8	92.4	95.2	11
12	65.3	68.8	71.8	74.6	77.0	79.2	81.2	82.9	84.5	85.9	91.2	94.5	12
13	60.4	64.3	67.8	71.0	73.7	76.2	78.5	80.5	82.3	83.9	90.0	93.7	13
14	55.0	59.5	63.4	67.0	70.2	73.0	75.5	77.8	79.9	81.7	88.6	92.9	14
15	49.1	54.1	58.6	62.7	66.2	69.5	72.3	74.9	77.2	79.3	87.1	91.9	15
16	42.6	48.3	53.4	57.9	62.0	65.6	68.8	71.7	74.3	76.7	85.5	90.9	16
17	35.5	42.0	47.7	52.7	57.3	61.3	65.0	68.2	71.2	73.8	83.7	89.8	17
18	27.8	35.0	41.4	47.1	52.2	56.7	60.8	64.4	67.7	70.7	81.8	88.5	18
19	19.4	27.4	34.5	40.9	46.6	51.6	56.2	60.3	64.0	67.3	79.6	87.2	19
20	10.1	19.1	27.0	34.1	40.4	46.1	51.2	55.7	59.8	63.5	77.3	85.7	20
21	0.0	10.0	18.8	26.7	33.7	40.0	45.7	50.7	55.3	59.4	74.7	84.1	21
22	0.0	0.0	9.8	18.6	26.4	33.4	39.6	45.3	50.3	54.9	71.9	82.4	22
23	0.0	0.0	0.0	9.7	18.4	26.1	33.1	39.3	44.9	50.0	68.9	80.4	23
24	0.0	0.0	0.0	0.0	9.6	18.2	25.9	32.8	39.0	44.6	65.5	78.3	24
25	0.0	0.0	0.0	0.0	0.0	9.5	18.0	25.7	32.5	38.8	61.9	76.0	25
26	0.0	0.0	0.0	0.0	0.0	0.0	9.4	17.9	25.5	32.3	57.9	73.5	26
27	0.0	0.0	0.0	0.0	0.0	0.0	0.0	9.3	17.7	25.3	53.5	70.8	27
28	0.0	0.0	0.0	0.0	0.0	0.0	0.0	0.0	9.3	17.6	48.7	67.8	28
29	0.0	0.0	0.0	0.0	0.0	0.0	0.0	0.0	0.0	9.2	43.5	64.5	29
30	0.0	0.0	0.0	0.0	0.0	0.0	0.0	0.0	0.0	0.0	37.8	60.9	30
31	0.0	0.0	0.0	0.0	0.0	0.0	0.0	0.0	0.0	0.0	31.5	57.0	31
32	0.0	0.0	0.0	0.0	0.0	0.0	0.0	0.0	0.0	0.0	24.6	52.6	32
33	0.0	0.0	0.0	0.0	0.0	0.0	0.0	0.0	0.0	0.0	17.2	47.9	33
34	0.0	0.0	0.0	0.0	0.0	0.0	0.0	0.0	0.0	0.0	9.0	42.8	34
35	0.0	0.0	0.0	0.0	0.0	0.0	0.0	0.0	0.0	0.0	0.0	37.2	35
36	0.0	0.0	0.0	0.0	0.0	0.0	0.0	0.0	0.0	0.0	0.0	31.0	36
37	0.0	0.0	0.0	0.0	0.0	0.0	0.0	0.0	0.0	0.0	0.0	24.2	37
38	0.0	0.0	0.0	0.0	0.0	0.0	0.0	0.0	0.0	0.0	0.0	16.9	38
39	0.0	0.0	0.0	0.0	0.0	0.0	0.0	0.0	0.0	0.0	0.0	8.8	39

AGE OF LOAN	2.0	3.0	5.0	8.0	10.0	12.0	15.0	16.0	17.0	18.0	19.0	20.0	AGE OF LOAN
1	52.3	69.7	83.5	91.1	93.6	95.2	96.8	97.1	97.5	97.7	98.0	98.2	1
2	0.0	36.4	65.4	81.4	86.6	90.0	93.2	94.0	94.7	95.2	95.7	96.2	2
3	0.0	0.0	45.6	70.8	79.0	84.2	89.3	90.5	91.6	92.5	93.3	94.0	3
4	0.0	0.0	23.8	59.1	70.5	77.9	85.1	86.8	88.2	89.5	90.6	91.6	4
5	0.0	0.0	0.0	46.3	61.3	71.0	80.4	82.6	84.6	86.2	87.7	89.0	5
6	0.0	0.0	0.0	32.3	51.2	63.5	75.3	78.1	80.5	82.6	84.5	86.1	6
7	0.0	0.0	0.0	16.9	40.1	55.2	69.6	73.1	76.1	78.7	81.0	82.9	7
8	0.0	0.0	0.0	0.0	27.9	46.1	63.5	67.6	71.2	74.4	77.1	79.5	8
9	0.0	0.0	0.0	0.0	14.6	36.1	56.7	61.6	65.9	69.6	72.9	75.7	9
10	0.0	0.0	0.0	0.0	0.0	25.1	49.3	55.1	60.1	64.4	68.2	71.5	10
11	0.0	0.0	0.0	0.0	0.0	13.1	41.2	47.9	53.7	58.7	63.1	67.0	11
12	0.0	0.0	0.0	0.0	0.0	0.0	32.2	40.0	46.6	52.4	57.5	62.0	12
13	0.0	0.0	0.0	0.0	0.0	0.0	22.5	31.3	39.0	45.6	51.4	56.5	13
14	0.0	0.0	0.0	0.0	0.0	0.0	11.7	21.8	30.5	38.1	44.7	50.5	14
15	0.0	0.0	0.0	0.0	0.0	0.0	0.0	11.4	21.3	29.8	37.3	43.9	15
16	0.0	0.0	0.0	0.0	0.0	0.0	0.0	0.0	11.1	20.8	29.2	36.6	16
17	0.0	0.0	0.0	0.0	0.0	0.0	0.0	0.0	0.0	10.9	20.4	28.7	17
18	0.0	0.0	0.0	0.0	0.0	0.0	0.0	0.0	0.0	0.0	10.6	20.0	18
19	0.0	0.0	0.0	0.0	0.0	0.0	0.0	0.0	0.0	0.0	0.0	10.4	19

AGE OF LOAN	21.0	22.0	23.0	24.0	25.0	26.0	27.0	28.0	29.0	30.0	35.0	40.0	AGE OF LOAN
1	98.4	98.5	98.7	98.8	98.9	99.0	99.1	99.2	99.3	99.4	99.6	99.8	1
2	96.6	96.9	97.2	97.5	97.8	98.0	98.2	98.3	98.5	98.6	99.2	99.5	2
3	94.6	95.2	95.7	96.1	96.5	96.8	97.1	97.4	97.6	97.9	98.7	99.2	3
4	92.5	93.2	93.9	94.5	95.1	95.5	96.0	96.3	96.7	97.0	98.2	98.9	4
5	90.1	91.1	92.0	92.8	93.5	94.1	94.7	95.2	95.7	96.1	97.6	98.5	5
6	87.5	88.8	89.9	90.9	91.8	92.6	93.3	93.9	94.5	95.0	96.9	98.1	6
7	84.7	86.3	87.6	88.9	89.9	90.9	91.8	92.6	93.3	93.9	96.2	97.7	7
8	81.6	83.5	85.1	86.6	87.9	89.1	90.1	91.1	91.9	92.7	95.5	97.2	8
9	78.2	80.4	82.4	84.1	85.7	87.0	88.3	89.4	90.4	91.3	94.7	96.7	9
10	74.5	77.0	79.3	81.4	83.2	84.8	86.3	87.6	88.8	89.8	93.7	96.1	10
11	70.4	73.4	76.0	78.4	80.5	82.4	84.1	85.6	87.0	88.2	92.7	95.5	11
12	65.9	69.3	72.4	75.1	77.6	79.7	81.7	83.4	85.0	86.4	91.6	94.8	12
13	60.9	64.9	68.4	71.5	74.3	76.8	79.0	81.0	82.8	84.4	90.4	94.0	13
14	55.5	60.1	64.1	67.6	70.8	73.6	76.1	78.4	80.5	82.3	89.1	93.2	14
15	49.6	54.7	59.3	63.3	66.9	70.1	73.0	75.5	77.8	79.9	87.6	92.3	15
16	43.1	48.9	54.0	58.6	62.6	66.2	69.5	72.4	75.0	77.3	86.1	91.3	16
17	36.0	42.5	48.3	53.4	57.9	62.0	65.7	68.9	71.9	74.5	84.3	90.2	17
18	28.2	35.5	41.9	47.7	52.8	57.4	61.5	65.1	68.4	71.4	82.4	89.1	18
19	19.7	27.8	35.0	41.4	47.2	52.3	56.9	61.0	64.7	68.C	80.3	87.8	19
20	10.3	19.4	27.4	34.6	41.0	46.7	51.8	56.4	60.5	64.2	78.0	86.3	20
21	0.0	10.1	19.1	27.1	34.2	40.6	46.3	51.4	56.0	60.1	75.5	84.8	21
22	0.0	0.0	10.0	18.9	26.8	33.9	40.2	45.9	51.1	55.6	72.7	83.0	22
23	0.0	0.0	0.0	9.9	18.7	26.6	33.6	39.9	45.6	50.7	69.7	81.2	23
24	0.0	0.0	0.0	0.0	5.8	18.5	26.3	33.3	39.6	45.3	66.3	79.1	24
25	0.0	0.0	0.0	0.0	0.0	9.7	18.3	26.1	33.1	39.4	62.7	76.8	25
26	0.0	0.0	0.0	0.0	0.0	0.0	9.6	18.2	25.9	32.9	58.7	74.3	26
27	0.0	0.0	0.0	0.0	0.0	0.0	0.0	9.5	18.1	25.8	54.3	71.6	27
28	0.0	0.0	0.0	0.0	0.0	0.0	0.0	0.0	9.4	17.9	49.5	68.6	28
29	0.0	0.0	0.0	0.0	0.0	0.0	0.0	0.0	0.0	9.4	44.2	65.3	29
30	0.0	0.0	0.0	0.0	0.0	0.0	0.0	0.0	0.0	0.0	38.4	61.7	30
31	0.0	0.0	0.0	0.0	0.0	0.0	0.0	0.0	0.0	0.0	32.1	57.8	31
32	0.0	0.0	0.0	0.0	0.0	0.0	0.0	0.0	0.0	0.0	25.1	53.5	32
33	0.0	0.0	0.0	0.0	0.0	0.0	0.0	0.0	0.0	0.0	17.5	48.7	33
34	0.0	0.0	0.0	0.0	0.0	0.0	0.0	0.0	0.0	0.0	9.1	43.5	34
35	0.0	0.0	0.0	0.0	0.0	0.0	0.0	0.0	0.0	0.0	0.0	37.8	35
36	0.0	0.0	0.0	0.0	0.0	0.0	0.0	0.0	0.0	0.0	0.0	31.6	36
37	0.0	0.0	0.0	0.0	0.0	0.0	0.0	0.0	0.0	0.0	0.0	24.7	37
38	0.0	0.0	0.0	0.0	0.0	0.0	0.0	0.0	0.0	0.0	0.0	17.2	38
39	0.0	0.0	0.0	0.0	0.0	0.0	0.0	0.0	0.0	0.0	0.0	9.0	39

AGE OF LOAN	2.0	3.0	5.0	8.0	10.0	12.0	15.0	16.0	17.0	18.0	19.0	20.0	AGE OF LOAN
1	52.4	69.8	83.6	91.2	93.7	95.3	96.8	97.2	97.5	97.8	98.0	98.2	1
2	0.0	36.5	65.6	81.6	86.8	90.1	93.4	94.1	94.8	95.4	95.9	96.3	2
3	0.0	0.0	45.7	71.0	79.2	84.5	89.5	90.7	91.8	92.7	93.5	94.2	3
4	0.0	0.0	23.5	59.3	70.8	78.2	85.3	87.0	88.5	89.8	90.9	91.8	4
5	0.0	0.0	0.0	46.5	61.6	71.4	80.7	82.9	84.9	86.5	88.0	89.3	5
6	0.0	0.0	0.0	32.5	51.5	63.8	75.6	78.4	80.9	83.0	84.8	86.4	6
7	0.0	0.0	0.0	17.0	40.4	55.5	70.0	73.5	76.5	79.1	81.3	83.3	7
8	0.0	0.0	0.0	0.0	28.2	46.4	63.9	68.1	71.7	74.8	77.5	79.9	8
9	0.0	0.0	0.0	0.0	14.8	36.4	57.1	62.1	66.4	70.1	73.3	76.2	9
10	0.0	0.0	0.0	0.0	0.0	25.4	49.7	55.5	60.6	64.9	68.7	72.0	10
11	0.0	0.0	0.0	0.0	0.0	13.3	41.6	48.3	54.2	59.2	63.6	67.5	11
12	0.0	0.0	0.0	0.0	0.0	0.0	32.6	40.4	47.1	53.0	58.1	62.5	12
13	0.0	0.0	0.0	0.0	0.0	0.0	22.7	31.7	39.4	46.1	51.9	57.0	13
14	0.0	0.0	0.0	0.0	0.0	0.0	11.9	22.1	30.9	38.5	45.2	51.0	14
15	0.0	0.0	0.0	0.0	0.0	0.0	0.0	11.6	21.6	30.2	37.8	44.4	15
16	0.0	0.0	0.0	0.0	0.0	0.0	0.0	0.0	11.3	21.1	29.6	37.1	16
17	0.0	0.0	0.0	0.0	0.0	0.0	0.0	0.0	0.0	11.0	20.7	29.1	17
18	0.0	0.0	0.0	0.0	0.0	0.0	0.0	0.0	0.0	0.0	10.8	20.3	18
19	0.0	0.0	0.0	0.0	0.0	0.0	0.0	0.0	0.0	0.0	0.0	10.6	19

AGE OF LOAN	21.0	22.0	23.0	24.0	25.0	26.0	27.0	28.0	29.0	30.0	35.0	40.0	AGE OF LOAN
1	98.4	98.6	98.7	98.5	99.0	99.1	99.2	99.2	99.3	99.4	99.6	99.8	1
2	96.7	97.0	97.3	97.6	97.8	98.1	98.2	98.4	98.6	98.7	99.2	99.5	2
3	94.8	95.3	95.8	96.2	96.6	96.9	97.2	97.5	97.7	98.0	98.8	99.2	3
4	92.7	93.4	94.1	94.7	95.2	95.7	96.1	96.5	96.8	97.1	98.3	98.9	4
5	90.4	91.4	92.3	93.0	93.7	94.3	94.9	95.4	95.8	96.2	97.7	98.6	5
6	87.9	89.1	90.2	91.2	92.1	92.9	93.6	94.2	94.7	95.3	97.1	98.2	6
7	85.1	86.6	88.0	89.2	90.3	91.2	92.1	92.9	93.5	94.2	96.4	97.8	7
8	82.0	83.9	85.5	87.0	88.3	89.4	90.5	91.4	92.2	93.0	95.7	97.4	8
9	78.7	80.9	82.8	84.5	86.1	87.5	88.7	89.8	90.8	91.7	94.9	96.9	9
10	75.0	77.5	79.8	81.9	83.7	85.3	86.7	88.0	89.2	90.2	94.0	96.3	10
11	70.9	73.9	76.6	78.9	81.0	82.9	84.6	86.1	87.4	88.6	93.1	95.7	11
12	66.4	69.9	73.0	75.7	78.1	80.3	82.2	83.9	85.5	86.9	92.0	95.1	12
13	61.5	65.5	69.0	72.1	74.9	77.4	79.6	81.6	83.4	85.0	90.8	94.4	13
14	56.1	60.7	64.7	68.2	71.4	74.2	76.7	79.0	81.0	82.8	89.6	93.6	14
15	50.2	55.3	59.9	63.9	67.5	70.7	73.6	76.2	78.5	80.5	88.1	92.7	15
16	43.7	49.5	54.6	59.2	63.3	66.9	70.1	73.0	75.6	78.0	86.6	91.8	16
17	36.5	43.1	48.9	54.0	58.6	62.7	66.3	69.6	72.5	75.2	84.9	90.7	17
18	28.6	36.0	42.5	48.3	53.5	58.0	62.2	65.8	69.1	72.1	83.0	89.6	18
19	20.0	28.2	35.5	42.0	47.8	53.0	57.6	61.7	65.4	68.7	80.9	88.3	19
20	10.5	19.7	27.9	35.1	41.6	47.4	52.5	57.1	61.3	65.0	78.7	86.9	20
21	0.0	10.3	19.4	27.6	34.8	41.2	47.0	52.1	56.7	60.9	76.2	85.4	21
22	0.0	0.0	10.2	19.2	27.3	34.4	40.9	46.6	51.8	56.4	73.4	83.7	22
23	0.0	0.0	0.0	10.1	19.0	27.0	34.2	40.6	46.3	51.4	70.4	81.8	23
24	0.0	0.0	0.0	0.0	10.0	18.8	26.8	33.9	40.3	46.0	67.1	79.8	24
25	0.0	0.0	0.0	0.0	0.0	9.9	18.7	26.6	33.7	40.0	63.5	77.6	25
26	0.0	0.0	0.0	0.0	0.0	0.0	9.8	18.5	26.4	33.5	59.5	75.1	26
27	0.0	0.0	0.0	0.0	0.0	0.0	0.0	9.7	18.4	26.2	55.1	72.4	27
28	0.0	0.0	0.0	0.0	0.0	0.0	0.0	0.0	9.6	18.3	50.3	69.4	28
29	0.0	0.0	0.0	0.0	0.0	0.0	0.0	0.0	0.0	9.6	45.0	66.2	29
30	0.0	0.0	0.0	0.0	0.0	0.0	0.0	0.0	0.0	0.0	39.1	62.6	30
31	0.0	0.0	0.0	0.0	0.0	0.0	0.0	0.0	0.0	0.0	32.7	58.7	31
32	0.0	0.0	0.0	0.0	0.0	0.0	0.0	0.0	0.0	0.0	25.6	54.3	32
33	0.0	0.0	0.0	0.0	0.0	0.0	0.0	0.0	0.0	0.0	17.9	49.6	33
34	0.0	0.0	0.0	0.0	0.0	0.0	0.0	0.0	0.0	0.0	9.4	44.3	34
35	0.0	0.0	0.0	0.0	0.0	0.0	0.0	0.0	0.0	0.0	0.0	38.6	35
36	0.0	0.0	0.0	0.0	0.0	0.0	0.0	0.0	0.0	0.0	0.0	32.2	36
37	0.0	0.0	0.0	0.0	0.0	0.0	0.0	0.0	0.0	0.0	0.0	25.3	37
38	0.0	0.0	0.0	0.0	0.0	0.0	0.0	0.0	0.0	0.0	0.0	17.6	38
39	0.0	0.0	0.0	0.0	0.0	0.0	0.0	0.0	0.0	0.0	0.0	9.2	39

AGE OF LOAN	2.0	3.0	5.0	8.0	10.0	12.0	15.0	16.0	17.0	18.0	19.0	20.0	AGE OF LOAN
						ORIGINAL TERM IN YEARS							
1	52.4	65.8	83.7	91.3	93.8	95.4	96.9	97.3	97.6	97.8	98.1	98.3	1
2	0.0	36.6	65.7	81.7	86.9	90.3	93.5	94.3	94.9	95.5	96.0	96.4	2
3	0.0	0.0	45.9	71.2	79.4	84.7	89.7	90.9	92.0	92.9	93.7	94.3	3
4	0.0	0.0	24.1	59.6	71.1	78.5	85.6	87.3	88.7	90.0	91.1	92.1	4
5	0.0	0.0	0.0	46.8	61.9	71.7	81.0	83.2	85.2	86.8	88.3	89.5	5
6	0.0	0.0	0.0	32.7	51.8	64.2	76.0	78.8	81.2	83.3	85.2	86.8	6
7	0.0	0.0	0.0	17.1	40.7	55.9	70.4	73.9	76.9	79.5	81.7	83.7	7
8	0.0	0.0	0.0	0.0	28.4	46.8	64.3	68.5	72.1	75.2	78.0	80.3	8
9	0.0	0.0	0.0	0.0	14.9	36.7	57.6	62.5	66.8	70.6	73.8	76.6	9
10	0.0	0.0	0.0	0.0	0.0	25.6	50.1	56.0	61.0	65.4	69.2	72.5	10
11	0.0	0.0	0.0	0.0	0.0	13.4	42.0	48.8	54.6	59.7	64.1	68.0	11
12	0.0	0.0	0.0	0.0	0.0	0.0	32.9	40.8	47.6	53.5	58.6	63.1	12
13	0.0	0.0	0.0	0.0	0.0	0.0	23.0	32.0	39.8	46.6	52.4	57.6	13
14	0.0	0.0	0.0	0.0	0.0	0.0	12.1	22.4	31.3	39.0	45.7	51.5	14
15	0.0	0.0	0.0	0.0	0.0	0.0	0.0	11.7	21.8	30.6	38.2	44.9	15
16	0.0	0.0	0.0	0.0	0.0	0.0	0.0	0.0	11.4	21.4	30.0	37.6	16
17	0.0	0.0	0.0	0.0	0.0	0.0	0.0	0.0	0.0	11.2	21.0	29.5	17
18	0.0	0.0	0.0	0.0	0.0	0.0	0.0	0.0	0.0	0.0	11.0	20.6	18
19	0.0	0.0	0.0	0.0	0.0	0.0	0.0	0.0	0.0	0.0	0.0	10.8	19

AGE OF LOAN	21.0	22.0	23.0	24.0	25.0	26.0	27.0	28.0	29.0	30.0	35.0	40.0	AGE OF LOAN
						ORIGINAL TERM IN YEARS							
1	98.5	98.6	98.8	99.0	99.1	99.1	99.2	99.3	99.4	99.4	99.6	99.8	1
2	96.8	97.1	97.4	97.7	97.9	98.1	98.3	98.5	98.6	98.8	99.3	99.5	2
3	94.9	95.5	95.9	96.4	96.7	97.1	97.3	97.6	97.8	98.1	98.8	99.3	3
4	92.9	93.6	94.3	94.9	95.4	95.9	96.3	96.6	97.0	97.3	98.4	99.0	4
5	90.0	91.6	92.5	93.3	93.9	94.6	95.1	95.6	96.0	96.4	97.8	98.7	5
6	88.2	89.4	90.5	91.5	92.3	93.1	93.8	94.4	95.0	95.3	97.3	98.3	6
7	85.4	87.0	88.3	89.5	90.6	91.5	92.4	93.1	93.8	94.4	96.6	98.0	7
8	82.4	84.3	85.9	87.3	88.6	89.8	90.8	91.7	92.5	93.3	95.9	97.5	8
9	79.1	81.3	83.2	85.0	86.5	87.8	89.1	90.1	91.1	92.0	95.2	97.1	9
10	75.5	78.0	80.3	82.3	84.1	85.7	87.1	88.4	89.6	90.6	94.3	96.6	10
11	71.4	74.4	77.1	79.4	81.5	83.4	85.0	86.5	87.8	89.0	93.4	96.0	11
12	67.0	70.4	73.5	76.2	78.6	80.8	82.7	84.4	86.0	87.3	92.4	95.4	12
13	62.1	66.1	69.6	72.7	75.5	77.9	80.1	82.1	83.9	85.4	91.2	94.7	13
14	56.7	61.2	65.3	68.8	72.0	74.8	77.3	79.6	81.6	83.4	90.0	93.9	14
15	50.8	55.9	60.5	64.5	68.1	71.3	74.2	76.8	79.0	81.1	88.6	93.1	15
16	44.2	50.1	55.2	59.8	63.9	67.5	70.8	73.7	76.3	78.6	87.1	92.2	16
17	37.0	43.6	49.4	54.6	59.2	63.3	67.0	70.3	73.2	75.8	85.4	91.2	17
18	29.0	36.5	43.1	48.9	54.1	58.7	62.8	66.5	69.8	72.8	83.6	90.0	18
19	20.3	28.6	36.0	43.2	48.4	53.6	58.2	62.4	66.1	69.4	81.6	88.8	19
20	10.6	20.0	28.3	35.6	42.2	48.0	53.2	57.8	62.0	65.7	79.3	87.5	20
21	0.0	10.5	19.8	28.0	35.3	41.8	47.6	52.8	57.4	61.6	76.9	86.0	21
22	0.0	0.0	10.3	19.5	27.7	35.0	41.5	47.3	52.5	57.1	74.2	84.3	22
23	0.0	0.0	0.0	10.2	19.3	27.5	34.7	41.2	47.0	52.1	71.2	82.5	23
24	0.0	0.0	0.0	0.0	10.1	19.2	27.2	34.4	40.9	46.7	67.9	80.5	24
25	0.0	0.0	0.0	0.0	0.0	10.0	19.0	27.0	34.2	40.7	64.3	78.3	25
26	0.0	0.0	0.0	0.0	0.0	0.0	10.0	18.9	26.9	34.0	60.3	75.9	26
27	0.0	0.0	0.0	0.0	0.0	0.0	0.0	9.9	18.8	26.7	55.9	73.2	27
28	0.0	0.0	0.0	0.0	0.0	0.0	0.0	0.0	9.8	18.6	51.0	70.3	28
29	0.0	0.0	0.0	0.0	0.0	0.0	0.0	0.0	0.0	9.8	45.7	67.0	29
30	0.0	0.0	0.0	0.0	0.0	0.0	0.0	0.0	0.0	0.0	39.8	63.4	30
31	0.0	0.0	0.0	0.0	0.0	0.0	0.0	0.0	0.0	0.0	33.3	59.5	31
32	0.0	0.0	0.0	0.0	0.0	0.0	0.0	0.0	0.0	0.0	26.1	55.1	32
33	0.0	0.0	0.0	0.0	0.0	0.0	0.0	0.0	0.0	0.0	18.2	50.3	33
34	0.0	0.0	0.0	0.0	0.0	0.0	0.0	0.0	0.0	0.0	9.5	45.1	34
35	0.0	0.0	0.0	0.0	0.0	0.0	0.0	0.0	0.0	0.0	0.0	39.3	35
36	0.0	0.0	0.0	0.0	0.0	0.0	0.0	0.0	0.0	0.0	0.0	32.8	36
37	0.0	0.0	0.0	0.0	0.0	0.0	0.0	0.0	0.0	0.0	0.0	25.8	37
38	0.0	0.0	0.0	0.0	0.0	0.0	0.0	0.0	0.0	0.0	0.0	18.0	38
39	0.0	0.0	0.0	0.0	0.0	0.0	0.0	0.0	0.0	0.0	0.0	9.4	39

AGE OF LOAN	2.0	3.0	5.0	8.0	10.0	12.0	15.0	16.0	17.0	18.0	19.0	20.0	AGE OF LOAN
1	52.5	69.9	83.8	91.4	93.9	95.5	97.0	97.3	97.6	97.9	98.1	98.3	1
2	0.0	36.7	65.8	81.9	87.1	90.4	93.6	94.4	95.0	95.6	96.1	96.5	2
3	0.0	0.0	46.0	71.4	79.6	84.9	89.9	91.1	92.1	93.0	93.8	94.5	3
4	0.0	0.0	24.2	59.8	71.3	78.8	85.8	87.5	89.0	90.2	91.3	92.3	4
5	0.0	0.0	0.0	47.0	62.2	72.0	81.3	83.5	85.5	87.1	88.5	89.8	5
6	0.0	0.0	0.0	32.9	52.1	64.5	76.3	79.1	81.6	83.7	85.5	87.1	6
7	0.0	0.0	0.0	17.3	41.0	56.2	70.8	74.3	77.3	79.9	82.1	84.1	7
8	0.0	0.0	0.0	0.0	28.6	47.1	64.7	68.9	72.5	75.7	78.4	80.7	8
9	0.0	0.0	0.0	0.0	15.0	37.0	58.0	63.0	67.3	71.0	74.3	77.1	9
10	0.0	0.0	0.0	0.0	0.0	25.9	50.6	56.5	61.5	65.5	69.7	73.0	10
11	0.0	0.0	0.0	0.0	0.0	13.6	42.4	49.2	55.1	60.2	64.7	68.5	11
12	0.0	0.0	0.0	0.0	0.0	0.0	33.3	41.2	48.1	54.0	59.1	63.6	12
13	0.0	0.0	0.0	0.0	0.0	0.0	23.3	32.4	40.3	47.1	53.0	58.1	13
14	0.0	0.0	0.0	0.0	0.0	0.0	12.2	22.7	31.6	39.4	46.2	52.1	14
15	0.0	0.0	0.0	0.0	0.0	0.0	0.0	11.9	22.1	31.0	38.7	45.4	15
16	0.0	0.0	0.0	0.0	0.0	0.0	0.0	0.0	11.6	21.7	30.4	38.0	16
17	0.0	0.0	0.0	0.0	0.0	0.0	0.0	0.0	0.0	11.4	21.3	29.9	17
18	0.0	0.0	0.0	0.0	0.0	0.0	0.0	0.0	0.0	0.0	11.2	20.9	18
19	0.0	0.0	0.0	0.0	0.0	0.0	0.0	0.0	0.0	0.0	0.0	11.0	19

AGE OF LOAN	21.0	22.0	23.0	24.0	25.0	26.0	27.0	28.0	29.0	30.0	35.0	40.0	AGE OF LOAN
1	98.5	98.7	98.8	98.9	99.1	99.1	99.2	99.3	99.4	99.4	99.7	99.8	1
2	96.9	97.2	97.5	97.8	98.0	98.2	98.4	98.6	98.7	98.8	99.3	99.6	2
3	95.1	95.6	96.1	96.5	96.9	97.2	97.5	97.7	97.9	98.2	98.9	99.3	3
4	93.1	93.8	94.5	95.1	95.6	96.0	96.4	96.8	97.1	97.4	98.5	99.1	4
5	90.9	91.9	92.7	93.5	94.2	94.8	95.3	95.8	96.2	96.6	98.0	98.8	5
6	88.5	89.7	90.8	91.8	92.6	93.4	94.0	94.6	95.2	95.7	97.4	98.4	6
7	85.8	87.3	88.6	89.8	90.9	91.8	92.7	93.4	94.1	94.6	96.8	98.1	7
8	82.8	84.7	86.3	87.7	89.0	90.1	91.1	92.0	92.8	93.5	96.1	97.7	8
9	79.6	81.7	83.7	85.4	86.9	88.2	89.4	90.5	91.4	92.3	95.4	97.2	9
10	75.9	78.5	80.8	82.8	84.6	86.1	87.6	88.8	89.9	90.9	94.6	96.8	10
11	71.9	74.9	77.6	79.9	82.0	83.8	85.5	87.0	88.3	89.4	93.7	96.2	11
12	67.5	71.0	74.1	76.8	79.2	81.3	83.2	84.9	86.4	87.8	92.7	95.6	12
13	62.7	66.6	70.2	73.3	76.0	78.5	80.7	82.6	84.4	85.9	91.6	95.0	13
14	57.3	61.8	65.5	69.4	72.6	75.4	77.9	80.1	82.1	83.9	90.4	94.2	14
15	51.3	56.5	61.1	65.2	68.8	72.0	74.8	77.4	79.6	81.7	89.1	93.4	15
16	44.7	50.6	55.8	60.5	64.5	68.2	71.4	74.3	76.9	79.2	87.6	92.6	16
17	37.5	44.2	50.0	55.3	59.9	64.0	67.7	70.9	73.8	76.5	86.0	91.6	17
18	29.5	37.0	43.6	49.5	54.7	59.4	63.5	67.2	70.5	73.4	84.2	90.5	18
19	20.6	29.1	36.6	43.2	49.0	54.3	58.9	63.1	66.8	70.1	82.2	89.3	19
20	10.8	20.3	28.7	36.2	42.8	48.6	53.9	58.5	62.7	66.4	80.0	88.0	20
21	0.0	10.7	20.1	28.4	35.8	42.4	48.3	53.5	58.2	62.3	77.6	86.5	21
22	0.0	0.0	10.5	19.9	28.2	35.5	42.1	47.9	53.2	57.8	74.9	84.9	22
23	0.0	0.0	0.0	10.4	19.7	27.9	35.2	41.8	47.6	52.9	71.9	83.2	23
24	0.0	0.0	0.0	0.0	10.3	19.5	27.7	35.0	41.5	47.4	68.7	81.2	24
25	0.0	0.0	0.0	0.0	0.0	10.2	19.4	27.5	34.8	41.3	65.1	79.0	25
26	0.0	0.0	0.0	0.0	0.0	0.0	10.2	19.2	27.3	34.6	61.1	76.6	26
27	0.0	0.0	0.0	0.0	0.0	0.0	0.0	10.1	19.1	27.2	56.7	74.0	27
28	0.0	0.0	0.0	0.0	0.0	0.0	0.0	0.0	10.0	19.0	51.8	71.1	28
29	0.0	0.0	0.0	0.0	0.0	0.0	0.0	0.0	0.0	10.0	46.4	67.8	29
30	0.0	0.0	0.0	0.0	0.0	0.0	0.0	0.0	0.0	0.0	40.5	64.3	30
31	0.0	0.0	0.0	0.0	0.0	0.0	0.0	0.0	0.0	0.0	33.9	60.3	31
32	0.0	0.0	0.0	0.0	0.0	0.0	0.0	0.0	0.0	0.0	26.6	56.0	32
33	0.0	0.0	0.0	0.0	0.0	0.0	0.0	0.0	0.0	0.0	18.6	51.1	33
34	0.0	0.0	0.0	0.0	0.0	0.0	0.0	0.0	0.0	0.0	9.8	45.8	34
35	0.0	0.0	0.0	0.0	0.0	0.0	0.0	0.0	0.0	0.0	0.0	40.0	35
36	0.0	0.0	0.0	0.0	0.0	0.0	0.0	0.0	0.0	0.0	0.0	33.5	36
37	0.0	0.0	0.0	0.0	0.0	0.0	0.0	0.0	0.0	0.0	0.0	26.3	37
38	0.0	0.0	0.0	0.0	0.0	0.0	0.0	0.0	0.0	0.0	0.0	18.4	38
39	0.0	0.0	0.0	0.0	0.0	0.0	0.0	0.0	0.0	0.0	0.0	9.7	39

AGE OF LOAN	2.0	3.0	5.0	8.0	10.0	12.0	15.0	16.0	17.0	18.0	19.0	20.0	AGE OF LOAN
1	52.5	70.0	83.9	91.5	93.9	95.5	97.0	97.4	97.7	98.0	98.2	98.4	1
2	0.0	36.8	66.0	82.1	87.2	90.6	93.7	94.5	95.1	95.7	96.2	96.6	2
3	0.0	0.0	46.2	71.6	79.8	85.1	90.1	91.3	92.3	93.2	94.0	94.7	3
4	0.0	0.0	24.3	60.1	71.6	79.0	86.1	87.8	89.2	90.4	91.5	92.5	4
5	0.0	0.0	0.0	47.3	62.5	72.3	81.6	83.8	85.7	87.4	88.8	90.1	5
6	0.0	0.0	0.0	33.1	52.4	64.8	76.7	79.5	81.9	84.0	85.8	87.4	6
7	0.0	0.0	0.0	17.4	41.2	56.6	71.2	74.7	77.7	80.2	82.5	84.4	7
8	0.0	0.0	0.0	0.0	28.9	47.5	65.1	69.3	73.0	76.1	78.8	81.2	8
9	0.0	0.0	0.0	0.0	15.2	37.3	58.4	63.4	67.7	71.5	74.7	77.5	9
10	0.0	0.0	0.0	0.0	0.0	26.1	51.0	56.9	62.0	66.4	70.2	73.5	10
11	0.0	0.0	0.0	0.0	0.0	13.7	42.8	49.7	55.6	60.7	65.2	69.1	11
12	0.0	0.0	0.0	0.0	0.0	0.0	33.6	41.6	48.5	54.5	59.6	64.1	12
13	0.0	0.0	0.0	0.0	0.0	0.0	23.6	32.8	40.7	47.5	53.5	58.7	13
14	0.0	0.0	0.0	0.0	0.0	0.0	12.4	22.9	32.0	39.9	46.7	52.6	14
15	0.0	0.0	0.0	0.0	0.0	0.0	0.0	12.0	22.4	31.4	39.1	45.9	15
16	0.0	0.0	0.0	0.0	0.0	0.0	0.0	0.0	11.8	22.0	30.8	38.5	16
17	0.0	0.0	0.0	0.0	0.0	0.0	0.0	0.0	0.0	11.5	21.6	30.3	17
18	0.0	0.0	0.0	0.0	0.0	0.0	0.0	0.0	0.0	0.0	11.3	21.2	18
19	0.0	0.0	0.0	0.0	0.0	0.0	0.0	0.0	0.0	0.0	0.0	11.1	19

AGE OF LOAN	21.0	22.0	23.0	24.0	25.0	26.0	27.0	28.0	29.0	30.0	35.0	40.0	AGE OF LOAN
1	98.6	98.7	98.9	99.0	99.1	99.2	99.3	99.3	99.4	99.5	99.7	99.8	1
2	97.0	97.3	97.6	97.9	98.1	98.3	98.5	98.6	98.8	98.9	99.3	99.6	2
3	95.2	95.8	96.2	96.6	97.0	97.3	97.6	97.8	98.0	98.2	99.0	99.4	3
4	93.3	94.0	94.7	95.2	95.7	96.2	96.6	96.9	97.2	97.5	98.5	99.1	4
5	91.2	92.1	93.0	93.7	94.4	95.0	95.5	95.9	96.4	96.7	98.1	98.9	5
6	88.8	90.0	91.1	92.0	92.9	93.6	94.3	94.9	95.4	95.9	97.6	98.6	6
7	86.1	87.6	89.0	90.1	91.2	92.1	92.9	93.6	94.3	94.9	97.0	98.2	7
8	83.2	85.0	86.6	88.1	89.3	90.4	91.4	92.3	93.1	93.8	96.3	97.8	8
9	80.0	82.2	84.1	85.8	87.3	88.6	89.8	90.8	91.8	92.6	95.6	97.4	9
10	76.4	79.0	81.2	83.2	85.0	86.6	87.9	89.2	90.3	91.3	94.9	97.0	10
11	72.5	75.4	78.1	80.4	82.5	84.3	85.9	87.4	88.7	89.8	94.0	96.4	11
12	68.1	71.5	74.6	77.3	79.7	81.8	83.7	85.4	86.9	88.2	93.1	95.9	12
13	63.2	67.2	70.7	73.8	76.6	79.0	81.2	83.1	84.9	86.4	92.0	95.2	13
14	57.8	62.4	66.4	70.0	73.2	76.0	78.5	80.7	82.6	84.4	90.8	94.6	14
15	51.9	57.1	61.7	65.8	69.4	72.6	75.4	77.9	80.2	82.2	89.5	93.8	15
16	45.3	51.2	56.4	61.1	65.2	68.8	72.0	74.9	77.5	79.8	88.1	92.9	16
17	38.0	44.7	50.6	55.9	60.5	64.6	68.3	71.6	74.5	77.1	86.5	92.0	17
18	29.9	37.5	44.2	50.1	55.4	60.0	64.2	67.9	71.1	74.1	84.7	90.9	18
19	20.9	29.5	37.1	43.7	49.7	54.9	59.6	63.7	67.5	70.8	82.8	89.8	19
20	11.0	20.6	29.2	36.7	43.3	49.3	54.5	59.2	63.4	67.1	80.6	88.5	20
21	0.0	10.8	20.4	28.9	36.3	43.0	48.9	54.2	58.8	63.0	78.2	87.1	21
22	0.0	0.0	10.7	20.2	28.6	36.0	42.7	48.6	53.8	58.5	75.6	85.5	22
23	0.0	0.0	0.0	10.6	20.0	28.4	35.8	42.4	48.3	53.6	72.7	83.8	23
24	0.0	0.0	0.0	0.0	10.5	19.8	28.2	35.5	42.1	48.0	69.4	81.8	24
25	0.0	0.0	0.0	0.0	0.0	10.4	19.7	28.0	35.3	41.9	65.8	79.7	25
26	0.0	0.0	0.0	0.0	0.0	0.0	10.3	19.6	27.8	35.2	61.8	77.3	26
27	0.0	0.0	0.0	0.0	0.0	0.0	0.0	10.3	19.5	27.7	57.4	74.7	27
28	0.0	0.0	0.0	0.0	0.0	0.0	0.0	0.0	10.2	19.4	52.5	71.8	28
29	0.0	0.0	0.0	0.0	0.0	0.0	0.0	0.0	0.0	10.2	47.1	68.6	29
30	0.0	0.0	0.0	0.0	0.0	0.0	0.0	0.0	0.0	0.0	41.1	65.1	30
31	0.0	0.0	0.0	0.0	0.0	0.0	0.0	0.0	0.0	0.0	34.5	61.1	31
32	0.0	0.0	0.0	0.0	0.0	0.0	0.0	0.0	0.0	0.0	27.1	56.7	32
33	0.0	0.0	0.0	0.0	0.0	0.0	0.0	0.0	0.0	0.0	19.0	51.9	33
34	0.0	0.0	0.0	0.0	0.0	0.0	0.0	0.0	0.0	0.0	10.0	46.6	34
35	0.0	0.0	0.0	0.0	0.0	0.0	0.0	0.0	0.0	0.0	0.0	40.6	35
36	0.0	0.0	0.0	0.0	0.0	0.0	0.0	0.0	0.0	0.0	0.0	34.1	36
37	0.0	0.0	0.0	0.0	0.0	0.0	0.0	0.0	0.0	0.0	0.0	26.8	37
38	0.0	0.0	0.0	0.0	0.0	0.0	0.0	0.0	0.0	0.0	0.0	18.8	38
39	0.0	0.0	0.0	0.0	0.0	0.0	0.0	0.0	0.0	0.0	0.0	9.8	39

AGE OF LOAN	2.0	3.0	5.0	8.0	10.0	12.0	15.0	16.0	17.0	18.0	19.0	20.0	AGE OF LOAN
1	52.6	70.1	83.9	91.6	94.0	95.6	97.1	97.5	97.8	98.0	98.2	98.4	1
2	0.0	36.9	66.1	82.2	87.4	90.7	93.9	94.6	95.3	95.8	96.3	96.7	2
3	0.0	0.0	46.3	71.8	80.0	85.3	90.3	91.5	92.5	93.4	94.1	94.8	3
4	0.0	0.0	24.4	60.3	71.9	79.3	86.3	88.0	89.4	90.7	91.7	92.7	4
5	0.0	0.0	0.0	47.5	62.8	72.6	81.9	84.1	86.0	87.7	89.1	90.3	5
6	0.0	0.0	0.0	33.3	52.7	65.2	77.0	79.8	82.2	84.3	86.1	87.7	6
7	0.0	0.0	0.0	17.5	41.5	57.0	71.6	75.1	78.0	80.6	82.8	84.8	7
8	0.0	0.0	0.0	0.0	29.1	47.8	65.6	69.8	73.4	76.5	79.2	81.6	8
9	0.0	0.0	0.0	0.0	15.3	37.7	58.9	63.9	68.2	71.9	75.2	78.0	9
10	0.0	0.0	0.0	0.0	0.0	26.4	51.4	57.4	62.5	66.9	70.7	74.0	10
11	0.0	0.0	0.0	0.0	0.0	13.9	43.2	50.1	56.1	61.2	65.7	69.6	11
12	0.0	0.0	0.0	0.0	0.0	0.0	34.0	42.1	49.0	55.0	60.1	64.7	12
13	0.0	0.0	0.0	0.0	0.0	0.0	23.8	33.1	41.1	48.0	54.0	59.2	13
14	0.0	0.0	0.0	0.0	0.0	0.0	12.5	23.2	32.4	40.3	47.2	53.2	14
15	0.0	0.0	0.0	0.0	0.0	0.0	0.0	12.2	22.7	31.8	39.6	46.4	15
16	0.0	0.0	0.0	0.0	0.0	0.0	0.0	0.0	11.9	22.3	31.2	39.0	16
17	0.0	0.0	0.0	0.0	0.0	0.0	0.0	0.0	0.0	11.7	21.9	30.7	17
18	0.0	0.0	0.0	0.0	0.0	0.0	0.0	0.0	0.0	0.0	11.5	21.5	18
19	0.0	0.0	0.0	0.0	0.0	0.0	0.0	0.0	0.0	0.0	0.0	11.3	19

AGE OF LOAN	21.0	22.0	23.0	24.0	25.0	26.0	27.0	28.0	29.0	30.0	35.0	40.0	AGE OF LOAN
1	98.6	98.8	98.9	99.0	99.1	99.2	99.3	99.4	99.4	99.5	99.7	99.8	1
2	97.1	97.4	97.7	97.9	98.2	98.4	98.5	98.7	98.8	98.9	99.4	99.6	2
3	95.4	95.9	96.3	96.7	97.1	97.4	97.7	97.9	98.1	98.3	99.0	99.4	3
4	93.5	94.2	94.8	95.4	95.9	96.3	96.7	97.1	97.4	97.6	98.6	99.2	4
5	91.4	92.3	93.2	93.9	94.6	95.1	95.7	96.1	96.5	96.9	98.2	98.9	5
6	89.1	90.3	91.3	92.3	93.1	93.8	94.5	95.1	95.6	96.0	97.7	98.6	6
7	86.5	88.0	89.3	90.4	91.5	92.4	93.2	93.9	94.5	95.1	97.1	98.3	7
8	83.6	85.4	87.0	88.4	89.7	90.8	91.7	92.6	93.4	94.1	96.5	98.0	8
9	80.4	82.6	84.5	86.2	87.6	89.0	90.1	91.2	92.1	92.9	95.9	97.6	9
10	76.9	79.4	81.7	83.7	85.4	87.0	88.3	89.6	90.7	91.6	95.1	97.1	10
11	73.0	76.0	78.6	80.9	82.9	84.8	86.4	87.8	89.1	90.2	94.3	96.7	11
12	68.6	72.1	75.1	77.8	80.2	82.3	84.2	85.8	87.3	88.6	93.4	96.1	12
13	63.8	67.8	71.3	74.4	77.1	79.6	81.7	83.6	85.3	86.9	92.4	95.5	13
14	58.4	63.0	67.0	70.6	73.7	76.5	79.0	81.2	83.2	84.9	91.2	94.8	14
15	52.4	57.7	62.3	66.4	70.0	73.2	76.0	78.5	80.8	82.8	90.0	94.1	15
16	45.8	51.8	57.0	61.7	65.8	69.4	72.7	75.5	78.1	80.4	88.6	93.3	16
17	38.5	45.2	51.2	56.5	61.2	65.3	68.9	72.2	75.1	77.7	87.0	92.4	17
18	30.3	38.0	44.8	50.7	56.0	60.7	64.8	68.5	71.8	74.7	85.3	91.4	18
19	21.2	29.9	37.6	44.3	50.3	55.6	60.3	64.4	68.1	71.4	83.4	90.2	19
20	11.2	21.0	29.6	37.2	43.9	49.9	55.2	59.9	64.1	67.8	81.2	89.0	20
21	0.0	11.0	20.7	29.3	36.9	43.6	49.5	54.8	59.5	63.7	78.9	87.6	21
22	0.0	0.0	10.9	20.5	29.0	36.6	43.3	49.2	54.5	59.2	76.3	86.1	22
23	0.0	0.0	0.0	10.8	20.4	28.8	36.3	43.0	49.0	54.3	73.4	84.4	23
24	0.0	0.0	0.0	0.0	10.7	20.2	28.6	36.1	42.8	48.7	70.1	82.5	24
25	0.0	0.0	0.0	0.0	0.0	10.6	20.1	28.4	35.9	42.6	66.6	80.4	25
26	0.0	0.0	0.0	0.0	0.0	0.0	10.6	19.9	28.3	35.7	62.6	78.1	26
27	0.0	0.0	0.0	0.0	0.0	0.0	0.0	10.5	19.8	28.1	58.3	75.5	27
28	0.0	0.0	0.0	0.0	0.0	0.0	0.0	0.0	10.4	19.7	53.3	72.6	28
29	0.0	0.0	0.0	0.0	0.0	0.0	0.0	0.0	0.0	10.4	47.8	69.4	29
30	0.0	0.0	0.0	0.0	0.0	0.0	0.0	0.0	0.0	0.0	41.8	65.9	30
31	0.0	0.0	0.0	0.0	0.0	0.0	0.0	0.0	0.0	0.0	35.1	61.9	31
32	0.0	0.0	0.0	0.0	0.0	0.0	0.0	0.0	0.0	0.0	27.6	57.5	32
33	0.0	0.0	0.0	0.0	0.0	0.0	0.0	0.0	0.0	0.0	19.4	52.7	33
34	0.0	0.0	0.0	0.0	0.0	0.0	0.0	0.0	0.0	0.0	10.2	47.3	34
35	0.0	0.0	0.0	0.0	0.0	0.0	0.0	0.0	0.0	0.0	0.0	41.3	35
36	0.0	0.0	0.0	0.0	0.0	0.0	0.0	0.0	0.0	0.0	0.0	34.7	36
37	0.0	0.0	0.0	0.0	0.0	0.0	0.0	0.0	0.0	0.0	0.0	27.3	37
38	0.0	0.0	0.0	0.0	0.0	0.0	0.0	0.0	0.0	0.0	0.0	19.2	38
39	0.0	0.0	0.0	0.0	0.0	0.0	0.0	0.0	0.0	0.0	0.0	10.1	39

AGE OF LOAN	2.0	3.0	5.0	8.0	10.0	12.0	15.0	16.0	17.0	18.0	19.0	20.0	AGE OF LOAN
1	52.7	70.2	84.0	91.7	94.1	95.7	97.2	97.5	97.8	98.1	98.3	98.5	1
2	0.0	37.0	66.3	82.4	87.5	90.9	94.0	94.7	95.4	95.9	96.4	96.8	2
3	0.0	0.0	46.5	72.0	80.2	85.5	90.5	91.7	92.7	93.5	94.3	95.0	3
4	0.0	0.0	24.5	60.5	72.1	79.5	86.6	88.2	89.7	90.9	92.0	92.9	4
5	0.0	0.0	0.0	47.7	63.1	72.9	82.2	84.4	86.3	87.9	89.3	90.6	5
6	0.0	0.0	0.0	33.5	53.0	65.5	77.4	80.2	82.6	84.6	86.4	88.0	6
7	0.0	0.0	0.0	17.6	41.8	57.3	72.0	75.4	78.4	81.0	83.2	85.1	7
8	0.0	0.0	0.0	0.0	29.3	48.2	66.0	70.2	73.8	76.9	79.6	82.0	8
9	0.0	0.0	0.0	0.0	15.4	38.0	59.3	64.3	68.6	72.4	75.6	78.4	9
10	0.0	0.0	0.0	0.0	0.0	26.6	51.8	57.8	62.9	67.3	71.1	74.5	10
11	0.0	0.0	0.0	0.0	0.0	14.0	43.6	50.6	56.5	61.7	66.2	70.1	11
12	0.0	0.0	0.0	0.0	0.0	0.0	34.4	42.5	49.5	55.5	60.7	65.2	12
13	0.0	0.0	0.0	0.0	0.0	0.0	24.1	33.5	41.6	48.5	54.5	59.7	13
14	0.0	0.0	0.0	0.0	0.0	0.0	12.7	23.5	32.8	40.8	47.7	53.7	14
15	0.0	0.0	0.0	0.0	0.0	0.0	0.0	12.4	23.0	32.1	40.1	47.0	15
16	0.0	0.0	0.0	0.0	0.0	0.0	0.0	0.0	12.1	22.5	31.6	39.5	16
17	0.0	0.0	0.0	0.0	0.0	0.0	0.0	0.0	0.0	11.9	22.2	31.1	17
18	0.0	0.0	0.0	0.0	0.0	0.0	0.0	0.0	0.0	0.0	11.7	21.8	18
19	0.0	0.0	0.0	0.0	0.0	0.0	0.0	0.0	0.0	0.0	0.0	11.5	19

AGE OF LOAN	21.0	22.0	23.0	24.0	25.0	26.0	27.0	28.0	29.0	30.0	35.0	40.0	AGE OF LOAN
1	98.7	98.8	98.9	99.1	99.2	99.3	99.3	99.4	99.5	99.5	99.7	99.8	1
2	97.2	97.5	97.8	98.0	98.2	98.4	98.6	98.7	98.9	99.0	99.4	99.7	2
3	95.5	96.0	96.5	96.9	97.2	97.5	97.8	98.0	98.2	98.4	99.1	99.5	3
4	93.7	94.4	95.0	95.6	96.0	96.5	96.9	97.2	97.5	97.8	98.7	99.3	4
5	91.6	92.6	93.4	94.1	94.8	95.3	95.8	96.3	96.7	97.0	98.3	99.0	5
6	89.4	90.6	91.6	92.5	93.3	94.1	94.7	95.3	95.8	96.2	97.8	98.7	6
7	86.8	88.3	89.6	90.7	91.8	92.6	93.4	94.1	94.8	95.3	97.3	98.4	7
8	84.0	85.8	87.4	88.8	90.0	91.1	92.0	92.9	93.6	94.3	96.7	98.1	8
9	80.9	83.0	84.9	86.5	88.0	89.3	90.5	91.5	92.4	93.2	96.1	97.7	9
10	77.4	79.9	82.1	84.1	85.8	87.4	88.7	89.9	91.0	91.9	95.4	97.3	10
11	73.5	76.4	79.1	81.4	83.4	85.2	86.8	88.2	89.4	90.6	94.6	96.9	11
12	69.1	72.6	75.6	78.3	80.7	82.8	84.6	86.3	87.7	89.0	93.7	96.3	12
13	64.3	68.3	71.8	74.9	77.7	80.1	82.2	84.1	85.8	87.3	92.7	95.8	13
14	58.9	63.6	67.6	71.2	74.3	77.1	79.5	81.7	83.7	85.4	91.6	95.1	14
15	53.0	58.2	62.9	67.0	70.6	73.7	76.6	79.1	81.3	83.3	90.4	94.4	15
16	46.3	52.3	57.6	62.3	66.4	70.0	73.3	76.1	78.7	80.9	89.0	93.6	16
17	38.9	45.8	51.8	57.1	61.8	65.9	69.6	72.8	75.7	78.3	87.5	92.8	17
18	30.7	38.5	45.3	51.3	56.6	61.3	65.5	69.2	72.4	75.3	85.8	91.8	18
19	21.5	30.3	38.1	44.9	50.9	56.2	60.9	65.1	68.8	72.1	83.9	90.7	19
20	11.3	21.3	30.0	37.7	44.5	50.5	55.8	60.5	64.7	68.5	81.8	89.5	20
21	0.0	11.2	21.1	29.7	37.4	44.2	50.2	55.5	60.2	64.4	79.5	88.1	21
22	0.0	0.0	11.1	20.9	29.5	37.1	43.9	49.9	55.2	59.9	76.9	86.6	22
23	0.0	0.0	0.0	11.0	20.7	29.3	36.9	43.6	49.6	54.9	74.1	85.0	23
24	0.0	0.0	0.0	0.0	10.9	20.5	29.1	36.6	43.4	49.4	70.9	83.1	24
25	0.0	0.0	0.0	0.0	0.0	10.8	20.4	28.9	36.5	43.2	67.3	81.0	25
26	0.0	0.0	0.0	0.0	0.0	0.0	10.7	20.3	28.7	36.3	63.3	78.7	26
27	0.0	0.0	0.0	0.0	0.0	0.0	0.0	10.7	20.2	28.6	58.9	76.2	27
28	0.0	0.0	0.0	0.0	0.0	0.0	0.0	0.0	10.6	20.1	54.0	73.3	28
29	0.0	0.0	0.0	0.0	0.0	0.0	0.0	0.0	0.0	10.6	48.5	70.2	29
30	0.0	0.0	0.0	0.0	0.0	0.0	0.0	0.0	0.0	0.0	42.4	66.6	30
31	0.0	0.0	0.0	0.0	0.0	0.0	0.0	0.0	0.0	0.0	35.7	62.7	31
32	0.0	0.0	0.0	0.0	0.0	0.0	0.0	0.0	0.0	0.0	28.1	58.3	32
33	0.0	0.0	0.0	0.0	0.0	0.0	0.0	0.0	0.0	0.0	19.7	53.5	33
34	0.0	0.0	0.0	0.0	0.0	0.0	0.0	0.0	0.0	0.0	10.4	48.0	34
35	0.0	0.0	0.0	0.0	0.0	0.0	0.0	0.0	0.0	0.0	0.0	42.0	35
36	0.0	0.0	0.0	0.0	0.0	0.0	0.0	0.0	0.0	0.0	0.0	35.3	36
37	0.0	0.0	0.0	0.0	0.0	0.0	0.0	0.0	0.0	0.0	0.0	27.8	37
38	0.0	0.0	0.0	0.0	0.0	0.0	0.0	0.0	0.0	0.0	0.0	19.5	38
39	0.0	0.0	0.0	0.0	0.0	0.0	0.0	0.0	0.0	0.0	0.0	10.3	39

AGE OF LOAN	ORIGINAL TERM IN YEARS												AGE OF LOAN
	2.0	3.0	5.0	8.0	10.0	12.0	15.0	16.0	17.0	18.0	19.0	20.0	
1	52.7	70.2	84.1	91.7	94.2	95.7	97.2	97.6	97.9	98.1	98.3	98.5	1
2	0.0	37.0	66.4	82.5	87.7	91.0	94.1	94.9	95.5	96.0	96.5	96.9	2
3	0.0	0.0	46.6	72.2	80.4	85.7	90.7	91.8	92.8	93.7	94.4	95.1	3
4	0.0	0.0	24.6	60.8	72.4	79.8	86.8	88.5	89.9	91.1	92.2	93.1	4
5	0.0	0.0	0.0	48.0	63.3	73.2	82.5	84.7	36.6	88.2	89.6	90.8	5
6	0.0	0.0	0.0	33.7	53.3	65.9	77.7	80.5	82.9	85.0	86.7	88.3	6
7	0.0	0.0	0.0	17.8	42.1	57.6	72.4	75.8	78.8	81.3	83.6	85.5	7
8	0.0	0.0	0.0	0.0	29.5	48.5	66.4	70.6	74.2	77.3	80.0	82.3	8
9	0.0	0.0	0.0	0.0	15.6	38.3	59.7	64.8	69.1	72.8	76.0	78.8	9
10	0.0	0.0	0.0	0.0	0.0	26.9	52.3	58.3	63.4	67.8	71.6	74.9	10
11	0.0	0.0	0.0	0.0	0.0	14.2	44.0	51.0	57.0	62.2	66.7	70.6	11
12	0.0	0.0	0.0	0.0	0.0	0.0	34.7	42.9	49.9	55.9	61.2	65.7	12
13	0.0	0.0	0.0	0.0	0.0	0.0	24.4	33.9	42.0	49.0	55.0	60.3	13
14	0.0	0.0	0.0	0.0	0.0	0.0	12.8	23.8	33.1	41.2	48.2	54.2	14
15	0.0	0.0	0.0	0.0	0.0	0.0	0.0	12.5	23.3	32.5	40.5	47.5	15
16	0.0	0.0	0.0	0.0	0.0	0.0	0.0	0.0	12.3	22.8	32.0	39.5	16
17	0.0	0.0	0.0	0.0	0.0	0.0	0.0	0.0	0.0	12.0	22.5	31.5	17
18	0.0	0.0	0.0	0.0	0.0	0.0	0.0	0.0	0.0	0.0	11.8	22.1	18
19	0.0	0.0	0.0	0.0	0.0	0.0	0.0	0.0	0.0	0.0	0.0	11.7	19

AGE OF LOAN	ORIGINAL TERM IN YEARS												AGE OF LOAN
	21.0	22.0	23.0	24.0	25.0	26.0	27.0	28.0	29.0	30.0	35.0	40.0	
1	98.7	98.9	99.0	99.1	99.2	99.3	99.4	99.4	99.5	99.5	99.7	99.9	1
2	97.3	97.6	97.9	98.1	98.3	98.5	98.7	98.8	98.9	99.0	99.5	99.7	2
3	95.7	96.2	96.6	97.0	97.3	97.6	97.9	98.1	98.3	98.5	99.1	99.5	3
4	93.9	94.6	95.2	95.7	96.2	96.6	96.9	97.3	97.6	97.9	98.8	99.3	4
5	91.9	92.8	93.6	94.3	95.0	95.5	96.0	96.4	96.8	97.2	98.4	99.1	5
6	89.6	90.8	91.9	92.8	93.6	94.3	94.9	95.5	95.9	96.4	97.9	98.8	6
7	87.2	88.6	89.9	91.0	92.0	92.9	93.7	94.4	95.0	95.5	97.4	98.5	7
8	84.4	86.2	87.7	89.1	90.3	91.4	92.3	93.1	93.9	94.5	96.9	98.2	8
9	81.3	83.4	85.3	86.9	88.4	89.7	90.8	91.8	92.7	93.5	96.3	97.9	9
10	77.8	80.3	82.6	84.5	86.2	87.7	89.1	90.3	91.3	92.3	95.6	97.5	10
11	74.0	76.9	79.5	81.8	83.8	85.6	87.2	88.6	89.8	90.9	94.8	97.0	11
12	69.7	73.1	76.1	78.8	81.2	83.2	85.1	86.7	88.1	89.4	94.0	96.5	12
13	64.9	68.9	72.4	75.5	78.2	80.6	82.7	84.6	86.3	87.7	93.0	96.0	13
14	59.5	64.1	68.2	71.7	74.9	77.6	80.1	82.2	84.2	85.9	92.0	95.4	14
15	53.5	58.8	63.5	67.5	71.1	74.3	77.1	79.6	81.8	83.8	90.8	94.7	15
16	46.8	52.9	58.2	62.9	67.0	70.6	73.8	76.7	79.2	81.5	89.4	94.0	16
17	39.4	46.3	52.4	57.7	62.4	66.5	70.2	73.4	76.3	78.9	88.0	93.1	17
18	31.1	39.0	45.8	51.9	57.2	61.9	66.1	69.8	73.1	76.0	86.3	92.2	18
19	21.8	30.7	38.6	45.4	51.5	56.8	61.5	65.7	69.4	72.7	84.5	91.1	19
20	11.5	21.6	30.4	38.2	45.1	51.1	56.5	61.2	65.4	69.1	82.4	89.9	20
21	0.0	11.4	21.4	30.2	37.9	44.7	50.8	56.1	60.9	65.1	80.1	88.6	21
22	0.0	0.0	11.3	21.2	29.9	37.6	44.5	50.5	56.0	60.6	77.6	87.2	22
23	0.0	0.0	0.0	11.2	21.0	29.7	37.4	44.2	50.2	55.6	74.7	85.5	23
24	0.0	0.0	0.0	0.0	11.1	20.5	29.5	37.2	44.0	50.0	71.6	83.7	24
25	0.0	0.0	0.0	0.0	0.0	11.0	20.7	29.3	37.0	43.8	68.0	81.7	25
26	0.0	0.0	0.0	0.0	0.0	0.0	10.9	20.6	29.2	36.8	64.0	79.4	26
27	0.0	0.0	0.0	0.0	0.0	0.0	0.0	10.9	20.5	29.1	59.6	76.9	27
28	0.0	0.0	0.0	0.0	0.0	0.0	0.0	0.0	10.8	20.4	54.7	74.0	28
29	0.0	0.0	0.0	0.0	0.0	0.0	0.0	0.0	0.0	10.7	49.2	70.9	29
30	0.0	0.0	0.0	0.0	0.0	0.0	0.0	0.0	0.0	0.0	43.1	67.4	30
31	0.0	0.0	0.0	0.0	0.0	0.0	0.0	0.0	0.0	0.0	36.2	63.5	31
32	0.0	0.0	0.0	0.0	0.0	0.0	0.0	0.0	0.0	0.0	28.6	59.1	32
33	0.0	0.0	0.0	0.0	0.0	0.0	0.0	0.0	0.0	0.0	20.1	54.2	33
34	0.0	0.0	0.0	0.0	0.0	0.0	0.0	0.0	0.0	0.0	10.6	48.7	34
35	0.0	0.0	0.0	0.0	0.0	0.0	0.0	0.0	0.0	0.0	0.0	42.7	35
36	0.0	0.0	0.0	0.0	0.0	0.0	0.0	0.0	0.0	0.0	0.0	35.9	36
37	0.0	0.0	0.0	0.0	0.0	0.0	0.0	0.0	0.0	0.0	0.0	28.3	37
38	0.0	0.0	0.0	0.0	0.0	0.0	0.0	0.0	0.0	0.0	0.0	19.9	38
39	0.0	0.0	0.0	0.0	0.0	0.0	0.0	0.0	0.0	0.0	0.0	10.5	39

AGE OF LOAN	2.0	3.0	5.0	8.0	10.0	12.0	15.0	16.0	17.0	18.0	19.0	20.0	AGE OF LOAN
						ORIGINAL TERM IN YEARS							
1	52.8	70.3	84.2	91.8	94.3	95.8	97.3	97.6	97.9	98.2	98.4	98.6	1
2	0.0	37.1	66.6	82.7	87.8	91.1	94.2	95.0	95.6	96.1	96.6	97.0	2
3	0.0	0.0	46.8	72.5	80.7	85.9	90.8	92.0	93.0	93.9	94.6	95.2	3
4	0.0	0.0	24.7	61.0	72.6	80.1	87.1	88.7	90.1	91.3	92.4	93.3	4
5	0.0	0.0	0.0	48.2	63.6	73.5	82.8	85.0	86.9	88.5	89.8	91.1	5
6	0.0	0.0	0.0	33.9	53.6	66.2	78.0	80.8	83.2	85.3	87.0	88.6	6
7	0.0	0.0	0.0	17.9	42.4	58.0	72.7	76.2	79.2	81.7	83.9	85.8	7
8	0.0	0.0	0.0	0.0	29.8	48.8	66.8	71.0	74.6	77.7	80.4	82.7	8
9	0.0	0.0	0.0	0.0	15.7	38.6	60.1	65.2	69.5	73.3	76.5	79.3	9
10	0.0	0.0	0.0	0.0	0.0	27.1	52.7	58.7	63.8	68.3	72.1	75.4	10
11	0.0	0.0	0.0	0.0	0.0	14.3	44.4	51.4	57.5	62.7	67.2	71.1	11
12	0.0	0.0	0.0	0.0	0.0	0.0	35.1	43.3	50.4	56.4	61.7	66.2	12
13	0.0	0.0	0.0	0.0	0.0	0.0	24.7	34.2	42.4	49.5	55.5	60.8	13
14	0.0	0.0	0.0	0.0	0.0	0.0	13.0	24.1	33.5	41.6	48.7	54.8	14
15	0.0	0.0	0.0	0.0	0.0	0.0	0.0	12.7	23.6	32.9	41.0	48.0	15
16	0.0	0.0	0.0	0.0	0.0	0.0	0.0	0.0	12.4	23.1	32.4	40.4	16
17	0.0	0.0	0.0	0.0	0.0	0.0	0.0	0.0	0.0	12.2	22.8	31.9	17
18	0.0	0.0	0.0	0.0	0.0	0.0	0.0	0.0	0.0	0.0	12.0	22.4	18
19	0.0	0.0	0.0	0.0	0.0	0.0	0.0	0.0	0.0	0.0	0.0	11.8	19

AGE OF LOAN	21.0	22.0	23.0	24.0	25.0	26.0	27.0	28.0	29.0	30.0	35.0	40.0	AGE OF LOAN
						ORIGINAL TERM IN YEARS							
1	98.8	98.5	99.0	99.1	99.2	99.3	99.4	99.5	99.5	99.6	99.8	99.9	1
2	97.4	97.7	97.9	98.2	98.4	98.6	98.7	98.9	99.0	99.1	99.5	99.7	2
3	95.8	96.3	96.7	97.1	97.4	97.7	98.0	98.2	98.4	98.6	99.2	99.5	3
4	94.1	94.7	95.3	95.9	96.3	96.7	97.1	97.4	97.7	98.0	98.9	99.4	4
5	92.1	93.0	93.8	94.5	95.1	95.7	96.2	96.6	97.0	97.3	98.5	99.1	5
6	89.9	91.1	92.1	93.0	93.8	94.5	95.1	95.6	96.1	96.6	98.1	98.9	6
7	87.5	88.9	90.2	91.3	92.3	93.2	93.9	94.6	95.2	95.7	97.6	98.6	7
8	84.7	86.5	88.1	89.4	90.6	91.7	92.6	93.4	94.1	94.8	97.1	98.3	8
9	81.7	83.8	85.7	87.3	88.7	90.0	91.1	92.1	93.0	93.7	96.5	98.0	9
10	78.3	80.8	83.0	84.9	86.6	88.1	89.4	90.6	91.6	92.6	95.8	97.6	10
11	74.5	77.4	80.0	82.3	84.3	86.0	87.6	89.0	90.2	91.3	95.1	97.2	11
12	70.2	73.6	76.7	79.3	81.6	83.7	85.5	87.1	88.5	89.8	94.3	96.7	12
13	65.4	69.4	72.9	76.0	78.7	81.1	83.2	85.1	86.7	88.2	93.3	96.2	13
14	60.0	64.7	68.7	72.3	75.4	78.2	80.6	82.7	84.6	86.3	92.3	95.6	14
15	54.1	59.4	64.0	68.1	71.7	74.9	77.7	80.2	82.3	84.3	91.2	95.0	15
16	47.4	53.5	58.8	63.5	67.6	71.2	74.4	77.3	79.8	82.0	89.9	94.3	16
17	39.9	46.9	52.9	58.3	63.0	67.1	70.8	74.0	76.9	79.4	88.4	93.4	17
18	31.5	39.5	46.4	52.5	57.8	62.6	66.7	70.4	73.7	76.6	86.8	92.5	18
19	22.2	31.2	39.1	46.0	52.1	57.5	62.2	66.4	70.1	73.4	85.0	91.5	19
20	11.7	21.9	30.9	38.7	45.6	51.7	57.1	61.9	66.1	69.8	83.0	90.4	20
21	0.0	11.6	21.7	30.6	38.4	45.3	51.4	56.8	61.6	65.8	80.7	89.1	21
22	0.0	0.0	11.5	21.5	30.4	38.2	45.1	51.1	56.5	61.3	78.2	87.7	22
23	0.0	0.0	0.0	11.4	21.4	30.2	37.9	44.8	50.9	56.3	75.4	86.1	23
24	0.0	0.0	0.0	0.0	11.3	21.2	30.0	37.7	44.6	50.7	72.3	84.3	24
25	0.0	0.0	0.0	0.0	0.0	11.2	21.1	29.8	37.6	44.4	68.7	82.3	25
26	0.0	0.0	0.0	0.0	0.0	0.0	11.1	21.0	29.7	37.4	64.8	80.1	26
27	0.0	0.0	0.0	0.0	0.0	0.0	0.0	11.1	20.9	29.6	60.4	77.6	27
28	0.0	0.0	0.0	0.0	0.0	0.0	0.0	0.0	11.0	20.8	55.4	74.8	28
29	0.0	0.0	0.0	0.0	0.0	0.0	0.0	0.0	0.0	11.0	49.9	71.6	29
30	0.0	0.0	0.0	0.0	0.0	0.0	0.0	0.0	0.0	0.0	43.7	68.1	30
31	0.0	0.0	0.0	0.0	0.0	0.0	0.0	0.0	0.0	0.0	36.8	64.2	31
32	0.0	0.0	0.0	0.0	0.0	0.0	0.0	0.0	0.0	0.0	29.1	59.8	32
33	0.0	0.0	0.0	0.0	0.0	0.0	0.0	0.0	0.0	0.0	20.5	55.0	33
34	0.0	0.0	0.0	0.0	0.0	0.0	0.0	0.0	0.0	0.0	10.8	49.5	34
35	0.0	0.0	0.0	0.0	0.0	0.0	0.0	0.0	0.0	0.0	0.0	43.4	35
36	0.0	0.0	0.0	0.0	0.0	0.0	0.0	0.0	0.0	0.0	0.0	36.5	36
37	0.0	0.0	0.0	0.0	0.0	0.0	0.0	0.0	0.0	0.0	0.0	28.8	37
38	0.0	0.0	0.0	0.0	0.0	0.0	0.0	0.0	0.0	0.0	0.0	20.3	38
39	0.0	0.0	0.0	0.0	0.0	0.0	0.0	0.0	0.0	0.0	0.0	10.7	39

AGE OF LOAN	ORIGINAL TERM IN YEARS												AGE OF LOAN
	2.0	3.0	5.0	8.0	10.0	12.0	15.0	16.0	17.0	18.0	19.0	20.0	
1	52.9	70.4	84.3	91.9	94.3	95.9	97.3	97.7	98.0	98.2	98.4	98.6	1
2	0.0	37.2	66.7	82.8	88.0	91.3	94.4	95.1	95.7	96.2	96.7	97.1	2
3	0.0	0.0	46.9	72.7	80.9	86.1	91.0	92.2	93.2	94.0	94.7	95.4	3
4	0.0	0.0	24.8	61.2	72.9	80.3	87.3	88.9	90.3	91.5	92.6	93.4	4
5	0.0	0.0	0.0	48.5	63.9	73.8	83.1	85.3	87.1	88.7	90.1	91.3	5
6	0.0	0.0	0.0	34.1	53.9	66.5	78.4	81.2	83.5	85.6	87.3	88.9	6
7	0.0	0.0	0.0	18.0	42.6	58.3	73.1	76.6	79.5	82.1	84.2	86.1	7
8	0.0	0.0	0.0	0.0	30.0	49.2	67.2	71.4	75.0	78.1	80.8	83.1	8
9	0.0	0.0	0.0	0.0	15.9	38.9	60.5	65.6	70.0	73.7	76.9	79.7	9
10	0.0	0.0	0.0	0.0	0.0	27.4	53.1	59.1	64.3	68.7	72.5	75.8	10
11	0.0	0.0	0.0	0.0	0.0	14.5	44.8	51.9	58.0	63.2	67.7	71.5	11
12	0.0	0.0	0.0	0.0	0.0	0.0	35.4	43.7	50.8	56.9	62.2	66.7	12
13	0.0	0.0	0.0	0.0	0.0	0.0	24.9	34.6	42.8	49.9	56.0	61.3	13
14	0.0	0.0	0.0	0.0	0.0	0.0	13.2	24.3	33.9	42.1	49.2	55.3	14
15	0.0	0.0	0.0	0.0	0.0	0.0	0.0	12.9	23.9	33.3	41.4	48.5	15
16	0.0	0.0	0.0	0.0	0.0	0.0	0.0	0.0	12.6	23.4	32.8	40.9	16
17	0.0	0.0	0.0	0.0	0.0	0.0	0.0	0.0	0.0	12.4	23.1	32.3	17
18	0.0	0.0	0.0	0.0	0.0	0.0	0.0	0.0	0.0	0.0	12.2	22.8	18
19	0.0	0.0	0.0	0.0	0.0	0.0	0.0	0.0	0.0	0.0	0.0	12.0	19

AGE OF LOAN	ORIGINAL TERM IN YEARS												AGE OF LOAN
	21.0	22.0	23.0	24.0	25.0	26.0	27.0	28.0	29.0	30.0	35.0	40.0	
1	98.8	98.5	99.1	99.2	99.3	99.3	99.4	99.5	99.5	99.6	99.8	99.9	1
2	97.4	97.7	98.0	98.3	98.4	98.6	98.8	98.9	99.0	99.1	99.5	99.7	2
3	95.9	96.4	96.8	97.2	97.5	97.8	98.0	98.3	98.5	98.6	99.2	99.6	3
4	94.2	94.9	95.5	96.0	96.5	96.9	97.2	97.5	97.8	98.1	98.9	99.4	4
5	92.3	93.2	94.0	94.7	95.3	95.8	96.3	96.7	97.1	97.4	98.6	99.2	5
6	90.2	91.3	92.3	93.2	94.0	94.7	95.3	95.8	96.3	96.7	98.2	99.0	6
7	87.8	89.2	90.5	91.6	92.5	93.4	94.1	94.8	95.4	95.9	97.7	98.7	7
8	85.1	86.9	88.4	89.7	90.9	91.9	92.9	93.7	94.4	95.0	97.2	98.4	8
9	82.1	84.2	86.0	87.7	89.1	90.3	91.4	92.4	93.2	94.0	96.7	98.1	9
10	78.7	81.2	83.4	85.3	87.0	88.5	89.8	90.9	92.0	92.9	96.0	97.8	10
11	74.9	77.9	80.5	82.7	84.7	86.4	88.0	89.3	90.5	91.6	95.3	97.4	11
12	70.7	74.1	77.1	79.8	82.1	84.1	85.9	87.5	88.9	90.2	94.5	96.9	12
13	65.9	69.9	73.4	76.5	79.2	81.6	83.7	85.5	87.1	88.6	93.6	96.4	13
14	60.6	65.2	69.3	72.8	75.9	78.7	81.1	83.2	85.1	86.8	92.6	95.9	14
15	54.6	59.9	64.6	68.7	72.3	75.4	78.2	80.7	82.9	84.8	91.5	95.3	15
16	47.9	54.0	59.4	64.1	68.2	71.8	75.0	77.8	80.3	82.5	90.3	94.6	16
17	40.4	47.4	53.5	58.9	63.6	67.7	71.4	74.6	77.5	80.0	88.9	93.8	17
18	31.9	39.9	46.9	53.1	58.5	63.2	67.4	71.0	74.3	77.2	87.3	92.9	18
19	22.5	31.6	39.6	46.5	52.7	58.1	62.8	67.0	70.7	74.0	85.5	91.9	19
20	11.9	22.2	31.3	39.2	46.2	52.3	57.7	62.5	66.7	70.4	83.6	90.8	20
21	0.0	11.7	22.0	31.0	38.9	45.9	52.0	57.4	62.2	66.4	81.3	89.6	21
22	0.0	0.0	11.6	21.8	30.8	38.7	45.6	51.8	57.2	62.0	78.8	88.2	22
23	0.0	0.0	0.0	11.5	21.7	30.6	38.5	45.4	51.5	56.9	76.1	86.6	23
24	0.0	0.0	0.0	0.0	11.4	21.5	30.4	38.3	45.2	51.3	72.9	84.8	24
25	0.0	0.0	0.0	0.0	0.0	11.4	21.4	30.3	38.1	45.0	69.4	82.9	25
26	0.0	0.0	0.0	0.0	0.0	0.0	11.3	21.3	30.1	37.9	65.5	80.7	26
27	0.0	0.0	0.0	0.0	0.0	0.0	0.0	11.2	21.2	30.0	61.1	78.2	27
28	0.0	0.0	0.0	0.0	0.0	0.0	0.0	0.0	11.2	21.1	56.1	75.4	28
29	0.0	0.0	0.0	0.0	0.0	0.0	0.0	0.0	0.0	11.1	50.6	72.3	29
30	0.0	0.0	0.0	0.0	0.0	0.0	0.0	0.0	0.0	0.0	44.4	68.9	30
31	0.0	0.0	0.0	0.0	0.0	0.0	0.0	0.0	0.0	0.0	37.4	65.0	31
32	0.0	0.0	0.0	0.0	0.0	0.0	0.0	0.0	0.0	0.0	29.6	60.6	32
33	0.0	0.0	0.0	0.0	0.0	0.0	0.0	0.0	0.0	0.0	20.8	55.7	33
34	0.0	0.0	0.0	0.0	0.0	0.0	0.0	0.0	0.0	0.0	11.0	50.2	34
35	0.0	0.0	0.0	0.0	0.0	0.0	0.0	0.0	0.0	0.0	0.0	44.0	35
36	0.0	0.0	0.0	0.0	0.0	0.0	0.0	0.0	0.0	0.0	0.0	37.1	36
37	0.0	0.0	0.0	0.0	0.0	0.0	0.0	0.0	0.0	0.0	0.0	29.3	37
38	0.0	0.0	0.0	0.0	0.0	0.0	0.0	0.0	0.0	0.0	0.0	20.6	38
39	0.0	0.0	0.0	0.0	0.0	0.0	0.0	0.0	0.0	0.0	0.0	10.9	39

AGE OF LOAN	2.0	3.0	5.0	8.0	10.0	12.0	15.0	16.0	17.0	18.0	19.0	20.0	AGE OF LOAN
						ORIGINAL TERM IN YEARS							
1	52.9	70.5	84.4	92.0	94.4	96.0	97.4	97.7	98.0	98.3	98.5	98.7	1
2	0.0	37.3	66.8	83.0	88.1	91.4	94.5	95.2	95.8	96.3	96.8	97.2	2
3	0.0	0.0	47.1	72.9	81.1	86.3	91.2	92.4	93.3	94.2	94.9	95.5	3
4	0.0	0.0	24.9	61.5	73.1	80.6	87.5	89.1	90.5	91.7	92.7	93.6	4
5	0.0	0.0	0.0	48.7	64.2	74.1	83.4	85.5	87.4	89.0	90.3	91.5	5
6	0.0	0.0	0.C	34.3	54.2	66.9	78.7	81.5	83.9	85.9	87.6	89.1	6
7	0.0	0.0	0.0	18.2	42.9	58.7	73.5	76.9	79.9	82.4	84.6	86.5	7
8	0.0	0.0	0.0	0.0	30.2	49.5	67.6	71.8	75.4	78.5	81.2	83.5	8
9	0.0	0.0	0.0	0.0	16.0	39.2	61.0	66.1	70.4	74.1	77.3	80.1	9
10	0.0	0.0	0.0	0.0	0.0	27.6	53.5	59.6	64.8	69.2	73.0	76.3	10
11	0.0	0.0	0.0	0.0	0.0	14.6	45.2	52.3	58.4	63.6	68.1	72.0	11
12	0.0	0.0	0.0	0.0	C.0	0.0	35.8	44.2	51.3	57.4	62.7	67.2	12
13	0.0	0.0	0.0	0.0	0.0	0.0	25.2	35.0	43.3	50.4	56.5	61.9	13
14	0.0	0.0	0.0	0.C	0.0	0.0	13.3	24.6	34.3	42.5	49.6	55.8	14
15	0.0	0.0	0.C	0.0	C.0	0.0	0.0	13.0	24.2	33.7	41.9	49.0	15
16	0.0	0.0	0.0	0.0	0.0	0.0	0.0	0.0	12.8	23.7	33.2	41.3	16
17	0.0	0.0	0.0	0.C	0.0	0.0	0.0	0.0	0.0	12.6	23.4	32.7	17
18	0.0	0.0	0.C	0.0	C.0	0.0	0.0	0.0	0.0	0.0	12.4	23.1	18
19	0.0	0.0	0.0	0.0	0.0	0.0	0.0	0.0	0.0	0.C	0.0	12.2	19

AGE OF LOAN	21.0	22.0	23.0	24.0	25.0	26.0	27.0	28.0	29.0	30.0	35.0	40.0	AGE OF LOAN
						ORIGINAL TERM IN YEARS							
1	98.8	99.0	99.1	99.2	99.3	99.4	99.4	99.5	99.6	99.6	99.8	99.9	1
2	97.5	97.8	98.1	98.3	98.5	98.7	98.8	99.0	99.1	99.2	99.6	99.8	2
3	96.1	96.5	96.9	97.3	97.6	97.9	98.1	98.3	98.5	98.7	99.3	99.6	3
4	94.4	95.1	95.7	96.2	96.6	97.0	97.3	97.7	97.9	98.2	99.0	99.4	4
5	92.5	93.4	94.2	94.9	95.5	96.0	96.5	96.9	97.2	97.5	98.7	99.3	5
6	90.5	91.6	92.6	93.5	94.2	94.9	95.5	96.0	96.5	96.9	98.3	99.0	6
7	88.1	89.5	90.8	91.8	92.8	93.6	94.4	95.0	95.6	96.1	97.8	98.8	7
8	85.5	87.2	88.7	90.0	91.2	92.2	93.1	93.9	94.6	95.2	97.4	98.5	8
9	82.5	84.6	86.4	88.0	89.4	90.6	91.7	92.7	93.5	94.2	96.8	98.2	9
10	79.2	81.7	83.8	85.7	87.4	88.8	90.1	91.3	92.3	93.1	96.2	97.9	10
11	75.4	78.3	80.9	83.2	85.1	86.8	88.4	89.7	90.9	91.9	95.6	97.5	11
12	71.2	74.6	77.6	80.3	82.6	84.6	86.4	87.9	89.3	90.5	94.8	97.1	12
13	66.5	70.5	74.0	77.0	79.7	82.1	84.1	85.9	87.5	89.0	93.9	96.6	13
14	61.1	65.8	69.8	73.4	76.5	79.2	81.6	83.7	85.6	87.2	93.0	96.1	14
15	55.1	60.5	65.2	69.3	72.9	76.0	78.8	81.2	83.3	85.2	91.9	95.5	15
16	48.4	54.6	60.0	64.7	68.8	72.4	75.6	78.4	80.9	83.0	90.7	94.8	16
17	40.9	47.9	54.1	59.5	64.2	68.4	72.0	75.2	78.0	80.5	89.3	94.1	17
18	32.4	40.4	47.5	53.7	59.1	63.8	68.0	71.7	74.9	77.7	87.8	93.2	18
19	22.8	32.0	40.1	47.1	53.3	58.7	63.5	67.6	71.3	74.6	86.0	92.3	19
20	12.1	22.6	31.7	39.8	46.8	52.9	58.4	63.1	67.4	71.1	84.1	91.2	20
21	0.0	11.9	22.4	31.5	39.5	46.5	52.7	58.1	62.9	67.1	81.9	90.0	21
22	0.0	0.0	11.8	22.2	31.3	39.2	46.2	52.4	57.8	62.6	79.5	88.6	22
23	0.0	0.0	0.0	11.7	22.0	31.1	39.0	46.0	52.2	57.6	76.7	87.1	23
24	0.0	0.0	0.0	0.0	11.7	21.9	30.9	38.8	45.8	52.0	73.6	85.4	24
25	0.0	0.0	0.0	0.0	0.0	11.6	21.8	30.7	38.7	45.6	70.1	83.5	25
26	0.0	0.0	0.C	0.0	0.0	0.0	11.5	21.7	30.6	38.5	66.2	81.3	26
27	0.0	0.0	0.0	0.0	0.0	0.0	0.0	11.5	21.6	30.5	61.8	78.9	27
28	0.0	0.0	0.0	0.0	0.0	0.C	0.0	0.0	11.4	21.5	56.8	76.1	28
29	0.0	0.0	0.0	0.0	0.0	0.0	0.0	0.0	0.0	11.4	51.3	73.0	29
30	0.0	0.0	0.0	0.0	0.0	0.0	0.0	0.0	0.0	0.0	45.0	69.6	30
31	0.0	0.0	0.0	0.0	0.0	0.C	0.0	0.0	0.0	0.0	38.0	65.7	31
32	0.0	0.0	0.0	0.0	0.0	0.C	0.0	0.0	0.0	0.0	30.1	61.3	32
33	0.0	0.0	0.0	0.0	0.0	0.0	0.0	0.0	0.0	0.0	21.2	56.4	33
34	0.0	0.0	0.0	0.0	0.0	0.C	0.0	0.0	0.0	0.0	11.2	50.9	34
35	0.0	0.0	0.0	0.0	0.0	0.C	0.0	0.0	0.0	0.0	0.0	44.7	35
36	0.0	0.0	0.0	0.0	0.0	0.0	0.0	0.0	0.0	0.0	0.C	37.7	36
37	0.0	0.0	0.C	0.0	0.0	0.0	0.0	0.0	0.0	0.0	0.0	29.9	37
38	0.0	0.0	0.0	0.0	C.0	0.0	0.0	0.0	0.0	0.0	0.0	21.0	38
39	0.0	0.0	0.0	0.0	C.0	0.0	0.0	0.0	0.0	0.0	0.0	11.1	39

AGE OF LOAN	2.0	3.0	5.0	8.0	10.0	12.0	15.0	16.0	17.0	18.0	19.0	20.0	AGE OF LOAN
1	53.0	70.6	84.5	92.1	94.5	96.0	97.5	97.8	98.1	98.3	98.5	98.7	1
2	0.0	37.4	67.0	83.1	88.3	91.5	94.6	95.3	95.9	96.4	96.9	97.3	2
3	0.0	0.0	47.2	73.1	81.3	86.5	91.4	92.5	93.5	94.3	95.0	95.6	3
4	0.0	0.0	25.0	61.7	73.4	80.8	87.7	89.4	90.7	91.9	92.9	93.8	4
5	0.0	0.0	0.0	48.9	64.5	74.4	83.6	85.8	87.6	89.2	90.6	91.7	5
6	0.0	0.0	0.0	34.5	54.5	67.2	79.0	81.8	84.2	86.2	87.9	89.4	6
7	0.0	0.0	0.0	18.3	43.2	59.0	73.8	77.3	80.2	82.8	84.9	86.8	7
8	0.0	0.0	0.0	0.0	30.5	49.9	68.0	72.2	75.8	78.9	81.5	83.8	8
9	0.0	0.0	0.0	0.0	16.1	39.5	61.4	66.5	70.8	74.5	77.7	80.5	9
10	0.0	0.0	0.0	0.0	0.0	27.9	53.9	60.0	65.2	69.6	73.5	76.7	10
11	0.0	0.0	0.0	0.0	0.0	14.8	45.6	52.8	58.9	64.1	68.6	72.5	11
12	0.0	0.0	0.0	0.0	0.0	0.0	36.1	44.6	51.7	57.5	63.2	67.7	12
13	0.0	0.0	0.0	0.0	0.0	0.0	25.5	35.3	43.7	50.9	57.0	62.4	13
14	0.0	0.0	0.0	0.0	0.0	0.0	13.5	24.9	34.6	43.0	50.1	56.3	14
15	0.0	0.0	0.0	0.0	0.0	0.0	0.0	13.2	24.4	34.1	42.3	49.5	15
16	0.0	0.0	0.0	0.0	0.0	0.0	0.0	0.0	12.9	24.0	33.6	41.8	16
17	0.0	0.0	0.0	0.0	0.0	0.0	0.0	0.0	0.0	12.7	23.7	33.1	17
18	0.0	0.0	0.0	0.0	0.0	0.0	0.0	0.0	0.0	0.0	12.5	23.4	18
19	0.0	0.0	0.0	0.0	0.0	0.0	0.0	0.0	0.0	0.0	0.0	12.4	19

AGE OF LOAN	21.0	22.0	23.0	24.0	25.0	26.0	27.0	28.0	29.0	30.0	35.0	40.0	AGE OF LOAN
1	98.9	99.0	99.1	99.2	99.3	99.4	99.5	99.5	99.6	99.6	99.8	99.9	1
2	97.6	97.9	98.2	98.4	98.6	98.7	98.9	99.0	99.1	99.2	99.6	99.8	2
3	96.2	96.6	97.0	97.4	97.7	98.0	98.2	98.4	98.6	98.8	99.3	99.6	3
4	94.6	95.2	95.8	96.3	96.7	97.1	97.5	97.8	98.0	98.2	99.0	99.5	4
5	92.8	93.6	94.4	95.1	95.7	96.2	96.6	97.0	97.4	97.7	98.7	99.3	5
6	90.7	91.8	92.8	93.7	94.4	95.1	95.7	96.2	96.6	97.0	98.4	99.1	6
7	88.4	89.8	91.0	92.1	93.0	93.9	94.6	95.2	95.8	96.3	98.0	98.9	7
8	85.8	87.5	89.0	90.3	91.5	92.5	93.4	94.1	94.8	95.4	97.5	98.6	8
9	82.9	85.0	86.8	88.4	89.7	90.9	92.0	92.9	93.8	94.5	97.0	98.4	9
10	79.6	82.1	84.2	86.1	87.8	89.2	90.5	91.6	92.6	93.4	96.4	98.0	10
11	75.9	78.8	81.4	83.6	85.5	87.2	88.7	90.0	91.2	92.2	95.8	97.7	11
12	71.7	75.1	78.1	80.7	83.0	85.0	86.8	88.3	89.7	90.9	95.0	97.3	12
13	67.0	71.0	74.5	77.5	80.2	82.5	84.6	86.4	88.0	89.3	94.2	96.8	13
14	61.7	66.3	70.4	73.9	77.0	79.7	82.1	84.2	86.0	87.6	93.3	96.3	14
15	55.7	61.1	65.7	69.8	73.4	76.5	79.3	81.7	83.8	85.7	92.2	95.8	15
16	48.9	55.1	60.5	65.2	69.4	73.0	76.1	78.9	81.4	83.5	91.0	95.1	16
17	41.3	48.4	54.6	60.1	64.8	68.9	72.6	75.8	78.6	81.1	89.7	94.4	17
18	32.8	40.9	48.0	54.2	59.7	64.4	68.6	72.2	75.5	78.3	88.2	93.6	18
19	23.1	32.4	40.6	47.7	53.9	59.3	64.1	68.3	71.9	75.2	86.5	92.6	19
20	12.2	22.9	32.2	40.3	47.3	53.5	59.0	63.8	68.0	71.7	84.6	91.6	20
21	0.0	12.1	22.7	31.9	40.0	47.1	53.3	58.7	63.5	67.7	82.5	90.4	21
22	0.0	0.0	12.0	22.5	31.7	35.7	46.8	53.0	58.5	63.3	80.0	89.1	22
23	0.0	0.0	0.0	11.9	22.4	31.5	39.5	46.6	52.8	58.3	77.3	87.6	23
24	0.0	0.0	0.0	0.0	11.8	22.2	31.3	39.3	46.4	52.6	74.2	85.9	24
25	0.0	0.0	0.0	0.0	0.0	11.8	22.1	31.2	39.2	46.2	70.8	84.0	25
26	0.0	0.0	0.0	0.0	0.0	0.0	11.7	22.0	31.1	39.0	66.9	81.9	26
27	0.0	0.0	0.0	0.0	0.0	0.0	0.0	11.6	21.9	31.0	62.5	79.5	27
28	0.0	0.0	0.0	0.0	0.0	0.0	0.0	0.0	11.6	21.8	57.5	76.8	28
29	0.0	0.0	0.0	0.0	0.0	0.0	0.0	0.0	0.0	11.6	51.9	73.7	29
30	0.0	0.0	0.0	0.0	0.0	0.0	0.0	0.0	0.0	0.0	45.6	70.3	30
31	0.0	0.0	0.0	0.0	0.0	0.0	0.0	0.0	0.0	0.0	38.5	66.4	31
32	0.0	0.0	0.0	0.0	0.0	0.0	0.0	0.0	0.0	0.0	30.6	62.0	32
33	0.0	0.0	0.0	0.0	0.0	0.0	0.0	0.0	0.0	0.0	21.6	57.1	33
34	0.0	0.0	0.0	0.0	0.0	0.0	0.0	0.0	0.0	0.0	11.4	51.6	34
35	0.0	0.0	0.0	0.0	0.0	0.0	0.0	0.0	0.0	0.0	0.0	45.3	35
36	0.0	0.0	0.0	0.0	0.0	0.0	0.0	0.0	0.0	0.0	0.0	38.3	36
37	0.0	0.0	0.0	0.0	0.0	0.0	0.0	0.0	0.0	0.0	0.0	30.3	37
38	0.0	0.0	0.0	0.0	0.0	0.0	0.0	0.0	0.0	0.0	0.0	21.4	38
39	0.0	0.0	0.0	0.0	0.0	0.0	0.0	0.0	0.0	0.0	0.0	11.3	39

AGE OF LOAN	2.0	3.0	5.0	8.0	10.0	12.0	15.0	16.0	17.0	18.0	19.0	20.0	AGE OF LOAN
						ORIGINAL TERM IN YEARS							
1	53.0	70.6	84.6	92.2	94.6	96.1	97.5	97.9	98.1	98.4	98.6	98.8	1
2	0.0	37.5	67.1	83.3	88.4	91.7	94.7	95.4	96.0	96.5	97.0	97.4	2
3	0.0	0.0	47.4	73.3	81.5	86.7	91.5	92.7	93.6	94.5	95.2	95.8	3
4	0.0	0.0	25.1	62.6	73.6	81.1	88.0	89.6	90.9	92.1	93.1	94.0	4
5	0.0	0.0	0.0	49.2	64.8	74.7	83.9	86.1	87.9	89.5	90.8	92.0	5
6	0.0	0.0	0.0	34.7	54.8	67.5	79.4	82.1	84.5	86.5	88.2	89.7	6
7	0.0	0.0	0.0	18.4	43.5	59.4	74.2	77.7	80.6	83.1	85.2	87.1	7
8	0.0	0.0	0.0	0.0	30.7	50.2	68.4	72.6	76.2	79.3	81.9	84.2	8
9	0.0	0.0	0.0	0.0	16.3	39.9	61.8	66.9	71.3	75.0	78.2	80.9	9
10	0.0	0.0	0.0	0.0	0.0	28.2	54.4	60.5	65.7	70.1	73.9	77.2	10
11	0.0	0.0	0.0	0.0	0.0	14.9	46.0	53.2	59.3	64.6	69.1	73.0	11
12	0.0	0.0	0.0	0.0	0.0	0.0	36.5	45.0	52.2	58.4	63.7	68.2	12
13	0.0	0.0	0.0	0.0	0.0	0.0	25.8	35.7	44.1	51.4	57.5	62.9	13
14	0.0	0.0	0.0	0.0	0.0	0.0	13.7	25.2	35.0	43.4	50.6	56.8	14
15	0.0	0.0	0.0	0.0	0.0	0.0	0.0	13.4	24.7	34.5	42.8	50.0	15
16	0.0	0.0	0.0	0.0	0.0	0.0	0.0	0.0	13.1	24.3	34.0	42.3	16
17	0.0	0.0	0.0	0.0	0.0	0.0	0.0	0.0	0.0	12.9	24.0	33.6	17
18	0.0	0.0	0.0	0.0	0.0	0.0	0.0	0.0	0.0	0.0	12.7	23.7	18
19	0.0	0.0	0.0	0.0	0.0	0.0	0.0	0.0	0.0	0.0	0.0	12.6	19

12.25

AGE OF LOAN	21.0	22.0	23.0	24.0	25.0	26.0	27.0	28.0	29.0	30.0	35.0	40.0	AGE OF LOAN
						ORIGINAL TERM IN YEARS							
1	98.9	99.0	99.2	99.3	99.4	99.4	99.5	99.6	99.6	99.7	99.8	99.9	1
2	97.7	98.0	98.2	98.4	98.6	98.8	98.9	99.1	99.2	99.3	99.6	99.8	2
3	96.3	96.8	97.2	97.5	97.8	98.1	98.3	98.5	98.7	98.8	99.4	99.7	3
4	94.7	95.4	95.9	96.4	96.9	97.2	97.6	97.9	98.1	98.3	99.1	99.5	4
5	93.0	93.8	94.6	95.2	95.8	96.3	96.8	97.1	97.5	97.8	98.8	99.4	5
6	91.0	92.1	93.0	93.9	94.6	95.3	95.8	96.3	96.8	97.1	98.5	99.2	6
7	88.7	90.1	91.3	92.4	93.3	94.1	94.8	95.4	96.0	96.4	98.1	99.0	7
8	86.2	87.9	89.3	90.6	91.8	92.8	93.6	94.4	95.0	95.6	97.6	98.7	8
9	83.3	85.3	87.1	88.7	90.1	91.2	92.3	93.2	94.0	94.7	97.2	98.5	9
10	80.0	82.5	84.6	86.5	88.1	89.5	90.8	91.9	92.8	93.7	96.6	98.2	10
11	76.3	79.3	81.8	84.0	85.9	87.6	89.1	90.4	91.5	92.5	96.0	97.8	11
12	72.2	75.6	78.6	81.2	83.5	85.4	87.2	88.7	90.0	91.2	95.3	97.4	12
13	67.5	71.5	75.0	78.0	80.7	83.0	85.0	86.8	88.4	89.7	94.5	97.0	13
14	62.2	66.9	70.9	74.4	77.5	80.2	82.6	84.6	86.5	88.0	93.6	96.5	14
15	56.2	61.6	66.3	70.4	74.0	77.1	79.8	82.2	84.3	86.2	92.6	96.0	15
16	49.5	55.7	61.1	65.8	69.9	73.5	76.7	79.5	81.9	84.0	91.4	95.4	16
17	41.8	49.0	55.2	60.6	65.4	69.5	73.2	76.3	79.1	81.6	90.1	94.7	17
18	33.2	41.4	48.6	54.8	60.3	65.0	69.2	72.8	76.1	78.9	88.7	93.9	18
19	23.4	32.9	41.1	48.2	54.5	59.9	64.7	68.9	72.6	75.8	87.0	93.0	19
20	12.4	23.2	32.6	40.8	47.9	54.1	59.6	64.4	68.6	72.3	85.1	92.0	20
21	0.0	12.3	23.0	32.4	40.5	47.6	53.9	59.3	64.2	68.4	83.0	90.8	21
22	0.0	0.0	12.2	22.9	32.1	40.3	47.4	53.6	59.1	63.9	80.6	89.5	22
23	0.0	0.0	0.0	12.1	22.7	32.0	40.1	47.2	53.4	58.9	77.9	88.1	23
24	0.0	0.0	0.0	0.0	12.0	22.6	31.8	39.9	47.0	53.2	74.9	86.4	24
25	0.0	0.0	0.0	0.0	0.0	12.0	22.5	31.7	39.7	46.8	71.4	84.6	25
26	0.0	0.0	0.0	0.0	0.0	0.0	11.9	22.4	31.5	39.6	67.6	82.5	26
27	0.0	0.0	0.0	0.0	0.0	0.0	0.0	11.9	22.3	31.4	63.2	80.1	27
28	0.0	0.0	0.0	0.0	0.0	0.0	0.0	0.0	11.8	22.2	58.2	77.4	28
29	0.0	0.0	0.0	0.0	0.0	0.0	0.0	0.0	0.0	11.8	52.6	74.4	29
30	0.0	0.0	0.0	0.0	0.0	0.0	0.0	0.0	0.0	0.0	46.3	71.0	30
31	0.0	0.0	0.0	0.0	0.0	0.0	0.0	0.0	0.0	0.0	39.1	67.1	31
32	0.0	0.0	0.0	0.0	0.0	0.0	0.0	0.0	0.0	0.0	31.1	62.8	32
33	0.0	0.0	0.0	0.0	0.0	0.0	0.0	0.0	0.0	0.0	21.9	57.8	33
34	0.0	0.0	0.0	0.0	0.0	0.0	0.0	0.0	0.0	0.0	11.6	52.3	34
35	0.0	0.0	0.0	0.0	0.0	0.0	0.0	0.0	0.0	0.0	0.0	46.0	35
36	0.0	0.0	0.0	0.0	0.0	0.0	0.0	0.0	0.0	0.0	0.0	38.9	36
37	0.0	0.0	0.0	0.0	0.0	0.0	0.0	0.0	0.0	0.0	0.0	30.9	37
38	0.0	0.0	0.0	0.0	0.0	0.0	0.0	0.0	0.0	0.0	0.0	21.8	38
39	0.0	0.0	0.0	0.0	0.0	0.0	0.0	0.0	0.0	0.0	0.0	11.6	39

AGE OF LOAN	2.0	3.0	5.0	8.0	10.0	12.0	15.0	16.0	17.0	18.0	19.0	20.0	AGE OF LOAN
1	53.1	70.7	84.6	92.2	94.6	96.2	97.6	97.9	98.2	98.4	98.6	98.8	1
2	0.0	37.5	67.2	83.4	88.6	91.8	94.8	95.5	96.1	96.6	97.1	97.4	2
3	0.0	0.0	47.6	73.5	81.7	86.9	91.7	92.8	93.8	94.6	95.3	95.9	3
4	0.0	0.0	25.2	62.2	73.9	81.3	88.2	89.8	91.1	92.3	93.3	94.2	4
5	0.0	0.0	0.0	49.4	65.1	75.0	84.2	86.3	88.2	89.7	91.0	92.2	5
6	0.0	0.0	0.0	34.9	55.1	67.8	79.7	82.4	84.8	86.8	88.5	89.9	6
7	0.0	0.0	0.0	18.5	43.7	59.7	74.6	78.0	80.9	83.4	85.6	87.4	7
8	0.0	0.0	0.0	0.0	30.9	50.6	68.8	73.0	76.6	79.7	82.3	84.5	8
9	0.0	0.0	0.0	0.0	16.4	40.2	62.2	67.3	71.7	75.4	78.6	81.3	9
10	0.0	0.0	0.0	0.0	0.0	28.4	54.8	60.9	66.1	70.5	74.3	77.6	10
11	0.0	0.0	0.0	0.0	0.0	15.1	46.4	53.6	59.8	65.1	69.6	73.4	11
12	0.0	0.0	0.0	0.0	0.0	0.0	36.8	45.4	52.7	58.8	64.2	68.7	12
13	0.0	0.0	0.0	0.0	0.0	0.0	26.0	36.1	44.6	51.8	58.0	63.4	13
14	0.0	0.0	0.0	0.0	0.0	0.0	13.8	25.5	35.4	43.9	51.1	57.3	14
15	0.0	0.0	0.0	0.0	0.0	0.0	0.0	13.5	25.0	34.8	43.3	50.5	15
16	0.0	0.0	0.0	0.0	0.0	0.0	0.0	0.0	13.3	24.6	34.4	42.7	16
17	0.0	0.0	0.0	0.0	0.0	0.0	0.0	0.0	0.0	13.1	24.3	34.0	17
18	0.0	0.0	0.0	0.0	0.0	0.0	0.0	0.0	0.0	0.0	12.9	24.0	18
19	0.0	0.0	0.0	0.0	0.0	0.0	0.0	0.0	0.0	0.0	0.0	12.7	19

12.50

AGE OF LOAN	21.0	22.0	23.0	24.0	25.0	26.0	27.0	28.0	29.0	30.0	35.0	40.0	AGE OF LOAN
1	99.0	99.1	99.2	99.3	99.4	99.5	99.5	99.6	99.6	99.7	99.8	99.9	1
2	97.8	98.0	98.3	98.5	98.7	98.8	99.0	99.1	99.2	99.3	99.6	99.8	2
3	96.4	96.9	97.3	97.6	97.9	98.1	98.4	98.6	98.7	98.9	99.4	99.7	3
4	94.9	95.5	96.1	96.6	97.0	97.4	97.7	98.0	98.2	98.4	99.2	99.6	4
5	93.2	94.0	94.8	95.4	96.0	96.5	96.9	97.3	97.6	97.9	98.9	99.4	5
6	91.2	92.3	93.3	94.1	94.8	95.4	96.0	96.5	96.9	97.3	98.6	99.2	6
7	89.0	90.4	91.6	92.6	93.5	94.3	95.0	95.6	96.1	96.6	98.2	99.0	7
8	86.5	88.2	89.6	90.9	92.0	93.0	93.9	94.6	95.2	95.8	97.8	98.8	8
9	83.7	85.7	87.5	89.0	90.4	91.5	92.6	93.5	94.2	94.9	97.3	98.6	9
10	80.4	82.9	85.0	86.9	88.5	89.9	91.1	92.2	93.1	93.9	96.8	98.3	10
11	76.8	79.7	82.2	84.4	86.3	88.0	89.4	90.7	91.8	92.8	96.2	98.0	11
12	72.7	76.1	79.1	81.6	83.9	85.8	87.6	89.1	90.4	91.5	95.5	97.6	12
13	68.0	72.0	75.5	78.5	81.1	83.4	85.4	87.2	88.7	90.1	94.7	97.2	13
14	62.7	67.4	71.4	74.9	78.0	80.7	83.0	85.1	86.9	88.4	93.9	96.7	14
15	56.7	62.1	66.8	70.9	74.5	77.6	80.3	82.7	84.8	86.6	92.9	96.2	15
16	50.0	56.2	61.6	66.4	70.5	74.1	77.2	80.0	82.4	84.5	91.8	95.6	16
17	42.3	49.5	55.8	61.2	66.0	70.1	73.7	76.9	79.7	82.1	90.5	94.9	17
18	33.6	41.9	49.1	55.4	60.8	65.6	69.8	73.4	76.6	79.4	89.1	94.2	18
19	23.8	33.3	41.6	48.8	55.0	60.5	65.3	69.5	73.1	76.4	87.4	93.3	19
20	12.6	23.5	33.0	41.3	48.5	54.7	60.2	65.0	69.2	72.9	85.6	92.3	20
21	0.0	12.5	23.3	32.8	41.0	48.2	54.5	60.0	64.8	69.0	83.5	91.2	21
22	0.0	0.0	12.4	23.2	32.6	40.8	48.0	54.2	59.7	64.6	81.2	90.0	22
23	0.0	0.0	0.0	12.3	23.0	32.4	40.6	47.8	54.0	59.5	78.5	88.5	23
24	0.0	0.0	0.0	0.0	12.2	22.9	32.2	40.4	47.6	53.9	75.5	86.9	24
25	0.0	0.0	0.0	0.0	0.0	12.2	22.8	32.1	40.3	47.4	72.1	85.1	25
26	0.0	0.0	0.0	0.0	0.0	0.0	12.1	22.7	32.0	40.1	68.2	83.0	26
27	0.0	0.0	0.0	0.0	0.0	0.0	0.0	12.0	22.6	31.9	63.8	80.7	27
28	0.0	0.0	0.0	0.0	0.0	0.0	0.0	0.0	12.0	22.5	58.9	78.0	28
29	0.0	0.0	0.0	0.0	0.0	0.0	0.0	0.0	0.0	12.0	53.3	75.0	29
30	0.0	0.0	0.0	0.0	0.0	0.0	0.0	0.0	0.0	0.0	46.9	71.7	30
31	0.0	0.0	0.0	0.0	0.0	0.0	0.0	0.0	0.0	0.0	39.7	67.8	31
32	0.0	0.0	0.0	0.0	0.0	0.0	0.0	0.0	0.0	0.0	31.5	63.5	32
33	0.0	0.0	0.0	0.0	0.0	0.0	0.0	0.0	0.0	0.0	22.3	58.5	33
34	0.0	0.0	0.0	0.0	0.0	0.0	0.0	0.0	0.0	0.0	11.8	52.9	34
35	0.0	0.0	0.0	0.0	0.0	0.0	0.0	0.0	0.0	0.0	0.0	46.6	35
36	0.0	0.0	0.0	0.0	0.0	0.0	0.0	0.0	0.0	0.0	0.0	39.4	36
37	0.0	0.0	0.0	0.0	0.0	0.0	0.0	0.0	0.0	0.0	0.0	31.3	37
38	0.0	0.0	0.0	0.0	0.0	0.0	0.0	0.0	0.0	0.0	0.0	22.2	38
39	0.0	0.0	0.0	0.0	0.0	0.0	0.0	0.0	0.0	0.0	0.0	11.8	39

AGE OF LOAN	2.0	3.0	5.0	8.0	10.0	12.0	15.0	16.0	17.0	18.0	19.0	20.0	AGE OF LOAN
					ORIGINAL TERM IN YEARS								
1	53.2	70.8	84.7	92.3	94.7	96.2	97.6	98.0	98.2	98.5	98.7	98.8	1
2	0.0	37.6	67.4	83.6	88.7	91.9	94.9	95.6	96.2	96.7	97.1	97.5	2
3	0.0	0.0	47.7	73.7	81.9	87.1	91.9	93.0	93.9	94.7	95.4	96.0	3
4	0.0	0.0	25.4	62.4	74.1	81.5	88.4	90.0	91.3	92.5	93.5	94.3	4
5	0.0	0.0	0.0	49.6	65.3	75.3	84.5	86.6	88.4	89.9	91.3	92.4	5
6	0.0	0.0	0.0	35.1	55.4	68.2	80.0	82.7	85.1	87.0	88.7	90.2	6
7	0.0	0.0	0.0	18.7	44.0	60.1	74.9	78.4	81.3	83.8	85.9	87.7	7
8	0.0	0.0	0.0	0.0	31.2	50.6	69.2	73.4	77.0	80.0	82.6	84.9	8
9	0.0	0.0	0.0	0.0	16.6	40.5	62.6	67.7	72.1	75.8	79.0	81.7	9
10	0.0	0.0	0.0	0.0	0.0	28.7	55.2	61.3	66.5	71.0	74.8	78.0	10
11	0.0	0.0	0.0	0.0	0.0	15.2	46.8	54.1	60.3	65.5	70.0	73.9	11
12	0.0	0.0	0.0	0.0	0.0	0.0	37.2	45.8	53.1	59.3	64.7	69.2	12
13	0.0	0.0	0.0	0.0	0.0	0.0	26.3	36.4	45.0	52.3	58.5	63.9	13
14	0.0	0.0	0.0	0.0	0.0	0.0	14.0	25.8	35.8	44.3	51.6	57.9	14
15	0.0	0.0	0.0	0.0	0.0	0.0	0.0	13.7	25.3	35.2	43.7	51.0	15
16	0.0	0.0	0.0	0.0	0.0	0.0	0.0	0.0	13.5	24.9	34.8	43.2	16
17	0.0	0.0	0.0	0.0	0.0	0.0	0.0	0.0	0.0	13.3	24.6	34.4	17
18	0.0	0.0	0.0	0.0	0.0	0.0	0.0	0.0	0.0	0.0	13.1	24.3	18
19	0.0	0.0	0.0	0.0	0.0	0.0	0.0	0.0	0.0	0.0	0.0	12.9	19

12.75

AGE OF LOAN	21.0	22.0	23.0	24.0	25.0	26.0	27.0	28.0	29.0	30.0	35.0	40.0	AGE OF LOAN
					ORIGINAL TERM IN YEARS								
1	99.0	99.1	99.2	99.3	99.4	99.5	99.5	99.6	99.6	99.7	99.8	99.9	1
2	97.8	98.1	98.3	98.6	98.7	98.9	99.0	99.1	99.3	99.3	99.7	99.8	2
3	96.5	97.0	97.4	97.7	98.0	98.2	98.4	98.6	98.8	98.9	99.4	99.7	3
4	95.0	95.7	96.2	96.7	97.1	97.5	97.8	98.0	98.3	98.5	99.2	99.6	4
5	93.4	94.2	94.9	95.6	96.1	96.6	97.0	97.4	97.7	98.0	98.9	99.4	5
6	91.5	92.5	93.5	94.3	95.0	95.6	96.2	96.6	97.0	97.4	98.6	99.3	6
7	89.3	90.6	91.8	92.8	93.7	94.5	95.2	95.8	96.3	96.7	98.3	99.1	7
8	86.8	88.5	89.9	91.2	92.3	93.2	94.1	94.8	95.4	96.0	97.9	98.9	8
9	84.0	86.1	87.8	89.3	90.7	91.8	92.8	93.7	94.5	95.1	97.5	98.7	9
10	80.9	83.3	85.4	87.2	88.8	90.2	91.4	92.5	93.4	94.2	96.9	98.4	10
11	77.3	80.1	82.6	84.8	86.7	88.3	89.8	91.0	92.1	93.1	96.4	98.1	11
12	73.2	76.6	79.5	82.1	84.3	86.3	87.9	89.4	90.7	91.8	95.7	97.7	12
13	68.5	72.5	76.0	79.0	81.6	83.9	85.9	87.6	89.1	90.4	95.0	97.4	13
14	63.3	67.9	72.0	75.5	78.5	81.2	83.5	85.5	87.3	88.8	94.1	96.9	14
15	57.3	62.7	67.4	71.5	75.0	78.1	80.8	83.2	85.2	87.0	93.2	96.4	15
16	50.5	56.8	62.2	66.9	71.0	74.6	77.8	80.5	82.9	85.0	92.1	95.8	16
17	42.8	50.0	56.3	61.8	66.5	70.7	74.3	77.4	80.2	82.6	90.9	95.2	17
18	34.0	42.4	49.6	55.9	61.4	66.2	70.4	74.0	77.2	80.0	89.5	94.5	18
19	24.1	33.7	42.1	49.3	55.6	61.1	65.9	70.1	73.7	76.9	87.9	93.6	19
20	12.8	23.9	33.5	41.8	49.0	55.3	60.8	65.6	69.8	73.5	86.1	92.7	20
21	0.0	12.7	23.7	33.2	41.5	48.8	55.1	60.6	65.4	69.6	84.1	91.6	21
22	0.0	0.0	12.6	23.5	33.0	41.3	48.5	54.9	60.4	65.2	81.7	90.4	22
23	0.0	0.0	0.0	12.5	23.4	32.9	41.1	48.3	54.7	60.2	79.1	89.0	23
24	0.0	0.0	0.0	0.0	12.4	23.3	32.7	41.0	48.2	54.5	76.1	87.4	24
25	0.0	0.0	0.0	0.0	0.0	12.4	23.2	32.6	40.8	48.0	72.7	85.6	25
26	0.0	0.0	0.0	0.0	0.0	0.0	12.3	23.1	32.5	40.7	68.9	83.6	26
27	0.0	0.0	0.0	0.0	0.0	0.0	0.0	12.3	23.0	32.4	64.5	81.3	27
28	0.0	0.0	0.0	0.0	0.0	0.0	0.0	0.0	12.2	22.9	59.5	78.7	28
29	0.0	0.0	0.0	0.0	0.0	0.0	0.0	0.0	0.0	12.2	53.9	75.7	29
30	0.0	0.0	0.0	0.0	0.0	0.0	0.0	0.0	0.0	0.0	47.5	72.3	30
31	0.0	0.0	0.0	0.0	0.0	0.0	0.0	0.0	0.0	0.0	40.3	68.5	31
32	0.0	0.0	0.0	0.0	0.0	0.0	0.0	0.0	0.0	0.0	32.0	64.1	32
33	0.0	0.0	0.0	0.0	0.0	0.0	0.0	0.0	0.0	0.0	22.7	59.2	33
34	0.0	0.0	0.0	0.0	0.0	0.0	0.0	0.0	0.0	0.0	12.1	53.6	34
35	0.0	0.0	0.0	0.0	0.0	0.0	0.0	0.0	0.0	0.0	0.0	47.3	35
36	0.0	0.0	0.0	0.0	0.0	0.0	0.0	0.0	0.0	0.0	0.0	40.0	36
37	0.0	0.0	0.0	0.0	0.0	0.0	0.0	0.0	0.0	0.0	0.0	31.8	37
38	0.0	0.0	0.0	0.0	0.0	0.0	0.0	0.0	0.0	0.0	0.0	22.5	38
39	0.0	0.0	0.0	0.0	0.0	0.0	0.0	0.0	0.0	0.0	0.0	12.0	39

Selected Financial Tables   **A-217**

AGE OF LOAN	2.0	3.0	5.0	8.0	10.0	12.0	15.0	16.0	17.0	18.0	19.0	20.0	AGE OF LOAN
					ORIGINAL TERM IN YEARS								
1	53.2	70.9	84.8	92.4	94.8	96.3	97.7	98.0	98.3	98.5	98.7	98.9	1
2	0.0	37.7	67.5	83.7	88.8	92.1	95.0	95.7	96.3	96.8	97.2	97.6	2
3	0.0	0.0	47.9	73.9	82.1	87.3	92.0	93.1	94.1	94.9	95.6	96.1	3
4	0.0	0.0	25.5	62.6	74.4	81.8	88.6	90.2	91.5	92.7	93.6	94.5	4
5	0.0	0.0	0.0	49.6	65.6	75.6	84.7	86.9	88.6	90.2	91.5	92.6	5
6	0.0	0.0	0.0	35.3	55.7	68.5	80.3	83.0	85.4	87.3	89.0	90.4	6
7	0.0	0.0	0.0	18.8	44.3	60.4	75.3	78.7	81.6	84.1	86.2	88.0	7
8	0.0	0.0	0.0	0.0	31.4	51.2	69.5	73.8	77.4	80.4	83.0	85.2	8
9	0.0	0.0	0.0	0.0	16.7	40.8	63.0	68.2	72.5	76.2	79.4	82.1	9
10	0.0	0.0	0.0	0.0	0.0	28.9	55.6	61.8	67.0	71.4	75.2	78.5	10
11	0.0	0.0	0.0	0.0	0.0	15.4	47.2	54.5	60.7	66.0	70.5	74.4	11
12	0.0	0.0	0.0	0.0	0.0	0.0	37.5	46.2	53.6	59.8	65.1	69.7	12
13	0.0	0.0	0.0	0.0	0.0	0.0	26.6	36.8	45.4	52.8	59.0	64.4	13
14	0.0	0.0	0.0	0.0	0.0	0.0	14.2	26.1	36.2	44.7	52.1	58.4	14
15	0.0	0.0	0.0	0.0	0.0	0.0	0.0	13.9	25.6	35.6	44.2	51.5	15
16	0.0	0.0	0.0	0.0	0.0	0.0	0.0	0.0	13.6	25.2	35.2	43.7	16
17	0.0	0.0	0.0	0.0	0.0	0.0	0.0	0.0	0.0	13.4	24.9	34.8	17
18	0.0	0.0	0.0	0.0	0.0	0.0	0.0	0.0	0.0	0.0	13.3	24.6	18
19	0.0	0.0	0.0	0.0	0.0	0.0	0.0	0.0	0.0	0.0	0.0	13.1	19

13.00

AGE OF LOAN	21.0	22.0	23.0	24.0	25.0	26.0	27.0	28.0	29.0	30.0	35.0	40.0	AGE OF LOAN
					ORIGINAL TERM IN YEARS								
1	99.0	99.1	99.3	99.4	99.4	99.5	99.6	99.6	99.7	99.7	99.8	99.9	1
2	97.9	98.2	98.4	98.6	98.8	98.5	99.1	99.2	99.3	99.4	99.7	99.8	2
3	96.6	97.1	97.4	97.8	98.1	98.3	98.5	98.7	98.9	99.0	99.5	99.7	3
4	95.2	95.8	96.4	96.8	97.2	97.6	97.9	98.1	98.4	98.6	99.3	99.6	4
5	93.6	94.4	95.1	95.7	96.3	96.7	97.1	97.5	97.8	98.1	99.0	99.5	5
6	91.7	92.8	93.7	94.5	95.2	95.8	96.3	96.8	97.2	97.5	98.7	99.3	6
7	89.6	90.9	92.1	93.1	94.0	94.7	95.4	95.9	96.5	96.9	98.4	99.2	7
8	87.1	88.8	90.2	91.5	92.5	93.5	94.3	95.0	95.6	96.2	98.0	99.0	8
9	84.4	86.4	88.1	89.6	91.0	92.1	93.1	93.9	94.7	95.4	97.6	98.7	9
10	81.3	83.7	85.8	87.6	89.1	90.5	91.7	92.7	93.6	94.4	97.1	98.5	10
11	77.7	80.6	83.1	85.2	87.1	88.7	90.1	91.3	92.4	93.4	96.6	98.2	11
12	73.6	77.0	80.0	82.5	84.7	86.6	88.3	89.8	91.0	92.1	95.9	97.9	12
13	69.0	73.0	76.5	79.4	82.0	84.3	86.3	88.0	89.5	90.8	95.2	97.5	13
14	63.8	68.4	72.5	76.0	79.0	81.6	83.9	85.9	87.7	89.2	94.4	97.1	14
15	57.8	63.2	67.9	72.0	75.5	78.6	81.3	83.6	85.7	87.4	93.5	96.6	15
16	51.0	57.3	62.8	67.5	71.6	75.2	78.3	81.0	83.3	85.4	92.4	96.1	16
17	43.2	50.5	56.9	62.3	67.1	71.2	74.8	78.0	80.7	83.1	91.2	95.4	17
18	34.4	42.9	50.2	56.5	62.0	66.8	70.9	74.5	77.7	80.5	89.9	94.7	18
19	24.4	34.1	42.5	49.8	56.2	61.7	66.5	70.7	74.3	77.5	88.3	93.9	19
20	13.0	24.2	33.9	42.3	49.6	55.9	61.4	66.2	70.4	74.1	86.6	93.0	20
21	0.0	12.9	24.0	33.7	42.0	49.3	55.7	61.2	66.0	70.2	84.6	91.9	21
22	0.0	0.0	12.8	23.8	33.5	41.8	49.1	55.4	61.0	65.8	82.3	90.8	22
23	0.0	0.0	0.0	12.7	23.7	33.3	41.6	48.9	55.3	60.8	79.7	89.4	23
24	0.0	0.0	0.0	0.0	12.6	23.6	33.2	41.5	48.8	55.1	76.7	87.9	24
25	0.0	0.0	0.0	0.0	0.0	12.6	23.5	33.0	41.3	48.6	73.3	86.1	25
26	0.0	0.0	0.0	0.0	0.0	0.0	12.5	23.4	32.9	41.2	69.5	84.1	26
27	0.0	0.0	0.0	0.0	0.0	0.0	0.0	12.4	23.3	32.8	65.2	81.8	27
28	0.0	0.0	0.0	0.0	0.0	0.0	0.0	0.0	12.4	23.3	60.2	79.3	28
29	0.0	0.0	0.0	0.0	0.0	0.0	0.0	0.0	0.0	12.4	54.5	76.3	29
30	0.0	0.0	0.0	0.0	0.0	0.0	0.0	0.0	0.0	0.0	48.1	73.0	30
31	0.0	0.0	0.0	0.0	0.0	0.0	0.0	0.0	0.0	0.0	40.8	69.2	31
32	0.0	0.0	0.0	0.0	0.0	0.0	0.0	0.0	0.0	0.0	32.5	64.8	32
33	0.0	0.0	0.0	0.0	0.0	0.0	0.0	0.0	0.0	0.0	23.0	59.9	33
34	0.0	0.0	0.0	0.0	0.0	0.0	0.0	0.0	0.0	0.0	12.2	54.3	34
35	0.0	0.0	0.0	0.0	0.0	0.0	0.0	0.0	0.0	0.0	0.0	47.9	35
36	0.0	0.0	0.0	0.0	0.0	0.0	0.0	0.0	0.0	0.0	0.0	40.6	36
37	0.0	0.0	0.0	0.0	0.0	0.0	0.0	0.0	0.0	0.0	0.0	32.3	37
38	0.0	0.0	0.0	0.0	0.0	0.0	0.0	0.0	0.0	0.0	0.0	22.9	38
39	0.0	0.0	0.0	0.0	0.0	0.0	0.0	0.0	0.0	0.0	0.0	12.2	39

AGE OF LOAN	ORIGINAL TERM IN YEARS												AGE OF LOAN
	2.0	3.0	5.0	8.0	10.0	12.0	15.0	16.0	17.0	18.0	19.0	20.0	
1	53.3	71.0	84.9	92.5	94.8	96.4	97.7	98.1	98.3	98.6	98.7	98.9	1
2	0.0	37.8	67.7	83.5	89.0	92.2	95.2	95.8	96.4	96.9	97.3	97.7	2
3	0.0	0.0	48.0	74.1	82.3	87.4	92.2	93.3	94.2	95.0	95.7	96.3	3
4	0.0	0.0	25.6	62.5	74.6	82.0	88.8	90.4	91.7	92.9	93.8	94.6	4
5	0.0	0.0	0.0	50.1	65.9	75.8	85.0	87.1	88.9	90.4	91.7	92.8	5
6	0.0	0.0	0.0	35.6	55.9	68.8	80.6	83.3	85.6	87.6	89.3	90.7	6
7	0.0	0.0	0.0	18.5	44.6	60.8	75.6	79.1	81.9	84.4	86.5	88.3	7
8	0.0	0.0	0.0	0.0	31.6	51.6	69.9	74.2	77.7	80.8	83.3	85.6	8
9	0.0	0.0	0.0	0.0	16.9	41.1	63.4	68.6	72.9	76.6	79.7	82.4	9
10	0.0	0.0	0.0	0.0	0.0	29.2	56.0	62.2	67.4	71.9	75.6	78.9	10
11	0.0	0.0	0.0	0.0	0.0	15.5	47.6	54.9	61.2	66.4	71.0	74.8	11
12	0.0	0.0	0.0	0.0	0.0	0.0	37.9	46.6	54.0	60.3	65.6	70.2	12
13	0.0	0.0	0.0	0.0	0.0	0.0	26.9	37.2	45.8	53.2	59.5	64.9	13
14	0.0	0.0	0.0	0.0	0.0	0.0	14.3	26.4	36.5	45.2	52.6	58.9	14
15	0.0	0.0	0.0	0.0	0.0	0.0	0.0	14.1	25.9	36.0	44.6	52.0	15
16	0.0	0.0	0.0	0.0	0.0	0.0	0.0	0.0	13.8	25.6	35.6	44.1	16
17	0.0	0.0	0.0	0.0	0.0	0.0	0.0	0.0	0.0	13.6	25.2	35.2	17
18	0.0	0.0	0.0	0.0	0.0	0.0	0.0	0.0	0.0	0.0	13.4	25.0	18
19	0.0	0.0	0.0	0.0	0.0	0.0	0.0	0.0	0.0	0.0	0.0	13.3	19

13.25

AGE OF LOAN	ORIGINAL TERM IN YEARS												AGE OF LOAN
	21.0	22.0	23.0	24.0	25.0	26.0	27.0	28.0	29.0	30.0	35.0	40.0	
1	99.1	99.2	99.3	99.4	99.5	99.5	99.6	99.6	99.7	99.7	99.9	99.9	1
2	98.0	98.2	98.5	98.7	98.8	99.0	99.1	99.2	99.3	99.4	99.7	99.8	2
3	96.7	97.2	97.5	97.9	98.1	98.4	98.6	98.8	98.9	99.1	99.5	99.7	3
4	95.3	96.0	96.5	96.9	97.3	97.7	98.0	98.2	98.4	98.6	99.3	99.6	4
5	93.7	94.6	95.3	95.9	96.4	96.9	97.3	97.6	97.9	98.2	99.1	99.5	5
6	91.9	93.0	93.9	94.7	95.4	96.0	96.5	96.9	97.3	97.6	98.8	99.4	6
7	89.8	91.2	92.3	93.3	94.2	94.9	95.6	96.1	96.6	97.0	98.5	99.2	7
8	87.5	89.1	90.5	91.7	92.8	93.7	94.5	95.2	95.8	96.3	98.1	99.0	8
9	84.8	86.7	88.5	90.0	91.2	92.4	93.3	94.2	94.9	95.6	97.7	98.8	9
10	81.7	84.1	86.1	87.9	89.5	90.8	92.0	93.0	93.9	94.6	97.3	98.6	10
11	78.1	81.0	83.5	85.6	87.4	89.0	90.4	91.6	92.7	93.6	96.7	98.3	11
12	74.1	77.5	80.4	82.9	85.1	87.0	88.7	90.1	91.4	92.4	96.1	98.0	12
13	69.5	73.5	76.9	79.9	82.5	84.7	86.7	88.4	89.8	91.1	95.4	97.7	13
14	64.3	69.0	73.0	76.5	79.5	82.1	84.4	86.4	88.1	89.6	94.7	97.2	14
15	58.3	63.8	68.5	72.5	76.0	79.1	81.8	84.1	86.1	87.8	93.8	96.8	15
16	51.5	57.8	63.3	68.0	72.1	75.7	78.8	81.5	83.8	85.8	92.7	96.3	16
17	43.7	51.1	57.4	62.5	67.7	71.8	75.4	78.5	81.2	83.6	91.6	95.7	17
18	34.8	43.4	50.7	57.1	62.6	67.3	71.5	75.1	78.2	81.0	90.3	95.0	18
19	24.7	34.6	43.0	50.4	56.7	62.3	67.1	71.2	74.9	78.0	88.7	94.2	19
20	13.2	24.5	34.3	42.8	50.1	56.5	62.0	66.8	71.0	74.7	87.0	93.3	20
21	0.0	13.1	24.3	34.1	42.5	49.9	56.2	61.8	66.0	70.8	85.0	92.3	21
22	0.0	0.0	13.0	24.2	33.9	42.3	49.7	56.0	61.6	66.4	82.8	91.1	22
23	0.0	0.0	0.0	12.9	24.1	33.8	42.2	49.5	55.9	61.4	80.2	89.8	23
24	0.0	0.0	0.0	0.0	12.8	23.9	33.6	42.0	49.3	55.7	77.3	88.3	24
25	0.0	0.0	0.0	0.0	0.0	12.8	23.8	33.5	41.9	49.2	74.0	86.6	25
26	0.0	0.0	0.0	0.0	0.0	0.0	12.7	23.8	33.4	41.8	70.2	84.6	26
27	0.0	0.0	0.0	0.0	0.0	0.0	0.0	12.7	23.7	33.3	65.8	82.4	27
28	0.0	0.0	0.0	0.0	0.0	0.0	0.0	0.0	12.6	23.6	60.8	79.8	28
29	0.0	0.0	0.0	0.0	0.0	0.0	0.0	0.0	0.0	12.6	55.2	76.9	29
30	0.0	0.0	0.0	0.0	0.0	0.0	0.0	0.0	0.0	0.0	48.7	73.6	30
31	0.0	0.0	0.0	0.0	0.0	0.0	0.0	0.0	0.0	0.0	41.4	69.8	31
32	0.0	0.0	0.0	0.0	0.0	0.0	0.0	0.0	0.0	0.0	33.0	65.5	32
33	0.0	0.0	0.0	0.0	0.0	0.0	0.0	0.0	0.0	0.0	23.4	60.6	33
34	0.0	0.0	0.0	0.0	0.0	0.0	0.0	0.0	0.0	0.0	12.5	54.9	34
35	0.0	0.0	0.0	0.0	0.0	0.0	0.0	0.0	0.0	0.0	0.0	48.5	35
36	0.0	0.0	0.0	0.0	0.0	0.0	0.0	0.0	0.0	0.0	0.0	41.2	36
37	0.0	0.0	0.0	0.0	0.0	0.0	0.0	0.0	0.0	0.0	0.0	32.8	37
38	0.0	0.0	0.0	0.0	0.0	0.0	0.0	0.0	0.0	0.0	0.0	23.3	38
39	0.0	0.0	0.0	0.0	0.0	0.0	0.0	0.0	0.0	0.0	0.0	12.4	39

AGE OF LOAN	ORIGINAL TERM IN YEARS												AGE OF LOAN
	2.0	3.0	5.0	8.0	10.0	12.0	15.0	16.0	17.0	18.0	19.0	20.0	
1	53.3	71.0	85.0	92.5	94.9	96.4	97.8	98.1	98.4	98.6	98.8	98.9	1
2	0.0	37.9	67.8	84.0	89.1	92.3	95.3	95.9	96.5	97.0	97.4	97.7	2
3	0.0	0.0	48.2	74.3	82.5	87.6	92.4	93.4	94.4	95.1	95.8	96.4	3
4	0.0	0.0	25.7	63.1	74.9	82.3	89.0	90.6	91.9	93.0	94.0	94.8	4
5	0.0	0.0	0.0	50.4	66.2	76.1	85.3	87.4	89.1	90.6	91.9	93.0	5
6	0.0	0.0	0.0	35.8	56.2	69.1	80.9	83.6	85.9	87.9	89.5	90.9	6
7	0.0	0.0	0.0	19.1	44.9	61.1	76.0	79.4	82.3	84.7	86.8	88.6	7
8	0.0	0.0	0.0	0.0	31.9	51.9	70.3	74.5	78.1	81.1	83.7	85.9	8
9	0.0	0.0	0.0	0.0	17.0	41.4	63.8	69.0	73.3	77.0	80.1	82.8	9
10	0.0	0.0	0.0	0.0	0.0	29.4	56.4	62.6	67.8	72.3	76.1	79.3	10
11	0.0	0.0	0.0	0.0	0.0	15.7	47.9	55.3	61.6	66.9	71.4	75.3	11
12	0.0	0.0	0.0	0.0	0.0	0.0	38.3	47.0	54.4	60.7	66.1	70.7	12
13	0.0	0.0	0.0	0.0	0.0	0.0	27.2	37.5	46.3	53.7	60.0	65.4	13
14	0.0	0.0	0.0	0.0	0.0	0.0	14.5	26.7	36.9	45.6	53.0	59.4	14
15	0.0	0.0	0.0	0.0	0.0	0.0	0.0	14.2	26.2	36.4	45.1	52.5	15
16	0.0	0.0	0.0	0.0	0.0	0.0	0.0	0.0	14.0	25.8	36.0	44.6	16
17	0.0	0.0	0.0	0.0	0.0	0.0	0.0	0.0	0.0	13.8	25.5	35.6	17
18	0.0	0.0	0.0	0.0	0.0	0.0	0.0	0.0	0.0	0.0	13.6	25.3	18
19	0.0	0.0	0.0	0.0	0.0	0.0	0.0	0.0	0.0	0.0	0.0	13.5	19

13.50

AGE OF LOAN	ORIGINAL TERM IN YEARS												AGE OF LOAN
	21.0	22.0	23.0	24.0	25.0	26.0	27.0	28.0	29.0	30.0	35.0	40.0	
1	99.1	99.2	99.3	99.4	99.5	99.5	99.6	99.7	99.7	99.7	99.9	99.9	1
2	98.0	98.3	98.5	98.7	98.9	99.0	99.2	99.3	99.4	99.4	99.7	99.9	2
3	96.9	97.3	97.6	97.9	98.2	98.4	98.6	98.8	99.0	99.1	99.5	99.8	3
4	95.5	96.1	96.6	97.0	97.4	97.8	98.1	98.3	98.5	98.7	99.3	99.7	4
5	93.9	94.7	95.4	96.0	96.5	97.0	97.4	97.7	98.0	98.3	99.1	99.6	5
6	92.1	93.2	94.1	94.9	95.5	96.1	96.6	97.0	97.4	97.8	98.9	99.4	6
7	90.1	91.4	92.5	93.5	94.4	95.1	95.7	96.3	96.8	97.2	98.6	99.3	7
8	87.8	89.4	90.8	92.0	93.0	93.9	94.7	95.4	96.0	96.5	98.2	99.1	8
9	85.1	87.1	88.8	90.2	91.5	92.6	93.6	94.4	95.1	95.7	97.8	98.9	9
10	82.1	84.4	86.5	88.3	89.8	91.1	92.3	93.2	94.1	94.9	97.4	98.7	10
11	78.6	81.4	83.6	86.0	87.8	89.4	90.7	91.9	93.0	93.9	96.9	98.4	11
12	74.6	77.9	80.8	83.4	85.5	87.4	89.0	90.4	91.7	92.7	96.3	98.1	12
13	70.0	74.0	77.4	80.4	82.9	85.1	87.1	88.7	90.2	91.4	95.7	97.8	13
14	64.8	69.5	73.5	76.9	79.9	82.5	84.8	86.8	88.5	89.9	94.9	97.4	14
15	58.8	64.3	69.0	73.0	76.5	79.6	82.2	84.5	86.5	88.2	94.0	97.0	15
16	52.0	58.4	63.8	68.6	72.7	76.2	79.3	81.9	84.3	86.3	93.0	96.5	16
17	44.2	51.6	58.0	63.5	68.2	72.3	75.9	79.0	81.7	84.0	91.9	95.9	17
18	35.2	43.8	51.2	57.6	63.1	67.9	72.0	75.6	78.8	81.5	90.6	95.2	18
19	25.0	35.0	43.5	50.9	57.3	62.8	67.6	71.8	75.4	78.6	89.1	94.5	19
20	13.3	24.8	34.3	43.3	50.7	57.0	62.6	67.4	71.6	75.2	87.4	93.6	20
21	0.0	13.2	24.7	34.5	43.0	50.4	56.8	62.4	67.2	71.4	85.5	92.6	21
22	0.0	0.0	13.2	24.5	34.3	42.8	50.2	56.6	62.2	67.0	83.3	91.5	22
23	0.0	0.0	0.0	13.1	24.4	34.2	42.7	50.1	56.5	62.0	80.8	90.2	23
24	0.0	0.0	0.0	0.0	13.0	24.3	34.1	42.5	49.9	56.3	77.9	88.7	24
25	0.0	0.0	0.0	0.0	0.0	12.9	24.2	33.9	42.4	49.8	74.6	87.1	25
26	0.0	0.0	0.0	0.0	0.0	0.0	12.9	24.1	33.8	42.3	70.8	85.1	26
27	0.0	0.0	0.0	0.0	0.0	0.0	0.0	12.8	24.0	33.7	66.4	82.9	27
28	0.0	0.0	0.0	0.0	0.0	0.0	0.0	0.0	12.8	24.0	61.5	80.4	28
29	0.0	0.0	0.0	0.0	0.0	0.0	0.0	0.0	0.0	12.8	55.8	77.5	29
30	0.0	0.0	0.0	0.0	0.0	0.0	0.0	0.0	0.0	0.0	49.3	74.2	30
31	0.0	0.0	0.0	0.0	0.0	0.0	0.0	0.0	0.0	0.0	41.9	70.5	31
32	0.0	0.0	0.0	0.0	0.0	0.0	0.0	0.0	0.0	0.0	33.4	66.1	32
33	0.0	0.0	0.0	0.0	0.0	0.0	0.0	0.0	0.0	0.0	23.8	61.2	33
34	0.0	0.0	0.0	0.0	0.0	0.0	0.0	0.0	0.0	0.0	12.7	55.6	34
35	0.0	0.0	0.0	0.0	0.0	0.0	0.0	0.0	0.0	0.0	0.0	49.1	35
36	0.0	0.0	0.0	0.0	0.0	0.0	0.0	0.0	0.0	0.0	0.0	41.7	36
37	0.0	0.0	0.0	0.0	0.0	0.0	0.0	0.0	0.0	0.0	0.0	33.3	37
38	0.0	0.0	0.0	0.0	0.0	0.0	0.0	0.0	0.0	0.0	0.0	23.6	38
39	0.0	0.0	0.0	0.0	0.0	0.0	0.0	0.0	0.0	0.0	0.0	12.6	39

REMAINING BALANCE
IN PERCENT OF ORIGINAL LOAN AMOUNT

AGE OF LOAN	ORIGINAL TERM IN YEARS												AGE OF LOAN
	2.0	3.0	5.0	8.0	10.0	12.0	15.0	16.0	17.0	18.0	19.0	20.0	
1	53.4	71.1	85.1	92.6	95.0	96.5	97.8	98.1	98.4	98.6	98.8	99.0	1
2	0.0	38.0	67.9	84.2	89.2	92.4	95.4	96.0	96.6	97.1	97.5	97.8	2
3	0.0	0.0	48.3	74.5	82.7	87.8	92.5	93.6	94.5	95.3	95.9	96.5	3
4	0.0	0.0	25.8	63.3	75.1	82.5	89.3	90.8	92.1	93.2	94.1	94.9	4
5	0.0	0.0	0.0	50.6	66.4	76.4	85.5	87.6	89.4	90.8	92.1	93.2	5
6	0.0	0.0	0.0	36.0	56.5	69.4	81.2	83.9	86.2	88.1	89.8	91.2	6
7	0.0	0.0	0.0	19.2	45.1	61.4	76.3	79.7	82.6	85.0	87.1	88.9	7
8	0.0	0.0	0.0	0.0	32.1	52.2	70.7	74.9	78.5	81.5	84.0	86.2	8
9	0.0	0.0	0.0	0.0	17.1	41.7	64.2	69.4	73.7	77.4	80.5	83.2	9
10	0.0	0.0	0.0	0.0	0.0	29.7	56.8	63.0	68.3	72.7	76.5	79.7	10
11	0.0	0.0	0.0	0.0	0.0	15.8	48.3	55.8	62.0	67.3	71.8	75.7	11
12	0.0	0.0	0.0	0.0	0.0	0.0	38.6	47.4	54.9	61.2	66.5	71.1	12
13	0.0	0.0	0.0	0.0	0.0	0.0	27.4	37.9	46.7	54.1	60.5	65.9	13
14	0.0	0.0	0.0	0.0	0.0	0.0	14.6	26.9	37.3	46.0	53.5	59.8	14
15	0.0	0.0	0.0	0.0	0.0	0.0	0.0	14.4	26.5	36.8	45.5	52.9	15
16	0.0	0.0	0.0	0.0	0.0	0.0	0.0	0.0	14.1	26.1	36.3	45.0	16
17	0.0	0.0	0.0	0.0	0.0	0.0	0.0	0.0	0.0	14.0	25.8	36.0	17
18	0.0	0.0	0.0	0.0	0.0	0.0	0.0	0.0	0.0	0.0	13.8	25.6	18
19	0.0	0.0	0.0	0.0	0.0	0.0	0.0	0.0	0.0	0.0	0.0	13.6	19

13.75

AGE OF LOAN	ORIGINAL TERM IN YEARS												AGE OF LOAN
	21.0	22.0	23.0	24.0	25.0	26.0	27.0	28.0	29.0	30.0	35.0	40.0	
1	99.1	99.2	99.3	99.4	99.5	99.6	99.6	99.7	99.7	99.8	99.9	99.9	1
2	98.1	98.4	98.6	98.8	98.9	99.1	99.2	99.3	99.4	99.5	99.7	99.9	2
3	97.0	97.4	97.7	98.0	98.3	98.5	98.7	98.9	99.0	99.1	99.6	99.8	3
4	95.6	96.2	96.7	97.2	97.5	97.9	98.1	98.4	98.6	98.8	99.4	99.7	4
5	94.1	94.9	95.6	96.2	96.7	97.1	97.5	97.8	98.1	98.3	99.2	99.6	5
6	92.4	93.4	94.3	95.0	95.7	96.3	96.7	97.2	97.5	97.9	98.9	99.5	6
7	90.4	91.7	92.8	93.7	94.6	95.3	95.9	96.4	96.9	97.3	98.6	99.3	7
8	88.1	89.7	91.1	92.2	93.3	94.2	94.9	95.6	96.2	96.7	98.3	99.2	8
9	85.5	87.4	89.1	90.5	91.8	92.9	93.8	94.6	95.3	95.9	98.0	99.0	9
10	82.4	84.8	86.8	88.6	90.1	91.4	92.5	93.5	94.3	95.1	97.5	98.8	10
11	79.0	81.8	84.2	86.3	88.1	89.7	91.0	92.2	93.2	94.1	97.1	98.5	11
12	75.0	78.4	81.3	83.8	85.9	87.8	89.4	90.8	92.0	93.0	96.5	98.2	12
13	70.5	74.5	77.9	80.8	83.3	85.5	87.4	89.1	90.5	91.7	95.9	97.9	13
14	65.3	70.0	74.0	77.4	80.4	83.0	85.2	87.1	88.8	90.3	95.1	97.6	14
15	59.3	64.8	69.5	73.5	77.0	80.1	82.7	84.9	86.9	88.6	94.3	97.1	15
16	52.5	58.9	64.4	69.1	73.2	76.7	79.8	82.4	84.7	86.7	93.3	96.6	16
17	45.6	52.1	58.5	64.0	68.7	72.9	76.4	79.5	82.2	84.5	92.2	96.1	17
18	35.7	44.3	51.7	58.1	63.7	68.5	72.6	76.2	79.3	82.0	91.0	95.5	18
19	25.3	35.4	44.0	51.4	57.9	63.4	68.2	72.4	76.0	79.1	89.5	94.7	19
20	13.5	25.1	35.1	43.8	51.2	57.6	63.2	68.0	72.1	75.8	87.9	93.9	20
21	0.0	13.4	25.0	34.9	43.5	51.0	57.4	63.0	67.8	72.0	86.0	92.9	21
22	0.0	0.0	13.3	24.8	34.8	43.3	50.8	57.2	62.8	67.6	83.8	91.8	22
23	0.0	0.0	0.0	13.3	24.7	34.6	43.2	50.6	57.0	62.6	81.3	90.6	23
24	0.0	0.0	0.0	0.0	13.2	24.6	34.5	43.0	50.5	56.9	78.4	89.2	24
25	0.0	0.0	0.0	0.0	0.0	13.1	24.5	34.4	42.9	50.3	75.1	87.5	25
26	0.0	0.0	0.0	0.0	0.0	0.0	13.1	24.4	34.3	42.8	71.4	85.6	26
27	0.0	0.0	0.0	0.0	0.0	0.0	0.0	13.0	24.4	34.2	67.1	83.4	27
28	0.0	0.0	0.0	0.0	0.0	0.0	0.0	0.0	13.0	24.3	62.1	80.9	28
29	0.0	0.0	0.0	0.0	0.0	0.0	0.0	0.0	0.0	13.0	56.4	78.1	29
30	0.0	0.0	0.0	0.0	0.0	0.0	0.0	0.0	0.0	0.0	49.9	74.8	30
31	0.0	0.0	0.0	0.0	0.0	0.0	0.0	0.0	0.0	0.0	42.5	71.1	31
32	0.0	0.0	0.0	0.0	0.0	0.0	0.0	0.0	0.0	0.0	33.9	66.8	32
33	0.0	0.0	0.0	0.0	0.0	0.0	0.0	0.0	0.0	0.0	24.1	61.8	33
34	0.0	0.0	0.0	0.0	0.0	0.0	0.0	0.0	0.0	0.0	12.9	56.2	34
35	0.0	0.0	0.0	0.0	0.0	0.0	0.0	0.0	0.0	0.0	0.0	49.7	35
36	0.0	0.0	0.0	0.0	0.0	0.0	0.0	0.0	0.0	0.0	0.0	42.3	36
37	0.0	0.0	0.0	0.0	0.0	0.0	0.0	0.0	0.0	0.0	0.0	33.8	37
38	0.0	0.0	0.0	0.0	0.0	0.0	0.0	0.0	0.0	0.0	0.0	24.0	38
39	0.0	0.0	0.0	0.0	0.0	0.0	0.0	0.0	0.0	0.0	0.0	12.8	39

AGE OF LOAN	ORIGINAL TERM IN YEARS												AGE OF LOAN
	2.0	3.0	5.0	8.0	10.0	12.0	15.0	16.0	17.0	18.0	19.0	20.0	
1	53.5	71.2	85.1	92.7	95.1	96.5	97.9	98.2	98.5	98.7	98.9	99.0	1
2	0.0	38.1	68.1	84.3	89.4	92.6	95.5	96.1	96.7	97.1	97.5	97.9	2
3	0.0	0.0	48.5	74.7	82.9	88.0	92.7	93.7	94.6	95.4	96.0	96.6	3
4	0.0	0.0	25.9	63.6	75.3	82.7	89.5	91.0	92.3	93.4	94.3	95.1	4
5	0.0	0.0	0.0	50.8	66.7	76.7	85.8	87.8	89.6	91.1	92.3	93.4	5
6	0.0	0.0	0.0	36.2	56.8	69.7	81.5	84.2	86.5	88.4	90.0	91.4	6
7	0.0	0.0	0.0	19.3	45.4	61.8	76.7	80.1	82.9	85.3	87.4	89.1	7
8	0.0	0.0	0.0	0.0	32.3	52.6	71.1	75.3	78.8	81.8	84.4	86.5	8
9	0.0	0.0	0.0	0.0	17.3	42.0	64.6	69.8	74.1	77.8	80.9	83.5	9
10	0.0	0.0	0.0	0.0	0.0	29.9	57.2	63.5	68.7	73.1	76.9	80.1	10
11	0.0	0.0	0.0	0.0	0.0	16.0	48.7	56.2	62.5	67.8	72.3	76.1	11
12	0.0	0.0	0.0	0.0	0.0	0.0	39.0	47.9	55.3	61.6	67.0	71.6	12
13	0.0	0.0	0.0	0.0	0.0	0.0	27.7	38.3	47.1	54.6	60.9	66.4	13
14	0.0	0.0	0.0	0.0	0.0	0.0	14.8	27.2	37.7	46.5	54.0	60.3	14
15	0.0	0.0	0.0	0.0	0.0	0.0	0.0	14.6	26.8	37.2	46.0	53.2	15
16	0.0	0.0	0.0	0.0	0.0	0.0	0.0	0.0	14.3	26.5	36.7	45.5	16
17	0.0	0.0	0.0	0.0	0.0	0.0	0.0	0.0	0.0	14.1	26.2	36.4	17
18	0.0	0.0	0.0	0.0	0.0	0.0	0.0	0.0	0.0	0.0	14.0	25.9	18
19	0.0	0.0	0.0	0.0	0.0	0.0	0.0	0.0	0.0	0.0	0.0	13.8	19

14.00

AGE OF LOAN	ORIGINAL TERM IN YEARS												AGE OF LOAN
	21.0	22.0	23.0	24.0	25.0	26.0	27.0	28.0	29.0	30.0	35.0	40.0	
1	99.2	99.3	99.4	99.5	99.5	99.6	99.6	99.7	99.7	99.8	99.9	99.9	1
2	98.2	98.4	98.6	98.8	99.0	99.1	99.2	99.3	99.4	99.5	99.8	99.9	2
3	97.1	97.5	97.8	98.1	98.4	98.6	98.8	98.9	99.1	99.2	99.6	99.8	3
4	95.8	96.3	96.8	97.3	97.6	97.9	98.2	98.5	98.7	98.8	99.4	99.7	4
5	94.3	95.1	95.7	96.3	96.8	97.2	97.6	97.9	98.2	98.4	99.2	99.6	5
6	92.6	93.6	94.5	95.2	95.8	96.4	96.9	97.3	97.7	98.0	99.0	99.5	6
7	90.6	91.9	93.0	93.9	94.8	95.5	96.1	96.6	97.0	97.4	98.7	99.4	7
8	88.4	90.0	91.3	92.5	93.5	94.4	95.1	95.8	96.3	96.8	98.4	99.2	8
9	85.8	87.7	89.4	90.8	92.1	93.1	94.0	94.8	95.5	96.1	98.1	99.0	9
10	82.8	85.2	87.2	88.9	90.4	91.7	92.8	93.7	94.6	95.3	97.7	98.8	10
11	79.4	82.2	84.6	86.7	88.5	90.0	91.3	92.5	93.5	94.3	97.2	98.6	11
12	75.5	78.8	81.7	84.2	86.3	88.1	89.7	91.1	92.2	93.3	96.7	98.3	12
13	71.0	74.9	78.3	81.2	83.8	85.9	87.8	89.4	90.8	92.0	96.1	98.0	13
14	65.8	70.5	74.5	77.9	80.9	83.4	85.6	87.5	89.2	90.6	95.4	97.7	14
15	59.8	65.3	70.0	74.0	77.5	80.5	83.1	85.4	87.3	89.0	94.5	97.3	15
16	53.0	59.4	64.9	69.6	73.7	77.2	80.2	82.9	85.1	87.1	93.6	96.8	16
17	45.1	52.6	59.0	64.5	69.3	73.4	76.9	80.0	82.6	84.9	92.5	96.3	17
18	36.1	44.8	52.3	58.7	64.2	69.0	73.1	76.7	79.8	82.4	91.3	95.7	18
19	25.7	35.8	44.5	52.0	58.4	64.0	68.8	72.9	76.5	79.6	89.9	95.0	19
20	13.7	25.5	35.6	44.3	51.7	58.2	63.7	68.5	72.7	76.3	88.3	94.2	20
21	0.0	13.6	25.3	35.4	44.0	51.5	58.0	63.5	68.4	72.5	86.4	93.3	21
22	0.0	0.0	13.5	25.2	35.2	43.9	51.3	57.8	63.4	68.2	84.3	92.2	22
23	0.0	0.0	0.0	13.5	25.1	35.1	43.7	51.2	57.6	63.2	81.8	91.0	23
24	0.0	0.0	0.0	0.0	13.4	25.0	34.9	43.6	51.0	57.5	79.0	89.6	24
25	0.0	0.0	0.0	0.0	0.0	13.3	24.9	34.8	43.5	50.9	75.7	87.9	25
26	0.0	0.0	0.0	0.0	0.0	0.0	13.3	24.8	34.7	43.4	72.0	86.1	26
27	0.0	0.0	0.0	0.0	0.0	0.0	0.0	13.3	24.7	34.7	67.7	83.9	27
28	0.0	0.0	0.0	0.0	0.0	0.0	0.0	0.0	13.2	24.7	62.7	81.5	28
29	0.0	0.0	0.0	0.0	0.0	0.0	0.0	0.0	0.0	13.2	57.1	78.7	29
30	0.0	0.0	0.0	0.0	0.0	0.0	0.0	0.0	0.0	0.0	50.5	75.4	30
31	0.0	0.0	0.0	0.0	0.0	0.0	0.0	0.0	0.0	0.0	43.0	71.7	31
32	0.0	0.0	0.0	0.0	0.0	0.0	0.0	0.0	0.0	0.0	34.4	67.4	32
33	0.0	0.0	0.0	0.0	0.0	0.0	0.0	0.0	0.0	0.0	24.5	62.5	33
34	0.0	0.0	0.0	0.0	0.0	0.0	0.0	0.0	0.0	0.0	13.1	56.8	34
35	0.0	0.0	0.0	0.0	0.0	0.0	0.0	0.0	0.0	0.0	0.0	50.3	35
36	0.0	0.0	0.0	0.0	0.0	0.0	0.0	0.0	0.0	0.0	0.0	42.9	36
37	0.0	0.0	0.0	0.0	0.0	0.0	0.0	0.0	0.0	0.0	0.0	34.3	37
38	0.0	0.0	0.0	0.0	0.0	0.0	0.0	0.0	0.0	0.0	0.0	24.4	38
39	0.0	0.0	0.0	0.0	0.0	0.0	0.0	0.0	0.0	0.0	0.0	13.0	39

AGE OF LOAN		ORIGINAL TERM IN YEARS											AGE OF LOAN
	2.0	3.0	5.0	8.0	10.0	12.0	14.0	15.0	16.0	17.0	18.0	19.0	20.0	
1	53.5	71.3	85.2	92.8	95.1	96.6	97.6	97.9	98.2	98.5	98.7	98.9	99.0	1
2	0.0	38.1	68.2	84.4	89.5	92.7	94.8	95.6	96.2	96.8	97.2	97.6	98.0	2
3	0.0	0.0	48.6	74.8	83.0	88.2	91.5	92.8	93.9	94.8	95.5	96.1	96.7	3
4	0.0	0.0	26.0	63.8	75.6	83.0	87.8	89.7	91.2	92.5	93.5	94.5	95.2	4
5	0.0	0.0	0.0	51.1	67.0	77.0	83.6	86.0	88.1	89.8	91.3	92.5	93.6	5
6	0.0	0.0	0.0	36.4	57.1	70.1	78.6	81.8	84.5	86.8	88.7	90.3	91.6	6
7	0.0	0.0	0.0	19.5	45.7	62.1	72.9	77.0	80.4	83.2	85.6	87.7	89.4	7
8	0.0	0.0	0.0	0.0	32.6	52.9	66.4	71.4	75.6	79.2	82.2	84.7	86.8	8
9	0.0	0.0	0.0	0.0	17.4	42.4	58.9	65.0	70.2	74.5	78.2	81.2	83.9	9
10	0.0	0.0	0.0	0.0	0.0	30.2	50.2	57.6	63.9	69.1	73.5	77.3	80.5	10
11	0.0	0.0	0.0	0.0	0.0	16.1	40.2	49.1	56.6	62.9	68.2	72.7	76.6	11
12	0.0	0.0	0.0	0.0	0.0	0.0	28.6	39.3	48.3	55.8	62.1	67.5	72.0	12
13	0.0	0.0	0.0	0.0	0.0	0.0	15.3	28.0	38.6	47.5	55.0	61.4	66.8	13
14	0.0	0.0	0.0	0.0	0.0	0.0	0.0	15.0	27.5	38.0	46.9	54.4	60.8	14
15	0.0	0.0	0.0	0.0	0.0	0.0	0.0	0.0	14.7	27.1	37.5	46.4	53.9	15
16	0.0	0.0	0.0	0.0	0.0	0.0	0.0	0.0	0.0	14.5	26.7	37.1	45.9	16
17	0.0	0.0	0.0	0.0	0.0	0.0	0.0	0.0	0.0	0.0	14.3	26.5	36.8	17
18	0.0	0.0	0.0	0.0	0.0	0.0	0.0	0.0	0.0	0.0	0.0	14.2	26.2	18
19	0.0	0.0	0.0	0.0	0.0	0.0	0.0	0.0	0.0	0.0	0.0	0.0	14.0	19

14.25

AGE OF LOAN		ORIGINAL TERM IN YEARS											AGE OF LOAN
	21.0	22.0	23.0	24.0	25.0	26.0	27.0	28.0	29.0	30.0	35.0	40.0	
1	99.2	99.3	99.4	99.5	99.5	99.6	99.7	99.7	99.7	99.8	99.9	99.9	1
2	98.2	98.5	98.7	98.9	99.0	99.2	99.3	99.4	99.5	99.5	99.8	99.9	2
3	97.2	97.5	97.9	98.2	98.4	98.6	98.8	99.0	99.1	99.2	99.6	99.8	3
4	95.9	96.5	97.0	97.4	97.7	98.0	98.3	98.5	98.7	98.9	99.5	99.7	4
5	94.5	95.2	95.9	96.4	96.9	97.3	97.7	98.0	98.3	98.5	99.3	99.6	5
6	92.8	93.8	94.6	95.4	96.0	96.5	97.0	97.4	97.8	98.3	99.1	99.5	6
7	90.9	92.1	93.2	94.1	94.9	95.6	96.2	96.7	97.2	97.5	98.8	99.3	7
8	88.7	90.2	91.6	92.7	93.7	94.6	95.3	95.9	96.5	97.0	98.5	99.3	8
9	86.1	88.0	89.7	91.1	92.3	93.3	94.2	95.0	95.7	96.3	98.2	99.1	9
10	83.2	85.5	87.5	89.2	90.7	91.9	93.0	94.0	94.8	95.5	97.8	98.9	10
11	79.8	82.6	85.0	87.0	88.8	90.3	91.6	92.8	93.7	94.6	97.3	98.7	11
12	75.9	79.3	82.1	84.5	86.7	88.5	90.0	91.4	92.5	93.5	96.8	98.4	12
13	71.4	75.4	78.8	81.7	84.2	86.3	88.2	89.8	91.1	92.3	96.2	98.2	13
14	66.3	70.9	74.9	78.4	81.3	83.8	86.0	87.9	89.5	90.9	95.6	97.8	14
15	60.3	65.8	70.5	74.5	78.0	81.0	83.5	85.8	87.7	89.4	94.8	97.4	15
16	53.5	59.9	65.4	70.1	74.2	77.7	80.7	83.3	85.5	87.5	93.9	97.0	16
17	45.6	53.1	59.5	65.1	69.8	73.9	77.4	80.5	83.1	85.4	92.8	96.5	17
18	36.5	45.3	52.8	59.2	64.8	69.5	73.7	77.2	80.3	82.9	91.6	95.9	18
19	26.0	36.2	45.0	52.5	59.0	64.5	69.3	73.4	77.0	80.1	90.3	95.2	19
20	13.9	25.8	36.0	44.7	52.3	58.7	64.3	69.1	73.3	76.8	88.7	94.4	20
21	0.0	13.8	25.6	35.8	44.5	52.0	58.5	64.1	68.9	73.1	86.8	93.5	21
22	0.0	0.0	13.7	25.5	35.6	44.4	51.9	58.4	64.0	68.8	84.7	92.5	22
23	0.0	0.0	0.0	13.6	25.4	35.5	44.2	51.7	58.2	63.8	82.3	91.3	23
24	0.0	0.0	0.0	0.0	13.6	25.3	35.4	44.1	51.6	58.1	79.5	89.4	24
25	0.0	0.0	0.0	0.0	0.0	13.5	25.2	35.3	44.0	51.5	76.3	88.4	25
26	0.0	0.0	0.0	0.0	0.0	0.0	13.5	25.1	35.2	43.9	72.6	86.5	26
27	0.0	0.0	0.0	0.0	0.0	0.0	0.0	13.4	25.1	35.1	68.3	84.4	27
28	0.0	0.0	0.0	0.0	0.0	0.0	0.0	0.0	13.4	25.0	63.3	82.0	28
29	0.0	0.0	0.0	0.0	0.0	0.0	0.0	0.0	0.0	13.4	57.6	79.2	29
30	0.0	0.0	0.0	0.0	0.0	0.0	0.0	0.0	0.0	0.0	51.1	76.0	30
31	0.0	0.0	0.0	0.0	0.0	0.0	0.0	0.0	0.0	0.0	43.5	72.3	31
32	0.0	0.0	0.0	0.0	0.0	0.0	0.0	0.0	0.0	0.0	34.8	68.0	32
33	0.0	0.0	0.0	0.0	0.0	0.0	0.0	0.0	0.0	0.0	24.8	63.1	33
34	0.0	0.0	0.0	0.0	0.0	0.0	0.0	0.0	0.0	0.0	13.3	57.4	34
35	0.0	0.0	0.0	0.0	0.0	0.0	0.0	0.0	0.0	0.0	0.0	50.9	35
36	0.0	0.0	0.0	0.0	0.0	0.0	0.0	0.0	0.0	0.0	0.0	43.4	36
37	0.0	0.0	0.0	0.0	0.0	0.0	0.0	0.0	0.0	0.0	0.0	34.7	37
38	0.0	0.0	0.0	0.0	0.0	0.0	0.0	0.0	0.0	0.0	0.0	24.7	38
39	0.0	0.0	0.0	0.0	0.0	0.0	0.0	0.0	0.0	0.0	0.0	13.2	39

REMAINING BALANCE
IN PERCENT OF ORIGINAL LOAN AMOUNT

AGE OF LOAN	\multicolumn{12}{c}{ORIGINAL TERM IN YEARS}											AGE OF LOAN
	2.0	3.0	5.0	8.0	10.0	12.0	15.0	16.0	17.0	18.0	19.0	20.0	
1	53.6	71.3	85.3	92.8	95.2	96.7	98.0	98.3	98.5	98.7	98.9	99.1	1
2	0.0	38.2	68.4	84.6	89.6	92.8	95.7	96.3	96.8	97.3	97.7	98.0	2
3	0.0	0.0	48.8	75.0	83.2	88.3	93.0	94.0	94.9	95.6	96.3	96.8	3
4	0.0	0.0	26.1	64.0	75.8	83.2	89.9	91.4	92.6	93.7	94.6	95.4	4
5	0.0	0.0	0.0	51.3	67.3	77.2	86.3	88.3	90.0	91.5	92.7	93.7	5
6	0.0	0.0	0.0	36.6	57.4	70.4	82.1	84.8	87.0	88.9	90.5	91.8	6
7	0.0	0.0	0.0	19.6	46.0	62.4	77.3	80.7	83.5	85.9	88.0	89.7	7
8	0.0	0.0	0.0	0.0	32.8	53.3	71.8	76.0	79.5	82.5	85.0	87.1	8
9	0.0	0.0	0.0	0.0	17.6	42.7	65.4	70.6	74.9	78.5	81.6	84.2	9
10	0.0	0.0	0.0	0.0	0.0	30.4	58.0	64.3	69.5	74.0	77.7	80.9	10
11	0.0	0.0	0.0	0.0	0.0	16.3	49.5	57.0	63.3	68.7	73.2	77.0	11
12	0.0	0.0	0.0	0.0	0.0	0.0	39.7	48.7	56.2	62.6	67.9	72.5	12
13	0.0	0.0	0.0	0.0	0.0	0.0	28.3	39.0	47.9	55.5	61.9	67.3	13
14	0.0	0.0	0.0	0.0	0.0	0.0	15.2	27.8	38.4	47.3	54.9	61.3	14
15	0.0	0.0	0.0	0.0	0.0	0.0	0.0	14.9	27.4	37.9	46.8	54.4	15
16	0.0	0.0	0.0	0.0	0.0	0.0	0.0	0.0	14.7	27.1	37.5	46.4	16
17	0.0	0.0	0.0	0.0	0.0	0.0	0.0	0.0	0.0	14.5	26.8	37.2	17
18	0.0	0.0	0.0	0.0	0.0	0.0	0.0	0.0	0.0	0.0	14.3	26.5	18
19	0.0	0.0	0.0	0.0	0.0	0.0	0.0	0.0	0.0	0.0	0.0	14.2	19

14.50

AGE OF LOAN	\multicolumn{12}{c}{ORIGINAL TERM IN YEARS}											AGE OF LOAN
	21.0	22.0	23.0	24.0	25.0	26.0	27.0	28.0	29.0	30.0	35.0	40.0	
1	99.2	99.3	99.4	99.5	99.6	99.6	99.7	99.7	99.8	99.8	99.9	100.0	1
2	98.3	98.5	98.7	98.9	99.1	99.2	99.3	99.4	99.5	99.6	99.8	99.9	2
3	97.2	97.6	98.0	98.2	98.5	98.7	98.9	99.0	99.2	99.3	99.6	99.8	3
4	96.0	96.6	97.1	97.5	97.8	98.1	98.4	98.6	98.8	99.0	99.5	99.8	4
5	94.6	95.4	96.0	96.6	97.0	97.5	97.8	98.1	98.4	98.6	99.3	99.7	5
6	93.0	94.0	94.8	95.5	96.2	96.7	97.1	97.5	97.9	98.2	99.1	99.6	6
7	91.1	92.4	93.4	94.3	95.1	95.8	96.4	96.9	97.3	97.7	98.9	99.5	7
8	89.0	90.5	91.8	93.0	93.9	94.8	95.5	96.1	96.6	97.1	98.6	99.3	8
9	86.5	88.4	90.0	91.4	92.6	93.6	94.5	95.2	95.9	96.4	98.3	99.2	9
10	83.6	85.9	87.8	89.5	91.0	92.2	93.3	94.2	95.0	95.7	97.9	99.0	10
11	80.2	83.0	85.4	87.4	89.1	90.6	91.9	93.0	94.0	94.8	97.5	98.8	11
12	76.4	79.7	82.5	84.9	87.0	88.8	90.3	91.7	92.8	93.8	97.0	98.5	12
13	71.9	75.9	79.2	82.1	84.6	86.7	88.5	90.1	91.4	92.6	96.4	98.3	13
14	66.8	71.4	75.4	78.8	81.7	84.2	86.4	88.3	89.9	91.2	95.8	97.9	14
15	60.8	66.3	71.0	75.0	78.5	81.4	84.0	86.2	88.1	89.7	95.0	97.6	15
16	54.0	60.4	65.9	70.7	74.7	78.2	81.2	83.7	86.0	87.9	94.1	97.2	16
17	46.0	53.6	60.1	65.6	70.3	74.4	77.9	80.9	83.5	85.8	93.1	96.7	17
18	36.9	45.7	53.3	59.8	65.3	70.1	74.2	77.7	80.7	83.4	92.0	96.1	18
19	26.3	36.6	45.5	53.0	59.5	65.1	69.9	74.0	77.5	80.6	90.6	95.5	19
20	14.1	26.1	36.4	45.2	52.8	59.3	64.9	69.7	73.8	77.4	89.1	94.7	20
21	0.0	14.0	26.0	36.2	45.0	52.6	59.1	64.7	69.5	73.6	87.3	93.8	21
22	0.0	0.0	13.9	25.9	36.1	44.9	52.4	58.9	64.5	69.3	85.2	92.8	22
23	0.0	0.0	0.0	13.9	25.7	35.9	44.7	52.3	58.8	64.4	82.8	91.7	23
24	0.0	0.0	0.0	0.0	13.8	25.6	35.8	44.6	52.2	58.7	80.0	90.3	24
25	0.0	0.0	0.0	0.0	0.0	13.7	25.6	35.7	44.5	52.0	76.8	88.8	25
26	0.0	0.0	0.0	0.0	0.0	0.0	13.7	25.5	35.6	44.4	73.1	87.0	26
27	0.0	0.0	0.0	0.0	0.0	0.0	0.0	13.7	25.4	35.6	68.9	84.9	27
28	0.0	0.0	0.0	0.0	0.0	0.0	0.0	0.0	13.6	25.4	63.9	82.5	28
29	0.0	0.0	0.0	0.0	0.0	0.0	0.0	0.0	0.0	13.6	58.3	79.8	29
30	0.0	0.0	0.0	0.0	0.0	0.0	0.0	0.0	0.0	0.0	51.7	76.6	30
31	0.0	0.0	0.0	0.0	0.0	0.0	0.0	0.0	0.0	0.0	44.1	72.9	31
32	0.0	0.0	0.0	0.0	0.0	0.0	0.0	0.0	0.0	0.0	35.3	68.6	32
33	0.0	0.0	0.0	0.0	0.0	0.0	0.0	0.0	0.0	0.0	25.2	63.7	33
34	0.0	0.0	0.0	0.0	0.0	0.0	0.0	0.0	0.0	0.0	13.5	58.1	34
35	0.0	0.0	0.0	0.0	0.0	0.0	0.0	0.0	0.0	0.0	0.0	51.5	35
36	0.0	0.0	0.0	0.0	0.0	0.0	0.0	0.0	0.0	0.0	0.0	43.9	36
37	0.0	0.0	0.0	0.0	0.0	0.0	0.0	0.0	0.0	0.0	0.0	35.2	37
38	0.0	0.0	0.0	0.0	0.0	0.0	0.0	0.0	0.0	0.0	0.0	25.1	38
39	0.0	0.0	0.0	0.0	0.0	0.0	0.0	0.0	0.0	0.0	0.0	13.5	39

AGE OF LOAN	2.0	3.0	5.0	8.0	10.0	12.0	15.0	16.0	17.0	18.0	19.0	20.0	AGE OF LOAN
						ORIGINAL TERM IN YEARS							
1	53.7	71.4	85.4	92.9	95.3	96.7	98.0	98.3	98.6	98.8	99.0	99.1	1
2	0.0	38.3	68.5	84.7	89.8	92.9	95.7	96.4	96.9	97.4	97.8	98.1	2
3	0.0	0.0	48.5	75.2	83.4	88.5	93.1	94.1	95.0	95.7	96.4	96.9	3
4	0.0	0.0	26.2	64.3	76.1	83.4	90.0	91.6	92.8	93.9	94.8	95.5	4
5	0.0	0.0	0.0	51.5	67.5	77.5	86.5	88.5	90.2	91.7	92.9	93.9	5
6	0.0	0.0	0.0	36.8	57.7	70.7	82.4	85.1	87.3	89.1	90.7	92.1	6
7	0.0	0.0	0.0	19.7	46.3	62.8	77.7	81.0	83.8	86.2	88.2	89.9	7
8	0.0	0.0	0.0	0.0	33.0	53.6	72.2	76.4	79.9	82.8	85.3	87.4	8
9	0.0	0.0	0.0	0.0	17.7	43.0	65.8	71.0	75.3	78.9	82.0	84.6	9
10	0.0	0.0	0.0	0.0	0.0	30.7	58.4	64.7	69.9	74.4	78.1	81.2	10
11	0.0	0.0	0.0	0.0	0.0	16.5	49.9	57.5	63.8	69.1	73.6	77.4	11
12	0.0	0.0	0.0	0.0	0.0	0.0	40.0	49.1	56.6	63.0	68.4	72.9	12
13	0.0	0.0	0.0	0.0	0.0	0.0	28.6	39.3	48.4	55.9	62.3	67.8	13
14	0.0	0.0	0.0	0.0	0.0	0.0	15.3	28.1	38.8	47.8	55.4	61.8	14
15	0.0	0.0	0.0	0.0	0.0	0.0	0.0	15.1	27.7	38.3	47.3	54.9	15
16	0.0	0.0	0.0	0.0	0.0	0.0	0.0	0.0	14.9	27.4	37.9	46.9	16
17	0.0	0.0	0.0	0.0	0.0	0.0	0.0	0.0	0.0	14.7	27.1	37.6	17
18	0.0	0.0	0.0	0.0	0.0	0.0	0.0	0.0	0.0	0.0	14.5	26.8	18
19	0.0	0.0	0.0	0.0	0.0	0.0	0.0	0.0	0.0	0.0	0.0	14.4	19

14.75

AGE OF LOAN	21.0	22.0	23.0	24.0	25.0	26.0	27.0	28.0	29.0	30.0	35.0	40.0	AGE OF LOAN
						ORIGINAL TERM IN YEARS							
1	99.2	99.3	99.4	99.5	99.6	99.6	99.7	99.7	99.8	99.8	99.9	100.0	1
2	98.4	98.6	98.8	99.0	99.1	99.2	99.3	99.4	99.5	99.6	99.8	99.9	2
3	97.3	97.7	98.0	98.3	98.5	98.8	98.9	99.1	99.2	99.3	99.7	99.8	3
4	96.2	96.7	97.2	97.6	97.9	98.2	98.4	98.7	98.8	99.0	99.5	99.8	4
5	94.8	95.5	96.2	96.7	97.2	97.6	97.9	98.2	98.4	98.7	99.4	99.7	5
6	93.2	94.2	95.0	95.7	96.3	96.8	97.3	97.6	98.0	98.2	99.2	99.6	6
7	91.4	92.6	93.6	94.5	95.3	96.0	96.5	97.0	97.4	97.8	98.9	99.5	7
8	89.2	90.8	92.1	93.2	94.1	95.0	95.7	96.3	96.8	97.2	98.7	99.4	8
9	86.8	88.7	90.3	91.6	92.8	93.8	94.7	95.4	96.0	96.6	98.4	99.2	9
10	83.9	86.2	88.2	89.8	91.2	92.5	93.5	94.4	95.2	95.8	98.0	99.1	10
11	80.6	83.4	85.7	87.7	89.4	90.9	92.2	93.3	94.2	95.0	97.6	98.9	11
12	76.8	80.1	82.9	85.3	87.4	89.1	90.6	91.9	93.1	94.0	97.1	98.6	12
13	72.4	76.3	79.6	82.5	85.0	87.1	88.9	90.4	91.7	92.9	96.6	98.4	13
14	67.3	71.9	75.9	79.3	82.2	84.7	86.8	88.6	90.2	91.5	96.0	98.1	14
15	61.3	66.8	71.5	75.5	78.9	81.9	84.4	86.6	88.4	90.0	95.2	97.7	15
16	54.5	60.9	66.4	71.2	75.2	78.6	81.6	84.2	86.4	88.2	94.4	97.3	16
17	46.5	54.1	60.6	66.1	70.9	74.9	78.4	81.4	84.0	86.2	93.4	96.8	17
18	37.3	46.2	53.8	60.3	65.8	70.6	74.7	78.2	81.2	83.8	92.3	96.3	18
19	26.6	37.0	45.9	53.5	60.0	65.6	70.4	74.8	78.0	81.1	91.0	95.7	19
20	14.3	26.5	36.8	45.7	53.3	59.8	65.4	70.2	74.3	77.9	89.4	94.9	20
21	0.0	14.2	26.3	36.7	45.5	53.1	59.6	65.2	70.0	74.2	87.7	94.1	21
22	0.0	0.0	14.1	26.2	36.5	45.4	53.0	59.5	65.1	69.9	85.6	93.1	22
23	0.0	0.0	0.0	14.0	26.1	36.4	45.2	52.8	59.3	65.0	83.3	92.0	23
24	0.0	0.0	0.0	0.0	14.0	26.0	36.3	45.1	52.7	59.2	80.5	90.7	24
25	0.0	0.0	0.0	0.0	0.0	13.9	25.9	36.2	45.0	52.6	77.4	89.2	25
26	0.0	0.0	0.0	0.0	0.0	0.0	13.9	25.8	36.1	44.9	73.7	87.4	26
27	0.0	0.0	0.0	0.0	0.0	0.0	0.0	13.8	25.8	36.0	69.5	85.4	27
28	0.0	0.0	0.0	0.0	0.0	0.0	0.0	0.0	13.8	25.7	64.5	83.0	28
29	0.0	0.0	0.0	0.0	0.0	0.0	0.0	0.0	0.0	13.8	58.8	80.3	29
30	0.0	0.0	0.0	0.0	0.0	0.0	0.0	0.0	0.0	0.0	52.2	77.1	30
31	0.0	0.0	0.0	0.0	0.0	0.0	0.0	0.0	0.0	0.0	44.6	73.5	31
32	0.0	0.0	0.0	0.0	0.0	0.0	0.0	0.0	0.0	0.0	35.8	69.2	32
33	0.0	0.0	0.0	0.0	0.0	0.0	0.0	0.0	0.0	0.0	25.5	64.3	33
34	0.0	0.0	0.0	0.0	0.0	0.0	0.0	0.0	0.0	0.0	13.7	58.7	34
35	0.0	0.0	0.0	0.0	0.0	0.0	0.0	0.0	0.0	0.0	0.0	52.1	35
36	0.0	0.0	0.0	0.0	0.0	0.0	0.0	0.0	0.0	0.0	0.0	44.5	36
37	0.0	0.0	0.0	0.0	0.0	0.0	0.0	0.0	0.0	0.0	0.0	35.7	37
38	0.0	0.0	0.0	0.0	0.0	0.0	0.0	0.0	0.0	0.0	0.0	25.5	38
39	0.0	0.0	0.0	0.0	0.0	0.0	0.0	0.0	0.0	0.0	0.0	13.6	39

INCOME CONVERSION

HOUR	WEEK	MONTH	YEAR	HOUR	WEEK	MONTH	YEAR
4.00	160.00	693.33	8320.00	17.00	680.00	2946.67	35360.00
4.25	170.00	736.67	8840.00	17.25	690.00	2990.00	35880.00
4.50	180.00	780.00	9360.00	17.50	700.00	3033.33	36400.00
4.75	190.00	823.33	9880.00	17.75	710.00	3076.67	36920.00
5.00	200.00	866.67	10400.00	18.00	720.00	3120.00	37440.00
5.25	210.00	910.00	10920.00	18.25	730.00	3163.33	37960.00
5.50	220.00	953.33	11440.00	18.50	740.00	3206.67	38480.00
5.75	230.00	996.67	11960.00	18.75	750.00	3250.00	39000.00
6.00	240.00	1040.00	12480.00	19.00	760.00	3293.33	39520.00
6.25	250.00	1083.33	13000.00	19.25	770.00	3336.67	40040.00
6.50	260.00	1126.67	13520.00	19.50	780.00	3380.00	40560.00
6.75	270.00	1170.00	14040.00	19.75	790.00	3423.33	41080.00
7.00	280.00	1213.33	14560.00	20.00	800.00	3466.67	41600.00
7.25	290.00	1256.67	15080.00	20.25	810.00	3510.00	42120.00
7.50	300.00	1300.00	15600.00	20.50	820.00	3553.33	42640.00
7.75	310.00	1343.33	16120.00	20.75	830.00	3596.67	43160.00
8.00	320.00	1386.67	16640.00	21.00	840.00	3640.00	43680.00
8.25	330.00	1430.00	17160.00	21.25	850.00	3683.33	44200.00
8.50	340.00	1473.33	17680.00	21.50	860.00	3726.67	44720.00
8.75	350.00	1516.67	18200.00	21.75	870.00	3770.00	45240.00
9.00	360.00	1560.00	18720.00	22.00	880.00	3813.33	45760.00
9.25	370.00	1603.33	19240.00	22.25	890.00	3856.67	46280.00
9.50	380.00	1646.67	19760.00	22.50	900.00	3900.00	46800.00
9.75	390.00	1690.00	20280.00	22.75	910.00	3943.33	47320.00
10.00	400.00	1733.33	20800.00	23.00	920.00	3986.67	47840.00
10.25	410.00	1776.67	21320.00	23.25	930.00	4030.00	48360.00
10.50	420.00	1820.00	21840.00	23.50	940.00	4073.33	48880.00
10.75	430.00	1863.33	22360.00	23.75	950.00	4116.67	49400.00
11.00	440.00	1906.67	22880.00	24.00	960.00	4160.00	49920.00
11.25	450.00	1950.00	23400.00	24.25	970.00	4203.33	50440.00
11.50	460.00	1993.33	23920.00	24.50	980.00	4246.67	50960.00
11.75	470.00	2036.67	24440.00	24.75	990.00	4290.00	51480.00
12.00	480.00	2080.00	24960.00	25.00	1000.00	4333.33	52000.00
12.25	490.00	2123.33	25480.00	25.25	1010.00	4376.67	52520.00
12.50	500.00	2166.67	26000.00	25.50	1020.00	4420.00	53040.00
12.75	510.00	2210.00	26520.00	25.75	1030.00	4463.33	53560.00
13.00	520.00	2253.33	27040.00	26.00	1040.00	4506.67	54080.00
13.25	530.00	2296.67	27560.00	26.25	1050.00	4550.00	54600.00
13.50	540.00	2340.00	28080.00	26.50	1060.00	4593.33	55120.00
13.75	550.00	2383.33	28600.00	26.75	1070.00	4636.67	55640.00
14.00	560.00	2426.67	29120.00	27.00	1080.00	4680.00	56160.00
14.25	570.00	2470.00	29640.00	27.25	1090.00	4723.33	56680.00
14.50	580.00	2513.33	30160.00	27.50	1100.00	4766.67	57200.00
14.75	590.00	2556.67	30680.00	27.75	1110.00	4810.00	57720.00
15.00	600.00	2600.00	31200.00	28.00	1120.00	4853.33	58240.00
15.25	610.00	2643.33	31720.00	28.25	1130.00	4896.67	58760.00
15.50	620.00	2686.67	32240.00	28.50	1140.00	4940.00	59280.00
15.75	630.00	2730.00	32760.00	28.75	1150.00	4983.33	59800.00
16.00	640.00	2773.33	33280.00	29.00	1160.00	5026.67	60320.00
16.25	650.00	2816.67	33800.00	29.25	1170.00	5070.00	60840.00
16.50	660.00	2860.00	34320.00	29.50	1180.00	5113.33	61360.00
16.75	670.00	2903.33	34840.00	29.75	1190.00	5156.67	61880.00

EQUITY BUILD-UP
IN PERCENT OF ORIGINAL LOAN AMOUNT
FOR FIRST 15 YEARS

15 YEAR TERM

YEAR	8% Int. Annual %	8% Int. Cum. %	8¼% Int. Annual %	8¼% Int. Cum. %	8½% Int. Annual %	8½% Int. Cum. %	8¾% Int. Annual %	8¾% Int. Cum. %
1	3.598	3.598	3.523	3.523	3.449	3.449	3.377	3.377
2	3.896	7.494	3.825	7.348	3.754	7.203	3.684	7.061
3	4.220	11.714	4.153	11.500	4.086	11.289	4.020	11.081
4	4.570	16.284	4.508	16.009	4.447	15.736	4.386	15.467
5	4.949	21.234	4.895	20.903	4.840	20.576	4.786	20.253
6	5.360	26.594	5.314	26.218	5.268	25.844	5.222	25.474
7	5.805	32.399	5.770	31.987	5.734	31.578	5.697	31.171
8	6.287	38.686	6.264	38.251	6.240	37.818	6.216	37.388
9	6.809	45.495	6.801	45.052	6.792	44.610	6.783	44.170
10	7.374	52.869	7.384	52.435	7.392	52.003	7.400	51.571
11	7.986	60.855	8.016	60.452	8.046	60.048	8.075	59.645
12	8.649	69.503	8.703	69.155	8.757	68.805	8.810	68.455
13	9.367	78.870	9.449	78.604	9.531	78.336	9.613	78.068
14	10.144	89.014	10.259	88.862	10.373	88.710	10.488	88.556
15	10.986	100.000	11.138	100.000	11.290	100.000	11.444	100.000

YEAR	9% Int. Annual %	9% Int. Cum. %	9¼% Int. Annual %	9¼% Int. Cum. %	9½% Int. Annual %	9½% Int. Cum. %	9¾% Int. Annual %	9¾% Int. Cum. %
1	3.305	3.305	3.235	3.235	3.166	3.166	3.098	3.098
2	3.615	6.921	3.547	6.783	3.480	6.647	3.414	6.513
3	3.955	10.875	3.890	10.673	3.826	10.473	3.763	10.275
4	4.326	15.201	4.265	14.938	4.206	14.678	4.146	14.421
5	4.731	19.932	4.677	19.615	4.623	19.301	4.569	18.991
6	5.175	25.107	5.128	24.743	5.082	24.383	5.035	24.026
7	5.661	30.768	5.624	30.367	5.586	29.969	5.548	29.574
8	6.192	36.959	6.166	36.533	6.141	36.110	6.114	35.688
9	6.772	43.732	6.762	43.295	6.750	42.860	6.738	42.426
10	7.408	51.139	7.414	50.709	7.420	50.279	7.425	49.851
11	8.103	59.242	8.130	58.839	8.156	58.436	8.182	58.033
12	8.863	68.105	8.915	67.753	8.966	67.402	9.016	67.049
13	9.694	77.799	9.775	77.528	9.856	77.257	9.936	76.985
14	10.603	88.402	10.719	88.247	10.834	88.091	10.949	87.934
15	11.598	100.000	11.753	100.000	11.909	100.000	12.066	100.000

YEAR	10% Int. Annual %	10% Int. Cum. %	10¼% Int. Annual %	10¼% Int. Cum. %	10½% Int. Annual %	10½% Int. Cum. %	10¾% Int. Annual %	10¾% Int. Cum. %
1	3.032	3.032	2.966	2.966	2.902	2.902	2.839	2.839
2	3.349	6.381	3.285	6.251	3.222	6.123	3.159	5.998
3	3.700	10.081	3.638	9.889	3.577	9.700	3.516	9.514
4	4.087	14.168	4.029	13.918	3.971	13.671	3.913	13.427
5	4.515	18.683	4.462	18.380	4.408	18.079	4.355	17.782
6	4.988	23.671	4.941	23.321	4.894	22.973	4.847	22.629
7	5.510	29.182	5.472	28.793	5.434	28.407	5.395	28.024
8	6.087	35.269	6.060	34.853	6.032	34.439	6.004	34.028
9	6.725	41.994	6.711	41.564	6.697	41.136	6.682	40.710
10	7.429	49.423	7.432	48.997	7.435	48.572	7.437	48.147
11	8.207	57.630	8.231	57.228	8.255	56.826	8.277	56.425
12	9.066	66.697	9.116	66.344	9.164	65.990	9.212	65.637
13	10.016	76.712	10.095	76.439	10.174	76.164	10.253	75.889
14	11.065	87.777	11.180	87.619	11.295	87.460	11.411	87.300
15	12.223	100.000	12.381	100.000	12.540	100.000	12.700	100.000

YEAR	11% Int. Annual %	11% Int. Cum. %	11¼% Int. Annual %	11¼% Int. Cum. %	11½% Int. Annual %	11½% Int. Cum. %	11¾% Int. Annual %	11¾% Int. Cum. %
1	2.776	2.776	2.715	2.715	2.655	2.655	2.596	2.596
2	3.098	5.874	3.037	5.752	2.977	5.633	2.919	5.515
3	3.456	9.330	3.397	9.149	3.338	8.971	3.281	8.795
4	3.856	13.186	3.799	12.949	3.743	12.714	3.687	12.483
5	4.302	17.488	4.250	17.198	4.197	16.911	4.145	16.628
6	4.800	22.289	4.753	21.951	4.706	21.617	4.659	21.287
7	5.356	27.644	5.316	27.267	5.277	26.894	5.237	26.524
8	5.975	33.619	5.946	33.214	5.916	32.810	5.886	32.410
9	6.667	40.286	6.651	39.864	6.634	39.444	6.617	39.027
10	7.438	47.724	7.439	47.303	7.438	46.883	7.437	46.464
11	8.299	56.023	8.320	55.623	8.340	55.223	8.360	54.824
12	9.259	65.283	9.306	64.929	9.352	64.575	9.397	64.220
13	10.331	75.614	10.408	75.337	10.486	75.060	10.562	74.783
14	11.526	87.140	11.642	86.979	11.757	86.817	11.872	86.655
15	12.860	100.000	13.021	100.000	13.183	100.000	13.345	100.000

YEAR	Annual %	Cum. %	Annual %	Cum. %	Annual %	Cum. %	Annual %	Cum. %
	12% Int.		12¼% Int.		12½% Int.		12¾% Int.	
1	2.539	2.539	2.482	2.482	2.426	2.426	2.371	2.371
2	2.861	5.399	2.804	5.285	2.747	5.174	2.692	5.064
3	3.223	8.623	3.167	8.452	3.111	8.285	3.056	8.120
4	3.632	12.255	3.577	12.030	3.523	11.808	3.469	11.589
5	4.093	16.348	4.041	16.071	3.990	15.798	3.939	15.528
6	4.612	20.960	4.565	20.636	4.518	20.316	4.471	19.999
7	5.197	26.156	5.157	25.793	5.116	25.432	5.076	25.075
8	5.856	32.012	5.825	31.618	5.794	31.226	5.762	30.837
9	6.599	38.611	6.580	38.198	6.561	37.787	6.541	37.378
10	7.435	46.046	7.433	45.631	7.430	45.216	7.426	44.804
11	8.378	54.425	8.396	54.027	8.413	53.630	8.430	53.233
12	9.441	63.866	9.485	63.512	9.528	63.157	9.570	62.803
13	10.638	74.504	10.714	74.226	10.789	73.946	10.864	73.667
14	11.998	86.492	12.103	86.328	12.218	86.164	12.333	86.000
15	13.508	100.000	13.672	100.000	13.836	100.000	14.000	100.000
	13% Int.		13¼% Int.		13½% Int.		13¾% Int.	
1	2.318	2.318	2.265	2.265	2.213	2.213	2.163	2.163
2	2.638	4.955	2.584	4.849	2.531	4.745	2.480	4.642
3	3.002	7.957	2.948	7.797	2.895	7.640	2.843	7.485
4	3.416	11.373	3.363	11.161	3.311	10.951	3.259	10.745
5	3.888	15.261	3.837	14.998	3.787	14.738	3.737	14.482
6	4.424	19.685	4.378	19.376	4.331	19.069	4.284	18.766
7	5.035	24.720	4.994	24.370	4.953	24.022	4.912	23.678
8	5.730	30.450	5.698	30.067	5.665	29.687	5.632	29.310
9	6.521	36.971	6.500	36.567	6.479	36.166	6.457	35.767
10	7.421	44.392	7.416	43.983	7.410	43.576	7.403	43.170
11	8.445	52.838	8.460	52.443	8.474	52.050	8.487	51.657
12	9.611	62.449	9.652	62.095	9.692	61.741	9.731	61.388
13	10.938	73.387	11.011	73.106	11.084	72.825	11.156	72.544
14	12.448	85.834	12.562	85.668	12.677	85.502	12.791	85.335
15	14.166	100.000	14.332	100.000	14.498	100.000	14.665	100.000
	14% Int.		14¼% Int.		14½% Int.		14¾% Int.	
1	2.113	2.113	2.064	2.064	2.017	2.017	1.970	1.970
2	2.429	4.542	2.378	4.443	2.329	4.346	2.281	4.250
3	2.791	7.333	2.740	7.183	2.690	7.036	2.641	6.891
4	3.208	10.541	3.158	10.341	3.107	10.143	3.058	9.949
5	3.687	14.229	3.638	13.979	3.589	13.732	3.541	13.489
6	4.238	18.467	4.192	18.171	4.146	17.878	4.100	17.589
7	4.871	23.338	4.830	23.000	4.788	22.666	4.747	22.336
8	5.598	28.936	5.565	28.565	5.531	28.197	5.496	27.832
9	6.434	35.370	6.411	34.976	6.388	34.585	6.364	34.196
10	7.395	42.766	7.387	42.364	7.378	41.963	7.369	41.565
11	8.500	51.266	8.511	50.875	8.522	50.486	8.532	50.098
12	9.769	61.035	9.807	60.682	9.844	60.329	9.880	59.977
13	11.228	72.263	11.299	71.981	11.370	71.699	11.440	71.417
14	12.905	85.168	13.019	85.000	13.132	84.832	13.246	84.663
15	14.832	100.000	15.000	100.000	15.168	100.000	15.337	100.000
	15% Int.		15¼% Int.		15½% Int.		15¾% Int.	
1	1.924	1.924	1.879	1.879	1.835	1.835	1.791	1.791
2	2.233	4.157	2.186	4.065	2.140	3.975	2.095	3.886
3	2.592	6.749	2.544	6.609	2.496	6.471	2.450	6.336
4	3.009	9.757	2.960	9.569	2.912	9.383	2.865	9.200
5	3.492	13.250	3.444	13.013	3.397	12.780	3.350	12.550
6	4.054	17.303	4.008	17.021	3.962	16.742	3.917	16.467
7	4.705	22.009	4.664	21.685	4.622	21.365	4.581	21.048
8	5.462	27.470	5.427	27.112	5.392	26.756	5.356	26.404
9	6.340	33.810	6.315	33.427	6.290	33.046	6.264	32.668
10	7.359	41.169	7.348	40.775	7.337	40.383	7.325	39.992
11	8.542	49.711	8.550	49.325	8.558	48.941	8.565	48.558
12	9.915	59.626	9.949	59.275	9.983	58.924	10.016	58.574
13	11.509	71.135	11.577	70.852	11.645	70.569	11.713	70.287
14	13.359	84.494	13.472	84.324	13.584	84.154	13.697	83.983
15	15.506	100.000	15.676	100.000	15.846	100.000	16.017	100.000

YEAR	8% Int. Annual %	Cum. %	8¼% Int. Annual %	Cum. %	8½% Int. Annual %	Cum. %	8¾% Int. Annual %	Cum. %
1	2.114	2.114	2.051	2.051	1.990	1.990	1.931	1.931
2	2.289	4.403	2.227	4.278	2.166	4.156	2.107	4.037
3	2.479	6.882	2.418	6.696	2.358	6.514	2.299	6.336
4	2.685	9.567	2.625	9.321	2.566	9.080	2.508	8.844
5	2.908	12.474	2.850	12.171	2.793	11.873	2.736	11.580
6	3.149	15.623	3.094	15.265	3.040	14.912	2.986	14.566
7	3.410	19.034	3.359	18.624	3.308	18.221	3.258	17.823
8	3.693	22.727	3.647	22.271	3.601	21.822	3.554	21.378
9	4.000	26.727	3.960	26.231	3.919	25.741	3.878	25.256
10	4.332	31.059	4.299	30.530	4.265	30.006	4.231	29.487
11	4.692	35.751	4.667	35.198	4.643	34.649	4.617	34.104
12	5.081	40.832	5.067	40.265	5.053	39.702	5.038	39.142
13	5.503	46.335	5.502	45.767	5.499	45.201	5.496	44.638
14	5.959	52.294	5.973	51.740	5.986	51.187	5.997	50.635
15	6.454	58.748	6.485	58.224	6.515	57.701	6.543	57.179

YEAR	9% Int. Annual %	Cum. %	9¼% Int. Annual %	Cum. %	9½% Int. Annual %	Cum. %	9¾% Int. Annual %	Cum. %
1	1.873	1.873	1.816	1.866	1.761	1.761	1.707	1.707
2	2.048	3.921	1.991	3.808	1.936	3.697	1.881	3.588
3	2.241	6.162	2.184	5.991	2.128	5.824	2.073	5.661
4	2.451	8.612	2.394	8.386	2.339	8.163	2.284	7.946
5	2.681	11.293	2.626	11.011	2.571	10.735	2.517	10.463
6	2.932	14.225	2.879	13.890	2.826	13.561	2.774	13.238
7	3.207	17.432	3.157	17.047	3.107	16.668	3.057	16.295
8	3.508	20.940	3.462	20.508	3.415	20.083	3.369	19.664
9	3.837	24.777	3.796	24.304	3.754	23.837	3.712	23.376
10	4.197	28.974	4.162	28.466	4.127	27.964	4.091	27.467
11	4.591	33.565	4.564	33.030	4.536	32.500	4.508	31.975
12	5.021	38.586	5.004	38.034	4.986	37.487	4.968	36.943
13	5.492	44.078	5.487	43.522	5.481	42.968	5.474	42.417
14	6.008	50.086	6.017	49.539	6.025	48.993	6.033	48.450
15	6.571	56.657	6.598	56.136	6.623	55.617	6.648	55.098

YEAR	10% Int. Annual %	Cum. %	10¼% Int. Annual %	Cum. %	10½% Int. Annual %	Cum. %	10¾% Int. Annual %	Cum. %
1	1.655	1.655	1.604	1.604	1.554	1.554	1.505	1.505
2	1.828	3.483	1.776	3.380	1.725	3.279	1.676	3.181
3	2.019	5.502	1.967	5.347	1.915	5.194	1.865	5.046
4	2.231	7.733	2.178	7.525	2.126	7.321	2.075	7.121
5	2.464	10.198	2.412	9.937	2.361	9.681	2.310	9.431
6	2.723	12.920	2.671	12.608	2.621	12.302	2.571	12.002
7	3.008	15.928	2.959	15.567	2.910	15.212	2.861	14.863
8	3.323	19.250	3.276	18.843	3.230	18.442	3.184	18.048
9	3.671	22.921	3.628	22.472	3.586	22.029	3.544	21.592
10	4.055	26.976	4.018	26.490	3.982	26.010	3.944	25.536
11	4.479	31.455	4.450	30.940	4.420	30.431	4.390	29.926
12	4.949	36.404	4.928	35.869	4.907	35.338	4.886	34.812
13	5.467	41.870	5.458	41.327	5.448	40.786	5.438	40.250
14	6.039	47.909	6.044	47.371	6.049	46.835	6.052	46.302
15	6.671	54.581	6.694	54.065	6.715	53.551	6.736	53.038

YEAR	11% Int. Annual %	Cum. %	11¼% Int. Annual %	Cum. %	11½% Int. Annual %	Cum. %	11¾% Int. Annual %	Cum. %
1	1.458	1.458	1.412	1.412	1.368	1.368	1.324	1.324
2	1.627	3.085	1.580	2.992	1.534	2.901	1.489	2.813
3	1.815	4.901	1.767	4.759	1.720	4.621	1.673	4.486
4	2.025	6.926	1.976	6.735	1.928	6.549	1.881	6.367
5	2.260	9.186	2.210	8.946	2.162	8.711	2.114	8.481
6	2.521	11.707	2.472	11.418	2.424	11.135	2.376	10.857
7	2.813	14.520	2.765	14.184	2.718	13.853	2.671	13.528
8	3.139	17.659	3.093	17.277	3.048	16.901	3.002	16.530
9	3.502	21.161	3.459	20.736	3.417	20.318	3.375	19.905
10	3.907	25.068	3.869	24.606	3.831	24.149	3.793	23.698
11	4.359	29.427	4.328	28.933	4.296	28.445	4.264	27.962
12	4.864	34.291	4.841	33.774	4.817	33.262	4.793	32.755
13	5.426	39.717	5.414	39.188	5.401	38.663	5.387	38.142
14	6.054	45.772	6.056	45.244	6.056	44.719	6.055	44.198
15	6.755	52.527	6.773	52.017	6.790	51.510	6.807	51.004

YEAR	Annual %	Cum. %	Annual %	Cum. %	Annual %	Cum. %	Annual %	Cum. %
	12% Int.		12¼% Int.		12½% Int.		12¾% Int.	
1	1.282	1.282	1.241	1.241	1.201	1.201	1.162	1.162
2	1.445	2.727	1.402	2.643	1.360	2.561	1.319	2.481
3	1.628	4.354	1.583	4.226	1.540	4.101	1.498	3.979
4	1.834	6.189	1.789	6.015	1.744	5.845	1.700	5.679
5	2.067	8.256	2.021	8.035	1.975	7.820	1.930	7.609
6	2.329	10.585	2.282	10.318	2.236	10.056	2.191	9.800
7	2.624	13.209	2.578	12.896	2.533	12.589	2.487	12.287
8	2.957	16.166	2.912	15.809	2.868	15.457	2.824	15.111
9	3.332	19.499	3.290	19.099	3.248	18.704	3.205	18.316
10	3.755	23.254	3.716	22.815	3.678	22.382	3.639	21.955
11	4.231	27.485	4.198	27.013	4.165	26.547	4.131	26.086
12	4.768	32.253	4.742	31.755	4.716	31.263	4.689	30.776
13	5.372	37.625	5.357	37.112	5.341	36.604	5.324	36.099
14	6.054	43.679	6.051	43.164	6.048	42.652	6.043	42.143
15	6.822	50.501	6.836	49.999	6.849	49.500	6.861	49.003
	13% Int.		13¼% Int.		13½% Int.		13¾% Int.	
1	1.124	1.124	1.088	1.088	1.052	1.052	1.017	1.017
2	1.280	2.404	1.241	2.328	1.203	2.255	1.166	2.184
3	1.456	3.860	1.416	3.744	1.376	3.631	1.337	3.521
4	1.657	5.517	1.615	5.359	1.574	5.205	1.533	5.054
5	1.886	7.403	1.842	7.202	1.800	7.005	1.758	6.812
6	2.146	9.549	2.102	9.304	2.058	9.063	2.015	8.828
7	2.442	11.992	2.398	11.702	2.354	11.417	2.311	11.139
8	2.780	14.771	2.736	14.438	2.692	14.110	2.649	13.788
9	3.163	17.935	3.121	17.559	3.079	17.189	3.037	16.825
10	3.600	21.534	3.561	21.119	3.522	20.711	3.482	20.308
11	4.097	25.631	4.062	25.182	4.028	24.738	3.993	24.300
12	4.662	30.293	4.635	29.816	4.606	29.344	4.577	28.878
13	5.306	35.599	5.287	35.104	5.268	34.612	5.248	34.126
14	6.038	41.637	6.032	41.136	6.025	40.637	6.017	40.143
15	6.872	48.509	6.882	48.017	6.891	47.528	6.899	47.041
	14% Int.		14¼% Int.		14½% Int.		14¾% Int.	
1	0.984	0.984	0.951	0.951	0.919	0.919	0.889	0.889
2	1.131	2.115	1.096	2.047	1.062	1.982	1.029	1.918
3	1.300	3.414	1.263	3.310	1.227	3.208	1.192	3.109
4	1.494	4.908	1.455	4.765	1.417	4.625	1.380	4.489
5	1.717	6.624	1.676	6.441	1.637	6.262	1.598	6.087
6	1.973	8.598	1.931	8.372	1.890	8.152	1.850	7.936
7	2.268	10.865	2.225	10.598	2.183	10.335	2.142	10.078
8	2.606	13.472	2.564	13.162	2.522	12.857	2.480	12.558
9	2.996	16.467	2.954	16.116	2.913	15.770	2.872	15.430
10	3.443	19.911	3.404	19.519	3.364	19.134	3.325	18.756
11	3.957	23.868	3.922	23.441	3.886	23.020	3.850	22.605
12	4.548	28.416	4.519	27.960	4.488	27.509	4.458	27.063
13	5.227	33.644	5.206	33.166	5.184	32.693	5.162	32.225
14	6.008	39.652	5.999	39.164	5.988	38.681	5.977	38.201
15	6.905	46.557	6.911	46.076	6.916	45.597	6.920	45.122
	15% Int.		15¼% Int.		15½% Int.		15¾% Int.	
1	0.859	0.859	0.830	0.830	0.802	0.802	0.775	0.775
2	0.997	1.856	0.966	1.796	0.935	1.737	0.906	1.681
3	1.157	3.013	1.124	2.920	1.091	2.829	1.059	2.740
4	1.343	4.357	1.308	4.227	1.273	4.102	1.239	3.979
5	1.559	5.916	1.522	5.749	1.485	5.586	1.449	5.428
6	1.810	7.726	1.771	7.520	1.732	7.319	1.694	7.122
7	2.101	9.827	2.060	9.580	2.020	9.339	1.981	9.103
8	2.439	12.265	2.398	11.978	2.357	11.696	2.317	11.420
9	2.831	15.096	2.790	14.768	2.749	14.445	2.709	14.129
10	3.286	18.382	3.246	18.014	3.207	17.652	3.168	17.297
11	3.814	22.196	3.778	21.792	3.741	21.394	3.704	21.001
12	4.427	26.622	4.396	26.187	4.364	25.757	4.332	25.333
13	5.139	31.761	5.115	31.302	5.091	30.848	5.066	30.399
14	5.965	37.726	5.952	37.254	5.938	36.786	5.924	36.322
15	6.924	44.649	6.926	44.180	6.927	43.713	6.927	43.250

EQUITY BUILD-UP
IN PERCENT OF ORIGINAL LOAN AMOUNT
FOR FIRST 15 YEARS

YEAR	Annual %	Cum. %	Annual %	Cum. %	Annual %	Cum. %	Annual %	Cum. %
	8% Int.		8¼% Int.		8½% Int.		8¾% Int.	
1	1.309	1.309	1.258	1.258	1.209	1.209	1.162	1.162
2	1.418	2.727	1.366	2.624	1.316	2.525	1.267	2.429
3	1.535	4.262	1.483	4.108	1.432	3.957	1.383	3.812
4	1.663	5.925	1.610	5.718	1.559	5.516	1.509	5.321
5	1.801	7.726	1.748	7.466	1.697	7.213	1.646	6.967
6	1.950	9.676	1.898	9.364	1.847	9.060	1.796	8.763
7	2.112	11.789	2.061	11.425	2.010	11.070	1.960	10.723
8	2.288	14.076	2.237	13.662	2.188	13.257	2.138	12.861
9	2.477	16.554	2.429	16.091	2.381	15.638	2.333	15.195
10	2.683	19.237	2.637	18.728	2.591	18.229	2.546	17.740
11	2.906	22.142	2.863	21.591	2.820	21.050	2.778	20.518
12	3.147	25.289	3.108	24.700	3.070	24.120	3.031	23.549
13	3.408	28.697	3.375	28.075	3.341	27.461	3.307	26.855
14	3.691	32.388	3.664	31.739	3.636	31.097	3.608	30.463
15	3.997	36.386	3.978	35.717	3.958	35.055	3.937	34.400
	9% Int.		9¼% Int.		9½% Int.		9¾% Int.	
1	1.116	1.116	1.071	1.071	1.028	1.028	0.987	0.987
2	1.220	2.336	1.175	2.246	1.130	2.159	1.088	2.075
3	1.335	3.671	1.288	3.534	1.243	3.401	1.199	3.273
4	1.460	5.131	1.412	4.946	1.366	4.767	1.321	4.594
5	1.597	6.728	1.549	6.495	1.502	6.269	1.455	6.049
6	1.747	8.474	1.698	8.193	1.651	7.919	1.604	7.653
7	1.911	10.385	1.862	10.055	1.814	9.734	1.767	9.421
8	2.090	12.475	2.042	12.097	1.994	11.728	1.948	11.368
9	2.286	14.761	2.239	14.336	2.192	13.921	2.146	13.515
10	2.500	17.261	2.455	16.791	2.410	16.331	2.365	15.880
11	2.735	19.996	2.692	19.483	2.649	18.980	2.606	18.486
12	2.991	22.987	2.952	22.435	2.912	21.892	2.872	21.358
13	3.272	26.259	3.237	25.671	3.201	25.093	3.165	24.523
14	3.579	29.838	3.549	29.221	3.519	28.612	3.488	28.011
15	3.915	33.752	3.892	33.112	3.868	32.480	3.843	31.855
	10% Int.		10¼% Int.		10½% Int.		10¾% Int.	
1	0.947	0.947	0.908	0.908	0.871	0.871	0.835	0.835
2	1.046	1.993	1.006	1.915	0.967	1.839	0.930	1.765
3	1.156	3.149	1.114	3.029	1.074	2.913	1.035	2.800
4	1.277	4.426	1.234	4.263	1.192	4.105	1.152	3.952
5	1.410	5.836	1.367	5.629	1.324	5.429	1.282	5.234
6	1.558	7.394	1.513	7.143	1.470	6.898	1.427	6.661
7	1.721	9.116	1.676	8.819	1.632	8.530	1.588	8.248
8	1.902	11.017	1.856	10.675	1.811	10.341	1.767	10.016
9	2.101	13.118	2.056	12.730	2.011	12.352	1.967	11.983
10	2.321	15.439	2.276	15.007	2.233	14.585	2.189	14.172
11	2.564	18.002	2.521	17.528	2.479	17.063	2.436	16.608
12	2.832	20.834	2.792	20.320	2.752	19.815	2.711	19.319
13	3.129	23.963	3.092	23.412	3.055	22.870	3.018	22.337
14	3.456	27.419	3.424	26.836	3.392	26.261	3.359	25.696
15	3.818	31.238	3.792	30.628	3.765	30.027	3.738	29.434
	11% Int.		11¼% Int.		11½% Int.		11¾% Int.	
1	0.801	0.801	0.768	0.768	0.736	0.736	0.705	0.705
2	0.894	1.695	0.859	1.626	0.825	1.560	0.792	1.497
3	0.997	2.692	0.960	2.587	0.925	2.485	0.890	2.387
4	1.112	3.804	1.074	3.661	1.037	3.522	1.001	3.388
5	1.241	5.045	1.201	4.862	1.163	4.685	1.125	4.513
6	1.385	6.430	1.344	6.206	1.304	5.989	1.265	5.778
7	1.545	7.975	1.503	7.709	1.462	7.450	1.421	7.199
8	1.724	9.699	1.681	9.390	1.639	9.089	1.598	8.797
9	1.923	11.622	1.880	11.270	1.838	10.927	1.796	10.593
10	2.146	13.768	2.103	13.373	2.061	12.988	2.019	12.611
11	2.394	16.162	2.352	15.725	2.310	15.298	2.269	14.880
12	2.671	18.833	2.631	18.356	2.591	17.889	2.550	17.431
13	2.980	21.813	2.943	21.299	2.905	20.794	2.867	20.297
14	3.325	25.138	3.291	24.590	3.257	24.051	3.222	23.520
15	3.710	28.848	3.684	28.271	3.652	27.703	3.622	27.142

YEAR	Annual %	Cum. %	Annual %	Cum. %	Annual %	Cum. %	Annual %	Cum. %
	12% Int.		12¼% Int.		12½% Int.		12¾% Int.	
1	0.675	0.675	0.646	0.646	0.619	0.619	0.592	0.592
2	0.761	1.436	0.730	1.377	0.701	1.320	0.673	1.265
3	0.857	2.293	0.825	2.201	0.794	2.113	0.764	2.029
4	0.966	3.259	0.932	3.133	0.899	3.012	0.867	2.895
5	1.088	4.347	1.053	4.186	1.018	4.030	0.984	3.879
6	1.226	5.573	1.189	5.375	1.153	5.183	1.117	4.996
7	1.382	6.955	1.343	6.718	1.305	6.488	1.268	6.264
8	1.557	8.512	1.517	8.235	1.478	7.966	1.440	7.704
9	1.755	10.267	1.714	9.949	1.674	9.639	1.634	9.338
10	1.977	12.244	1.936	11.885	1.895	11.535	1.855	11.193
11	2.228	14.471	2.187	14.072	2.146	13.681	2.106	13.299
12	2.510	16.982	2.470	16.542	2.430	16.112	2.391	15.690
13	2.829	19.811	2.791	19.333	2.752	18.864	2.714	18.404
14	3.187	22.998	3.152	22.485	3.117	21.981	3.081	21.485
15	3.592	26.590	3.561	26.046	3.530	25.510	3.498	24.983
	13% Int.		13¼% Int.		13½% Int.		13¾% Int.	
1	0.567	0.567	0.543	0.543	0.519	0.519	0.497	0.497
2	0.645	1.212	0.619	1.162	0.594	1.113	0.569	1.066
3	0.734	1.947	0.706	1.868	0.679	1.792	0.653	1.718
4	0.836	2.782	0.806	2.673	0.776	2.568	0.749	2.467
5	0.951	3.733	0.919	3.593	0.888	3.456	0.858	3.325
6	1.082	4.816	1.049	4.641	1.016	4.472	0.984	4.308
7	1.232	6.048	1.196	5.837	1.162	5.633	1.128	5.436
8	1.402	7.449	1.365	7.202	1.328	6.962	1.293	6.729
9	1.595	9.045	1.557	8.759	1.519	8.481	1.482	8.211
10	1.815	10.860	1.776	10.535	1.738	10.219	1.699	9.910
11	2.066	12.926	2.026	12.562	1.987	12.206	1.948	11.859
12	2.351	15.277	2.312	14.874	2.273	14.479	2.234	14.093
13	2.676	17.953	2.638	17.511	2.599	17.078	2.561	16.654
14	3.045	20.998	3.009	20.520	2.973	20.051	2.936	19.590
15	3.465	24.464	3.433	23.953	3.400	23.451	3.367	22.957
	14% Int.		14¼% Int.		14½% Int.		14¾% Int.	
1	0.475	0.475	0.454	0.454	0.434	0.434	0.415	0.415
2	0.546	1.021	0.523	0.977	0.501	0.935	0.480	0.895
3	0.627	1.648	0.603	1.580	0.579	1.514	0.556	1.452
4	0.721	2.369	0.694	2.274	0.669	2.183	0.644	2.096
5	0.829	3.197	0.800	3.074	0.773	2.956	0.746	2.841
6	0.952	4.150	0.922	3.996	0.892	3.848	0.864	3.705
7	1.095	5.244	1.062	5.059	1.031	4.879	1.000	4.705
8	1.258	6.502	1.224	6.283	1.190	6.069	1.158	5.862
9	1.446	7.948	1.410	7.693	1.375	7.444	1.341	7.203
10	1.662	9.610	1.625	9.317	1.588	9.032	1.552	8.755
11	1.910	11.520	1.872	11.189	1.834	10.867	1.797	10.552
12	2.195	13.715	2.157	13.346	2.119	12.986	2.081	12.633
13	2.523	16.238	2.485	15.831	2.447	15.433	2.410	15.043
14	2.900	19.138	2.863	18.695	2.827	18.260	2.790	17.833
15	3.333	22.471	3.299	21.994	3.265	21.525	3.231	21.063
	15% Int.		15¼% Int.		15½% Int.		15¾% Int.	
1	0.396	0.396	0.379	0.379	0.362	0.362	0.346	0.346
2	0.460	0.857	0.441	0.820	0.422	0.784	0.404	0.750
3	0.534	1.391	0.513	1.333	0.493	1.277	0.473	1.223
4	0.620	2.011	0.597	1.930	0.575	1.851	0.553	1.776
5	0.720	2.731	0.695	2.624	0.670	2.521	0.646	2.422
6	0.835	3.566	0.808	3.432	0.782	3.303	0.756	3.178
7	0.970	4.536	0.940	4.373	0.912	4.215	0.884	4.062
8	1.126	5.662	1.094	5.467	1.064	5.279	1.034	5.096
9	1.307	6.968	1.273	6.741	1.241	6.520	1.209	6.305
10	1.517	8.485	1.482	8.222	1.447	7.967	1.414	7.718
11	1.761	10.246	1.724	9.947	1.688	9.655	1.653	9.372
12	2.044	12.289	2.006	11.953	1.970	11.625	1.933	11.305
13	2.372	14.661	2.335	14.288	2.297	13.922	2.261	13.565
14	2.753	17.415	2.717	17.004	2.680	16.602	2.643	16.209
15	3.198	20.610	3.161	20.166	3.126	19.729	3.091	19.300

YEAR	Annual %	Cum. %	Annual %	Cum. %	Annual %	Cum. %	Annual %	Cum. %
	8% Int.		8¼% Int.		8½% Int.		8¾% Int.	
1	0.835	0.835	0.795	0.795	0.756	0.756	0.719	0.719
2	0.905	1.740	0.863	1.658	0.823	1.579	0.784	1.503
3	0.980	2.720	0.937	2.595	0.896	2.474	0.856	2.359
4	1.061	3.781	1.017	3.612	0.975	3.449	0.934	3.292
5	1.149	4.930	1.104	4.716	1.061	4.510	1.019	4.311
6	1.245	6.175	1.199	5.915	1.155	5.664	1.111	5.423
7	1.348	7.523	1.302	7.217	1.257	6.921	1.213	6.635
8	1.460	8.982	1.413	8.630	1.368	8.289	1.323	7.959
9	1.581	10.563	1.534	10.164	1.489	9.777	1.444	9.402
10	1.712	12.275	1.666	11.830	1.620	11.397	1.575	10.978
11	1.854	14.130	1.809	13.639	1.763	13.161	1.719	12.696
12	2.008	16.138	1.964	15.602	1.919	15.080	1.875	14.572
13	2.175	18.312	2.132	17.734	2.089	17.169	2.046	16.618
14	2.355	20.668	2.314	20.048	2.274	19.443	2.233	18.851
15	2.551	23.218	2.513	22.561	2.475	21.917	2.436	21.287
	9% Int.		9¼% Int.		9½% Int.		9¾% Int.	
1	0.683	0.683	0.649	0.649	0.617	0.617	0.586	0.586
2	0.747	1.430	0.712	1.361	0.678	1.294	0.645	1.231
3	0.817	2.248	0.781	2.142	0.745	2.040	0.711	1.942
4	0.894	3.142	0.856	2.997	0.819	2.859	0.784	2.726
5	0.978	4.120	0.938	3.936	0.900	3.759	0.864	3.589
6	1.070	5.190	1.029	4.965	0.990	4.749	0.952	4.541
7	1.170	6.360	1.128	6.093	1.088	5.837	1.049	5.599
8	1.280	7.639	1.237	7.331	1.196	7.033	1.156	6.745
9	1.400	9.039	1.357	8.687	1.315	8.347	1.273	8.018
10	1.531	10.570	1.488	10.175	1.445	9.792	1.403	9.421
11	1.675	12.245	1.631	11.807	1.589	11.381	1.546	10.968
12	1.832	14.077	1.789	13.595	1.746	13.127	1.704	12.672
13	2.004	16.081	1.961	15.557	1.919	15.046	1.878	14.549
14	2.192	18.272	2.151	17.708	2.110	17.156	2.069	16.619
15	2.397	20.670	2.358	20.066	2.319	19.476	2.280	18.899
	10% Int.		10¼% Int.		10½% Int.		10¾% Int.	
1	0.556	0.556	0.528	0.528	0.501	0.501	0.475	0.475
2	0.614	1.170	0.584	1.112	0.556	1.056	0.528	1.003
3	0.678	1.848	0.647	1.759	0.617	1.673	0.588	1.591
4	0.749	2.598	0.717	2.475	0.685	2.358	0.654	2.246
5	0.828	3.426	0.794	3.269	0.760	3.118	0.728	2.974
6	0.915	4.340	0.879	4.148	0.844	3.962	0.811	3.785
7	1.010	5.351	0.973	5.121	0.937	4.900	0.902	4.687
8	1.116	6.467	1.078	6.199	1.040	5.940	1.004	5.691
9	1.233	7.700	1.194	7.392	1.155	7.095	1.118	6.808
10	1.362	9.062	1.322	8.714	1.282	8.378	1.244	8.052
11	1.505	10.567	1.464	10.178	1.424	9.801	1.384	9.436
12	1.662	12.229	1.621	11.799	1.581	11.382	1.541	10.977
13	1.836	14.066	1.795	13.595	1.755	13.137	1.715	12.692
14	2.029	16.094	1.988	15.583	1.948	15.085	1.908	14.600
15	2.241	18.335	2.202	17.785	2.163	17.248	2.124	16.724
	11% Int.		11¼% Int.		11½% Int.		11¾% Int.	
1	0.450	0.450	0.427	0.427	0.404	0.404	0.383	0.383
2	0.502	0.952	0.477	0.904	0.453	0.858	0.431	0.814
3	0.560	1.513	0.534	1.438	0.508	1.366	0.484	1.298
4	0.625	2.138	0.597	2.035	0.570	1.936	0.544	1.842
5	0.698	2.835	0.668	2.703	0.639	2.575	0.612	2.453
6	0.778	3.614	0.747	3.449	0.717	3.292	0.687	3.141
7	0.868	4.482	0.835	4.285	0.804	4.096	0.773	3.914
8	0.969	5.451	0.934	5.219	0.901	4.997	0.869	4.782
9	1.081	6.532	1.045	6.264	1.010	6.007	0.976	5.758
10	1.206	7.737	1.169	7.433	1.133	7.140	1.097	6.856
11	1.345	9.083	1.307	8.741	1.270	8.410	1.234	8.089
12	1.501	10.584	1.462	10.203	1.424	9.834	1.387	9.476
13	1.675	12.259	1.636	11.839	1.597	11.431	1.558	11.034
14	1.869	14.128	1.829	13.668	1.790	13.221	1.752	12.786
15	2.085	16.213	2.046	15.714	2.008	15.229	1.969	14.755

YEAR	Annual %	Cum. %	Annual %	Cum. %	Annual %	Cum. %	Annual %	Cum. %
	12% Int.		12¼% Int.		12½% Int.		12¾% Int.	
1	0.363	0.363	0.344	0.344	0.325	0.325	0.308	0.308
2	0.409	0.772	0.388	0.732	0.368	0.694	0.350	0.657
3	0.461	1.233	0.438	1.170	0.417	1.111	0.397	1.054
4	0.519	1.752	0.495	1.666	0.472	1.583	0.450	1.505
5	0.585	2.337	0.560	2.225	0.535	2.118	0.511	2.016
6	0.659	2.996	0.632	2.857	0.606	2.724	0.581	2.597
7	0.743	3.739	0.714	3.571	0.686	3.410	0.659	3.256
8	0.837	4.576	0.807	4.378	0.777	4.187	0.748	4.004
9	0.943	5.519	0.911	5.289	0.880	5.067	0.849	4.853
10	1.063	6.582	1.029	6.318	0.996	6.063	0.964	5.817
11	1.198	7.780	1.163	7.480	1.128	7.191	1.094	6.912
12	1.350	9.129	1.313	8.793	1.278	8.469	1.242	8.154
13	1.521	10.650	1.483	10.277	1.447	9.915	1.411	9.565
14	1.714	12.363	1.676	11.953	1.638	11.553	1.601	11.166
15	1.931	14.294	1.893	13.845	1.855	13.409	1.818	12.984
	13% Int.		13¼% Int.		13½% Int.		13¾% Int.	
1	0.291	0.291	0.276	0.276	0.261	0.261	0.247	0.247
2	0.332	0.623	0.314	0.590	0.298	0.559	0.283	0.529
3	0.377	1.000	0.359	0.949	0.341	0.900	0.324	0.853
4	0.429	1.430	0.409	1.358	0.390	1.290	0.371	1.225
5	0.489	1.918	0.467	1.825	0.446	1.736	0.426	1.651
6	0.556	2.474	0.533	2.358	0.510	2.246	0.488	2.139
7	0.633	3.107	0.608	2.965	0.583	2.829	0.560	2.699
8	0.720	3.828	0.693	3.659	0.667	3.496	0.642	3.341
9	0.820	4.647	0.791	4.450	0.763	4.259	0.736	4.077
10	0.933	5.580	0.902	5.352	0.873	5.132	0.844	4.920
11	1.062	6.642	1.029	6.381	0.998	6.130	0.967	5.888
12	1.208	7.850	1.174	7.556	1.141	7.271	1.109	6.997
13	1.375	9.225	1.340	8.896	1.305	8.577	1.272	8.268
14	1.565	10.789	1.529	10.424	1.493	10.070	1.458	9.726
15	1.781	12.570	1.744	12.168	1.707	11.777	1.671	11.397
	14% Int.		14¼% Int.		14½% Int.		14¾% Int.	
1	0.233	0.233	0.220	0.220	0.208	0.208	0.197	0.197
2	0.268	0.501	0.254	0.474	0.240	0.449	0.228	0.424
3	0.308	0.809	0.292	0.766	0.278	0.726	0.264	0.688
4	0.354	1.163	0.337	1.103	0.321	1.047	0.305	0.993
5	0.407	1.569	0.388	1.492	0.370	1.417	0.353	1.347
6	0.467	2.037	0.447	1.939	0.428	1.845	0.409	1.756
7	0.537	2.574	0.515	2.454	0.494	2.340	0.474	2.230
8	0.617	3.191	0.594	3.048	0.571	2.910	0.549	2.779
9	0.710	3.901	0.684	3.732	0.659	3.570	0.635	3.414
10	0.816	4.716	0.788	4.520	0.762	4.331	0.736	4.150
11	0.937	5.654	0.908	5.428	0.880	5.211	0.852	5.002
12	1.077	6.731	1.046	6.475	1.016	6.227	0.986	5.988
13	1.238	7.969	1.206	7.680	1.174	7.401	1.142	7.130
14	1.423	9.393	1.389	9.069	1.356	8.756	1.322	8.453
15	1.636	11.028	1.600	10.670	1.566	10.322	1.531	9.984
	15% Int.		15¼% Int.		15½% Int.		15¾% Int.	
1	0.186	0.186	0.175	0.175	0.166	0.166	0.156	0.156
2	0.216	0.401	0.204	0.380	0.193	0.359	0.183	0.339
3	0.250	0.652	0.238	0.617	0.225	0.584	0.214	0.553
4	0.291	0.942	0.276	0.893	0.263	0.847	0.250	0.803
5	0.337	1.279	0.322	1.215	0.307	1.154	0.292	1.096
6	0.391	1.671	0.374	1.589	0.358	1.512	0.342	1.437
7	0.454	2.125	0.435	2.025	0.417	1.929	0.400	1.837
8	0.527	2.653	0.507	2.532	0.487	2.416	0.468	2.305
9	0.612	3.265	0.590	3.121	0.568	2.984	0.547	2.852
10	0.711	3.975	0.686	3.807	0.662	3.646	0.639	3.491
11	0.825	4.800	0.798	4.606	0.773	4.419	0.748	4.239
12	0.957	5.757	0.929	5.535	0.901	5.320	0.874	5.113
13	1.111	6.869	1.081	6.616	1.051	6.372	1.022	6.136
14	1.290	8.159	1.258	7.874	1.227	7.598	1.196	7.331
15	1.497	9.656	1.464	9.338	1.431	9.029	1.398	8.729

MEASUREMENTS

Computing Square Feet

SQ. FT.	ACRES	SQ. FT.	ACRES	SQ. FT.	ACRES	SQ. FT.	ACRES
1,742,400	40	217,800	5	26,136	0.6	3,049.2	0.07
1,306,800	30	174,240	4	21,780	0.5	2,613.6	0.06
871,200	20	130,680	3	17,424	0.4	2,178	0.05
435,600	10	87,120	2	13,068	0.3	1,742.4	0.04
392,040	9	43,560	1	8,712	0.2	1,306.8	0.03
348,480	8	39,204	0.9	4,356	0.1	871.2	0.02
304,920	7	34,848	0.8	3,920.4	0.09	435.6	0.01
261,360	6	30,492	0.7	3,484.8	0.08		

Number of Various Lots per Acre

For the purpose of subdivision, the number of lots
per acre given below must be adjusted to allow
for streets and other dedications.

LOT SIZE	Approx. No. of Lots per Acre	LOT SIZE	Approx. No. of Lots per Acre	LOT SIZE	Approx. No. of Lots per Acre	LOT SIZE	Approx. No. of Lots per Acre
25 × 100	17.42	30 × 100	14.52	50 × 100	8.71	100 × 100	4.35
25 × 120	14.52	30 × 120	12.1	50 × 120	7.26	100 × 120	3.63

Widths Times Depths Equaling One Acre

1 ACRE EQUALS		1 ACRE EQUALS		1 ACRE EQUALS	
Length	Width	Length	Width	Length	Width
16.5 ft.	2640. ft.	66. ft.	660. ft.	132. ft.	330. ft.
33.	1320.	75.	580.8	150.	290.4
50.	871.2	100.	435.6	208.71	208.71

Price Per Acre Produced by Certain Prices Per Square Foot

CENTS PER SQ. FOOT	$ PER ACRE	CENTS PER SQ. FOOT	$ PER ACRE	CENTS PER SQ. FOOT	$ PER ACRE	CENTS PER SQ. FOOT	$ PER ACRE
1¢	$ 435.60	9¢	$3,920.40	30¢	$13,068	70¢	$30,492
2	871.20	10	4,356.00	35	15,246	75	32,670
3	1,306.80	12	5,227.20	40	17,424	80	34,848
4	1,742.40	14	6,098.40	45	19,602	85	37,026
5	2,178.00	16	6,969.60	50	21,780	90	39,204
6	2,613.60	18	7,840.80	55	23,958	95	41,382
7	3,049.20	20	8,712.00	60	26,136	100	43,560
8	3,484.80	25	10,890.00	65	28,314		

1 Link = 7.92 Inches
1 Rod = 16½ Feet
5½ Yards = 25 Links
1 Chain = 66 Feet = 4 Rods = 100 Links
1 Furlong = 660 Feet = 40 Rods
1 Mile = 8 Furlongs = 320 Rods = 80 Chains = 5280 Feet
1 Square Mile = 1 Section = 640 Acres
1 Township = 36 Sections or square miles
1 Sq. Rod = 272¼ Sq. Feet = 30¼ Sq. Yards
1 Acre = 43560 Square Feet
1 Acre = 160 Square Rods
1 Acre is about 208¾ Feet Square
1 Acre is 8 Rods × 20 Rods (or any two numbers of rods whose product is 160)

ONE SECTION OF LAND CONTAINS ONE SQUARE MILE OR 640 ACRES

DETERMINING SQUARE FOOTAGE

a = area   b = base   h = height

① SQUARES

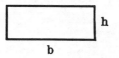

$$a = b \times h$$

② RECTANGLES

$$a = b \times h$$

③ PARALLELOGRAMS
(4-sided figure with parallel opposite sides)

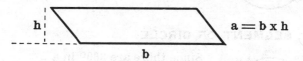

$$a = b \times h$$

④ TRAPEZOID
(4-sided figure with only 2 parallel sides)

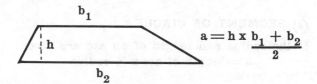

$$a = h \times \frac{b_1 + b_2}{2}$$

⑤ TRIANGLES WITH 90° ANGLE

$$a = \tfrac{1}{2}(b \times h)$$

⑥ TRIANGLES WITHOUT 90° ANGLE

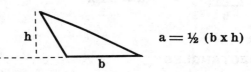

$$a = \tfrac{1}{2}(b \times h)$$

⑦ CIRCLE

R = radius

$a = R^2 \times 3.1416$

If radius is 14 ft.,

$a = 14 \times 14 \times 3.1416 = 615.75$

⑧ SEGMENT OF CIRCLE

Since there are 360° in a circle, the area of a 60° section is $\frac{60}{360}$, or $\frac{1}{6}$ of the entire circle.

⑨ SEGMENT OF CIRCLE

If the radius and length of an arc are given:

$$a = \text{length of arc} \times \tfrac{1}{2} \text{ radius}$$

METRIC MEASUREMENTS AND CONVERSIONS

DISTANCE

km = kilometer   cm = centimeter

m = meter   mm = millimeter

dm = decimeter

	km	m	dm	cm	mm	mile	yard	foot	inch
1 km	1	1000	10,000	100,000	1,000,000	0.6214	1,093.64	3280.9	
1 m	$\frac{1}{1000}$	1	10	100	1,000	0.00062	1.0936	3.2809	39.371
1 dm	$\frac{1}{10,000}$	$\frac{1}{10}$	1	10	100		0.1094	0.3281	3.9371
1 cm		$\frac{1}{100}$	$\frac{1}{10}$	1	10		0.0109	0.0328	0.3937
1 mm		$\frac{1}{1000}$	$\frac{1}{100}$	$\frac{1}{10}$	1			0.0033	0.0394
1 mile	1.6093	1609.33				1	1760	5280	63360
1 yard		0.9144	9.1438	91.438	914.38		1	3	36
1 foot		0.3048	3.0479	30.479	304.79		$\frac{1}{3}$	1	12
1 inch		0.0254	0.254	2.54	25.4		0.0277	0.0833	1

VOLUME

1 cu. yd = 0.7646 cu. m   1 cu. m = 1.308 cu. yd

1 cu. ft. = 0.0283 cu. m   1 cu. m = 35.31 cu. ft.

LIQUID VOLUME

10 milliliters = 1 centiliter = 0.338 fluid ounce

10 centiliters = 1 deciliter = 0.845 liquid gill

10 deciliters = 1 liter = 1.0567 liquid quarts

10 liters = 1 dekaliter = 2.6417 liquid gallons

10 dekaliters = 1 hectoliter = 2.8375 U.S. bu.

10 hectoliters = 1 kiloliter = 28.375 U.S. bu.

(or stere)

WEIGHT

kg = kilogram   g = gram

1 kg = 1000 grams

1 kg = 2.205 lbs   1 lb = 0.4536 kg

1 g = 0.0353 ounce   1 oz = 28.35 g

DISTANCE CONVERSIONS

Inches	Centimeters	Centimeters	Inches		Feet	Meters		Meters	Feet
1	2.54	1	.3937		1	.3048		1	3.281
2	5.08	2	.7874		2	.6096		2	6.562
3	7.62	3	1.181		3	.9144		3	9.843
4	10.16	4	1.575		4	1.219		4	13.12
5	12.70	5	1.969		5	1.524		5	16.40
6	15.24	6	2.362		6	1.829		6	19.69
7	17.78	7	2.756		7	2.133		7	22.97
8	20.32	8	3.150		8	2.438		8	26.25
9	22.86	9	3.543		9	2.743		9	29.53
10	25.40	10	3.937		10	3.048		10	32.81
20	50.80	20	7.874		20	6.096		20	65.62
30	76.20	30	11.81		30	9.144		30	98.43
40	101.6	40	15.75		40	12.19		40	131.2
50	127.0	50	19.69		50	15.24		50	164.0
60	152.4	60	23.62		60	18.29		60	196.9
70	177.8	70	27.56		70	21.33		70	229.7
80	203.2	80	31.50		80	24.38		80	262.5
90	228.6	90	35.43		90	27.43		90	295.3
100	254.0	100	39.37		100	30.48		100	328.1
200	508.0	200	78.74		200	60.96		200	656.2
300	762.0	300	118.1		300	91.44		300	984.3
400	1016	400	157.5		400	121.9		400	1312
500	1270	500	196.9		500	152.4		500	1640
600	1524	600	236.2		600	182.9		600	1969
700	1778	700	275.6		700	213.3		700	2297
800	2032	800	315.0		800	243.8		800	2625
900	2286	900	354.3		900	274.3		900	2953
1000	2540	1000	393.7		1000	304.8		1000	3281

TEMPERATURE

°F	°C	°F	°C		°C	°F		°C	°F
−10	−23.0	90	32.2		−20	− 4		40	104
0	−17.8	100	37.8		−10	14		50	122
10	−12.2	110	43		0	32		60	140
20	− 6.7	120	49		5	41		80	176
30	− 1.1	130	54		10	50		100	212
40	4.4	150	66		15	59		120	248
50	10	200	93		20	68		150	302
60	15.6	300	149		25	77		180	356
70	21.1	400	204		30	86		200	392
80	26.7	500	260		35	95		250	482

DISTANCE CONVERSIONS

Yards	Meters	Meters	Yards	Miles	Kilo-meters	Kilo-meters	Miles
1	.9144	1	1.094	1	1.609	1	.6214
2	1.829	2	2.188	2	3.218	2	1.243
3	2.743	3	3.282	3	4.828	3	1.864
4	3.658	4	4.376	4	6.437	4	2.486
5	4.572	5	5.470	5	8.047	5	3.107
6	5.486	6	6.564	6	9.656	6	3.728
7	6.401	7	7.658	7	11.27	7	4.350
8	7.315	8	8.752	8	12.87	8	4.971
9	8.230	9	9.846	9	14.48	9	5.592
10	9.144	10	10.94	10	16.09	10	6.214
20	18.29	20	21.88	20	32.18	20	12.43
30	27.43	30	32.82	30	48.28	30	18.64
40	36.58	40	43.76	40	64.37	40	24.86
50	45.72	50	54.70	50	80.47	50	31.07
60	54.86	60	65.64	60	96.56	60	37.28
70	64.01	70	76.58	70	112.7	70	43.50
80	73.15	80	87.52	80	128.7	80	49.71
90	82.30	90	98.46	90	144.8	90	55.92
100	91.44	100	109.4	100	160.9	100	62.14
200	182.9	200	218.8	200	321.8	200	124.3
300	274.3	300	328.2	300	482.8	300	186.4
400	365.8	400	437.6	400	643.7	400	248.6
500	457.2	500	547.0	500	804.7	500	310.7
600	548.6	600	656.4	600	965.6	600	372.8
700	640.1	700	765.8	700	1127	700	435.0
800	731.5	800	875.2	800	1287	800	497.1
900	823.0	900	984.6	900	1448	900	559.2
1000	914.4	1000	1094	1000	1609	1000	621.4

FRACTIONAL EQUIVALENTS

Fractional Inches	Decimal Inches	MM	Fractional Inches	Decimal Inches	MM
1/16	.0625	1.587	9/16	.5625	14.287
1/8	.1250	3.175	5/8	.6250	15.875
3/16	.1875	4.762	11/16	.6875	17.462
1/4	.2500	6.350	3/4	.7500	19.050
5/16	.3125	7.937	13/16	.8125	20.637
3/8	.3750	9.525	7/8	.8750	22.225
7/16	.4375	11.112	15/16	.9375	23.812
1/2	.5000	12.700	1	1	25.400

AREA CONVERSIONS

Sq. In.	Sq. CM	Sq. CM	Sq. In.	Square Yards	Square Meters	Square Meters	Square Yards
1	6.452	1	.1550	1	.8361	1	1.196
2	12.90	2	.3100	2	1.672	2	2.392
3	19.36	3	.4650	3	2.508	3	3.588
4	25.81	4	.6200	4	3.344	4	4.784
5	32.26	5	.7750	5	4.181	5	5.980
6	38.71	6	.9300	6	5.017	6	7.176
7	45.16	7	1.085	7	5.853	7	8.372
8	51.62	8	1.240	8	6.689	8	9.568
9	58.07	9	1.395	9	7.525	9	10.76
10	64.52	10	1.550	10	8.361	10	11.96
20	129.0	20	3.100	20	16.72	20	23.92
30	193.6	30	4.650	30	25.08	30	35.88
40	258.1	40	6.200	40	33.44	40	47.84
50	322.6	50	7.750	50	41.81	50	59.80
60	387.1	60	9.300	60	50.17	60	71.76
70	451.6	70	10.85	70	58.53	70	83.72
80	516.2	80	12.40	80	66.89	80	95.68
90	580.7	90	13.95	90	75.25	90	107.6
100	645.2	100	15.50	100	83.61	100	119.6
200	1290	200	31.00	200	167.2	200	239.2
300	1936	300	46.50	300	250.8	300	358.8
400	2581	400	62.00	400	334.4	400	478.4
500	3226	500	77.50	500	418.1	500	598.0
600	3871	600	93.00	600	501.7	600	717.6
700	4516	700	108.5	700	585.3	700	837.2
800	5162	800	124.0	800	668.9	800	956.8
900	5807	900	139.5	900	752.5	900	1076
1000	6452	1000	155.0	1000	836.1	1000	1196

AREA

1 sq. mile = 2.59 sq. km

1 acre = 4068.8 sq. m

1 sq. yd. = 0.836 sq. m

1 sq. ft. = 0.0929 sq. m = 929 sq. cm

HIGH-TECH SELLING

To receive advance notice of the
next *Realty Bluebook*® edition
(and information about
what's new), please call
1-800-428-3846
to register your name and address,
or visit the Bluebook Web Page at
www.deheer.com/bluebook

CONTENTS

HIGH-TECH SELLING

Modern Technology B-1

Listing Techniques B-14

MODERN TECHNOLOGY

A NEW ERA OF MARKETING REAL ESTATE

Technology has had a huge impact on the real estate industry. Using computers, electronic mail, cellular telephones, fax transmissions, and time/management software, an agent can with accuracy produce much more in less time than ever before.

A recent set of surveys conducted by the National Association of REALTORS® divided brokers into high, average and low technology users. The survey shows that high-technology users earned more than twice as much as low or infrequent users ($57,100 vs. $26,200). Among top producers, high-tech users had incomes that were 73% higher than their low-tech counterparts ($179,000 vs. $104,400).

The rapid acceptance of the Internet is perhaps the biggest catalyst for change in the real estate industry. Public access to national and regional real estate directories weakens the proprietary hold on property information heretofore held by multiple-listing services. National and regional real estate directories publish hundreds of thousands of properties listed for sale by brokers and multiple-listing services. While the sum total of properties for sale still far exceeds those published on the Internet, national and regional real estate directories on the Net may in fact go on to assume the function so far performed by multiple-listing services.

Does this mean real estate brokers are no longer needed? Far from it. Today's legal and inspection requirements demand the expertise of the professional more than ever.

Millions of home buyers and sellers are connected to the Internet and the numbers grow. As more sellers, brokerage firms and individual agents publish properties for sale on the Internet, buyers in growing numbers search the Net and contact real estate brokers and agents for information on their listings. The time is approaching rapidly when the Internet will be the premier medium of matching the needs of buyers and sellers. In fact, it may just be one of the most logical marketing functions the Internet has yet encountered.

HOW SUCCESSFUL AGENTS USE TECHNOLOGY

A top producer uses specialized computer programs including: a contact management system to keep track of customers; a database program to create mass mailings to prospects; a bookkeeping system to keep track of income, expenses, budgets and other financial aspects; and electronic mail to communicate rapidly with clients and brokers.

Although the real estate profession is still in its infancy on the Internet, a growing number of enterprising professionals are using e-mail (electronic mail) and the Internet with remarkable success. Many have created their own web sites to reach out to over 100 million people around the world browsing the Net.

The following examples are just a few of the many everyday experiences from the business life of real estate agents who use the Net and e-mail as regular tools to communicate with clients and colleagues.

- Agent Carol Sellmore receives an e-mail inquiry from a prospective buyer about one of the listings shown on her web site. Within less than an hour's time she replies by e-mail and attaches a description of the property with pictures and information on school districts and public transportation.
- Realtor Harold Bold has set up an e-mail network with out-of-state brokers. When a referral comes in he e-mails an acknowledgment with a referral agreement attached by simply clicking the reply button, then sends an introductory e-mail to the client with initial relocation data. It's all done in a matter of minutes.

- During a listing interview, Herb Toplister—well prepared with his laptop computer and modem connected to his cellphone—shows the prospective seller comparable properties on several web sites. Excited by Herb's efficiency, the sellers want to know if he would show a picture of their home on his web site as well when they list with him.

If you are considering joining this group of successful professionals, here is a simple roadmap to follow.

GET YOUR OWN LAPTOP COMPUTER WITH
MODEM & CELLPHONE
↓
GET THE SOFTWARE YOU NEED
↓
CONNECT TO THE INTERNET & INSTALL A
BROWSER (LIKE NETSCAPE)
↓
USE E-MAIL TO COMMUNICATE
↓
SEARCH THE INTERNET FOR PROPERTIES
↓
YOUR OWN WEB SITE

THE HARDWARE YOU NEED

- *Computer:* Laptop or notebook computers have the benefit of portability compared to a desktop system. As an agent, it is a distinct advantage having the computer in the field, at listing interviews, discussing properties with buyers and for e-mail communication, outweighing no doubt the advantage of a larger keyboard and display in a desktop system.
- A hard drive with at least 1 gigabyte and 16 megabytes of RAM is recommended to accommodate sophisticated software.
- *Modem:* Modern laptops with internal modems can easily be connected to other computers via a telephone line or a cellular telephone. This

enables you to download listings from MLSs, regional networks or the Internet; download forms from an office network; and to communicate with e-mail. The modem should be the fastest model available to save long distance telephone expenses in the long run.

- *CD drive:* The laptop should have a CD (compact disc) drive, as well as a floppy drive.
- *Back-up system:* Backing up vital data on your computer is easy and fast with modern Iomega Jaz drives and 1-gigabyte tapes.
- *Printer:* A laser or ink jet printer is indispensable.
- *Scanner:* A scanner allows importing documents and pictures into the computer, which can be edited and resized, saving a great deal of time in retyping.

The Internet is the ideal way to compare prices, performance and features of the latest computer products on the market.

THE SOFTWARE YOU NEED

Programs that perform tasks on a computer are called *software*. Some basic, as well as specialized, software for real estate professionals is listed below:

- *Word processing:* For preparing and editing letters, documents, promotional material, and so forth. The most popular programs include *Microsoft Word* and *WordPerfect.*
- *Spread sheet:* For preparing financial data, amortization schedules, statistics, charts, and more. The most popular programs include *Excel, Lotus 1-2-3* and *Quattro Pro.*
- *Bookkeeping:* For personal finances, check registers, budgets, financial reports, check writing, electronic bill payments, online banking, and other functions. The market leader is *Quicken;* other programs include *Managing Your Money* and *Money.* Accounting systems for businesses include *Peachtree Accounting.*

- *Database:* For preparing mailing lists and other lists and records that can be sorted by many different characteristics. Popular programs include *dBASE, Access* and *Paradox.*
- *Presentation programs:* For preparing listing and sales presentations. Beautiful color graphics, moving charts and sound bring excitement to the presentation. Outstanding programs include *PowerPoint, Freelance, Harvard Graphics* and *Astound.*
- *Time management software:* Functions include mailings, client follow-up, CMA preparation, presentations, flyers, postcards, and other items. Time management systems are key production enhancers. Agents with these programs are ready to present the most professional material available to the consumer. Those without such programs may find themselves at a disadvantage in a competitive marketplace. Outstanding programs include: *Top Producer, Howard & Friends, Super CMA, Prep Software, Power-Point* and others.

CONNECTING TO THE INTERNET

The Internet, or Net for short, is a world-wide network of computers connected by telephone lines. The Net is also referred to as the World Wide Web.

To access the Internet you need a computer, modem, telephone line and an account with an *Internet Service Provider* (ISP). At the very minimum, the Internet Service Provider furnishes you with communications software (a program that tells a modem how to work) and an e-mail address. But in most cases more sophisticated packages are offered, such as a web browser (e.g., Netscape Navigator). All ISPs provide technical support, often including house calls, to get you going. In addition to commercial online services, such as America Online, Prodigy, or Compu-Serve, there are local Internet Service Providers. ISPs generally can be found in the Yellow Pages under the heading "Computers-Online Services Internet."

Persons who wish to publish information on the Internet may do so by creating a *web site*. Each web site has a unique address, called URL (Universal Resource Locator). Most URLs start with: http:// www, followed by a unique name that identifies the web site on the Internet. A typical URL may look like this: http://www.infoseek.com

Web browsers, such as Netscape Navigator, Microsoft's Internet Explorer and NCSA Mosaic, are used to retrieve web sites from the Net. Imagine Santa as a browser, reaching into a huge sack (Internet) and producing a package (web site).

Once you have accessed a *home page* (the first page of a web site) you can jump to other pages of the site at a click of the mouse.

E-mail (Electronic Mail)

Electronic mail, or e-mail, is your personal connection to the world of the Net.

To send or receive e-mail messages you need an e-mail address, provided by your Internet Service Provider when opening an Internet account. Once you have your address you can communicate via e-mail with anyone who has an e-mail address. It is important for every agent in a real estate office to have his or her own e-mail address.

A typical e-mail address consists of the user's name followed by the symbol @ and the host name of the ISP ending in a three-letter identifier (e.g., com). An e-mail address generally is written in all lower case, such as: johnemailer@bestprovider.com.

Advantages of E-mail:
- Being able to reach the other side of the world in minutes is one advantage over regular mail (snail mail).
- You can send files and documents, and access databases.

- You send your message when it's convenient. Your recipients respond at their convenience. No more telephone tag.
- E-mail lets you exchange vast amounts of mail and attachments for only pennies. No more huge telephone bills.

What E-mail Can Do for You—It Lets You . . .

- communicate with buyers, send them information about your listings, even attach photos;
- keep sellers informed about market activity;
- handle relocation referrals promptly;
- follow up on closing activities with title and escrow companies, lenders, appraisers and inspectors;
- receive and send inspection reports, closing documents and letters;
- promote your listings with other brokers;
- use mail lists to search for buyers or properties.

Newsgroups

A *newsgroup* is a collection of messages with a related theme, stored in a host system that everybody with an account on the system can access. No matter how many people actually read a given message, each host system has to store only one copy of it. Think of it as a bulletin board. Subscribers to a real estate newsgroup are likely to be brokers and agents interested in promoting listings, looking for exchange properties, discussing a topic, etc. You can generally find newsgroups through your local ISP.

A newsgroup is not to be confused with a mail list (mailing list). In a newsgroup, messages go to a central location (bulletin board), for each subscriber to read. In a mail list each message goes to every one of the subscribers.

Search Engines

A *search engine* is a web site maintained by an organization whose business is to search for specific information provided by one or more web sites on the Internet. Like a librarian, a search engine assists in guiding you through a maze of information to find what you are looking for.

Some of the major search engines include Yahoo, Infoseek, Lycos, Excite, Alta Vista, Webcrawler, to mention just a few.

Real Estate Related Web Sites

Listed below are important web sites providing real estate related news and information.

- Becky Swann's Internet Real Estate Directory (IRED) (http://www.ired.com) is a comprehensive index of real estate sites and topics, broken down into: *Daily Updated News* and an *International Directory* of real estate related web links and sites (lenders, builders, associations, software, etc.), properties for sale, and buyers seeking sellers. News and features target the industry as well as consumers of real estate.
- Brad Inman's "Inman News Features" (http://www.inman.com/news) offers news analysis of real estate related topics.
- Professional Publishing (http://www.prof/pub.com) publishes a complete assortment of "Plain Language" real estate forms for use in most states, both in paper format and software for Windows, DOS or Macs. The site provides online form samples and online ordering.
- Buyer's Agent Network (http://www.bestagents.com) provides information for buyers seeking agents to represent them exclusively, and invites agents who want to represent buyers exclusively.
- American Relocation Center (http://www.sover.net/~relo/) offers an array of tools.

Real Estate Directories on the Internet

National and regional real estate directories function like search engines. Search criteria generally include: City:____ including cities within _____ miles, State/ Province:____, Type of House:____, Maximum Price:____, Minimum Price:____, Bedrooms:____, Baths:____, and many more features. In several directories you can zoom in on a succession of maps until you find the desired location.

The largest directories publish listings from individual real estate brokers and multiple-listing services. Almost all of the major real estate companies and franchises have their own web sites. Some web sites, not controlled by brokers, cater to properties for sale by owners, although most of them usually welcome the cooperation of brokers. Some sites show listings of individual agents, and even provide agents with e-mail addresses and their own individual web sites.

Some sites do not publish their own listings, but perform fast searches of other directories and web sites, even matching properties and buyers.

Typical search engines, such as Yahoo, Alta Vista and others, also include real estate topics. Type in "homes for sale" and you might find a myriad of listings.

At the time this edition goes to press, the major national and regional real estate networks include:

- The biggest national real estate directory, the official site of the National Association of REALTORS® (http://www.realtorads.com/) has more than 549,000 homes presented by 121 participating REALTOR® multiple-listing services in 41 states.
- LivingNetwork Web (http://www.ca.living.net) is a directory of California properties for sale, provided by virtually every REALTOR® multiple-listing service throughout California.
- HomeScout (http://www.homescout.com) provides access to over 350,000 homes from more than 130 real estate web sites in the U.S., Canada

and other countries. Both HomeScout and Match-Point take a buyer's requirements and speed-search the Net for listings that match, displaying a list of properties fitting the buyer's requirements. The buyer selects the home(s) of interest and is provided with the URL of the home page that includes the listing. In addition, HomeScout every 24 hours notifies the buyer by e-mail of new listings and changed listings.

- MatchPoint (http://www.nji.com/map) has sites in most states and in Canada. Like HomeScout, MatchPoint takes a buyer's requirements and speed-searches the Net for listings that match, displaying a list of properties that match the buyer's requirements. The buyer selects the home(s) of interest and is provided with the URL of the home page that includes the listing. In addition, Match-Point notifies the buyer every 24 hours by e-mail of new listings and changed listings. (Both Home-Scouts and MatchPoint are supported by advertising.)

- Homes & Land Magazine (http://www.homes. com), a network of regional magazines, claims to have 200,000 listings, including homes for sale and rentals.

- Home Web (http://www.us-digital.com:8080/ homeweb), with about 200,000 listings, will increase the total by over 50,000 listings that Better Home & Gardens agreed to add to Home Web, according to Chris Petty, V.P. of U.S. Digital Corp.

- Homeseekers (http://www.homeseekers.com) covers over 117,000 homes, with full support of local Boards of REALTORS® and multiple-listing services in Washington, California, Nevada, Iowa, Illinois, West Virginia, Virginia and Maryland, and is expanding.

- Cyberhomes (http://www.cyberhomes.com) provides a complete inventory of MLS listings in your search area, generally covering the midwestern states and Canada, and is expanding. (Individual brokers and agents may choose to withhold certain listings.) A mapping feature shows how selected homes are distributed within a general region, and then zooms into the county, city, and even street level.

- HomeNet (http://www.netprop.com) has most of its listings concentrated in the New York and New Jersey area.
- For Sale By Owner (http://www.human.com/mkt/fsbo/), where owners can post their own ads, buyers can view listings, and agents can work the FSBO market.

Your Own Web Site

There are untold success stories of real estate agents whose business skyrocketed as a direct result of having their own web site.

Reasons for having your own individual web site (independent of the company site):

- A web site of your own enables you to conduct business from your home.
- Any e-mail inquiries come directly to you.
- Your own web site establishes your name in the marketplace. It gains not only buyers, but also sellers.
- Your own web site affords you the opportunity to tell your story as only you can tell it, including *Your Personal Profile, What Past Clients Have to Say, Your Past Record,* plus *Active Listings, Relocation Tips* and more.
- If you have your own web site, buyers shopping the Internet are like walk-ins.
- As a relocation specialist, your own web site is a necessity.

How To Acquire Your Own Web Site

In order to have your own web site it must have a unique name. Domain Name Services (http://www.netbistro.com/synaptic/domain.html) lets you check which Internet domain names are still available.

- Building and maintaining your own page requires a considerable investment in time and money and may not turn out to be the site you envisioned. Your time is better spent selling real estate.
- Most commercial Internet Service Providers and some regional real estate networks offer a very basic skeleton web site for a small monthly fee. If none of the local providers offers a site geared to real estate, ask one of them to create one, which should include information of interest to home buyers, such as the location of schools and available community services. Most agents find this the most cost-effective alternative.
- The National Association of REALTORS® offers information on creating a personal home page.
- Creative Web, a division of Alta Vista Technology, Inc., designs and maintains web sites. Contact 800-480-ALTA, or FAX 408-364-8778. E-mail: sales@altavista.com
- A fully customized web site designed by a professional web designer, though costly and may take several months to complete, should produce the most successful type of site. You may find web site designers in the Yellow Pages under the heading "Computers-Online-Services-Internet," or you may wish to ask someone whose web site you admire to refer you to his or her designer.

Ways To Market Your Web Site

- Buyers surfing the Net rely on search engines. Get your web site listed in as many search engines as possible. Companies exist that will submit your web site to a number of search engines at a reasonable cost, including a service named Submit-It (http://www.submit-it.com).
- Wilson Internet Services (http://www.garlic.com/rfwilson/webmarket/) is a great source of information and ideas on Internet marketing.

- Print your URL and e-mail address on your business card, letterhead, For Sale sign, license plate frame, etc. Include your URL in your e-mail signature. Any postcards you mail should have your URL and e-mail address. Announce your URL to your newsgroup and in your mail lists.

Important features to include on your web site

- Prominently display your telephone number, fax number and street address.
- Provide a link to your e-mail page to make it easy for people to communicate with you.
- With a web site you can win buyers by including an e-mail link to a personal home profile questionnaire that effectively says "tell me what you're looking for."
- Offer something that gives a prospective buyer or seller an incentive to contact you.
- In addition to listings, your web site should include information about schools, community, area, home buyer tips, relocation tips, the market and other noteworthy data. Provide such information yourself; relying on links to other sites invites visitors to exit yours.
- By using a digital camera to produce pictures of your listings, your web site becomes a more powerful marketing tool.
- Tell Your Story: Your Personal Profile, Your Technology, What Past Clients Have To Say, Your Past Record.

LISTING TECHNIQUES

PREREQUISITES FOR SUCCESS

Important Personal Attributes

- Cultivate a positive attitude about yourself and genuine interest in people.
- Show confidence in your ability to market real estate. Be enthusiastic about your company and real estate in general. Your enthusiasm affects your clients and creates a good business atmosphere. (How can a client possibly be excited about a property if you, the expert, are just lukewarm about it?)
- Be relaxed.
- Address people by their names—pronounced correctly! Ask if in doubt.
- Maintain good eye contact.
- Be a good listener. Find out what the other person wants and help him or her find the best way to get it. Show understanding of clients' problems.
- Always be prompt; if delayed, be sure to call to apologize.
- Be tactful and courteous at all times.
- Be honest and fair to all parties involved in the transaction.

LISTING GOALS

Striving toward a goal makes your listing efforts more exciting and more effective.

1. Begin by setting a goal of the annual income you plan to earn from your listing efforts, taking into account how much of your total real estate effort you plan to devote to listing.
2. Calculate the number of properties you need to list per year in order to achieve your goal by using the formula in the example shown

below, substituting your own numbers for income goal and commission splits.

A. Listing income goal: $ 50,000
B. Average sale price: 140,000
C. Average seller's commission: 6% of B _____
D. Listing broker's commission*: 50% of C _____
E. Average agent's share: 60% of D _____
F. Average agent's commission:
   B × C × D × E
   $140,000 × 0.06 × 0.5 × 0.6   2,520
G. Average percentage of listings sold: 60%
   Number of listings needed per year:
   A ÷ F ÷ G
   $50,000 ÷ $2,520 ÷ 0.6   **33**

Therefore, you need to list 33 properties per year in order to attain your goal of $50,000 in listing commissions.

*Based on co-op sales.

TIME MANAGEMENT

Distinguish Serious Sellers from Maybe Sellers

Identify maybe sellers quickly or you'll waste precious time.

- Real sellers have specific reasons for selling (transfer, retirement, marriage, birth, divorce, death, financial, tax).
- Real sellers have a time frame for selling (transfer, closing date of new home).
- Real sellers accept the concept of fair market value (as opposed to maybe sellers who sell only if they get their price).

- Real sellers cooperate in providing needed documentation and disclosures (as opposed to maybe sellers who balk at such inconvenience).

Distinguish Serious Buyers from Shoppers

- Serious buyers are motivated, ready, willing and able to enter into and fulfill a contract.
- Serious buyers are prompt and forthright in providing needed information (for loan qualification, family needs, etc.).
- Serious buyers have specific reasons for buying.
- Serious buyers have a time frame for buying a home.
- Serious buyers accept the concept of fair market value.

Prioritize Your Work

- List your activities in priority groups (A, B, C, etc.), in the order of importance.
- Schedule the majority of your time for contacts with clients and prospective buyers.
- If possible, delegate unproductive detail work to hired assistants.
- Every evening, prepare a priority list of tasks for the next day.
- Check your priority list often, especially between appointments and during lulls in your business day.
- Always carry productive reading material in case you are kept waiting.

FARMING

Two Types of Farms

1. Territorial or geographical farm. The objective of territorial farming is to build a clientele through a concentrated effort in a limited geo-

graphic territory in which the agent develops an expertise.

2. Social or sphere of influence farm. In social farming, the agent concentrates listing efforts within social groups or organizations in which he or she is extremely active.

Considerations in Selecting a Territorial Farm

- Turnover in the territory.
- Average selling price in the territory.
- Whether you can relate easily to the people in the farm or share similar interests.
- Competition from other agents. If you see a number of different real estate signs in the territory, you may assume that no agent has as yet been able to establish a beachhead. However, if the signs of one broker are dominating the territory, you are probably up against considerable competition.
- In a new subdivision, you will find less competition than in a more established neighborhood, but you may have to wait a few years for the first listings.

Establishing the Size of a Farm

Limit the farm to a number of properties that make in-person contacts feasible every four to six months and telephone contacts every three months. Between 150 to 400 homes should be an acceptable range depending on these factors:

1. The number of listings you expect your farm to yield. The example under the heading Listing Goals shows 33 listings per year to achieve a $50,000 annual listing income from all sources. Estimate how many of these listings you expect to come from farming and how many from other sources.

2. The turnover rate of the farm. Compute the turnover rate by dividing the number of homes sold during the previous year in the MLS district in which the farm is located by the total number of homes in that district.
3. Your estimated share of homes listed in the farm. Your share of the homes listed will depend upon your efforts, such as the amount of time devoted to farming, diligence, attitude and use of hired help or computer for direct mail. The results are necessarily lower in a newly initiated farm but should increase after the first year.

Based on these three factors, you can calculate the size of your farm using the formula in the example below:

Number of listings the farm is expected
to yield: 10   [A]
Number of sales in MLS district in
previous year: 150
Number of homes in MLS district: 1,400
Annual turnover:
150 ÷ 1,400 = 0.107   [B]
Estimated share of homes listed in farm:
45% = .45   [C]
Size of farm needed:
[A] ÷ [B] ÷ [C]
10 ÷ 0.107 ÷ 0.45 = 208 Homes

Therefore, you need a farm of 208 homes in order to attain your goal of ten listings per year.

Farm Mailing List

Commercial services, including *Real Estate Date, Inc.*, and others, provide names of property owners on disk that can be readily downloaded into any of various computer software products.

Outstanding time management software products that maintain farm mailing lists include *Top Producer, Howard & Friends, Super CMA, Prep Software, PowerPoint* and others.

Be a Specialist in Your Farm

- Become thoroughly familiar with the type of homes in the farm, floor plans, construction, sale prices; public transportation, shopping facilities, schools (college, private, parochial), churches, recreational facilities; any proposed changes in zoning, proposed construction (commercial, churches, sports arenas, industrial, etc.).
- Attend neighborhood functions, get involved in PTA, etc.
- Drive through the territory at least once a week— look for new signs, construction, changes, new landscaping.
- Keep up with current events in the farm (local newspapers).

Rejection-Free Method of Farming

Because most of us fear being rejected, develop an approach that makes rejection extremely unlikely.

- Offer service, make positive statements, do not ask favors.
- Never ask for a listing when knocking on someone's door. Introduce yourself as a specialist, and offer your services whenever needed. Ask if anyone in the neighborhood has plans to move.
- Write letters of introduction and follow up with telephone calls before making personal contacts.

1. Letter of Introduction
- Introduce yourself as the specialist in the territory.
- You plan to provide a service to homeowners by keeping them informed on matters concerning real estate, especially in the neighborhood.
- Provide service by offering to:
  - Answer questions concerning real estate.
  - Provide information on properties listed by any broker.
  - Prepare a free market analysis.

- Remember to mention if you can be reached evenings at home.
- Provide a brief background of your company, including its track record.
- Provide a brief background of yourself.
- Ask for referral of friends who may plan to move.
- Mention that you hope to introduce yourself in person in the very near future.

2. Telephone Follow-Up—Three to Four Days after the Mailing Arrives

   "Mr./Mrs. Owner, I'm with ABC Realty. My name is Jim Ross. I mailed you a card [letter] telling you about [subject matter]. Is this a convenient time to talk for a minute or two? Real estate in Westlake is my specialty. I'd be happy to be of service if you have any questions concerning any Westlake home that has a For Sale sign. . . ."

   With any favorable response, offer to look at the house and give a complimentary market analysis.

3. Mail Handwritten Note

   "I enjoyed our telephone conversation yesterday. Thank you for taking time from your daily schedule."

   Include a business card and confirm an appointment, if any.

4. Personal Contact At Least Twice a Year
- Knock on door.
- Stand away from the door.
- Look relaxed.
- Wait until acknowledged.
- Introduce yourself.
- "You probably received my postcard—I specialize in homes in this area."
- Be complimentary.
- Do not solicit listing!
- Do ask about anyone considering moving in the neighborhood.

- "Do you happen to know of anyone interested in buying or selling?"
- Examples of handouts to offer:
  - New listing cards (Choose your neighbor cards)
  - Open house invitations
  - Newsletter (see Topics for Newsletters)
  - Real estate–related handout
  - Consumer discount program with local businesses
  - Baseball, football or basketball schedules
  - After leaving, make notes of conversation, names, and so on to add to your records later.

5. Mail Handwritten Note

"I enjoyed meeting you and (other persons) on Wednesday. (Compliment owner on any particularly attractive feature of the house or garden, etc.) Any interested buyers or sellers you may wish to refer will be assured of prompt professional attention. Sincerely,".

Individual Farming Newsletters

A number of publishers produce monthly real estate newsletters that can be personalized with your name and photo. Because of quantity production, they are reasonable and quite convenient. However, there is no substitute for the individual style and personal touch of your own newsletter. You may find the following guidelines helpful should you decide to produce your own. Today's desktop publishing (using personal computers and laser printers) makes production of quality newsletters a breeze, individually addressed with matching envelopes, to boot. An individual newsletter mailed every other month should be more effective than a commercially produced one mailed monthly.

Topics for Newsletters

- Current neighborhood real estate news (recent sales, new homes for sale–not only your own listings)—Ask if owner knows of any potential purchasers for these new listings.

- Annual summary sheet or card of neighborhood activities
    - Homes listed by your company
    - Homes sold by your company
    - Homes listed and sold by your company
- Real estate market and tax information
    - Interest rates
    - Price trends (sellers' or buyers' market)
    - New types of financing
    - Real estate statistics
    - Purchasing a home as income property
    - Recent tax news affecting property owners
- A glimpse into the life of a real estate agent
    - Professional services free for the asking
    - Advantages of working with your own agent
    - How the real estate profession is organized
    - Types of listings, advantages and disadvantages
- Answers to common questions about real estate
    - Types of home improvements that add value to a home in terms of sale price
    - What to look for in floor plans
    - News about energy conservation
    - Security in the home
    - Safety in the home
- Thumbnail sketches of articles or ideas of interest to homeowners—new products, fix-it ideas, storage ideas, gardening, home improvement, maintenance, repairs, consumer information, recipes. Your imagination is the only limit. Always identify your source ("I just read in *XYZ Magazine, Readers Digest, New York Times* or saw on TV or heard from Joe the Chef or Mary the Gardener, etc.").
- Monthly bulletin offering free ads
- Neighborhood directory of hobbies, services, interests

- Discount coupons from new (or established) neighborhood businesses
- Remember to ask for referrals of friends or relatives who may be moving.
- Always offer to
  - prepare a complimentary market analysis,
  - provide information on properties listed by any broker, and
  - answer questions concerning real estate.
- Give your home phone number in case you cannot be reached in the office.
- Enclose a self-addressed, stamped return postcard.

Style and Technique for Writing a Newsletter

- Write in a personal, conversational style as one individual to another. Create a friendly tone.
- Put yourself in the readers' shoes and try to read your story from their point of view.
- Avoid real estate lingo.
- Use short, easy-to-read sentences (maximum 15 words per sentence) and short paragraphs.
- Write interesting stories.
- Present your case in an understandable manner.
- Use specifics, not generalities ("Interest rates have dropped from 10% to 9% during the last three months" instead of "Interest rates have been going down").
- Emphasize the benefits to the client of the topic under discussion instead of listing its features, qualities or statistics. (Example: "Over 100 L&H sales associates are in contact with many prospective buyers; what this means to you is immediate exposure to an active portion of the market!" instead of saying: "L&H Realty Company has over 100 sales associates.")
- Make sure what you write is believable.
- Use a bold headline as an attention getter:
  - Year's Real Estate Activity in Westlake
  - Is It Worth Improving Your Home?
  - You Asked Me about Real Estate . . .

- Free Homebuyers' Guide
- Use informal language (try simple words instead of intellectual ones). Your letter will run smoother and have a more emotional effect on a reader.
- Salutation—be specific: "Dear Westlake Neighbor" or "Dear Westlake Homeowner" (instead of just "Dear Neighbor").
- Start your letter with an attention getter.
  - "As I drove through Westlake this morning . . . ."
  - "If you are like most of your neighbors. . . ."
  - "Have you noticed. . . ?"
  - "Remember the days when. . . ?"
  - "The other day I read an interesting article in. . . ."
- Use transition phrases to lead into the next paragraph:
  - "That's why. . . ."
  - "In short. . . ."
  - "You too. . . ."
  - "Here's how . . ."

  (Refer to a topic of the newsletter)

- End your letter with an appropriate closing—"Sincerely yours" or "Sincerely" with your first and last name.
- Always add a postscript, an effective call for action!
  - P.S. If you miss me at the office, don't hesitate to call me at home: 123-4567.
  - P.S. There is no obligation for a market analysis.
  - P.S. Return the enclosed card now while you're thinking about it.
  - P.S. When you have a minute, don't forget to read. . . .
  - For ethical reasons (which will also impress an owner), add: P.S. Please disregard this letter if your home is listed with another broker.

- Always enclose a stamped, self-addressed return postcard with printed check blocks for easy replies.

Telephone Consumer Protection Act of 1991 (TCPA)

REALTORS® who use the telephone to contact potential clients and customers must comply with a regulation effective December 20, 1992, on telephone solicitations.

The regulation, issued October 16, 1992, by the Federal Communications Commission, implements portions of the TCPA and applies to all telemarketers. The use of automated telephone dialing systems and prerecorded voice messages is severely restricted by the regulation, which places only minor limitations on person-to-person telephone solicitations.

A rundown of the regulation's restriction and the steps real estate brokers and sales associates must take to comply with them are listed below.

Person-to-Person Calls

- No calls may be made to residences before 8 A.M. or after 9 P.M.
- A solicitor must identify himself or herself and the company, and provide the company's telephone number. If an established business relationship exists with a consumer, a solicitor is exempt from this requirement. An established business relationship exists when there has been prior, voluntary two-way communication between a business entity and a consumer, whether or not the contact results in an actual business transaction involving the services offered by the solicitor.
- A real estate firm whose sales associates conduct live cold calling must honor consumers' request not to be called again by maintaining in writing a do-not-call list of residences. A company must also have a written policy for maintaining its list.

- A firm must advise employees and independent contractors engaged in any aspect of telephone solicitation about its do-not-call list and must train employees and independent contractors how to maintain the list as required by the firm's written policy.
- A consumer's request not to be called applies to the business entity making the call and not affiliated business entities, unless the consumer reasonably would expect the affiliated businesses to be included, given the identification of the caller and the product or service being advertised.

Autodialers and Faxes

- No calls may be made to any residential telephone line using an automatic telephone dialing system or artificial or prerecorded voice to deliver a message unless there is prior consent from the called party, an established business relationship exists, the call is an emergency or the call is made by a tax-exempt nonprofit organization.
- Audodialers may not be used in such a way that two or more telephone lines of a multiple-line business are engaged simultaneously.
- All automatic systems shall identify the name and address or telephone number of the person or firm making the call.
- No individual or firm may use a telephone fax machine, computer or other device to send unsolicited advertisements to a telephone fax machine.

Penalties

- Consumers, state authorities and the FCC may fine telemarketers up to $500 in damages for violating the regulation. Telemarketers who have established a record of compliance with the regulation may present examples of this compliance—such as a do-not-call list and a written policy for maintaining the list—as a defense to alleged violations.

Telephone Techniques for Farming

- Call at appropriate times.
- Make the maximum number of calls in the shortest possible time.
- The purpose of the call is to get an appointment.
- Set the appointment for a time when both owners are at home.
- Keep calls short and simple.
- Keep asking questions beginning with *how, what, when, where, why, who* or *which;* such questions prompt specific answers, whereas questions beginning with *are, is, have* or *do* merely require a yes or no answer.
- Know when to stop talking.
- Listen carefully—do not occupy yourself with anything but paying attention to what the other person has to say.
- Never interrupt or finish someone's sentence.
- Never argue.
- Speak into the mouthpiece so your words are clearly heard.
- Smile while talking on the phone.
- Use everything you know about people and their homes.
- Never patronize or talk down to people (never use expressions like "my friend" or "you understand" or "you see").
- Do not put a client on hold if at all possible.
- Never hang up first; wait for your client to hang up.
- If you call at an inconvenient time, apologize and reschedule.
- Wrap up a conversation as soon as you have an appointment.
- If the prospect is not interested, end the conversation in a pleasant way, such as "it was nice talking with you."

Effective Words and Phrases To Use

- The word *you* and a person's name are sweet music in the listener's ear; use them often.
- Pronounce names correctly—ask if in doubt.
- Use *please* and *thank you*.
- Thank the prospect for his or her time.
- Thank the prospect for waiting.

Openers

Begin with a friendly, casual greeting.

- "Mrs. Whitmore, good evening. I'm with Sunshine Realty here in Westlake. My name is Terry Ross. Do you have a minute to talk?"
- "Hello, is Mr. Goodman at home? Mr. Goodman, my name is Patricia Riley, do you have a moment to talk on the phone?"
- "Mr. Bentley, I'm Tammy Bowman with Star Realty. Did you receive my letter?"

Telephone Topics

Make an outline of topics that will stir the prospect's interest.

- Talk about peoples' hobbies, children, schools, college and their homes. Get to know people.
- Offer free home evaluations.
- Offer financing and refinancing information.
- Discuss income property.
- Discuss the possibility for renters to own a home.
- Remember to ask for referrals of friends or relatives who may be moving.
- Offer to answer questions concerning real estate.

FOR SALE BY OWNER (FSBO)

Sources for Leads

- Search the classifieds daily for FSBO ads, and update as you obtain information (reason for selling, deadline, property data, asking price, contacts, appointments, etc.).
- Look for FSBO signs.

First Contact with Seller

Put the seller at ease during the first conversation, whether it is on the phone or in person. Speak calmly, listen attentively and show understanding for the seller's problems in order to establish a relaxed climate. It takes an average of four to five weeks for a FSBO to be ready to list, so take it easy.

Qualifying the Seller

Find out if the listing is worth pursuing by discovering

- the reason for selling (unless the FSBO—the seller—has a strong motivation to sell, you will probably waste your time);
- if they have found (purchased) another home;
- where they are moving;
- if there is any deadline for moving;
- if there are any meaningful commitments to other brokers, agents or buyers (a friend or relative in the business? Find out a name, to check if it is an excuse.); and
- if the property is in excessively poor condition.

Asking Permission To See the House and Meet the FSBO

Once the seller is qualified, your objective is to gain permission to see the seller in his or her home.

Techniques and Dialogue

- Show understanding of the seller's problems.
- Emphasize your expertise.
- FSBO: "Why do you want to see the house?"
  Agent: "For the benefit of several of my buyers."
  FSBO: "We're not interested."
  Agent: "If I had a good offer on your house today, would you turn it down?"
  FSBO: "Do you have an interested buyer? I've never heard of your firm."

Agent: "I'm sure I'll be able to show evidence that we have an excellent reputation."

The First Meeting Inside the Home

Your first impression, which includes personality, appearance, manners, dress and automobile, counts. Be positive and confident in your ability to successfully market properties. Show understanding of the seller's problems and offer assistance even though he or she is not prepared to list with you. It may take several weeks before a FSBO is ready.

Leading questions to ask in a subtle manner:

- Have you sold a home before?
- How long did it take?
- How much time do you have to make a sale?
- If you have not sold by then, have you considered retaining a professional real estate person?
- What qualities would you expect in a real estate person to entrust him or her with the marketing of your property?
- Do you want me to do a market analysis for you—without obligation? (If the answer is yes, set up a listing appointment. CAUTION: Do not make this offer unless or until you feel the seller is ready to list.)

Be sure to ask the sellers for a commitment to meet with you before they decide to list the property for sale. Follow up with a handwritten note thanking them for their commitment. Make weekly follow-up telephone calls asking about their progress and offer continued assistance.

To List or Not To List

"Mr. and Mrs. Seller, selling a house and carrying the transaction through to a successful completion is no easy task. You can, of course, retain a professional to do the job or you can try to save the commission by making the sale yourself. Remember, though, the typical direct-from-owner buyer expects you to knock off the commission for his own benefit and is likely to have experience in such negotiations. Before you decide to go the for-sale-by-owner route, ask yourself the following questions (listed on pages B-31 and B-32). Unless you can answer yes to most of them, it will be to your advantage to list your home with the best real estate professional you can find."

YES   NO

❏   ❏   Do you have ample time to sell your house?

❏   ❏   Is your house easy to find?

❏   ❏   Do you have the know-how to price your house at the highest figure that will attract buyers?

❏   ❏   Are you capable of running an effective advertising campaign? Do you have time to answer phone calls at all hours and to keep your house in top condition ready for prospects at any time?

❏   ❏   Do you know how to show your house to best advantage?

❏   ❏   Can you answer objections and criticism without showing irritation?

❏   ❏   Are you familiar with today's disclosure laws?

❏   ❏   Do you know how to protect yourself against the legal liabilities sellers are subject to as a result of numerous recent court decisions?

❏   ❏   Can you tell the difference between a prospective buyer answering your ad by phone and a criminal disguised as a buyer, using ads to get into homes?

❏   ❏   Are you able to call back prospects without placing yourself in a poor bargaining position to negotiate an offer?

❏   ❏   Can you show prospects comparable properties, so they can see why your home is worth the money you ask?

❏   ❏   Do you have the ability to bargain successfully for price, terms, moving date and so on?

YES	NO	
❏	❏	Are you familiar with today's financing techniques and sources?
❏	❏	Do you have an outlet for second mortgages?
❏	❏	Do you have the professional skill necessary to draw legally binding contracts?
❏	❏	Can you handle all the details and paperwork required to close the transaction?

EXPIRED LISTINGS

Seller Qualification by Telephone

- Is your home off the market?
- Would you sell it if you had a buyer?
- Why do you think it has not sold?
- How was it exposed to the market?
- How many showings did you have?
- Did you have any offers?
- At what price and terms?
- What will you do when it is sold?
- May I come by between three and four o'clock this afternoon to see your home?

The Appointment

- Find some feature in the house to admire.
- Show understanding for their situation.
- Do you think your house was realistically priced?
- Do you think your terms were attractive to a typical buyer?
- Do you feel your house was in a condition to attract buyers?
- What qualities would you expect in a real estate person to entrust him or her with marketing your property?

PERSONAL REFERRALS

National statistics show that personal referrals account for almost half the listings generated. A successful referral system, built over the years, will replace the hard work necessary in the early years of one's career.

Up-to-Date Records

Constant updating of your records is essential in building an effective personal referral system. It requires an efficient record system, one that can be maintained with a minimum expenditure of time.

Personal and Telephone Contacts

It is vital to make regular contacts by telephone (at least every 60 days) and in person (three to four times per year) with everyone in your personal referral system.

Always remember to send a thank-you note for the referral. Keep the referring source informed of the transaction status at regular intervals.

Mailings, Handouts, Special Promotions

- Anniversary cards
- Birthday cards to all family members on a regular basis
- Personal brochures
- Choose-your-neighbor cards
- New-neighbor cards
- Open house invitations
- Monthly informative newsletters (local developments, taxes, storage ideas, home maintenance suggestions, etc.)
- Consumer discount programs with local businesses
- Short investment seminars (two or three hours)
- Promotional products calendars, key tags, etc.

PREPARATION FOR LISTING INTERVIEW

Armed with facts and knowledge, an agent reflects professionalism and credibility, causing most sellers to give serious consideration to what agents have to say. The result is usually a more salable listing.

Research

- Become thoroughly familiar with
  - the type of homes in the neighborhood, floor plans, construction and recent sale prices; and
  - public transportation, shopping facilities, schools (elementary, junior high, high school, college, private), churches, recreational facilities, as well as any proposed changes in zoning, proposed construction (commercial, churches, sports arenas, industrial etc.).

Comparative Market Analysis

Determine a realistic price range and terms; establish a price limit beyond which the listing becomes unattractive. The market analysis should show

- properties for sale,
- properties sold in the past 12 months, and
- expired listings.

LISTING APPOINTMENT

Listing Kit

- Presentation software
- Completed residential market analysis
- Current *Realty Bluebook*® and **Financial Tables**
- The following forms:
  - Listing contract
  - Estimated seller's proceeds
  - Seller's property disclosure statement
  - Agency disclosure statement
  - FIRPTA nonforeign seller affidavit
  - Home warranty forms
- Listing presentation manual
- Visual aids
- Legal pad
- Lock box and lock box agreement
- Tape measure

- Camera with film
- Calculator
- Ballpoint pen
- Business cards

Seller's Motivation

Find out the seller's needs (if not discussed previously).

- Why are they selling?
- Where are they moving?
- Have they purchased another home?
- Do they need their equity to close the new house?
- When do they plan to move?
- Any deadline for selling their house?

Seller's Prior Experience in Selling Real Estate

- Sold by owner?
- Through a broker?
- Was experience good or bad?

Inspecting the Home

- Most salable features—Have seller point them out and make notes.
- Problem areas—Discuss with seller, reinspect later for red flags.
- Fixtures that are not to be included in the sale— A fixture is anything permanently affixed to real estate and that, therefore, goes with the house. Fixtures usually include trees, shrubs and plants, built-in appliances, drapery hardware, wall-to-wall carpets, light fixtures, chandeliers, TV antennae. If any of such fixtures are not to go with the house, they should be replaced with something comparable now or, at least, specifically excluded from the sale.
- Improvements that help the sale—Certain improvements add value to a home in terms of sale price; others do not.

- Expensive improvements, such as a spa or swimming pool, should be avoided because their cost usually does not increase the sale price enough to warrant the effort.
- To bring top dollars, a home should be in top physical condition. Listed below are some cost-effective improvements.
  - Clean if and where needed; wash off fingerprints on doors.
  - Painting, if needed, increases salability.
  - Remove/replace stained or torn wallpaper.
  - Remove stains from kitchen and bathroom counters.
  - Replace worn kitchen and bathroom floor coverings.
  - Shampoo carpets.
  - Replace missing or broken door and cupboard hardware.
  - Use soap to lubricate sticking windows and drawers.
  - Oil creaking door hinges.
  - Repair broken windows, shower doors, shutters and storm windows.
  - Repair clogged plumbing lines, leaky faucets and leaks underneath sinks.
  - Fix creaky floors.
  - Make sure all mechanical systems and appliances are in good working order; make repairs where needed.
  - Repair roof, if needed.
  - Repair worn and leaky rain gutters and downspouts.
  - Fix and paint fence, if needed.

Remodeling Job	Average Job Cost	Average Resale Value	Cost Recouped
Minor Kitchen Remodel	$ 6,234	$ 6,551	104%
Bath Addition	10,552	10,020	95
Major Kitchen Remodel	19,261	18,021	94
Bath Remodel	7,207	6,109	85
Family Room Addition	28,455	24,069	85
Master Bedroom Suite	22,060	18,320	83
Attic Bedroom	21,904	17,715	81
Deck Addition	5,731	4,456	78
Replace Windows	7,315	5,289	72
Replace Siding	9,052	6,403	71
Sun Space Addition	24,929	17,416	70

Source: *Realtor News*, week of May 24, 1993

Reasons for Listing with You and Your Firm

- Be positive, demonstrate your confidence in your ability to fill the seller's most important needs:
    - To net them the most money
    - In the shortest possible time
    - With the least amount of inconvenience to the owner
- Company's sources of buyers:
    - Current list of prospective buyers
    - Multiple listing
    - Classified and display advertising
    - Personal referrals
    - Corporate relocation referrals
    - National referral organizations
    - Open houses
    - For Sale signs
- Visual Aids
    - Track record (listings sold by you and your firm showing listed price, sold price, time on the market)
    - Company background
    - Company sales activities

The Right Asking Price

Present Comparative Market Analysis:

The following excerpt, "The Right Asking Price" is reproduced from *Home Sellers Guide* by Professional Publishing.

"Establishing the right price range is a critical consideration in marketing real property. Overpricing, as well as underpricing, can be detrimental to the sale.

"Many sellers tend to price their house far above market value for a number of reasons: sentimental attachment, expensive improvements made over the years (not necessarily always appreciated by prospective buyers), false rumors of high priced sales in the neighborhood, and often unrealistic opinions of well meaning friends.

"An overpriced house discourages serious buyers and real estate people. It usually remains on the market too long causing people to wonder if something is wrong with the house.

"On the other hand, unfamiliarity with the market may cause sellers to underprice their home, only to find it snapped up by a speculator for quick resale at a profit."

AGENCY RELATIONSHIPS

An increasing number of states are requiring real estate agents to disclose their intended agency relationship with sellers and buyers.

Need for Property Inspections and Disclosures

Real estate brokers and agents have always been responsible for faithfully representing the condition of a property without concealing any known defects. In the 1980s, the courts and legislatures of various states, notably California, required brokers and agents to inspect a property for any visible defects, also called red flags, that may affect its value or desirability and to disclose them to prospective buyers.

Closing

Obtaining the sellers' signatures should be no more than the logical result of a well-prepared, smooth listing interview with all the sellers' questions and objections convincingly answered. When that point has arrived, it is up to the agent to take the initiative by filling in the listing contract and asking the necessary questions in the process. All that remains is simply to hand the contract to the sellers for their signatures—with a pen!

MARKETING AND SERVICING THE LISTING

Marketing a real property efficiently involves exposure of the property's benefits to the ultimate extent via a maximum number of channels in order to reach the greatest possible number of potential buyers.

Channels

- Current list of prospective buyers in contact with your firm
- Multiple listing
- Classified and display advertising
- Personal referrals
- Corporate relocation referrals
- National referral organizations
- Open houses
- For Sale signs

Product Knowledge

Intimate knowledge of the home is not only a prerequisite of successful marketing, but also a sign of professionalism. The Listing Data checklists (see Checklist section) provide the data you need to market almost any type of real estate.

SERVICING THE LISTING

An essential part of servicing the listing entails

- constant communication with the seller;
- adjusting the listing price, if needed;
- making sure landscaping, exterior and interior of the home are in top condition;
- preparing the best possible financing packages for the typical buyer;
- exposing the property to the market through all available channels;
- enthusiastically discussing the listing at every opportunity; and
- seeing to insurance requirements, lights, water, maintenance, and so on;
- keeping an eye on the vacant house.

SELLING TECHNIQUES

AGENCY RELATIONSHIPS

Definitions

Agency is a relationship in which one person (the agent) is authorized to act on behalf of the best interests of another (the principal or client) in business dealings with third persons.

A fiduciary is a person in a position of trust and confidence. Fiduciary duties are obligations a fiduciary owes to a principal under the law of agency, including loyalty; obedience to (lawful) instructions; and honesty, full disclosure, utmost care and diligence in working for the principal's best interests within the scope of business for which he or she has been retained. An agent must avoid any conflicts of interest that might compromise his or her undivided loyalty. An agent is duty bound to disclose to his or her principal all relevant information concerning the agency relationship and to protect the principal's confidences (such as a seller's confidentially expressed willingness to sell below the listed price or a buyer-client's confidentially expressed willingness to pay a price higher than is offered).

Real Estate Agency Alternatives

Subagency versus Buyer Agency. This is, of course, a policy choice for the broker to make.

Until April 1992, traditional MLS policy in most states was a blanket unilateral offer of subagency, making any MLS member automatically a subagent of the seller, unless subagency was specifically rejected.

On April 28, 1992, NAR changed its MLS policy to delete the mandatory offer of subagency and make offers of subagency optional. Participants submitting listings to the MLS must, however, offer cooperation to other MLS participants in the form of subagency or cooperation with buyer-agents or both. All offers of subagency or cooperation made through an MLS must include an offer of compensation.

While subagency in the MLS has a definite marketing advantage to sellers, it also creates liability because a seller is bound by the acts, representations and misrepresentations of a subagent. Thus, the new MLS policy of optional subagency offers a choice to reject subagency to both sellers and MLS members—to sellers because they may not want the added liability that goes hand in hand with subagency, to agents who may prefer to represent buyers rather than be subagents of sellers.

Subagency. A seller's agent (and subagent) under a listing agreement with the seller acts as the agent for the seller only. A seller's agent has the following obligations to the seller:

- A fiduciary duty of loyalty, utmost care, integrity and honesty in dealings with the seller
- A duty to obey all lawful instructions from the seller within scope of authority
- A duty not to disclose confidential information that may weaken the seller's bargaining position
- A duty to disclose
  - the identity of all potential buyers
  - information about what price or terms the buyer may be willing to offer other than those contained in the written offer
  - the buyer's intention to subdivide or resell the property at a profit
  - any business or family relationship between agent and buyer

A seller's agent has the following obligations to a buyer:

- Diligent exercise of reasonable skill and care in the performance of the agent's duties
- A duty of honest and fair dealing and good faith
- A statutory duty to present all offers
- A duty to disclose all facts known to the agent materially affecting the value or desirability of the

property that are not known to, or within the diligent attention and observation of, the parties (including disclosure of material facts the broker knew or should have known)

- A duty to verify critical information received from the seller

SUGGESTION: To avoid falling into the trap of accidental undisclosed dual agency, it would be well for agents to caution buyers to avoid any discussion of what they might be willing to pay or anything they would not tell the seller directly.

Buyer Agency. A selling agent can enter into an agreement with a buyer to represent the buyer only. As such, the agent is not the agent or subagent of the seller.

A buyer's agent has the following obligations to the buyer:

- A fiduciary duty of loyalty, utmost care, integrity and honesty in dealings with the buyer
- A duty to obey all lawful instructions from the buyer within scope of authority
- A duty not to disclose confidential information that may weaken the buyer's bargaining position
- A duty to disclose
  - information about what price or terms a seller might be willing to accept other than the listed price or terms
  - any facts relating to the urgency of seller's need to dispose of the property
  - the length of time the property has been on the market and any other offers or counteroffers that have been made on the property
  - all facts known to the agent materially affecting the value or desirability of the property that are not known to, or within the diligent attention and observation of, the buyer

Buyer-Broker Contract. Unless the buyer employs his or her own agent to protect and represent him or her, the buyer is without adequate representation.

The buyer retains the agent for the purpose of locating property acceptable to the buyer and conducting negotiations on the buyer's behalf. The agent must advise the seller and the seller's agent that he or she is the agent of the buyer and not the agent of the seller.

The greatest benefit to a buyer in employing his or her own agent is that the buyer's best interests are represented in negotiations with sellers. Another important benefit is that the agent's search for the right property for the buyer is no longer limited to listed properties. Because his or her fee is protected, a buyer's agent can negotiate on properties that are for sale by owner or seek out properties that are not on the market or are in foreclosure or probate.

Buyer's Choice. After explaining subagency and buyer agency, an agent should offer the buyers a choice: "I can represent the sellers, or I can represent you as the buyers. Which do you prefer?"

Dual Agency. Dual agency situations can arise with in-house sales if a buyer-client, represented by one of the broker's agents, becomes interested in one of the broker's listings. A real estate broker can legally be the agent of both the seller and the buyer in a transaction, provided full disclosure is made and both parties give their informed consent. Because the seller and buyer in a transaction have conflicts of interest, the dual agent can only act as an intermediary between them. Provided both parties give their informed consent to such limited agency, the broker is obligated not to disclose any information of a confidential nature that could harm one party's bargaining position or benefit the other's.

A New Class Of Broker Legislated in Some States. Recent legislation in some states has attempted to eliminate the fiduciary relationship between broker and customer by creating a new class of real estate broker, mostly referred to as *intermediary, facilitator,* or *designated agent.* The effect of such legislation has not yet been passed upon by the courts. Specific local laws should always be consulted.

SOURCES OF BUYERS

- Past clients
- Relatives
- Acquaintances
- Referrals
- Service people (professionals, tradespeople, etc.)
- Farming owners
- Farming tenants
- Relocation contacts
- Neighbors of listings
- Ad and sign calls
- Walk-ins
- Open houses
- Investors
- Enrollees at your investment seminars
- Groups such as homeowners' association, PTA, Little League, service clubs, etc.

TIME MANAGEMENT IN SELLING

Show Fewer Properties to More Buyers

Preview the market before making a sales presentation. It is less time consuming, more professional and more effective than wasting your buyers' time by dragging them needlessly from house to house.

QUALIFYING THE BUYER

Prequalifying Questions

A prospect's time frame and reason for buying are the most important clues for telling a real buyer from a shopper.

- How soon do they need occupancy?
- Do they own or rent?
- How many in their family live with them?

- Do they have to sell their present home before they purchase?
- Do they have their home listed with another real estate broker?
- What price range do they have in mind?
- How much have they set aside for an initial investment?
- How much have they budgeted for monthly loan payments?
- How long have they been looking?
- Are they looking for a house as an investment?

Before taking a prospect on a home showing tour, it is highly recommended to have a further qualifying session to establish a realistic price range. Explain to the prospects the need for obtaining answers to a number of questions prior to looking at homes in the interest of saving them valuable time and zeroing in on the right home.

A buyer should not give a seller's agent too much information, especially with respect to motivation and time frame. As a buyer's agent, however, the more you know about the buyer's needs, family, likes and dislikes, living style, background and financial situation, the better equipped you will be to help him or her. It is, therefore, important to establish a pleasant, frank relationship. Meeting buyers in their home can provide valuable clues about their living style.

At this stage, it is not practical nor possible to gather all the information a lender needs to underwrite a loan. However, you can determine the buyer's stable income, recurring monthly obligations and funds available for down payment. It generally is desirable for the buyer to be prequalified by a lender.

You should be familiar with the debt-to-income ratios for the type of financing prevalent in your area (FHA, VA, Fannie Mae, Freddie Mac).

For detailed information, please refer to Loan Underwriting and Qualifying Ratios under Conventional, FHA and VA in the Financing section.

KNOWING THE MARKET

Knowing your market is not only your obligation to your clients, it is essential to a successful selling career.

- Be informed about every aspect of your listings and the needs of your sellers.
- Have a working knowledge of every property listed by your company.
- On a regular basis, drive by and inspect as many other brokers' listings within your farm and/or within the realm of your specialty as practicable.
- Inspect new listings of interest to any of your prospective buyers.

FLOOR CALL TECHNIQUES

Advertising is by far the biggest item on most brokers' budgets, so each ad call represents more dollars than most agents realize.

Advance Preparation

Prepare an ad sheet, and be sure you have familiarized yourself with these properties as well. Inspect them prior to your floor time.

Objective

- The primary purpose is to get an appointment.
- You must show excitement about a property to make your client want to see it.
- Follow your answers with your own qualifying questions—then be a good listener.

General Telephone Tips

- The purpose of the call is to get an appointment!
- Keep calls short and simple.
- Keep asking qualifying questions beginning with *how, what, when, where, why, who* or *which;* such questions prompt specific answers whereas questions beginning with *are, is, have* or *do* merely require a yes or no answer.

- Listen carefully—do not occupy yourself with anything but paying attention to what the other person has to say.
- Never interrupt or finish someone's sentence.
- Know when to stop talking.
- Never argue.
- Speak into the mouthpiece so your words are clearly heard.
- Smile while talking on the telephone.
- Remember to use *please* and *thank you*.
- Frequently use the word *you* and the person's name.
- Pronounce names correctly—always ask if in doubt.
- Do not put a client on hold if you can possibly help it.
- Never hang up first. Wait for your client to hang up the phone.
- If you call at an inconvenient time, apologize and reschedule.
- Wrap up a conversation as soon as you have an appointment.
- End a call politely if the prospect is not interested.

Openers

Begin with a friendly, casual greeting.

- "Mrs. Whitmore, good evening. I'm with Sunshine Realty here in Westlake. My name is Terry Ross. Do you have a minute to talk?"
- "Hello, is Mr. Goodman at home? Mr. Goodman, my name is Patricia Riley, do you have a moment on the phone?"
- "Mr. Bentley, I'm Tammy Bowman with Star Realty. Did you receive my letter?"

How to Talk on the Phone with a Prospect

- "Good morning, Star Realty. How can I help you?"

- "Yes, that's one of the best listings we've had in the area, let me pull the detail folder for you. By the way, I'm Julie Goodman, who am I speaking with?"
- "By the way, my name is, . . . , and your name please?"
- "Incidentally, if you have any other ads circled in your paper, I could save time by checking them out. I can report back to you within the hour. We cooperate with all brokers and there would be no cost or obligation. If you would just read the ads to me please."
- "May I show you the home now or would this afternoon be better?"
- "Let me give you my home phone number, in case you need to call after office hours . . . What's your number?"

Make an Outline of Topics That Will Stir the Prospect's Interest

Talk about prospects' hobbies, children, schools, college and their homes. Get to know people.

- Offer free home evaluations.
- Offer financing and refinancing information.
- Discuss income property.
- Discuss the possibility for renters to own a home.
- Remember to ask for referrals of friends or relatives who may be moving.
- Offer to answer questions concerning real estate.

What If the Caller Wants the Address?

A problem most agents have to deal with is the buyer who keeps asking for the address of the property. Because giving out the address means essentially losing the prospect, the trick is to obtain an appointment without giving out an address.

Demonstrated below is a telephone dialogue between a most persistent buyer wanting to know the address of the property advertised and a real estate agent equally determined to obtain an appointment without giving the address. Notice how the agent follows each answer with a significant question (underlined).

Agent: **Good morning, Blue Sky Realtors, how may I help you?**

Buyer: I'm calling on your ad in. . . .

Agent: **Oh, I'm glad you called. This is one of the more interesting homes we have had in this area.**

Buyer: What's the address?

Agent: **If you'll pardon me for just a moment, I'll get the folder that has all the information. By the way, my name is Fred Drake. May I <u>ask your name?</u>**

Buyer: Mr. Friendly.

Agent: **Mr. Friendly, when we listed this home we searched the market to find other properties for sale similar to this one. I think you will be interested in seeing one or two of these. But before I take up your time in giving you the details of these homes, let me just ask you a few questions that will help me to understand your needs. (Fill in the answers on your sheet.)**

Buyer: What is the price?

Agent: **$. . . , <u>what price range did you have in mind?</u>**

Buyer: What down payment?

Agent: **<u>What did you have available as an initial investment? Do you have to sell your present home before you purchase?</u>**

Buyer: How many bedrooms?

Agent: **This home has four bedrooms. <u>May I ask how many you have in your family living with you?</u>**

Buyer:	Where is the property located?
Agent:	**(Give general area; near college, park, major intersection, etc.—do not give the address.) Is this an area you would consider?**
Buyer:	Yes.
Agent:	**May I show you the home now or would this afternoon be better?**
Buyer:	What is the exact address?
Agent:	**I would be glad to give you the address; however, one of the conditions of our contract with the sellers is that we accompany each client to their home. I would be glad to show it to you now, or this afternoon between two and three. Which time would be more convenient for you?**
Buyer:	I just want to drive by the property.
Agent:	**It's always a good idea to see the exterior of a home first as well as the neighborhood. When do you plan to drive by?**
Buyer:	Oh, say 5 p.m.
Agent:	**Fine, in order to save you time, I'll be available at 5 p.m. to answer any questions you may have about this home. Shall I pick you up or would you prefer to stop by the office?**
Buyer:	I would prefer to drive by the home myself first.
Agent:	**Mr. Friendly, maybe this home is not for you . . . but then again, maybe it is. . . . The only way I can assist you is to show you a home and let you tell me your likes and dislikes. After all, it is difficult to determine your true needs over the telephone, isn't it?**

Buyer: I don't have time to look with you.

Agent: **I understand your frustration. Buying a home is an important decision, one that takes a great deal of time. When you are busy time is hard to find. Printed detailed information on several homes, as well as professional guidance, can save you time and money. <u>Where would you like me to mail this information?</u>**

Buyer: The last broker showed me a bunch of real dogs. Are you going to waste my time?

Agent: **Mr. Friendly, to assure you that your time will not be wasted, I'll prepare detailed information on several excellent homes that fit your requirements. I'll drop these off for your consideration before you visit the properties. <u>What is your address and phone number?</u>**

Buyer: I prefer not to give you my phone number. I don't want to be hounded.

Agent: **I know how you feel. No one likes to be pressured. However, I feel that overeager selling is an unnecessary act. The important skill I can offer you is to find the home you want and show you how you can own it. <u>Suppose such a home becomes available tomorrow, how can I reach you?</u>**

Buyer: I only want information. I have my own broker.

Agent: **May I suggest it sounds as if you need a broker, one that will do the work for you. <u>Are there any other ads you would like information on? I'd be happy to obtain the information for you and call you back if you would let me know how I can get in touch with you.</u>**

SHOWING THE HOME

Preparation

Upon qualifying the buyers and determining their needs, it is your job to conscientiously search the market before making a sales presentation. You will show fewer homes to more satisfied buyers. Try not to show more than three homes in any one session.

Bear in mind that most homebuyers base their decision primarily on emotion. They often purchase homes entirely different from their original specifications, so do not hesitate introducing them to a home you feel would suit their fancy even though it is not what they said they were looking for.

Ask the buyer to take notes. Let them know that you will be discussing with them what they liked most, what they liked least, what they would change . . . and that before looking at another home they will be eliminating one property. That means they are constantly selecting a property, and when they have found the right one, you'll be able to say, "I think we've found your home . . . Let's see how it looks on paper."

Planning

- Plan appointments to allow enough time between properties.
- Obtain keys or lock-box combinations, where needed.
- Arrange for the home to look inviting—lights on, draperies open, soft music, a roaring fire in the fireplace in the winter, windows open or air-conditioning on in the summer.
- Decide on the sequence in which to show the homes you have selected.
  - Showing your best choice last generally works better with buyers who are inexperienced and need to be educated or buyers who have not looked before and need to compare homes in the area before making a decision.

- Showing the best choice first, and additional homes only if necessary, is the correct method for buyers who are familiar with the market and know what they want.
- Select the route and approach to the property that shows off the home to its best advantage.

On the Way to the Home

- Meet the buyers (preferably both of them if there are two) at your office or pick them up at their home. Do not meet them at the property.
- At this time, confirm your agency relationship with the buyers (if required by state law).
- Do not tell your buyers how many homes you have selected to show them (you may not want to show more once you have found the right one).
- Set them at ease by making them feel you will stay at their side in their search for the right home. Let them know your feelings are not hurt by negative comments.
- Keep asking qualifying questions.
- On the way to the home tell them about people living in the neighborhood, community, schools, shopping centers and transportation. Remember to disclose obvious negatives.
- Parking across the street often provides the best position from which to favorably display the setting and exterior of the home.

Let the Buyers Discover the Home

- If the sellers are home, introduce the buyers.
- Precede the buyers to the area of the home you want them to see first. It is usually a good idea to save the most attractive part of the home until last.
- Let them discover the home at their own pace.
- Keep quiet, except to point out features that are not obvious.
- Observe and listen carefully for any positive or negative reactions and comments.

- Make mental notes for later use in closing.
- If they show signs of real interest, encourage them to go through the home again, and leave them alone.
- If they show signs that this is not the house they want, cut the inspection short. Do it in a manner that will not hurt the sellers' feelings.
- If they don't know, try to make them decide. "How soon will you know? . . . How will you know?"

Tips

- If the home is occupied, knock on bedroom doors before entering.
- Do not stand in the way of a scenic view.
- Do not argue if the buyers voice objections.
- If you answer objections, do it in the form of a question.

OBTAINING THE OFFER

At this point, you have identified the prospects as real buyers with a strong motivation to purchase; you have successfully established a relationship of trust, qualified the buyers and found them a home they like. The culmination of these actions should simply be the writing and signing of an offer to purchase.

For most of us, the purchase of a home is a big decision and it usually takes some type of initiative by the agent to get the process started, such as:

- "I can tell you love the house. You do, don't you? Shall I write it up?"
- "Why don't we make them an offer?"
- "I have the impression this is the home you want. Right?"
- "You like the house, don't you? Let's see what it looks like on paper."

Whether you are sitting at a kitchen table or at a computer in your office, simply ask the questions you need answered to fill in the blanks of the deposit receipt and start writing. Once completed, review the offer with the buyers and hand it to them, with a pen, for the signature. It's as simple as that.

What If They Cannot Decide?

There may be valid reasons why the house is not right for your buyers. If that is the case, find out the reasons and search for another home. In most cases, however, the indecision is caused by a fear of making a decision. This is a normal reaction and may be easily resolved by using one of these proven methods:

- Repeat previously acknowledged benefits.
  - "How important is the quality of the schools to you?"
  - "Would you agree this is the only home you've seen that has the spaciousness and privacy your family needs?"
  - "Didn't you mention that the proximity to shopping and transportation would mean the need for only one car?"
  - "I'm afraid you're not the only people attracted by the comfortable family room with its cozy fireplace and the pleasant patio to spend a cool evening. It wouldn't be the first time more than one buyer makes an offer on a house, which would put you at a serious negotiating disadvantage."
- Use the Ben Franklin approach.

Assist the client in making a decision by weighing the advantages against the disadvantages, a method used by Ben Franklin and referred to as the Ben Franklin method. Divide a sheet of paper in two by drawing a vertical line in the center with a horizontal line at the top. Write the heading REASONS FOR on the left and REASONS AGAINST on the right. Then help the client list all the reasons for buying the home on the left side of the sheet and the reasons against buying on the right. If the reasons against buying outweigh those in favor, you will probably need to find another house. If the opposite occurs, you might say,

"It sure seems the reasons in favor of buying outweigh those against. Shall we go ahead?"

PREPARING THE OFFER AND COUNTEROFFER

Need for Property Inspections and Disclosures

Real estate brokers and agents have always been responsible for faithfully representing the condition of a property without concealing any known defects. In the 1980s, the courts and legislatures of various states required brokers and agents to inspect a property for any visible defects—also called red flags—that may affect its value or desirability and to make appropriate disclosures to prospective buyers.

NEGOTIATING THE TRANSACTION

If you are the selling agent, you should call the listing agent as soon as you have a signed deposit receipt and request an appointment with the seller to present the offer. As a general rule, letting the seller know the price and terms of an offer on the telephone is not recommended. Therefore, the listing agent would be wise to have a secretary or an associate call the seller for the appointment because that person can honestly say he or she has no knowledge of the terms of the offer.

Preparation for Presentation of the Offer

The listing agent should ask himself or herself these questions:

- Is it a fair offer?
- What does my comparative market analysis say?
- Have market conditions changed?
- Have I prepared a seller's proceeds sheet?
- Am I thoroughly familiar with the details of the offer—price, terms, dates of closing and occupancy, etc.?

- What are the benefits of the offer?
- Is the possibility of a slightly higher price worth the burden of keeping the home on the market?
- Can I honestly recommend this offer to the seller?
- What is my agency relationship with the seller? Whom do I represent?

Tips

- Select a quiet room with plenty of light, such as the kitchen or dining room, where you will undisturbed by children, TV or radio.
- Never seat yourself between husband and wife.

Presenting the Offer

- Tell the sellers about the buyers; portray them as real people with real needs, not as someone waiting to take advantage of them.
- Tell the seller how you obtained the offer, that the buyers were interested in several homes but finally favored this one.
- Point out the benefits of the offer.
- Ask if the possibility of a slightly higher price is worth the burden of keeping the home on the market.
- The benefits of a second mortgage, if offered, include:
  - High interest
  - Security commensurate with a buyer's cash investment
  - A buyer's credit check by the lender
  - Its use as collateral
  - Its potential sale to an investor for cash at a discount (refer to yield Tables with Examples in the *Realty Bluebook® Financial Tables*).
- If sellers stall, are undecided, need more information, object or give reason why they can't accept, ask:
  - "I can respect (appreciate). . . ."
  - "Does that mean. . . ?"

- "Other than. . . , is there anything else preventing you from. . . ?"
- "If I could. . . , would you. . . ?"
- If seller wants to think it over:
  - Ask what part of the proposal they are uncomfortable with.
  - Point out the buyers may also be thinking it over and have the right to withdraw the offer.
- Get seller to accept, reject or counter.
- If the offer contains provisions not in the best interest of the sellers, it is your obligation to recommend a counteroffer with the necessary corrections.
- It is not only your obligation to represent the best interest of the sellers, it is also good business sense. After all, you want their referral business.
- If the offer is unacceptable in its present form, try to obtain a counteroffer on the best possible terms.

Multiple Offers

Occasionally, more than one offer is received simultaneously on the same property. In such an event, each offer should be presented separately by only the listing agent and the respective selling agent. If one of the offers is procured by the listing agent, the broker or manager of the listing office should take the agent's place.

TRANSACTION FOLLOW-THROUGH

Reiterating a statement from earlier in this section: Personal referrals account for almost half the listings generated, according to national statistics. Without conscientiously taking care of your clients' interests until the transaction is successfully completed, all the good efforts put forth so far may be wasted.

Much detail work needs to be done to ascertain that all conditions of the contract are carried out in a proper and timely fashion. This is where professional assistants can be worth their weight in gold. Keeping clients happy by remaining in constant touch until the transaction is satisfactorily completed provides an effective path to profitable referrals. Furthermore, it frees the agent to pursue more productive activities.

ASSISTANTS

More and more sales agents find that hiring one or more assistants increases their net income, reduces stress and leaves more time for family and recreation. A great deal of work can be delegated to skilled assistants, leaving the agent free to spend more time on prospecting and/or selling.

Assisting real estate salespeople is becoming a profession unto itself. Many personal assistants are growing into their own careers as professional assistants specializing in marketing, business management, and other areas of expertise.

Licensed assistants are allowed to perform the same tasks as the employing agent, while unlicensed assistants are restricted in their function by state licensing laws.

WHEN TO HIRE AN ASSISTANT

When the number of neglected leads can support an average real estate agent, it's time to hire an assistant. Just keep track of all the people you cannot get back to.

According to research by *Real Estate Insider*, March, 1996, it is time to hire an assistant when an agent averages more than four to six transactions per month.

TASKS FOR UNLICENSED ASSISTANTS

A professional assistant should have communication, technological and/or administrative skills, and be able to handle such tasks as:
- Computer programs including bookkeeping, word processing, database, time management
- Communicating with sellers on a regular basis
- Correspondence
- Qualifying buyers

- Handling closings
- Preparing brochures
- Handling all types of mailings
- Ad writing
- Preparing CMAs
- Meeting appraisers and inspectors
- Following up on loans in process
- Mailing FSBO letters and making follow-up calls
- Telemarketing
- Matching homes with buyers
- Open houses
- General secretarial work

EMPLOYMENT STATUS

Unlicensed assistants are salaried employees and are subject to federal or state minimum wage laws. Income taxes and FICA taxes have to be withheld and paid by the employing agent, who must file all required withholding tax reports on a timely basis.

Agents should also be aware of the liability that goes with having employees. An accident on the job could make the agent/employer liable. If the employee injures another person while running errands for the agent, the agent could also be held liable.

Licensed assistants may be paid a commission and act as independent contractors.

GLOSSARY OF TECHNOLOGICAL TERMS

Baud The number of bits a modem can send or receive per second.

Bit (Binary DigIT) The smallest unit of computerized data.

BPS (Bits-Per-Second) A 28.8 modem can move 28,800 bits per second.

Browser Software used to look at various kinds of Internet resources.

Byte A set of bits that represents a single character. Usually there are eight bits in a byte.

Client A software program used to contact and obtain data from a *Server* software program on another computer. Each *Client* program is designed to work with one or more specific kinds of *Server* programs, and each *Server requires a specific kind of* Client. A web browser is a specific kind of client.

Communications Software A program that tells a modem how to work.

Cyberspace The whole range of information resources available through computer networks.

Domain Name The unique name that identifies an Internet site.

Download Copy a file from a host system to your computer.

FTP (File Transfer Protocol) A very common method of moving files between two Internet sites.

Gopher A widely successful method of making menus of material available over the Internet.

Home Page The main page of a web site.

Host Any computer on a network that is a repository for services available to other computers on the network.

HTML (HyperText Markup Language) The coding language used to create Hypertext documents for use on the World Wide Web.

HTTP (HyperText Transport Protocol) The protocol for moving Hypertext files across the Internet.

Hypertext Generally, any text that contains links to other documents—words or phrases in the document that can be chosen by the reader and that cause another document to be retrieved and displayed.

Internet The collection of interconnected networks that connects roughly 60,000 independent networks into a vast global internet (as of July 1995).

Intranet A private network of computers inside a company or organization.

ISP (Internet Service Provider) An organization that provides access to the Internet.

Java A programming language invented by Sun Microsystems, specifically designed for writing programs that can be safely downloaded to your computer through the Internet and immediately run without fear of viruses or other harm to your computer of files.

LAN (Local Area Network) A computer network limited to the immediate area, usually the same building or floor or a building.

Login The act of entering a computer system.

Mail List A system that allows people to send e-mail to one address, whereupon their message is copied and sent to all of the other subscribers of the mail list.

Megabyte A million bytes or a thousand kilobytes.

MIME (Multipurpose Internet Mail Extensions) The standard for attaching non-text files to standard Internet mail messages. Non-text files include graphics, spreadsheets, formatted word-processor documents, sound files, etc.

Modem (MOdulator DEModulator) A device that allows a computer to talk to other computers through the phone system.

Netiquette The etiquette on the Internet.

Netscape A WWW browser and the name of a company.

Newsgroup The name for discussion groups on USENET.

Node A single computer connected to a network.

PPP (Point to Point Protocol) A protocol that allows a computer to use a regular telephone line and a *modem* to make *TCP/IP* connections.

Server A computer, or a software package, that provides a specific kind of service to *Client* software running on other computers.

TCP/IP (Transmission Control/Internet Protocol) The suite of protocols that defines the Internet.

URL Uniform Resource Locator.

USENET A world-wide system of discussion groups, with comments passed among hundreds of thousands of machines.

WWW World Wide Web.

RISK MANAGEMENT

To receive advance notice of the
next *Realty Bluebook®* edition
(and information about
what's new), please call
1-800-428-3846
to register your name and address,
or visit the Bluebook Web Page at
www.deheer.com/bluebook

CONTENTS

RISK MANAGEMENT

RISK
C

RISK MANAGEMENT

MANAGING RISK

Risk management can be defined as a plan of action to minimize the real estate broker's risk of liability and generally involves four components: (1) education, (2) risk shifting, (3) risk anticipation and (4) risk control.

EDUCATION

Educating the sales staff should be the number one concern of a broker's efforts in reducing legal liability, which has become an increasingly serious risk of doing business. A sales staff able to recognize and deal with the situations that most frequently result in litigation is without a doubt a broker's best insurance to stay out of court. The following sections are designed to assist in achieving this goal.

RISK SHIFTING

Several approaches are available to shift the risk of liability from the broker.

Errors and Omissions Insurance Coverage

Brokers should plan to devote more time and attention to risk management and their own professional liability insurance needs. To assist in this effort, some tips from insurance experts are offered here.

- E&O policies vary substantially among insurance carriers. It is important to consider the insured activities, exclusions, conditions and definitions.
- Premium savings should be accomplished by taking a higher deductible, not by opting for an inadequate insurance amount. Keep in mind that the primary purpose of E&O insurance is protection against catastrophic, business-threatening lawsuits.

- Read all fine print in the policy.
- Complete the application in every detail, including information on operations, personnel, revenues, descriptive brochures, standard contracts used, resumes and any prior claims.
- Any material misrepresentation made by an applicant for insurance, even though made innocently, whether verbal or written, renders the insurance contract voidable. A misrepresentation is material when the insurance company would not have entered the contract had the complete facts been known at the time the policy was issued. The company has the legal right to rescind or cancel the policy in such an event.
- Liability that may not be covered by E&O insurance includes claims based upon fraud and antitrust violations.

Inspections or Evaluations by Third Party Experts

"I am not qualified to give you an expert opinion on the condition of.... A structural engineer could best answer your question." Such conversations should be documented by a follow-up note or letter to the buyer. Real estate professionals should be cautioned that if they hold themselves out to be experts in a certain trade or profession by answering questions, for example, on structural soundness, they may be held to the same performance standards as a structural engineer.

RISK ANTICIPATION

Risk anticipation involves identifying the source of problems and taking steps to ensure that such problems do not arise.

Seller Disclosure Statements

The seller is generally in a better position than the real estate broker to know of and provide information about any defects in the property. The National Association of REALTORS® strongly recommends the use of seller disclosure statements, and a majority of states have adopted laws requiring sellers of residential property to provide to buyers a disclosure statement of property condition. These disclosures result in fewer surprises to buyers after closing, and less liability for both the real estate licensee and the seller.

Seller's Agents' Duty To Inspect for Red Flags

The law, through court decisions, imposes a duty upon real estate licensees to exercise care in obtaining information about the property. Some courts have noted that this duty is limited to a visual inspection and does not necessarily include an obligation to verify facts related by the seller unless there are indications to the contrary.

Verbal Representations To Be Confirmed In Writing

Verbal representations of material facts must be confirmed in writing, by letter or in the body of the contract.

Protective Clauses

BOUNDARIES, SIZE AND AGE OF IMPROVEMENTS:

> *Any oral or written representations by Seller or Broker with respect to location of property lines, size and square footage of parcel and building, or age of the improvements may not be accurate. Apparent boundary line indicators such as fences, hedges, walls or other barriers may not represent the true boundary lines. Only a surveyor can determine the actual boundary lines. If any of these issues are important to Buyer's decision to purchase, Buyer should obtain a survey.*

CONDITION OF PROPERTY:

Buyer acknowledges that he/she has not relied on any representations by either Broker or Seller with respect to the condition of the property which are not contained in this agreement or in any disclosure statements. Both parties are advised that Broker does not investigate the status of permits, zoning or code compliance; the parties are to satisfy themselves concerning these issues.

PREVIOUSLY OWNED PERSONAL PROPERTY AND FIXTURES:

The personal property and/or fixtures referred to in this agreement may not be new and may have been subject to normal wear and tear. Buyer understands that, except as may be provided otherwise in this agreement, Seller makes no express or implied warranty with respect to the condition of such property included in the sale and Seller assumes no obligation to repair any item that may fail after possession is delivered.

HAZARDOUS MATERIALS:

Buyer understands that the Broker has no expertise with respect to toxic wastes, hazardous materials or undesirable substances including, but not limited to, asbestos, formaldehyde, lead-based paint, radon gas or underground storage tanks. No representations, either expressed or implied, have been or will be made with respect to the existence or non-existence of such materials on the property. Buyers who are concerned about the presence of such materials should have the property inspected by qualified experts.

TAX LIABILITY:

Buyer and Seller acknowledge that they have not received or relied upon any statements or representations by the Broker with respect to the effect of this transaction on their tax liability.

SALE OF UNIMPROVED LAND:

> *Buyers acknowledge that they have not relied upon any representations by Broker to determine the environmental condition of the property or its suitability for the intended projects.*

NOTE: Real estate licensees are not expected to be experts in areas such as land-use planning, surveying, toxic waste, hazardous materials, tax or law. They are not required to advise clients in these disciplines. But if a broker or agent undertakes to make a statement about a material fact, however innocent it may be, he or she then becomes responsible for the accuracy of the representation. For example, if the agent produces a flyer containing statements as to the size (e.g., "5-parcel"), the agent has a duty of verification. Similarly, if the agent represents, by inference or otherwise, that the information contained in the listing is accurate, then he or she may be liable if the information later proves inaccurate. Some courts go so far as to hold that an agent has a duty to tell his or her principal if any material information being relied upon has not been verified.

RISK CONTROL

Brokers should establish procedures to identify the first clue of grievances and set up written policies to deal with complaints before they turn into litigation.

- Salespersons and office staff should be required to immediately report the first clues of a buyer's dissatisfaction or "buyer's remorse" to the broker or a designated manager.
- All sales and office staff should be made aware of the importance of answering any complaints with respect and consideration, no matter how ill-founded they may appear.

- Prompt action by the broker is essential, showing understanding, but emphasizing all the positive points of the property. In case of "buyer's remorse," it may be necessary to sell the property all over again. Often an expert opinion may lay a buyer's concerns to rest.
- If the firm is responsible and likely to incur liability, the broker and his or her attorney may consider the possibility of a settlement rather than risk litigation.

MISREPRESENTATION AND NONDISCLOSURE

A broker judged liable for misrepresenting or failing to disclose a material fact could be ordered to pay severe actual damages, punitive damages and even criminal penalties in case of fraud. Other penalties may include disciplinary sanctions for violating the REALTORS® Code of Ethics and suspension or revocation of real estate license.

Misrepresentation imposes liability on several bases of law:

1. Intentional misrepresentation (active fraud): Knowingly making a false statement about a material fact
2. Intentional concealment (constructive fraud or passive fraud): Knowingly failing to disclose a material fact
3. Negligent misrepresentation: Making a false statement about a material fact that the broker did not know but should have known was false
4. Negligent nondisclosure: Failure to disclose a material fact for lack of exercising adequate care in obtaining information about the property
5. Negligent advice: Giving incorrect professional advice when the agent should have known the advice was wrong

INTENTIONAL MISREPRESENTATION (ACTIVE FRAUD)

Active fraud imposes liability for knowingly making a false statement about a material fact with the intention to deceive the buyer. A fact is material if it would affect a reasonable buyer's decision to purchase the property or how much to pay for it.

In *Loch Ridge Construction, Inc. v. Barra*, 291 Ala 312, 280 S2d 745 (1973), the buyer claimed the salesperson had fraudulently misrepresented the house to be in perfect condition, constructed in a good and workmanlike manner and in compliance with plans and specifications approved by FHA. The court ruled in favor of the buyer.

In *Pumphrey v. Quillen*, Ohio St 343, 135 NE2d 328 (1956), the court ruled that brokers may be held liable for fraudulent misrepresentation if they make a statement they know they cannot justify and the statement is found to be false.

INTENTIONAL CONCEALMENT (CONSTRUCTIVE FRAUD)

Constructive fraud imposes liability for intentionally concealing known material defects to a buyer, particularly if one or more of the following is true:

- The buyer is unable or unlikely to discover such a defect without assistance, sometimes referred to as a latent defect. *Cooper v. Jevne*, 128 Cal. Rpt. 724 (Cal. App. 1976); *Lynn v. Taylor*, 642 P.2d 131 (Kan. App. 1982).
- The defect relates to a health or safety matter. *Cashion v. Ahmadi*, 345 So. 2d 268 (Ala 1977); *Gozon v. Henderson-Dewey & Assoc., Inc.*, 458 A. 2d 605 (Pa. Sup. 1983).
- The real estate agent has led the buyer away from discovering the defect.
- The real estate agent has made a false statement, believing it to be true when made, but later discovering it to be false without correcting it. *Mammas v. Oro Valley Townhouses, Inc.*, 638 P.2d 1367 (Ariz. App. 1981).

In *May v. Hopkinson*, 347 S.E.2d 508 (S.C. App. 1986), the real estate agent obtained two estimates for repair work on a window. One estimate did not include repairs to the wall's structural damage. The agent did not disclose this estimate, and despite the fact that there were other indications of termites and additional problems, he informed the purchasers that the house was structurally sound. The South Carolina Court of Appeals held that the agent's actions supported a finding of fraud.

In *Lynn v. Taylor,* 7 Kan. App. 369, 642 P2d 131 (1982), the buyer of a termite-damaged residence sued the seller and broker for delivering a clean pest control inspection report while fraudulently concealing a negative report previously obtained by the broker. The appellate court confirmed judgment against the broker and seller and explained a general principle that a party is under legal obligation to disclose information, including existing reports, if it has knowledge the other party would not or could not reasonably be expected to have. Failure to do so can constitute fraud, especially if the other party relies on the first party's advice.

In *Century 21 Page One Realty v. Naghad,* 760 S.W.2d 305 (Tex. App. 1988), the sellers listed their property with a real estate agency. A neighbor promptly called the agency and informed them of a sewage problem and threatened suit if it was not fixed before the property was sold. The real estate agent sold the property without disclosing the problem. Soon after the purchasers moved in, raw sewage leaked into their yard. The Texas Court of Appeal affirmed judgment against the agent and the seller for failing to disclose the problem.

NEGLIGENT MISREPRESENTATION

Negligent misrepresentation imposes liability for false statements that the real estate agent did not know were false but that reasonable care in observation would have revealed to be untrue. In general, a broker may rely on statements made by the seller unless the broker or agent has observed or otherwise knows of facts or conditions on the property that give reason to believe the seller's statements are untrue. Some courts go so far as to hold that an agent has a duty to tell his or her principal if any material information being relied upon has not been verified.

To avoid liability on the basis of negligence, a broker should conduct at least a visual examination of the property. That examination should focus on those property conditions, features and potential defects that brokers in that market area are ordinarily expected and trained to recognize and understand. It is important to recognize that the inspection should not and need not extend to defects or conditions that are reasonably discoverable only by professional inspectors in areas including land-use, planning, surveying, toxic waste, hazardous materials, tax or law. Any defects or red flags discovered should be discussed with the seller, investigated further and disclosed to the buyer.

The Alaska Supreme Court noted that real estate professionals "hold themselves out to the public as having specialized knowledge of the realty they sell" and "a purchaser who relies on a material misrepresentation, even though innocently made, has a cause of action against the broker originating or communicating the misrepresentation."

NEGLIGENT NONDISCLOSURE

Negligent nondisclosure imposes liability for failure to exercise adequate care to discover a material defect and disclose it to the buyer.

In *Easton v. Strassburger*, 152 3rd 90, 199 Cal. Rpt 383 (Cal. App. 1984), the plaintiff purchased a house that was later severely damaged by a massive landslide. Although the property had in the past experienced some earth movement and the listing broker was aware of certain red flags indicating the need for soil testing, no warning was given to the buyer. The California Court of Appeals ruled that in light of certain red flags, the seller's agent was negligent in failing to perform a reasonably competent inspection (or having such an inspection performed by appropriate professionals) and revealing to the buyer the problems that would have been discovered in the course of such an inspection.

NOTE: This decision imposed a duty on the seller's agent to disclose defects to the buyer even though no fiduciary relationship existed between the seller's agent and the buyer.

In *Robinson v. Grossman* (1997) 57 Cal. App. 4th 634, 67 Cal. Rptr. 2d 380, the Court reaffirmed the holding in *Padgett v. Phariss* (1997) 54 Cal. App. 4th 1270, 63 Cal. Rptr. 2d 273, that neither common law nor statute imposes upon real estate agents representing the seller a duty to independently verify the accuracy of representations made by the seller (unless contradicted by the agent's visual observations), or tell the buyer that the matters have not been verified.

However, in *Salahutdin v. Valley of California, Inc.* (1994) 24 Cal. App. 4th 555, 29 Cal. Rptr. 2d 463, the court held that, because of the fiduciary relationship, an agent representing the buyer does have a duty to verify facts (e.g., the size of the parcel), or advise the buyer that he or she has not verified the representation, if the agent knows that the matter is of concern to the buyer.

In *Gouveia v. Citycorp Person to Person Financial Center Inc.* (N.M. App. 1984), the buyer sued the listing broker who had described the property in "all top shape," when in fact it was "replete with major defects," which were not apparent until after the buyer had moved in. The New Mexico Court of Appeals, ruling in favor of the buyer, concluded that a listing broker has a legal obligation to prospective buyers to disclose defects discoverable by reasonable inspection.

In *Provost v. Miller,* 144 Vt. 67, 473 A2d 1162 (1984), the court noted that, as seller's agents, brokers are guilty of negligent misrepresentation only if they pass along information that they know, or have reason to know, may not be true.

In *Hoffman v. Connell*, 108 Wash. 2d 69, 736 P2d 242 (1987), the Supreme Court of Washington ruled in favor of a broker who innocently misrepresented a property's location and boundary lines by telling the buyer what the seller had told him. The court held that the broker would be liable for passing the seller's misinformation only if something had occurred to alert the broker of a problem, in which case the broker would have been negligent in failing to investigate. The court characterized brokers and salespeople as "marketing agents," not "structural engineers or contractors" and explained that brokers have "no duty" to verify a seller's independent representations unless they are aware of facts that "tend to indicate such representations are false." However, it is always prudent to verify information regarding acreage, boundary lines and permitted uses of the property.

In *Amato v. Rathbun Realty, Inc.*, 98 NM 231, 647 P2d 433 (NM Ct. App. 1982), a buyer sued a selling broker for negligent misrepresentation and failure to disclose information. The court ruled for the buyer, noting "a broker is a fiduciary in a position of great trust and confidence and must exercise the utmost good faith." Breaching such a duty can give rise to a cause of action against the broker for both negligence and constructive fraud.

New legislation in this area is constantly being enacted and brokers should become familiar with new developments in their state through local associations and other sources.

NEGLIGENT ADVICE

Negligent advice imposes a liability for giving incorrect professional advice when the agent should have known the advice was wrong. Advice differs from a representation in that advice is a suggestion, whereas a representation is a statement of fact. In *Gerard v. Peterson*, 448 N.W. 2d 669 (Iowa 1989), a real estate agent, who had casually advised the buyer that it "probably wasn't necessary" to include a financing contingency in the purchase agreement, was held liable for giving the buyer negligent advice.

FREQUENT CAUSES OF LITIGATION AND HOW TO AVOID THEM

- Failure to disclose to a buyer that an addition or alteration was performed without a building permit and/or not in compliance with code requirements. Courts have held agents liable for failing to verify that a seller obtained a building permit and final inspection, if necessary by inquiring with the local building department.
- Agents should advise sellers to disclose water leaks or drainage problems even though they have been fixed. Complaints for concealment can be avoided by disclosure of all leaks including when, by whom and how they were repaired.
- Agents should refrain from making representations with respect to boundary lines. Surveying is beyond the expertise of real estate brokers and agents.
- Agents should recommend having a qualified inspector check the septic system including the leach lines. Simply pumping out is not sufficient.
- Failure to disclose pet urine contamination. Buyers should be advised to retain a qualified expert if such contamination is suspected.
- Failure to investigate and disclose red flags pointing to prior land movements or excessive settling, such as sloping floors, distorted garage frames, cracks at window or door corners or cracks in fireplaces.

SUMMARY

To minimize liability for misrepresentation and nondisclosure of material facts, brokers should:

I. Conduct a careful visual inspection of the property. Discuss any red flags with the seller and investigate further. Discuss any known material defects, any red flags and the results of investigations with the buyer.

II. Have sellers complete a *Seller Property Disclosure Form,* whether required by law or on a voluntary basis. If there is reason to believe the seller's statements are incorrect or incomplete, the broker should investigate and resolve any inconsistency before relaying the seller-provided information to prospective buyers.

III. Encourage the use of other professionals to determine the condition of the property.

IV. Make only statements of fact that have been verified and confirm them in writing to the buyer.

V. Document answers to the buyer's questions.

DISCLOSURE OF ENVIRONMENTAL HAZARDS

The following section, Disclosure of Environmental Hazards, is an integral part of the course outline Risk Management III, produced by and reprinted with permission of the Hawaii Association of REALTORS®.

The series of courses, titled Risk Management I, II and III, is based on material provided by NAR during their Risk Reduction Instructors Training Seminar in Chicago. The courses are available for purchase from the Hawaii Association of REALTORS®.

The information contained herein is accurate, reliable and current as of the date of publication. Because the regulations change often, readers are advised to be certain they are looking at the most current version before relying on its information for any type of decision making. This information is not intended as legal or technical advice. Readers are advised to consult appropriate experts or licensed professionals on questions concerning its applicability to their particular factual circumstances or situation.

THE REAL ESTATE AGENT'S ROLE

Real estate agents cannot and are not required to understand complicated environmental legislation. This is a field for specialized attorneys and environmental experts. The real estate agent's primary responsibility in this area is (1) to recognize potential environmental hazards in commercial, industrial, agricultural or residential properties, and (2) to recommend that the seller retain appropriate experts to evaluate those hazards. Should the agent discover a potential environmental hazard, an attorney ought to be involved in drafting the required disclosure. This may shift any liability from the agent to the respective experts. When representing the buyer, the broker should recommend that any contamination be properly cleaned up. The potential liability resulting from environmental problems is so great that most buyers should not be encouraged to take such risk. A real estate agent representing a buyer who insists on purchasing a property that has potential environmental problems should strongly advise the buyer in writing, with the assistance of an attorney, not to proceed with the purchase.

MAJOR FEDERAL ENVIRONMENTAL LEGISLATION

Hazardous Substances and Environmental Laws

A number of federal and state laws (1) regulate the storage, use, transportation and disposal of hazardous substances, and (2) require the removal of hazardous wastes by the owners of real property. One important federal law that affects the real estate industry is the Comprehensive Environmental Response, Compensation and Liability Act of 1980 (CERCLA), which was amended as the Superfund Amendment and Reauthorization Act of 1986.

A major concern of real estate brokers are those laws that make owners of real property responsible for the cleanup of hazardous substances found on the property. Under CERCLA, there is no financial limit to an owner's obligation for the cleanup of hazardous wastes found on his or her property. The current owner may be strictly or absolutely liable for the costs of the cleanup whether he or she caused the problem or not. However, CERCLA states that a defense to this liability, known as the *innocent landowner defense*, may be satisfied if an assessment is performed prior to acquisition of the property, which constitutes "all appropriate inquiry into the previous ownership and uses of the property consistent with good commercial or customary practice" as defined in 42 USC Section 9601(35)(B).

In agreements for the sale of real property, buyers will want a comprehensive warranty and indemnity from the seller with respect to the existence of hazardous wastes. Sellers ordinarily will want to limit their representations to facts of which they have actual knowledge and require the buyer to make his or her own investigation. Although an indemnity agreement can be helpful, an indemnification is only good if the indemnifying parties still exist and have the funds to back it up. Some states require sellers of commercial property to notify the buyer of the existence of any hazardous substance known to the seller.

Lenders are concerned with the effect of hazardous wastes upon the value of their security. Because of this, they normally require a comprehensive inspection and report with respect to the environmental integrity of the property. Many lenders require that an environmental inspection be performed by an environmental professional prior to agreeing to lend money on a parcel of real property. This is more often the case with properties zoned commercial or industrial, or those that have a history warranting an investigation.

Current commercial leases commonly include a provision prohibiting the use or storage of hazardous substances on the premises, or requiring that the lessee comply with all the environmental laws. Some states require a lessee to notify the lessor of the existence of any hazardous substance on the premises.

The Resource Conservation and Recovery Act of 1976 (RCRA)

RCRA enables the EPA to regulate hazardous waste generators, hazardous waste facilities and the transportation of hazardous wastes.

Under RCRA, a waste is hazardous if it

- is specifically listed as hazardous or

- fails specific characteristic tests that result in it being considered either toxic, corrosive, reactive or ignitable.

A real estate agent should be aware that a transporter of hazardous wastes must be registered. If a potentially hazardous waste is found on a property, it should be left in place until picked up by a certified hauler; a real estate agent is not normally a registered hazardous waste transporter. Additionally, strict documentation requirements apply.

Environmental Responsibilities under CERCLA/Superfund

Environmental liability extends to those who violate environmental quality laws and to those who somehow become responsible for the cleanup of contaminated property. Keep in mind that the issue is not fairness. It is a question of who has "deep pockets" and might be able to afford to pay for the cleanup. The government will seek cleanup costs from innocent purchasers of real estate if the original wrongdoer is insolvent or cannot be found. In other words, this legislation is based on strict liability. It doesn't matter if the contamination was not the owner's fault.

NAR advises that brokers should familiarize themselves with hazards known to be common in their market area. The broker's investigation should include signs of environmental problems readily apparent to a real estate broker, but the broker should not be expected to discover problems apparent only to the trained eye or judgment of an environmental expert.

When there is a *release* (spill, leak, etc.) of hazardous substances, CERCLA gives the Environmental Protection Agency (EPA) the right to have the substances cleaned up either by

1. cleaning up a release using Superfund resources and suing to recover costs from any responsible party on a strict liability basis, or

2. ordering through injunction that responsible parties have to clean up the release. EPA has the right to fine violators at $25,000 per day.

Note that no minimum amount is required for the definition of a *release*. Even the threat of a release is sufficient to trigger EPA action to require payment for a cleanup.

Liability for Clean-Up

Who can become liable for cleaning up contaminated property? Property owners, lenders who foreclose on contaminated property, parties who have the equivalency of ownership through a sale-leaseback and others can become responsible for cleanup costs. Superfund Section 107(a) imposes liability on persons known as *potentially responsible parties* (PRPs).

1. Those who have operations and processes that release regulated materials or wastes must pay to clean up the contaminated property or property where the wastes were improperly (illegally) disposed. This could include problems from leaking tanks affecting the soil or groundwater. It could range from contamination resulting from illegal dumping of materials to legal disposal of a waste that later caused a problem.
2. The current owner or purchaser may have to pay for cleanup of contamination from previous owners, even if the current owner had nothing to do with past contamination.
3. The current owner may have to pay for disposal of wastes illegally disposed without the consent of the owner by an unknown third party.
4. An owner of land may be responsible to pay for the cleanup of wastes that have leached in from an adjoining property.
5. Landlords may be liable for actions of their tenants whenever a tenant improperly disposes of hazardous waste onto a property.

6. Tenants may assume liability for property conditions or may be required to correct a condition they did not create or contribute to, such as cleanup of a prior tenant's waste or the removal of asbestos necessary for renovation.

Current owners can become responsible for cleanup costs when hazardous substances are discovered, unless they can prove they meet the requirements of the *innocent landowner defense* under CERCLA at 42 USC 9601(35)(A). They can also be liable for pre-existing hazardous substances if these are later released into the environment.

Congress has issued regulations describing when lenders and fiduciaries are liable for cleanup costs under CERCLA. Under these regulations, secured lenders are not considered to be in the chain of title for liability purposes even if they foreclose on a trust deed and briefly own the property, unless they participate in the management of the property.

Limiting a Landowner's Liability

Defenses include an act of God, an act of war and/or act of an unrelated third party of an innocent owner.

The so-called innocent landowner defense may not stop the purchaser from losing the contaminated asset. It will merely protect other income and assets from being attached for the cleanup costs. The general rule is: To avoid liability for cleanup costs, a purchaser must make all appropriate and customary inquiries into the past ownership and use of the property. If contamination is found later, liability for cleanup costs might not attach, although one's equity in the property might be lost. The process of taking all appropriate and reasonable steps to ascertain that there is no contamination is part of what is called *environmental due diligence*.

Example

Part of environmental due diligence is to become aware of red flags that might suggest the possibility of contamination. In *BCW Assoc. Ltd. v. Occidental Chem Corp.*, 3 Toxics Law Reporter 943, No. 88-5847 (E.D. PA September 29, 1988), a purchaser relied solely on an engineer's report of no contamination. Dust had accumulated in the building; the purchaser decided not to have the dust tested even though it was an indication of possible problems. The dust was later found to contain lead, and the purchaser was ordered by the federal court to pay some of the cleanup costs for ignoring an "obvious red flag of contamination."

The Environmental Protection Agency is willing to consider a *de minimis settlement* with innocent landowners that would limit the amount the landowner had to contribute to the cost of hazardous waste cleanup.

1. To meet the requirements of such a settlement the following question must be answered affirmatively: "Did the landowner acquire the property without knowledge or reason to know of the disposal of hazardous substances?"
2. To meet this test, the landowner must show that he or she has conducted "all appropriate inquiry." Factors listed under Section 101(35)(B) for consideration in determining if all appropriate inquiry has been made include
   a. any specialized knowledge of an experienced defendant,
   b. relationship of purchase price to value of the property if uncontaminated,
   c. commonly known or reasonably ascertainable information about the property,
   d. the obviousness of the presence or likely presence of contamination at the property and

e. the ability to detect such contamination by appropriate inspection.
3. IMPORTANT OBSERVATION: The ability of a purchaser to demonstrate "all appropriate inquiry" and thus be able to receive a de minimis settlement may be based on the issue of whether the real estate agent was diligent in ascertaining and disclosing material facts.
4. The EPA publishes a National Priorities List of sites that require action through the Superfund. There are potentially 30,000 such sites nationally.

SPECIFIC ENVIRONMENTAL HAZARDS

Asbestos

Basically, there is no safe level of asbestos exposure. It is a fibrous material that has been used as construction material because it is a good fire retardant and efficient insulator. When inhaled, asbestos can cause asbestosis, a fibrotic scarring in the lung; lung cancer; and mesothelioma, a cancer of the chest cavity. A 1988 random survey by the EPA found asbestos in about 20% of buildings surveyed. A national hotline on asbestos is 1-202-554-1404 (8:30 A.M. to 5 P.M., EST).

Asbestos or asbestos-containing material (ACM) can be classified into two general categories: friable and nonfriable.

Friable products are materials that can easily crumble, usually with little mechanical activity. This is considered the most dangerous because when this asbestos becomes airborne, asbestos fibers can be easily inhaled. Activities that can cause friable products to become airborne include routine cleaning, repair and maintenance, renovation, operation of air-conditioning and general deterioration over time.

Nonfriable products typically contain bonding agents like cements, plastics and so on that prevent asbestos from being released into the air. However, problems can occur if the material is physically altered through sanding, drilling and so forth. The owner or operator of a demolition or renovation activity must first thoroughly inspect the pertinent facility area for the presence of asbestos-containing material prior to any construction activities. Any contractor working near a potential ACM should be notified of its presence.

The use of asbestos in buildings has been generally prohibited since 1978, with some restrictions as early as 1973. A building constructed prior to 1979, therefore, becomes a red flag property and should be evaluated for asbestos danger.

The EPA has indicated that many homes built during the past 20 years probably do contain asbestos products. (It should be noted that asbestos still may be present in a building constructed after 1979 if older building materials were used.) According to experts, some places where asbestos might be found in the home include

- around pipes and furnaces in older homes as insulating jackets and sheeting;
- in some vinyl flooring material;
- in ceiling tiles and sprayed ceilings;
- in exterior roofing, shingles and siding;
- in some wallboards;
- mixed with other materials and sprayed around pipes, ducts and beams;
- in patching compounds or textured paints; and
- in door gaskets of stoves, furnaces and ovens.

Both the EPA and the Occupational Safety and Health Administration (OSHA) have authority in issues concerning asbestos.

On July 26, 1986, the *permissible exposure limit* (PEL) for an eight-hour period was lowered by OSHA to 0.2 fibers per cubic centimeter.

Removal of asbestos should be performed by experts. Projects involving more than 230 square feet or 160 linear feet of asbestos-carrying materials require notification to the EPA regional office. On July 20, 1990, OSHA proposed new standards that would only exempt repair or removal of asbestos on pipes of less than 21 linear feet and repair and removal of an asbestos panel of less than 9 square feet (see Zachary S. Cowan, "New Asbestos Rules on the Horizon for Building Owners," *Building Operating Management,* January 1991, p. 34).

Experts indicate that "if the material is in good condition and in an area where it is not likely to be disturbed, leave the asbestos-containing material in place." Extreme care should be exercised in handling, cleaning or working with material suspected of containing asbestos. The owner or operator of a demolition or renovation activity must first thoroughly inspect the pertinent facility area for the presence of asbestos-containing material prior to any construction activities. Any contractor working near a potential ACM should be notified of its presence.

Formaldehyde

Formaldehyde is a colorless, gaseous chemical compound that was used for home insulation until the early 1980s. It is also used in some glues, resins, preservatives and bonding agents.

In homes, the most likely source of formaldehyde is adhesives in pressed-wood building materials (used in furniture, kitchen cabinets, etc.) and insulation.

Health risks to humans are undetermined, but it has been found to cause cancer in animals, while humans exposed to sufficient quantities have been affected with skin rash, breathing difficulties and other symptoms.

Formaldehyde emissions decrease over the first two or three years; experts say that older urea-formaldehyde building materials are probably not a significant source of formaldehyde emissions.

Radon

Radon is a naturally occurring, odorless, tasteless radioactive gas. It is the second largest cause of lung cancer after cigarette smoking. Radon is one of the few known Group A carcinogens. It occurs in regions that contain uranium. It also has been discovered in soils with phosphate, granite and certain types of shale. Problems occur when radon passes through cracks and spaces in the foundation and becomes concentrated in tight buildings that do not allow the gas to escape and dissipate to the outside. Radon can also seep into well water, but the likelihood is reduced for homes supplied with municipal water supply. According to the National Council on Radiation Protection and Measurement, radon represents 55% of all radiation sources. A national hotline is 1-800-SOS-RADON.

Radon problems can be corrected by sealing cracks in foundations and by increasing ventilation.

Indoor Air Quality

A broader issue, of which asbestos, formaldehyde and radon are a part, is the problem of indoor air quality in commercial and industrial buildings.

As part of due diligence in the purchase of a commercial building, clients should be advised to consider hiring experts to perform indoor air quality surveys. Buildings that are sealed to promote energy efficiency also can seal in pollution and facilitate radon problems.

One authority, J. M. Kuvalanka, has described something called sick- or tight-building syndrome with symptoms including headaches, fatigue, skin and eye irritations, allergies and upper respiratory problems. An indoor air quality survey can include some or all of the following: tenant and employee questionnaires, ventilation studies, CO_2 profiling, temperature and relative humidity measurements, and specific contaminant sampling and analysis.

Lead

Lead poisoning, usually caused by the presence of lead in paint and drinking water, can cause permanent damage to the brain and many other organs, and may cause reduced intelligence and behavioral problems. Lead can also cause abnormal fetal development in pregnant women.

The hazard of contaminated drinking water has ceased to be a health concern in the United States since the Safe Drinking Water Act of 1986 required the use of lead-free solder, pipes and flux for any facilities connected to a public water system.

Lead-Based Paint. Approximately three-quarters of the nation's housing built before 1978 contains lead-based paint, usually found on walls, woodwork, door and window frames. Lead-based paint is especially hazardous to children who tend to absorb more lead than adults and are more likely to exhibit hand-to-mouth behavior.

To protect families from exposure to lead from paint, dust, and soil, Congress passed the Residential Lead-Based Paint Hazard Reduction Act of 1992. In accordance with the act, HUD and EPA promulgated regulations requiring the disclosure of known information on lead-based paint and lead-based paint hazards before a sale or lease agreement becomes binding. Target housing under the act is housing built prior to 1978, except:

- zero-bedroom units, such as efficiency units, lofts and dormitories;
- leases for less than 100 days where no lease renewal can occur, such as vacation houses or short-term rentals;
- housing for the elderly (unless children live there);
- housing for the handicapped (unless children live there);

- rental housing that has been inspected by a certified inspector and found to be free of lead-based paint; and
- foreclosure sales.

REQUIREMENTS

Before a contract for the sale or lease becomes binding:

- Sellers and landlords must give buyers and renters the pamphlet, developed by EPA and HUD, titled *Protect Your Family from Lead in Your Home.*
- Sellers/landlords must disclose to buyers/tenants and to each agent in the transaction any known lead-based paint and lead-based paint hazards. The regulations do not require any testing or removal of lead-based paint by sellers or landlords.
- Sellers/landlords must provide to buyers/renters available reports concerning lead-based paint and lead-based paint hazards on the property.
- If this information is provided after the seller/lessor receives an offer, he or she must allow the buyer/lessee an opportunity to review the information and possibly amend the offer.
- Home buyers must be given a ten-day (or any other agreed upon time period) opportunity to conduct a lead-based paint inspection or risk assessment at their own expense.
- A Certification and Acknowledgment of Disclosure must be attached to the purchase agreement in which the buyer acknowledges, among other things, that he or she has received an opportunity to conduct a risk assessment or inspection within ten days (or other agreed upon period) or has waived the opportunity. (Form 110.74, *Certification and Acknowledgment of Disclosure,* available from Professional Publishing, fulfills these requirements.)

- Both listing and selling agent (except a selling agent who is paid solely by the buyer or lessee), must inform the seller or lessor of his or her obligations and ensure: (a) that the required disclosures are given; (b) that the buyer is permitted the opportunity to inspect, unless waived; and (c) that the Certification and Acknowledgment is completed. If the agent does this, he or she will not be liable for the seller's or lessor's failure to disclose.
- A copy of the Certification and Acknowledgment must be kept by the seller and both agents for three years after closing or the commencement of the lease.

In addition to civil and criminal sanctions, any person who knowingly violates the provisions will be jointly and severally liable to the purchaser or lessee in an amount equal to three times the amount of damages actually incurred, together with attorney fees, expert witness fees and costs.

Waste Disposal Sites

Americans produce vast quantities of garbage every day. Despite public and private recycling and composting efforts, huge piles of waste materials—from beer cans, junk mail and diapers to food, paint and toxic chemicals—must be disposed of. Landfill operations have become the main receptacles for garbage and refuse. Special hazardous waste disposal sites have been established to contain radioactive waste from nuclear power plants, toxic chemicals and waste materials produced by medical, scientific and industrial processes.

Perhaps the most prevalent method of common waste disposal is to simply bury it. A landfill is an enormous hole, either excavated for the purpose of waste disposal or left over from surface mining operations. The hole is lined with clay or a synthetic liner to prevent leakage of waste material into the water supply. A system of underground drainage pipes permits monitoring of leaks and leaching. Waste is laid on the liner at the bottom of the excavation, and a layer of topsoil is then compacted onto the waste. The layering procedure is repeated again and again until the landfill is full, the layers mounded up sometimes as high as several hundred feet over the surrounding landscape. Capping is the process of laying two to four feet of soil over the top of the site and then planting grass or some other vegetation to enhance the landfill's aesthetic value and to prevent erosion. A ventilation pipe runs from the landfill's base through the cap to vent off accumulated natural gases created by the decomposing waste.

Federal, state and local regulations govern the location, construction, content and maintenance of landfill sites. Test wells around landfill operations are installed to constantly monitor the groundwater in the surrounding area, and soil analyses can be used to test for contamination. Completed landfills have been used for such purposes as parks and golf courses. Rapid suburban growth has resulted in many housing developments and office campuses being built on landfill sites.

For Example

A suburban office building constructed on an old landfill site was very popular until its parking lot began to sink. While the structure itself was supported by pylons driven deep into the ground, the parking lot was unsupported. As the landfill beneath it compacted, the wide concrete lot sank lower and lower around the building. Each year, the building's management had to relandscape to cover the exposed foundations. The sinking parking lot eventually severed underground phone and power lines and water mains, causing the tenants considerable inconvenience. Computers were offline for hours, and flooding was frequent on the ground floor. Finally, leaking gases from the landfill began causing unpleasant odors. The tenants moved out, and the building was left vacant, a victim of poorly conceived landfill design.

Hazardous and radioactive waste disposal sites are subject to strict state and federal regulation to prevent the escape of toxic substances into the surrounding environment. Some materials, such as radioactive waste, are sealed in containers and placed in "tombs" buried deep underground. The tombs are designed to last thousands of years, built according to strict federal and state regulations. These disposal sites are usually limited to extremely remote locations, well away from populated areas or farmland.

The *Midwest Interstate Compact on Low-Level Radioactive Waste* is one example of a regional approach to the disposal of hazardous materials. The states of Delaware, Illinois, Indiana, Iowa, Kansas, Kentucky, Maryland, Michigan, Minnesota, Missouri, Nebraska, North Dakota, Ohio, South Dakota, Virginia and Wisconsin have agreed to cooperate in establishing and managing regional low-level radioactive waste sites. This approach allows the participants to share the costs, benefits, obligations and inconveniences of radioactive waste disposal in a fair and reasonable way.

Environmental issues have a significant impact on the real estate industry. In 1995, a jury awarded $6.7 million to homeowners whose property values had been reduced because of the defendant tire company's negligent operation and maintenance of a hazardous waste dump site. The 1,713 plaintiffs relied on testimony from economists and a real estate appraiser to demonstrate how news stories about the site had lowered the market values of their homes. Nationwide, some landfill operators now offer price guarantees to purchasers of homes near waste disposal sites.

Underground Storage Tanks (USTs)

Underground storage tanks have been used to store petroleum products, chemicals and liquid wastes since the early 1900s for the convenience of owners and for what was then considered "safety." However, corrosion, stress, and faulty construction or installation have caused tanks to leak after 20 years or sooner, depending on the corrosiveness of the soil. Some estimates place the number of USTs in the United States between 3 and 5 million, and the EPA estimates that on a national scale about 40% of USTs are leaking—discharging gasoline, petroleum products and other hazardous liquids into the soil and potential groundwater sources.

Under federal law, a UST is defined as any tank system, including its piping, that has at least 10% of its volume underground. Federal law regulates only those tanks that are used to store petroleum or those hazardous chemicals regulated under CERCLA (Superfund). The following tanks are exempt:

- Farm and residential tanks holding 1,100 gallons or less motor fuel used for noncommercial purposes
- Tanks storing heating oil used on the premises where stored
- Tanks on or above the floor of underground areas, such as basements or tunnels
- Septic tanks and systems for collecting storm water and waste water
- Flow-through process tanks and emergency spill and over-fill tanks

Under Superfund, both current and former owners are responsible for the maintenance of a UST. Therefore, responsibility for complying with federal UST requirements can continue even after ownership of the UST is terminated.

Above-ground spills from a UST, which either releases 25 gallons of a petroleum substance, or which cause an oil sheen on nearby water surfaces, must be reported to the local administering agency within 24 hours. Below-ground releases must be reported within 24 hours after discovery. Failure to report a spill or release can result in civil or criminal penalties or both. Owners should consult legal counsel when dealing with property containing a UST.

Clues indicating the possible presence of a UST:

- Air vents or piping sticking out of the ground above the tank
- Oil sheens in wet areas
- Traces of concrete, metal or asphalt that may indicate former commercial use of the property

Where such indicators are observed, the seller should be questioned concerning any knowledge he or she may have about the presence of a UST.

The presence of a UST should be a red flag, triggering advice to the client that further investigation by a qualified expert is needed. Real estate licensees should be familiar with disclosure laws in their state so they can properly advise buyers and sellers.

In states where sellers are not required to make written disclosures, including knowledge of USTs on their property, a buyer would be well advised to ask the seller about the presence of underground storage tanks and to include the seller's statement in the sales agreement. The existence of a UST can often be discovered by fill pipes or vent lines protruding from or flush with the ground, stained soil and odors or fumes, such as fuels or solvents, seemingly coming from nowhere. If the presence of a UST is suspected, a trained consultant should be retained to perform further studies. It should be noted that there may not be any visual signs of a UST, such as vent and fill pipes. In some cases, detailed historical investigation may be required to identify a potential UST.

Once it has been established that a UST is in the ground, further steps need to be taken to determine (1) whether the tank is leaking, (2) the extent of any contamination caused by the leakage and (3) the cost of remediating the contamination.

The first step is a *Phase I Assessment.* This may include a physical examination of the property, review of the property's history, examination of records showing reported incidents and potential problems, and investigation into nearby potential off-site locations of contamination. Sampling is not normally performed during a Phase I Assessment. If it is known that a UST exists, a tank tightness test may be able to determine whether a tank is leaking and to what extent. The result of a Phase I Assessment will help determine if an environmental contamination problem potentially exists. If it appears that a potential problem exists, it usually is verified in a Phase II Assessment.

During a *Phase II Assessment,* sampling is performed to verify the potential problem. If the potential problem is a UST, it is often removed, and samples are taken from under it. If a release has been verified, the pertinent regulatory agencies must be informed. If necessary, the extent of contamination is normally characterized in a *Phase III Assessment.* In this phase, sampling is performed to determine how far the problem has migrated.

Once reported, the pertinent regulatory agency will usually provide guidance on remediation. For a leaking tank, this may include removal of the tank and cleanup of affected soils and/or groundwater. Affected nearby properties must also be cleaned up. Usually, final samples are required to verify that a contaminated site has been properly cleaned up.

It should be noted that different entities may call the assessment phases by different names. For example, a Phase I is sometimes called an ESA (Environmental Site Assessment), and so on. This can result in confusion. It is therefore recommended that any assessment be carefully screened to ensure that the contractors are professional, certified when required, and reputable. A mistake by the contractor can ultimately be at the cost of the landowner.

Water Quality and Groundwater Contamination

Surface water and groundwater contamination can result from many sources, including leaking tanks, surface spills, hazardous wastes and materials, mining waste and runoff, agricultural chemicals, septic and sewer systems and boat traffic. The EPA Safe Drinking Water Hotline may be contacted at 1-800-426-4791 for additional information.

Polychlorinated Biphenyls (PCBs)

PCBs are used in electrical equipment because they provide a good insulating medium. The EPA has determined that "PCBs may cause adverse reproductive effects, developmental toxicity, and tumor development in humans" (Freeman, 1989, pp. 4–13). PCBs have been found to remain in the environment for a long time and have been shown to be passed on with the food chain and offspring of contaminated species.

PCBs are used in electrical transformers, capacitors, fluorescent light ballasts, heat transfer and hydraulic systems, and other electrical equipment.

A real estate agent should be aware of the types of equipment that may contain PCBs. PCBs may remain in place as long as the equipment they are contained in does not appear to be leaking. For example, older light ballasts may contain PCBs. These do not represent a contamination problem unless they are leaking or are disposed of improperly. If a piece of equipment containing PCBs is observed to be leaking, the local regulatory agency may be contacted for direction. It should also be noted that specific record-keeping requirements apply to threshold quantities of PCBs.

HANDLING ENVIRONMENTAL PROBLEMS

General Precautionary Measures To Avoid Liability for Environmental Problems

Real estate agents may advise their clients to obtain environmental audits before purchasing property in order to

1. discover the extent of any environmental contamination and
2. be able to utilize the innocent landowner defense under CERCLA if contamination is subsequently discovered.

Avoid Advising Parties on Environmental Issues. Sellers and real estate agents should avoid making any representations or offering any advice, not only about the environmental condition of the property, but also about the status of the law or the meaning of any environmental provision contained in a contract.

Listing Agreements/Engagement Letters. These documents should include language stating that no warranties, representations or characterizations as to the environmental condition of the property are made that are not expressed in writing.

Environmental Questionnaires. Language requiring sellers to disclose any information known to them about the environmental condition of the property is sometimes added to the disclosure checklists presently used by many real estate agents. These questionnaires can be the basis for communicating information regarding environmental problems to prospective buyers. However, completion of a questionnaire should not be solely relied upon to determine whether a site is clean, as the seller may not know enough to answer all the questions.

Environmental Site Assessments. Only an environmental assessment performed by a competent environmental professional in accordance with good commercial or customary practice should be relied upon. In some instances, even with the use of a competent environmental professional, a problem may not be uncovered. No environmental assessment can wholly eliminate uncertainty regarding the potential for recognized environmental conditions in connection with a property. An environmental assessment is intended to reduce, but not to eliminate, uncertainty regarding the existence of recognized environmental conditions, recognizing reasonable limits of time and cost.

Buy and Sell Agreements. Provisions may be included in the buy and sell agreement allocating the risk of environmental problems among the parties to the agreement. Contingencies also may be included in the buy and sell agreement making the sale conditional upon a satisfactory environmental audit.

Vacant Land. Real estate agents who represent buyers seeking vacant land for a particular project should be careful not to make representations about the suitability of the land for the project. A buyer representation agreement should contain explicit language stating:

> *Buyer does not rely on any representation by the agent to determine the environmental condition of the property, or its suitability for the intended project.*

Visual Inspections. If a real estate agent spots certain red flags indicating possible environmental problems, the agent should recommend that the buyer obtain an environmental audit.

DRUG PROPERTY FORFEITURES

The real estate agent's role in this area is similar to the role in environmental hazards, except that no amount of disclosure will compensate for a seizure of the property. A buyer should obviously be discouraged from purchasing a property that could conceivably be subject to seizure. A seller cannot sell a property that could conceivably be subject to seizure. In short, the property should not be listed or sold until the condition subjecting the property to drug seizure has been corrected and eliminated.

If illegal drug activity is taking place on real property, that property could be seized even though the actual owner of the property was not in any way involved with such activity. The right of the federal drug enforcement authorities to seize this property is contained in the Federal Drug Enforcement Act of 1988 (Title 21 USC Section 853). Property subject to criminal forfeiture includes real property and tangible and intangible personal property.

To avoid seizure, a property owner would use the *innocent owner* defense and must demonstrate that either

1. he or she had no knowledge of the use of the property for illegal drug activity, or
2. he or she had knowledge and made reasonable efforts to keep the property from being used for such illegal activity.

The burden of proof is on the property owner or lessor.

AGENCY

Agency is a relationship in which one person (the agent) is authorized to represent the interests of another (the principal or client) in business dealings with third parties.

AGENCY PROBLEMS IN REAL ESTATE

Many buyers, sellers and even professionals still wrongly believe that selling agents represent the buyer, when in fact they may be subagents of the seller.

CONSEQUENCES OF BREACH OF AGENCY DUTIES

- Loss of commission
- Rescission of transaction
- Loss or suspension of license
- Actual damages
- Punitive damages over and above actual damages in severe cases
- Criminal penalties in severe cases of fraud

RISK REDUCTION RECOMMENDATIONS

- Education and training in agency relationships
- Use of disclosure forms
- A written company policy addressing agency relationships (as recommended by NAR, April 28, 1992)

A NEW CLASS OF BROKER LEGISLATED IN SOME STATES

Recent legislation in some states has attempted to eliminate the fiduciary relationship between broker and customer by creating a new class of real estate broker, mostly referred to as *intermediary, facilita-*

tor, or *designated agent.* The effect of such legislation has not yet been passed upon by the courts. Specific local laws should always be consulted.

SUBAGENCY VERSUS BUYER AGENCY

With the exception of some states, traditional MLS policy has been a blanket unilateral offer of subagency, making any MLS member automatically a subagent of the seller unless subagency was specifically rejected.

On April 28, 1992, NAR changed its MLS policy to read:

"NAR's multiple listing policy shall be modified to delete the mandatory offer of subagency and make offers of subagency optional. Participants submitting listings to the MLS must, however, offer cooperation to other MLS participants in the form of subagency or cooperation with buyer agents or both. All offers of subagency or cooperation made through an MLS must include an offer of compensation."

While subagency in MLS has a definite marketing advantage to sellers, it also creates liability because a seller is bound by the acts, representations and misrepresentations of a subagent. Thus, the new MLS policy of optional subagency offers a choice to reject subagency to both sellers and MLS members; sellers may reject subagency because they may not want the added liability that goes hand in hand with subagency; agents may reject it because they prefer to represent buyers rather than be subagents of sellers.

SUBAGENCY

A subagent, under a listing agreement with a seller, acts as the agent for the seller only. A seller's agent, or a subagent of that agent, has the affirmative obligations listed below.

Duties of a Seller's Agent to the Seller

Fiduciary Duties. Fiduciary duties include loyalty, utmost care, integrity and honesty in dealings with the seller.

Duty of Obedience. The seller's agent must obey all lawful instructions from the seller within the scope of his or her authority.

Duty of Confidentiality. The seller's agent must keep secrets that may weaken the seller's position.

Duty of Disclosure. The seller's agent is obliged to disclose to the seller

- at time of listing, the fact that subagency is optional and that the seller is responsible for the subagents' acts and representations,
- the identity of all potential buyers,
- information about the willingness of a buyer to complete the sale or offer a higher price,
- the buyer's intention to subdivide or resell property at a profit and
- any business or family relationship between agent and buyer.

Duty of Accounting. The seller's agent must

- account for all monies entrusted to the agent, and
- keep accurate and complete records of all.

Duties of a Seller's Agent to the Buyer

- Diligent exercise of reasonable skill and care in the performance of the agent's duties
- A duty of honest and fair dealing and good faith
- A statutory duty to present all offers
- A duty to disclose all facts known to the agent materially affecting the value or desirability of the property that are not known to, or within the diligent attention and observation of, the parties (including disclosure of material facts the broker knew or should have known)

- A duty to verify critical information received from the seller

SUGGESTION: To avoid falling into the trap of accidental undisclosed dual agency, it is good for agents to caution buyers to avoid any discussion of what they might be willing to pay or anything they would not tell the seller directly.

BUYER AGENCY

A selling agent can, with a buyer's consent, agree to act as agent for the buyer only. As such, the agent is not the agent or subagent for the seller. A buyer's agent has the affirmative obligations listed below.

Duties of the Buyer's Agent to the Buyer

Fiduciary Duties. Fiduciary duties include loyalty, utmost care, integrity and honesty in dealings with the buyer.

Duty of Obedience. The buyer's agent must obey all lawful instructions from the buyer within the scope of his or her authority.

Duty of Confidentiality. The buyer's agent must keep secrets that may weaken the buyer's position.

Duty of Disclosure. The buyer's agent is obliged to disclose to the buyer

- the willingness of a seller to accept a lower price,
- any facts relating to the urgency of a seller's need to dispose of the property,
- the length of time a property has been on the market and any other offers or counteroffers that have been made on the property,
- all facts known to the agent materially affecting the value or desirability of the property that are not known to, or within the diligent attention and observation of, the buyer, and
- any business or family relationship between agent and seller.

Duty of Accounting. The buyer's agent must account for all monies entrusted to the agent.

Duties of the Buyer's Agent to the Seller

- Diligent exercise of reasonable skill and care in the performance of the agent's duties
- A duty of honest and fair dealing and good faith

Recent legislation in some states has attempted to eliminate the fiduciary relationship between broker and customer by creating a new class of real estate broker, mostly referred to as facilitator, intermediary, designated agent, or transaction broker.

THE CHOICE

After explaining subagency and buyer agency, an agent may offer the buyer a choice: "I can represent the seller, or I can represent you as the buyer. Which do you prefer?"

Client vs. Customer

A *Client* is a person who employs an agent to perform a service for a fee. A *Customer*, in real estate brokerage, is a prospective buyer not represented by an agent. An agent or subagent of a seller is duty bound not to disclose to a customer any confidential information that might harm the seller's bargaining position, or give advice on matters of price, etc.

Buyers Who Should or Must Be Clients

In the event an agent's close relative, or any other type of buyer listed below, becomes interested in a property listed by the agent's broker, can such a purchaser be treated in any way other than a client?

- Buyers who require anonymity, such as famous or wealthy people or corporations moving into the area
- Relatives

- Close friends
- Close business associates or partners
- Buyers who want to be represented
- Former clients and former customers
- First-time buyers who need help
- Out-of-town buyers who need help with property values and location

BUYER REPRESENTATION AGREEMENT

A buyer representation agreement provides for the exclusive right to represent the buyer for a certain period, to assist the buyer in locating real property of a specific nature and to negotiate terms for its acquisition acceptable to the buyer. The form also includes clauses such as possible dual agency, possible conflicts with other buyer clients, compensation options, optional retainer fee and binding arbitration.

Disclosures to Listing Broker, Seller and Closing (Escrow) Agent

In a transaction in which the broker represents a buyer, the listing broker should be informed of the buyer-broker arrangement at first contact, again at the time the appointment is made and once more when the offer is presented. The closing agent should also understand the representation arrangements.

Compensation

Payment of commission does not necessarily establish agency. It makes no difference who pays the commission–the seller, the buyer or both. Commissions are disbursed at closing as part of the transaction as any other closing cost. The closing document should clearly show two commissions–one marked "on behalf of the sellers" to the listing office, the other marked "on behalf of the buyers" to the selling office.

Advantages of Buyer Brokerage

- No liability for subagents
- Closer control over buyers
- No marketing expenses

DUAL AGENCY

Dual agency situations can arise with in-house sales if a buyer-client, represented by one of the broker's agents, becomes interested in one of the broker's listings. Exchanges, syndications and purchases by real estate agents for their own account are other potential dual agency situations. A real estate broker can legally be the agent of both the seller and the buyer in a transaction, provided full disclosure is made and both parties give their informed consent. Because seller and buyer in a transaction have conflicts of interest, the dual agent can only act as an intermediary between the parties. A *dual agency disclosure addendum* form is designed to present the predicament to seller and buyer and to provide full disclosure of the limitation in services the agent is able to provide in such a dual agency situation. Provided both parties give their informed consent to such dual agency, the broker is under obligation not to disclose any information of a confidential nature that could harm one party's bargaining position or benefit the other's. For example, the broker could not disclose to the seller information about what price or terms the buyer might be willing to pay other than what is offered in writing, or disclose to the buyer information about what price or terms the seller might accept other than what is contained in the listing agreement.

Duties of a Dual Agent to Both Seller and Buyer

Fiduciary Duties. Fiduciary duties include utmost care, integrity, honesty and loyalty in dealings with the seller and the buyer.

Duty of Disclosure and Honest and Fair Dealings

- A dual agent has a duty to disclose all material facts required by law and information the agent believes might affect the principals' decisions with respect to the transaction.
- A dual agent has a duty to disclose any business or family relationship between the agent and either the seller or the buyer.
- A dual agent may not disclose to the seller information about what price or terms the buyer may offer other than those offered in writing by buyer.
- A dual agent may not disclose to the buyer information about what price or terms the seller may accept other than the listed price or terms.
- A dual agent may not disclose any information of a confidential nature that could harm one party's bargaining position or benefit the other's.

Unintended or Accidental Undisclosed Dual Agency. Undisclosed dual agency is unlawful, whether intended, unintended or accidental. The broker who fails to disclose dual agency is likely to (1) violate both state licensing law and general agency law, (2) jeopardize any right to a commission and (3) justify having either the seller or the buyer rescind the underlying transaction. The broker is then potentially liable for monetary damages. This right of rescission exists even if there is no injury, the transaction is fair and the agent acts in good faith. Even though the dual agent obtains the required consents, the agent must still be extremely careful not to favor one side over the other.

Risk of Dual Agency. Because the dual agent owes the same fiduciary duties to both principals, the dual agent walks a legal razor's edge, trying to avoid situations in which the agent might unintentionally compromise one principal in favor of the other.

Dual agency has been described as a time bomb. As long as the buyer and the seller are happy with the transaction, the question of dual agency probably will never arise, but if either party becomes unhappy for whatever reason, even months after closing, undisclosed dual agency may provide the mechanism to undo the transaction. It is no legal defense that the dual agency was unintended or was performed with all good intentions to help both the buyer and the seller. Buyers and sellers generally neither care nor know about the subject of dual agency until one of them wants to back out of the deal and consults an attorney. Dual agency cases have a high rate of success for plaintiffs and a high value for settlement purposes.

DISCLOSURE OF AGENCY RELATIONSHIP

Written Disclosure with Informed Consent

Written disclosure of agency relationship with informed consent is an essential risk reduction tool. Most states have disclosure regulations (most of them oral).

Article 21 of the NAR Code of Ethics requires disclosure of agency relationship to buyers and sellers.

Timing of Disclosure

Disclosure to sellers should be made at time of listing; disclosure to buyers at first meaningful contact.

COMPANY AGENCY POLICIES

Seller Agency Exclusively

All sellers are clients; all buyers are customers.

Advantages

Both the public and real estate licensees are more familiar with this traditional method of conducting real estate transactions.

Drawbacks

- The agency may lose agents who want to represent buyers.
- The agency may lose buyers who want to be represented.
- There is a high risk potential of unintended undisclosed dual agency.
- Maximum liability exists for breach of subagents' fiduciary duty.

Buyer Agency Exclusively

All buyers are clients. Buyers do not list property.

Advantages

- There is a minimum risk policy legally.
- There is no liability for subagents.
- There is closer control over buyers.

Drawbacks

- A buyer agency discourages agents who want to list.
- Sellers do not contact buyer agencies, and thus, business is lost.

Single Agency Whether Listing or Selling

The agent represents either buyer or seller but never both in same transaction.

Advantages. There is no risk of undisclosed dual agency.

Drawbacks. A single agency whether listing or selling is difficult to manage and only works in very small firms.

Dual Agency for In-House Sales

One agent works with a seller-client while another agent works with a buyer-client. A listing agent selling his or her own listing to a buyer-client should be avoided.

Advantages. The flexibility allows for buyer brokerage and subagency.

Drawbacks. A dual agency for in-house sales requires extensive training, constant monitoring and consent of both parties. The liability of creating a dual agency exists.

For an in-depth coverage of agency relationships and office policies, refer to the following books:

Agency Disclosure: The Complete Office Policy Guide, John W. Reilly and Michael Somers

Agency Relationships in Real Estate, John W. Reilly

Consensual Dual Agency, John Reilly, Gail Lyons and Don Harlan

FEDERAL FAIR HOUSING LAWS

Title VIII of the Civil Rights Act of 1968, amended in 1988, is administered by the Department of Housing and Urban Development (HUD). The act is herein referred to as Title VIII.

The Secretary of HUD is authorized to review state and local statutes and certify those that are substantially equivalent to Title VIII. "Substantially equivalent" may include those statutes that provide broader protection than Title VIII.

Title VIII is a comprehensive fair housing law that prohibits discrimination on the basis of the following criteria:

1. Race
2. Color
3. Religion
4. Sex
5. National origin
6. Handicap* or
7. Familial status*

The 1988 amendment to Title VIII includes handicapped persons and families with children as so-called protected classes.

CONDUCT PROHIBITED BY THE FAIR HOUSING LAWS

Refusal To Sell or Rent

The following acts are illegal:

- Any refusal based on race, color, sex, religion, national origin, handicap or familial status to sell, rent or otherwise make unavailable a dwelling after receipt of a bona fide offer
- Discrimination in terms, conditions, privileges or services in the sale or rental of a dwelling based on prohibited criteria
- Representation that a dwelling is not available when in fact it is, based on prohibited criteria

- Denial of access to or participation in a multiple-listing service based on prohibited criteria
- Discrimination in granting requested financial assistance based on prohibited criteria

Racial Steering

Racial steering, or influencing a person's housing choice based on prohibited criteria, is, for example, directing minority prospects to integrated or all-minority neighborhoods and white prospects to all-white neighborhoods. Evidence of steering is often gathered through the use of testers.

Advertising That Expresses a Preference

Publishing any material or advertisement that indicates a preference, limitation or discrimination based on prohibited criteria is illegal. HUD has promulgated advertising guidelines designed to clarify permissible and nonpermissible real estate advertising. It is also inappropriate to make explicit reference to the proximity of the dwelling to a commonly known racial or ethnic landmark, such as a synagogue, ethnic center or predominantly black institution.

Blockbusting

Blockbusting or panic selling refers to the suggestion when soliciting a listing that crime is increasing or that persons of a minority are moving into the neighborhood.

Handicapped Discrimination

The law defines handicap as a "physical or mental impairment which substantially limits one or more of a person's major life activities."

NOTE: A physical or mental impairment includes any physiological disorder or condition, cosmetic disfigurement or anatomical loss, mental and/or psychological disorders, specifically including alcoholics and persons with HIV virus, AIDS and other diseases that cannot be transmitted by casual contact. However, the handicap classification specifically excludes "those who are illegally using or are addicted to a controlled substance and those whose tenancy would constitute a direct threat to the health or safety of other individuals," or those "whose tenancy would result in substantial physical damage to the property of others."

NOTE: Major life activities include caring for oneself, performing manual tasks, walking, seeing, hearing, speaking, breathing and learning.

HUD regulations state that real estate brokers or agents may not inquire whether a person has a handicap or the extent of any handicap in evaluating a person's qualifications to buy or rent a dwelling. A broker or agent may, however, ask questions about a prospect's rent history as long as the same questions are asked of every prospect. For example, a broker may inquire whether a prospect will be able to meet the monthly payments or whether the prospect is a current abuser of or addict of a controlled substance.

Title VIII prohibits property owners from refusing to allow a tenant to make reasonable structural modifications to a unit, at the tenant's expense, to allow the handicapped tenant full enjoyment of the premises. The property owner may, however, condition any structural modifications to the interior of a unit on the tenant's agreement to restore the unit to its original condition upon termination of occupancy.

Title VIII requires property owners to make reasonable accommodations in any rules or regulations governing the housing development that are necessary to permit the tenant to fully enjoy the premises (e.g., allowing a seeing eye dog notwithstanding a no pet rule, assignment of a parking space to a handicapped tenant near a building entrance, a waiver of a rule banning vans in a building's parking lot when a van is necessary to a handicapped person's transportation).

Title VIII further provides that all new *covered multifamily dwellings* meet certain basic accessibility and adaptability requirements. A covered multifamily dwelling includes all units in a building of four or more dwelling units if the building has an elevator, and ground floor dwelling units in buildings of four or more dwelling units without an elevator.

Covered multifamily dwellings must meet the following design and construction requirements:

- Public and common use areas readily accessible to handicapped
- Doors wide enough to allow passage by a wheelchair
- An accessible route into and through the unit
- Reinforcements in bathroom walls to allow later installation of grab bars around toilet, tub, shower, stall and shower seat, where provided
- Kitchens and bathrooms allowing an individual in a wheelchair to maneuver about the space
- Light switches, electrical outlets, thermostats and other environmental controls in accessible locations

Families with Children

Familial status means a parent or guardian in the legal custody of children under the age of eighteen, and pregnant women.

Title VIII forbids property owners or agents from refusing to sell or rent a dwelling to an otherwise qualified prospect simply because the prospect has children under the age of eighteen in his or her household. While Title VIII prohibits discrimination based upon familial status, the statute does not preempt reasonable state or local regulations limiting the number of persons who may occupy a particular dwelling.

According to HUD regulations, property owners may not establish dual purpose facilities where certain sections of a housing complex are reserved for adults only and other sections for families with children.

Housing for Older Persons

Title VIII specifically authorizes the exclusion of children from housing for older persons, notwithstanding the prohibition of discrimination against families with children. The exemption was amended by the Housing for Older Persons Act of 1995. The following is now required for housing to qualify for the "55 and older" senior housing exemption:

  I. At least 80% of the occupied units must be occupied by persons 55 and older;

  II. The housing facility must publish and adhere to policies and procedures that demonstrate an intent to be housing for seniors; and

  III. The facility must comply with rules issued by the secretary of HUD for verification of occupancy.

CONSEQUENCES OF FAIR HOUSING LAWS VIOLATIONS

The potential penalties for violation of fair housing laws are so severe that responsible real estate brokers simply cannot assume the risk. Furthermore, fair housing cases are almost always excluded from errors and omissions policies.

An *aggrieved person* who believes himself or herself to be a victim of a discriminatory housing practice may bring an action directly in federal court or may file a complaint with HUD. If HUD finds reasonable cause, the case may be tried before a *HUD administrative law judge (ALJ)* or before a *federal district judge*. If state or local law is deemed by HUD to be substantially equivalent to Title VIII, HUD will refer all complaints from that jurisdiction to the state or local agency for processing.

Both ALJs and federal courts may award *actual damages,* attorneys fees and issue injunctions to prevent any further discriminatory practices. An ALJ may also assess *civil penalties* limited to $10,000 with no prior offense, $25,000 with one prior offense within five years and $50,000 with two prior offenses within seven years. A federal court judge may also impose an unlimited amount in punitive damages plus attorneys fees and costs.

Also, the United States attorney general may bring an action where a pattern of practice of discrimination has occurred, as opposed to a single isolated act, and secure *injunctive relief and damages,* together with civil penalties of $50,000 for the first offense and $100,000 for any subsequent offense.

To highlight the importance of complying with federal fair housing laws, in July 1992 a jury ordered a Washington, D.C., area property management company to pay $2.41 million in damages to a woman who said the company refused to rent an apartment to her because she has children. In 1990, after being told for the second time that the building in which she and her children had hoped to rent was an "all adult" building, plaintiff Carrie H. Timus sued the management company, claiming it violated federal fair housing laws that prohibit discrimination on the basis of familial status.

NAR General Counsel Laurene K. Janik noted that the damages award underscores the seriousness with which juries are viewing cases that involve discrimination against families with children. "The extraordinary amount of the damages award sends a message that society is not going to tolerate discrimination against families with children," said Janik.

RISK REDUCTION RECOMMENDATIONS

Education and Training

Risk will be reduced by

- providing education and training to all sales associates, directly or through the board, and making available the NAR "Fair Housing Handbook."
- educating individual clients, who may put the greatest source of pressure on a broker to discriminate or steer. Sellers must understand that the broker will not accept a listing on any conditions that are in violation with the fair housing laws. NAR developed an informative brochure titled "What Everyone Should Know about Equal Opportunity in Housing" that can be given to clients and customers.

Documentation

When an agent is confronted with a complaint of discriminatory housing practice, especially when the complaint is grounded upon the use of a tester, it is imperative to have records showing the prospect's name, address, telephone number, race, stated requirements for housing, price range, as well as dates and addresses of properties offered and/or shown.

The agent may have only a hazy memory of the prospect as one of hundreds encountered in the last month or year. Without a written record to refresh his or her recollection, the agent has no basis to establish whether the prospect was in fact afforded equal professional service. A paper trail is the strongest defense!

As part of its Fair Housing Initiatives Program, HUD has committed to fund a $1 million contract with the National Fair Housing Alliance in Washington, D.C.

THE AMERICANS WITH DISABILITIES ACT (ADA)

The Americans with Disabilities Act (ADA), signed by President George Bush in 1990, is intended to protect individuals with disabilities from various forms of discrimination in employment, public services, transportation, public accommodations and telecommunications services. The requirements of the law pertaining to employment discrimination and removal of barriers in public accommodations are of particular importance to real estate brokers.

TITLE I—EMPLOYMENT

Title I of the ADA became effective July 26, 1992, for employers with more than 25 employees, and on July 26, 1994, for employers with 15 or more employees. It is enforced by the Equal Employment Opportunity Commission.

Title I prohibits employers from discriminating against "qualified individuals with disabilities."

A qualified individual with a disability is one who meets the skill, experience, education and other job-related requirements of a position held or desired and who, with or without "reasonable accommodation," can perform the "essential functions of a job."

Disability means a physical or mental impairment that "substantially limits" one or more of a person's major life activities. This also includes a record of such impairment or being regarded as having such impairment.

Reasonable accommodation is a logical adjustment made to a job or the work environment that enables a qualified person with a disability to perform the functions of that employment position. It is considered to be discrimination under the ADA to refuse to make a reasonable accommodation to the known physical or mental limitations of a qualified applicant or employee with the disability unless the accommodation would pose an undue hardship on the business.

Examples of Reasonable Accommodations

- Reserved parking spaces that must be accessible and clearly labeled
- Level or ramped entrance
- Access to conference rooms, restrooms and cafeterias
- Widening doorways for wheelchair access
- Job restructuring
- Providing readers to blind employees
- Providing interpreters for conferences and training courses for hearing-impaired persons
- Schedule modifications
- Retraining
- Reassignment to vacant positions
- Adjusting or modifying examinations, training materials or policies
- Buying special equipment and devices

Essential functions of a job are fundamental job duties and not just the marginal functions of a particular position.

Major life activities are functions such as caring for oneself, performing manual tasks, walking, seeing, hearing, speaking, learning and working.

"Substantially limits" means unable to perform a major life activity that the average person in the general population can perform or being significantly restricted as to the condition, manner or duration under which an individual can perform a particular major life activity.

The Federal Government has developed a number of guidelines for undue hardships under a previous law known as the Rehabilitation Act of 1973. In judging what an undue hardship is, the government looks at business activity; financial cost and expenses; overall size of the firm including number of employees and budget; the structure of the workforce and the nature and cost of the accommodations needed.

Also protected is anyone associated with an individual who has a disability. A person currently on illegal drugs or engaged in alcohol abuse is not considered by the ADA provisions to be impaired, but a person who has been rehabilitated and is not using drugs or a person currently in a drug rehabilitation program may be protected under ADA.

An employer is not required to hire a person who poses a direct threat to health or safety. This threat, however, must create "a significant risk of substantial harm" and not just slightly increase the risk. The burden of proof is on the employer.

Pointers for Avoiding Claims of Discrimination under the ADA

- Employers should not ask job applicants about their medical condition. However, employers may require them to undergo a medical exam as a condition of a job offer.
- Employers should not ask applicants how many days they missed from work last year due to illness. However, it is all right to ask how many days they were absent from work.
- Employers should not ask applicants whether they would need reasonable accommodation or what type of accommodation they would need to perform the job. However, employers may ask applicants whether they can perform the specific job-related functions with or without reasonable accommodation.
- Alcoholism is considered a disability, so employers should not ask applicants how much alcohol they drink or if they have ever been treated for alcoholism. However, it is correct to ask applicants if they drink alcohol.
- Psychiatric disorders are also considered disabilities. Asking applicants if they have ever sought treatment for an inability to handle stress is not

allowable. Instead, employers may ask them how well they handle stress or if they work better or worse under pressure.

Even if applicants volunteer information about their disability, employers should not follow up with questions about the disability.

For more information on complying with the ADA, contact the local office of the Equal Employment Opportunity Commission (EEOC).

TITLE III–PUBLIC ACCOMMODATIONS AND COMMERCIAL FACILITIES

Title III of the ADA, effective January 26, 1992, prohibits discrimination against persons with a disability in places of public accommodation and commercial facilities.

The law requires removal of architectural and communications barriers in existing privately owned places of public accommodations.

A privately owned public accommodation includes virtually all commercial facilities, such as office buildings, convention centers, hotels, restaurants, theaters, museums, retail establishments, day care centers and medical buildings. ADA applies to private entities that own, lease or operate such public accommodations.

The requirement to remove architectural and communications barriers assumes that these changes are readily achievable. The obligation to remove barriers does not require extensive restructuring or burdensome expense. However, there is no specific monetary formula to determine that an action is readily achievable. Factors to be considered in determining whether removal of a barrier is readily achievable include the nature and cost of the work needed, the overall financial resources of the facility itself and the overall financial resources of the parent corporation.

An employer who takes the position that an accommodation needed by a disabled person is not readily achievable has the burden of proof.

In examining the "readily achievable" test, the government has suggested priorities to remove barriers where all accessibility goals might not be readily achievable, in this order:

1. Providing access to site from public sidewalks, parking or public transportation
2. Providing access to all areas where goods and services are made available to the public
3. Providing access to restroom facilities
4. Providing access to all remaining areas

Tax Credits

Real estate brokers and clients should consult an accountant about possible tax relief to offset any financial burden resulting from ADA requirements. Tax credits for up to 50% of eligible expenditures greater than $250 but less than $10,250 are available to businesses with annual gross receipts not exceeding $1 million or fewer than 30 full-time workers. Eligible expenditures include costs for removing barriers and providing auxiliary aids. A tax deduction of up to $15,000 per year for qualified removal of architectural and transportation barriers may be taken by any business regardless of its size.

New Buildings

A new building intended for first occupancy after January 26, 1993, must for all practical purposes be barrier free or readily accessible to people with disabilities.

The readily accessible standard does not require elevators to be installed in facilities less than three stories high and less than 3,000 square feet in area unless these facilities are shopping centers or offices of a health care provider.

REDUCING RISK OF ADA LIABILITY

Noncompliance with the ADA exposes violators to stiff penalties and significant liability.

Steps Brokers Can Take To Avoid Legal Problems with the ADA

- Brokers may advise building owners, tenants and property managers to review their leases to determine who is responsible for compliance mandated by legislation or regulation.
- If a lease is due to expire, ADA compliance might be discussed during renewal negotiations.
- Brokers should have their offices inspected by an architect familiar with ADA regulations.
- Brokers might alert their commercial clients to the existence of the ADA and suggest they have their buildings inspected by a knowledgeable architect.
- Brokers and their commercial clients should document their awareness of the legislation and any steps they have taken or costs they have incurred to comply, including all discussions, correspondence, reports, costs of inspections, building modifications and purchases of auxiliary aids.

ADA REQUIREMENTS FACT SHEET

(U.S. Department of Justice)

Employment

- Employers may not discriminate against an individual with a disability in hiring or promotion if the person is otherwise qualified for the job.
- Employers can ask about one's ability to perform a job but cannot inquire if someone has a disability or subject a person to tests that tend to screen out people with disabilities.
- Employers must provide reasonable accommodation to individuals with disabilities. This includes

steps such as job restructuring and modification of equipment.

- Employers do not need to provide accommodations that impose an undue hardship on business operations.
- Who needs to comply: All employers with 15 or more employees must comply effective July 26, 1994.

Public Accommodations

- Private entities—such as restaurants, hotels and retail stores—may not discriminate against individuals with disabilities effective January 26, 1992.
- Auxiliary aids and services must be provided to individuals with vision or hearing impairments or individuals with other disabilities unless an undue burden would result.
- Physical barriers in existing facilities must be removed if removal is readily achievable. If not, alternative methods of providing the services must be offered if they are readily achievable.
- All new construction and alterations of facilities must be accessible.

Transportation

- New public transit buses ordered after August 26, 1990, must be accessible to individuals with disabilities.
- Unless an undue burden would result, transit authorities must provide comparable paratransit or other special transportation services to individuals with disabilities who cannot use fixed route bus services.
- Existing train systems must have one accessible car per train by July 26, 1995.
- New rail cars ordered after August 26, 1990, must be accessible.
- New bus and train stations must be accessible.

- Key stations in rapid, light and commuter trail systems must be made accessible by July 26, 1993, with extensions up to 20 years for commuter rail (30 years for rapid and light rail).
- Who needs to comply: Effective July 26, 1994, all employers with 15 or more employees must comply.

State and Local Governments

- State and local governments may not discriminate against qualified individuals with disabilities.
- All government facilities, services and communications must be accessible consistent with the requirements of Section 504 of the Rehabilitation Act of 1973.

Telecommunications

- Companies offering telephone service to the general public must offer telephone relay services to individuals who use telecommunications devices for the deaf (TDDs) or similar devices.

Examples

The following fact situations were prepared by the Hawaii Real Estate Research & Education Center, University of Hawaii.

Fact Situation A. Ms. X is in a wheelchair. She holds a real estate sales license and has applied to work in the residential sales division of Broker B's office, a firm with 45 salespersons. Because of the wheelchair, Broker B does not think that Ms. X will be effective in showing houses to prospective buyers and advises her that she is not qualified to apply for a job with his firm. Broker B is also concerned that Ms. X's wheelchair is too big to fit through the door of the conference room in which the firm's sales meetings are held.

Fact Situation B. Mr. Y is a prospective buyer of a small, four-story medical office building. Mr. Y is very,

very rich. The building does not have an elevator and the stairs are narrow. The current owner has had a negative cash flow problem for the past three years and is seeking to sell the property. Mr. Y tells Broker B that he plans to keep the property. Mr. Y tells Broker B that he plans to keep the building in its existing condition for a few years until he can tear it down and develop a high rise hotel in its place.

In both fact situations, Broker B has problems created by the passage of ADA. In the Fact Situation A, Broker B is guilty of employment discrimination in violation of Title I. Ms. X has the right to file a charge of discrimination with the U.S. Equal Employment Opportunity Commission.

In Fact Situation B, Mr. Y will need to spend capital to remove barriers that discriminate against the disabled. This may be an expense he may not have expected. Having failed to disclose the provisions of ADA as they apply to this situation, Broker B may be sued by Mr. Y.

DISCLAIMER

The material presented in this section is for general education purposes and is not intended to provide specific legal advice. Because the ADA requirements are very technical, licensees are advised to consult their attorney for guidance.

Other Sources of Information

For information concerning Title I, Employment Discrimination:

Equal Employment Opportunity Commission
Telephone: 1-800-669-EEOC

For information concerning Title III, Public Accommodations and Commercial Facilities:

U.S. Department of Justice
Telephone: 1-202-514-0301

The Americans with Disabilities Act
Title III Technical Assistance Manual

Job Accommodation Network (JAN)
Telephone: 1-800-232-9675
Civil Rights Division

Accessibility Guidelines for Buildings and Facilities
U.S. Architectural & Transportation Barriers Compliance Board
Telephone: 1-202-653-7834
Fax: 1-202-653-7863

ANTITRUST LAWS

Antitrust laws protect competition and prevent monopolies. Violation of federal and/or state antitrust laws result in severe sanctions the law can inflict upon a business, its partners and corporate officers. Therefore, real estate brokers and sales associates must have a basic understanding of antitrust laws and how they are applied to the real estate industry. Antitrust violations are generally not covered by errors and omissions policies.

THE SHERMAN ACT

Section 1 of the Sherman Act (1890) provides: "Every contract combination in the form of trust or otherwise, or conspiracy, in restraint of trade or commerce among several states, or with foreign nations, is declared to be illegal."

Conspiracy means that two or more separate business entities participate in a *common scheme or plan* and that the effect of the scheme is *restraint of trade*.

Conspiracies To Fix Real Estate Commission Rates or Commission Splits

In *United States v. National Association of Real Estate Boards (NAREB)*, the Supreme Court in 1950 held that the concept of *trade* as used in the Sherman Act included real estate brokerage, and that mandatory fee schedules that were promulgated and enforced by a real estate board through disciplinary proceedings violated Section 1 of the Sherman Act.

While commission rates are the most common object of price fixing allegations against real estate brokers, a conspiracy among brokers to fix the duration of listing agreements, the form of compensation or the type of listings that will be accepted are also in violation of the Sherman Act.

Restraint of Trade

The 1980 decision in *McLain v. New Orleans Real Estate Board* held that a conspiracy to fix real estate commissions can have the necessary effect upon interstate commerce because the transaction that results from the successful marketing effort often involves the use of out-of-state mortgage lenders or insurers. As such, an artificially inflated real estate brokerage commission raises the total cost of closing a real estate transaction that in turn affects interstate commerce in mortgage lending and insurance. This decision established without a doubt that the federal antitrust laws apply to the real estate brokerage business despite the local character of the real estate being sold or leased.

The language in the Sherman Act that *every* contract or combination in restraint of trade is declared to be illegal brought about a dispute that was decided in *Standard Oil v. United States.* Reasoning that every business contract is a restraint upon the commercial freedom of the parties, the Supreme Court interpreted the words *in restraint of trade* to mean only those contracts, combinations or conspiracies that unreasonably restrain trade. This judicial editing of the Sherman Act is known as the *Rule of Reason.*

Applying the Rule of Reason to various types of trade restraints, the Supreme Court eventually identified that their anticompetitive effects can be presumed. This conclusive presumption of an anticompetitive effect is known as the *per se rule.* If a particular restraint is found to be within the per se category, the antitrust laws do not allow any evidence, justification or excuse to be presented in defense of a per se offense. Thus, the issue in a per se case is not to determine if there is a conspiracy but whether the defendant is found to have participated in the conspiracy.

There are two categories of restraints subject to the per se rule that are of most concern to real estate brokers: (1) conspiracies to fix commission rates or commission splits and (2) group boycotts.

In *United States v. Foley,* a conspiracy to fix real estate commissions was found when a member of the Montgomery County (Maryland) Board of REAL-TORS® announced at a board function that he was raising his gross commission rate and that "he did not care what others did." The announcement was construed as an invitation to conspire, and the subsequent action by the other competitors was construed as an acceptance of this invitation. This case demonstrates that an inference of conspiracy based upon the actions of alleged conspirators is permissible as evidence without proving that alleged conspirators actually consulted with each other concerning a fee structure.

Group Boycotts

Group boycotts, having the primary objective of harming or destroying a competitor or a supplier of goods and services, occur in the real estate business when two or more brokers agree to refuse to cooperate or to cooperate on less favorable terms with a third broker, often a discount broker, in order to force a change in the competitor's behavior or to drive the competitor out of business. Such boycotts are per se (as a matter of law) illegal under the antitrust laws.

Real estate brokers or salespeople who act as if there were a conspiracy to boycott a competitor are just as vulnerable to an antitrust lawsuit as those who actually participate in the conspiracy.

Tying Agreements

The Supreme Court has defined a tying agreement as "an agreement to sell one product, only on the condition that the buyer also purchases a different (or tied) product . . ."

Courts have concluded that when the effect of a tying arrangement is to extend the seller's market power in the tying product into the market for the tied product, the tying arrangement is per se illegal under the antitrust laws.

As a result of *Northern Pacific Railway Co. v. United States,* real estate brokers should treat with caution any contract for the sale of land that conditions the sale on the buyer's agreement that he or she will engage the services of the seller or the seller's subsidiary.

Examples of possible antitrust violations are

- a list-back clause in an agreement for the sale of subdivision lots whereby the developer sells a subdivision lot to a builder conditioned upon the builder's agreement to list back the improved property with the developer's brokerage firm for subsequent sale to homebuyers.
- a property management agreement that binds the owner to list the property with the broker-manager.

ANTITRUST ENFORCEMENT

The Department of Justice

The U.S. attorney general, through the Antitrust Division of the Department of Justice, may bring criminal and civil actions to enforce the Sherman Act.

The Antitrust Division has brought criminal antitrust indictments against real estate brokers, all of which have alleged that the defendants engaged in a conspiracy to fix real estate commissions.

A corporation found guilty of violating the Sherman Act may be fined up to $1 million. An individual may be fined up to $100,000 and imprisoned up to three years, or both.

Private Enforcement

Section 4 of the Clayton Act authorizes private persons to recover damages for injuries to their business or property by reason of anything forbidden by the antitrust laws.

Under the act, injured persons may recover three times actual damages plus reasonable attorney's fees.

REDUCING RISK OF ANTITRUST LIABILITY

Office Policies

Education. Education is imperative because brokers are held accountable and liable for the actions and statements of their sales associates. Each new salesperson should attend an orientation program. For this purpose NAR has prepared a videotape, *Antitrust and Real Estate,* as well as a booklet entitled "Antitrust and Real Estate Compliance Program for REALTORS® and REALTOR®-ASSOCIATES®."

Training. When discussing fees with actual or prospective clients, sales associates should use language conveying the impression that the firm sets commission rates unilaterally and independently.

Sales associates should provide positive reasons for the firm's fee structure when sellers ask to lower the commission rate. Any suggestion that commissions are established by agreement among brokers or that an individual competitor is the object of a boycott must definitely be avoided.

Brokers or salespeople who find themselves in the midst of a prohibited discussion of commission rates with competitors must immediately take affirmative steps to disavow any connection with it. Being silent may imply that the silent broker participated in the price-fixing conspiracy.

To avoid antitrust liability, real estate brokers and salespeople should be particularly careful to avoid any communications or discussions with their competitors that relate in any way to the commission rates charged to sellers or the compensation levels paid to other firms for cooperative brokerage services.

Sales associates should report any suggestions by salespeople from other firms that could imply an invitation to fix commissions or boycott a competitor.

Standard Forms. Printed forms should *not* contain *preprinted* commission rates, predetermined listing periods, automatic renewal clauses or predetermined protection periods. There should be blanks to be filled out in each transaction.

Antitrust Investigations or Complaints. In the event of an antitrust investigation or complaint, the matter should be referred immediately to the firm's attorney. The local board or Association of REALTORS®, state association and the general counsel's office of NAR may also provide legal assistance.

What To Do

- The key to avoiding inferences of antitrust conspiracy is to establish independently fees and other listing policies, including commission rates (flat fee or percentage of sales price), commission splits, length of listing, length of protected period after expiration and type of listing without consulting any competing brokerage firms.
- Documenting that commission rates and commission splits are set and/or adjusted as a result of independent business judgment is recommended. Such documentation may take the form of a confidential memo restricted solely to sales associates of the firm and to the office file.
- In the event a broker finds it necessary to deviate from his or her cooperative compensation split to one particular cooperating broker, it is essential to document that the deviation is based upon an independent evaluation of the circumstances. Such documentation would be necessary to rebut a possible inference of conspiracy in the event one or more other firms also lowered their cooperative compensation to the same firm.

What Not To Do

Real estate brokers must never

- mention or intimate intentions concerning commissions, fees or other business plans to competitors.
- refer to pricing policies of competitors when responding to questions about fees.
- include representatives of a third office when discussing a commission split with a cooperating broker.
- tell prospective clients they should not work with another firm because other brokers will not do business with that firm.
- suggest that other brokers have agreed not to cooperate for less than a particular commission split.

Dangerous Words and Phrases

(From the booklet entitled "Antitrust and Real Estate Compliance Program for REALTORS® and REALTOR-ASSOCIATES®," 1st and 3rd editions, by permission of the National Association of REALTORS®. All rights reserved.)

The following are examples of words or phrases occasionally used by salespeople that would permit a judge or jury to infer that real estate brokers are engaged in an illegal conspiracy:

- "I'd like to lower the commission rate, but the board has a rule . . ."
- "The MLS will not accept less than a 120-day listing."
- "Before you list with XYZ Realty, you should know that nobody works on their listings."
- "If John Doe was really professional (or ethical), he would have joined the board."
- "The board requires all REALTORS® to make their salespeople join."
- "The best way to deal with John Doe is to boycott him."

- "If you valued your services as a professional, you wouldn't cut your commission."
- "No board member will accept a listing for less than ninety days."
- "Let him stay in his own market. This is our territory."
- "If he was really a professional, he wouldn't use part-timers."
- "This is the rate every firm charges."
- "I'd like to lower the commission, but no one else in the MLS will show your house unless the commission is X%."
- "Before you decide to list with XYZ Realty, you should know that because they are a 'discount' broker, members of the board won't show their listings."
- "I'd like to (reduce the commission . . . shorten the listing term . . . accept an exclusive agency listing), but if I do the MLS won't accept the listing."
- "This is what all brokers do."
- "No one else will cooperate unless you accept the listing on these terms."

UNAUTHORIZED PRACTICE OF LAW

PRACTICE OF LAW

Quoting John Reilly's *The Language of Real Estate*, practice of law is defined as: "Rendering services that are peculiar to the law profession, such as preparing legal documents, giving legal advice and counsel, or construing contracts by which legal rights are secured. A real estate broker's license can be suspended or revoked for the unauthorized practice of law, regardless of whether or not fees are charged. The broker also has an ethical duty to recommend that legal counsel be obtained when the interest of either buyer or seller requires it.

"There is universal uncertainty as to whether the broker's use of certain forms constitutes the practice of law. While it is permissible for the broker to help complete certain standard forms, such as a sales contract, the broker has a duty to do so with accuracy and with certainty. Such completion of forms is permissible only where it is incidental to the broker's earning a commission and not where he or she makes a separate charge for filling in the form. In most states the broker may not prepare documents such as contracts for deed, deeds, mortgages, deeds of trust, options and certain leases.

"Only attorneys and the parties to a transaction are authorized to prepare legal instruments. However, many state Associations of REALTORS® and Bar Associations have broker-lawyer accords that recognize that the real estate broker must have authority to secure some kind of agreement between buyer and seller, evidence of the transaction, and provisions for payment of the broker's compensation. This usually gives a broker the authority to fill in the blanks of preprinted documents only, and not to draft legal documents or close transactions (as some states recognize these acts as the practice of law)."

Thus, in many states real estate licensees may fill in the blanks in printed, standardized forms approved by a lawyer and in connection with transactions handled by the broker in the usual course of business. However, the broker may not charge for filling in the blanks or give advice or counsel as to the legal effect and validity of such documents.

The standard of care demanded of an attorney will be the standard applied to a real estate licensee who practices law.

In an effort to help resolve the unauthorized practice of law problem, the National Association of REALTORS® adopted Article 17 of the Code of Ethics: "The REALTOR® shall not engage in activities that constitute the unauthorized practice of law and shall recommend that legal counsel be obtained when the interest of any party to the transaction requires it." This article has been introduced in court [*Crutchley v. First Trust & Savings Bank*, 450 N.W. 2d 877 (Iowa 1990)] as the standard of a case against which a salesperson's conduct should be measured. Proof of a violation of this standard is evidence upon which the judge and jury may find a salesperson negligent.

Legal Advice or Judgment

Exercising legal judgment as to which competing real estate form to use or giving advice about legal effects of executing a joint tenancy deed constitutes a practice of law [*State Bar of New Mexico v. Guardian Abstract and Title Company, Inc.*, 575 P.2d 943 (NM 1978)].

A real estate broker who counseled a seller on the tax consequences of various forms of property transfer engaged in unauthorized practice of law [*Wolfenberger v. Madison*, 357 N.E.2d 656 (IL 1976)].

BIBLIOGRAPHY

Agency: Challenges, Choices and Opportunities, ©1993 by NAR

Agency Disclosure: The Complete Office Policy Guide by John W. Reilly and Michael Somers

Agency Relationships in Real Estate by John W. Reilly

Antitrust and Real Estate Compliance Program for REALTORS® and REALTOR®-ASSOCIATES® by NAR

Buyer Agency by Gail G. Lyons and Donald L. Harlan

Buyer Brokering by James B. Warkentin

Buyer's Broker Registry, P.O. Box 23275, Ventura, CA 93002; 1-800-729-5147

Consensual Dual Agency by John Reilly, Gail G. Lyons and Donald L. Harlan

Don't Risk It: A Broker's Guide to Risk Management, ©1996 by NAR

Fair Housing: Opening Doors to Equal Opportunity, ©1995 by NAR

Leading Guide to Buyer Brokering by Barry M. Miller

Property Disclosures: What You Need to Know, ©1995 by NAR

Reference Handbook: Antitrust and Real Estate by NAR

Risk Management I, course outline by the Hawaii Association of REALTORS®

Risk Management II, course outline by the Hawaii Association of REALTORS®

Risk Management III, course outline by the Hawaii Association of REALTORS®

The How & Why of Buyer Agency by Pat M. Goodover II

The Language of Real Estate by John W. Reilly

TAX
INFORMATION

To receive advance notice of the
next *Realty Bluebook*® edition
(and information about
what's new), please call
1-800-428-3846
to register your name and address,
or visit the Bluebook Web Page at
www.deheer.com/bluebook

CONTENTS

TAX INFORMATION

The real estate broker is generally not trained or licensed to give tax advice and cannot take the resulting responsibility. This field belongs to the professional tax consultant—the attorney at law or the public accountant—who by virtue of his or her profession is trained and licensed to give tax advice and holds himself or herself responsible for the consequences of that advice.

Buyers and sellers of real property often fail to consult a professional tax consultant when real estate is concerned. It is then that the real estate broker is often the only one in a position to recognize certain opportunities or pitfalls with respect to the client's real estate holdings or transactions that could have serious consequences on the client's tax liability. If able to recognize such opportunities and pitfalls, the broker can perform an invaluable service for clients by pointing out tax effects resulting from certain situations and by urging clients to consult their tax advisers. While the broker has thus not given tax advice, he or she may well have saved clients from making a move that could otherwise have resulted in costly tax consequences; or the broker may have caused clients to make a profitable move tax-wise that they otherwise might not have made.

The broker should protect himself or herself—and the client—by ascertaining that the client does not rely upon any statements or representations made by the broker with respect to the client's tax liability. It may be prudent to insert a clause to that effect into sales and exchange agreements.

BASIS

Basis (tax book value of property) has significant tax consequences to the owner.

1. It is the starting point for computing cost recovery deductions.

2. It determines the amount of gain or loss realized upon disposition of the property.
3. It controls the amount of any casualty losses.

During ownership of property, the basis is adjusted upward by adding any capital expenditures the owner may have made. Basis is adjusted downward by subtracting any cost recovery (depreciation) deductions.

The *Sale Price* less *Selling Expenses* is the *Amount Realized*.

The *Amount Realized* less *Adjusted Basis* is termed *Gain Realized*.

The taxable portion of the *realized gain* is called *recognized gain*.

I. Acquisition by Purchase

Basis is the cost of acquisition (purchase price plus purchase costs).

II. Acquisition by Gift

Basis is the donor's adjusted basis plus gift tax, but does not exceed the fair market value at the time of the gift for the purpose of computing loss on sale.

III. Acquisition by Inheritance

When the property is included in the transferor's gross estate for federal estate tax purposes, and when basis is the fair market value at the date of death or at the alternate valuation date* if the alternate valuation date was elected for federal estate tax purposes, acquisition is by inheritance or other transfer.

Alternate valuation date is six months after death or the date of sale or distribution if prior to this date.

There is a limited exception to this rule for property acquired from a decedent who died between January 1, 1977, and November 7, 1978, when the executor of the estate elected to use the carryover basis provisions that were in effect at that time. The election would have been made only if the market value of the property passing from the decedent was less than the amount of the basis that could be established under the carryover basis provisions.

When property is held as community property and one spouse dies, both the descendant's and survivor's one-half interests receive a new basis (determined as previously stated), even though only one half of the community property is included in the gross estate for federal estate tax purposes. However, this advantage is not available when the property is held in joint tenancy. Only that portion of the property that is included in the decedent's estate receives a new basis, and the basis of the survivor's interest is equal to his or her adjusted cost.

IV. Acquisition in Tax-Deferred Transactions

These include exchanges, sale and purchase of personal residences and involuntary conversions (replacement of property condemned, requisitioned, destroyed or sold under threat of condemnation). In these transactions, the taxpayer is permitted to defer recognition of all or part of the gain realized on the old property. In general, the basis of the new property is equal to the basis of the old property plus any additional boot paid (such as cash, notes and other assets) minus any recognized (taxable) gain. Alternatively, the basis of the new property may be determined by subtracting that deferred gain from the cost of the acquired property. (See Tax-Deferred Exchanges and Personal Residences in this section.)

V. Acquisition as Compensation for Services

Basis is the fair market value of the services at time of transfer.

VI. Acquisition Through Exercise of an Option

Basis is the cost of acquisition of the property plus the cost of the option.

VII. Basis Increase

Basis is increased by:

1. additions and improvements (as distinguished from repairs);
2. cost of insuring, perfecting and defending the title, and other purchase expenses; and
3. special assessments.

CAPITAL IMPROVEMENTS VERSUS REPAIRS

Capital improvements increase the basis and are subject to annual cost recovery deductions spread over the life of the asset, whereas repairs are fully deductible expenses. The basic distinction between capital improvement and repair is that the former normally involves a relatively permanent increase in the value of the building or a lengthening of its useful life, whereas the latter is usually a recurring type of expenditure to keep the property in operating condition and will not cause an increase in value or in useful life. Please refer to Deductible Expenses under Personal Residences.

Type of Expenditure	Capital	Expense
Foundation–new	X	
Foundation–repair		X
Pest control		X
New front	X	
Painting–outside		X
Painting–inside		X
Papering		X
Plastering		X
Floors–new	X	
Floors–resurfacing and patching	X	
Floors–replacing with tile	X	
Roof–replacement	X	
Roof–reshingling	X	
Roof–repair broken portions		X

Type of Expenditure	Capital	Expense
Ratproofing.............	X	
Fire escapes—new........	X	
Fire escapes rails replaced.		X
Stairway—new supports ...		X
Electric wiring—new......	X	
Electric wiring—replaced (defective).............		X
Iron water pipes replaced by copper	X	
Plumbing—replaced (defective).............		X
Stopping plumbing leaks..		X
Heating—permanent conversion	X	
Furnace—relining	X	
Furnace—enameling		X
Insulating		X
Air-conditioning compressor replaced		X
Wells—cleaning and repairing		X
Maintenance of property ..		X
Casualties—repairs resulting from		X
Damaged property restored to normal		X
Damaged property restored to something better and different	X	
Restoration of property purchased in rundown condition	X	
Alterations to suit taxpayer's use	X	

Type of Expenditure	Capital	Expense
Repairs and improvements as part of a general plan of remodeling	X	
Alteration of building	X	
Architect's fee–addition . . .	X	
Assessments for improvements	X	
Enlarging and adding bathrooms.	X	
Office layout nonpermanent change.	X	
Residence–converting upper floor for rental	X	
Keeping building in safe condition.		X
Shoring up building to prevent collapse		X
Installation of a swimming pool or landscaping	X	

Fees and Commissions*	Capital	Expense
For management and collecting rent.		X
For negotiating lease deductible over original term of lease	X	
Points or discount in lieu of interest in whole or part deductible by cash basis taxpayer over the period of repayment of loan.	X	

Fees and Commissions*	Capital	Expense
Loan fee, if an expense for obtaining the loan and not interest, deductible as a business or investment expense.	X	
For negotiating a sale or purchase.	X	
Selling commission paid by dealers		X
Legal and accounting for acquisition of property or protection of title.	X	
Legal and accounting, except as above		X
Tax advice, tax return, litigation.	X	X
Title search and title insurance	X	
Cost of removing clouds on title.	X	
Cost of survey.	X	
Appraisal fee.	X	
Mortgage interest and prepayment fees.		X

*For investment properties.

CLASSIFICATION OF REAL ESTATE

For tax purposes, real estate can be classified into the following types of holdings:

1. R.E. Held for Investment or for Production of Income
   Gain is capital gain.
   Loss is capital loss.
   Expenses are deductible.

Depreciation is allowed (if rented or available for rent).

2. R.E. Held for Use in Trade or Business
   Gain is capital gain.
   Loss is ordinary loss.
   Expenses are deductible.
   Depreciation is allowed.

3. R.E. Held as a Personal Residence
   Gain is capital gain.
   Loss is nondeductible.
   Expenses are nondeductible, except interest, property taxes and casualty losses.
   Depreciation is not allowed.

4. R.E. Held Primarily for Sale to Customers
   Gain is ordinary gain.
   Loss is ordinary loss.
   Expenses are deductible.
   Depreciation is not allowed unless property produces income or is held for the purpose of producing income.

R.E. Held for Investment or for Production of Income

These two categories include real property held as an investment, such as unimproved land or property that requires little or no supervision or maintenance.

Investment property is a capital asset. As such, profits are capital gains and losses are capital losses. Capital losses reduce the amount of capital gain if they occur in the same year. If the capital loss exceeds the capital gain, then the resulting deduction for net capital loss is limited to the lesser of $3,000 or taxable income per year; the remainder is carried forward to the next succeeding year until it is used up.

R.E. Held for Use in Trade or Business

This category includes real property used by the taxpayer in his or her trade or business. Generally, rental property falls into this category as the property is used in the trade or business of producing rental income.

Real estate in this category falls outside the definition of capital asset and qualifies for tax treatment that is especially advantageous.

1. If in any one year gains exceed losses on trade or business property, all gains or losses are treated as gain or loss from the sale of a capital asset, resulting in a net capital gain.
2. If in any one year losses exceed gains, all such gains and losses are treated as arising from the sale of noncapital assets, resulting in a fully deductible ordinary loss.

R.E. Held as a Personal Residence

When a personal residence is sold or exchanged, any resulting profit is treated as capital gain, but losses cannot be deducted against income.

If a personal residence has been converted to income-producing property, it may become trade or business real estate and, as such, qualifies for capital gain or ordinary loss treatment upon disposition. Special rules apply to calculation of losses in this situation.

Refer also to Personal Residences in this section.

R.E. Held Primarily for Sale to Customers

Real estate under this classification can be compared to merchandise on a dealer's shelf. Taxpayers who deal in real estate so classified are called *dealers*. Gains or losses resulting from the disposition of dealers' realty are ordinary gains or ordinary losses.

Rules as to whether a taxpayer is classified as a dealer have evolved from court decisions. Among the factors considered by the courts in the classification of taxpayers as dealers are the following:

1. The degree of activity in the purchase and sale of real estate. Merely reducing the frequency of real estate turnover is not sufficient to remove

the dealer status once the taxpayer has been so classified.

2. The intent of purchasing and holding the property as an investment or as part of an inventory held for resale. It is important to make the intent a matter of record at the time of acquisition and to act consistently with such intent during the term the property is held.

3. The length of time the property is held.

4. The extent of involvement in real estate activity by the owner, such as promotion, advertising, listing the property with a real estate broker, and so forth.

5. The reason for purchasing or selling the property; whether the purchase or sale was voluntary or involuntary (because of a drop in rents, increase in maintenance costs, sudden rise in land values, etc.).

6. Undeveloped real estate is subdivided.

7. The extent income from real estate sales compares with income from another full-time occupation.

8. Real estate brokers, builders and subdividers need additional evidence to establish that any of their real estate holdings are investments.

It should be noted that nonprofessional investors are not protected from being classified as dealers by the IRS, even though they are in an entirely different business.

CAPITAL GAIN

Capital gain is the taxable profit derived from the sale or exchange of a capital asset. Real property generally is a capital asset unless the property is held for sale in the ordinary course of business by a taxpayer commonly described as a dealer.

THE TAXPAYER RELIEF ACT OF 1997

Reduced Capital Gains Tax Rates

The Taxpayer Relief Act of 1997, effective retroactively to May 7, 1997, provides for a capital gains rate of 20% (reduced from 28%) for taxpayers in upper brackets and 10% (down from 15%) for those in lower brackets. (Taxpayers in upper brackets are those with gross incomes upwards of $150,000 if filing jointly and upwards of $75,000 for those filing singly.) Effective July 29, 1997, assets must be held at least 18 months to qualify for the new rates.

While the reduced capital gains rates also apply to investment properties, gains due to recapture of depreciation deductions are taxable at 25%. The tax-deferred exchange rules under IRC Sec. 1031 remain unchanged.

Beginning in the year 2001, home buyers who occupy their homes for more than five years may qualify for the even lower capital gains rate of 18%.

Capital Gains Exclusion for Homeowners

In the sale of a principal residence where the owner has resided for two of the last five years, the Act provides for a capital gains tax exclusion of $500,000 for taxpayers filing jointly and $250,000 for those filing singly. Taxpayers may take advantage of this capital gains tax exclusion every two years for an unlimited number of transactions. The measure eliminates existing rollover provisions and the one-time exclusion for those 55 years old or older.

Penalty-Free IRA Withdrawals for Down Payment

The measure allows first-time home buyers to make penalty-free early withdrawals of up to $10,000 from newly created *American Dream* Individual Retirement Accounts to help with the down payment and closing costs on a first-time home purchase.

Exemption on Estate Taxes

The exemption on estate taxes would increase to $1 million (up from $600,000), phased in over ten years. For family-owned farms and small businesses, the exemption is immediately increased to $1,300,000.

Home Office

The term "principal place of business" will now specifically include a place of business that is used by the taxpayer for business-related administrative or management activities, if there is no other fixed location of the business where the taxpayer conducts substantial administrative or management activities. REALTORS® should contact their tax advisor to determine how the new definition impacts them.

ALTERNATIVE MINIMUM TAX

A taxpayer is subject to payment of the *alternative minimum tax* if such tax exceeds the taxpayer's regular income tax for the year.

The alternative minimum tax is 26% of alternative minimum taxable income up to $175,000 and 28% of alternative minimum taxable income in excess of $175,000.

Alternative minimum taxable income for most taxpayers will be the *adjusted gross income* plus *items of tax preference* minus *Alternative Tax Itemized Deductions*.

Alternative tax itemized deductions include (1) casualty and theft losses in excess of 10% of adjusted gross income; (2) charitable deductions; (3) medical deductions in excess of 10% of adjusted gross income; (4) interest paid on indebtedness for acquisition, construction or substantial improvement of taxpayer's principal residence or second home; and (5) investment interest to the extent of net investment income of the taxpayer. *Items of tax preference* include accelerated depreciation in excess of straight-line depreciation on real property and net loss from a passive activity. (As explained hereafter, net loss from the ownership of rental real property is a passive activity loss.)

The alternative minimum taxable income is reduced by an exemption of $45,000 for joint returns, $33,750 for single taxpayers and $22,500 for married taxpayers filing separately. However, the exemption amount is reduced by 25% of the amount by which the alternative minimum taxable income exceeds $150,000 for joint returns, $112,500 for single individuals and $75,000 for married taxpayers filing separately.

Example

Taxpayers file a joint return with an ordinary income of $100,000 and rental (passive activity) loss of $20,000. Their adjusted gross income is $80,000. Assume they have alternative minimum tax itemized deductions of $48,000 and nonalternative minimum itemized deductions of $2,000. Excess accelerated depreciation deducted is $23,333. Their regular income tax for the year is $4,504.

The alternative minimum tax would be computed as follows:

Adjusted gross income			$80,000
less			
alt. tax itemized deductions		$48,000	
plus			
Allowable rental loss	$20,000		
Excess depreciation	23,333		
		43,333	
			−4,667
Alternative minimum taxable income			$75,333

| Exemption | 45,000 |
| Less 25% AMTI excess over $150,000 | None |

$$-45,000$$
$$30,333$$

Alternative minimum tax at 26% $7,887

NOTE: *The alternative minimum tax is $3,383 greater than the regular tax.*

DEPRECIATION–COST RECOVERY

Historically, the law permitted taxpayers investing in depreciable property to take regular tax deductions for the amount of annual depreciation of an asset. Depreciation was computed on the basis of an asset and was spread systematically over its estimated useful life.

The Economic Recovery Tax Act of 1981 introduced the Accelerated Cost Recovery System (ACRS) for property placed in service after December 31, 1980. The new system substitutes the term *cost recovery* for *depreciation*. ACRS enables taxpayers to recover the cost of eligible (depreciable) property more rapidly than was formerly permitted. However, the TRA '86 substantially lengthened the period of time over which taxpayers can recover costs.

Cost recovery tax deductions do not result from current cash expenses; yet they reduce taxpayers' tax liability and thus increase the cash return on investments.

Eligible (depreciable) property. To be eligible for cost recovery, property must be held for production of income or for use in the taxpayer's trade or business.

Persons entitled to cost recovery (depreciation). To be entitled to cost recovery deductions, the taxpayer must have an economic interest in the property; just holding title to the property is not sufficient.

Elements of Cost Recovery (Depreciation)

To compute annual cost recovery tax deductions, one must determine the tax basis of the property and the recovery period.

Basis. In the case of real property, only the improvements are subject to cost recovery, not the land. Therefore, the basis of the improvements must be allocated. This is often done by using the assessment ratio of land to improvements or by using comparable sales or appraisals.

Adjusted basis. The original basis is adjusted by adding capital improvements and subtracting cost recovery deductions.

Recovery period and method. The recovery period for residential real property is 27½ years. The recovery period for nonresidential real property acquired after May 12, 1993, is 39 years. Cost recovery must be taken on a straight-line basis for all property acquired after December 31, 1986.

Component Depreciation

Component depreciation is no longer available. When a taxpayer makes a substantial improvement to a building, the substantial improvement is treated as a separate building rather than a component. An improvement is a substantial improvement if (1) the amounts added to the capital account of the building over a two-year period are at least 25% of the adjusted basis of the building (disregarding depreciation and amortization adjustments) as of the first day of that two-year period. and (2) the improvement is made at least three years after the building was placed in service.

LIMITATION ON INTEREST AND OTHER DEDUCTIONS

Loss Limitation from Passive Activities

A passive activity is a trade or business in which the tax-payer does not materially participate. Section 469 of the Internal Revenue Code disallows the deduction of losses and tax credits of passive activities to individuals, estates, trusts, closely held Subchapter C corporations and personal service corporations. This is true subject to certain exceptions, including closely held Subchapter C corporations, which may offset passive losses against net active business income, but not against portfolio income (dividends, interest and royalties).

The following discussion is limited to the disallowance or allowance of losses attributable to real estate rental activities. With certain exceptions, the rental of real estate is considered a passive activity for many taxpayers, even though they may actually participate materially in the activity.

There is an exception for losses not exceeding $25,000 in any tax year incurred by an individual who actively participates in the management of his or her property. The $25,000 amount is phased out between $100,000 and $150,000 of modified adjusted gross income (determined without regard to passive losses).

Low-income housing credits may be taken (upon a deduction equivalent basis) under the $25,000 allowance against nonpassive income without regard to whether the individual actively participates.

The active participation with respect to the $25,000 allowance does not require regular, continuous and substantial involvement in operations. The requirement may be satisfied if the taxpayer participates in the making of management decisions, such as approval of new tenants or deciding on rental real estate activity if he or she owns less than 10% of the value of all interest in the activity.

There is a special exception for taxpayers in the real estate business. This exception applies to the taxpayer for a taxable year if more than one-half of the personal services performed in trades or business by the taxpayer during the year are performed in real pro-perty trades or business in which the taxpayer materially participates, and if the taxpayer performs more than 750 hours of services during the taxable year in real property trades or business in which the taxpayer materially participates. The term *real property trade or business* means any real property development, redevelopment, construction, reconstruction, acquisition, conversion, rental, operation, management, leasing or brokerage trade or business. With respect to a closely held Subchapter C corporation, the requirements are satisfied if more than 50% of the gross receipts of such a corporation for the taxable year are derived from real property trades or businesses in which the corporation materially participates. The personal services of an employee are not treated as performed in real property trades or businesses unless such employee is a 5% or greater owner of the employer.

Interest deductions attributable to passive activities are treated as passive activity deductions, not as investment interest (see explanation of investment interest under the subhead that follows). Thus, such interest deductions are subject to limitation under the passive activity loss rule, not under the investment interest limitation. Similarly, income and loss from passive activities generally are not treated as investment income or loss in calculating the amount of the investment interest limitation.

To the extent that passive activity losses are not deductible in any one year, they are carried forward from year to year. They may be deducted in subsequent years against passive activity income. When the passive activity is disposed of, the losses from prior years become deductible (offset by any gain).

Investment Interest

The allowable deduction for interest paid by a taxpayer was substantially changed by the TRA '86. (See also Residence Interest.)

Investment interest means interest paid or accrued on indebtedness on property held for investment. Interest on debt used to purchase or hold rental real property is *not* investment interest. If the taxpayer materially participates in the operation of the rental property, the interest is incurred on a trade or business. If the taxpayer does not materially participate in the operation of the rental property, interest is an expense in computing taxable income from a passive activity. Property subject to a net lease is not treated as investment property because it is treated as a passive activity under the passive loss rules.

The deduction for investment interest is limited to the amount of net investment income. In the event the net investment interest exceeds the net investment income in any one year, such excess is carried forward and treated as investment interest in the succeeding tax year.

Net investment income means the excess of investment income over investment expenses.

Investment income includes gross income from property held for investment, gains attributable to the disposition of property held for investment and gross portfolio income.

Portfolio income means dividends, interest and royalties.

Investment expenses are deductible expenses (other than interest) directly connected with the production of investment income.

INVESTMENT TAX CREDIT

Low-Income Housing

Commencing in 1987, a tax credit is allowed for investments in low-income housing. The credit may be claimed annually for a period of ten years. The credit rate is set so that the annualized credit amounts have a present value of 70% for qualified new construction and rehabilitation expenditures that are not federally subsidized and a 30% credit for other qualifying low-income housing expenditures. Expenditures qualifying for the 30% present value credit consist of the cost of acquisition, certain rehabilitation expenditures incurred in connection with the acquisition of an existing building and federally subsidized new construction or rehabilitation expenditures. The taxpayer's credit amount in any taxable year is computed by applying the appropriate credit%age to the appropriate qualified basis amount in such year.

For buildings placed in service in 1987, the credit%ages are 9% annually over ten years for the 70% present value credit and 4% annually over ten years for the 30% present value credit. For buildings placed in service after 1987, these credit percentages are to be adjusted monthly by the Treasury to reflect the present values of 70% and 30% at the time the building is placed in service.

The qualified basis amounts with respect to which the credit amount is computed are determined as the proportion of the eligible basis in a qualified low-income building attributable to the low-income rental units. This proportion is the lesser of (1) the proportion of low-income units to all residential units or (2) the proportion of floor space of the low-income units to the floor space of all rental units. Generally, in these calculations, low-income units are those units presently occupied by qualifying tenants, whereas residential rental units are all units, whether presently occupied or not.

Eligible basis consists of (1) the cost of new construction, (2) the cost of rehabilitation or (3) the cost of acquisition of existing buildings acquired through purchase and the cost of rehabilitation, if any, to such buildings incurred before the close of the first taxable year of the credit. Only the adjusted basis of the building may be included in the eligible basis. The cost of land is not included.

The cost of residential units in buildings that are not low-income units may be included in the eligible basis only if such units are not above the average quality standard of the low-income units. Residential real property may qualify for credit even though a portion of the building in which the residential rental units are located is used for commercial purposes. No portion of the cost of such nonresidential rental property may be included in eligible basis. The qualified basis attributable to rehabilitation expenditures not claimed in connection with the acquisition of an existing building must equal at least $3,000 per low-income unit or 10% of the building's adjusted basis, whichever is greater, in order for rehabilitation expenditures to qualify for the credit.

Residential rental projects providing low-income housing qualify for the credit only if (1) 20% or more of the aggregate residential rental units in the project are occupied by individuals with incomes of 50% of the area median income as adjusted for family size, or (2) 40% or more of the aggregate residential rental units in the project are occupied by individuals with incomes of 60% or less of the area median income as adjusted for family size. The owner must irrevocably elect the minimum set-aside requirement at the time the project is placed in service. The gross rent paid by families in units included in the qualified basis may not exceed 30% of the applicable qualifying income for a family of its size. Gross rent is to include the cost of any utilities other than telephone.

Subject to provision for correction of inadvertent noncompliance, if a low-income housing project fails to continue to qualify during the 15-year compliance period, the credits allowed in the prior years are recaptured. Buildings will not receive credit allocations unless an extended low-income housing agreement is entered into between the allocating agency and the taxpayer. The extended agreement would be for an additional 15 years but may be terminated if the taxpayer requests the agency to find a buyer at a formula price contained in the agreement and the agency is unable to do so. Notwithstanding termination, the taxpayer may not increase the rent for three years after the agreement terminates. The effect of this is to extend the compliance period to 18 years if the allocating agency is unable to find a buyer pursuant to a request received one year before the end of the initial 15-year compliance period. If there is a change in ownership of the building, this is a recapture event unless the seller posts a bond to the Secretary of the Treasury in a satisfactory amount to ensure compliance during the balance of the 15-year term. For partnerships consisting of more than 35 individual taxpayers and at the partnership's election, no change in ownership is deemed to occur provided that within a 12-month period at least 50% in value of the original ownership is unchanged. A purchaser of a low-income housing project is eligible to continue to receive the credits based upon the original qualified basis.

Limitations are placed on the number of low-income housing projects qualifying for the credit in each state. In the case of projects financed with tax-exempt bonds, this limitation arises on account of the statewide limitation on the number of bonds that are financed for the tax exemption. With respect to projects not financed by tax-exempt bonds, there is a procedure for the state to approve a limited number of units. The annual dollar limit for each state on the total amount of qualifying projects is $1.25 for each individual resident of the state.

Rehabilitation of Nonresidential Buildings

The tax credit for rehabilitation expenditures of older nonresidential buildings was modified by the TRA '86 with respect to property placed in service after December 31, 1986. The credit%age is 20% for rehabilitations of certified historic structures and 10% for rehabilitation of buildings other than certified historic structures originally placed in service before 1936. Expenditures incurred by a lessee do not qualify for the credit unless the remaining lease term on the date the rehabilitation is completed is at least as long as the applicable cost recovery period under the general cost recovery rules.

There must be a substantial rehabilitation requiring that the rehabilitation expenditures during a 24-month period ending on the last day of the taxable year exceed the greater of the adjusted basis of the property or $5,000. At least 75% of existing external walls, as well as 75% of the building's interior structural framework must remain in place. This limitation does not apply to historic structures.

EXCHANGE AGREEMENTS

BALANCING EQUITIES

Before an exchange agreement can be written, the equities of both parties must be balanced.

Case 1: Two-Way Exchange

Jones offers to exchange his property at 101 Atlantic for Brown's property at 505 Pacific.

Jones' property has an FMV (fair market value) of $100,000, and he has a first loan of $50,000, giving him an equity in Atlantic of $50,000.

Brown's property has an FMV of $200,000, and he owes $30,000 on it, which gives him an equity in Pacific of $170,000.

Jones proposes to obtain a new loan on 505 Pacific of $130,000; he has $15,000 cash to give to Brown and proposes to execute a second mortgage on Pacific in favor of Brown for the balance of $5,000.

Jones		Gives	Gets
Atlantic FMV	$100,000		
Minus existing loan balance	−50,000		
Equity in Atlantic		$50,000	
Cash		15,000	
2nd mortgage on Pacific		5,000	
Pacific FMV	200,000		
Minus new loan	−130,000		
Equity in Pacific			70,000
		$70,000	$70,000

Brown		Gives	Gets
Pacific FMV	$200,000		
Minus existing loan balance	−30,000		
Equity in Pacific		170,000	
Atlantic FMV	100,000		

Minus existing loan balance	−50,000	
Equity in Atlantic		50,000
Proceeds of new loan on Pacific	130,000	
Minus payoff existing loan	−30,000	
Net loan proceeds		100,000
Cash from Jones		15,000
2nd mortgage from Jones on Pacific		5,000
	$170,000	$170,000

Case 2: Three-Way Exchange

Uses the same example as above but with this difference: Brown is not interested in Atlantic but wants to cash out. A buyer, Smith, offers to buy Atlantic for $100,000 on the following terms: $30,000 cash, conditioned upon Smith's ability to assume the $50,000 loan and with Brown to carryback a second loan on Atlantic for the balance of $20,000.

Brown		Gives	Gets
Pacific FMV	$200,000		
Minus existing loan balance	−30,000		
Equity in Pacific		170,000	
Proceeds of new loan on Pacific	130,000		
Minus payoff existing loan	−30,000		
Net loan proceeds			100,000
Cash from Jones			15,000
Cash from Smith			30,000
2nd mortgage from Jones on Pacific			5,000
2nd mortgage from Smith on Atlantic			20,000
		$170,000	$170,000

Case 3: Four-Way Exchange

Use the example of Cash 1 but with the following complications: Brown wants to cash out. He is not interested in Atlantic. Builder Green offers a property at Sierra Avenue in exchange for the Atlantic property. Green's property has an FMV of $80,000 with an assumable first loan of $60,000. Green proposes to pay $30,000 cash in addition to his $20,000 equity in the Sierra property. Green would acquire Atlantic at the FMV of $100,000 and assume the $50,000 loan. Brown still is not interested in exchanging but says he would sign if a buyer is found for the Sierra property, provided he would not incur any extra expenses on account of the exchange. Before long, buyer Black makes an offer on the Sierra property for $80,000 with $20,000 cash, assuming the $60,000 loan.

Brown		Gives	Gets
Pacific FMV	$200,000		
Minus existing loan balance	–30,000		
Equity in Pacific		170,000	
Proceeds of new loan on Pacific	130,000		
Minus payoff existing loan	–30,000		
Net loan proceeds			100,000
Cash from Jones			15,000
Cash from Green			30,000
Cash from Black			20,000
2nd mortgage from Jones on Pacific			5,000
		$170,000	$170,000

TAX-DEFERRED EXCHANGES

Tax-Deferred Exchange versus Sale and Purchase

The following illustration demonstrates the benefit of a tax-deferred exchange over sale and purchase of real estate held for investment or for productive use in trade or business.

Case 1: Sale and Purchase

Assume someone sells a property for $800,000, purchased a number of years earlier for $600,000, and that the tax basis is depreciated down to $500,000. The seller would have a federal tax liability of $84,000 (28% of $300,000), which would reduce the sale proceeds available for reinvestment.

Case 2: Tax-Deferred Exchange

In a tax-deferred exchange, the $84,000, which would otherwise go to Uncle Sam, can be fully used for reinvestment, provided the taxpayer acquires like-kind real property of equal or greater value, held for investment or for productive use in trade or business, and provided further that the taxpayer owes at least as much on the property acquired as he or she owed on the property exchanged, and that he or she did not receive any cash, notes, personal property or other assets referred to as boot.

Internal Revenue Code Section 1031

Under Internal Revenue Code Sec. 1031, gain or loss realized is not recognized (taxable) in an exchange if property held for productive use in trade or business or for investment is exchanged solely for property of like kind that is to be held for productive use in trade or business or for investment.

The taxpayer, however, has merely deferred (not avoided) tax on nonrecognized gain realized in a so-called tax-deferred exchange.

Real property of like kind includes improved and unimproved property, fixtures and leaseholds with a remaining term of at least 30 years. (If improved real property is exchanged for unimproved, gain is not recognized except for that portion of the gain treated as ordinary income under IRC Recapture rules of Sec. 1250.)

The Revenue Reconciliation Act of 1989 provides that exchanges between U.S. and foreign property are no longer like kind.

Boot-Recognized Gain

Property not qualifying as like-kind property, if transferred partly in exchange for like-kind property, is termed *boot* and includes:

1. Mortgage boot (existing liens on the properties exchanged)
2. Other boot:
   a. Cash (including loan proceeds)
   b. Third-party notes
   c. Notes executed in escrow by one of the parties to the exchange
   d. Furniture, equipment and other personal property transferred in the exchange
   e. dealer property
   f. Property used as taxpayer's residence

Gain may be recognized to the extent of the fair market value of such boot. (Rev. Rul. 72-456, 1972-2, C.B. 468 provides that in determining the amount of gain to be recognized by the taxpayer, the brokerage commission paid from the cash boot may be deducted.)

Because various kinds of boot may be given and/or received in such a partly tax-deferred exchange, the rule is that the taxable (recognized) portion of the gain realized is equal to the net boot received. However, part of the rule is that mortgage boot received (mortgage relief) can be offset by other boot given, but that mortgage boot given (new or assumed mortgages) cannot be offset by other boot received. Therefore, the mortgage boot must be netted first before the other boot is netted. From these principles, the following formula has evolved to determine the recognized portion of the gain realized:

Recognized Gain = (1) *Net Mortgage Relief** plus *Other Boot received* or less *Other Boot given* or (2) *Gain Realized,* whichever is lower.

**Net Mortgage Relief—Any excess of existing mortgages on the real property transferred over existing mortgages on the property acquired.*

The following examples illustrate the application of the above formula:

Example 1

Jones	Gives	Gets
Fair market values	$100,000	$200,000
Less Existing mortgages	($25,000)	($150,000)
Equities	75,000	$75,000
Cash		25,000
Net mortgage relief (25,000–150,000)		0
Plus other boot (cash) received		$25,000 (1)
Gain realized is assumed to be		$70,000 (2)
Recognized gain [the lower of (1) and (2)]		**$25,000**

Example 2

Brown	Gives	Gets
Fair market values	$150,000	$200,000
Less Existing mortgages	($120,000)	($120,000)
Equities	$ 30,000	$100,000
Third party note	70,000	
	$100,000	$100,000
Net mortgage relief (120,000–100,000)		$ 20,000
Less other boot given		($70,000)
		0 (1)
Realized gain is assumed to be		$60,000 (2)
Recognized gain [the lower of (1) and (2)]		**$0**

Example 3

Smith	Gives	Gets
Fair market value	$250,000	$225,000
Less Existing mortgages	($130,000)	(100,000)
Equities	$120,000	$125,000
Furniture		40,000
Cash	45,000	
	$165,000	$165,000

Smith buys the furniture for $40,000 in a separate transaction and gives $5,000 in the exchange, thus eliminating boot on one side.

Net mortgage relief ($130,000–$100,000)		$30,000
Less other boot given		($5,000)
		$25,000 (1)
Realized gain is assumed to be		$70,000 (2)

Recognized Gain

[the lower of (1) or (2)]	**$25,000**

Where properties of unequal equities are exchanged, recognition of gain can be reduced by avoiding payment of cash in escrow. This can be accomplished—as illustrated below—by reducing the loan on the property with the smaller equity before the exchange agreement is executed.

	Existing Position		Alternate Position	
	Jones	Smith	Jones	Smith
Fair market values	$100,000	$120,000	$100,000	$120,000
Less Loans	(40,000)	(90,000)	(40,000)	(60,000)
Equities	60,000	30,000	60,000	60,000
Cash transfer		30,000		0
Recognized gain	**30,000**	20,000	**0**	20,000

Regulation 1.1031 (b)-1(c) provides that mortgage boot given by the taxpayer cannot be offset by mortgage boot incurred by the taxpayer in anticipation of the exchange. There is some court authority that would permit such refinancing. However, refinancing should not be undertaken without the advice of a qualified tax professional.

Transfer of Basis

Transferring the basis from the old to the new property becomes more complex as existing loans are involved and boot of various kinds is given.

Basis of New Property =
Fair Market Value of New Property
less *Realized Gain*
plus *Recognized Gain*

Basis of New Property =
Adjusted Basis of Old Property
plus *Boot given*
plus *Mortgages on New Property*
plus *Recognized Gain*
less *Boot received*
less *Mortgages on Old Property*

The following examples will demonstrate how—under increasingly complicated conditions—bases are transferred and to what extent gain is recognized by applying the above formula.

1. A taxpayer owns a real property free and clear with an adjusted basis of $20,000 and an FMV (fair market value) of $30,000. She exchanges her property plus $10,000 boot for another property of like kind worth $40,000.
   Realized gain = $10,000
   Recognized gain = None
   New basis = $20,000 + $10,000 = $30,000
2. The same taxpayer exchanges her property for another property of like kind worth $40,000. This time she gives no boot but assumes a loan of $10,000.

Realized gain = $10,000
Recognized gain = None
New basis = $20,000 + $10,000 = $30,000

3. The same taxpayer exchanges her property for another property of like kind worth $22,000 and receives $8,000 boot.
Realized gain = $10,000
Recognized gain = $8,000
New basis = $20,000 + $8,000 - $8,000 = $20,000

4. A taxpayer owns real property with a loan balance of $15,000, an adjusted basis of $20,000 and an FMV of $30,000. He exchanges his property for another property of like kind worth $50,000, assuming a $30,000 loan and giving the other party $5,000 boot.
Realized gain = $10,000
Recognized gain = None
New basis = $20,000 + $5,000 + $30,000 - $15,000 = $40,000

5. A taxpayer owns real property with a loan balance of $15,000, an adjusted basis of $20,000 and an FMV of $30,000. He exchanges his property for another property of like kind worth $19,000, assuming a loan of $10,000 and receiving $6,000 boot.
Realized gain = $10,000
Recognized gain = $10,000
New basis = $20,000 + $10,000 + $10,000 - $6,000 - $15,000 = $19,000
Because in this example all of the realized gain is recognized (taxable), there is no tax advantage of an exchange over a sale and a purchase.

6. A taxpayer owns real property with a loan of $10,000, an adjusted basis of $20,000 and an FMV of $30,000. He exchanges his property for another property of like kind worth $44,000, assuming a loan of $30,000 and receiving $6,000 boot.
Realized gain = $10,000

Recognized gain = $6,000

New basis = $20,000 + $30,000 + $6,000 – $6,000 – $10,000 = $40,000

Multiple Exchanges

It is highly unlikely that two property owners will wish to exchange their properties with each owner retaining the property received from the other.

The usual situation arises when a taxpayer, owning Property A, wishes to make a tax-deferred exchange for Property B, owned by a seller who is not interested in Property A.

The taxpayer may enter into an exchange agreement with the owner of Property B, conditioned upon the sale at a specified price of Property A to a third party within a period acceptable to the owner of Property B.

Supposing the owner of Property B is unwilling to wait until the taxpayer has found a buyer for Property A, can the taxpayer still make a tax-deferred exchange of Property A for Property B?

The answer is yes, but it would probably be necessary to use a third-party facilitator, and additional financing will be required until Property A is sold. The taxpayer can enter into an exchange agreement with a facilitator for the exchange of Property A for Property B. The facilitator could purchase Property B and make a simultaneous exchange with the taxpayer for Property A. Alternatively, the facilitator could purchase Property B and exchange it for Property A when a buyer is found to purchase Property A. In either event, the facilitator will need funds with which to purchase Property B. The funds would ordinarily be borrowed and repaid from the sale proceeds of Property A.

In an alternative situation, the taxpayer receives an acceptable offer to purchase Property A before she has located a suitable Property B. Because buyers are often hard to come by, the taxpayer may enter into a *binder agreement*, whereby the party wishing to purchase Property A agrees to purchase Property B, to be selected by the taxpayer within a specified period, and then exchange it with the taxpayer for Property A.

Supposing the buyer is unwilling to wait until the taxpayer has found Property B, can the taxpayer still effect a tax-deferred exchange of Property A for Property B and allow the buyer to purchase Property A without delay? The answer is yes, by effecting a delayed exchange.

Starker Delayed Exchanges

The term *Starker Exchange* stems from the famous 1979 Starker case, in which T. J. Starker survived an IRS attack. The case was legislatively sanctioned by the TRA '84 in amending Section 1031(a) (3). Final regulations of the IRS were published in May 1991.

The rules of a Starker Exchange are outlined in three basis steps:

1. The exchanger finds a cash buyer for the smaller *like kind* property. When the sale closes, the cash must be held by a third-party *qualified intermediary*. (If the seller has access to that cash, called *constructive receipt*, the sale proceeds are taxable to the seller.)
2. Within 45 days of closing the sale, the exchanger must designate the property to be acquired, with the sales proceeds being held by the intermediary (plus any cash to be added).
3. The purchase of the designated property must be completed within 180 days after selling the old property.

A Starker delayed exchange agreement should be prepared by a tax or real estate attorney.

Definitions

A *deferred exchange* is an exchange in which, pursuant to an agreement, the taxpayer (*exchanger*) transfers property held for productive use in trade or business or for investment (*relinquished property*) and subsequently receives property to be held either for productive use in trade or business or for investment (*replacement property*).

A deferred exchange is entitled to the same benefits under Section 1031 as a simultaneous exchange as long as two additional requirements are met: (1) The replacement property must be identified within 45 days after the date of the original transfer of the delinquished property (*identification period*) and (2) the replacement property must be received within 180 days of the transfer of the relinquished property or before the due date (including extensions) of the exchanger's return, whichever occurs sooner (*exchange period*).

NOTE: It is important that the documents be drawn properly so that the transaction does not appear to be merely a sale and purchase. The exchange documents should be drawn by an experienced real estate or tax practitioner and not by the broker. Brokers involved in an exchange should recommend that their clients be represented by experienced real estate or tax counsel.

Identification of Replacement Property

Replacement property received after the end of the identification period must be identified either in a written document signed by the exchanger and hand delivered, mailed, telecopied or otherwise sent before the end of the identification period to the person obligated to transfer the replacement property or any other person involved in the exchange other than the taxpayer or a disqualified person. The replacement property must be unambiguously described by a legal description, street address or assessor's parcel number. Any replacement property received by the exchanger before the end of the identification period is deemed to have been timely identified.

The maximum number of replacement properties the exchanger may identify (regardless of the number of relinquished properties in the same deferred exchange) is either (1) three properties without regard to the fair market values of the properties (the three-property rule) or (2) any number of replacement properties as long as their aggregate fair market value at the end of the identification period does not exceed 200% of the aggregate fair market value of all the relinquished properties (the 200% rule). If more properties than allowed under these two rules are identified, the exchange will be disallowed unless the exchanger acquires at least 95% of the aggregate fair market value of the identified replacement properties. If the exchanger receives like-kind replacement property simultaneously with the disposition of the relinquished property, that property is counted as replacement property for the purpose of both the three-property rule and the 200% rule.

The exchanger may revoke a designation of a replacement property at any time before the end of the identification period. The revocation must be in a written document signed by the exchanger and sent before the end of the identification period to the person to whom the identification was previously made. If the identification was made in a written agreement, then the revocation must be made in a written amendment to such agreement or in a written document signed by the exchanger and sent to all parties to the agreement before the end of the identification period. If a revocation is timely and properly made, the exchanger may identify new replacement properties, provided that the total number of identified replacement properties at the end of the identification period satisfies either the three-property rule or the 200% rule.

Incidental personal property (furniture or equipment) need not be identified separately nor counted separately in applying the three-property rule or the 200% rule. Personal property is treated as incidental if its value does not exceed 15% of the value of the real property it accompanies. Even if personal property is treated as incidental in a real property exchange, it is still treated as money or other property, and the exchanger's gain is recognized to the extent of its fair market value.

The replacement property received must be substantially the same property as the property that was identified. Although *substantially* is not defined, the regulations provide an example in which the exchanger acquires a parcel with a size and value of 75% of the property identified. Furthermore, when the identified real property consists of real property with improvements to be constructed, that property generally qualifies as being substantially the same property even if improvements are not completed by the time the property is received by the exchanger.

Actual or Constructive Receipt

Gain is recognized to the extent the exchanger is in actual or constructive receipt of money or other non-like-kind property. An exchanger is in actual receipt of money if he or she actually receives such money or receives the economic benefits thereof. An exchanger is in constructive receipt of money at such time as money is credited to the exchanger's account, set apart for the exchanger or otherwise made available so the exchanger might draw upon it at any time. However, if the exchanger's control over the receipt of monies is subject to substantial limitations or restrictions, then the exchanger is not in constructive receipt of such monies. If such restrictions lapse, expire or are waived before the exchanger receives the replacement property, the exchange is disallowed. Although the term *substantial restrictions and limitations* is not defined, an exchange agreement is considered suitably restrictive if it permits the exchanger to receive money or other property only at the following times: (1) If replacement property is not identified, then after the end of the identification period; (2) If replacement property is identified, then after the exchanger has received all of the replacement property to which he or she is entitled, or at the end of the exchange period. In addition, actual constructive receipt of money by an agent or the exchanger is actual or constructive receipt by the exchanger.

Safe Harbors

The regulations allow for the following four *safe harbors* to avoid actual or constructive receipt, which may be provided for in the exchange agreement:

1. Security or guaranty arrangements
2. Qualified escrow accounts and qualified trusts
3. Qualified intermediaries
4. Interest or growth factors

Qualified Intermediaries

The use of qualified intermediaries is probably the most important safe harbor in the regulations. For a person to be a qualified intermediary, the following conditions must be met:

1. He or she may not be a related party to the exchanger.
2. He or she receives a fee for facilitating the deferred exchange.
3. He or she acquires the relinquished property from the exchanger and transfers it to a buyer.
4. He or she acquires the replacement property and transfers it to the exchanger.

Related parties include the exchanger's spouse, ancestors, descendants, siblings, entities in which the exchanger owns at least 10% interest, the exchanger's employees and, under certain circumstances, his or her attorneys and brokers. The exchanger's attorney or broker is not considered a related party if his or her only relationship with the exchanger is as a provider of services with respect to exchanges of property. The exchanger's regular attorney is considered a related party. A wide range of people with whom the exchanger has a pre-existing relationship (such as business associates, aunts, uncles and certain in-laws) qualify as qualified intermediaries. Other qualified intermediaries include financial institutions and professional exchange companies. Exchangers can obtain greater security by requiring security in the form of a standby letter of credit issued by a financial institution, or by insisting that the exchange proceeds be impounded in a qualified escrow account.

The regulations permit direct deeding when the qualified intermediary safe harbor structure is used. The exchanger may deed the relinquished property directly to its ultimate buyer, and the owner of the replacement property may deed that property directly to the exchanger. Use of direct deeding saves transfer taxes and avoids exposing the intermediary to risks of ownership.

The regulations also permit assignment to the intermediary of the agreement to sell the relinquished property and the agreement to purchase the replacement property if all parties to the agreement are notified of the assignment. This eliminates the need of novation of these agreements by a superseding exchange agreement and enables the exchanger to retain the intermediary just prior to close of escrow.

Important Factors

Regardless of the timing of the transactor or of the form in which the transaction is set up, it is important to specify the balances of the encumbrances on the respective properties at the time of the transaction and the expected balances at the time of closing so that the mortgage relief may be properly calculated, for the mortgage relief is a trap for the unwary in an otherwise tax-deferred exchange and must be protected against. An otherwise tax-deferred exchange might generate mortgage relief.

Proper planning can eliminate any taxable profit in the exchange. For example, the owner of Property A may pay down the principal of the encumbrance on Property A so there is no mortgage relief. An alternative might be for the owner of Property B to further encumber his or her property prior to consummation of the exchange to eliminate mortgage relief.

One can see that in order to accomplish a tax-deferred exchange with its attendant benefits, knowledge and timing are prime requisites, together with precise analysis of all factors involved in the transaction. All the facts relating to the transaction should be thoroughly analyzed, and the agreement should spell out all the elements of the transaction and especially, as mentioned, the intention to enter into a tax-deferred exchange should be stated.

EXCHANGE ANALYSIS

The Comparative Exchange Analysis, Form 122, is reprinted with permission from Professional Publishing (see page D–41). The form is designed to determine the feasibility of an exchange by computing the client's cash flow and net equity income before and after the exchange. If the comparison is favorable, the broker will have a strong argument in favor of the exchange.

The form is unique in that it has built-in directions for completing all calculations, including balancing the equities, computing recognized gain, transferring the basis, computing cost recovery and, most important, the net equity income. Each pad of forms comes with a built-in example and simple directions. The form teaches anyone to complete a professional exchange analysis in a matter of minutes, a subject that takes many hours to learn in an exchange course.

Directions for Use of Form 122

1. Obtain and fill in the data needed to complete the analysis, where indicated by the arrows at the left margins of columns A and B.
2. The numbers in the column Guide Numbers refer to the line numbers in the far left column.
3. To balance the equities on lines 1 through 13 in columns A and B, compute (and tentatively write in with pencil) the amounts on line 8, column A

and line 13, column B. Because these two amounts must balance, erase the smaller of the two and substitute the larger. The difference must now be made up in either: Boot Given (lines 4, 5, 6 or 7 in column A) or in Boot Received (lines 9, 10, 11 or 12 in column B), as the case may be.

In the following example, 8A amounted to $300,000 and 13B to $350,000. In order to balance 8A and 13B, $350,000 was then substituted for $300,000 in equity plus $30,000 in cash. Therefore, make up the balance of $20,000 in some form of boot; in this case a note for $20,000 was offered.

4. Now complete column A from line 14 to line 48 as directed by the guide numbers. Rereading the sections Recognition of Gain and Transfer of Basis under the heading Tax-Deferred Exchanges in this Tax section of the **Realty Bluebook®** is recommended.

5. Upon completion of column A, complete column B, beginning at line 16 down to line 48 as directed by the guide numbers.

6. Finally, show the result of the analysis, by computing the Increase or Decrease in Cash Flow and Net Equity Income after the Exchange in lines 28 and 48 in the last column. An increase in cash flow and/or net equity income should be a strong argument in favor of the proposed exchange.

INSTALLMENT SALES

The taxpayer's use of the installment sale method under Internal Revenue Code Sec. 453 provides a way to spread tax on profit from the sale of an asset over a number of years. This avoids paying tax on the entire gain in the year of sale. The installment sale method is used unless the taxpayer elects not to use it by reporting the entire gain in the year of sale.

COMPARATIVE EXCHANGE ANALYSIS

PREPARED BY	JOHN REAL ESTATE		DATE:
PREPARED FOR:	MR BROWN		

			CLIENT'S PROPERTY A		EXCHANGE PROPERTY B	
PROPERTY ADDRESS			100 GREEN ST		22 OCEAN AVE	
TYPE OF PROPERTY			OFFICE WAREHSE		OFFICES	

		For vital pertinent data and tables refer to the REALTY BLUEBOOK I & II published annually by Professional Publishing Corp	GUIDE NUMBERS	CLIENT'S PROPERTY A	CAP RATE	EXCHANGE PROPERTY B	CAP RATE	INCREASE (+) or DECREASE (-) of B over A	CAP RATE
BALANCING OF EQUITIES	1	Market Values		480,000		800,000			
	2	Less Existing Mortgages		180,000		450,000			
	3	EQUITIES	1 - 2	300,000		350,000			
	4	Personal Property							
	5	Personal Residence							
	6	Notes		20,000					
	7	Cash		30,000					
	8	EQUITY AND BOOT GIVEN	3 + 4 + 5 + 6 + 7	350,000					
	9	Personal Property							
	10	Personal Residence							
	11	Notes							
	12	Cash							
	13	EQUITY AND BOOT RECEIVED	3 + 9 + 10 + 11 + 12			350,000			

(LINES 8 AND 13 MUST BALANCE)

			GUIDE NUMBERS	A	CAP RATE	B	CAP RATE	B over A	CAP RATE
RECOGNIZED GAIN	14	Transaction Costs		5,000					
	15	Adjusted Basis		300,000					
	16	Realized (Indicated) Gain	1 - 14 - 15	175,000					
	17	Any Net Mortgage Relief	Excess of 2 over 2 B			0			
	18	Cash or Other Boot Received	9 + 10 + 11 + 12			0			
	19	Total Boot Received	17 + 18			0			
	20	Cash or Other Boot Given	4 + 5 + 6 + 7 + 14			55,000			
	21	Net Boot Received	Excess of 19 over 20			0			
	22	RECOGNIZED (TAXABLE) GAIN	The lower of 18A or 21B			0			

			GUIDE NUMBERS	A	CAP RATE	B	CAP RATE	B over A	CAP RATE
INCOME	23	SCHEDULED ANNUAL INCOME		94,800		190,000			
	24	Less Vacancy and Credit Losses		2,844		7,600			
	25	GROSS OPERATING INCOME	23 - 24	91,956		182,400			
	26	Less Operating Expenses		8,600		17,000			
	27	NET OPERATING INCOME	25 - 26	83,356		165,400			
	28	Less Annual Loan Payments		28,440		66,828			
	29	GROSS SPENDABLE INCOME (Cash Flow)	27 - 28	54,916	18.3	98,572	28.1	+ 43,656	

			GUIDE NUMBERS	A	CAP RATE	B	CAP RATE	B over A	CAP RATE
Transfer Basis	30	Market Value of Property B	1B			800,000			
	31	Less Realized (Indicated) Gain	16A			175,000			
	32	Plus Recognized Gain	22B			0			
	33	BASIS OF PROPERTY B	30 - 31 + 32			625,000			

			GUIDE NUMBERS	A	CAP RATE	B	CAP RATE	B over A	CAP RATE
AFTER — TAX INCOME	34	Allocation to Improvements	INFO			75 %			
	35	Cost Recovery Period				31.5 Years			
	36	Cost Recovery Method				S L			
	37	Cost Recovery Rate p/year				3.1746 %			
	38	Depreciation Allowance	33 × 34 × 37	23,017		14,880			
	39	Interest		25,200		63,000			
	40	Taxable Income from Property	27 - 38 - 39	35,139		87,520			
	41	Other Taxable Income		60,000		60,000			
	42	Total Taxable Income	40 + 41	95,139		147,520			
	43	Total Federal Tax Liability (See Bluebook II)	Tax Rate x 42	23,933		41,219			
	44	Tax Liability Other Income	Tax Rate x 41	12,933		12,933			
	45	Tax Liability due to Property	43 - 44	11,000		28,286			
	46	NET SPENDABLE INCOME	29 - 45	43,916		70,286			
	47	Plus Equity Build-up (See Bluebook II)		3,240		3,828			
	48	NET EQUITY INCOME	46 + 47	47,156	13.5	74,114	21.2	26,958	

OTHER DATA									

FORM 122 (10-88)   COPYRIGHT · 1987 BY PROFESSIONAL PUBLISHING CORP 122 PAUL DR SAN RAFAEL CA 94903 (415) 472 1964   PROFESSIONAL PUBLISHING

Year of sale is usually the year in which title passes. Payments during the year of sale would include the down payment (in whatever form) and the principal portion of installment payments received during the year. In the event that property is sold subject to a mortgage that exceeds the seller's basis, the difference between the principal amount of the mortgage and the adjusted basis of the seller would be treated as a payment made during the year of sale.

This method may be to the advantage of a particular client's overall tax situation. The broker's task is not to advise his or her client in the matter but to alert the client to the fact that the Internal Revenue Code provides for such a method and to refer the client to a tax consultant for advice.

The installment sale method is not available to persons classified as dealers in real property.

Realized Gain

Realized gain is the net selling price (after selling expense) less adjusted basis.

Contract Price

The contract price is the gross selling price (before commission) less mortgages assumed by the purchaser, except to the extent that such mortgages exceed the seller's adjusted basis.

Reportable Gain

The reportable gain in each year, including the year of sale, is equal to the amount paid to the principal multiplied by the realized gain and divided by the contract price.

Gain may be capital or ordinary. If the sale resulted in capital gain, then the gain portion of installment payments in subsequent years is also capital gain, and vice versa.

If a portion of the gain is ordinary gain due to excess depreciation as defined in Internal Revenue

Code Section 1250, then the entire ordinary gain must be reported in the year of sale, irrespective of the amount received. The amount thus recognized is added to the basis of the property disposed of for the purpose of determining the gross profit ratio and calculating how much of each installment payment is included in income.

The Internal Revenue Code provides that interest will be imputed where no interest is stated or where the interest is too low. If a portion of the installments in future years is held to be interest rather than principal, then such reduction in principal would, of course, also reduce the sales price.

See Imputed Interest in this Tax section.

Computations

Example

Gross selling price	$100,000
Commission	5,000
Adjusted basis	65,000
Loan balance	40,000
Purchaser assumes the existing loan of	40,000
Seller takes back a second mortgage of	34,000
Down payment	26,000

Installment payments in the year of sale $1,500 of which $1,000 is interest.

Down payment	$26,000
Plus principal payments in year of sale	500
Total paid to principal in year of sale	**$26,500**
Gross selling price	100,000
Less commission	5,000
Net selling price	$95,000
Less adjusted basis	65,000
Realized gain	**$30,000**
Gross selling price	100,000
Less mortgage assumed by purchaser	40,000

Contract price   **$60,000**

Profit Ratio = Realized Gain ÷ Contract Price =
$30,000 ÷ $60,000 = 0.5
Recognized Gain = Profit Ratio ×
Principal Payments Received =
0.5 × $26,500 = $13,250

Mortgages Assumed in Installment Sales

Any amount of mortgage assumed or taken subject to is considered part of the initial payments in installment sale reporting only to the extent that the mortgage exceeds the adjusted basis.

Sellers should be cautioned that in the event the seller encumbers the property to the extent of the adjusted basis immediately before the sale with the intention of obtaining tax-free cash, the IRS may take the position that the refinancing is undertaken in connection with the sale and should therefore be regarded as a single transaction, and that consequently the proceeds from the refinancing should be considered as part of the initial payments.

Disposition and Hypothecation of Installment Sale Contracts

With certain limited exceptions, the disposition of the note or contract evidencing the deferred payments in an installment sale results in the recognition of gain or loss. The basis of the note or contract right is the amount of the unrecovered cost of the property sold. The gain or loss recognized is the difference between the amount received for the obligation and its basis. If the disposition is made by gift, the amount to be recognized is the difference between the basis of the obligation and its fair market value at the date of the gift.

If an installment obligation is used as collateral for a loan, the full amount of the loan proceeds is considered to be a payment.

The transfer of an installment obligation on account of the death of a seller does not result in immediate recognition of gain. There are also exceptions relating to various tax-free transfers under the Internal Revenue Code.

Prepayment of Installment Contract by Buyer

Ordinarily, a seller is not required to accept a prepayment under an installment note or contract that does not allow prepayment by its terms. However, a state statute may permit such prepayment and substantially diminish the tax advantages of the installment sale to the seller. For example, Sec. 2954.9 of the California Civil Code permits a buyer to prepay a real estate loan for residential property of four units or less that is taken back by the seller as part of the purchase price. Under the statute the buyer is not permitted to make such prepayment in the year of sale unless the seller has taken back four or more such loans during that calendar year. The California statute permits a lender to charge a prepayment penalty if specified in the note.

Imputed Interest

When there is a sale of property and a portion of the sale price is deferred, interest is imputed where no interest is stated or where the interest is less than the minimum allocable.

Subject to the limit set forth below, the interest rate is equal to the applicable federal rate. When the transaction is a sale and leaseback by the seller, the imputed interest is 110% of the applicable federal rate.

The applicable federal rate depends upon the term of the note. There is a rate for notes due in three years or less, one for notes due in more than three years but not more than nine years, and one for notes due in more than nine years. The rates are determined by the IRS and published monthly. The lowest rate in effect during the three-month period ending on the first day of the month in which a binding contract is executed will be the applicable federal rate for the transaction.

Ordinarily, both the buyer and seller must report the interest income and deductions on the accrual method. However, when the principal amount does not exceed a specified statutory maximum and when the parties jointly elect, the seller does not use the accrual method of accounting and is not a dealer with respect to the property sold. Then the transaction may be reported by both the buyer and seller on the cash method of accounting.

Section 1274A of the IRC provides that when the deferred payment does not exceed $2.8 million, increased by inflation adjustments after the calendar year 1989, the maximum interest rate is 9%. Said section provides that the maximum amount permitted under the preceding paragraph for use of the cash method is $2 million, which is also adjusted for inflation after 1989. In 1993, the inflation adjusted amount in order to qualify for the 9% limitation was $3,332,400 and the maximum amount that would quality for the cash method of accounting was $2,380,300.

PERSONAL RESIDENCES

The Taxpayer Relief Act of 1997

Capital Gains Exclusion for Homeowners

The *Taxpayer Relief Act of 1997* provides a $500,000 capital gains exclusion for the sale of a principal residence where the owner has resided for at least five years for taxpayers filing jointly and $250,000 for those filing singly. Any profit derived from the sale in excess of this exclusion is taxable at the reduced capital gains rates under the Act. Taxpayers may take advantage of this capital gains tax exclusion every two years for an unlimited number of transactions. The measure eliminates existing rollover provisions and the one-time exclusion for those 55 years old or older.

Reduced Capital Gains Tax Rates

The new captal gains tax rates under the At are 20% (reduced from 28%) for taxpayers in upper brackets and 10% (down form 15%) for those in lower brackets. (Taxpayers in upper brackets are those with gross incomes upwards of $150,000 if filing jointly and upwards of $75,000 for those filing singly.) Effective July 29, 1997, assets must be held at least 18 months to qualify for the new capital gains tax rates.

Penalty-Free IRA Withdrawals for Down Payments

The measure allows first-time home buyers to make penalty-free early withdrawals of up to $10,000 from newly created *American Dream.* Individual Retirement Accounts to help with the down payment and closing costs on a first-time home purchase.

Residence Interest

Qualified residence interest is deductible as an itemized deduction against ordinary income. Qualified residence interest is defined as interest on debt secured by either the taxpayer's principal residence or a second residence of the taxpayer.

Where the taxpayer is a tenant/stockholder of a housing cooperative, debt secured by stock of the cooperative is treated as debt secured by the residence of the taxpayer. When stock may not be used as security by virtue of restrictions pursuant to local or state law or reasonable restrictions in the cooperative agreement, the stock may be treated as securing such debt if the taxpayer established that the debt was incurred to acquire the stock.

A second residence is a residence owned by the taxpayer that is (1) used by the taxpayer for personal purposes for a number of days exceeding the greater of 14 days or 10% of the number of days during such year as such unit is rented at fair rental or (2) neither used nor rented by the taxpayer during the taxable year.

The amount of interest deductible as residential interest is limited to *acquisition indebtedness* or *home equity indebtedness*. Acquisition indebtedness means indebtedness incurred in acquiring, constructing or substantially improving a qualified residence of the taxpayer secured by such residence. The term also includes any indebtedness secured by such residence resulting from the refinancing of indebtedness meeting the requirements of the definition, but only to the extent that the amount of the indebtedness resulting from such refinancing does not exceed the amount of the refinanced indebtedness. There is a $1 million limitation on acquisition indebtedness.

Home equity indebtedness is indebtedness, other than qualified acquisition indebtedness secured by a qualified residence, that does not exceed the fair market value of the qualified residence less the amount of the acquisition indebtedness. There is a limit of $100,000 on home equity indebtedness.

All indebtedness existing on October 13, 1987, is treated as acquisition indebtedness, and the $1 million limitation does not apply. Pre-October 13, 1987, indebtedness also includes indebtedness incurred to refinance such debt. However, the refinancing indebtedness cannot exceed the pre-October 13, 1987, indebtedness existing at the time of the refinancing. The foregoing rule with respect to indebtedness existing on October 13, 1987, means that interest on loans existing on that date remains fully deductible if they are secured by a qualified residence. However, as the principal amount of the loan is paid down, if the refinancing amount exceeds the amount due at the time of refinancing, the interest is deductible only to the extent that it qualifies as home equity indebtedness that is limited to $100,000. This rule with respect to refinancing also applies to acquisition indebtedness incurred after October 13, 1987, for which the principal amount is reduced and the principal amount of the refinancing exceeds the amount of the reduced principal.

It is not necessary that the home equity indebtedness be the subject of a separate loan. The principal amount of the indebtedness for which interest is deductible is determined by adding the acquisition indebtedness to the home equity indebtedness.

However, the $1 million limitation on acquisition indebtedness is reduced by the amount of outstanding pre-October 13, 1987, indebtedness.

Deductible Expenses

The following expenses do not adjust the homeowner's basis but may be deducted against ordinary income:

1. Residence interest (both primary and second homes).
2. Discount points to be deductible must:
   - show on settlement statement as loan origination, loan discount, or discount points;
   - be computed as a% age of the loan amount;
   - conform to an established business practice with respect to home financing in the area in which the residence is located and must not exceed the amount generally charged in that market area; and
   - be paid for financing a principal residence.
   - NOTE: In March 1994, the IRS announced that homebuyers are now permitted to deduct points paid on their behalf by sellers for a mortgage to purchase their principal residence. The change is retroactive to homes purchased since 1991. Buyers who purchased since 1991 and did not deduct any seller paid points should contact the IRS about obtaining the deduction.

Points are deductible over the term of the loan if paid in the following situations:
- for refinancings or lines of credit;

- for home improvement loans when the amount borrowed has no connection with an acquisition of a principal residence;
- for loans on second or vacation homes, business or investment properties; and
- in connection with purchases of a principal residence that are allocable to a loan amount exceeding the $1 million limit.

Nondeductible Expenses

Acquisition expenses may not be deducted against ordinary income but are added to the basis. Examples include appraisal fees, credit reports, inspection fees, title fees, attorney fees, property taxes and mortgage insurance premiums.

Fixing-up expenses are the cost of work to assist the sale, performed within 90 days before the sale and paid within 30 days after the sale. Fixing-up expenses are not deductible against ordinary income.

Partial Occupancy by Owner

The sale of a small residential income property, partially occupied by the owner, can result in both capital gain and a nondeductible loss. The sales price and the basis must be apportioned to the owner's unit and the rental portion of the property. Because only the rental portion of the property is depreciable, the basis allocated to the owner's unit is higher. In the following example, an owner occupied one of three flats that he bought for $75,000 and sold at an adjusted sales price of $60,000.

	Total	Rental	Personal
Adjusted sales price	$60,000	$40,000	$20,000
Cost basis	75,000	50,000	25,000
Less depreciation		12,000	
Adjusted basis		38,000	
Gain (or loss)		2,000	(5,000)*

The $5,000 loss is a nondeductible personal loss and cannot be offset against the $2,000 gain from the rental portion of the building.

Conversion of a Personal Residence to Income-Producing Property

Homeowners cannot deduct maintenance expenses, nor can they take depreciation deductions on personal residences. However, if they convert a home to rental property, maintenance expenses become deductible nonbusiness expenses under IRC Sec. 212; the owners can also take depreciation deductions while the property is held for the production of income or for investment under IRC Sec. 167(a)(2).

However, by converting a home to rental property, homeowners can lose their Sec. 1034 nonrecognition of gain benefits. The property then only qualifies for nonrecognition of gain under Sec. 1031. (See section on Tax-Deferred Exchanges.)

Business Use of a Home

A taxpayer is entitled to deduct certain business expenses attributable to a portion of the home used exclusively and regularly as a principal place of business or as a place of business that is used by patients, clients or customers in meeting or dealing with the taxpayer in the ordinary course of business.

In addition, employees must establish that they are required for their employer's convenience to provide their own space and facilities for the performance of their duties and are not doing so merely because it is appropriate and helpful in their employment. These limitations also apply when an employee leases a portion of his or her home to his or her employer.

Deductible expenses include those made exclusively for the business portion of the home and expenses that must be allocated to the portion of the home used for business, such as utilities, real estate taxes, insurance, mortgage interest, and so on.

In addition, deductions for depreciation may be claimed on the business portion of the home.

Tax Savings the Homebuyer Should Know About

The tax deductions of interest and property taxes, as well as reduction of the principal loan amount, can considerably reduce the homeowner's actual monthly housing cost, depending upon his or her tax bracket. This is a powerful closing argument with a buyer who finds monthly payments excessive, as the following example illustrates. (The tax benefits as shown in the example are only applicable if the homeowner itemizes deductions. The allowed standard deduction may be higher than the actual deductible items).

Loan amount	$80,000
Term	30 Years
Interest	9%
Monthly payment	$644
Taxes	$200/mo
Insurance	$40/mo
Total monthly payment	$884

First month's interest:	
9% × 80,000 ÷ 12	$600
Property taxes per month	+200
Total tax deduction per mo.	$800
Monthly tax savings @ Client's tax bracket of 28%:	
$800 × 28%	−224
Effective monthly cost	$660
Monthly equity build-up (See Section A, Equity Build-Up Tables)	
$80,000 × 0.683% ÷ 12	−46
Actual monthly cost	$614

Tax-Deductible Moving Expenses

Certain specified expenses connected with the move to a new principal place of employment are deductible. All employees, old or new, reimbursed or unreimbursed, are treated alike, and the self-employed are allowed comparable deductions as well.

Deductible expenses include cost of moving household goods and personal effects and the expense of traveling (including lodging) from the old home to the new home of the taxpayer and members of his or her household. If traveling is done by car, expenses can be deducted either by itemizing or by a standard deduction of $.09 per mile plus tolls and parking.

The foregoing expenses are deductible only if the new principal place of work is at least 50 miles farther from the old residence than the old place of work was. This distance is measured by the shortest of the more commonly traveled routes between two points.

The taxpayer must be employed full-time (not necessarily by one employer only) at the new location for a minimum of 39 weeks during the 12 months following the move. This test is waived if employment is terminated due to certain circumstances beyond his or her control. On a joint return, the deduction is allowed if either husband and or wife meet this 39-week test. The self-employed must work at the new location either as a self-employed person or as an employee for at least 78 weeks during the 24 months following the move of which at least 39 weeks must be during the first 12 months.

Reimbursements of any of the above expenses must be included in the taxpayer's gross income.

Energy Tax Credit

A 10% energy credit is allowed to a business for equipment that uses solar power to generate electricity or to heat or cool, and for equipment to produce, distribute or use geothermal energy.

Information Reporting on Real Estate Transactions

The TRA '86 requires that real estate transactions be reported to the IRS. The primary responsibility for reporting is on the person or entity responsible for closing the transaction, including any title company or attorney conducting the settlement. If there is no person or entity responsible for closing the transaction, the reporting must be done by the mortgage lender. If there is no mortgage lender, the reporting must be done by the seller's broker. If there is no seller's broker, the reporting must be done by the buyer's broker.

Form 1099 is used to report the necessary information. The provision is effective for real estate transactions that close on or after January 1, 1987.

CHECKLISTS

To receive the next edition of the Rigby Blue Book edition and information about what's new, please call

1-800-424-1844

to register your name and address or visit the Blue Book Web Page at www.bluebook.com/bluebook

To receive advance notice of the
next *Realty Bluebook*® edition
(and information about
what's new), please call
1-800-428-3846
to register your name and address,
or visit the Bluebook Web Page at
www.deheer.com/bluebook

CONTENTS

CHECKLISTS

Checklists E–1

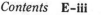

Instructions E-63

CHECKLISTS

RESPA INFO TO LENDER WITH COMMITMENT REQUEST

- ☐ Copy sales contract
- ☐ Name of escrow holder with buyers' and sellers' fees
- ☐ Name of title company with buyers' and sellers' fees
- ☐ Commission split information
- ☐ Name, address and phone number of buyer
- ☐ Request lender to delete from seller's copy of advance disclosure statement confidential information of concern only to the buyer and vice versa
- ☐ Request lender to allow agent to look over advance disclosure statement before mailing to principals
- ☐ Request copy of statement to be mailed to broker
- ☐ Title report, if available
- ☐ Pest control report, if available

CHECKLIST OF BUYER'S CLOSING COSTS

Nonrecurring Costs

- ☐ Title insurance (where payable by buyer)
- ☐ Escrow fee (where applicable)
- ☐ Legal fee (where applicable)
- ☐ Survey fee (where applicable)
- ☐ Loan fee
- ☐ Appraisal fee
- ☐ Tax service
- ☐ Credit report
- ☐ Notary fee
- ☐ Recording fee
- ☐ Pest control inspection
- ☐ Document preparation fee
- ☐ Review fee
- ☐ Application fee
- ☐ Underwriting fee
- ☐ Courier fee
- ☐ Verification fee
- ☐ Warehousing fee

Recurring Costs

- ☐ Hazard insurance
- ☐ Trust fund or impound account
- ☐ Prorated taxes (if paid beyond recordation)
- ☐ Prorated interest (if charged in arrears, to end of month; if charged in advance, to date of first payment)

Credits, If Any

- ☐ Prorated taxes (if not paid to recordation)
- ☐ Prorated rents, if any
- ☐ Security deposits on hand, if any

CHECKLIST OF SELLER'S CLOSING COSTS AND CREDITS

Costs

- ☐ Selling commission
- ☐ Title insurance (where payable by seller)
- ☐ Escrow fee (where applicable)
- ☐ Survey fee (where applicable)
- ☐ Legal fee (where applicable)
- ☐ Prepayment penalty, if any
- ☐ State or local revenue stamps or transfer tax, if any
- ☐ Pest control inspection fee, in case of VA loan
- ☐ Pest control work, if any
- ☐ Recording fee
- ☐ FHA or VA points, if any
- ☐ Forwarding fee
- ☐ Reconveyance fees (on any deeds of trust to be reconveyed)
- ☐ Notary fee
- ☐ Prorated taxes (if not paid to date of recordation)
- ☐ Personal property tax
- ☐ Interest, if paid in arrears (from date of last payment to date of recordation)
- ☐ Prorated rents, if any
- ☐ Security deposits on hand, if any

Credits

- ☐ Interest, if paid in advance (from recordation to date of next loan payment)
- ☐ Refund existing trust fund (impound account), if any
- ☐ Prorated taxes (if paid beyond recordation)

ESCROW CHECKLIST FOR SELLING BROKER

- ☐ Obtain increase of deposit
- ☐ Open an escrow
- ☐ Order credit report on buyer (if required)
- ☐ Order pest control inspection
- ☐ Order other inspections (roof, etc., if required)
- ☐ Check on any contingencies to be eliminated
- ☐ Check occupancy permit
- ☐ Order loan commitment
- ☐ Assist buyer with loan application and submit to lender
- ☐ Arrange for hazard insurance
- ☐ Have closing instructions prepared and signed by buyer

ESCROW CHECKLIST FOR LISTING BROKER

- ☐ Notice of sale to multiple-listing office
- ☐ Check on increase of deposit
- ☐ Examine preliminary title report and assist in eliminating clouds on the title, if any
- ☐ Check on any contingencies to be eliminated
- ☐ Request title or escrow company to order payoff demand or statement of condition and assumption papers from lender(s)
- ☐ Check with selling office on buyer's loan
- ☐ If income property, obtain: rent schedule, rent due dates, security deposits, copies of leases, names and phone numbers of tenants
- ☐ Have seller's instructions prepared and signed
- ☐ If seller carries a second loan, have seller record a request for copy of notice of default and subscribe to a tax agency
- ☐ Obtain seller's future address and phone number

DATA CHECKLIST FOR SINGLE-FAMILY DWELLINGS

1	Date information was obtained
2	Property location
3	Type of home
100	**OWNERSHIP**
101	Owner's name, address (if other than above), residence phone, business phone
102	Occupation
103	Title vested in (list all persons having an interest in the title)
104	To inspect property
105	Acquisition date/cost of acquisition
106	Previously listed/how long/at what price
107	Reason for selling/degree of urgency
108	Date occupancy can be given
200	**LOCATION**
201	Nearest cross street
202	District/subdistrict/tract
203	Public transportation
204	Shopping facilities
205	Schools (elementary, junior high, high school, college, private)
206	Churches
207	Recreational facilities
208	View
300	**SITE**
301	Lot size
302	Corner
303	Zoning
304	Legal description
305	Utilities and street improvements in
306	Yard (front, rear)/fenced/condition
307	Patio/lanai
308	Lawn sprinklers
309	Pool
310	Condition of grounds
400	**IMPROVEMENTS**
401	Estimated age
402	Style

403	Attached or detached
404	Type and quality of construction
405	Builder
406	Exterior finish/condition
407	Stories/levels
408	Type of roof/condition
409	Basement
410	Garage/number of cars
411	Storage space
412	Wiring (110 or 220 volt)/condition
413	Plumbing (copper or galvanized)/condition
414	Sewer
415	Type of heating
416	Air-conditioning
417	Insulation
418	Weather stripping
419	Type of flooring
420	Window screens
421	Storm windows
422	Intercom system
500	**INTERIOR**
501	Floor plan
502	Square footage of living space
503	Number of bedrooms/sizes
504	Number of bathrooms/tubs/stall showers/ over tub showers
505	Living room/size/fireplace
506	Dining room/size/separate or combination
507	Breakfast room
508	Family room/social room
509	Kitchen/gas or electric/built-in range or oven/disposal/dishwasher/other
510	Laundry room
511	Carpeting
512	Draperies
513	Other personal property included/inventory
514	Unusual extras
515	Interior condition
600	**EXISTING FINANCING** (List first and junior liens)

	601	Loan balance/as of what date
	602	Monthly payments (taxes and insurance included)
	603	Interest rate
	604	Lender/address/phone number
	605	Loan number
	605-A	Loan owned by FNMA
	605-B	Blended interest rate
	606	Prepayment penalty
	607	Transferable/assumption fee/can loan be taken subject to
	608	Due date/balloon payment
	609	Original amount/term/year of inception
	610	If there is a second loan, can it be bought at a discount/what discount
	611	Improvement bond/prepayment penalty

700 POTENTIAL FINANCING

701 Loan commitment/amount/term/interest/ payments/loan fee/lender
702 Will seller pay FHA or VA points
703 Will seller help finance/if so, amount/ interest/monthly pay-off rate/due date
704 Is seller interested in installment sale

800 COMPETITIVE MARKET ANALYSIS

801 For sale now
802 Sold past year
803 Expired past year

900 PRICE

901 Listed price
902 Predicted probable sale price (Use comparative market approach)
903 Possible rental value
904 Taxes 19__ /19__
905 Assessed value

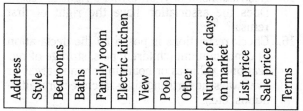

CONDOMINIUM BUYER'S CHECKLIST

1. Hazard and liability insurance included in association fee? What limits of liability?
2. Amount of association fee. Is fee guaranteed fixed for a certain period?
3. In case of a resale unit, check with the association regarding possible problems with the unit, such as unapproved changes or alterations, delinquent fees, etc.
4. Common areas owned or leased?
5. Is maintenance budget realistic?
6. Obtain comprehensive listing of which items are standard and which are optional.
7. If purchase includes extras, obtain written work orders with price quotations signed by a responsible person.
8. Check completion date of unit and common areas. Are penalties provided for delay in completion?
9. Security: intercom, closed-circuit TV?
10. Parking space designated, ample, how close to unit? Guest parking?
11. Storage space ample?
12. Soundproofing adequate?
13. Warranties covering structural defects, equipment, systems and appliances in effect until what date?
14. In case of a conversion, obtain copy of engineer's report on condition of building and its equipment (roof, foundations, heating and cooling systems, elevators, plumbing and electrical systems).
15. Restrictions, if any, on owner's right to resell? Does the association have the right of first refusal?
16. Check restrictions imposed by the declaration of condominium (children, pets, storage of recreational vehicles or boats in common areas or driveways, advertising signs, architectural alterations, etc.).

Condominium Documents

- [ ] CC&Rs or declaration of condominium (also referred to as master regulations or master deed). The declaration authorizes the board of directors of the owners' association, through the bylaws, to manage the affairs of the development with regard to the common areas and facilities.

  The declaration establishes the ratio of each unit to the total of all units affecting the assessments for common expenses, votes in the association and real estate taxes apportioned to each unit. The declaration further deals with the description of the units and the common areas, common expenses, the owners' and the association's obligations, use restrictions, options in case of partial or total destruction, rules for amending the declaration, remedies for violation of the declaration and termination of the condominium by the members.
- [ ] Bylaws of the association of owners set forth certain rules and regulations for the internal government of the condominium development.
- [ ] Financial statement of the association.
- [ ] Operating budget and schedule of monthly assessments.
- [ ] Regulatory agreement, used only in FHA-financed condominium projects.
- [ ] Engineer's report on condition of building and equipment in case of a condominium conversion.

In addition, state law may require other documents, such as:

- [ ] Articles of incorporation of the owners' association
- [ ] Final subdivision report

DATA CHECKLIST FOR MANUFACTURED (MOBILE) HOMES

1   Date information obtained
2   Property location
3   Type/brand name

100 OWNERSHIP
101 Registered owner(s)
102 Legal owner's name, address and phone number
103 Title vested in (list all persons having an interest in title)
104 Title information/serial number, year, model, license number
105 How to inspect property
106 Acquisition date and cost
107 If previously listed, for how long and at what price
108 Reason for selling/degree of urgency
109 Date occupancy can be given

200 LOCATION
201 Name of park
202 Address
203 Space
204 Public transportation
205 Shopping facilities
206 Schools (elementary, junior high, high, college, private)
207 Churches
208 Recreation facilities, clubhouse, pool, playground

300 SITE
301 Park/poor, standard, excellent
302 Children
303 Pets
304 Number of spaces/% occupancy
305 Space rental cost
306 Manager's name and phone number
307 Laundry/showers

400 IMPROVEMENTS

401	Estimated age
402	Brand name, manufacturer, year, width, length
403	Construction quality/economy, average, good, custom
404	Skirting
405	Patio size
406	Carport size
407	Window awnings/number
408	Front porch/size/awnings
409	Rear porch/size/awnings
410	Hitch/detachable/missing
500	**INTERIOR**
501	Square footage
502	Bedrooms
503	Bathrooms/shower/tub
504	Living room
505	Dining/breakfast area
506	Kitchen/gas or electric
507	Appliances and equipment/refrigerator, range, oven, dishwasher, disposal, other
508	Air conditioner/serial number and tonnage
509	Furniture
600	**EXISTING FINANCING**
	(List all loans)
601	Loan balance/date
602	Monthly payments
603	Interest rate
604	Lender/address/phone number
605	Loan numbers
606	Prepayment penalty
607	Transferable/assumption fee/can loan be taken subject to
608	Balloon payment/due date
609	Original amount/term/year of inception
610	If there is a second, can it be bought at a discount
700	**POTENTIAL FINANCING**
701	Loan commitment/amount/term/interest/ payments/loan fee lender

702   Will seller pay points
703   Will seller help finance, and if so, under what terms and conditions

800   COMPETITIVE MARKET ANALYSIS

Address - Park	Brand name - Year	Width - Length	Bedrooms	Baths	Appliances	Other	How long on market	List price	Sale price	Terms

801   For sale now
802   Sold past year
803   Expired past year

900   PRICE

901   Listed
902   Probable sale price
903   Possible rental value
904   Taxes

DATA CHECKLIST FOR APARTMENT HOUSES

1   Date information was obtained
2   Property location
3   Number of units

100 **OWNERSHIP**

101 Owner's name, address, residence phone, business phone
102 Owner's occupation
103 Property operated by owner or manager/manager's duties
104 Title vested in (list all persons having an interest in the title)
105 Adjusted basis/depreciation reduction/depreciation method/useful life
106 Owner's tax bracket/legal status
107 Owner's attorney/tax counsel/accountant
108 Resident manager's name, apartment number, phone number
109 To inspect property
110 Acquisition date/cost of acquisition
111 Previously listed/how long/at what price
112 Reason for disposition/degree of urgency
113 Investment objective
    a. Tax shelter
    b. Estate building
    c. Equity return (how much)
    d. Spendable (how much)
    e. Other

200 **LOCATION**

201 Proximity to central business district
202 Public transportation
203 Access to arterial roads, freeways, etc.
204 Shopping facilities
205 Churches
206 Schools
207 Recreational facilities
208 Other

300 **SITE**

301 Lot size

302	Zoning
303	Legal description
304	Off-street parking
305	Pool
306	Patios
307	Lawn sprinklers
308	Condition of grounds
400	**IMPROVEMENTS**
401	Builder
402	Age of building
403	Architectural design
404	Number of stories
405	Type of construction
406	Type of roof/condition
407	Exterior finish/condition
408	Basement/foundations
409	Storage facilities for tenants
410	Laundry facilities (owned or leased)
411	Garbage chutes
412	Elevator
413	Separate meters
414	Wiring/condition
415	Plumbing (copper or galvanized)/condition
416	Type of heating/age/condition
417	Air-conditioning/age/condition
418	Adequate sprinklers and fireproofing system
419	Recent pest control clearance
420	Interior halls/type of floor covering/ condition
500	**APARTMENTS**
501	View
502	Floors
503	Carpeting
504	Draperies
505	Stoves/built-in
506	Refrigerators
507	Dishwashers
508	Garbage disposals
509	Bathrooms/tubs/showers over tub/stall showers

510 Amount of storage space and closets
511 Intercom system
512 TV antenna/outlets
513 Fireplaces
514 Decks, balconies, patios
515 General condition of apartments
516 Furniture/condition
517 Inventory of personal property
518 General size of rooms (large/average/small)
519 General quality of interior (deluxe/average/economy)
520 Typical occupants/families/couples/single people/age groups/occupation (economic level)
521 Other

600 RENTALS

Apartment No.	No. of bedrooms	No. of baths	Furnished	Leased	Rent per month	Square footage	Rent per square foot	Tenant turnover last 12 months	Vacancy period per turnover	Rent loss due to vacancies	Potential rent

601 Totals of above schedule
602 Income from garages and/or laundry
603 Scheduled annual gross income (based on unfurnished units; adjust if furnished)
604 Total rent loss due to vacancies last 12 months in dollars
605 Vacancy factor in percent of scheduled annual gross income
606 Last two or three years' audited rental income
607 Normal source for new tenants
608 Check prepaid rents, security deposits, rent arrears, side agreements, concessions

609	Are rents comparable, higher or lower than average rents of similar units in neighborhood
700	**EXPENSES**
701	Taxes 19__ /19__
702	Operating license fee
703	Hazard insurance/premium/coverage
704	Liability insurance/premium/coverage
705	Workmen's compensation insurance
706	Social Security
707	Electricity
708	Gas
709	Water
710	Garbage collection
711	Sewer service charge
712	Elevator inspection service
713	Pool maintenance service
714	Janitor and/or gardener
715	Resident manager's salary or rent allowance; list duties
716	Legal and accounting fees
717	Administrative management
718	Reserve for maintenance, repairs and supplies/does property show signs of substandard maintenance/what needs to be done soon
719	Reserve for replacement of personal property/what needs replacement soon
720	Are expenses in keeping with similar expense items in neighborhood
721	Other
800	**EXISTING FINANCING** (List all loans on real and personal property)
801	Loan balance/as of what date
802	Monthly payments, including taxes and insurance
803	Interest rate
804	Annual debt service/interest payments/ equity build-up
805	Lender/address/phone number

806	Loan number
807	Prepayment penalty
808	Loan locked in/until when
809	Transferable/assumption fee/Can loan be taken subject to
810	Due date/balloon payment
811	Original amount/term/year of inception
812	If there is a second loan, can it be bought at a discount/if so, what discount

900 POTENTIAL FINANCING

901	Loan commitment/amount/interest/term/payments/loan fee/lender
902	Will seller help finance/amount/interest/payoff rate/due date
903	Is seller interested in installment sale

1000 YIELD COMPUTATION ON FIRST YEAR'S INCOME

1001		Scheduled annual income
1002	Less	Vacancy reserve
1003	Equals	Gross operating income
1004	Less	Operating cost
1005	Equals	Net operating income
1006	Less	Annual debt service (payments on principal and interest
1007	Equals	Cash flow (gross spendable income)
1008	Plus	Equity build-up (annual principal payments)
1009	Equals	Equity return

(See the section on Tax Effects for computations of after-tax equity return and after-tax cash flow)

1100 NEIGHBORHOOD AND MARKET ANALYSIS

1101	Economic level of people in area (typical occupation)*
1102	Average income per family/per capita*
1103	Typical family size in area*
1104	Ratio of homeowners to tenants in area*
1105	Population growth in area*

1106	Number of competitive apartment houses in area
1107	Level of rent in comparable competitive buildings
1108	Gross multipliers of comparable properties recently sold

For sources of information, contact public utility companies, lending institutions, local building department, chamber of commerce, telephone company, local newspapers and U.S. Department of Commerce (Census Bureau)

1200 PRICE

1201	Listed price
1202	Predicted probable sale price/apply average gross multiplier to scheduled annual gross income of subject property/Make adjustments for higher than average rents due to exceptionally efficient management and for lower than average rents due to poor management.

1300 IMPORTANT EXHIBITS

1301	Preliminary title report (Watch for and examine covenants, conditions and restrictions on record.)
1302	Survey report
1303	Plot plan
1304	Photographs of property
1305	Area map with property plotted
1306	Recent inspection reports (pest control, roof, heating system, elevators, etc.)
1307	Certified operating statements for last few years
1308	Copies of leases and rental agreements
1309	Copies of management contracts
1310	Inventory of personal property
1311	Statistical reports on economic and population growth of area

DATA CHECKLIST FOR OFFICE BUILDINGS

1   Date information was obtained
2   Property location
3   Number of stories
100   OWNERSHIP
101   Owner's name, address, residence phone, business phone
102   Owner's occupation/is owner occupant of property
103   Building operated by owner or manager
104   Title vested in (list all persons having an interest in the title)/ground lease
105   Adjusted basis/depreciation deduction/depreciation method/useful life
106   Owner's tax bracket/legal status
107   Is owner classified as dealer
108   Owner's attorney/tax counsel/accountant
109   Manager's name, address, phone number
110   To inspect property
111   Acquisition date/cost of acquisition
112   Previously listed/how long/at what price
113   Reason for disposition/degree of urgency
114   Investment objective
     a.   Tax shelter
     b.   Estate building
     c.   Equity return (how much)
     d.   Spendable (how much)
     e.   Other
115   Sale and leaseback/tax-deferred exchange/installment sale
200   LOCATION
201   Quality of location: 100% location (main business section in town); 90% location, etc.
202   Proximity to: transportation/freeways/financial institutions/service facilities/restaurants/stores/etc.
203   Parking facilities nearby
204   Any foreseeable trends toward shift in business section

300 SITE

301 Lot size
302 Corner
303 Zoning
304 Legal description
305 Off-street parking
306 Landscaping

400 IMPROVEMENTS

401 Number of stories
402 Basement/foundations
403 Type of entrance and lobby
404 Parking garage in building
405 Square feet of rentable office space
406 Number of offices
407 Age of building
408 Architectural design
409 Condition/functional obsolescence
410 Recent pest control clearance
411 Type of construction
412 Type of roof/condition
413 Exterior finish/condition
414 Type of floors/load factors/floor coverings/condition
415 Type of ceilings/concealed lighting
416 Ceiling height
417 Interior halls/floor coverings/condition
418 Design/potential for altering size and layouts of offices
419 Storage facilities for tenants
420 Elevators/automatic/service elevators
421 Wiring/voltages/condition
422 Plumbing (copper, galvanized)/condition
423 Size of windows
424 View
425 Lighting/intensity level
426 Type of heating/age/condition
427 Air-conditioning/age/condition
428 Ventilation
429 Adequate sprinklers and fireproofing system/fire alarm system

430 Adequate locks and burglar alarm system
431 Toilet facilities
432 Special equipment
433 Special facilities

500 TENANCIES

Floor	Tenant	Type business	Financial rating	Lease term	Lease expiration	Square feet	Rent per month	Rent per sq. foot	Vacant

501 Income from parking garage
502 Scheduled annual gross income
503 Last few years audited gross income
504 Are rents comparable, higher or lower than average rents in similar buildings with equal location?

600 EXPENSES
601 Taxes 19
602 Hazard insurance
603 Liability insurance
604 Workmen's compensation insurance
605 Social Security
606 Electricity
607 Gas
608 Water
609 Garbage collection
610 Elevator inspection service
611 Janitor/window cleaning
612 Manager/list duties
613 Legal and accounting fees
614 Adminstrative management/leasing fees/ signs of substandard maintenance/what needs to be done soon
615 Replacement reserve for personal property

| 616 | Are expenses in keeping with similar expense items in comparable buildings with equal location |
| 617 | Other |

700 EXISTING FINANCING
(List first and junior liens)

701	Loan balance/as of what date
702	Monthly payments
703	Interest rate
704	Annual debt service/interest payments/ equity build-up
705	Lender/address/phone number
706	Loan number
707	Prepayment penalty
708	Loan locked in/until when
709	Transferable/assumption fee/can loan be taken subject to
710	Due date/balloon payment
711	Original amount/term/year of inception
712	If there is a second loan, can it be bought at a discount/if so, what discount

800 POTENTIAL FINANCING

801	Loan commitment/amount/interest/term/ payments/loan fee/lender
802	Will seller help finance/amount/interest/ payoff rate/due date
803	Is seller interested in installment sale

900 PRICE

| 901 | Listed price |
| 902 | Predicted probable sale price/use capitalization approach (usually for lack of sufficient comparable buildings)/make adjustments for above-average income due to over-efficient management or below-average expenses due to poor management |

1000 IMPORTANT EXHIBITS
See items 1301 through 1311

DATA CHECKLIST FOR COMMERCIAL PROPERTIES

1   Date information was obtained
2   Property location
3   Type of property

100   OWNERSHIP

101   Owner's name, address, residence phone, business phone
102   Owner's occupation/is owner occupant of property
103   Title vested in (list all persons having an interest in title)/ground lease
104   Adjusted basis/depreciation deduction/ depreciation method/useful life
105   Owner's tax bracket/legal status
106   Is owner classified as dealer
107   Owner's attorney/tax counsel/accountant
108   To inspect property
109   Acquisition date/cost of acquisition
110   Previously listed/how long/at what price
111   Reason for disposition/degree of urgency
112   Investment objective
     a.   Tax shelter
     b.   Estate building
     c.   Equity return (how much)
     d.   Spendable (how much)
     e.   Other property to occupy
     f.   Other
113   Sale and leaseback/tax-deferred exchange/ installment sale

200   LOCATION

201   Median strip/left-turn lane
202   Advertising value of property
203   Public transportation
204   Proximity to main arteries and freeways
205   Traffic patterns/projected streets/street widening
206   If shopping center/neighborhood center/ community center/regional center

300   SITE

301	Lot size/square footage or acreage
302	Zoning
303	Legal description
304	Deed restrictions
305	Parking lot/number of cars/paving/ condition
306	Access for loading
307	Landscaping
308	Room for expansion
400	**IMPROVEMENTS**
401	Square footage/front footage/depth/ layout
402	Number of stories or levels
403	Basement/foundations
404	Use restrictions, if any
405	Expansion possibilities
406	Age of building
407	Architectural design
408	Condition/functional obsolescence
409	Recent pest control clearance
410	Type of construction
411	Exterior finish/condition
412	Type of roof/condition
413	Type of floors/condition/load factor of each floor
414	Ceiling height
415	Wiring/voltage
416	Lighting/intensity level
417	Heating/age/condition
418	Air-conditioning/age/condition
419	Number and location of toilets
420	Adequate sprinklers and fireproofing system
421	Adequate locks/burglar alarm
422	Any special equipment
423	Loading dock height
500	**INCOME**
501	Lessee's name/original or sublessee
502	Type of business/how long in business
503	Capital
504	Dun & Bradstreet rating

505	Bank reference
506	Other financial and/or credit information
507	Monthly rent/monthly rent per square foot/ per front foot
508	Percentage lease/method of computing coverage
509	Overage last few years
510	Number of years remaining on lease/option to renew, at what rent
511	Tax clause in lease
512	Owner responsible for exterior maintenance
513	Other terms of lease (including option to buy, option to renew, right of first refusal)
514	Annual gross income
600	**EXPENSES**
601	Taxes 19__/19__ (assessed value land and improvements)
602	Hazard and liability insurance (classification)/coverage/premium
603	Services
604	Utilities
605	Salaries
606	Reserve for maintenance and repairs/signs of substandard maintenance/what needs to be done soon
607	Promotion
608	Legal and accounting fees
700	**EXISTING FINANCING** (List first and junior liens)
701	Loan balance/as of what date
702	Monthly payments
703	Interest rate
704	Annual debt service/interest payments/ equity build-up
705	Lender/address/phone number
706	Loan number
707	Prepayment penalty
708	Loan locked in/until when
709	Transferable/assumption fee/can loan be taken subject to

710	Due date/balloon payment
711	Original amount/term/year of inception
712	If there is a second loan, can it be bought at a discount/if so, what discount

800 POTENTIAL FINANCING

801	Loan commitment/amount/interest/term/ loan fee/lender
802	Will seller help finance/amount/interest/ pay-off rate/due date
803	Is seller interested in installment sale

900 AREA SURVEY

901	Traffic count in front and at nearest intersection (per day, week, month, year)
902	Distance to nearest competitive business
903	Estimated number of families within service radius of business*
904	Average family size*
905	Average income per family*
906	Trend of population growth*
907	Is area, district or street deteriorating*

For sources of information contact public utility companies, chamber of commerce, lending institutions, local building department, telephone company, local newspapers and U.S. Department of Commerce (Census Bureau)

1000 IMPORTANT EXHIBITS

1001	Preliminary title report (watch for and examine covenants, conditions and restrictions on record)
1002	Survey report
1003	Plot plan
1004	Photographs of property
1005	Area map with property plotted
1006	Recent inspection reports (pest control, roof, heating system, elevators, etc.)
1007	Certified operating statements last few years
1008	Copies of leases and rental agreements
1009	Copies of management contracts
1010	Inventory of personal property
1011	Statistical reports on economic and population growth of area

DATA CHECKLIST FOR INDUSTRIAL PROPERTIES

1 Date information was obtained
2 Property location
3 Type of property/present use/highest and best use

100 OWNERSHIP

101 Owner's name, address, residence phone, business phone
102 Owner's occupation
103 Is owner occupant or absentee owner
104 Title vested in (list all persons having an interest in the title)/ground lease
105 Adjusted basis/depreciation deduction/ depreciation method/useful life
106 Owner's tax bracket/legal status
107 Is owner classified as dealer
108 Owner's attorney/tax counsel/accountant
109 To inspect property
110 Acquisition date/cost of acquisition
111 Previously listed/how long/at what price
112 Reason for disposition/degree of urgency
113 Investment objective
   a. Tax shelter
   b. Estate building
   c. Equity return (how much)
   d. Spendable (how much)
   e. Other property to occupy
   f. Other
114 Sale and leaseback/tax-deferred exchange/ installment sale

200 LOCATION

201 Proximity to nearest city or metropolitan area
202 Proximity to major highways, freeways, etc./ highway weight, height and length limitations of vehicles
203 Advertising value of property
204 Railroad sidings/spots/team-track service

404 Population growth trend*
405 Projected growth,* due to new industries (list), new military contracts or bases, new tracts, freeways, rapid transit, other

*For sources of information, contact public utility companies, chamber of commerce, lending institutions, local building department, local planning commissions, U.S. Army Corps of Engineers, U.S. Department of Commerce (Census Bureau), telephone company and local newspapers.

500 CLIMATE AND NATURAL HAZARDS
501 Temperatures/average/minimum/maximum
502 Average length of frost period
503 Rainfall in inches/rainy season
504 Humidity/average/minimum/maximum
505 Fog conditions
506 Fire hazards
507 Storm hazards
508 Inundation hazards
509 Earthquake faults

600 LABOR MARKET
601 Total estimated employment*
602 Breakdown:* agriculture/construction/manufacturing/transportation/trade/finance/insurance/real estate/service/government/military
603 Availability of skilled and unskilled labor*
604 Union or nonunion/history of strikes*
605 Wage rates/hours overtime/fringe benefits*

*For sources of information, contact the Census Bureau, U.S. Department of Commerce.

700 SITE
701 Lot dimensions and square footage, shape, plot
702 Size of off-street loading, parking and expansion areas
703 Zoning/heavy or light industry/foreseeable shift in zoning
704 Building code requirements
705 Legal description

706	Easements
707	Deed restrictions and covenants: use/ construction/zoning/setbacks/signs/ parking/storage/waste disposal/ maintenance of building grounds/loading
708	Topography/grading needed/cost of grading
709	Elevation relative to highest known high water level
710	Soil/load-bearing characteristics/subsoil/ depth to bedrock/depth to groundwater
711	Drainage/natural run-off capacity for industrial waste/need for artificial drainage/need for flood protection
712	Type of paving/condition
713	Landscaping
800	**IMPROVEMENTS**
801	Building dimensions and square footage/ layout/stories
802	Office dimensions and square footage/ number of private offices/condition
803	Expansion possibilities/master plan for development
804	Adaptability for various uses
805	Age of building
806	Architectural design
807	General condition of building/functional obsolescence
808	Type of construction (tilt-up, concrete, concrete blocks, corrugated metal, other)
809	Building code classification of structure
810	Type of roof/condition
811	Type of floors/condition/load factor
812	Ceiling height
813	Clear span or posts/column space
814	Floor/truss clearance
815	Number of skylights/sizes
816	Exhaust vents
817	Wiring/voltage/amps/H.P.
818	Lighting/intensity level

819	Number of drains
820	Number and location of toilets
821	Adequate sprinkler and fireproofing system
822	Adequate locks/burglar alarm
823	Number of truck doors/size
824	Number of rail doors/interval
825	Dock height/excavated loading dock/covered

900 UTILITIES AND FUEL

901	Power/availability/capacity/connections/rates
902	Gas/availability/capacity/storage factors/connections/rates
903	Water/source/capacity/pressure/rates/chemical analysis
904	Telephone
905	Cost of coal and oil

1000 EQUIPMENT

1001	Number of freight elevators/size/capacity/passenger elevator
1002	In-plant rail
1003	Cranes/type/capacity in tons/clearance
1004	Type of heating
1005	Air-conditioning
1006	Boiler(s)/type/rating in BTUs
1007	Air and steam lines
1008	Transformers/capacity/location/bus ducts
1009	Auxiliary power generator
1010	Condition of equipment/obsolescence

1100 INCOME

1101	Lessee's name/original or sublessee
1102	Type of business/how long in business
1103	Capital
1104	Dun & Bradstreet rating
1105	Bank reference
1106	Other financial and/or credit information
1107	Monthly rent
1108	Number of years remaining on lease/option to renew, at what rent
1109	Tax clause in lease

1110	Owner responsible for exterior maintenance
1111	Other terms of lease (including option to buy, option to renew, right of first refusal)
1112	Annual gross income
1200	**EXPENSES**
1201	Taxes 19__/19__ (assessed value land and improvements)
1202	Hazard and liability insurance (classification)/coverage/premium
1203	Reserve for maintenance and repairs/signs of substandard maintenance/what needs to be done soon
1204	Legal and accounting fees
1205	Other
1300	**EXISTING FINANCING** (List all loans on real property and equipment)
1301	Loan balance/as of what date
1302	Monthly payments
1303	Interest rate
1304	Annual debt service/interest payments/equity build-up
1305	Lender/address/phone
1306	Loan number
1307	Prepayment penalty
1308	Loan locked in/until when
1309	Loan transferable/assumption fee
1310	Due date/balloon payment
1311	Original loan amount/term/year of inception
1312	If there is a second loan, can it be bought at a discount/what discount
1400	**POTENTIAL FINANCING**
1401	Loan commitment/amount/interest/term/payments/loan fee/lender
1402	Will seller help finance/amount/interest/payoff rate/due date
1403	Is seller interested in installment sale
1500	**PRICE**
1501	Listed price, price per acre

1502	Price range per acre of comparable sites recently sold
1503	Predicted probable sale price
1600	**IMPORTANT EXHIBITS**
1601	Preliminary title report (watch for and examine covenants, conditions and restrictions on record)
1602	Survey report
1603	Plot plan
1604	Photographs of property
1605	Area map with property plotted
1606	Recent inspection reports (pest control, roof, heating system, elevators, etc.)
1607	Certified operating statements last few years
1608	Copies of leases and rental agreements
1609	Copies of management contracts
1610	Inventory of personal property
1611	Statistical reports on economic and population growth of area

DATA CHECKLIST FOR MOTELS

1 Date information was obtained
2 Name of motel
3 Property location
4 Number of units
5 Type/resort motel/roadside motel/ perimeter motel/in-city motel

100 OWNERSHIP

101 Owner's name/address/residence phone/ business phone
102 Owner's occupation
103 Motel operated by owner or manager
104 Franchise chain/motel chain
105 Independent operator/affiliation with recommending organization
106 Title vested in (all persons having an interest in the title)
107 Adjusted basis/depreciation deduction/ depreciation method/useful life
108 Owner's tax bracket/legal status
109 Is owner classified as dealer
110 Owner's attorney/tax counsel/accountant
111 Manager's name/phone
112 To inspect property
113 Acquisition date
114 Acquisition cost/land/construction/ furniture and fixtures/total
115 Previously listed/how long/at what price
116 Reason for disposition/degree of urgency
117 Investment objective
   a. Tax shelter
   b. Estate building
   c. Equity return (how much)
   d. Spendable (how much)
   e. Other motel to operate
   f. Other
118 Sale and leaseback/tax-deferred exchange/ installment sale/sale of an operating lease

200 GROUND LEASE

201 Ground rent
202 Expiration date of lease
203 Option/what rent/length of option
204 Subordination clause in lease
205 Who pays land taxes/amount
206 Summary of lease terms
207 Can land be purchased/when/at what price
300 LOCATION
301 Traffic counts per day, week, month, year, season
302 Traffic patterns/present road conditions/ projected road improvements/ contemplated rerouting of traffic
303 Adequacy of signs/on site/highway signs/ how many/owned or rented
310 **Resort Motels:**
311 Scenic and/or recreational values
312 Self-contained resort
313 Closest tourist attractions
314 Visibility to entering traffic
320 **Roadside Motels:**
321 On main interstate route
322 Is route part of national master road plan
323 Accessibility to freeway on and off ramps
324 Strategic location between major cities
325 Proximity to resort area, industrial, manufacturing and financial centers, and military installations
330 **Perimeter Motels:**
331 Proximity to airport/central business district
332 On downtown feeder road
333 Access to freeways
340 **In-City Motels:**
341 Proximity to central business district
342 Proximity to tourist attractions
343 Proximity to convention centers
344 Access to freeways
345 Fire and police protection
346 Adjoining properties

533 Shape of rooms/square/greater in depth/ greater in width
534 Number of baths/tubs/showers over tubs/ twin basins
535 Private dressing alcoves
536 Number of kitchens in units
537 Picture windows overlooking grounds and pool area
538 Decks, patios, cabanas
540 **Public Facilities:**
541 Lobby/size/how furnished
542 Office/size/equipment
543 Pool/size/children's pool/pool equipment
544 Children's play area
545 Patios/cabanas
546 Ice and beverage machine
547 Restaurant/seating capacity/leased/who owns equipment
548 Cocktail lounge/leased/who owns equipment
549 Meeting facilities
550 Banquet facilities
551 Gift shop/barber shop/beauty salon/ newsstand/leased
552 Manager's living quarters/size/furnishings included
600 FURNISHINGS AND FIXTURES
601 Quality and style of furnishings/condition
602 TVs/how many/age/make/condition
603 Radios
604 Room telephones
605 Other equipment
606 Linens owned or rented/5-day minimum linen inventory
607 Detailed inventory
700 SERVICES
701 Valet and laundry service
702 Babysitter
703 Bellhop service
704 Free continental breakfast

705	Room service
706	Pool lifeguard
707	Number of maids used/salaries/how long employed
708	Clerical employees/salaries
709	Maintenance employees/salaries
800	**INCOME STATEMENT (3 years)**
801	Number of rooms
802	Asking price
803	Gross multiplier
804	Total room gross income
805	Gross income per room
806	Cost per room
807	Other income
808	Income bar and food
809	Rate schedules
810	Occupancy percentages
811	Is income in keeping with room gross income per unit and occupancy percentages of comparable motels in area
900	**EXPENSES**
901	Taxes 19__ /19__
902	Hazard and liability insurance/premium/ coverage
903	Workmen's compensation insurance
904	Social Security
905	Payrolls
906	Utilities
907	Water
908	Garbage collection
909	Supplies
910	Linen service or laundry
911	Elevator inspection service
912	Pool maintenance service
913	Payrolls/clerical/maids/service/ maintenance
914	Legal and accounting fees
915	Advertising/sign on property/roadside signs/AAA

916	Maintenance and repairs/signs of substandard maintenance/what needs to be done soon
917	Reserve for replacement of personal property
918	Are expenses in keeping with similar expense items of comparable motels in area
1000	**EXISTING FINANCING** (List all loans on real and personal property)
1001	Loan balance/as of what date
1002	Monthly payments/taxes and insurance included
1003	Interest rate
1004	Annual debt service/interest payments/ equity build-up
1005	Lender/address/phone number
1006	Loan number
1007	Prepayment penalty
1008	Loan locked in/until when
1009	Transferable/assumption fee/can loan be taken subject to
1010	Due date/balloon payment
1011	Original amount/term/year of inception
1012	If there is a second loan, can it be bought at a discount/if so, what discount
1100	**POTENTIAL FINANCING**
1101	Loan commitment/amount/interest term/ payments/loan fee/lender
1102	Will seller help finance/amount/interest/ payoff rate/due date
1103	Is seller interested in installment sale
1200	**PRICE**
1201	Listed price (times-earnings ratio applied to net income before debt service and depreciation)
1202	Overall rates and occupancy percentages of comparable motels in area
1203	Predicted probable sale price/apply to subject property average times-earnings ratios of comparable motels recently sold/

make adjustments for above-average income due to over-efficient management or below-average expenses due to poor management and vice versa

1400 IMPORTANT EXHIBITS

1401 Preliminary title report (watch for and examine covenants, conditions and restrictions on record)

1402 Survey report

1403 Plot plan

1404 Photographs of property

1405 Area map with property plotted

1406 Recent inspection reports (pest control, roof, heating system, elevators, etc.)

1407 Certified operating statements last few years

1408 Copies of leases and rental agreements

1409 Copies of management contracts

1410 Inventory of personal property

1411 Statistical reports on economic and population growth of area

DATA CHECKLIST FOR FARM PROPERTIES

1. Date information was obtained
2. Property location
3. Type of farm/grain/livestock/special purpose
4. Highest and best use

100 OWNERSHIP

101. Owner's name/address/residence phone/business phone
102. Owner's occupation/absentee owner
103. Farm operated by owner or manager
104. Title vested in (list all persons having an interest in the title)
105. Tax basis/owner's tax bracket/legal status
106. Owner's attorney/tax counsel/accountant
107. Manager's name/address/phone number
108. Acquisition date/cost of acquisition
109. Previously listed/how long/at what price
110. Reason for disposition/degree of urgency
111. Investment objective
    a. Expansion of operation
    b. Tax shelter
    c. Estate building
    d. Equity return (how much)
    e. Spendable (how much)
    f. Other
112. Sale and leaseback/tax-deferred exchange/installment sale

200 LOCATION

201. Proximity to metropolitan area or nearest town
202. Proximity to recreational area/lakes/reservoirs
203. Potential alternative use of land/subdivision/industrial/recreational
204. Proximity to local grain, livestock and other markets
205. Proximity to canneries, dairies, grain or cereal plants

206	Proximity to farm equipment service
207	Access to arterial roads, freeways, etc.
208	Access to waterways
209	Access to railroads
210	Proximity of schools, school bus, churches, shopping center, recreational facilities
211	Availability of farm labor/wages
300	**CLIMATE AND HAZARDS**
301	Length of growing season
302	Temperatures/average/minimum/ maximum
303	Average length of frost period/begin and end
304	Rainfall in inches/rainy season
305	Humidity/average/high/low
306	Fog conditions
307	Fire hazards
308	Storm hazards
309	Inundation hazards
310	Diseases
311	Weeds
400	**LAND**
401	Legal description/easements/deed restrictions
402	Neighbors
403	Total acreage/boundary lines
404	Tillable land/orchards/pasture/ timberland/waste land
405	Fences/type/condition
406	Soil/type and quality of topsoil and subsoil/ crops most adaptable to soil/productivity/ soil test
407	Topography/level/degree of slope/rolling/ can tractor be used
408	Drainage/natural, surface or tile drainage/ adequacy for peak rainfalls/assessment drainage district
409	Adequacy of water supply/chemical composition/safe for human consumption

410	Source of water supply/well/riparian rights to river or creek
411	Irrigation/method/irrigation district/cost
412	Utilities/electricity/gas/telephone
413	Livestock/dairy/cattle breeding/hog/poultry/other
414	Special purpose/orchard/vegetable/berry/timber/other
415	Crop history/rotation of crops/type of crops
416	Government allotted acreage to crops, if any
417	Annual yield per acre of common crops/average annual yield per acre in area
418	Fertilizer/type/average annual amount used/average annual cost

500 IMPROVEMENTS

501	Buildings/use/construction/size/roof/foundation/age/condition/value
502	Dwelling/type/age/construction/exterior/roof/basement/foundation/stories/flooring/wiring/plumbing/heat/air-conditioning/insulation/weather stripping/window screens/storm windows/number of rooms/kitchen (built-ins)/baths/extras/condition
503	Roads/paving/blacktop/gravel/other

600 PERSONAL PROPERTY INCLUDED

601	Machinery/other equipment
602	Growing crops
603	Livestock/ancestry

700 TENANCY

701	Lessee's name/address/phone number/experience/capital/credit rating
702	Lease/length/terms
703	Monthly rent

800 INCOME AND EXPENSES

801	Annual gross income past few years
802	Taxes 19__ /19__
803	Insurance coverage and premium/hazard/liability/crop/workmen's compensation/Social Security

804	Utilities
805	Maintenance of buildings and personal property/signs of substandard maintenance/what needs to be done soon
806	Soil and water conservation
807	Fertilizer
808	Development/clearing land
809	Wages
810	Are income and expenses in keeping with comparable items in the area/if so, does it reflect over-efficient or poor management

900 FINANCING

901	Private mortgage
902	Land contract of sale (installment contract)
903	Federal Land Bank Loan
904	Bank/insurance company loan
905	Farmer's Home Administration loan (FHA)
906	Terms: Cash down payment required/ payments/interest/term/subordination/ due-on-sale/prepayment penalty/lock-in/ due date

1000 PRICE

1001	Listed price/price per acre
1002	Prices per acre of comparable farm land recently sold in the area (excluding buildings and personal property)

1100 IMPORTANT EXHIBITS

1101	Preliminary title report
1102	Survey report
1103	Plot plan
1104	Photographs of property
1105	Area map with property plotted
1106	Recent inspection reports (pest control, roof, heating system, elevators, etc.)
1107	Certified operating statements last few years
1108	Copies of leases and rental agreements
1109	Copies of management contracts
1110	Inventory of personal property

DATA CHECKLIST FOR UNDEVELOPED LAND

1   Date information was obtained
2   Property location
3   Present land use

100 OWNERSHIP

101 Owner's name/address/residence phone/ business phone
102 Owner's occupation
103 Title vested in (list all persons having an interest in the title)
104 Tax basis/owner's tax bracket/legal status
105 Is owner classified as dealer
106 Acquisition date/cost of acquisition
107 Previously listed/how long/at what price
108 Tax-deferred exchange/installment sale
109 Reason for disposition/investment objective
110 Will owner sell in parcels or only as a whole
111 Will owner sell only, lease or build to lease
112 Investment objective
    a. Tax shelter
    b. Estate building
    c. Equity
    d. Spendable (how much)
    e. Other

200 SIZE AND DESCRIPTION

201 Size of parcel/dimensions/boundaries/plot or survey map
202 Legal description
203 Deed restrictions/covenants/easements

Surveyors Terminology/Abbreviations

IPF Iron pin found by surveyor
IPP Iron pin placed by surveyor
LLL Land lot line
BL Building line
DE Draining easement
MH Manhole
R/W Right of way

300   CHARACTERISTICS AND UTILITIES
301   Highest and best use (recommendations from qualified engineer or land planner)
   a.   Farm, ranch or timberland
   b.   Recreation or resort property
   c.   Industrial property
   d.   Commercial property
   e.   Residential property
302   Topography of terrain (contour map)
303   Elevation relative to highest known high water level
304   Drainage/natural run-off capacity/need for artificial drainage/need for flood protection
305   Sanitary sewerage system/adequacy/proximity
306   Subsoil (soil engineer's report)/depths to bedrock and groundwater
307   Estimate of clearing, grading and cut and fill operations, if any
308   Cost estimates of off-site and on-site improvements to obtain finished lots or plots
309   Pure drinking water/adequacy of supply
310   Source of water supply/well/riparian rights to river or creek
311   Spot location of the following items on a general location map:
   a.   Existing easements/size and purpose
   b.   Sanitary sewer outfall lines
   c.   Storm sewer outfall lines
   d.   Drainage directions
   e.   Existing water service lines/sizes
   f.   Existing gas service lines
   g.   Existing electrical lines
312   Letters from public utilities or governmental agencies regarding present or projected services to the property
400   LOCATION
401   Proximity to what metropolitan area, city or district

402	Proximity to central business district and regional shopping center*
403	Proximity to neighborhood shopping centers*
404	Proximity to and quality of schools (grade, junior high, high, college, private)*
405	Proximity to churches/recreational centers/parks/theatres/hospital/medical center*
406	Industrial or cemetery property nearby
407	Public transportation
408	Access to main traffic arteries and freeways
409	Contemplated new roads, freeways, transportation facilities
410	Traffic count/in front and at nearest intersection (if commercial lot)
411	Median strip/left turn lane (if commercial lot)
412	Located in city or county/fire and police protection
413	Type and quality of adjoining properties
414	Other site and neighborhood characteristics

Generally acceptable maximum distances from homes:
Regional shopping center 4 miles
Neighborhood shopping center 3/4 mile
Recreation facilities 4 miles
Public school 1 mile
High school 12 miles
Church 4 miles
Work 45 minutes

500 SOCIAL REGULATIONS

501	Zoning/existing and proposed
502	Dedication of land to public use
503	Requirements as to location and width of streets
504	Requirements as to curbs, gutters, sidewalks
505	Requirements as to lot size
506	Use restrictions
507	Building restrictions
508	Bond required for improvements

600 TAXATION
601 Tax rate
602 Assessment policies and trends
603 Assessed value
604 Taxes 19__ /19__
605 Special assessments
700 POPULATION
701 Present population in above area*
702 Average income per family and family size*
703 Present sources of income in percentages*:
    a. Industry
    b. Farming
    c. Government
    d. Military
    e. Other
704 Projected growth due to the following factors*:
    a. New industries (list)
    b. New military contracts
    c. New military bases
    d. Freeways
    e. Rapid transit
    f. Other
705 Ratio of homeowners to tenants in area*
800 CLIMATE AND NATURAL HAZARDS
801 Temperatures/average/minimum/maximum
802 Average length of frost period
803 Rainfall in inches/rainy season
804 Humidity/average/minimum/maximum
805 Fog conditions
806 Fire hazards
807 Storm hazards
808 Inundation hazards
809 Earthquake faults
900 LOCAL BUILDING TRENDS
901 Number of new subdivisions in area/location
902 Number of new homes under construction in area*/finished home costs

903   Number of new apartment houses under construction in area*

904   Number of existing shopping centers in area*

For sources of above data, contact chamber of commerce, local building department, public utilities (for number of recent and planned installations), title insurance companies, lending institutions, local planning commission, U.S. Department of Commerce and U.S. Army Corps of Engineers.

1000   PRICE

1001   Listed price/price per acre

1002   Price range per acre of comparable land recently sold

1003   Predicted probable sale price

1100   IMPORTANT EXHIBITS

1101   Preliminary report

1102   Survey report

1103   Plot plan

1104   Photographs of property

1105   Area map with property plotted

1106   Recent inspection reports (pest control, roof, heating system, elevators, etc.)

1107   Certified operating statements last few years

1108   Copies of leases and rental agreements

1109   Copies of management contracts

1110   Inventory of personal property

1111   Statistical reports of economic and population growth in the area

CHECKLIST FOR PURCHASE OF DEVELOPMENT LOTS

(Courtesy of Colonial Mortgage Company, Fort Wayne, Indiana)

1. Are there large, successful builders nearby (especially on the same road closer to town) who will provide very tough competition?
2. Have any builders failed recently in the immediate neighborhood?
3. Have out-of-town builders considered moving here (taken options, etc.) and then changed their minds?
4. Are efficient subcontractors and labor available?
5. Is the market so competitive that you could not afford to do as much advertising or as expensive a job of merchandising as other nearby builders?
6. Has a qualified engineer walked over the property and, if necessary, made soil tests and other studies to assure you this is buildable land?
7. Has this parcel been peddled to other builders and rejected?
8. Do you understand the zoning and can you live with it?
9. Are there easements over the property?
10. Can you solve any drainage problems?
11. Are there mosquitoes, fog, smog, noise, or smells?
12. Is that part of town a one-industry area that could be hurt badly by layoffs?
13. Is the area heavily dependent on Army, Navy, or Air Force units that might be withdrawn?
14. Is the area overbuilt with apartments that offer serious competition to new houses?
15. Is it likely that real estate taxes soon will be increased substantially?
16. Are new highways with uncertain locations planned, which might tie up the whole area for a year or more?

17. Is nearby land zoned for outdoor movies, commercial buildings, or any other purpose that homeowners would consider a liability?
18. Has the property a poor approach?
19. Are there nearby shack towns or other undesirable elements?
20. Are you surrounded by subdivisions where houses sell for several thousand dollars less than yours?
21. Are you so far out of town that you need to sell for $2,000 less than builders closer in?
22. Can you offer as much house for the money as nearby competitive builders?
23. Has a big local builder, or an out-of-town builder, an option on land nearby that could spoil your sales once he opens up?
24. Would an experienced local broker refuse to try to sell houses here?
25. What is the tax rate now? Two years ago?
26. How many foreclosures are there in the area?

DATA CHECKLIST FOR MOBILE HOME PARK SITES

1	Date information was obtained
2	Property location
3	Present land use

100 OWNERSHIP

101	Owner's name/address/residence phone/business phone
102	Owner's occupation
103	Title vested in (list all persons having an interest in the title)
104	Acquisition date/cost of acquisition
105	Previously listed/how long/at what price
106	Tax-deferred exchange/installment sale
107	Reason for disposition/investment objective
108	Will owner sell in parcels or only as a whole

200 SIZE AND DESCRIPTION

201	Size of parcel/dimensions/boundaries/plot or survey map
202	Legal description
203	Deed restrictions/covenants/easements

300 CHARACTERISTICS AND UTILITIES

301	Topography: level, rolling, hilly, rough, low, rocky
302	Existing structures on property
303	Elevation relative to highest known high water level
304	Drainage/natural run-off capacity/need for artificial drainage/need for flood protection
305	Sewer at property line/proximity
306	Subsoil (soil engineer's report)/depths to bedrock and groundwater
307	Estimate of clearing, grading and cut and fill operations, if any
308	Cost estimate of off-site and on-site improvements to obtain finished lots or plots
309	Water at property line/pure drinking water/proximity
310	Source of water supply/well/riparian rights to river or creek

311 Gas at property line/proximity
312 Power at property line/proximity
313 Spot location of the following items on a general location map:
   a. Existing easements/size and purpose
   b. Sanitary sewer outfall lines
   c. Storm sewer outfall lines
   d. Drainage directions
   e. Existing water service lines/sizes
   f. Existing gas service lines
   g. Existing electrical lines
314 Letters from public utilities or governmental agencies regarding present or projected services to the property

400 LOCATION

401 Proximity to what metropolitan area, city or district
402 Proximity to central business district and regional shopping centers*
403 Proximity to neighborhood shopping centers*
404 Proximity to and quality of schools (grade, junior high, high, college, private)*
405 Proximity to churches/recreation centers/parks/theatres/hospital/medical center*
406 Industrial or cemetery property nearby
407 Public transportation
408 Access to main traffic arteries and freeways
409 Contemplated new roads, freeways, transportation facilities
410 Located in city or county/fire and police protection

*For sources of above data, contact chamber of commerce, local building department, public utility companies (for number of recent and planned installations), title insurance companies, lending institutions, local planning commission, U.S. Department of Commerce and U.S. Army Corp of Engineers.

500 ZONING

501 Present zoning
502 Proposed zoning
503 Purchase subject to zoning

504	Planning department opinion of chances to obtain zoning for mobile home site
600	**TAXATION**
601	Tax rate
602	Assessment policies and trends
603	Assessed value
604	Taxes 19__ /19__
605	Special assessments
700	**POPULATION**
701	Present population in above area*
702	Average income per family and family size*
703	Present sources of income in percentages*
	a. Industry
	b. Farming
	c. Government
	d. Military
	e. Other
704	Projected growth due to the following factors*
	a. New industries (list)
	b. New military contracts
	c. New military bases
	d. Freeways
	e. Rapid transit
	f. Other
705	Ratio of homeowners to tenants in area*
800	**CLIMATE AND NATURAL HAZARDS**
801	Temperatures/average/minimum/maximum
802	Average length of frost period
803	Rainfall in inches/rainy season
804	Humidity/average/minimum/maximum
805	Fog conditions
806	Fire hazards
807	Storm hazards
808	Inundation hazards
809	Earthquake faults
900	**LOCAL BUILDING TRENDS**
901	Number of mobile home parks in area/proximity/quality/other characteristics

902	Number of new subdivisions in area/location
903	Number of new homes under construction in area*/finished home costs
904	Number of new apartment houses under construction in area*
905	Number of existing shopping centers in area*
1000	**PRICE**
1001	Listed price/price per acre
1002	Price range per acre of comparable land recently sold
1003	Predicted probable sale price
1100	**TERMS**
1101	Loan balance, if any/interest rate/payments/due date/prepayment penalty
1102	Lender/loan number
1103	Loan assumable
1104	Can loan be subordinated
1105	Will seller help finance/amount/interest/pay-back rate/due date/subordinate
1106	Amount of cash required
1200	**IMPORTANT EXHIBITS**
1201	City or county map with location of property
1202	Assessor's or parcel map with dimensions
1203	Topographical map
1204	Aerial photo
1205	Survey report
1206	Statistical reports on economic and population growth of area

For sources of above data, contact chamber of commerce, local building department, public utility companies (for number of recent and planned installations), title insurance companies, lending institutions, local planning commission, U.S. Department of Commerce and U.S. Army Corp of Engineers.

SELLER'S PROPERTY DISCLOSURE STATEMENT

1. Title and Access

a. Is the property currently leased? If so, when does the lease expire? Does the lessee have an option to extend the lease?

b. Does anyone have a first right of refusal to buy, option or lease the property? If so, who?

c. Do you know of any existing, pending or potential legal actions concerning the property or the homeowners' association?

d. Has there been a notice of default filed against your property? If yes, please explain.

e. Are there any bonds, assessments or judgments that are either liens upon the property or that limit its use?

f. Do you own real property adjacent to, across the street from or in the same subdivision as the subject property? If yes, please describe.

g. Do you know of any encroachments, easements, licenses, boundary disputes or third party claims affecting the property (rights of other people to interfere with the use of the property in any way)? If so, explain.

h. Are you aware of any pending real estate development in your area (such as condominiums, planned unit developments, subdivisions or property for commercial, educational or religious use)?

i. Do you experience any excessive noises, for example, airplanes, trains, trucks, freeway, etc.?

j. Are you aware of any other conditions that could affect the value or desirability of the property?

2. Land

a. Does the property have any filled ground? If so, is the house built on filled or unstable ground?

b. Do you know of any past or present settling or soil movement problems on the property or on adjacent properties? If so, have they resulted in any structural damage? What was the extent of damage?

c. Do you know of any past or present drainage or flooding problem on your property or adjacent properties? If so, explain on separate sheet. Is there water standing on the property after rainfall? Any active springs?

d. Is the property in a designated flood zone?

e. Is the property in a Special Studies Zone as provided by the Alquist-Priolo Geological Hazard Zones Act?

f. Are you aware of any past or present problems with driveways, walkways, patios or retaining walls on your property or adjacent properties due to drainage, flooding or soil movement (such as large cracks, potholes, raised sections)? If so, please describe.

3. Structural Disclosures

a. Do you know of any structural additions or alterations or the installation, alteration, repair or replacement of significant components of the structures upon the property completed during the term of your ownership or that of a prior owner with or without an appropriate permit or other authority for construction from a public agency having jurisdiction?

☐ Explanation attached

b. Approximate age of structure: Do you know of any condition in the original or existing design or workmanship of the structure that would be considered substandard? If so, please explain.

c. Are you aware of excessive settling, slanted floors, large cracks in walls, foundations, garage floors, driveways, chimneys or fireplaces? If so, explain.

d. Are you aware of any structural wood members, including mudsills, being below soil level?

e. Is crawlspace, if any, below soil level?

f. Do you know of any inspection reports, surveys, studies, notices and so on concerning the property? If so, please list each one, even if you have already made them available.

g. Date of last structural pest control inspection? By whom?

h. Do you prefer a presale structural pest control inspection?

i. Date of last city/county mandatory inspection report?

j. Have you any notice(s) of violations relating to the property from any city, county or state agencies? If so, please explain.

k. Do you know of any violations of government regulations, ordinances or zoning laws regarding this property? If so, explain.

4. Roof, Gutters, Downspouts

a. Type of roof: ❑ Tar and gravel, ❑ Asphalt shingle, ❑ Wood shingle, ❑ Tile, ❑ Other. Age of roof?

b. Has roof been resurfaced? If so, what year? Is there a guarantee on the roof? For how long? By whom?

c. Has roof ever leaked since you owned the property? If so, what was done to correct the leak?

d. Are gutters and downspouts free of holes and excessive rust?

e. Do downspouts empty into drainage system or onto splash blocks? Is water directed away from structure?

5. Plumbing System

a. Source of water supply: ❑ Public, ❑ Private well. If well water, when was water sample last checked for safety? Result of test?

b. Well water pump? Date installed? Condition? Sufficient water during late summer?

c. Are water supply pipes copper or galvanized?

d. Are you aware of below normal water pressure in your water supply lines (normal is 50 to 70 lbs.)?

e. Are you aware of excessive rust stains in tubs, lavatories and sinks?

f. Are you aware of water standing around any of the lawn sprinkler heads?

g. Are there any plumbing leaks around and under sinks, toilets, showers, bathtubs and lavatories? If so, where?

h. Pool? Age? Pool heater: ❑ Gas, ❑ Electric, ❑ Solar. Pool sweep? Date of last inspection? By whom? Regular maintenance?

i. Hot tub/spa? Date of last inspection? By whom?

j. ❑ City sewer, ❑ Septic tank: ❑ Fiberglass, ❑ Concrete, ❑ Redwood. Capacity? Is septic tank in good working order?

6. Electrical System

a. 220 Volt?

b. Are there any damaged or malfunctioning receptacles?

c. Are you aware of any damaged or malfunctioning switches?

d. Are there any extension cords stapled to baseboards or underneath carpets or rugs?

e. Does outside TV antenna have a ground connection?

f. Are you aware of any defects, malfunctioning or illegal installation of electrical equipment in or outside the house?

7. Heating, Air-Conditioning, Other Equipment

a. Is the house insulated?
b. Type of heating system?
c. Is furnace room or furnace closet adequately vented?
d. Are fuel-consuming heating devices adequately vented to the outside directly or through a chimney?
e. Date of last inspection of heating equipment? By whom?
f. Solar heating? In working order?
g. Air-conditioning? Date of last inspection? By whom?
h. Does fireplace have a damper?
i. Provision for outside venting of clothes dryer?
j. Approximate age of water heater? Capacity? Is your water heater equipped with temperature pressure relief valve, which is a required safety device?
k. Electric garage door opener? Condition? Number of controls?
l. Burglar alarm? Make? In working order? Owned? Leased? Rented?
m. Smoke detectors? How many? ❏ 110V, ❏ Battery. In working order?
n. Lawn sprinklers? Automatic clock? In working order?
o. Water softener? In working order?
p. Sump pump? In working order?
q. Are you aware of any of the above equipment that is in need of repair or replacement or is illegally installed?

8. Built-In Appliances

a. Are you aware of any built-in appliances that are in need of repair or replacement? If so, which?

9. Personal Property Included in the Purchase Price

a. List items of personal property that are included in the purchase price.

b. Are there any liens against any of these items? If so, please explain.

10. Home Protection Program

11. Condominiums

a. Please check availability of copies of the following documents: ❑ CC&Rs, ❑ Condominium declaration, ❑ Association bylaws, ❑ Articles of incorporation, ❑ Subdivision report, ❑ Current financial statement, ❑ Regulations currently in force.

b. Does the condominium declaration contain any resale restrictions?

c. Does the homeowners' association have the first right of refusal?

d. Please check occupancy restrictions imposed by the association, including but not limited to: ❑ Children, ❑ Pets, ❑ Storage of recreational vehicles or boats on driveways or in common areas, ❑ Advertising or For Sale signs, ❑ Architectural or decorative alterations subject to association approval, ❑ Other.

e. In case of a conversion, do you have an engineer's report on the condition of the building and its equipment?

f. Monthly/annual association dues? How much? What is included in the association dues?

g. Has your association notified you of any future dues increases or special assessments? If so, please give details.

h. Are all dues, assessments and taxes current?

i. I shall provide a statement from the condominium homeowners' association documenting the amount of any delinquent assessments, including penalties, attorney's fees and any other charges provided for in the management documents to be delivered to Buyer.

j. Security: ☐ Intercom, ☐ Closed circuit TV, ☐ Guards, ☐ Electric gate, ☐ Other.

k. Parking? Does each unit have its own designated parking spaces? How close to unit? Is space ample? Guest parking?

l. Is soundproofing adequate? Are there noisy trash chutes?

m. Property management company.

12. Newly Constructed Residences

a. Is deposit held in trust fund?

b. Bond guaranteeing completion of unit and common area and facilities?

c. Is builder a member of Home Builders Association? Is Home Owners' Warranty (HOW) available?

d. Will carpets, draperies and appliances be identical to those shown in model unit?

e. Please list expiration dates of warranties covering appliances and equipment. Final inspection date? Occupancy permit date? Contractor? License?

13. Ownership

a. Are you a builder or developer?

b. Are you a licensed real estate agent?

c. Have all persons on the title signed the listing agreement?

d. Please list all persons on the title who are not U.S. citizens.

e. Are you aware of anything else you should disclose to a prospective buyer? If so, please explain. (Use addendums if necessary.)

The foregoing answers and explanations are true and complete to the best of my/our knowledge and I/we have retained a copy hereof. I/we herewith authorize the Agent in this transaction to disclose the information set forth above to other real estate brokers, real estate agents and prospective buyers of the property.

Dated:_____ Seller:_____ Seller:_____:

I/we acknowledge receipt of this Seller's Property Disclosure Statement, including additional explanations, if any, attached hereto.

Dated:_____ Buyer:_____ Buyer:_____

I am satisfied with the above Seller's property disclosure statement.

Dated: [_____] Buyer: [_____] Buyer: [_____]

I am not satisfied with the above Seller's property disclosure statement and herewith rescind my offer to purchase above property.

Dated: [_____] Buyer: [_____] Buyer: [_____]

I reserve the right to have the property inspected by the following professional(s) and to submit a copy of the inspection report(s) to Seller's Agent on or before_____.

Dated: [_____] Buyer: [_____] Buyer: [_____]

INSTRUCTIONS

The law in some jurisdictions requires that the broker make a physical inspection of the property and that notice of any defects observed during such an inspection be disclosed to buyers.

The purpose of the Seller's Property Disclosure Statement (Forms 110.11, 110.12 and 110.13) is to give a buyer such notice.

RED FLAGS INSPECTION CHECKLIST

	CIRCLE APPROPRIATE SYMBOL OR MARK ☒		
Property _____			
Agent _____	⌐	⌐	🌀
Date _____			
Red Flags Property Inspection Guide page numbers provided for reference.	Red Flag	Possible Red Flag	Nothing Observed or Not Applicable

1. INSPECTING FOR RED FLAGS OUTSIDE THE HOME

	Red Flag	Possible Red Flag	Nothing Observed
Cracks in sidewalks, driveways, or decks? (2/4)	⌐	⌐	☐
Cracks in foundation? (2/5)	⌐	⌐	☐
Cracks in fireplace? (2/26)	⌐	⌐	☐
Visually distorted structure? (2/7)	⌐	⌐	☐
Visual evidence of drainage problems? (2/8)	⌐	⌐	☐
Building ventilation screens damaged? (2/10)	⌐	⌐	☐
Visual evidence of hillside instability, landsliding? (2/11)	⌐	⌐	☐
Visual evidence of erosion? (2/12)	⌐	⌐	☐
Visual evidence of roof deterioration? (2/15)	⌐	⌐	☐
Hazardous vegetation observed? (2/16)	⌐	⌐	☐
Hazardous deck or stair railings? (2/18)	⌐	⌐	☐
Hazardous stairs? (2/19)	⌐	⌐	☐
Hazardous walkways or steps? (2/20)	⌐	⌐	☐
Visual evidence of failing retaining walls? (2/39)	⌐	⌐	☐
Swimming pool out-of-level? (2/40)	⌐	⌐	☐
Cracks in swimming pool? (2/40)	⌐	⌐	☐
Hazardous play structure or treehouse? (2/41)	⌐	⌐	☐
_____	⌐	⌐	☐

2. INSPECTING FOR RED FLAGS INSIDE THE HOME

	Red Flag	Possible Red Flag	Nothing Observed
Cracks in basement walls? (2/21)	⌐	⌐	☐
Water stains, or white powdery deposits on basement walls? (2/21)	⌐	⌐	☐
Sump pump(s)? (2/21)	⌐	⌐	☐
Water stains on ceiling or around windows? (2/14)	⌐	⌐	☐
Wall or ceiling cracks? (2/22)	⌐	⌐	☐
Hidden wall cracks? (2/23)	⌐	⌐	☐
Any noticeable sloping floors? (2/24)	⌐	⌐	☐
Cracks in tile floors? (2/24)	⌐	⌐	☐
Sticking doors or windows? (2/25)	⌐	⌐	☐
Uneven spaces between doors and frames? (2/26)	⌐	⌐	☐
Cracks in fireplace? (2/26)	⌐	⌐	☐
Hazardous fireplace hearth? (2/27)	⌐	⌐	☐
Visual evidence of sagging beams? (2/28)	⌐	⌐	☐
Burned or damaged electrical outlets? (2/29)	⌐	⌐	☐
Any extension cords under carpet or stapled to wall? (2/29)	⌐	⌐	☐
Any exposed wiring? (2/30)	⌐	⌐	☐
Electrical panel accessible and intact? (2/30)	⌐	⌐	☐
Gas shut-off valve accessible? (2/32)	⌐	⌐	☐
Hazardous water heater? (ie. no pressure valve, etc.) (2/33)	⌐	⌐	☐
Visual evidence of illegal additions? (2/34)	⌐	⌐	☐
Hazardous steps? (2/35)	⌐	⌐	☐
_____	⌐	⌐	☐

3. DURING YOUR INSPECTION DID YOU OBSERVE?

CIRCLE YES OR NO

Safety glass emblem on sliding doors (2/36)	Yes	No
Ground fault interrupters (2/31)	Yes	No
Safety wire on garage door springs (2/37)	Yes	No
Smoke alarm(s) (2/37)	Yes	No
_____	Yes	No

This form is designed to be used in conjunction with the **Red Flags Property Inspection Guide**. In California the completed checklist may be made an attachment to the Real Estate Transfer Disclosure Statement (Statutory Form) part 3 or 4 as applicable (PPC 109.3 & 109.4 CAL)

FORM   109 RF   (10-87)   COPYRIGHT F 1987 BY PROFESSIONAL PUBLISHING CORP 122 PAUL DR SAN RAFAEL, CA 94903 (415)472 1964   **PROFESSIONAL PUBLISHING**

INDEX

settlement: **A**: 163

shared appreciation mortgage (*see* mortgage, shared appreciaiton)

shared equity mortgage (*see* mortgage, shared equity)

Sherman Act: **C**: 66–69

showing home: **B**: 53–55

single agency: **C**: 47

single-family dwellings: **E**: 5–7

site: **E**: 10, 13–14, 20, 23–24, 29–30, 36, 46

size: **E**: 45, 52

Small Residential Income Property Appraisal Report: **A**: 51

social regulations: **B**: 17

software programs: **B**: 4–5, 18

social/sphere of influence farm: **E**: 5

solar power: **A**: 81 **C**: 64

special information booklet: **A**: 164

specialist: **B**: 19

special promotions: **B**: 33

spousal maintenance income: **A**: 36

spread: **A**: 10

spread sheet software: **B**: 4

square footage: **A**: 235, 237–38

Starker exchange: **D**: 33

start-up mortgage (*see* mortgage, start-up)

stocks: **A**: 39 **D**: 47

streamline refinances: **A**: 90

structural disclosures: **E**: 57–58

subagency: **B**: 41–43 **C**: 39–41

subagent: **C**: 39–40

Subchapter C corporations: **D**: 15–16, 17

subject to: **A**: 5–6 **D**: 44

subordination clause: **A**: 2–3

substantial restrictions and limitations: **D**: 36–37

substitution of entitlement: **A**: 119, 133

success attributes: **B**: 14

Summary Report: **A**: 45

Superfund Amendment and Reauthorization Act: **C**: 16, 18–22, 31

NOTES

NOTES

NOTES